THE WAITE GROUP'S

Visual Basic® 6
Client/Server

How-To

Noel Jerke
George Szabo
David Jung
Don Kiely

SAMS

A Division of Macmillan Computer Publishing
201 West 103rd St., Indianapolis, Indiana, 46290 USA

The Waite Group's Visual Basic® 6 Client/Server How-To

Copyright © 1999 by Sams Publishing

International Standard Book Number: 1-57169-154-5

Library of Congress Catalog Card Number: 98-84686

Printed in the United States of America

First Printing: October 1998

00 99 98   4   3   2   1

Trademarks

Warning and Disclaimer

EXECUTIVE EDITOR
Brian Gill

ACQUISITIONS EDITOR
Ron Gallagher

DEVELOPMENT EDITOR
Scott Warner

MANAGING EDITOR
Jodi Jensen

PROJECT EDITOR
Tonya Simpson

COPY EDITORS
Fran Blauw
Geneil Breeze
Gail Burlakoff
Pat Kinyon

INDEXER
Rebecca Salerno

PROOFREADER
Linda Knose

TECHNICAL EDITOR
Sakhr Youness

SOFTWARE DEVELOPMENT SPECIALIST
John Warriner

TEAM COORDINATOR
Carol Ackerman

INTERIOR DESIGNER
Gary Adair

COVER DESIGNER
Karen Ruggles

LAYOUT TECHNICIANS
Tim Osborn
Staci Somers
Mark Walchle

CONTENTS AT A GLANCE

CONTENTS

Noel Jerke is an Internet enthusiast and currently works in the Internet industry at Judd's OnLine, Inc. (`http://www.juddsonline.com`) in Winchester, VA. As the Senior Vice President of Operations, he manages a great team that is helping publishers, catalogers, and many other businesses move to the Internet. Some of Judd's OnLine's customers include Martha Stewart, Reba McEntire, and the American Diabetes Association. His background includes receiving a B.S. degree in Computer Science and Economics from Trinity University, San Antonio, TX, developing banking applications, and being the Manager of Research and Development for a graphics company. Noel is an experienced developer familiar with SQL Server, Active Server Pages, and Visual Basic. Currently his interests include writing about client/server programming, Internet programming, and developing Web sites for the Internet. Noel has also authored Waite Group Press's *Visual Basic Multimedia How-To*, *Visual Basic Interactive Course*, and *Visual Basic API How-To* and is working on several other book projects. Noel is married with no children (yet), but is kept busy with an energetic dog and freelance writing. His other interests include basketball, politics, and church activities.

Noel can be reached at `noelj@juddsonline.com` or you can visit his Web site at `http://www.activepubs.com`.

George Szabo is currently working for Universal Studios, Inc. helping develop and implement enterprise-wide project management for the IT organization. Since 1994 George has specialized in the appropriate use of new and emerging technologies as well as the development of enterprise-wide information systems and infrastructure. He has been working with Visual Basic since its original release in 1989 and has been a guest speaker on topics revolving around Web-based technologies. When he is not glued to the computer screen or fooling around with some new gadget, George and his wife Felicia enjoy waterskiing and snowskiing as well as a good game of Quake Deathmatch to settle an argument. George has four wonderfully supportive siblings, Leandra, Marcel, Elizabeth, and Sophia, who are thrilled that he mentioned their names in his book.

David Jung has been developing programs in BASIC ever since he discovered personal computers back in the early 1980s. A graduate of California State Polytechnic University, Pomona, David has a Bachelor of Science degree in Business Administration emphasizing computer information systems. His development expertise is in architecting and constructing cross-platform client/server and distributed database solutions using Visual Basic, Java, Access, SQL Server, Oracle, DB2, and Internet technology. He is a member of the Pasadena IBM Users Group's technical staff and leads its Visual Basic Special Interest Group. He is a frequent speaker at seminars and users groups showing how Visual Basic, Java, and the Internet can be integrated into business solutions. David has co-authored several Waite Group Press books, including *Visual Basic 5 Client/Server How-To*, *Visual Basic 4 Superbible*, *Visual Basic 5 Superbible*, and the *Visual Basic 6 Interactive Course*. When he's not programming, writing, and presenting, he can be found on the bike trails in Southern California or the golf course, and with his wife, Joanne, and two dogs (that he pretends he likes). He can be reached at `davidj@vb2java.com` (`http://www.vb2java.com`).

Don Kiely is the Director of Technology for SkyFire Group in Fairbanks, Alaska, developing Visual Basic, Web, and Internet applications for businesses in rural Alaska. He is a frequent contributor to several industry publications. He has a B.S. in Civil Engineering from the University of Notre Dame and an MBA from the University of Colorado, Boulder, but fortunately has learned the error of his ways. In his spare time he works on tourism and economic development projects throughout Alaska, with a particular interest in shifts from a subsistence to cash economy. He has written and co-authored several Visual Basic and Visual C++ books, including *Visual Basic Programmer's Guide to the Windows Registry* from Mabry Software, as well as *Visual Basic Database How-To* from Waite Group Press. You can reach him at `donkiely@computer.org`.

DEDICATIONS

I would like to dedicate this book to my Grandma Edna and my Father. Thank you for taking such good care of me when growing up. Thank you both for setting such a good example for me and loving me so much. And, thank you for your prayers and care, I could not have made it with out you. God bless.

—Noel Jerke

I would like to dedicate this book to my loving and supportive wife Felicia and our furry pets, Bailey and Laila. It's great to know I'm where I belong.

—George Szabo

To David Mendlen, for showing me the true power of Visual Basic.

—David Jung

To my father Paul and stepmother Sue. You showed me the value of hard work, strong ethics, and believing in the cause. I've had a fascinating life so far, and I owe much of it to you.

—Don Kiely

A C K N O W L E D G M E N T S

First I would like to thank an excellent writing team for the great work they did on the previous version of this book. Obviously it was well received or we would not be working on this rewrite! Once again I am very thankful for my wife who has been very supportive and encouraging. Many hours go into learning, coding, testing, writing, and editing a book. Maria has been there through each hour with love and GREAT patience. I would like to also thank the great team we have at Judd's OnLine. Thank you for the hard work and dedication. May we have continued success! Last but certainly not least I thank the Lord Jesus for providing me with the skills and capabilities to write this book.

—Noel Jerke

No one knows how much pain goes into writing a book until they write one. When it is complete you swear you'll never do it again. Then a season later you're starting all over. Fortunately I didn't write this book alone. I truly appreciate the patience and support given by Ron Gallagher and Brian Gill as well as the staff of people who help to review, improve, and prepare the technical subject matter. Books are truly a team project. Thanks for letting me be a part of the team.

—George Szabo

I want to thank my wife, Joanne, for her enduring love and support. As crazy as things might have gotten, she was always there with positive encouragement and support (and understood when I couldn't take the dogs for their walk). Thanks to the rest of my family and friends who understood that I "couldn't come out and play." A special thanks to everyone at Waite Group Press/Macmillan Computer Publishing for their support and putting this project together. And last but certainly not least, I would like to thank David Mendlen. Without his encouragement and guidance, I would have never discovered the true power of Visual Basic.

—David Jung

Any book project, particularly one that has unyielding deadlines, is the collective effort of several people. My coauthors are some of the best in the business, and it has been an honor to once again collaborate with them. Margot Maley at Waterside has been a big help in smoothing my participation in this project and slaying the beast. I've had the pleasure of meeting a few of the members of the VB, VBA, and Office teams at Microsoft over the last year, and I am impressed with their dedication to producing nothing less than excellent development tools. And I continue to be eternally grateful to Julia and Tom for helping me understand what I should do with my life.

—Don Kiely

TELL US WHAT YOU THINK!

As the reader of this book, *you* are our most important critic and commentator. We value your opinion and want to know what we're doing right, what we could do better, what areas you'd like to see us publish in, and any other words of wisdom you're willing to pass our way.

As the Executive Editor for the Programming and Borland Press team at Macmillan Computer Publishing, I welcome your comments. You can fax, email, or write me directly to let me know what you did or didn't like about this book—as well as what we can do to make our books stronger.

Please note that I cannot help you with technical problems related to the topic of this book, and that due to the high volume of mail I receive, I might not be able to reply to every message.

When you write, please be sure to include this book's title and author as well as your name and phone or fax number. I will carefully review your comments and share them with the author and editors who worked on the book.

Fax: 317-817-7070
E-mail: `prog@mcp.com`
Mail: Brian Gill, Executive Editor
         Programming and Borland Press Team
         Macmillan Computer Publishing
         201 West 103rd Street
         Indianapolis, IN 46290 USA

INTRODUCTION

Visual Basic 6 Client/Server How-To is a practical step-by-step guide to implementing distributed client/server solutions, including the Internet and intranet, using the tools provided in Visual Basic 6.0. This book addresses the needs of programmers looking for answers to real-world questions and assures them that what they create really works. It also helps simplify the client/server development process by providing a framework for solutions development.

Question-and-Answer Format

The How-To format of this book clearly defines the question of the tasks tackled in each section. Every How-To includes an overview of how the task will be accomplished, followed by an explanation of the project code, and finalized by a thorough demonstration of the techniques used. At the end of each How-To are comments on how to accomplish additional variations on the task performed.

Expected Level of the Reader

This book is designed to be used by all levels of readers. However, basic knowledge of Visual Basic programming is assumed. Each How-To is given a complexity rating at the beginning of the discussion. The three levels are Beginning, Intermediate, and Advanced. The How-To's with a Beginning rating are straightforward for any entry-level Visual Basic programmer. The Intermediate How-To's go more in depth while the advanced How-To's employ more difficult techniques and are intended for experienced Visual Basic programmers.

How This Book Is Organized

Visual Basic 6 Client/Server How-To is divided into 10 chapters as follows.

Chapter 1, "Client/Server Basics"

This chapter provides an introduction to client/server basics and is especially helpful in explaining client/server development. It also gives a general overview of Visual Basic 6's strategic role in the client/server world.

Chapter 2, "Getting Connected"

The How-To's in this chapter demonstrate the various ways you can make a connection to a database. Because the Enterprise Edition's Active Data Object and Remote Data Objects are based on ODBC, the examples here discuss the different ways to make a connection with connect strings, the ODBC API, and other ODBC techniques. The final How-To discusses ways to determine the best connection for your particular application given the existing hardware, software, and network setup.

Chapter 3, "Data Objects"

In this chapter you will explore basic methods for ADO and RDO methods, along with more advanced topics such as stored procedures, resultset management, and asynchronous queries.

Chapter 4, "User Interface Design"

The How-To's in this chapter demonstrate the standard user interface design for your client-tier applications. Each How-To builds on the last to produce a fully integrated and feature-rich application interface. The sample application used throughout the chapter is a simple image-tracking database. This program will allow you to categorize and track all bitmap (BMP) and icon (ICO) format fields on your system. In addition, this chapter discusses how to display large amounts of data to the user. Through the use of business components, optimizing your applications can become much easier. Several of the How-To's demonstrate different data-displaying methods for a fictitious hotel chain.

Chapter 5, "Object-Oriented Application Development"

This chapter provides an introduction to the basic fundamentals of object-oriented analysis and design and, most importantly, how to apply these techniques to your client/server programs. You will discover how to implement an object model and build a simple three-tier application utilizing ActiveX components.

Chapter 6, "Business Objects"

The toughest part of building business objects is knowing where to start. This chapter shows how to set up an ActiveX project that you can use as the starting point for all your business objects.

Chapter 7, "Basic SQL Server Management"

This chapter focuses on the basics of building a database using Microsoft SQL Server 6.5, as well as optimizing its tips and tricks. This chapter's How-To's guide you through the graphical user interface portion of the SQL Enterprise manager. The Data Definition Language (DDL) equivalents are discussed in the "How It Works" sections.

Chapter 8, "Visual Basic and Active Server Pages on the Web"

Building Internet and intranet applications is becoming important in the corporate environment. With Active Server Pages you can use a flavor of Visual Basic, Visual Basic Scripting Edition, to build client/server applications. On the server is Internet Information Server 4.0 and the ASP pages as well as SQL Server. On the client end is the Web browser. And, with Visual Basic 6.0 you can build components for use in the Active Server Pages.

Chapter 9, "Building IIS Applications with Visual Basic 6.0"

One of the key new features in Visual Basic 6.0 is the capability to create applications that run in Internet Information Server (IIS) and are accessed from a Web browser. Instead of relying on scripting code as the primary programming tool for the Web, you can build robust client/server applications that run on the Web with Visual Basic. This chapter demonstrates how to build several different kinds of IIS applications.

Chapter 10, "Reporting and Data Connection Support"

This chapter provides a series of How-To's for the decision support aspect of client/server development. Because Microsoft Access has opened up its reporting facilities to Visual Basic through the use of OLE, this chapter provides special solutions crafted around the use of Visual Basic 6, Microsoft Office, Microsoft Access, and Crystal Reports.

NOTE

Chapters 8 and 9 require that either the Personal Web Server for Windows 95/98 or Internet Information Server 3.0 or higher be installed on the system.

About the CD-ROM

The CD-ROM bundled with *Visual Basic 6 Client/Server How-To* contains all the source code from the How-To's developed in the book, as well as additional third-party utilities. Please refer to the file `readme.1st` on the root level of the CD-ROM to learn more.

What follows are directions for copying files to your hard drive for Windows 95/98 and Windows NT 4.0. The easiest way to copy files using Windows 95/98 and Windows NT 4.0 is by using the desktop.

1. Double-click the My Computer icon. Your drives will appear in a window on the desktop.

2. Double-click your hard drive and create a new folder, such as VB 6 Client Server How-To, by selecting File, New, Folder from the window menu. A folder called New Folder will be created on your hard drive with the name highlighted. Type the name you want and press Enter.

3. Go back to your drive window and double-click the icon that represents your CD-ROM drive. You will see a window that has a SOURCE folder in it. Double-click the SOURCE folder to open it.

4. Select the directories you want to copy (Ctrl+click the folders if you're not copying all of them) and drag your selection to the directory you created on your hard drive. You might need to reposition your windows to make your hard drive windows visible.

NOTE

When Windows copies a CD-ROM, it does not change the read-only attribute for the files it copies. You can view the files, but you cannot edit them until you remove this attribute. To do this, select the files. Right-click and select Properties, then click the Read-only check box to deselect it and then click OK.

CHAPTER 1

CLIENT/SERVER BASICS

CLIENT/SERVER BASICS

by George Szabo

How do I...

Clearly, the future of application development lies in standardized distributed components where the business logic can reside within its own tier and be located on centralized servers. Rather than recompiling and deploying 1,000 client applications, you would modify and redeploy your business services on their own centralized servers. How will client applications be able to use business logic that exists on another machine? An object framework is essential to achieving this goal. This object framework is embodied in the Component Object Model (COM) and Microsoft's ActiveX standard. The Visual Basic 6 Professional and Enterprise Edition enables developers to exploit this object framework as they create a new generation of client/server solutions that take advantage of the latest technologies.

Microsoft has crafted Visual Basic to allow the creation of reusable components—invisible to the client—that can be deployed and accessed on remote machines of the components' services. This is done through support for the distributed Component Object Model as well as HTTP. Services can be grouped into three logical categories: user services, business services, and data services. These logical areas can contain numerous physical components that can reside anywhere from the client's machine to a remote server across the world, depending on what business problem needs to be solved. Robust, scalable, maintainable systems are what it's all about.

1.1 Discover Client/Server and Other Computing Architectures

This section introduces three system architectures: centralized, file server, and client/server. You will explore a high-level view of these architectures and the weaknesses that encouraged the introduction of a client/server option.

1.2 Understand File Server Versus Client/Server Database Deployment

Some developers believe you can develop a client/server application by using a Microsoft Access database file (MDB) placed on a network file server. This chapter reviews the significant differences between deploying a database file on a file server and deploying an SQL database engine on a network server.

1.3 Learn About the Two-Tier Versus Three-Tier Client/Server Model

Many client/server systems have been developed and deployed. Most of them have been two-tier applications. The two-tier model has benefits as well as drawbacks. This section explores the advantages and disadvantages of a two-tier versus a three-tier approach.

1.4 Investigate the Component Object Model

The key to a distributed client/server application is the capability to break apart the physical restrictions of a single compiled EXE and to partition the business model into sharable, reusable components. This section explores the critical importance of the Component Object Model (COM) in making this possible.

1.5 Discover the Service Model

When an application is no longer a single physical entity but rather consists of a collection of partitioned logic, it is important to have a design strategy that allows a structured approach to the creation of client/server applications. The service model promotes the idea that, based on the services they provide, all physical components fall into one of three categories: user services, business services, and data services.

1.6 Understand Client/Server Deployments Using Components

Understanding that application logic must be partitioned into physical components and that these components should be designed logically according to the service model, this section illustrates three typical client/server deployments: single tier, two tier, and a multitier distributed deployment model.

1.7 Learn More About the Client/Server Development Tools Included with Visual Basic 6

To help implement new ideas, you need new tools. Visual Basic 6 Enterprise Edition comes with some special tools that enable you to create and remotely deploy components. This section introduces you to these tools and to their roles in the development of a Visual Basic 6 client/server solution.

1.8 Create a SourceSafe Project

Developing component-based client/server applications provides the opportunity for powerful teamwork. Each person will build a piece of the puzzle. Visual Basic comes with Visual SourceSafe, which enables you to catalog code as well as manage team projects in Visual Basic. This section provides a glimpse of this useful tool, which extends Visual Basic into a new league of application development tools.

COMPLEXITY
BEGINNING

1.1 How do I...

Discover client/server and other computing architectures?

COMPATIBILITY: VISUAL BASIC 4, 5, 6

Contrary to many predictions over the past decade, the mainframe computer is here and is not going away any time soon. During the '60s and '70s, companies that needed real computing power turned to the mainframe computer, which represents a "centralized" system architecture. Figure 1.1 shows a diagram of two critical components: the server and the client machines.

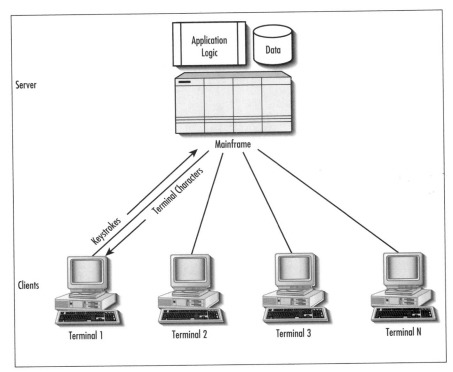

Figure 1.1 The centralized architecture

Of course, in this centralized architecture the only thing that moves between the client and the host machine is the marshaling of keystrokes and the return of terminal characters. *Marshaling* is the process of packaging interface parameters and sending them across process boundaries. In the mainframe environment, keystrokes are marshaled from the terminal to the host. This is arguably not what people are referring to when they discuss client/server implementations. Pros for a centralized architecture include excellent security and centralized administration because both the application logic and the data reside on the same machine. Cons begin with the price tag. Mainframe computers are expensive to buy, lease, maintain, use—the list goes on. Another disadvantage of this centralized architecture is the limitation that both the application and database live within the same mainframe process. There is no way to truly partition an application's logic beyond the mainframe's physical limitations.

During the 1980s, the personal computer charged into the business world. With it came a wealth of computing resources like printers, modems, and hard-disk storage. Businesses that could never have afforded a mainframe solution embraced the personal computer. Soon after the introduction of the personal computer to the business world came the introduction of the local area network (LAN) and the use of file server architectures. Figure 1.2 demonstrates a simple file server architecture.

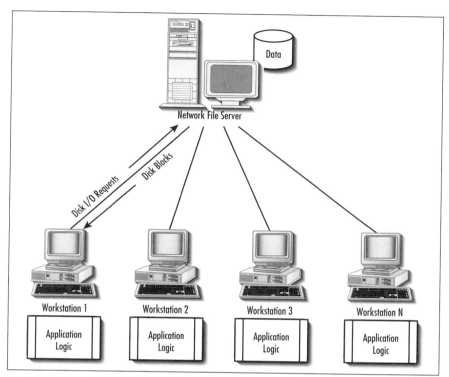

Figure 1.2 File server architecture

The file server system created a 180-degree change in implementation from the mainframe. As depicted in Figure 1.2, application logic was now executed on the client workstation rather than on the server. In the file server architecture, a centralized server, or servers, provided access to computing resources such as printers and large hard drives. Pros of this architecture are a low-cost entry point and flexible deployment. A business could buy a single computer, then two, and so on. A file server architecture is flexible; it enables you to add and reduce computer resources as necessary. Cons of a file server architecture include the fact that all application logic is executed on the client machine. The file server serves files; that is its job. Even though an application's files might be located on a network drive, the application actually runs in the client machine's memory space and using the client's processor. This means that the client machine must have sufficient power to run whatever application is needed or perform whatever task needs to be performed. Improving the performance and functionality of business applications is always a hot topic until the discussion includes the need to upgrade personal computers to take advantage of new application enhancements.

Even after personal computers became a powerful force in the business workplace, they still lacked the powerful computing resources available in a mainframe. The client/server application architecture was introduced to address issues of cost and performance. Client/server applications allowed for applications to run on both the user workstation and the server—no longer referred to as a file server (see Figure 1.3).

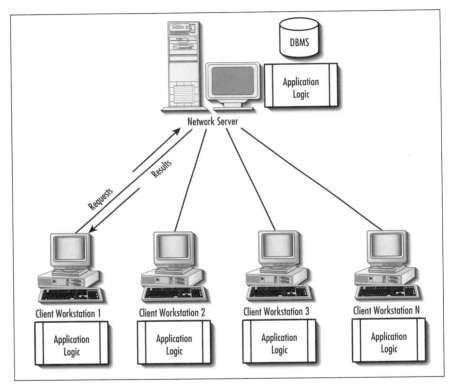

Figure 1.3 The client/server architecture

In this architecture, two separate applications, operating independently, could work together to complete a task. A well-known implementation of this concept is SQL-based database management systems (DBMS). SQL stands for structured English query language. In Figure 1.3 you can see that, unlike the file server architecture, the request that goes out to the server is not simply a request for a file (in the form of disk input/output requests, which are returned as a series of input/output blocks). Instead, actual instructions can be communicated to an application running on the server, and the server can execute those instructions itself and send back a response.

Client/server refers to a process involving at least two independent entities, one a client and the other a server. The client makes a request of the server, and the server services the request. A request can take the form of an SQL query submitted to an SQL database engine. The database engine in turn processes the request and returns a resultset. In this example, two independent processes work together to accomplish a single task. This exemplifies the client/server relationship.

Windows printing and the Print Manager is an example of a client/server relationship. A Windows application, such as Word or Excel, prepares your document and submits it to the Print Manager. The Print Manager provides the service of queuing up requests and sending them to your printer, monitors the job's progress, and then notifies the application when the job is complete. In this example, the Print Manager is the server; it provides the service of queuing and processing your print job. The application submitting the document for printing is the client. This example demonstrates how a client/server relationship can exist between applications that might not be database-related.

The most popular client/server applications today revolve around the use of SQL database management systems (DBMS) such as Oracle and Microsoft SQL Server. These applications, often referred to as *back ends*, provide support for the storage, manipulation, and retrieval of the businesses' persistent data. These systems use structured query language (SQL) as a standard method for submitting client requests. If you are not familiar with SQL, you can learn more from several good books that are available, such as Sams Publishing's *Sams Teach Yourself SQL in 21 Days*. Microsoft's SQL Server comes with an online help file that also can help you with proper SQL syntax.

Comments

Although both the mainframe and file server-based systems continue to provide service to business, they fail to provide a truly scalable framework for building competitive business solutions. The major factor is that logic must be executed on either the mainframe in a centralized architecture, or on the client in a file server-based architecture.

As stated earlier, a client/server application is composed of at least two pieces: a client that makes requests and a server that services those requests. For faster, more cost-effective application performance these pieces can be separated and application logic can be distributed between them. In the next section you will review a critical difference between database deployment on a file server and implementing a database system such as SQL Server or Oracle on a network server that explains why the performance difference can be so dramatically better for client/server applications.

1.2 How do I...
Understand file server versus client/server database deployment?

COMPATIBILITY: VISUAL BASIC 4, 5, 6

With the popularity of Microsoft Access and the proliferation of systems that use the Microsoft database file (MDB) to store data, it must be mentioned that even though the MDB allows multiuser access, it is not a true client/server implementation. When you use an MDB as part of your application, you are using a file server implementation. To take full advantage of what a client/server architecture has to offer, you must understand the difference between a file server-based implementation and a client/server-based implementation. Figures 1.4 and 1.5 demonstrate the fundamental difference between these two architectures.

In Figure 1.4, the query is never sent to the server; instead, the query is evaluated and processed at the client. The query logic to access the MDB realizes that it needs a table of data to process the request, so it requests the entire 30,000-row table across the network before it applies the WHERE clause of the Select statement, which specifies that you are looking for a record with a Social Security Number equal to 555-55-5555. When an SQL statement is used against an MDB, it is processed by the client machine and only a file I/O request is sent across the network to retrieve the required data in the form of disk blocks. No logic is executed on the server except the transferring of file disk blocks. This is not what is referred to as "client/server," but is simply a file server. Placing an MDB out on a network drive does allow multiuse, but only because of client-side logic that references a shared record-locking file for the MDB file in question. The lock file is comprised of the MDB name and an extension of .LDB.

> **NOTE**
> Don't confuse Microsoft Access the application with Microsoft Access the database. In the example used here the MDB refers to a situation in which you use Access to store and retrieve information directly in its own proprietary database format. Access also allows you to attach to real DBMS systems like SQL or Oracle databases. In this case you can achieve true client/server performance.

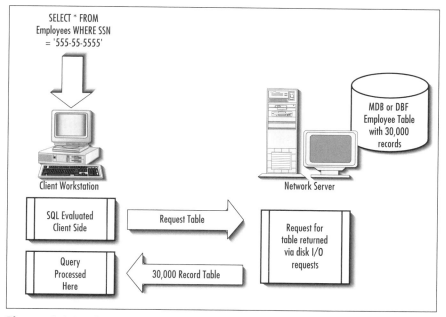

Figure 1.4 An SQL process on a file server-based system using an MDB

In the server-based architecture, the actual SQL statement is sent across the network and processed by an application running locally on the server machine, as shown in Figure 1.5. Because the SQL statement is processed on the server, only the results must be sent back to the client. This is a vast improvement over the file-based architecture. If your query is looking to find an individual based on Social Security Number, a resultset of one matching record (rather than the whole 30,000-record table) would be passed back over the network. A major benefit of a client/server application is reduced network traffic and, in most cases, an incredibly faster execution time.

The differences shown in Figures 1.4 and 1.5 clearly illustrate a significant advantage of a client/server implementation.

Consider the following: It would be impractical to give each employee a high-speed duplex laser printer but, by centralizing the printer and allowing people to share it as a resource, everyone benefits from it. The same is true with the database server. Because the query is processed by the server where the database engine is located and not on the clients' machine, a company can throw money into a powerful server and all the clients will benefit from the extra muscle.

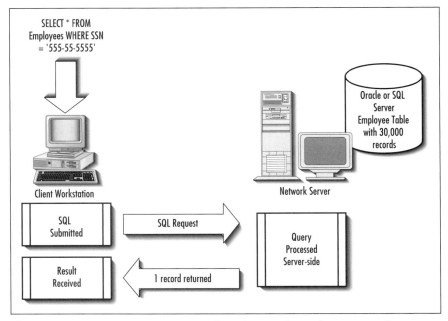

Figure 1.5 An SQL process on a client/server-based system using an SQL database management system

Comments

Use of an MDB on a file server does not mean that queries are actually processed by the server. Only when full back-end database systems like Oracle and SQL Server are deployed does a query actually get processed by the server instead of the client.

Deploying an MDB on a network file server is not always the wrong thing to do. Implementation of true back-end database systems requires higher levels of expertise than a simple Microsoft Access MDB deployment. If the amount of data being stored and retrieved is small (you must be the judge of this), then a file server solution might be a better solution. Clearly, network traffic will become an issue as a system grows, but you can always graduate your MDB file to an SQL Server database when the time is right.

Tools like the Upsizing Wizard (available from Microsoft) make the migration easier. After you decide that implementing a client/server solution is the right choice, you will need to choose between a two-tier and three-tier model. In the next section you will review the differences between two-tier and three-tier or n-tier client/server models.

1.3   How do I...
Learn about the two-tier versus three-tier client/server model?

COMPATIBILITY: VISUAL BASIC 4, 5, 6

It is becoming clear that the issue is not one of simply processing transactions and generating reports, but rather of creating an information system that can change with business needs—needs that mandate tighter budgets and higher quality. To respond to the challenges being presented by the business environment as well as by the Web, a new three-tier or n-tier client/server approach has been introduced. *n-tier* refers to the idea that there are no limits to the number of tiers that could be introduced to the client/server model. To begin this discussion, it is important to review the current two-tier approach.

Two-Tier Client/Server Model

The two-tier model is tied to the physical implementation: a desktop machine operating as a client, and a network server housing the back-end database engine. In the two-tier model, logic is split between these two physical locations, the client and the server. In a two-tier model, the front-end piece is commonly being developed in PowerBuilder, Visual Basic, or some other 4GL. The key point to remember is that, in a two-tier model, business logic for your application must physically reside on the client or be implemented on the back end within the DBMS in the form of triggers and stored procedures. Both triggers and stored procedures are precompiled collections of SQL statements and control-of-flow statements. Consider a situation in which you set up a series of stored procedures to support a particular application's needs. Meanwhile, the developers of five other applications are making similar efforts to support their own needs, all in the same database. Sure, there are naming conventions and definitions that indicate who owns what object, but the bottom line is that this scenario makes implementing and maintaining business rules downright ugly.

Paradigms, which implement a strict two-tier architecture, make the process of developing client/server applications look easy, such as the data window in PowerBuilder where a graphical window of fields is magically bound to the back-end data source. In Visual Basic, use of any data controls that provide a graphical link to the back-end data source creates a two-tier client/server application because these implementations of application development directly tie the graphical user interface to back-end data access. The upside is that data access is simplified, and very rapid development of applications is therefore possible. The GUI is bound directly to the data source, and all the details of data manipulation are handled automatically. However, this strength is also a weakness. Although data access is simplified, it is also less flexible. Often you will not have complete control over your interactions with the data source because they are being managed for you. Of course, this extra management uses additional resources on the client and can result in poor performance of your applications.

A two-tier client/server model has several critical limitations:

✔ Not scalable. The inability of a two-tier approach to grow beyond the physical boundaries of a client machine and a server machine prevents this model from being scalable.

✔ Unmanageable. Because you cannot encapsulate business rules and deploy them centrally, sharing common processes and reusing your work is difficult at best.

✔ Poor performance. The binding of the graphical interface to the data source consumes major resources on the client machine, which results in poor performance and, unfortunately, unhappy clients.

Three-Tier Client/Server Model

The limited effectiveness of two-tier client/server solutions ushered in an improved model for client/server development. The three-tier client/server model is based on the capability to build partitioned applications. Partitioning an application breaks up your code into logical components. The service model, discussed in How-To 1.5, suggests that these components can be logically grouped into three tiers: user services, business services, and data services. After an application has been developed by using this model and technique, each component can then be deployed to whichever machine will provide the best performance, depending on your situation and the current business need. Figure 1.6 shows a physical implementation of the three-tier client/server model. How-To's 1.4 and 1.5 discuss partitioning, components, and the service model in depth.

The following benefits illustrate the value of distributed three-tier client/server development:

✔ Reuse. The time you invest in designing and implementing components is not wasted because you can share them among applications.

✔ Performance. Because you can deploy your components on machines other than the client workstation, you have the ability to shift processing load from a client machine that might be underpowered to a server with extra horsepower. This flexibility in deployment and design enables you, as a developer, to take advantage of the best possible methods for each aspect of your application's execution, and results in better performance.

✔ Manageability. Encapsulation of your application's services into components enables you to break down large, complex applications into more manageable pieces.

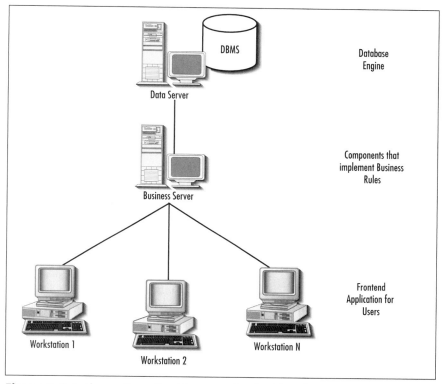

Figure 1.6 A three-tier client/server physical implementation

✔ Maintenance. The centralization of components for reuse has an added benefit. They become easier to redeploy when modifications are made, thus keeping pace with business needs.

Comments

Three-tier development is not the answer to every situation. Good partitioning and component design take time and expertise, both of which are in short supply. Additionally, three-tier client/server development, like any development, requires the support and commitment of the enterprise's powers that be. Two-tier client/server development is a much quicker way of taking advantage of SQL database engines and can fit the bill if both money and time are running out.

On the other hand, if you are looking to create systems to support a business as it grows and competes in today's marketplace, or a Web-based application that must be ready for success, a component-based client/server model gives a great return on investment. As mentioned earlier, the benefits of a three-tier approach are the ability to reuse your work, manage large projects, simplify maintenance, and improve overall performance of your business solutions. The following section introduces you to the Component Object Model and the concept of partitioning, which play a key role in making three-tier client/server applications possible.

COMPLEXITY
INTERMEDIATE

1.4 How do I...
Investigate the Component Object Model?

COMPATIBILITY: VISUAL BASIC 4, 5, 6

The Component Object Model (COM) is a general architecture for component software. This means that it is a standard, not an implementation. COM says this is how you should allow components to intercommunicate, but someone else (ActiveX) has to do it. ActiveX accomplishes the physical implementation of COM. Originally, ActiveX was called OLE (Object Linking and Embedding). ActiveX not only includes the OLE implementation of COM but also improves on the OLE implementation by extending capabilities to take advantage of the Internet. This is done in the form of ActiveX controls, as well as support for DCOM (Distributed Component Object Model), discussed in the "Distributed Component Object Model (DCOM)" section of this How-To.

Why is this important? So far, the discussion of client/server has shown the need for a design model that allows encapsulation of critical business logic away from the mire of database design and front-end code. An example of logic used to support the business could be a rule that prohibits orders for amounts of more than $500 to be placed without a manager's approval. This business rule can now be implemented with code in a component that is centralized on its own server, which makes it easier to modify if necessary. If the rule changes to also allow supervisors to approve orders of more than $500, the change can be made much more easily and quickly to a centralized component of code rather than by redeploying a new executable to every desktop.

So the answer suggested here is to partition the business logic out of the front-end and back-end applications and into its own set of components. The question is, how are these components supposed to talk to each other? How are you going to install these components on a network where your client applications can use them as if they were running locally on their computers? OLE and the Component Object Model are the answer.

In creating the COM, Microsoft sought to solve these specific problems:

✔ Interoperability. How can developers create unique components that work seamlessly with other components regardless of who creates them?

✔ Versioning. When a component is being used by other components or applications, how can you alter or upgrade the component without affecting all the components and applications that use it?

✔ Language independence. How can components written in different languages still work together?

✔ Transparent cross-process interoperability. How can developers write components to run in-process or out-of-process (and eventually cross-network), using one simple programming model?

If you are using Visual Basic today, then you have no doubt experienced the benefits of COM. All the third-party controls, as well as Visual Basic itself, take advantage of standards set by COM and implemented through what are referred to as *ActiveX technologies*. What this means to you is that objects based on the Component Object Model—objects you can write in Visual Basic, C++, or some other language—have the capability to work together regardless of the language used to create them. Because all these components know how to work together, you can purchase components from others or build them yourself and reuse them at any time during the business-system life cycle.

In-Process and Out-of-Process Servers

A component, also referred to as a *server*, is either *in-process*, which means that its code executes in the same process space as the client application (this is a DLL), or *out-of-process*, which means that it runs in another process on the same machine or in another process on a remote machine (this is an .EXE file). From these scenarios you can see that three types of servers can be created: in-process, local, and remote. Both local and remote servers must be out-of-process.

As you create components you will need to choose the type of server, based on the requirements of implementation and deployment. Components can be of any size—from those that encapsulate a few functions to larger, very robust implementations of a company's way of doing business. The powerful aspect of these component objects is that they look the same to client applications as well as to fellow components. The code used to access a component's services is the same, regardless of whether the component is deployed as in-process, local, or remote.

Distributed Component Object Model (DCOM)

The Distributed Component Object Model (DCOM) was previously referred to as Network OLE. DCOM is a protocol that enables applications to make object-oriented *remote procedure calls* (RPC) in *distributed computing environments* (DCE). Using DCOM, an ActiveX component or any component that supports DCOM can communicate across multiple network transport protocols, including the Internet Hypertext Transport Protocol (HTTP). DCOM provides a framework for the following:

✔ Data marshaling between components

✔ Client- and server-negotiated security levels, based on the capabilities of distributed computing environments' (DCEs) remote procedure calls (RPCs)

✔ Versioning of interfaces through the use of universally unique identifiers (UUIDs)

Comments

It is interesting to note that originally OLE was said to stand for Object Linking and Embedding. Microsoft backed off that definition and said that objects written to support the Component Object Model are collectively called *component objects*. Because OLE supports the Component Object Model, OLE objects are referred to as component objects. Now Microsoft refers to these component objects as *ActiveX*. ActiveX components have been extended to support DCOM.

ActiveX is a physical implementation of the Component Object Model that provides the foundation for the creation of components which can encapsulate logic and be distributed to operate in-process, local, or remote. Visual Basic 6 has been extended to enable the creation of ActiveX servers. Visual Basic's capability to create components in the form of ActiveX DLLs (in-process servers) and ActiveX EXEs (local or remote servers) makes three-tier client/server applications easier to create than ever before.

Using Visual Basic, you can create applications that are partitioned into several separate physical components. Those components can then be placed transparently on any machine within your network, as well as across the Internet, and they can talk to each other. The following section introduces you to the service model, which suggests a logical rather than a physical way of viewing how applications should be partitioned into components.

COMPLEXITY
INTERMEDIATE

1.5 How do I...
Discover the service model?

COMPATIBILITY: VISUAL BASIC 4, 5, 6

The service model is a logical way to group the components you create. Although this model is not language specific, this book discusses the service model and how it is implemented by using what is available in Visual Basic 6. The service model is based on the concept that every tier is a collection of components that provide a common type of service either to each other or to components in the tier immediately adjacent.

The following three types of services are used in the creation of business solutions:

✔ User services

✔ Business services

✔ Data services

Each of these types correlates to a tier in a three-tier client/server architecture. Figure 1.7 shows physical components (DLLs, EXEs, database triggers, and database-stored procedures) grouped logically into the three service types. Note that DLL components and EXE components can be used to encapsulate logic in any tier. In fact, the only objects that are not in every tier are triggers and stored procedures because they are database specific.

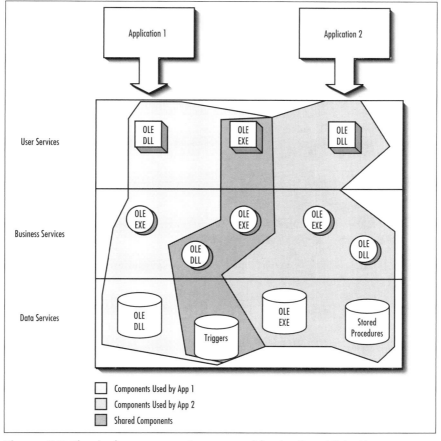

Figure 1.7 Physical components grouped logically within the services tiers

Figure 1.7 also shows a very important benefit of using components, which is the ability to make a component's services available to more than a single application. Notice that the shaded areas overlap where components are used by both application 1 and application 2. Reuse is a powerful aspect of the service model. The following basic rules for intercomponent communication must be followed in the service model:

✔ Components can request services from fellow components in their current tier and any tier below or above a component's tier.

✔ Requests cannot skip tiers. User services components cannot communicate directly with components in the data services tier and vice versa.

Often the service model is referred to as a layered approach. The typical use of the term *layer* refers to a process in which one layer must speak to the next layer and move from top to bottom and then back up. This does not correctly describe the way components communicate within the service model because a component can interact with other components in the same layer as well as those above and below it. The service model is meant to help you decide how to partition application logic into physical components, but it does not deal with the actual physical deployment of the software components. By understanding the three service tiers, you can begin to make decisions about which application logic you should encapsulate within a single component as well as within the various tiers. The following sections discuss the different types of services defined in the service model.

User Services

Components in the user services tier provide the visual interface that a client will use to view information and data. Components in this layer are responsible for contacting and requesting services from other components in the user services tier or in the business services tier. It is important to note that even though a component resides in the user services tier, one of the services provided to a user is the ability to perform business functions. User services play a role in doing business. Even though the business logic may be encapsulated in components of the business services tier, the user services component enables the user to have access to the whole process.

User services are normally, but not always, contained in the user application. A user service such as common company dialog boxes could be compiled into a DLL and made available locally on a client's machine. Perhaps you want to implement a standard set of error messages, but you don't want to deploy it to every machine. You could take that user service, compile it into an ActiveX EXE, and deploy it remotely on a shared server so that everyone could use it.

WARNING

If the Error message component is placed on a central server, it should only contain text string error messages and should not display a dialog box. If a remote ActiveX server displays a dialog box, it appears on the server rather than on the user's workstation. Refer to Chapter 6, "Business Objects," for more information on this topic.

Business Services

Because user services cannot directly contact the data services tier, it is the responsibility of the business services components to serve as bridges to alternative tiers. Business components provide business services that complete business tasks such as verifying that a customer is not over his or her credit limit. Rather than implementing business rules through a series of triggers and stored procedures, business components provide the service of implementing formal procedures and defined business rules. So why go through all the trouble of encapsulating the business logic in a business component or set of components? For robust, reusable, maintainable applications.

Business services components also serve to buffer the user from direct interaction with the database. The business tasks that will be executed by business services components, such as entering a patient record or printing a provider list, should be defined by the application's requirements. One overwhelming reason to partition out business services into components is the knowledge that business rules have the highest probability for change and, in turn, have the highest probability for requiring the rewriting and redeployment of an application.

Business rules are defined as policies that control the flow of business tasks. An example of a business rule might be a procedure that applies a late charge to a person's bill if payment is not received by a certain date. It is very common for business rules to change more frequently than the tasks they support. For this reason, business rules are excellent targets for encapsulation into components, thus separating the business logic from the application logic itself. The advantage here is that if the policy for applying late charges changes to include the stipulation that they cannot be sent to relatives of the boss, then you will need to change the logic in your shared business component only, rather than in every client application.

Data Services

Data services involve all the typical data chores, including the retrieval and modification of data as well as the full range of other database-related tasks. The key to data services is that the rules of business are not implemented here. Although a data service component is responsible for managing and satisfying the requests submitted by a business component, or even a fellow data services component, implementing the rules of business is not a responsibility.

Data services can be implemented as objects in a particular database management system (DBMS) in the form of triggers or stored procedures. Alternatively, the data services could provide access to heterogeneous data sources on multiple platforms on any number of servers or mainframes. A properly implemented data services tier should allow changes to take place in the data services tier and related data sources without affecting the services being provided to business services components.

Comments

The service model is a logical—not a physical—view of working with components and application partitioning. Sometimes physical deployment of components might parallel the component's tier assignments, but this is neither necessary nor desired. In Figure 1.8, components in the service model have been mapped to one of three physical locations. They can reside on the client, on a network server (typically a business server), or on a second network server (typically a database engine server).

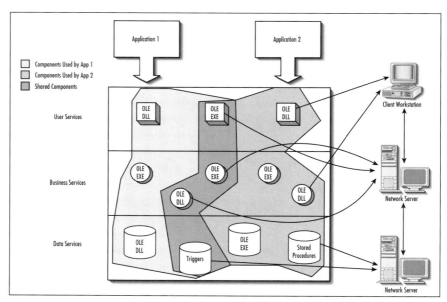

Figure 1.8 Simple physical deployment of components on a network

Figure 1.8 helps to illustrate the following key points with regard to the service model and physical deployment:

✔ Triggers and stored procedures from the data services tier must be deployed in the database back end. The reason is that these objects are

direct implementations of the database engine and are stored within the
database itself. This is shown by the direct mapping of the stored
procedures and triggers symbols within the data services tier to the
database server.

✔ To share a single common source of services, a component must be an
out-of-process remote Automation Server (ActiveX EXE) and be deployed
on a central server so that everyone can access it. In Figure 1.8, an ActiveX
EXE within the user services tier is mapped to the business server so that
multiple users can access it.

✔ Not all business logic is best deployed remotely. Due to performance
considerations, an in-process DLL provides better performance than an
ActiveX EXE and might be a wiser choice. In Figure 1.8, a DLL in the
business services tier represents this type of scenario. DLLs generally
cannot be utilized remotely, so the business services DLL must be
deployed to the user's workstation rather than to the business server.

One final comment about the idea of dual personality is that dual personality
is a powerful aspect of components that affects their design. Any component can
be both a client and a server. Consider a situation in which you design a
business services component to calculate book royalties. The royalty calculation
is a service that the Visual Basic component provides to any requester. To create
the calculation, the business component must have information about the
author's contract with the publisher. Your business services component becomes
a client of services rather than a server as it requests contract information from a
data services component. In this example, the royalty component is acting not
only as a server of royalty information but also as a client of data services. This is
a much more powerful implementation than the typical and more rigid
client/server relationship in which a client can't be a server, and vice versa. In
the next section you will review three physical deployment scenarios available
for client/server applications that utilize a three-tier client/server architecture.

COMPLEXITY
ADVANCED

1.6 How do I...
Understand client/server deploy-
ments using components?

COMPATIBILITY: VISUAL BASIC 4, 5, 6

The service model encourages the creation of components that encapsulate
common reusable functionality in a physical package—the ActiveX DLL or
ActiveX EXE. VB6 makes possible also the creation of ActiveX controls in the
form of OCXs, as well as the creation of ActiveX documents which are

applications that live inside a browser. Compiled into these physical formats, these pieces can be deployed on a practically infinite number of topologies. Before you review deployment options, you should understand the characteristics of the ActiveX DLL and ActiveX EXE. Both are ActiveX component objects and share a common interface based on the standards defined by the Component Object Model.

When considering which is the proper container for a particular component, you should consider the following about these two physical component implementations. A DLL is an in-process server. *In-process* refers to the fact that the DLL operates in the same process space as the application using it. Because a DLL is operating in the same process, it loads much more quickly than an EXE would. Additionally, a DLL cannot be deployed remotely, at least not without a trick or two. The trick being referred to here is that a DLL can be deployed remotely if the DLL is parented by an EXE component. The EXE would instantiate the DLL on the remote machine and provide an interface to the DLL's methods and properties. This process is referred to as *containment*. The parent component marshals requests between a client and the DLL.

In the case of an EXE, it is important to know that there are basically two types of ActiveX EXEs. The first type of EXE is deployed locally on a client machine (local ActiveX Automation Server); the second is a remotely deployed EXE (remote ActiveX Automation Server). ActiveX EXEs are always out-of-process servers, which means that they run in their own process space. Out-of-process servers can be deployed remotely on a network server and shared among all applications that have access to that server. On the downside, ActiveX EXEs take significantly longer to load than a DLL. Access to methods and properties of an ActiveX EXE component is much slower than when you're working with a DLL. After you place the EXE on a server, network traffic becomes an additional concern with regard to execution speed.

One final consideration is crash protection. This is an important consideration when you design components. A DLL operates in-process; if it dies, it takes the application with it because they share the same process space. On the other hand, an ActiveX EXE runs out-of-process; if a problem occurs, it might die but the application or component calling it will not die. This enables the calling application or component to handle the problem by either restarting the EXE or performing some other type of recovery. Fault tolerance can be designed into your systems to provide greater support for mission-critical execution. Finally, it is important to note that ActiveX EXEs can run on separate threads, while DLLs can only run within the thread of execution of the application or component calling it. Table 1.1 highlights the considerations presented thus far. You should keep these in mind when selecting the physical container for your component.

Table 1.1   ActiveX server types

COMPONENT	TYPE	PROS	CONS
DLL	In-process	Quick execution in-process	Local deployment only; no crash protection
EXE	Local out-of-process	Crash protection	Slower than DLL
EXE	Remote out-of-process	Remote execution, crash protection	Up to 100 times slower; affected by network traffic

Physical Deployments

The following four client/server deployments use the three-tier strategy shown here:

✔ Single server

✔ Business server

✔ Transaction server

✔ Web server

All figures in this section include the service model diagram from How-To 1.5. Each component has been given a letter (from A to L) to uniquely identify it. There is no specification as to whether the component is a DLL or EXE but you can refer to Figures 1.7 or 1.8 to reference this attribute.

Single-Server Deployment

In the single-server model shown in Figure 1.9, all components are split between the client machine and the network server. B, E, F, and J are all shared items; therefore, they had to be deployed on the network server so that others could have access to them.

It is true that components installed on a workstation can be shared with other workstations in a peer-to-peer configuration, but this is a very poor implementation idea. A workstation usually has less processing power than a server. Another reason to avoid deploying shared components on workstations is the headache it causes when you are trying to keep track of it all.

The single-server deployment model also runs the DBMS back-end engine on the network server. All the data services components are deployed on the network server as well. Application 1 is shown running on workstation 1. Notice that not only is there a user services component on workstation 1, but there is also a business services component, identified by the letter D. This is to suggest that there might be a need for locally deployed business services components, perhaps due to the need for speed of execution. Although it is not a good idea to partition components based on speed, which is not one of the factors considered on a logical service model level, you might find yourself in a situation in which speed is the number one concern. In this case, either local or in-process deployment of a component is possible. It doesn't take much to change a component from a DLL to an EXE with Visual Basic. For additional information, see Chapter 6, "Business Objects."

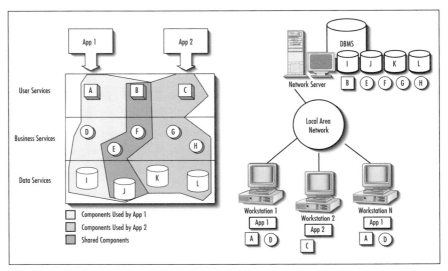

Figure 1.9 Single-server deployment of components on a network

Application Server Deployment

A second step in the deployment scenario is the business server deployment plan. Figure 1.10 shows the same service model diagram, but this time the physical deployment includes an additional network server, referred to as an *application server*. Its purpose is obvious: to provide a centralized location for all shared business components. Although meant as a home for your business components, the Application server usually houses all components that must be centrally shared. This might include user services components as well as those shown by component B in Figure 1.10.

Notice in Figure 1.10 that a user service component represented by the letter B is on the Application server. This makes sense because the Application server is a good centralized location for deployment and maintenance in this scheme.

All the data services components have been deployed to the Data server. If you refer to Figure 1.7 or 1.8 in the previous section, you will note that two of the four data services, trigger and store procedures, are labeled J and L in Figure 1.10. These components must be deployed on the same machine as the DBMS because they are integrated objects of the DBMS. In this deployment, all data services have been kept together to allow centralized administration of these pieces.

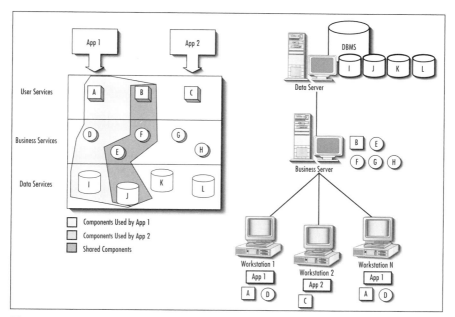

Figure 1.10 Business server deployment of components on a network

The components kept on each workstation have not changed from the previous deployment scenario to this one. This is worth noting because it suggests that after you set up your workstations and their applications, you can continue to enhance deployment schemes in the server arena transparent to the workstations. This powerful feature is made possible by the Remote Automation Connection Manager utility, which is discussed in the "Distributed Transaction Server Deployment" section.

One last point about this deployment diagram is that the connections of all workstations lead to the Application server. This might or might not be the actual physical implementation. Both the Business server and the Data server could be on the same network and be just as available, in which case Figure 1.10 simply shows the allowed communication path: User services talk to business services that talk to data services, and so on. This does not have to be only a logical deployment, however. If open database connectivity (ODBC) drivers are not installed on any of the workstations, and all communication with the data services components requires ODBC, then you have physically prevented this path. By eliminating a workstation's capability to directly access data you can create a much more secure environment, if that is a primary concern for your deployment. Remember that after ODBC is installed on a user's workstation a person could effectively install any number of data accessing packages that utilize ODBC drivers, thus providing a potential security risk. There are several security measures that you could take to prevent a renegade user from directly accessing production or warehouse data. Avoiding the installation of ODBC on every workstation is one step you could take.

Distributed Transaction Server Deployment

The third scenario discussed in this section is transaction server deployment. The word *distributed* is used in the name of this scenario to differentiate it from the use of Microsoft Transaction Server services, which can be utilized in all scenarios. Figure 1.11 shows a distributed transaction server deployment scheme. What does a transaction server do? It is an application whose purpose is to maintain and provide a pool of ActiveX server component objects in memory while providing security and context to the use of these components in a transaction. Remember that EXE components must be started and loaded into their own process space each time they are used. This is a huge cost to incur when you need to use one.

To offset the load-time cost of ActiveX EXEs, a transaction server creates a pool of these components. The transaction server then stands ready to pass clients an object reference to these preloaded components. After the client receives a reference to a preloaded component, the client can use the component directly without funneling requests through the transaction server. This is an important point. If all requests had to be funneled through the transaction server, the transaction server would soon become a bottleneck. The transaction server simply preloads components and hands out their addresses on request. When the client is finished with it, the component is released and a new instance of the component is loaded into the pool to await the next client request for a component.

What is a transaction? A transaction is a unit of work. If you make your components available, using Microsoft Transaction Server, you can create transactions using multiple components; if any of them fails you can roll all your actions backward. Let's take a banking transaction as an example. If you go to an automated teller machine and request money, it is very important that all the parts of that transaction be successful; otherwise, it's not a successful transaction (unit of work). Imagine your reaction if you inserted your card, entered your PIN number, and the machine debited your account but never gave you your money. Obviously, that would be an unsuccessful transaction. The understanding that a successful transaction contains multiple actions that must all be successful is what Microsoft Transaction Server provides. Of course, you must code the components and the transaction properly.

Figure 1.11 introduces the use of a transaction server. The transaction server becomes a type of switchboard operator, passing component references to requesting clients. If workstation 1 in Figure 1.11 requested use of component E, then workstation 1 would be able to use component E directly until the reference was released. This is depicted by the dotted line from workstation 1 to component E.

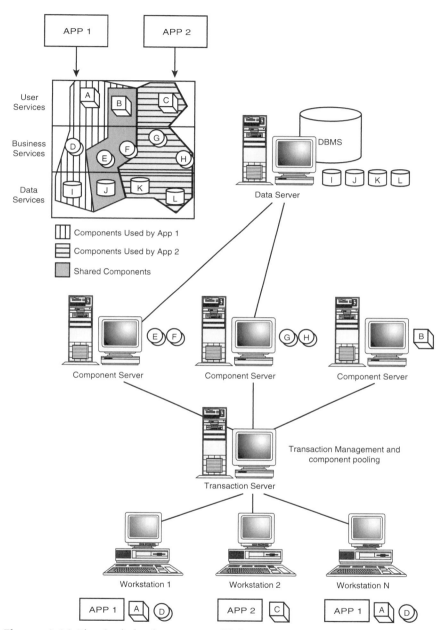

Figure 1.11 Physical deployment utilizing a transaction server and distributed components

Another important aspect of the transaction server deployment scenario is that components can be moved from one component server to another, based on load, in order to improve performance. As the components are moved from one location to another, you will only need to register the new location with the transaction server. The transaction server has the following responsibilities:

✔ Keeping a pool of ActiveX servers instantiated

✔ Passing requesting applications a reference to these servers

✔ Terminating references to the ActiveX server when it is no longer being used

✔ Validating usage of a component

✔ Managing the transaction participation of components

The transaction server sits between the workstations and the application servers.

Keep a Pool of ActiveX Servers Instantiated

In order for the transaction server to do its job, it must first be able to instantiate the components that it must maintain on the server. You will need to set up the transaction server machine so that it has access to all the other component servers. Additionally, you will need to use the Remote Connection Manager application to configure the network locations of these components. The benefit of this scenario is that you configure the location of the components at the transaction server machine. If a component is moved, you reconfigure the address at the transaction server, not at the workstation level. This is of huge importance in large deployments.

Pass References to These Servers to Requesting Applications

When a client requests a service of a component being maintained by the transaction server, the transaction server hands a reference to an available component in the pool. Depending on how many different components are being managed by the transaction server, this might not be a minor activity. This introduces the question of granularity when designing and implementing components in your system.

Granularity refers to how finely you will partition your services. For example, will you put 100 services in a single component because they all have to do with financial calculations, or will you give each calculation its own component? The larger component is easier to locate because all the calculations are in a single physical package, but giving each calculation its own physical package makes it easier to test and debug. And smaller components or more granular components seem to have a higher probability for reuse. To truly benefit from Microsoft Transaction Server you must create small stateless components and allow MTS to maintain the context of what is going on. This is covered in more detail in Chapter 6, "Business Objects."

Terminate References to the ActiveX Server when It Is No Longer Being Used

When a client finishes using a component, it drops all references to the component. When there are no references to an ActiveX server, this causes termination and it shuts down. When a component is terminated, the transaction server must adjust the pool and prepare for more requests. The transaction server can be configured to maintain pool levels at different values throughout the day, depending on expected demand.

Validate Usage of a Component

Another aspect of the transaction server is its capability to implement security. Part of the transaction server's design can and should be to know who is requesting a service. This information can be used to implement a security model. The transaction server could use the login and password to validate use of a component. Microsoft Transaction Server provides a management tool that enables you to define access to components based on roles. If a person belongs to a particular role, like administrator, then the rules and security context assigned to the administrator role are given to this person along with access to the component.

Manage the Transaction Participation of Components

When you create components that will participate in a transaction it is important to make the components as atomic and stateless as possible, thus enabling them to be used and released quickly. If a transaction requires more than one component, which it usually does, then Microsoft Transaction Server provides the necessary transaction management. The participation of components is managed and actions are either committed or rolled back based on overall success of the total transaction. Remember that components must be coded to take advantage of participation in a transaction. Only some Database ODBC drivers, level three and above, provide this type of transaction participation support. SQL Server provides transaction commit and rollback via MTS. If you are using a different DBMS you must verify that it will work properly through MTS. For more information about components and MTS please refer to Chapter 6, "Business Objects."

Web Server Deployment

The Web server deployment scenario is the fourth and final one discussed in this section. Figure 1.12 shows a Web server deployment scheme. This scenario can be as simple as a browser making a request for static pages or as complex as providing online banking. Unfortunately, the simplicity that the browser gives the user in accessing and using Web sites and applications translates directly into hard work for the developer. The key difference that the Web-based application architecture introduces into the picture is a standard application container on the client machine, usually a browser and the capability to download components to the user machine on demand.

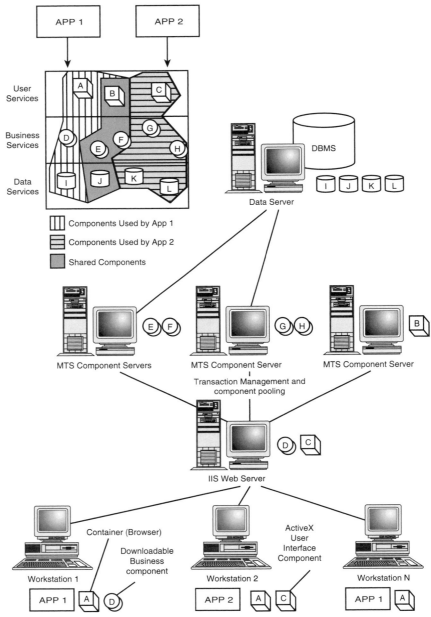

Figure 1.12 Physical deployment utilizing IIS Web Server, MTS application servers, and distributed components

What does this mean? Well, it means that the first three scenarios focused on keeping business rules on centralized servers to make it easier to deploy changes. Because the Web server automatically downloads components to the client's machine, the need to run business logic from centralized servers is no longer as important. Now the focus is on running components of logic where they make the most sense from an execution standpoint. If you are running over the Internet, you probably will want to download anything you can to the client and let it run locally with as few requests to the server as possible. This is recommended because you can't guarantee bandwidth and connectivity. If you are running on an intranet—a Web server available on a company's internal network—you might choose to mix up your deployment, based on the power of the client machines, your servers, and available bandwidth.

Comments

In the single-server, application server, and distributed transaction server deployment scenarios, the components deployed to the workstations did not change. This emphasizes the goal, which is to centralize the application logic that must be maintained and updated. It is much more cost effective to maintain components on a centralized server than to change the configuration on 100 workstations. This comes at a cost in execution time, however, so it is not a cure-all. Some components might have to be distributed to every workstation. The point here is that the physical deployment opportunities are vast. Unfortunately, they are also fraught with uncertainty.

The Web server deployment strategy adds a new twist to this whole understanding of where components can and should be deployed. Consider that components are not permanently installed on the client's machine but instead are downloaded and used as they are needed. The Web server can easily automate the installations of needed components and manage versioning on the client's machine, effectively reducing the need for centralized servers to run the components. The true value of this will be realized when the Web servers and application transaction servers can perform true load balancing by dynamically choosing where components should run best. In this scenario things like network traffic and server load and availability would play a role in deciding whether the component runs on server 1, server 2, or is downloaded to the client and run locally. Unfortunately, today's systems are not yet to this point—but they are moving in this direction. Be aware that until automatic load balancing is a reality, each situation in which you must deploy a component architecture and three-tier client/server application will require its own solution. Hopefully, this section has given you some ideas.

COMPLEXITY
INTERMEDIATE

1.7 How do I...
Learn more about client/server development tools included with Visual Basic 6?

COMPATIBILITY: VISUAL BASIC 6

There is a significant difference between what takes place in a two-tier client/server application and the implementation and deployment of a three-tier application. In a two-tier approach, business logic is integrated into the application that sits on the user's workstation, or the logic is integrated into the back-end database system in the form of triggers and stored procedures. With a three-tiered approach, the business logic that represents what the company is all about is given its own tier. This tier is made possible by facilitating the capability to partition executable logic out of both the front-end application and the back-end database engine. The difference resides in the partitioning of applications and the creation of components. The use of components, both on the local machine and deployed remotely, introduces a serious need for new tools. Visual Basic 6 comes with a variety of new tools:

- ✔ Microsoft Visual Modeler
- ✔ Application Performance Explorer
- ✔ Visual Component Manager
- ✔ Remote Automation Connection Manager
- ✔ Automation Manager
- ✔ Client Registration Utility
- ✔ Microsoft Transaction Server and NT Option Pack 4.0
- ✔ SQL Server 6.5 (Developer Edition)
- ✔ SQL Server debugging service
- ✔ Microsoft Data Access Controls
- ✔ Posting Acceptor
- ✔ SNA Server
- ✔ Database Access Methods and Tools
- ✔ Visual SourceSafe Client and Server Components

The rest of this section provides a brief overview of the above-mentioned tools and data access methods that accompany Visual Basic 6.0 Enterprise Edition. These tools play a vital role in making three-tier client/server application development feasible and desirable.

Microsoft Visual Modeler

Developing systems with components requires a great deal of planning. It is critical to understand both the logical and the physical aspects of the solutions you are designing. This tool is a subset of a fuller-featured product, Rational Rose 8.0, from a company called Rational.

Visual Modeler enables you to create a logical view of your solution that contains the classes and their relationships to each other. You can also create a component view that describes the physical structure of the system being created; finally, you can roll all this into a deployment view that shows the physical location of the components and how they will connect. Figure 1.13 shows Microsoft Visual Modeler with its three-tiered diagram. When you are ready, Visual Modeler can translate your work into Visual Basic classes and code. You can reverse-engineer into the modeler, as well.

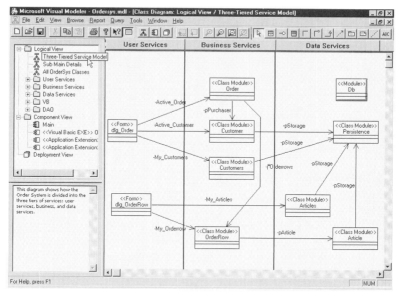

Figure 1.13 Visual Modeler in 3-tier presentation mode

Application Performance Explorer (APE)

Testing the performance of component-based systems has been a difficult if not impossible task. The Application Performance Explorer (APE) enables you to specify different scenarios to get a true gauge of performance on your equipment over your network. Figure 1.14 shows the Application Performance Explorer running a test. It is critical that you understand the benefits and consequences of your design decisions. The Application Performance Explorer enables you to do this in a test environment. You can set up tests to run automatically and even target peak times on your network.

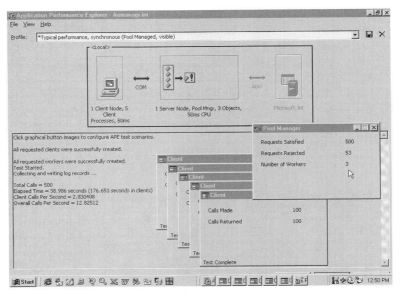

Figure 1.14 Application Performance Explorer (APE) running a test

Visual Component Manager

The promise of components is that they will make the long hours of work you put into building them pay off by letting you reuse them. The sad truth is that reuse is not a sure thing. For reuse to take place, you must make sure that everyone can easily find components that can be reused and then, having found them, that everyone can use them. The Visual Component Manager, shown in Figure 1.15, is provided as a tool to help you accomplish this task.

The Visual Component Manager enables you to add and remove components from a catalog that everyone can share. You can also track important information about each component, allowing people to reuse the component. Finding the component is only half the trick to using it; the other half is understanding the component's interface.

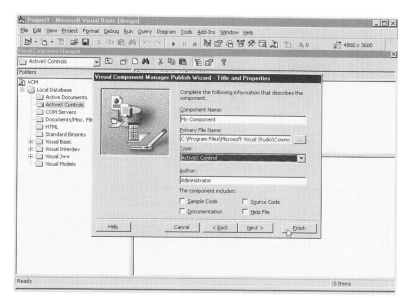

Figure 1.15 Visual Component Manager in tree view with wizard

Each component has a property sheet that enables you to enter information that describes the component and its interface. Importing components into the Visual Component Manager registers them for use. You and the people who will be creating and reusing components will have to decide how to implement the Component Manager's features. This is well worth the effort, even if the person you are sharing the components with is yourself.

Client Registration Utility

The Registry of both NT and Windows 95 provides a library in which all objects used are registered. In order for a component to be available for use under Windows 95 or NT, it must be registered in the Registry. This registration can take place in several ways. If the component is an EXE, you simply execute it; it will register itself on your system. If you have Visual Basic on your machine and compile a component into an EXE or DLL, that component will be registered automatically. You can also use the Setup Wizard to create a setup program that not only installs the component and registers it in the Registry, but also provides a method for uninstalling it.

The Client Registration Utility provided with Visual Basic enables you to register components from the command line. To use the Client Registration Utility, you must compile your components with the Remote Server Support Files option checked. This option is available when you generate an EXE in Visual Basic by choosing the Options button. The Remote Server Support Files option will generate a file with the .VBR extension. This file provides a client machine's Windows Registry with information it needs to run an ActiveX server that exists on a remote computer.

In today's world of choice, you get two versions of the Client Registration Utility: `CLIREG32.EXE` and `CLIREG16.EXE`. `CLIREG32.EXE` allows for registration that enables 32-bit applications to access the component you are registering. `CLIREG16.EXE` is used to register your component for use by 16-bit applications. If you will be using both 16- and 32-bit applications to reference this component on a single machine, you must run both registration utilities. If you must register a DLL on a client machine to run locally, you should use `Regsvr32.exe` for 32-bit Windows environments or `Regsvr16.exe` for 16-bit machines. This utility allows for local registration of ActiveX servers. Because a DLL cannot be executed like an EXE, nor accessed directly via Remote Automation, you must install it by using this utility. Regsvr32 and Regsvr16 can be found under your Visual Basic directory in the `Clisvr` subdirectory.

Remote Automation Connection Manager

The Remote Connection Manager is similar to a phone directory; it is provided as an easy way to tell your system where to find a component. Figure 1.16 shows the Remote Automation Connection Manager's Server Connection tab and ActiveX classes list. You put in the connection information and this utility stores it in the Registry. When an application or component tries to contact a component, it looks in the Registry to find the information about the component. In this case, the important information is security related.

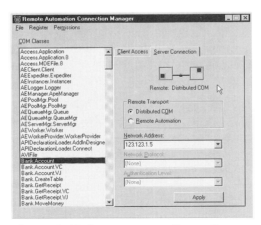

Figure 1.16 A remote configuration, using the Remote Automation Connection Manager

The list contains all the ActiveX classes that have been registered. To use the Remote Automation Connection Manager to set up access to a remote component class, you highlight the component's class name on the list and enter the network address, network protocol, and authentication level to be used (see Table 1.2). Additionally, you can use either standard Remote Automation or the distributed component object protocol by simply selecting it from the Server Connection tab.

Table 1.2 Sample entries for the Remote Automation Connection Manager

OPTION	SAMPLE ENTRIES
Network Address	IP Address or Associated Name
Network Protocol	TCP/IP, Named Pipes, or other installed option
Authentication Level	No Authentication

The real power of the Remote Automation Connection Manager is in its capability to easily repoint the Registry from a local reference to a remote reference of your component. Figure 1.16 shows the Remote Automation Connection Manager highlighting a component set up to be accessed remotely.

When the component's address in the Registry has been changed to a remote machine, the Remote Automation Connection Manager displays two component symbols connected by a line, and the label saying "remote." Switching from local to remote access of a component is easy; you simply select Local or Remote from the Register menu list. What is taking place is that entries are being changed in the Registry to point requests for service to a remote or local location. When you call someone on the phone, it really doesn't matter where they are as long as you have the phone number and they pick up the phone when you call. That is the idea with Remote Automation and components. Everyone uses a phone to talk to others. Even if you are in the same house (on the same computer), you use the phone to talk. Doing this enables components to be deployed anywhere, and all that must be done is to change the number in the phone book (Registry) to the current phone number.

Security is worth mentioning here. The two types of security in Remote Automation are as follows:

✔ Access control. This type of security ensures that only certain types of objects are remotely available. You can also make sure that only specified users can have access to certain objects.

✔ Authentication. This type of security, which ensures that data sent from one application is identical to the data received by the other, protects against someone intercepting your data as it goes from one point to another.

There are many ways to implement security. On one end of the spectrum, you could implement no security and just trust that people won't access things they shouldn't. This method is easy to maintain because you simply ignore the risk.

On the other end of the spectrum, you could lock everything up and assign access to only the logged-on person at a single station. Figure 1.17 shows the contents of the Client Access tab of the Remote Automation Connection Manager.

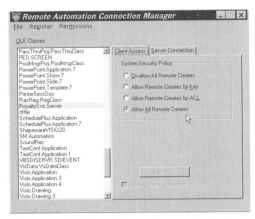

Figure 1.17 The Client Access tab of the Remote Automation Connection Manager

If you are running Windows NT, you will want to set the System Security Policy to Allow Remote Creates by ACL. ACL stands for *Access Control List* and is a method used by NT to determine whether a user running an application has adequate permission to access the class. This is very powerful because it enables the NT operating system's security model to kick in, allowing for a centralized method for handling security.

With Allow Remote Creates by ACL selected, a request for a remote ActiveX component object will be processed as usual by the Automation Manager (as discussed later in this section). The Automation Manager impersonates the client user and tries to open the remotely deployed object's class identification (CLSID) key with query permissions. If the open fails, the Automation Manager returns an error. On the other hand, if the open succeeds the Automation Manager no longer impersonates the client user. It creates the requested object and returns a reference as usual.

If you are using Windows 95, the client's ACL is not a valid choice; you can only specify Allow Remote Creates by Key. If you select this option in the Remote Automation Connection Manager on the client and also check the Allow Remote Activation, then the system will grant access to an application that has the correct value stored under the object's CLSID in the Registry. If you use Windows 95 as a server, you should also set the authentication level to No Authentication. Windows 95 does not support the full security model that NT does.

Automation Manager

The Automation Manager is an application responsible for connecting remote clients to ActiveX automation servers. This multithreaded application must be running on a machine that acts as a server for components, making them available for use by other machines. Figure 1.18 shows the Automation Manager and the two visible values it presents. If you are not using Microsoft Transaction Server to provide access to components, you will need to use this program.

Figure 1.18 The Automation Manager waiting for a client request

The Automation Manager must be running on the server machine. As requests are received, the Automation Manager tracks and increments the number of connections. As ActiveX component references are passed, the object's count will be incremented and as the referenced objects are released, the counts are correspondingly reduced. The Automation Manager (a 32-bit application) can be found in your Windows systems directory with the name AUTMGR32.EXE.

Database Management Tools

Communication between the business services components and the data services tier is a critical piece of the client/server puzzle. Visual Basic comes with five data access methods: Data Access Objects (DAOs), Remote Data Objects (RDOs), Open Database Connectivity API (ODBC), Active Data Objects, and OLE DB. Following is a brief description of each method. Microsoft is recommending movement to ADO and OLE DB for the future. Be aware that not all functionality found in DAO, RDO, and ODBC data access formats is found currently in ADO and OLE DB, although future releases will change this. For a fuller discussion of these access methods, see Chapter 3, "Data Objects."

Data Access Objects (DAO)

Visual Basic 6 comes with support for the *Joint Engine Technology* (JET). JET provides an object-oriented implementation of data access called *Data Access Objects* (DAOs). This method of accessing data enables a developer to use data objects and collections to handle the tasks of data access. The implementation of data access objects is closely tied to the Microsoft database file structure called MDB. The MDB allows the storage of tables as well as query definitions, macros, forms, reports, and code. Data access objects enable you to get at only the tables and queries stored in the MDB. Data access objects automate much of the task of dealing with data, including managing connections, record locking, and fetching resultsets; DAOs also provide for access to ODBC-compliant data sources.

Remote Data Objects

Optimizing the methods for accessing ODBC-compliant data sources, while at the same time simplifying the process, is a huge task. Remote Data Objects (RDO)—a thin layer that sits on top of the ODBC API—is provided to accomplish this task. Because this layer is thin, it does not impact the speed of execution for performing data access. This is critical to a production environment in which one of the evaluating factors is the speed of execution. Remote Data Objects is similar to the DAO object model and enables developers to use objects and collections to execute data-related tasks like submitting a query, processing results, and handling errors.

Open Database Connectivity (ODBC) API

Of all the methods for accessing data, the Open Database Connectivity (ODBC) API is the most efficient in terms of execution speed. In terms of programming, it requires the most time and the most caution. Because this is an *application programming interface* (API) you have full control over the very intimate details of data access.

Both the DAO and the RDO use the ODBC API layer when accessing ODBC-compliant database engines like Oracle and Microsoft SQL Server. The ODBC API is cryptic and difficult to use but provides more control and better execution speed. It is generally recommended that remote data objects be used because it is the best-balanced method. Its data access speed rivals that of using the ODBC API directly, and object-oriented syntax makes programming easy. But if you are looking to the future, you might want to pay special attention to ActiveX Data Objects (ADO) (covered in more detail in Chapter 3, "Data Objects").

Microsoft Data Access Components (MDAC)

With all this discussion of data access objects, remote data objects, and open database connectivity, the real story is found in what Microsoft is calling "universal data access." Microsoft Data Access Components are the cornerstone technologies that will allow universal data access. These technologies include ActiveX data objects (ADO), remote data service (RDS, which was previously known as advanced data connector, or ADC), open database connectivity (ODBC), and OLE DB.

Posting Acceptor

Component development relies on the capability to deploy solutions easily to a variety of servers. To deploy solutions with components that need to be installed and registered on the server to Windows NT machines, Microsoft is providing a solution that utilizes Internet Explorer 4.0 and Posting Acceptor 2.0 on the server machines where components will be deployed. Internet Information Server is necessary as well. If the components you are placing on a server will only be used locally by Active Server Pages, you won't need to use this solution. It is more likely, however, that components will be used in many more solutions than simply by local Active Server Pages.

SNA Server

Most companies have their share of legacy systems. Microsoft is providing SNA Server to ease the integration of legacy applications and data with modern network systems. You can install services for host connectivity and the SNA Server Software Development Kit. The version of SNA Server that comes with Visual Basic 6 includes the OLE DB Provider for VSAM and AS/400 as well as an ODBC driver for DB2, and COM Transaction Integrator for CICS and IMS. Serious enterprise solutions can use this functionality to create complete solutions that can leverage existing systems.

SQL Server 6.5 (Developer Edition)

A completely functional version of SQL Server is now included with Visual Basic 6. This version, called the Microsoft SQL Server 6.5 Developer Edition, is limited to a maximum of five simultaneous users. The license specifies that it is intended for use in designing, developing, and testing software products that are designed to operate in conjunction with Microsoft SQL Server.

SQL Server Debugging Service

One of the greatest challenges to developers is debugging. Distributed environments and toolsets only make it worse. Visual Basic 5 came with an SQL Server debugging service. Visual Basic 6 adds the capability to debug SQL code from within the Visual Basic programming environment itself. This is a very powerful step toward fully integrated debugging capabilities.

Visual SourceSafe Client and Server Components

With the release of Visual Basic 6, Microsoft included a complete system for team development of enterprise-wide solutions. Of course, this requires that the environment provide a mechanism for organizing team development. Visual SourceSafe provides the capability to manage large-scale team development.

SourceSafe comprises two applications. The first is the administrative module, shown in Figure 1.19, that enables you to maintain a roster of developers who work on various projects.

The following rights can be assigned per user and per project:

✔ Read. User can use the file in read-only mode.

✔ Check Out/Check In. User can check out files for use and make modifications, and can also check the files back in.

✔ Add/Rename/Delete. User has the ability to add files to the project as well as to rename and delete files within the project.

✔ Destroy. User has the ability to permanently remove files from the project and physically destroy them.

The second application is the SourceSafe Explorer, shown in Figure 1.20, which enables you to use a window that resembles the Windows Explorer.

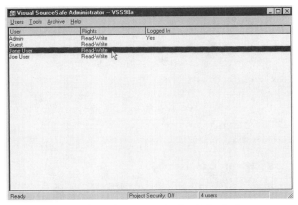

Figure 1.19 Visual SourceSafe Administrator

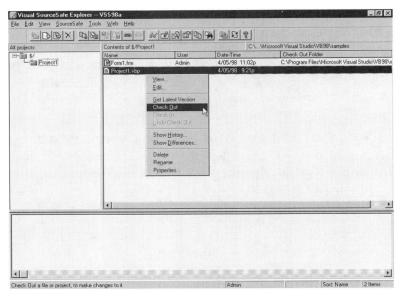

Figure 1.20 The Visual SourceSafe Explorer

You can use this application to check in and check out files for a project. You can also view the history of activity with a file, see the differences between files that have been changed, and create reports that enable you to manage a project.

Visual SourceSafe has also been provided as an add-in to the Visual Basic development environment. You can add it by using the Add-In Manager from the Visual Basic menu bar. Visual SourceSafe adds the following options to your Tools menu:

✔ Get Latest Version. Enables you to bring physical copies of files from the storage library maintained by SourceSafe on your network drive.

✔ Check Out. Used for selecting files that you want to work with exclusively. Optionally, you can keep them checked out or release the files so that other people can check them out.

✔ Check In. After you have finished working on a file or project, you use the Check In command to update the SourceSafe code library with your changes.

✔ Undo Check Out. This option enables you to effectively cancel a check out on the files you are working with. In a situation in which you check out a file or project, make changes, and then decide that you want to begin again, you can cancel the check-out process.

Comments

The development of components is a very powerful idea whose time has come. Creating components is facilitated by the additional tools that make management and implementation possible. It is important to note that some of these tools are available only with the Enterprise Edition of Visual Basic. As a way to get started, the next section walks you through the process of installing and adding a project to Visual SourceSafe.

COMPLEXITY
BEGINNING

1.8 How do I...
Create a SourceSafe project?

COMPATIBILITY: VISUAL BASIC 5, 6

Problem

I would like to use a simple and integrated source code control process with my team but I don't know where to start.

Technique

Using source code control is an important part of team development. It also provides the individual developer with the benefit of having a secure place for code, the ability to share files between projects, an online history of changes, and more. Visual SourceSafe is provided as part of Visual Studio. There are two methods for adding a project to Visual SourceSafe. The first method involves the use of the Visual SourceSafe Explorer; the second is performed in the Visual Basic environment when you have the Visual SourceSafe Add-In installed. For this quick start on using Visual SourceSafe, you will use the Add-In method from Visual Basic.

Steps

To use Visual SourceSafe from the Visual Basic development environment, you must make sure that Visual SourceSafe has been installed on your machine and that a valid login for you exists in the SourceSafe Administrator. To add a login to SourceSafe, start the Visual SourceSafe Administrator program. Press Ctrl+A to add a user. Enter your name and password and press OK. Now you have a valid login with SourceSafe. After that is finished, complete the following steps:

1. Start Visual Basic. You do not need to specify a project at this time.

2. Select Add-Ins from the menu, and then select Add-In Manager. A dialog box appears, showing the add-ins available on your system. If you do not see Source Code Control Add-In, then Visual SourceSafe has not been properly installed on your system. You will need to reinstall it before you can proceed.

3. Select Source Code Control, make sure that the Load Behavior is Startup/Loaded, and then click OK.

4. Open a project that you would like to add to Visual SourceSafe. As the project loads, you will be prompted automatically to add it to SourceSafe. For this How-To, reply No.

5. Select the Tools menu. You will notice an entry on the menu for SourceSafe. Select this option (see Figure 11.21).

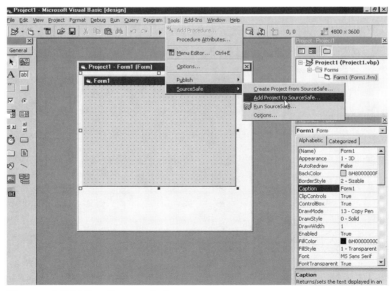

Figure 1.21 The SourceSafe menu

The SourceSafe Add-In menu has the following options:

✔ Create Project from SourceSafe. This option enables you to open a project already in SourceSafe but that has never been checked out to you.

✔ Add Project to SourceSafe. This adds the current project to the SourceSafe Code library.

✔ Run SourceSafe. This runs the Visual SourceSafe Explorer.

✔ Options. Use this to set options for SourceSafe.

6. Select Add Project to SourceSafe. You will be prompted by a login screen. Enter a valid login and password.

7. When presented with a SourceSafe dialog box, enter the name of this project in the Project field and click OK.

8. You will be prompted to select the files that make up the project. Select them and click OK. SourceSafe adds your project to the source code control library.

How It Works

When you install Visual SourceSafe on your machine, it also installs the Source Code Control Add-In. When you install this add-in into the Visual Basic development environment it enables you to add a project from the Visual Basic menus instead of starting the Visual SourceSafe Explorer and creating the project there. By selecting to add the currently open project to Source Code Control, you automatically start Visual SourceSafe and are prompted to create a project entry in the source code library. After the entry is made, you are prompted to add the files that make up the project, and then you are finished.

Comments

The add-in for Visual SourceSafe does a great deal to simplify the process of using source code control. Much of the process is automated, including prompts that urge you to add projects to the source code library. After a project becomes part of Visual SourceSafe, you will be able to check files in and out right from the Visual Basic development environment. Simply highlight the file in the Project window and use the right mouse button to see a menu of options for checking files in and out from SourceSafe (see Figure 1.22).

First, before you add your projects, you might want to add all developers to the SourceSafe Administrator. In this way, you can set access rights for them on the projects. The SourceSafe Administrator does allow you to set individual rights by project. A shortcoming of Visual SourceSafe is the lack of group rights. Everything is on an individual basis, which can be difficult if you deal with a large number of people or projects and want to control access to the code.

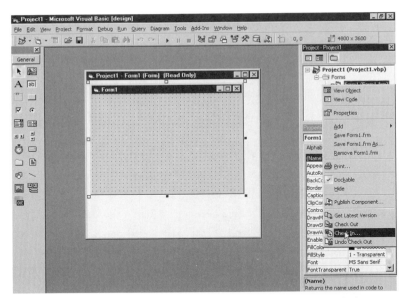

Figure 1.22 Menu choices available when you right-click on a file in the Project window

CHAPTER 2
GETTING CONNECTED

2

GETTING CONNECTED

by Don Kiely

How do I...

The How-To's in this chapter demonstrate how to use several of the most common database connections used in Visual Basic. Most of the examples aren't sophisticated database applications but are intended to showcase the connection techniques and related issues. Four of the How-To's produce essentially the same small application, highlighting the differences among the four connections used.

Microsoft has designed Jet so you can use it to directly access the `.MDB` or ISAM databases only, so you can't use the Jet engine and ODBC together to access database files. You can, however, use the ODBC API or Remote Data Objects alone, without Jet, to access these databases.

The How-To's in this chapter demonstrate the various ways you can make a connection to a database. Because the Enterprise Edition's remote data objects are based on ODBC, the examples here discuss the different ways to make a connection with connect strings, the ODBC API, and other ODBC techniques. The final How-To discusses ways to determine the best connection for your particular application given the hardware, software, and network setup you have.

Some of the How-To's in this chapter use an SQL Server ODBC driver, so you'll need to have both SQL Server and this driver installed so you can use them either on the local machine or on the network. If not, you'll need to modify the code to use the ODBC data source and driver you do have. You can see a list of ODBC drivers installed by running the ODBC Administrator, `ODBCAD32.EXE`, and clicking the ODBC Drivers tab.

You'll need access to a SQL Server database for these How-To's, either on the local machine or over the network. SQL Server 6.5 can be installed and run only on Windows NT machines, but SQL Server 7.0 includes a version that can run on Windows 95. If you don't have access to a network that has SQL Server, or don't have an NT machine, with a little work you can modify the applications to use Access databases.

The How-To's in this chapter assume that you are using the ODBC SDK 3.0 or later. If you are using version 2.x or earlier, you can download the latest version from Microsoft's Web site or get it from the Microsoft Developer Network CD-ROMs.

2.1 Display Errors Generated by Remote Data Objects and the RemoteData Control

The error message returned from any database engine, including ODBC, can be complex and hierarchical sets of information. This is because each database request can be handled by several layers on its way to the engine that ultimately handles the request. This How-To develops a method of retrieving and displaying error information.

2.2 Write a Connect String

With a fully formed connect string, your application can connect directly to any ODBC data source name available on the local computer. The trick is discovering what information ODBC needs to make the connection, and the driver's documentation often doesn't provide enough information. This How-To shows how you can discover this string and even paste it directly into your application.

2.3 Access Data with the Jet Engine, ODBC, and the Data Control

One of the simplest ways to connect to databases through ODBC is with the good old Visual Basic Data control. You'll see how to make the connection in this How-To and discover some of the limitations of doing things this way.

2.4 Make a Connection with the Jet Engine, ODBC, and DAO

Whereas the Visual Basic Data control provides an easy but limited way to connect to data, Visual Basic's data access objects (DAOs) provide a flexible method that takes some coding work. This How-To creates the same small application as How-To 2.3 but with DAOs instead of the Data control so you can explore the differences between the two techniques.

2.5 Use the SQL Passthrough Option

Most modern client/server databases use some form of structured query language (SQL) to retrieve and update information stored in the server. The SQL dialects are almost as varied as the number of database servers. This How-To shows you how to make sure your SQL statements are executed by the right tier in your enterprise application.

2.6 Make a Connection Using the RemoteData Control

When Microsoft first introduced the Visual Basic Enterprise Edition in 1995, it gave the world a new RemoteData control. This control has been described as "the regular VB Data control on steroids," giving you much more flexibility and power. This How-To rebuilds the application of How-To's 2.3 and 2.4 to use the RemoteData control and shows how its new features make your code simpler and more reliable.

2.7 Make a Connection Using Remote Data Objects

Although the RemoteData control substantially improved upon the Visual Basic Data control, it still has its limitations. Remote data objects, however, provide both power and flexibility to data access. This How-To demonstrates how to use RDOs and shows some of the features they offer.

2.8 Benchmark My Connection Options

The number of ways to access data seems to be growing exponentially, making it harder to decide what method to use in a particular application. The answer is highly dependent on the data and your network setup, but you can benchmark database connections by using your own live data to discover the best way to connect.

COMPLEXITY
INTERMEDIATE

2.1 How do I...
Display errors generated by remote data objects and the RemoteData control?

COMPATIBILITY: VISUAL BASIC 6

Problem

Because errors can originate in any one or several tiers of the application, the `rdoErrors` collection can contain several errors, any of which can be crucial for understanding and tracking down the source of the problem.

Technique

Several How-To's in this chapter use the Visual Basic RemoteData control, remote data objects (RDOs), or both. When an error occurs with a remote connection, Visual Basic will update the `rdoErrors` collection of `rdoError` objects with information about the source of the error, a brief description, and so on to help you track down the source of the error. All these objects and the errors collection are made available to your application when you select Project, References, and choose Microsoft Remote Data Object 2.0 from the Visual Basic main menu.

Steps

This How-To creates a form you can use in any application to display all the details about an RDO error. All the How-To's in this chapter that use remote data objects or the remote data control will use this form to report and handle connection errors.

Complete the following steps to create this form:

1. Insert a new form into a Visual Basic project, saving it as `ERRORRDO.FRM` and naming it `frmRDOErrors`. Add the controls shown in Figure 2.1 to this form, with property settings as listed in Table 2.1. From the Visual Basic menu select Project, Components. Add the Microsoft Outline Control by checking the box to the left of the name and clicking OK to close the window.

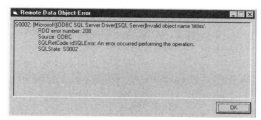

Figure 2.1 Reporting multiple remote data object errors.

Table 2.1 Objects and properties for ERRORRDO.FRM

OBJECT	PROPERTY	SETTING
Form	Name	frmRDOErrors
	Caption	"Remote Data Object Error"
	MaxButton	0 'False
CommandButton	Name	cmdQuit
	Caption	"OK"
TextBox	Name	txtErrors
	BackColor	&H8000000B& (Light gray to match form's client area
	Locked	-1 'True
	MultiLine	-1 'True

2. Add the following code to the declarations section of the form. `Option Explicit` tells Visual Basic to make sure you declare all variables and objects before using them to avoid naming problems. You can have VB automatically add this statement to your code modules by checking the Require Variable Declaration check box in Tools, Options under the Editor tab. The form will use a **Property Let** procedure to receive the `rdoErrors` collection when an error occurs.

```
Option Explicit

'PRIVATE: ****************************************
'Private data members
Private mrdoErrs As rdoErrors
```

3. Add the following code, which centers the form, to the form's **Load** event procedure:

```
Private Sub Form_Load()
    'Center the form
    Me.Top = (Screen.Height - Me.Height) / 2
    Me.Left = (Screen.Width - Me.Width) / 2
End Sub
```

4. The form uses a `Resize` event procedure so that the end user can stretch or shrink the form to view the error data. Even though the text box control is loaded with one piece of information per line, some ODBC drivers insist on returning long lines of data. This can make the information hard to read, sometimes made worse by word wrapping in the text box's multiline mode, and even harder to format. This way the end user can at least stretch the form to see all the error data.

```
Private Sub Form_Resize()
    If Me.WindowState = vbNormal Then
        If Me.ScaleHeight < (4 * cmdQuit.Height) Then
            Me.Height = (6 * cmdQuit.Height)
        End If
        If Me.ScaleWidth < (4 * cmdQuit.Width) Then
            Me.Width = (4 * cmdQuit.Width)
        End If

        'Redraw the controls
        cmdQuit.Top = Me.ScaleHeight - (1.25 * cmdQuit.Height)
        cmdQuit.Left = Me.ScaleWidth _
            - (cmdQuit.Width + 0.25 * cmdQuit.Height)

        txtErrors.Top = 0.25 * cmdQuit.Height
        txtErrors.Left = 0.25 * cmdQuit.Height
        txtErrors.Width = Me.ScaleWidth - 0.5 * cmdQuit.Height
        txtErrors.Height = cmdQuit.Top - 0.5 * cmdQuit.Height
    End If
End Sub
```

5. Enter the following code to the `Public ErrorColl Property Let` procedure. Using a `Property Let` procedure like this lets you set a property of a form, in this case to communicate the `rdoErrors` collection to the form for processing.

Because this error collection can include several errors from different tiers of the link to the database, this procedure builds a string, `sText`, with information about each error. By using a `for...next` loop through the collection, the code adds information to the `sText` string for each error using the properties of the `rdoError` object. Table 2.2 lists these properties. After the `sText` string is fully populated with the error information, the text box's `Text` property is set to `sText`.

Table 2.2   Properties of the `RDOError` object

NAME	DESCRIPTION
Description	A terse description of the error.
Number	The error number, from the tier causing the error.
Source	The source of the error. This will help identify the tier causing this error.
SQLRetcode	The ODBC error code associated with this problem. See the code for the `ReturnCode` procedure.
SQLState	The ODBC `SQLState` code, providing more information about the problem.

```vb
Public Property Let ErrorColl(rdoEr As rdoErrors)
Dim sText As String
Dim rdoE As rdoError
Dim i As Integer

    Set mrdoErrs = rdoEr

    'Load the Outline control with error members
    For Each rdoE In mrdoErrs
        sText = sText & rdoE.Description & vbCrLf
        sText = sText & Chr(9) & _
            "RDO error number: " & rdoE.Number & vbCrLf

        If rdoE.Source = "" Then
            sText = sText & Chr(9) & "Source: Unknown" & vbCrLf
        Else
            sText = sText & Chr(9) & "Source: " & rdoE.Source _
            & vbCrLf
        End If

        sText = sText & Chr(9) & ReturnCode(rdoE.SQLRetcode) _
            & vbCrLf
        sText = sText & Chr(9) & "SQLState: " & rdoE.SQLState _
            & vbCrLf

Next

    'Set the Text property to the error string
    txtErrors.Text = sText

    Me.Show vbModal

End Property
```

6. The rdoError object used in the ErrorColl Property Let procedure contains a return code with information about the nature of the error. The ReturnCode procedure converts this return code to text that will be at least slightly more intelligible to the end user.

```vb
Private Function ReturnCode(iRetCode As Integer) As String
Dim sText As String

    Select Case iRetCode
        Case rdSQLSuccess
            sText = "SQLRetCode rdSQLSuccess: " _
                & "The operation is successful."
        Case rdSQLSuccessWithInfo
            sText = "SQLRetCode rdSQLSuccessWithInfo: " _
                & "The operation is successful, and additional " _
                & "information is available."
        Case rdSQLNoDataFound
            sText = "SQLRetCode rdSQLNoDataFound: No " _
                & "additional data is available."
        Case rdSQLError
```

continued on next page

continued from previous page

```
                sText = "SQLRetCode rdSQLError: An error occurred " _
                    & "performing the operation."
            Case rdSQLInvalidHandle
                sText = "SQLRetCode rdSQLInvalidHandle: " _
                    & "The handle supplied is invalid."
            Case Else
                sText = "SQLRetCode: Unknown Return Code"
        End Select

        ReturnCode = sText
End Function
```

7. Add this code to the **cmdQuit** command button's **Click** procedure to unload this form when the end user is finished viewing the error information:

```
Private Sub cmdQuit_Click()
    Unload Me
End Sub
```

To use the **frmRDOErrors** form, check for errors in the normal Visual Basic way by using an **On Error** statement around statements that use RDOs. In the error handler, call **frmRDOErrors** like the following:

```
FormLoadError:
    frmRDOErrors.ErrorColl = rdoErrors
```

This statement assigns the **rdoErrors** collection to the **ErrorColl** property of the form, which executes the **ErrorColl Property Let** procedure listed previously, displaying the error information. I demonstrate this technique in each of the How-To's that use this error form.

How It Works

Although the code in this How-To is a bit complex, all it does is iterate through the error collection returned from the ODBC system and format and display it in a multiline text box. Most How-To's in this chapter use either ODBC or one of its wrappers, such as remote data objects. The techniques covered herein will work in any of the How-To's.

One issue you must decide for your own applications, however, is whether you really want to present the user with the cryptic error messages, even as modified in this How-To, returned by ODBC. As with any error-handling code, you'll want to let the user know a bit more clearly just what the problem was. That way, the user can fix it or at least communicate to you what went wrong.

COMPLEXITY
INTERMEDIATE

2.2 How do I...
Write a connect string?

COMPATIBILITY: VISUAL BASIC 6

Problem

I need to connect to a remote database using ODBC, but the driver documentation is just no help in giving me the information it needs to make a connection. I need my application to make the connection (if at all possible) without users making any decisions about how to respond to the dialog boxes. How can I write a connect string without wasting time guessing?

Technique

The ODBC Manager, an integral part of ODBC and used by several of Visual Basic's data access methods, is designed so that it will prompt the end user for any information it needs to make a connection to a database. Simply by structuring the **OpenDatabase** method, ODBC will respond by prompting for information about what data source you want (from those data sources installed on the system). Then you can make the connection and examine the Visual Basic **Connect** property, which applies to the DAO DBEngine and Workspace objects. The **Connect** property at that point contains the fully formed connect string required to make a connection to that data source and can be copied and used directly in future attempts to connect to the database.

Steps

Open and run the **CONNSTR.VBP** Visual Basic project file. The Retrieve ODBC Connect String window will open. Click the Connect to Data Source command button, and the ODBC Select Data Source window will appear, prompting you to select an installed data source name. Click the Machine Data Source tab and select one of the listed data sources. Visual Basic and ODBC will obtain a list of tables available from this data source and put them in the Tables Available list box on the main form.

After closing the Data Sources windows, either double-click one of the tables or select one and click the Get Connect String command button. The application will establish a connection to that database table and return the complete connect string, placing it in the Connect String text box, as shown in Figure 2.2. Click the Copy Connect String command button to put the string in the Windows Clipboard, and then paste it into your application.

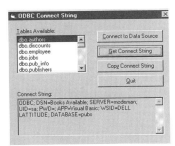

Figure 2.2 The ODBC connect string for a data source using an Access ODBC driver

To create this project, complete the following steps:

1. Create a new project called `CONNSTR.VBP`.

2. Select Project, Components from the Visual Basic main menu, and then select the custom controls shown in Table 2.3.

Table 2.3 Custom controls used in `CONNSTR.VBP`

CONTROL
Microsoft Outline Control
Microsoft Windows Common Controls 6.0

3. Select Project, References from the Visual Basic main menu, and then select the following references:

Microsoft Visual Basic For Applications
Visual Basic Runtime Objects and Procedures
Visual Basic Objects and Procedures
Microsoft DAO 3.51 Object Library

Uncheck all others so your project isn't cluttered with DLLs you aren't using and so the Setup Wizard doesn't include a lot of extra dead weight with your application.

4. Name the default form `frmConnect` and save the file as `CONNSTR.FRM`. Add the controls shown in Figure 2.2, setting the properties shown in Table 2.4.

Table 2.4 Objects and properties for CONNSTR.FRM

OBJECT	PROPERTY	SETTING
Form	Name	frmConnect
	BackColor	&H00C0C0C0&
	BorderStyle	3 'Fixed Dialog
	Caption	"ODBC Connect String"
	MaxButton	0 'False
	MinButton	0 'False
	ShowInTaskbar	0 'False
CommandButton	Name	cmdCopyConnect
	Caption	"Cop&y Connect String"
	Enabled	0 'False
CommandButton	Name	cmdGetConnect
	Caption	"&Get Connect String"
	Enabled	0 'False
CommandButton	Name	cmdQuit
	Caption	"&Quit"
TextBox	Name	txtConnect
	BackColor	&H00C0C0C0&
	Locked	-1 'True
	MultiLine	-1 'True
	ScrollBars	2 'Vertical
	TabStop	0 'False
CommandButton	Name	cmdConnect
	Caption	"&Connect to DataSource"
ListBox	Name	lstTables
	Sorted	-1 'True
Label	Name	Label2
	BackColor	&H00C0C0C0&
	Caption	"Connect String:"
Label	Name	Label1
	BackColor	&H00C0C0C0&
	Caption	"&Tables Available:"

5. Add the following code to the declarations section of frmConnect. Option Explicit tells Visual Basic to make sure that you declare all variables and objects before using them to avoid naming problems. You can have VB automatically add this statement to your code modules by checking the

Require Variable Declaration check box in Tools, Options under the Editor tab. The two module-level global variables will contain the connection information so the records can be used throughout the module.

```
Option Explicit

'PUBLIC:  *****************************************
'Public data members

'PRIVATE: *****************************************
'Private data members

'Module level globals to hold connection info
Private mDB As Database
Private mTbl As Recordset
```

6. Add the following code to the form's **Load** event. This code simply centers the form and shows itself.

```
Private Sub Form_Load()
Dim iTop As Integer, iLeft As Integer

    'Center the form
    iLeft = (Screen.Width - Me.Width) / 2
    iTop = (Screen.Height - Me.Height) / 2
    Me.Move iLeft, iTop

    Me.Show
End Sub
```

7. Add the following code to the **cmdConnect** command button's **Click** event. Before getting the connection data, the end user must select a data source name for connection information. For this procedure, the built-in ODBC dialog boxes do all the work. The code that comes with the dialog boxes includes the following **OpenDatabase** statement:

```
Set mDB = OpenDatabase("", False, False, "ODBC;")
```

This line tells Visual Basic to open a database but gives no information about which one, other than the fact that it is an ODBC database. ODBC responds by opening its Select Data Source dialog box for selection of a data source, as shown in Figure 2.3.

After the end user selects a data source name, the procedure loops through all the tables in the database—the **TableDefs** collection—using a Visual Basic **for each...next** loop, retrieves the table name of each table available in that data source, and adds each to the **lstTables** list box. If a connection is made and there are any tables available, the **cmdGetConnect** command button is enabled for the next step of retrieving the connection information.

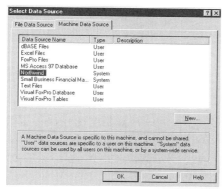

Figure 2.3 The ODBC dialog box
for data source selection.

```
Private Sub cmdConnect_Click()
'Connect to a data source and populate lstTables
Dim i As Integer
Dim iSaveCursor As Integer
Dim td As TableDef

    iSaveCursor = Screen.MousePointer
    Screen.MousePointer = vbHourglass

    lstTables.Clear

    On Error GoTo ErrHandler
    Set mDB = OpenDatabase("", False, False, "ODBC;")
    On Error GoTo 0

    For Each td In mDB.TableDefs
       lstTables.AddItem td.Name
    Next

    Screen.MousePointer = iSaveCursor

    If lstTables.ListCount Then
       cmdGetConnect.Enabled = True
    Else
       MsgBox "No tables available. Please connect " _
          & "to another data source."
    End If

    Exit Sub

ErrHandler:
    Screen.MousePointer = iSaveCursor
    Select Case Err.Number
       Case 3059
          'The user clicked on Cancel
          Exit Sub
```

continued on next page

continued from previous page

```
                Case Else
                    'The error is something else, so send it back to
                    'the VB exception handler
                    Err.Raise Err.Number
                    Resume
            End Select
    End Sub
```

8. Add the following code to the **cmdGetConnect**'s **Click** event. This command button is enabled only after a connection is made and tables are available for selection. Assuming that a table name has been selected, a connection is made to that table by creating a recordset. This makes the connection information available. It can be retrieved by copying the value of the database's **Connect** property to the **txtConnect** text box, running it through the **AddSpaces** function shown in step 9. Finally, the **cmdCopyConnect** command button is enabled.

```
Private Sub cmdGetConnect_Click()
Dim iSaveCursor As Integer

    iSaveCursor = Screen.MousePointer
    Screen.MousePointer = vbHourglass

    txtConnect.Text = ""

    If Len(lstTables.Text) Then
        Set mTbl = mDB.OpenRecordset(lstTables.Text)
        txtConnect.Text = AddSpaces(mDB.Connect)
    Else
        MsgBox "Please select a table first."
    End If

    cmdCopyConnect.Enabled = True
    Screen.MousePointer = iSaveCursor
End Sub
```

9. Add the following **Sub** procedure to the code section of **frmConnect**. After the program gets the raw connect string back from ODBC after making the connection to the database table, it is strung together with no spaces unless a space happens to be in any of the strings enclosed in double quotes. Sometimes the connect string is quite long, so the text box has the **MultiLine** property set to **True**. But even with that, an unbroken string with no spaces can exceed any text box width. So this function simply loops through the length of the string, replacing all the semicolon separators with a semicolon-space pair of characters. ODBC uses semicolons to separate the different phrases in a connect string.

```
Function AddSpaces(sConnect As String)
Dim i As Integer
Dim sNew As String
Dim sNextChar As String
```

```
   For i = 1 To Len(sConnect)
      sNextChar = Mid$(sConnect, i, 1)
      If sNextChar = ";" Then
         sNew = sNew & sNextChar & " "
      Else
         sNew = sNew & sNextChar
      End If
   Next
   AddSpaces = sNew
End Function
```

10. Add the code for **cmdCopyConnect**'s **Click** event shown next. This is added as a convenience for the programmer. After you have connected to the data source and have received the connect string, just click the Copy Connect String command button, and the full string is copied to the Windows Clipboard, ready to paste into your application wherever you need to set up the connection.

```
Private Sub cmdCopyConnect_Click()

   'Select the text in txtConnect
   txtConnect.SetFocus
   txtConnect.SelStart = 0
   txtConnect.SelLength = Len(txtConnect.Text)

   'Copy selected text to Clipboard.
   Clipboard.SetText Screen.ActiveControl.SelText

End Sub
```

11. Add the following code to the **cmdQuit** command button's **Click** event. The **cmdQuit** command button ends the program by unloading the form.

```
Private Sub cmdQuit_Click()
   Unload Me
End Sub
```

12. Add the following code to the **DblClick** event procedure of the **lstTables** list box. This simply adds the convenience of double-clicking a table in **lstTables** to retrieve the connect string, saving the work of also clicking the **cmdGetConnect** command button.

```
Private Sub lstTables_DblClick()
   cmdGetConnect_Click
End Sub
```

13. In the Project, [Project Name] Properties menu item, set the startup form to **frmConnect**. You can also set an application description, but that is not required for the operation of this application.

How It Works

Three ODBC API functions make a connection to a data source: `SQLConnect`, `SQLBrowseConnect`, and `SQLDriverConnect`, shown in Table 2.5. These functions are used by the `OpenDatabase` command demonstrated in this How-To.

Table 2.5 ODBC functions for establishing data source connections

FUNCTION	VERSION	CONFORMANCE	PRIMARY ARGUMENTS
`SQLConnect`	1.0	Core	hDbc, data source name, user ID, authorization string
`SQLDriverConnect`	1.0	1	hDbc, window handle (hwnd), connect string in, connect string out, completion option
`SQLBrowseConnect`	1.0	2	hDbc, connect string in, connect string out

`SQLConnect` is the standard way to connect to an ODBC data source. All the arguments must be complete and correct because if anything is wrong, ODBC generates an error. If everything is right, a connection is established. Valid return codes are `SQL_SUCCESS`, `SQL_SUCCESS_WITH_INFO`, `SQL_ERROR`, or `SQL_INVALID_HANDLE`. The only flexibility `SQLConnect` provides is that if the specified data source name can't be found, the function looks for a default driver and loads that if one is defined in `ODBC.INI`. If not, `SQL_ERROR` is returned and more information about the problem can be obtained with a call to `SQLError`. `SQLConnect` is the workhorse function of ODBC connections.

`SQLDriverConnect` offers a bit more flexibility for making ODBC connections. This function can handle data sources that require more information than the three arguments of `SQLConnect` (other than the connection handle `hDbc`, which all three functions require). It provides dialog boxes to prompt for any missing information needed for the connection and can handle connections not defined in the `ODBC.INI` file or Registry. `SQLDriverConnect` provides three connection options:

✔ A connection string provided in the function call that contains all the data needed, including data source name, multiple user IDs, multiple passwords, and any other custom information required by the database.

✔ A connection string that provides only some of the data required to make the connection. The ODBC Driver Manager and the driver then can prompt for any additional information that each needs to make the connection.

✔ A connection that is not defined in `ODBC.INI` or the Registry. If any partial information is provided, the function will make whatever use of it that it can.

When a connection is successfully established, the function will return SQL_SUCCESS and returns a completed connection string that can be used to make future connections to that database. It is a safe bet that SQLDriverConnect is the function Visual Basic uses to discover the connect string when this How-To is employed because of the similarity in their operation.

SQLDriverConnect can return SQL_SUCCESS, SQL_SUCCESS_WITH_INFO, SQL_NO_DATA_FOUND, SQL_ERROR, or SQL_INVALID_HANDLE. Valid choices for the completion option argument are SQL_DRIVER_PROMPT, SQL_DRIVER_COMPLETE, SQL_DRIVER_COMPLETE_REQUIRED, or SQL_DRIVER_NOPROMPT.

The third function, SQLBrowseConnect, is perhaps the most interesting of the three functions. This function initiates an interactive method of discovering what it takes to connect to a particular database. Each time SQLBrowseConnect is called, the function returns additional attributes that are needed to make a connection. An application making the call can parse out the resulting string containing missing attributes (which are marked as required or optional), and return successively more fully complete connect strings. Attributes that involve selection from a fixed list of items are returned as that full list, so an application can present a list box of choices to the end user.

Comments

You can't make an ODBC connection through an attached table to a Jet database that Visual Basic natively supports, like a Microsoft Access .MDB file or ISAM databases like Btrieve and dBase files. There normally isn't any reason to do so, although it can always be done by using the ODBC API directly, bypassing Jet.

COMPLEXITY
BEGINNING

2.3 How do I...
Access data with the Jet Engine, ODBC, and the Data control?

COMPATIBILITY: VISUAL BASIC 6

Problem

I have a database I need to use in my application for simple browsing and updating data. How can I link to the data without spending a lot of time writing data access code and learning a whole new API?

Technique

The Visual Basic Data control provides a quick and easy way to link your application to a database, at the cost of speed and flexibility. The steps to bind the Visual Basic Data control and other bound controls to an ODBC data source are quite simple, not that much different from connecting to one of Visual Basic's native data formats using the Jet database engine. This How-To shows exactly what is necessary to set up the controls to make the connection.

Steps

Open and run the **BOOKS.VBP** project file as shown in Figure 2.4. Use the Visual Basic Data control's navigation buttons at the bottom of the form to move through the SQL Server PUBS database; click Quit when you are finished.

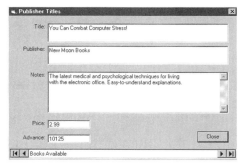

Figure 2.4 Using ODBC with the Visual Basic Data control to review a book database

This How-To uses an ODBC SQL Server driver and the sample PUBS database included with SQL Server. You can use any other ODBC data source or database, but you'll need to change the fields connected to the form's text boxes. Complete the following steps to create this project:

1. Create a data source name in ODBC for the PUBS database. Previous versions of ODBC required that you use the ODBC Data Source Adminstrator, **ODBCAD32.EXE**, usually located in the Windows System directory in Windows 95 or the System32 directory in Windows NT. The latest versions of ODBC install the Administrator as a Control Panel applet, listed either as 32bit ODBC or simply as ODBC. (If you are using an older version of ODBC, the steps you take will differ from those listed here. Check the ODBC documentation for information.) ODBC Administrator loads the ODBC Data Source Administrator window as shown in Figure 2.5. Here you define and maintain data source names available on this system.

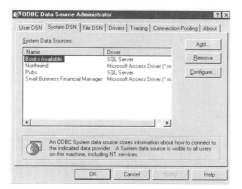

Figure 2.5 Main ODBC Data Source
Administrator window

2. Select the System DSN tab so that this data source name will be available
to any user on the system. Click Add, and the Create a New Data Source
window appears. The driver you need will be listed as something like SQL
Server or SQL Server (32-bit). Click this driver, and then click Finish so
the Create a New Data Source to SQL Server Wizard appears.

3. Each ODBC driver has its own version of this wizard, prompting for the
particular information the driver needs to make a connection with its
database. Enter the information as shown in Table 2.6 as you step through
the wizard. Use the defaults for any items not listed in the table. You might
have to adjust other entries not listed in the table for your system setup.
When you reach the last screen in the wizard, click Finish to create the
data source name.

Table 2.6   Books available data source name setup information

PROMPT	INFORMATION TO ENTER
Data Source Name	Books Available
Description	[Optional description information to identify the data source]
Server	[The server where SQL Server is located]
Database Name	PUBS
Login ID authenticity	[Check with your database administrator for this information]
Default Database	[Click the check box to enable the list box] PUBS

4. The ODBC Microsoft SQL Server Setup dialog box will appear, as shown
in Figure 2.6. The text box lists all the settings for this new data source
name. Click the Test Data Source button to test the connection to SQL
Server. If you receive an error message, go back and verify the settings,

particularly those for authenticating the login ID. Click OK when everything works.

Figure 2.6 ODBC SQL Server validation and test dialog box for a new data source name

5. The new Books Available data source name will appear in the Data Sources window as something like Books Available with a driver listed as SQL Server. Click OK to end the ODBC Data Source Administrator.

6. Start Visual Basic. Create a new project **BOOKS.VBP**.

7. Select Project, Components from the Visual Basic main menu and then unselect all the custom controls listed so your project isn't cluttered with controls you aren't using, and so the Setup Wizard doesn't include unneeded files with your application. This Visual Basic project uses only the native custom controls.

8. Select Project, References from the Visual Basic main menu and choose the following references:

Microsoft Visual Basic for Applications

Visual Basic Runtime Objects and Procedures

Visual Basic Objects and Procedures

Microsoft DAO 3.51 Object Library

Uncheck all others so your project isn't cluttered with DLLs you aren't using and so the Setup Wizard doesn't include unneeded files with your application.

9. Add the controls shown in Figure 2.4 to the default form in the new project, with the property settings listed in Table 2.7. Save the form as file BOOKS.FRM.

Table 2.7   Objects and properties for BOOKS.FRM

OBJECT	PROPERTY	SETTING
Form	Name	frmBooks
	BackColor	&H00C0C0C0&
	BorderStyle	3 'Fixed Dialog
	Caption	"Publisher Titles"
	MaxButton	0 'False
	MinButton	0 'False
TextBox	Name	txtPublisher
	DataSource	"Data1"
	MultiLine	-1 'True
CommandButton	Name	cmdClose
	Caption	"Close"
	Default	-1 'True
TextBox	Name	txtAdvance
	DataSource	"Data1"
TextBox	Name	txtPrice
	DataSource	"Data1"
TextBox	Name	txtNotes
	DataSource	"Data1"
	MultiLine	-1 'True
	ScrollBars	2 'Vertical
TextBox	Name	txtTitle
	DataSource	"Data1"
	MultiLine	-1 'True
Data	Name	Data1
	Align	2 'Align Bottom
	Caption	"Books Available"
	Connect	""
	DatabaseName	""
	Exclusive	0 'False
	Options	0
	ReadOnly	0 'False

continued on next page

Table 2.7   continued

OBJECT	PROPERTY	SETTING
	RecordsetType	1 'Dynaset
	RecordSource	" "
Label	Name	Label9
	Alignment	1 'Right Justify
	BackColor	&H00C0C0C0&
	Caption	"Publisher:"
Label	Name	Label6
	Alignment	1 'Right Justify
	BackColor	&H00C0C0C0&
	Caption	"Advance:"
Label	Name	Label5
	Alignment	1 'Right Justify
	BackColor	&H00C0C0C0&
	Caption	"Price:"
Label	Name	Label3
	Alignment	1 'Right Justify
	BackColor	&H00C0C0C0&
	Caption	"Notes:"
Label	Name	Label1
	Alignment	1 'Right Justify
	BackColor	&H00C0C0C0&
	Caption	"Title:"

10. Add the following code to the declarations section of the form. `Option Explicit` tells Visual Basic to make sure that you declare all variables and objects before using them in order to avoid naming problems. You can have Visual Basic automatically add this statement to your code modules by checking the Require Variable Declaration check box in Tools, Options under the Editor tab.

```
Option Explicit
```

11. Add the following code to the form's `Load` event procedure. After centering the form, the Data control's `Connect` property is set to the ODBC connection string and the `RecordSource` property is set to the SQL query to execute. Then the text boxes' `DataField` properties are set to the fields that each will hold. This is the step that links each field to the text boxes that hold each record's data. These properties could be set at design time, but when the Data control is not bound to a physical table, the code is less confusing.

```
Private Sub Form_Load()
'Set up the form and connect to data source
Dim db As Database
Dim rs As Recordset
Dim sSQL As String

    'Center the form
    Me.Top = (Screen.Height - Me.Height) / 2
    Me.Left = (Screen.Width - Me.Width) / 2

    'Connect to the database.
    Data1.Connect = "ODBC;DSN=Books Available;UID=sa;PWD="

    'Set the data control's RecordSource property
    sSQL = _
       "SELECT titles.*, publishers.* " _
       & "FROM titles, publishers " _
       & "WHERE publishers.pub_id = titles.pub_id " _
       & "ORDER BY titles.Title ASC;"
    Data1.RecordSource = sSQL

    'Connect each of the text boxes with the appropriate
    'fieldname
    txtAdvance.DataField = "Advance"
    txtNotes.DataField = "Notes"
    txtPrice.DataField = "Price"
    txtPublisher.DataField = "Pub_Name"
    txtTitle.DataField = "Title"

End Sub
```

12. Add the following code to the **Click** event of the **cmdQuit** command button. This is the exit point that terminates the program.

```
Private Sub cmdClose_Click()
    Unload Me
End Sub
```

13. In the Project, [Project Name] Options menu item, set the startup form to **frmBooks**. You can also set an application description, but that is not required for the operation of this application.

How It Works

This is all the code required to use ODBC with Visual Basic's Data control. When the form is loaded, you can move about the database with the built-in navigation buttons.

There are several important details in setting up this procedure for use with ODBC. Note that I chose to do most of the setup and initialization in code in this How-To, but you can also set the properties of the Data control and bound text boxes when designing the form and then simply load the form. In this case,

Visual Basic will make the connection for you and display the data directly, and you don't even need any code in the form's **Load** event.

The key to the success of this method is to properly orchestrate the various properties of the controls on the form:

✔ The Data control's **DatabaseName** property must be left blank to use an ODBC data source. If you enter a database name here, Visual Basic attempts to open the database using its native data format before you can set it to an empty string in code.

✔ The **Connect** property of the Data control is set to the connect string that ODBC needs to connect to the database. This is the same connect string that other How-To's in this chapter use to set up other uses of ODBC directly. You can also simply set this property to ODBC. ODBC will prompt the end user at runtime for information it needs to make the connection.

✔ The Data control's **RecordSource** property is set to the SQL statement used to select the data from the database. This can be any SQL statement that creates a resultset that Visual Basic can use to populate the bound text boxes.

✔ Each text box's **DataSource** is set to the name of the data control; in this How-To, **Data1**. This is the normal Visual Basic way of binding a control to a Data control. You can have as many Data controls on a form as you want, with different sets of controls bound to different bound controls and therefore to different databases.

✔ Each text box's **DataField** property is set to the particular field name in the resultset of data records. Note that this may be the name of the field in the database itself, but it is actually the name of the field returned in the recordset. The two can be the same, but the SQL statement can rename the fields or even return calculated fields that don't exist in the database.

Comments

You can actually perform some complex operations using the Visual Basic Data control, but you usually must do a lot more coding to get around its limitations than if you used other techniques such as data access objects (DAOs). Some of the later How-To's in this chapter cover these other techniques.

COMPLEXITY
INTERMEDIATE

2.4   How do I...
Make a connection with the Jet Engine, ODBC, and DAO?

COMPATIBILITY: VISUAL BASIC 6

Problem

I have a database I need to use in my application for data entry and editing. The Visual Basic Data control is easy to use, but I end up writing a ton of code to get around its limitations. Isn't there some way to code more flexibility into my application?

Technique

When the VB Data control falls short of your needs—and it will for any sophisticated, modern application—Visual Basic provides data access objects (DAOs), which let you have almost complete flexibility accessing data. Coding it is more work, but many of the routines can be used repeatedly in different forms in different applications. The biggest change is that you must code retrieving a record's data and putting it into controls on a form, and then code saving changed data back to the record. It is harder to describe the process than to actually do it, though. When you have a basic understanding of how DAOs work in this How-To, you should have no trouble using them in your own applications.

This How-To implements the same user interface used in How-To 2.3, which used the Visual Basic Data control, but modifies the code to use DAOs and adds a few features to demonstrate how to use DAOs.

Steps

Open and run the **BOOKS.VBP** project file. Use the navigation buttons at the bottom of the form to move through the database and then add, delete, and update records. Click Quit when you are finished. The Publisher Titles window is shown in Figure 2.7.

This How-To uses an ODBC SQL Server driver and the sample PUBS database included with SQL Server. You can use any other ODBC data source or database, but you'll need to change the fields connected to the form's text boxes. To create this project, complete the following steps:

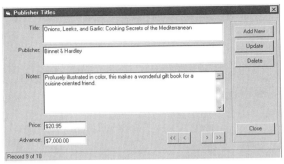

Figure 2.7 Using ODBC with Visual Basic data access objects to review a book database

1. Create a data source name in ODBC for the PUBS database. Previous versions of ODBC required that you use the ODBC Data Source Adminstrator, **ODBCAD32.EXE**, usually located in the Windows System directory in Windows 95 or the System32 directory in Windows NT. The latest versions of ODBC install the Administrator as a Control Panel applet, listed either as 32bit ODBC or simply as ODBC. (If you are using an older version of ODBC, the steps you take will differ from those listed here. Check the ODBC documentation for information.) ODBC Administrator loads the ODBC Data Source Administrator window as shown in Figure 2.5. Here you define and maintain data source names available on this system.

2. Select the System DSN tab so this data source name will be available to any user on the system. Click the Add button so the Create a New Data Source window appears. The driver you need will be listed as something like SQL Server or SQL Server (32-bit). Click this driver, and then click Finish so the Create a New Data Source to SQL Server Wizard appears.

3. Each ODBC driver has its own version of this wizard, prompting for the particular information the driver needs to make a connection with its database. Enter the information as shown in Table 2.6 as you step through the wizard. Use the defaults for any items not listed in the table. You might have to adjust other entries not listed in the table for your system setup. When you reach the last screen in the wizard, click Finish to create the data source name.

4. The ODBC Microsoft SQL Server Setup dialog box will appear, as shown in Figure 2.6. The text box lists all the settings for this new data source name. Click the Test Data Source button to test the connection to SQL Server. If you receive an error message, go back and verify the settings, particularly those for authenticating the login ID. Click OK when everything works.

5. The new Books Available data source name will appear in the Data Sources window as something like Books Available with a driver listed as SQL Server. Click OK to end the ODBC Data Source Administrator.

6. Start Visual Basic. Create a new project BOOKS.VBP.

7. Select Project, Components from the Visual Basic main menu and choose Microsoft Windows Common Controls 6.0.

8. Select Project, References from the Visual Basic main menu, and then choose the following references:

Microsoft Visual Basic for Applications
Visual Basic Runtime Objects and Procedures
Visual Basic Objects and Procedures
Microsoft DAO 3.51 Object Library

Uncheck all others so your project isn't cluttered with DLLs you aren't using, and so the Setup Wizard doesn't include unneeded files with your application.

9. Add the controls shown in Figure 2.7 to the form in the new project with property settings listed in Table 2.8. Save the form as file BOOKS.FRM.

Table 2.8   Objects and properties for BOOKS.FRM

OBJECT	PROPERTY	SETTING
Form	Name	frmBooks
	BackColor	&H00C0C0C0&
	BorderStyle	3 'Fixed Dialog
	Caption	"Publisher Titles"
	MaxButton	0 'False
	MinButton	0 'False
TextBox	Name	txtTitle
	MultiLine	-1 'True
TextBox	Name	txtNotes
	MultiLine	-1 'True
	ScrollBars	2 'Vertical
TextBox	Name	txtPrice
TextBox	Name	txtAdvance
TextBox	Name	txtPublisher
	MultiLine	-1 'True
Frame	Name	Frame1

continued on next page

Table 2.8 continued

OBJECT	PROPERTY	SETTING
CommandButton	Name	cmdClose
	Caption	"Close"
CommandButton	Name	cmdDelete
	Caption	"Delete"
CommandButton	Name	cmdUpdate
	Caption	"Update"
CommandButton	Name	cmdAddNew
	Caption	"Add New"
CommandButton	Name	cmdMove
	Caption	">>"
	Index	3
	TabStop	0 'False
CommandButton	Name	cmdMove
	Caption	">"
	Index	2
	TabStop	0 'False
CommandButton	Name	cmdMove
	Caption	"<"
	Index	1
	TabStop	0 'False
CommandButton	Name	cmdMove
	Caption	"<<"
	Index	0
	TabStop	0 'False
Label	Name	Label1
	Alignment	1 'Right Justify
	BackColor	&H00C0C0C0&
	Caption	"Title:"
Label	Name	Label3
	Alignment	1 'Right Justify
	BackColor	&H00C0C0C0&
	Caption	"Notes:"
Label	Name	Label5
	Alignment	1 'Right Justify
	BackColor	&H00C0C0C0&
	Caption	"Price:"

OBJECT	PROPERTY	SETTING
Label	Name	Label6
	Alignment	1 'Right Justify
	BackColor	&H00C0C0C0&
	Caption	"Advance:"
Label	Name	Label9
	Alignment	1 'Right Justify
	BackColor	&H00C0C0C0&
	Caption	"Publisher:"
StatusBar	Name	StatusBar1
	Align	2 'Align Bottom
	AlignSet	-1 'True
	Style	1
	SimpleText	" "

10. Add the following code to the declarations section of the form. `Option Explicit` tells Visual Basic to make sure that you declare all variables and objects before using them in order to avoid naming problems. You can have Visual Basic automatically add this statement to your code modules by checking the Require Variable Declaration check box in Tools, Options under the Editor tab. The first two variables are references to database objects so code throughout the module can manipulate the data. The next two variables track the total number of records and the current location in the recordset. The last variable, `mDirty`, records whether the end user has made any changes to the current data.

```
Option Explicit

'Database and Recordset objects that will contain
'the books table.
Dim db As Database
Dim rs As Recordset

'Variables to track the position in recordset.
Dim lTotRec As Long
Dim lCurrRec As Long

'Variable to indicated if data needs to be saved.
Dim mDirty As Boolean
```

11. Add the following code to the form's `Load` event procedure. After centering the form, `OpenDatabase` makes a connection to the ODBC data source, and then the `rs` recordset is opened by using an SQL query. To prevent problems when there is no current record, a new record is added if the recordset is empty.

The code uses the `lCurrRec` and `lTotRec` to keep track of the position in the recordset. You can implement this technique when using the data control, but the logic gets to be a bit more convoluted because Visual Basic is handling part of the record navigation work for you. (Visual Basic and the Jet engine are oriented to work on sets of records rather than individual records, so keeping track of the current record number is a concept foreign to Visual Basic.)

Finally, the **Load** event procedure calls the **DataLoad** procedure to load the form's controls with data from the current record.

```
Private Sub Form_Load()
'Set up the form and connect to data source
Dim sSQL As String

    'Center the form
    Me.Top = (Screen.Height - Me.Height) / 2
    Me.Left = (Screen.Width - Me.Width) / 2

    'Connect to the database.
    Set db = OpenDatabase("Books Available", _
        False, False, "ODBC;UID=sa;PWD=")

    'Create the recordset.
    sSQL = _
        "SELECT DISTINCTROW titles.*, publishers.* " _
        & "FROM publishers " _
        & "INNER JOIN titles " _
        & "ON publishers.pub_id = titles.pub_id " _
        & "ORDER BY titles.Title;"
        Set rs = db.OpenRecordset(sSQL)

    'If the recordset is empty, add a record.
    If rs.EOF And rs.BOF Then
        rs.AddNew
        rs.Update
        lTotRec = 1
    Else
        rs.MoveLast
        lTotRec = rs.RecordCount
    End If

    rs.MoveFirst
    lCurrRec = 1
    SetRecNum

    DataLoad

'    txtTitle.SetFocus

End Sub
```

12. Because the Visual Basic code is handling all the data management details, it must take care of properly saving data that is dirty or has changed. You have several options: Let the end user worry about it, manually updating the data when he or she changes it, or you can handle it entirely in code. Or you can use some combination of the two, which is the way I've implemented this program. The code responds to the form's controls' Change events and the end user can manually save the data by clicking an Update button. Add the following code to the Change event procedure for all the text boxes on the form:

```
Private Sub txtAdvance_Change()
    mDirty = True
End Sub

Private Sub txtNotes_Change()
    mDirty = True
End Sub

Private Sub txtPrice_Change()
    mDirty = True
End Sub

Private Sub txtPublisher_Change()
    mDirty = True
End Sub

Private Sub txtTitle_Change()
    mDirty = True
End Sub
```

13. Add the following code to the DataLoad Sub procedure. This is the code that loads the current record's data into the form each time the end user moves to a new record. The procedure finishes by setting the mDirty flag to False because the data was just loaded, and then updating the record counter at the bottom of the form.

```
Private Sub DataLoad()
'Copy the record's data to the text boxes.

    txtAdvance.Text = Format$(rs("Advance") & "", "Currency")
    txtNotes.Text = rs("Notes") & ""
    txtPrice.Text = Format$(rs("Price") & "", "Currency")
    txtPublisher.Text = rs("Pub_Name") & ""
    txtTitle.Text = rs("Title") & ""

    mDirty = False
    SetRecNum
End Sub
```

14. What goes in must come out, so add the following code to the DataSave procedure, which saves the data in the form to the current record whenever the data is dirty or the end user clicks the Update button. The mDirty flag is also set to False here because the data in the form is again the same as that in the record.

```
Private Sub DataSave()
'Copy the current control contents to the record.
'ODBC driver and database has to support editing
'(most do).
   rs.Edit
   rs("Advance") = txtAdvance.Text
   rs("Notes") = txtNotes.Text
   rs("Price") = txtPrice.Text
   rs("Pub_Name") = txtPublisher.Text
   rs("Title") = txtTitle.Text
   rs.Update

   mDirty = False
End Sub
```

15. The form has an Update button the end user can use to manually update
data, which simply executes the **DataSave** procedure. The lines
commented out here can be used to protect the end user against himself or
herself by saving data only when it is dirty. This is a user interface issue. If
the user wants to save the data, you should go ahead and save it rather
than essentially ignore his or her wishes, whether or not the data is dirty.
You might, however, have a good programmatic reason to not save clean
data. In that case, and if you uncomment the two lines, at least let the end
user know that the data isn't being saved, and why.

```
Private Sub cmdUpdate_Click()
'    If mDirty Then
       DataSave
'    End If
End Sub
```

16. The next few procedures take care of navigating through the recordset.
The navigation keys, a control array of command buttons, execute this
Click event procedure that starts by checking whether the end user wants
to save any dirty data. Then it calls the **MoveRecord** procedure with the
control index to actually reposition the record. Because there is a new
current record, the **DataLoad** procedure loads the new data into the form.

```
Private Sub cmdMove_Click(Index As Integer)
Dim iResponse As Integer

    If mDirty Then
       iResponse = MsgBox("Dirty data. Save changes?", _
          vbYesNo + vbExclamation, "Update Data?")
       If iResponse = vbYes Then
          DataSave
       End If
    End If

    lCurrRec = MoveRecord(rs, Index, lCurrRec)

    DataLoad
End Sub
```

17. Enter the following code into the **MoveRecord Function** procedure. This code is a reusable function to move around a recordset, implementing code to move to the first, last, next, or previous records. If the first record is current and the end user clicks the Move Previous button, a beep sounds; a beep also sounds at the last record when the end user clicks the Move Next button. You can get as creative as you want here, allowing the end user to move forward or backward a fixed number of records or to go to a specific record number.

```
Public Function MoveRecord( _
    rs As Recordset, _
    Index As Integer, _
    Optional lCurrRec As Variant) As Long

    If IsMissing(lCurrRec) Then
        lCurrRec = 0
    End If

    Select Case Index
        Case 0 'MoveFirst
            rs.MoveFirst
            MoveRecord = 1

        Case 1 'MovePrevious
            rs.MovePrevious
            If rs.BOF Then
                Beep
                rs.MoveFirst
                MoveRecord = 1
            Else
                MoveRecord = lCurrRec - 1
            End If

        Case 2 'MoveNext
            rs.MoveNext
            If rs.EOF Then
                Beep
                rs.MoveLast
                MoveRecord = rs.RecordCount
            Else
                MoveRecord = lCurrRec + 1
            End If

        Case 3 'MoveLast
            rs.MoveLast
            MoveRecord = rs.RecordCount

    End Select
End Function
```

18. At the bottom of the form, a **StatusBar** control shows the end user where he is in the recordset, indicating Record 5 of 120 or whatever. Here the **lCurrRec** and **lTotRec** module variables finally become visibly useful.

```
Private Sub SetRecNum()
    StatusBar1.SimpleText = "Record " & _
        lCurrRec & " of " & lTotRec
End Sub
```

19. To add a new record, the **cmdAddNew** button's **Click** event checks to see whether dirty data should be saved, and then adds a new record to the recordset. After updating the **lTotRec** count and the **lCurrRec** position in the recordset, the **DataLoad** procedure loads data from the new record. Because it is a new record and has no data, this clears the form's controls, making them ready to accept the end user's input.

```
Private Sub cmdAddNew_Click()
Dim iResponse As Integer

    If mDirty Then
        iResponse = MsgBox("Dirty data. " _
            & "Save before adding a new record?", _
            vbYesNo + vbExclamation, "Dirty Data")
        If iResponse = vbYes Then
            DataSave
        End If
    End If

    rs.AddNew
    rs.Update
    rs.Move 0, rs.LastModified
    lTotRec = lTotRec + 1
    lCurrRec = rs.RecordCount

    DataLoad
End Sub
```

20. A Delete button allows the end user to remove records from the recordset. This is very similar to the **AddNew** procedure. If after deleting the record the recordset is empty, a new record is added so there is always at least one record. Either way, the position is moved to the first record, and its data is loaded into the form.

```
Private Sub cmdDelete_Click()
Dim iResponse As Integer

    iResponse = MsgBox("Are you sure that you " _
        & "want to delete this record?", _
        vbYesNo + vbExclamation, "Delete Record")
    If iResponse = vbYes Then
        rs.Delete
        lTotRec = lTotRec - 1
        If (rs.BOF And rs.EOF) Or lTotRec = 0 Then
            'If there aren't any records in the table, add an
            'empty record to avoid problems with "No current
            'record" errors.
            rs.AddNew
            rs.Update
```

```
        rs.MoveLast <moved statement below>
        lCurrRec = rs.RecordCount
        lTotRec = lCurrRec
    Else
        lCurrRec = 1
    End If
End If


rs.MoveFirst
DataLoad
End Sub
```

21. Add the following code to the **Click** event of the **cmdClose** command button. This is the exit point that terminates the program. After checking one last time whether dirty data should be saved, the procedure unloads itself.

```
Private Sub cmdClose_Click()
Dim iResponse As Integer

    If mDirty Then
        iResponse = MsgBox("Dirty data. Save before closing?", _
            vbYesNo + vbExclamation, "Dirty Data")
        If iResponse = vbYes Then
            DataSave
        End If
    End If
    Unload Me
End Sub
```

22. In the Project, [Project Name] Options menu item, set the startup form to **frmBooks**. You can also set an application description, but that is not required for the operation of this application.

How It Works

If you compare this code with that in How-To 2.3, you'll find that many of the features you might take for granted with the Data control must be handled by your code. This is a bit more work but gives you far greater flexibility with how your application uses and navigates data.

The details of using ODBC are similar to those when using the Data control. All the work of making the connection is handled in this code from the form's **Load** event procedure as shown here:

```
'Connect to the database.
   Set db = OpenDatabase("Books Available", _
      False, False, "ODBC;UID=sa;PWD=")

   'Create the recordset.
   sSQL = _
      "SELECT DISTINCTROW titles.*, publishers.* " _
      & "FROM publishers " _
      & "INNER JOIN titles " _
```

continued on next page

continued from previous page

```
        & "ON publishers.pub_id = titles.pub_id " _
        & "ORDER BY titles.Title;"
Set rs = db.OpenRecordset(sSQL)
```

If ODBC needs more information in the `Connect` string (the last parameter of the `OpenDatabase` method), include it after the `ODBC;` entry, separating multiple entries with semicolons. If you must figure out what connection information a database needs, see How-To 2.2 for code that makes a connection and then exposes the full connect string.

Incidentally, for larger applications, you should put this database initialization code in a separate procedure instead of in `Form_Load` to give you more flexibility connecting with the database, particularly to handle error conditions such as if the ODBC data source no longer points to the correct database location. This way, you can ask the user to correct any problems before getting into the application or gracefully exit the application, if necessary. In a small sample application like this, it works well in the `Load` procedure.

Comments

Visual Basic's DAOs give your application enormous flexibility compared to the limitations of the Data control, along with better speed if you code your applications carefully, at the cost of a bit more coding work. As a practical matter, the Data control is rarely used extensively in full-size applications, except perhaps for a simple form or two, because it just doesn't give you much help providing ease-of-use and data management features required of modern Windows applications.

COMPLEXITY
INTERMEDIATE

2.5 How do I...
Use the SQL passthrough option?

COMPATIBILITY: VISUAL BASIC 6

Problem

Every time I try to use the powerful features of my database server, I get error messages (from Jet, I think) saying that my SQL statements are not valid. Even if the statements work, it takes forever to process the query. How can I be sure that my SQL statements are passing directly to the database server so that Visual Basic won't protect me from myself?

Technique

In an n-tier client/server application, SQL statements and queries theoretically can be executed at any tier in the application. If you use DAO without the techniques described in this How-To, the Jet engine will attempt to process the query. Other native data access techniques in Visual Basic might automatically cause the query to execute on a different tier. But if you write an SQL statement customized to the unique features of the back-end database, such as SQL Server or Oracle, Jet or other tiers might not be able to process the query. So how do you "pass the query through" to the right tier?

With the different tiers of a typical client/server database application, it isn't always easy to get the right statement to the right tier in the system because each layer might try to execute the statement itself. This is a problem if you are using any specialized features of the database server. For example, the Access Jet database engine, left to its own way of doing things, will attempt to execute the SQL statements you pass its way. You must "pass the statement through" Jet, bypassing it but still letting Jet manage the connection, thus creating a passthrough query.

The passthrough technique uses Visual Basic's native data access methods as shown in this How-To, using **CreateQueryDef** and **OpenRecordset**. Using this technique, you can execute any SQL syntax supported by the database, including stored procedures in SQL Server and extensions to SQL.

Steps

Open and run the **PASSTHRU.VBP** Visual Basic project file. The project automatically connects with the ODBC database and loads the bound data grid with two fields selected in the SQL string. Click Quit to end the program.

This How-To uses an ODBC SQL Server driver and the sample PUBS database included with SQL Server. You can use any other ODBC data source or database, but you'll need to change the fields connected to the form's text boxes. Complete the following steps to create this project:

1. Create a data source name in ODBC for the PUBS database. Previous versions of ODBC required that you use the ODBC Data Source Adminstrator, **ODBCAD32.EXE**, usually located in the Windows System directory in Windows 95 or the System32 directory in Windows NT. The latest versions of ODBC install the Administrator as a Control Panel applet, listed either as 32bit ODBC or simply as ODBC. (If you are using an older version of ODBC, the steps you take will differ from those listed here. Check the ODBC documentation for information.) ODBC Administrator loads the ODBC Data Source Administrator window as shown in Figure 2.5. Here you define and maintain data source names available on this system.

2. Select the System DSN tab so that this data source name will be available to any user on the system. Click Add so the Create a New Data Source window appears. The driver you need will be listed as something like SQL Server or SQL Server (32-bit). Click this driver, and then click Finish so the Create a New Data Source to SQL Server Wizard appears.

3. Each ODBC driver has its own version of this wizard, prompting for the particular information that the driver must make a connection with its database. Enter the information as shown in Table 2.6 as you step through the wizard. For any items not listed in the table, use the defaults. You might have to adjust other entries not listed in the table for your system setup. When you reach the last screen in the wizard, click Finish to create the data source name.

4. The ODBC Microsoft SQL Server Setup dialog box will appear, as shown in Figure 2.6. The text box lists all the settings for this new data source name. Click the Test Data Source button to test the connection to SQL Server. If you receive an error message, go back and verify the settings, particularly those for authenticating the login ID. Click OK when everything works.

5. The new Books Available data source name will appear in the Data Sources window as something like Books Available with a driver listed as SQL Server. Click OK to end the ODBC Data Source Administrator.

6. Start Visual Basic and create a new project called `PASSTHRU.VBP`.

7. Select Project, Components from the Visual Basic main menu, and then choose Microsoft Data Bound Grid Control 5.0. Uncheck all others so your project isn't cluttered with controls you aren't using, and so the Setup Wizard doesn't include unused custom controls with your application.

8. Select Project, References from the Visual Basic main menu, and choose the following references:

Microsoft Visual Basic for Applications
Visual Basic Runtime Objects and Procedures
Visual Basic Objects and Procedures
Microsoft DAO 3.51 Object Library

Uncheck all others so your project isn't cluttered with DLLs you aren't using, and so the Setup Wizard doesn't include a lot of extra dead weight with your application.

9. Name the default form `frmPassThru` and save the file as `PASSTHRU.FRM`. Add the controls shown in Figure 2.8, setting the properties as shown in Table 2.9.

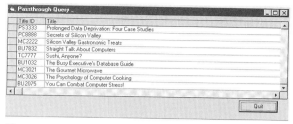

Figure 2.8 Dialog box to test SQL passthrough queries.

Table 2.9 Objects and properties for PASSTHRU.FRM

OBJECT	PROPERTY	SETTING
Form	Name	frmPassthru
	Caption	"Passthrough Query"
CommandButton	Name	cmdQuit
	Caption	"Quit"
Data	Name	Data1
	Caption	"Data1"
	Connect	" "
	DatabaseName	" "
	Exclusive	0 'False
	Options	0
	ReadOnly	0 'False
	RecordsetType	1 'Dynaset
	RecordSource	" "
DBGrid	Name	DBGrid1
	DataSource	Data1

10. Insert the following code in the declarations section of the form. Option Explicit tells Visual Basic to make sure that you declare all variables and objects before using them, in order to avoid naming problems. You can have Visual Basic automatically add this statement to your code modules by checking the Require Variable Declaration check box in Tools, Options under the Editor tab.

```
Option Explicit
```

11. Add the following code in the Load event procedure of the form. This code centers the form, and then sets the properties of the Data control to access the Books Available data source name.

```
Private Sub Form_Load()
```

```
'Dim dbPub As Database
'Dim qdPub As QueryDef
Dim sConnect As String
Dim iLeft As Integer
Dim iTop As Integer

    'Resize and center the form
    iLeft = (Screen.Width - Width) / 2
    iTop = (Screen.Height - Height) / 2

    Move iLeft, iTop

    sConnect = "ODBC;DSN=Books Available;UID=sa;PWD="
    data1.Options = dbSQLPassThrough
    data1.Connect = sConnect
    data1.RecordsetType = vbRSTypeSnapShot
    data1.RecordSource = "SELECT title_id AS 'Title ID', " _
        & "Title FROM Titles ORDER BY Title;"
    data1.Refresh
End Sub
```

12. Add the following code to the form's `Resize` event. This code expands and contracts the `DBGrid` control and relocates the `cmdQuit` command button as the end user resizes the form.

```
Private Sub Form_Resize()
    DBGrid1.Width = Me.ScaleWidth
    DBGrid1.Height = Me.ScaleHeight - 2 * cmdQuit.Height
    cmdQuit.Top = Me.ScaleHeight - 1.5 * cmdQuit.Height
    cmdQuit.Left = Me.ScaleWidth - 1.25 * cmdQuit.Width

    'Adjust the size of the data grid's columns
    DBGrid1.Columns(0).Width = 0.1 * Me.ScaleWidth
    DBGrid1.Columns(1).Width = 0.9 * Me.ScaleWidth
End Sub
```

13. Add the following code to the `Click` event of the `cmdQuit` command button:

```
Private Sub cmdQuit_Click()
    Unload Me
End Sub
```

14. In the Project, [Project Name] Options menu item, set the startup form to `frmPassThru`. You can also set an application description, but that is not required for the operation of the application.

How It Works

There are essentially three ways to execute a query in Visual Basic by using ODBC: execute the query using Visual Basic through the Jet database engine, pass the query straight through ODBC to the database system or driver and let

Jet manage the connection, or use remote data objects. This How-To showed how to pass the query directly to ODBC and the database system.

Visual Basic normally uses the Jet database engine to process queries before they are passed on to the database. When you use a passthrough query, however, the Jet engine is bypassed entirely, except that Visual Basic still uses its recordset processor to create and manage the resultsets of the query.

The major advantage of a passthrough query is to take advantage of any specific capabilities of the database. For example, you can execute SQL Server's stored procedures only by using a passthrough query. In this case, the grammar of the query is not valid under the SQL grammar used by either Visual Basic or ODBC, so an error would result if Visual Basic processed the query before sending it on.

Passthrough queries also are advantageous for databases located in distant locations over the network. Rather than passing a huge amount of data through the network, the database itself does all the processing, returning only a resultset (if there is one) to ODBC and Visual Basic.

This How-To used the Data control to make the connection, but you can also use these techniques with data access objects (DAOs). When using DAOs, all that is needed to execute a passthrough SQL statement is to use only a name argument in **CreateQueryDef**. You then assign the SQL command as a string to the SQL property of the **QueryDef**. The following code illustrates the general procedure:

```
Dim db as Database
Dim qd As QueryDef

'Use the first argument, name, only in CreateQueryDef:
Set qd = MyDb.CreateQueryDef("MYODbCQuery")

qd.Connect = "ODBC;" "DSN=MyServer;UID=sa;PWD=hithere;DATABASE=pubs"
qd.SQL = "Exec SELECT * FROM pubs"
qd.ReturnsRows = True

Dim rs As Recordset
Set rs = qd.OpenRecordset()
```

Note the use of the **ReturnsRows** property in this code. This property, when set to **True**, tells Visual Basic to use the Jet engine to be ready to receive and manage the recordset (if any) that ODBC and the database returns from the query. **ReturnsRows** should be set to **False** for action queries or other commands that do not return records to Visual Basic.

The SQL string assigned to the SQL property of the **QueryDef** object **qd** is the syntax of the external database, which might or might not be different from the syntax normally required by Visual Basic. This statement will be passed directly to the external database, as will all other SQL statements you make by using this instance of the **QueryDef** object. This also means that your application must be ready to handle any errors the database returns.

Note also that previous versions of Visual Basic included a DB_SQLPASSTHROUGH or dbSQLPassthrough (in Visual Basic 4) constant for use with CreateDynaset, CreateSnapshot, or ExecuteSQL methods. With the latest version of the Jet database engine, it is now recommended that you use the technique demonstrated earlier instead of using these constants.

Comments

Although the technique described in this How-To works, passing the query to a lower tier, the question remains as to why you might use this technique. If you intend to bypass the Jet database engine, why use it at all? One reason is that you might want Jet to provide features not supported by the back-end database, such as bidirectional cursors (see Chapter 1, "Client/Server Basics," for a discussion of cursors). You might also need to pass through only one or two specialized queries, but are otherwise using Jet normally, so it is easier to use the same techniques throughout your application rather than mixing DAO, RDO, and so on. Just remember that passthrough queries are, by their nature, nonportable because you are using the special capabilities of a single back-end database engine.

The following are other uses for passthrough queries:

✔ Creating a new database, table, or index on an external server

✔ Creating or managing triggers, defaults, rules, or stored procedures, all of which are different forms of small programs that are part of the back-end database

✔ Maintaining user accounts or performing other System Administrator tasks

✔ Running maintenance operations like Microsoft SQL Server's DBCC

✔ Executing multiple INSERT or UPDATE statements in a single batch command

In most cases, you'll be better off using remote data objects or other connection techniques instead of passthrough queries.

COMPLEXITY
INTERMEDIATE

2.6 How do I...
Make a connection using the RemoteData control?

COMPATIBILITY: VISUAL BASIC 6

Problem

I must access a database on another computer on the network. ODBC is too complex for a simple application, and the regular VB Data control can't handle the network well. How can I make a connection for simple database access?

Technique

The Visual Basic Enterprise Edition provides some nifty new tools for connecting with remote databases via ODBC. In this How-To, you'll modify the Books sample application used in How-To's 2.3 and 2.4 by using instead the RemoteData control available only in the Enterprise Edition. As you'll see, it is only slightly more complex than using a Visual Basic data control but reaps many benefits, not the least of which is performance.

Steps

Open and run the **BOOKS.VBP** project file. Use the Visual Basic RemoteData control's navigation buttons at the bottom of the form to move through the database, as shown in Figure 2.9. Click Close when you are finished. (These figures show vertical bars in some of the text notes of the **BIBLIO.MDB** file. These are embedded carriage-return and line-feed characters, which the Visual Basic **TextBox** doesn't handle elegantly. If they bother you, you can programmatically strip them out of the text.)

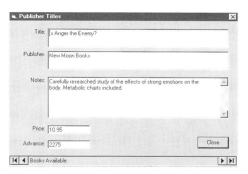

Figure 2.9 Using ODBC with the Visual Basic RemoteData control to review a book database

This How-To uses an ODBC SQL Server driver and the sample PUBS database included with SQL Server. You can use any other ODBC data source or database, but you'll need to change the fields connected to the form's text boxes. To create this project, complete the following steps:

1. Create a data source name in ODBC for the PUBS database. Previous versions of ODBC required that you use the ODBC Data Source Adminstrator, **ODBCAD32.EXE**, usually located in the Windows System directory in Windows 95 or the System32 directory in Windows NT. The latest versions of ODBC install the Administrator as a Control Panel applet, listed either as 32bit ODBC or simply as ODBC. (If you are using an older version of ODBC, the steps you take will differ from those listed here. Check the ODBC documentation for information.) ODBC Administrator loads the ODBC Data Source Administrator window as shown in Figure 2.5. Here you define and maintain data source names available on this system.

2. Select the System DSN tab so that this data source name will be available to any user on the system. Click Add so the Create a New Data Source window appears. The driver you need will be listed as something like SQL Server or SQL Server (32-bit). Click this driver, and then click Finish so the Create a New Data Source to SQL Server Wizard appears.

3. Each ODBC driver has its own version of this wizard, prompting for the particular information the driver needs to make a connection with its database. Enter the information as shown in Table 2.6 as you step through the wizard. Use the defaults for any items not listed in the table. You might have to adjust other entries not listed in the table for your system setup. When you reach the last screen in the wizard, click Finish to create the data source name.

4. The ODBC Microsoft SQL Server Setup dialog box will appear, as shown in Figure 2.6. The text box lists all the settings for this new data source name. Click the Test Data Source button to test the connection to SQL Server. If you receive an error message, go back and verify the settings, particularly those for authenticating the login ID. Click OK when everything works.

5. The new Books Available data source name will appear in the Data Sources window as something like Books Available with a driver listed as SQL Server. Click OK to end the ODBC Data Source Administrator.

6. Start Visual Basic. Create a new project `BOOKS.VBP`. Add the form `ERRORRDO.FRM` (see the introduction to this chapter for a description of this form) by using Visual Basic's Project, Add File menu command. This form handles RDO errors.

7. Select Project, Components from the Visual Basic main menu, and then choose Microsoft RemoteData Control 6.0. Uncheck all others so your project isn't cluttered with controls you aren't using, and so the Setup Wizard doesn't include a lot of extra dead weight with your application.

8. Select Project, References from the Visual Basic main menu and choose the following references:

Microsoft Visual Basic for Applications

Visual Basic Runtime Objects and Procedures

Visual Basic Objects and Procedures

Microsoft Remote Data Object 2.0

Uncheck all others so your project isn't cluttered with DLLs you aren't using, and so the Setup Wizard doesn't include a lot of extra dead weight with your application.

9. Add the controls shown in Figure 2.9 to the form in the new project with the property settings listed in Table 2.10. Save the form as file BOOKS.FRM.

Table 2.10   Objects and properties for BOOKS.FRM

OBJECT	PROPERTY	SETTING
Form	Name	frmBooks
	BackColor	&H00C0C0C0&
	BorderStyle	3 'Fixed Dialog
	Caption	"Publisher Titles"
	MaxButton	0 'False
	MinButton	0 'False
TextBox	Name	txtTitle
	DataSource	"rdcBooks"
	MultiLine	-1 'True
TextBox	Name	txtNotes
	DataSource	"rdcBooks"
	MultiLine	-1 'True
	ScrollBars	2 'Vertical
TextBox	Name	txtPrice
	DataSource	"rdcBooks"
TextBox	Name	txtAdvance
	DataSource	"rdcBooks"
CommandButton	Name	cmdClose
	Caption	"Close"
	Default	-1 'True
TextBox	Name	txtPublisher
	DataSource	"rdcBooks"
	MultiLine	-1 'True
Label	Name	Label1
	Alignment	1 'Right Justify
	BackColor	&H00C0C0C0&
	Caption	"Title:"
Label	Name	Label3
	Alignment	1 'Right Justify

continued on next page

Table 2.10   continued

OBJECT	PROPERTY	SETTING
	BackColor	&H00C0C0C0&
	Caption	"Notes:"
Label	Name	Label5
	Alignment	1 'Right Justify
	BackColor	&H00C0C0C0&
	Caption	"Price:"
Label	Name	Label6
	Alignment	1 'Right Justify
	BackColor	&H00C0C0C0&
	Caption	"Advance:"
Label	Name	Label9
	Alignment	1 'Right Justify
	BackColor	&H00C0C0C0&
	Caption	"Publisher:"
MSRDC	Name	rdcBooks
	Align	2 'Align Bottom
	DataSourceName	""
	RecordSource	""
	Connect	""
	ReadOnly	0 'False
	UserName	""
	Password	""
	Caption	"Books Available"

10. Add the following code to the declarations section of the form. `Option Explicit` tells Visual Basic to make sure that you declare all variables and objects before using them, in order to avoid naming problems. You can have Visual Basic automatically add this statement to your code modules by checking the Require Variable Declaration check box in Tools, Options under the Editor tab.

```
Option Explicit
```

11. Add the following code to the form's Load event procedure. After centering the form, the RemoteData control's **DataSourceName** property is set to connect to the Books Available ODBC data source name and the SQL property is set with the query to execute against the database. Other RemoteData control properties specify a **Keyset** resultset, optimistic locking, whether to use the ODBC or server-side cursors, options relating to the **Keyset** and **Rowset** sizes, and a synchronous query, all features of how the ODBC database responds to a query. Then the text boxes' **DataField** properties are set to the fields that each will hold. This is the step that links each field to use with the text boxes that hold each record's data.

If you want to test the RDO error handling form discussed at the beginning of this chapter, an easy way is to misspell one of the table names in the **sSQL** string, such as to change **titles** to **tittles**.

```
Private Sub Form_Load()
'Set up the form and connect to data source
Dim sSQL As String

    'Center the form
    Me.Top = (Screen.Height - Me.Height) / 2
    Me.Left = (Screen.Width - Me.Width) / 2

    sSQL = _
        "SELECT titles.*, publishers.* " _
        & "FROM titles, publishers " _
        & "WHERE publishers.pub_id = titles.pub_id " _
        & "ORDER BY titles.Title ASC;"

    rdcBooks.Connect = "DSN=Books Available;UID=sa;PWD="
    rdcBooks.SQL = sSQL
    rdcBooks.ResultsetType = rdOpenKeyset
    rdcBooks.LockType = rdConcurRowver
    rdcBooks.CursorDriver = rdUseIfNeeded
    rdcBooks.KeysetSize = 0
    rdcBooks.RowsetSize = 100
    rdcBooks.Options = 0

    'Connect each of the text boxes with the appropriate
    'fieldname
    txtAdvance.DataField = "Advance"
    txtNotes.DataField = "Notes"
    txtPrice.DataField = "Price"
    txtPublisher.DataField = "Pub_Name"
    txtTitle.DataField = "Title"

    On Error GoTo FormLoadError
    rdcBooks.Refresh

    Exit Sub

FormLoadError:
    frmRDOErrors.ErrorColl = rdoErrors
End Sub
```

12. Add the following code to the **Click** event of the **cmdQuit** command button. This is the exit point that terminates the program.

```
Private Sub cmdClose_Click()
   Unload Me
End Sub
```

13. In the Project, [Project Name] Options menu item, set the startup form to frmBooks. You can also set an application description, but that is not required for the operation of this application.

How It Works

If you worked with How-To 2.3, this How-To should have looked remarkably familiar. The only real difference is that the RemoteData control provides more options you can use to control the connection to the ODBC data source. And if you've ever used the ODBC API directly to code data applications, you'll never go back to coding the API directly because of the sheer amount of coding required, even if you use wrapper functions or VB classes.

Remote Data Objects and the RemoteData control are really just thin wrappers around the ODBC API, making it fairly easy to access any kind of ODBC data. And because ODBC has become the standard relational data access technology on the Windows platform, you have access to just about any data in the enterprise. This How-To showed a simple example of setting up and using the RemoteData control to present and update data.

COMPLEXITY
INTERMEDIATE

2.7 How do I...
Make a connection using remote data objects?

COMPATIBILITY: VISUAL BASIC 6

Problem

How can I use the remote data features of the Visual Basic Enterprise Edition to connect to and manage databases over a network? The most efficient way for me to code client/server applications is to have one basic data access technique.

Technique

The Visual Basic Enterprise Edition's remote data objects essentially provide a thin layer over the ODBC API by providing a set of objects that you can manipulate much like DAOs and other Visual Basic objects. As such, RDOs strike a balance between the two methods of accessing data, giving much of the best of both worlds. Figure 2.10 shows the hierarchy of remote data objects.

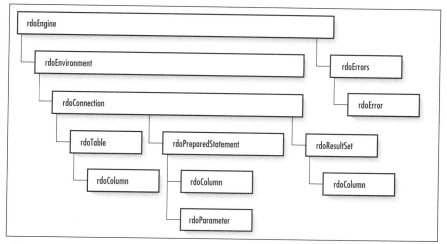

Figure 2.10 The remote data objects hierarchy

On the one hand, the hierarchy of remote data objects makes it relatively easy to create and manipulate objects, set their properties, and enumerate collections by using Visual Basic's collection objects. On the other hand, RDOs expose the underlying structure of the ODBC API, such as by providing environment, connection, and statement handles, so you can use individual API functions if you want. RDOs provide the rarest of benefits: the best of both worlds.

RDOs are a bit more complex than Jet's DAOs but in compensation they open many more options for remote data access than DAOs with ODBC.

Steps

Open and run the **BOOKS.VBP** project file. Use the navigation buttons at the bottom of the form to move through the database, and then add, delete, and update records. Click Close when you are finished. The Publisher Titles window is shown in Figure 2.11.

This How-To uses an ODBC SQL Server driver and the sample PUBS database included with SQL Server. You can use any other ODBC data source or database, but you'll need to change the fields connected to the form's text boxes. Complete the following steps to create this project:

1. Create a data source name in ODBC for the PUBS database. Previous versions of ODBC required that you use the ODBC Data Source Adminstrator, **ODBCAD32.EXE**, usually located in the Windows System directory in Windows 95 or the System32 directory in Windows NT. The latest versions of ODBC install the Administrator as a Control Panel applet, listed either as 32bit ODBC or simply as ODBC. (If you are using an older version of ODBC, the steps you take will differ from those listed here. Check the ODBC documentation for information.) ODBC Administrator loads the ODBC Data Source Administrator window as shown in Figure 2.5. Here you define and maintain data source names available on this system.

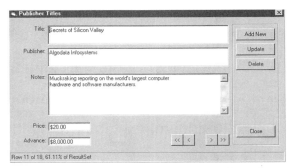

Figure 2.11 Using ODBC with Visual Basic remote data objects to review a book database

2. Select the System DSN tab so that this data source name will be available to any user on the system. Click Add so the Create a New Data Source window appears. The driver you need will be listed as something like SQL Server or SQL Server (32-bit). Click this driver, and then click Finish so the Create a New Data Source to SQL Server Wizard appears.

3. Each ODBC driver has its own version of this wizard, prompting for the particular information that the driver needs to make a connection with its database. Enter the information as shown in Table 2.6 as you step through the wizard. Use the defaults for any items not listed in the table. You might have to adjust other entries not listed in the table for your system setup. When you reach the last screen in the wizard, click Finish to create the data source name.

4. The ODBC Microsoft SQL Server Setup dialog box will appear, as shown in Figure 2.6. The text box lists all the settings for this new data source name. Click the Test Data Source button to test the connection to SQL Server. If you receive an error message, go back and verify the settings, particularly those for authenticating the login ID. Click OK when everything works.

5. The new Books Available data source name will appear in the Data Sources window as something like Books Available with a driver listed as SQL Server. Click OK to end the ODBC Data Source Administrator.

6. Start Visual Basic. Create a new project BOOKS.VBP. Add the form ERRORRDO.FRM (see the introduction to this chapter for a description of this form), using Visual Basic's Project, Add File menu command. This form handles RDO errors.

7. Select Project, Components from the Visual Basic main menu, and then choose Microsoft Windows Common Controls 6.0. Uncheck all others so your project isn't cluttered with controls you aren't using, and so the Setup Wizard doesn't include a lot of extra dead weight with your application.

8. Select Project, References from the Visual Basic main menu and choose the following references:

Microsoft Visual Basic for Applications

Visual Basic Runtime Objects and Procedures

Visual Basic Objects and Procedures

Microsoft Remote Data Object 2.0

Uncheck all others so your project isn't cluttered with DLLs you aren't using, and so the Setup Wizard doesn't include a lot of extra dead weight with your application.

9. Add the controls shown in Figure 2.11 to the default form in the new project with the property settings listed in Table 2.11. Save the form as file BOOKS.FRM.

Table 2.11   Objects and properties for BOOKS.VBP

OBJECT	PROPERTY	SETTING
Form	Name	frmBooks
	BackColor	&H00C0C0C0&
	BorderStyle	3 'Fixed Dialog
	Caption	"Publisher Titles"
	MaxButton	0 'False
	MinButton	0 'False
Frame	Name	Frame1
CommandButton	Name	cmdAddNew
	BackColor	&H80000005&
	Caption	"Add New"
CommandButton	Name	cmdUpdate
	BackColor	&H80000005&
	Caption	"Update"

continued on next page

Table 2.11 continued

OBJECT	PROPERTY	SETTING
CommandButton	Name	cmdDelete
	BackColor	&H80000005&
	Caption	"Delete"
CommandButton	Name	cmdClose
	Caption	"Close"
CommandButton	Name	cmdMove
	Caption	"<<"
	Index	0
	TabStop	0 'False
CommandButton	Name	cmdMove
	Caption	"<"
	Index	1
	TabStop	0 'False
CommandButton	Name	cmdMove
	Caption	">"
	Index	2
	TabStop	0 'False
CommandButton	Name	cmdMove
	Caption	">>"
	Index	3
	TabStop	0 'False
TextBox	Name	txtPublisher
	MultiLine	-1 'True
TextBox	Name	txtAdvance
TextBox	Name	txtPrice
TextBox	Name	txtNotes
	MultiLine	-1 'True
	ScrollBars	2 'Vertical
TextBox	Name	txtTitle
	MultiLine	-1 'True
Label	Name	Label9
	Alignment	1 'Right Justify
	BackColor	&H00C0C0C0&
	Caption	"Publisher:"

OBJECT	PROPERTY	SETTING
Label	Name	Label6
	Alignment	1 'Right Justify
	BackColor	&H00C0C0C0&
	Caption	"Advance:"
Label	Name	Label5
	Alignment	1 'Right Justify
	BackColor	&H00C0C0C0&
	Caption	"Price:"
Label	Name	Label3
	Alignment	1 'Right Justify
	BackColor	&H00C0C0C0&
	Caption	"Notes:"
Label	Name	Label1
	Alignment	1 'Right Justify
	BackColor	&H00C0C0C0&
	Caption	"Title:"
StatusBar	Name	StatusBar1
	Align	2 'Align Bottom
	AlignSet	-1 'True
	Style	1
	SimpleText	""

10. Add the following code to the declarations section of the form. Option Explicit tells Visual Basic to make sure you declare all variables and objects before using them, in order to avoid naming problems. You can have Visual Basic automatically add this statement to your code modules by checking the Require Variable Declaration check box in Tools, Options under the Editor tab. The mrdo* variables will hold the remote data object handles.

```
Option Explicit

'Remote Data Object variables
Private mrdoEnv As rdoEnvironment
Private mrdoConn As rdoConnection
Private mrdoRS As rdoResultset

'Variable to indicated if data needs to be saved.
Dim mDirty As Boolean
```

11. Add the following code to the form's Load event procedure. After centering the form, the remote data objects that will link the application to the database are created using the default `rdoEnvironment(0)` and the `OpenConnection` method. The method uses the `rdDriverNoPrompt` option so that if enough information is given in the connect string ODBC won't present the end user with dialog boxes to enter connect information. If the connect string is not complete, ODBC will prompt for whatever it needs.

Finally, the `Load` event procedure calls the `DataLoad` procedure to load the form's controls with data from the current record.

```
Private Sub Form_Load()
'Set up the form and connect to data source
Dim sSQL As String

    'Center the form
    Me.Top = (Screen.Height - Me.Height) / 2
    Me.Left = (Screen.Width - Me.Width) / 2

    'Allocate an ODBC environment handle
    Set mrdoEnv = rdoEnvironments(0)
    Set mrdoConn = mrdoEnv.OpenConnection("Books Available", _
        rdDriverNoPrompt, False, "ODBC;UID=sa;PWD=")

    sSQL = _
        "SELECT titles.*, publishers.* " _
        & "FROM titles, publishers " _
        & "WHERE publishers.pub_id = titles.pub_id " _
        & "ORDER BY titles.Title ASC;"
    On Error GoTo Form_LoadError
    Set mrdoRS = mrdoConn.OpenResultset(sSQL, _
        rdOpenKeyset, rdConcurRowver, 0)
    On Error GoTo 0

    mrdoRS.MoveFirst
    SetRecNum

    DataLoad

    Exit Sub

Form_LoadError:
    FrmRDOErrors.ErrorColl = rdoErrors

End Sub
```

12. Because your Visual Basic code is handling all the data management details, it must take care of properly saving data that is dirty or has changed. The code responds to the form's controls' `Change` events and the end user can manually save the data by clicking an Update button. Add the following code to the `Change` event procedure for all the text boxes on the form:

```
Private Sub txtAdvance_Change()
    mDirty = True
End Sub
```

```
Private Sub txtNotes_Change()
   mDirty = True
End Sub

Private Sub txtPrice_Change()
   mDirty = True
End Sub

Private Sub txtPublisher_Change()
   mDirty = True
End Sub

Private Sub txtTitle_Change()
   mDirty = True
End Sub
```

13. Add the following code to the **DataLoad Sub** procedure. This is the code that loads the current record's data into the form each time the end user moves to a new record. The procedure finishes by setting the **mDirty** flag to **False** because the data was just loaded, then updating the record counter at the bottom of the form.

```
Private Sub DataLoad()
'Copy the record's data to its text box.
   txtAdvance.Text = Format$(mrdoRS("Advance") _
      & "", "Currency")
   txtNotes.Text = mrdoRS("Notes") & ""
   txtPrice.Text = Format$(mrdoRS("Price") & "", "Currency")
   txtPublisher.Text = mrdoRS("Pub_Name") & ""
   txtTitle.Text = mrdoRS("Title") & ""

   mDirty = False
   SetRecNum
End Sub
```

14. Add the following code to the **DataSave** procedure, which saves the data in the form to the current record whenever the data is dirty or the end user clicks the Update button. The **mDirty** flag is also set to **False** here because the data in the form is again the same as that in the record. The procedure uses the **frmRDOErrors** form in case of an error when saving the data.

```
Private Sub DataSave()
'Copy the current control contents to the record.
'ODBC driver and database has to support editing
'(most do).

   mrdoRS.Edit
   mrdoRS("Advance") = txtAdvance.Text
   mrdoRS("Notes") = txtNotes.Text
   mrdoRS("Price") = txtPrice.Text
   mrdoRS("Pub_Name") = txtPublisher.Text
   mrdoRS("Title") = txtTitle.Text
   mrdoRS.Update
```

continued on next page

continued from previous page

```
        On Error GoTo DataSaveError
        mrdoRS.Update

        mDirty = False

        Exit Sub

    DataSaveError:
        frmRDOErrors.ErrorColl = rdoErrors

    End Sub
```

15. The form has an Update button the end user can use to manually update data, which simply executes the **DataSave** procedure. The lines commented out here can be used to protect the end user against himself by saving data only when it is dirty.

```
Private Sub cmdUpdate_Click()
'    If mDirty Then
        DataSave
'    End If
End Sub
```

16. The next few procedures take care of navigating through the recordset. The navigation keys, a control array of command buttons, execute this **Click** event procedure that starts by checking whether the end user wants to save any dirty data. Then it calls the **MoveRecord** procedure with the control index to actually reposition the record. Because there is a new current record, the **DataLoad** procedures loads the new data into the form.

```
Private Sub cmdMove_Click(Index As Integer)
Dim iResponse As Integer
Dim lRow As Long

    If mDirty Then
        iResponse = MsgBox("Dirty data. Save changes?", _
            vbYesNo + vbExclamation, "Update Data?")
        If iResponse = vbYes Then
            DataSave
        End If
    End If

    MoveRecord mrdoRS, Index

    DataLoad
End Sub
```

17. Enter the following code into the **MoveRecord Function** procedure. This code is a reusable function to move around a recordset, implementing code to move to the first, last, next, or previous records. If the first record is current and the end user clicks the Move Previous button, a beep sounds; a beep also sounds at the last record when the end user clicks the

Move Next button. You can get as creative as you want here, allowing the end user to move forward or backward a fixed number of records or to go to a specific record number.

```
Public Sub MoveRecord( _
    mrdoRS As rdoResultset, _
    Index As Integer)

    Select Case Index
        Case 0 'MoveFirst
            mrdoRS.MoveFirst

        Case 1 'MovePrevious
            mrdoRS.MovePrevious
            If mrdoRS.BOF Then
                Beep
                mrdoRS.MoveFirst
            End If

        Case 2 'MoveNext
            mrdoRS.MoveNext
            If mrdoRS.EOF Then
                Beep
                mrdoRS.MoveLast
            End If

        Case 3 'MoveLast
            mrdoRS.MoveLast

    End Select
End Sub
```

18. At the bottom of the form, a `StatusBar` control shows the end user where he is in the recordset, indicating Record 5 of 120, 4% of `ResultSet` or whatever. This code demonstrates two of the nice features of RDOs, the `AbsolutePosition` and `PercentPosition` properties. Rather than keeping track of the position in the resultset as the end user navigates about, RDOs keep track and expose the information in these two properties. This is "unSQL-like" behavior because it deals with individual rows rather than whole resultsets, but it is convenient if you must provide this information.

```
Private Sub SetRecNum()
    StatusBar1.SimpleText = "Row " _
        & mrdoRS.AbsolutePosition _
        & " of " & mrdoRS.RowCount _
        & ", " & Format$(mrdoRS.PercentPosition, "#0.00") _
        & "% of ResultSet"
End Sub
```

19. To add a new record, the `cmdAddNew` button's `Click` event checks to see whether dirty data should be saved, and then adds a new record to the recordset. The `DataLoad` procedure loads data from the new record. Because it is a new record and has no data, this clears the form's controls, ready to accept the end user's input. The error handler uses the frmRDOErrors form for RemoteData error handling.

```
Private Sub cmdAddNew_Click()
Dim iResponse As Integer

    If mDirty Then
       iResponse = MsgBox("Dirty data. " _
          & "Save before adding a new record?", _
          vbYesNo + vbExclamation, "Dirty Data")
       If iResponse = vbYes Then
          DataSave
       End If
    End If

    On Error GoTo AddNewError
    mrdoRS.AddNew
    mrdoRS.Update
    mrdoRS.Move 0, mrdoRS.LastModified

    DataLoad

    Exit Sub

AddNewError:
    frmRDOErrors.ErrorColl = rdoErrors

End Sub
```

20. A Delete button allows the end user to remove records from the recordset. This is very similar to the AddNew procedure. If after deleting the record the recordset is empty, a new record is added so there is always at least one record. Either way, the position is moved to the first record, and its data is loaded into the form. frmRDOErrors is again used for error handling.

```
Private Sub cmdDelete_Click()
Dim iResponse As Integer

    iResponse = MsgBox("Are you sure that you " _
       & "want to delete this record?", _
       vbYesNo + vbExclamation, "Delete Record")
    If iResponse = vbYes Then
       On Error GoTo DeleteError
       mrdoRS.Delete
       If (mrdoRS.BOF And mrdoRS.EOF) Or mrdoRS.RowCount = 0 _
          Then
          mrdoRS.AddNew
          mrdoRS.Update
          mrdoRS.MoveLast
       Else
          mrdoRS.MoveFirst
       End If
    End If

    DataLoad
```

```
      Exit Sub

DeleteError:
    frmRDOErrors.ErrorColl = rdoErrors
End Sub
```

21. Add the following code to the **Click** event of the **cmdClose** command
button. This is the exit point that terminates the program. After checking
one last time whether dirty data should be saved, the procedure unloads
itself.

```
Private Sub cmdClose_Click()
Dim iResponse As Integer

    If mDirty Then
        iResponse = MsgBox("Dirty data. Save before closing?", _
            vbYesNo + vbExclamation, "Dirty Data")
        If iResponse = vbYes Then
            DataSave
        End If
    End If
    Unload Me
End Sub
```

22. In the Project, [Project Name] Options menu item, set the startup form to
frmBooks. You can also set an application description, but that is not
required for the operation of this application.

How It Works

This How-To is essentially the same as the previous How-To, except that it uses
Remote Data Objects (RDO) instead of the RemoteData control. The main
difference between the two techniques is that you must write all the code for
every RDO operation (other than the underlying data access operations) while
the control does much of the work for you. But RDO gives you much more
flexibility in accessing data, so you can handle special situations without the
control limiting what you can do.

Comments

Using the Visual Basic remote data objects is similar in many ways to Jet DAOs
but provide much finer control over databases, particularly over a network. If
you compare the techniques used to navigate data in How-To's 2.3, 2.4, and 2.6
you'll find that the technique in this How-To is the most generally applicable to
virtually any data source you need to access with Visual Basic. In many cases, it
also gives the best performance.

COMPLEXITY
ADVANCED

2.8 How do I...
Benchmark my connection options?

COMPATIBILITY: VISUAL BASIC 6

Problem

I have so many different options for getting at my data on the server: attaching to Jet databases, ODBC, remote data objects, and so on. How can I decide the best way (usually meaning fastest) to make database connections?

Technique

This How-To sets up a simple form for comparing two database connections; one using ODBC through Jet and the other using RDOs. You can easily extend the application to include other connection techniques, such as including active data objects (ADO), directly using an OLE DB provider, or whatever makes sense for your application.

> **WARNING**
>
> Visual Basic's documentation can give the impression that the Timer function has a resolution of seconds. However, you can save times returned from the Timer function to single type variables to get timing granularity down to about 55 milliseconds.

One problem with benchmarking is that a network's performance, by its very nature, varies a great deal over time, and normal traffic fluctuates and causes bottlenecks. A reading you take now is unlikely to be the same as one you take in a minute. For this reason, it is important to run the tests several times under varying conditions to get an accurate picture of the best connections. The program developed in this How-To tackles these issues in two ways. First, it is designed to allow the user to set an unlimited number of repetitions that can be set independently, so you get reliable results through repetition. Second, it doesn't run all the RDO test repetitions and then all the Jet repetitions because network traffic can influence the results. Instead, it alternates the tests, reducing the likelihood that either set of results will be heavily influenced by network traffic.

This application uses the ODBC APIs directly to obtain the list of available ODBC data source names to list them in a list box for selection by the user. Included on the book's CD-ROM under the code for this chapter are two Visual Basic modules, **ODBCAPI.BAS** and **Errors.frm**. The code module includes all the function declarations in ODBC version 3.x and defines several support procedures, of which this How-To application uses `ODBCAllocateEnv`, along with some API functions in the `GetODBCdbs` procedure. The form handles and displays errors that are returned by ODBC. Feel free to spelunk the code for plenty of samples for using the ODBC API, although with all the universal data access techniques you can use with Visual Basic, you're unlikely to need to use the API directly very often, only when you need a specialized function.

Steps

Open and run the `PERFORM.VBP` Visual Basic project file. The Connection Performance window will open. Select an ODBC data source name from the combo box, enter a query in the Query text box, and enter the number of repetitions for each connection. Then click the Run Benchmark Tests button. The number of iterations will show in the Results section, including intermediate minimum, maximum, and average time for each connection. Figure 2.12 shows the results for one test using 10 repetitions.

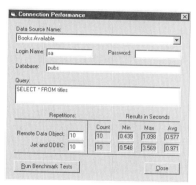

Figure 2.12 Results of benchmarking database connections using the PUBS SQL Server database over a Windows 95 and NT network

Complete the following steps to create this project:

1. Create a new project `PERFORM.VBP`. Add the form `ERRORS.FRM` and the code module `ODBCAPI.BAS` (these modules are available on the book's CD-ROM, but I discuss the procedures relevant to this How-To in the following steps), using Visual Basic's Project, Add File menu command. The code module contains all the declarations needed for the ODBC API functions and the constants used in many of the functions.

2. Select Project, Components from the Visual Basic main menu and clean any controls that are selected so your project isn't cluttered with controls you aren't using, and so the Setup Wizard doesn't include a lot of extra dead weight with your application. The code in this How-To uses only the intrinsic Visual Basic controls.

3. Select Project, References from the Visual Basic main menu, and then choose the following references:

Microsoft Visual Basic for Applications

Visual Basic Runtime Objects and Procedures

Visual Basic Objects and Procedures

Microsoft Remote Data Object 2.0

Microsoft DAO 3.51 Object Library

Uncheck all others so your project isn't cluttered with DLLs you aren't using, and so the Setup Wizard doesn't include a lot of extra dead weight with your application.

4. Name the default form `frmPerformance` and save the file as `PERFORM.FRM`. Add the controls as shown in Figure 2.12, setting the properties as shown in Table 2.12.

Table 2.12 Objects and properties for `PERFORM.FRM`

OBJECT	PROPERTY	SETTING
Form	Name	frmPerformance
	BorderStyle	3 'Fixed Dialog
	Caption	"Connection Performance"
	MaxButton	0 'False
	MinButton	0 'False
TextBox	Name	txtDatabase
TextBox	Name	txtPassword
TextBox	Name	txtLoginName
TextBox	Name	txtQuery
	MultiLine	-1 'True
TextBox	Name	txtJetResult
	BackColor	&H00C0C0C0&
	Locked	-1 'True
	TabStop	0 'False
TextBox	Name	txtRDOResult
	BackColor	&H00C0C0C0&
	Index	3

OBJECT	PROPERTY	SETTING
	Locked	-1 'True
	TabStop	0 'False
TextBox	Name	txtJetResult
	BackColor	&H00C0C0C0&
	Index	2
	Locked	-1 'True
	TabStop	0 'False
TextBox	Name	txtRDOResult
	BackColor	&H00C0C0C0&
	Index	2
	Locked	-1 'True
	TabStop	0 'False
TextBox	Name	txtJetResult
	BackColor	&H00C0C0C0&
	Index	1
	Locked	-1 'True
	TabStop	0 'False
TextBox	Name	txtRDOResult
	BackColor	&H00C0C0C0&
	Index	1
	Locked	-1 'True
	TabStop	0 'False
TextBox	Name	txtJetResult
	BackColor	&H00C0C0C0&
	Index	0
	Locked	-1 'True
	TabStop	0 'False
TextBox	Name	txtRDOResult
	BackColor	&H00C0C0C0&
	Index	0
	Locked	-1 'True
	TabStop	0 'False
TextBox	Name	txtJetCount
TextBox	Name	txtRDOCount
CommandButton	Name	cmdRDC
	Caption	"&Run Benchmark Tests"

continued on next page

Table 2.12   continued

OBJECT	PROPERTY	SETTING
CommandButton	Name	cmdClose
	Caption	"&Close"
ComboBox	Name	cmbDSN
	Sorted	-1 'True
	Style	2 'Dropdown List
Label	Name	Label13
	Caption	"Database:"
Label	Name	Label12
	Alignment	1 'Right Justify
	Caption	"Password:"
Label	Name	Label11
	Caption	"Login Name:"
Label	Name	Label10
	Caption	"Query:"
Label	Name	Label9
	Alignment	2 'Center
	Caption	"Count"
Label	Name	Label8
	Alignment	2 'Center
	Caption	"Avg"
Label	Name	Label6
	Alignment	2 'Center
	Caption	"Max"
Label	Name	Label5
	Alignment	2 'Center
	Caption	"Min"
Label	Name	Label7
	Alignment	2 'Center
	Caption	"Results in Seconds"
Label	Name	Label4
	Caption	"Repetitions:"
Label	Name	Label2
	Alignment	1 'Right Justify
	Caption	"Jet and ODBC:"

OBJECT	PROPERTY	SETTING
Label	Name	Label3
	Alignment	1 'Right Justify
	Caption	"Remote Data Object:"
Label	Name	Label1
	Caption	"Data Source Name:"
Line	Name	Line1
Line	Name	Line2
Line	Name	Line3
Line	Name	Line4

5. Add the following code to the declarations section of `frmPerformance`.
`Option Explicit` tells Visual Basic to make sure you declare all variables
and objects before using them, in order to avoid naming problems. You
can have Visual Basic automatically add this statement to your code
modules by checking the Require Variable Declaration check box in Tools,
Options under the Editor tab.

```
Option Explicit
```

6. Add this code to the form's **Load** event. After centering the form, the code
sets default values in the form's text boxes for the connection to be bench-
marked. Then it calls the `GetODBCdbs` procedure, which is discussed next.

```
Private Sub Form_Load()

    Me.Left = (Screen.Width - Me.Width) / 2
    Me.Top = (Screen.Height - Me.Height) / 2

    'Set the starting defaults.
    txtRDOCount.Text = 10
    txtJetCount.Text = 10
    txtQuery.Text = "SELECT * FROM titles"
    txtLoginName.Text = "sa"
    txtPassword.Text = ""
    txtDatabase.Text = "pubs"

    'Load the cmbDSN with data source names.
    GetODBCdbs

End Sub
```

7. The `GetODBCdbs` Sub procedure uses some of the ODBC wrapper
functions in **ODBCAPI.BAS** to obtain an environment handle, and then
queries ODBC for the list of available data source names. The
SQLDataSources API function enumerates the data source names,
providing information about each name. If the function call generates an

error, the ODBCErrors function in ODBCAPI.BAS loads a form displaying the error to the end user.

```
Private Sub GetODBCdbs()
'Variables for ODBC API calls
Dim cbDSNMax As Integer
Dim szDSN As String * 33
Dim pcbDSN As Long
Dim pcbDescription As Long
Dim szDescription As String * 512
Dim cbDescriptionMax As Integer

'Variables for procedure processing
Dim iResult As Integer
Dim iErrResult

    'Open a connection to an ODBC Environment handle
    iResult = ODBCAllocateEnv(ghEnv)
    If iResult <> SQL_SUCCESS Then
        MsgBox "Could not make connection to ODBC " _
            & "environment. Exiting application.", _
            vbOKOnly + vbCritical, "ODBC Problem"
        Unload Me
        End
    End If

    cbDSNMax = SQL_MAX_DSN_LENGTH + 1
    cbDescriptionMax = 512
    iResult = SQL_SUCCESS
    cmbDSN.Clear

    Screen.MousePointer = vbHourglass
    Do While iResult <> SQL_NO_DATA_FOUND
        'Get next data source (on the first call to
        'SQLDataSources, SQL_FETCH_NEXT gets the first
        'data source)
        iResult = SQLDataSources(ghEnv, _
            SQL_FETCH_NEXT, szDSN, cbDSNMax, pcbDSN, _
            szDescription, cbDescriptionMax, pcbDescription)

        If iResult = SQL_ERROR Then
            iErrResult = ODBCError("Env", ghEnv, 0, 0, _
                iResult, "Error getting list of data sources.")
            Screen.MousePointer = vbDefault
            Exit Sub
        End If

        cmbDSN.AddItem Left(szDSN, pcbDSN)
    Loop

    iResult = ODBCFreeEnv(ghEnv)

    cmbDSN.ListIndex = 0
    Screen.MousePointer = vbDefault

End Sub
```

8. The `ODBCAllocateEnv` function procedure, located in the `ODBCAPI.BAS`
code module, attempts to make an ODBC connection, displaying an error
form if anything goes wrong. The `ODBCLoadFuncs` loads a list of ODBC API
functions, and then the procedure calls a series of API functions to make
the connection. If the procedure is successful at making the connection, it
returns a connection handle. If it is unsuccessful, it calls the `ODBCError`
function to display the error message.

```
Function ODBCAllocateEnv(hEnv As Long)
Dim result As Integer
Dim saveCursor

    ODBCLoadFuncs
    LoadGetInfo
    ODBCAllocateEnv = SQL_SUCCESS

    saveCursor = Screen.MousePointer
    Screen.MousePointer = vbHourglass
    result = SQLAllocEnv(hEnv)
    Screen.MousePointer = vbDefault

    If result <> SQL_SUCCESS Then
        ODBCAllocateEnv = result
        result = ODBCError("Env", hEnv, 0, 0, _
            result, "Environment Allocation Error")
        Screen.MousePointer = saveCursor
        ODBCAllocateEnv = result
    End If
    Screen.MousePointer = saveCursor

End Function
```

9. Add the following code to the `Click` event of the `cmdRDC` command
button. After the end user has entered or changed any information for the
connection, he or she can click this button. The procedure starts by
verifying that it has all the information it needs to start the test: a DSN is
selected and the number of repetitions for each test is one or more. Entries
in the other controls are up to the end user, but all the information for a
valid connection is needed so that ODBC doesn't have to prompt for any
missing data. Then the procedure disables some of the controls for the
duration of the test so the user can't make any changes while it is running,
and calls the `Benchmark` procedure.

```
Private Sub cmdRDC_Click()
Dim iRDOCount As Integer
Dim iJetCount As Integer

    'Make sure that everything is set
    If cmbDSN.Text = "" Then
        MsgBox "Please select an ODBC data source name, " _
            & "then try again.", vbOKOnly + vbCritical, _
            "Data Source Name"
```

continued on next page

continued from previous page

```
                cmbDSN.SetFocus
        Exit Sub
    End If

    iRDOCount = Val(txtRDOCount.Text)
    iJetCount = Val(txtJetCount.Text)
    If iRDOCount < 1 Or iJetCount < 1 Then
        MsgBox "You must enter at least one repetition " _
            & "for each connection method.", _
            vbOKOnly + vbCritical, "Data Source Name"
        If iRDOCount Then
            txtJetCount.SetFocus
        Else
            txtRDOCount.SetFocus
        End If
        Exit Sub
    End If

    'Everything is hunky dory, so let's do it.
    txtRDOCount.Locked = True
    txtJetCount.Locked = True
    txtLoginName.Locked = True
    txtPassword.Locked = True
    txtQuery.Locked = True
    txtDatabase.Locked = True
    txtRDOCount.Locked = True
    txtJetCount.Locked = True
    cmdRDC.Enabled = False
    cmbDSN.Enabled = False
    cmdClose.Enabled = False

    Benchmark iRDOCount, iJetCount

    txtRDOCount.Locked = False
    txtJetCount.Locked = False
    txtLoginName.Locked = False
    txtPassword.Locked = False
    txtQuery.Locked = False
    txtDatabase.Locked = False
    txtRDOCount.Locked = False
    txtJetCount.Locked = False
    cmdRDC.Enabled = True
    cmbDSN.Enabled = True
    cmdClose.Enabled = True

End Sub
```

10. The `Benchmark Sub` procedure takes care of testing the connection string, recording benchmark values, and then running the `OpenRDO` and `OpenJet` procedures the specified number of repetitions. As each connection is made, this code records the elapsed time in single data types, `fRDOTime` and `fJetTime`, so that fractions of seconds are recorded. It is critical that you benchmark connections that have minimum durations greater than the timing resolution on your system (usually 10 milliseconds for

Windows NT and 55 milliseconds for Windows 95, according to the respective documentation). The statistics variables record information so that the minimum, maximum, and average times can be updated over the course of the test and displayed in the form.

Note that included are a couple of **DoEvents** statements outside the timing loops so that everything can catch up and stay in synch.

```
Private Sub Benchmark(iRDOReps As Integer, iJetReps As Integer)
Dim iRDOCount As Integer
Dim iJetCount As Integer
Dim iCount As Integer
Dim i As Integer
Dim sConnect As String

'Statistics variables
Dim fRDOTime As Single
Dim fJetTime As Single
Dim fRDOTotalTime As Double
Dim fJetTotalTime As Double
Dim fRDOMinTime As Single
Dim fJetMinTime As Single
Dim fRDOMaxTime As Single
Dim fJetMaxTime As Single
Dim fRDOAvgTime As Single
Dim fJetAvgTime As Single

    If iRDOReps > iJetReps Then
        iCount = iRDOReps
    Else
        iCount = iJetReps
    End If

    sConnect = "ODBC;DSN=" & cmbDSN.Text _
        & ";UID=" & txtLoginName.Text _
        & ";PWD=" & txtPassword.Text _
        & ";DATABASE=" & txtDatabase.Text

    sConnect = TestConnection(sConnect)
    If Len(sConnect) = 0 Then
        'Couldn't make the connection
        ClearResults
        Exit Sub
    End If

    For i = 1 To iCount
        If iRDOCount < iRDOReps Then
            fRDOTime = Timer

            If Not OpenRDO(sConnect) Then
                ClearResults
                Exit Sub
            End If

            fRDOTime = Timer - fRDOTime
```

continued on next page

continued from previous page

```
                fRDOTotalTime = fRDOTotalTime + fRDOTime
                iRDOCount = iRDOCount + 1
            End If

        DoEvents

        If iJetCount < iJetReps Then
            fJetTime = Timer

            If Not OpenJet(sConnect) Then
                ClearResults
                Exit Sub
            End If

            fJetTime = Timer - fJetTime
            fJetTotalTime = fJetTotalTime + fJetTime
            iJetCount = iJetCount + 1
        End If

        'Update statistics so far
        txtRDOResult(0).Text = iRDOCount
        txtJetResult(0).Text = iJetCount

        'Minimum time
        If fRDOMinTime = 0 Then
            fRDOMinTime = fRDOTime
        ElseIf fRDOMinTime > fRDOTime Then
            fRDOMinTime = fRDOTime
        End If
        txtRDOResult(1).Text = fRDOMinTime
        If fJetMinTime = 0 Then
            fJetMinTime = fJetTime
        ElseIf fJetMinTime > fJetTime Then
            fJetMinTime = fJetTime
        End If
        txtJetResult(1).Text = fJetMinTime

        'Maximum time
        If fRDOMaxTime < fRDOTime Then
            fRDOMaxTime = fRDOTime
        End If
        txtRDOResult(2).Text = fRDOMaxTime
        If fJetMaxTime < fJetTime Then
            fJetMaxTime = fJetTime
        End If
        txtJetResult(2).Text = fJetMaxTime

        txtRDOResult(3).Text = fRDOTotalTime / iRDOCount
        txtJetResult(3).Text = fJetTotalTime / iJetCount

        Me.Refresh
        DoEvents
    Next

End Sub
```

11. The `TestConnection` function tests the connect string built from the form's controls by establishing an RDO connection and using the `rdoConnection` object's `Connect` property to return a fully formed connection string. This is done before timing starts so that there are no false readings if there is a problem and no connection can be made. (The network might be down, the database pointed to by the ODBC data source name might be incorrect, or any of thousands of other problems can cause a failed connection.)

After allocating an ODBC environment handle through RDO, it attempts to make the connection by using the `OpenConnection` method of the `rdoEnvironment` object. One important argument to this method is the `Prompt` parameter in second position. This code uses `rdDriverComplete`, which tells ODBC to prompt the user for any missing information needed for a connection, such as a password. Table 2.13 lists the valid constants for this parameter.

Table 2.13 Valid constants for the `Prompt` argument to the `OpenConnection` method

CONSTANT	MEANING
rdDriverPrompt	Present dialog boxes to the user whether any additional information is required or not.
rdDriverNoPrompt	Do not show any dialog boxes at all, whether additional information is needed or not. If any information is missing for the connection, throw a trappable error.
rdDriverComplete	If all required information is already in the connect string, do not prompt the user. Otherwise, prompt for any missing information.
rdDriverCompleteRequired	Same as rdDriverComplete, except that the controls for any information not required to make the connection are disabled, letting the user make changes only to missing or incorrect information.

You have no need to return any records at this point, so it is not necessary to create and open a recordset. If a connection is successfully made—no error is thrown—the procedure uses the `Connect` property of the `rdoConnection` object to return a fully formed connect string. Some of the entries are usually not absolutely required to make a connection, but you are more assured of having a valid connection for the test.

While running this code from a network computer named Dell Lattitude, the `sConn` variable initially contained this connect string:

```
ODBC;DSN=Books Available;UID=sa;PWD=;DATABASE=pubs
```

After testing the connection, `rdoConn.Connect` returned this fully formed connect string:

```
DSN=Books Available;SERVER=modeman;UID=sa;PWD=;
APP=Visual Basic;WSID=DELL LATTITUDE;DATABASE=pubs
```

The Books Available data source name connects to the PUBS database in SQL Server located on the modeman server, running from a Visual Basic application.

If the test connection fails for any reason, the form assigns the **rdoErrors** collection to the **ErrorColl** property of the **frmRDOErrors** form, described in the introduction to this chapter. Then it assigns an empty string to **TestConnection**, which the calling procedure can test for success.

```
Private Function TestConnection(sConn As String) As String
'Test to make sure that the connection string is valid
Dim rdoEnv As rdoEnvironment
Dim rdoConn As rdoConnection

    On Error GoTo TestConnectionError

    'Allocate an ODBC environment handle
    Set rdoEnv = rdoEnvironments(0)

    'Make the connection, letting ODBC prompt for
    'and missing connection information.
    Set rdoConn = rdoEnv.OpenConnection("", _
        rdDriverComplete, False, sConn)

    'No error, so successfully connected
    TestConnection = rdoConn.Connect
    rdoConn.Close

    Set rdoEnv = Nothing
    Set rdoConn = Nothing

    Exit Function

TestConnectionError:
    frmRDOErrors.ErrorColl = rdoErrors
    'MsgBox "Error making RDO connection. Ending test.", _
    '   vbCritical, "Connect Error"
    TestConnection = ""

End Function
```

12. The **OpenJet Function** procedure actually opens the Jet connection by opening the database, creating a recordset, and then moving around a bit and recording some values. Because this is a timed test, if any error happens while making the connection, the test is ended by setting **OpenJet** to **False**. Note that the **db** and **rs** objects created are set to **Nothing** so their memory is released.

```
Private Function OpenJet(sConn As String) As Boolean
Dim db As Database
Dim rs As Recordset
```

```
Dim vValue As Variant

    On Error GoTo OpenJetError
    Set db = OpenDatabase("", False, False, sConn)

    'Create the recordset.
    Set rs = db.OpenRecordset(txtQuery.Text)

    rs.MoveLast
    vValue = rs(0)
    rs.MoveFirst
    vValue = rs(0)
    rs.MoveLast
    vValue = rs(0)

    Set db = Nothing
    Set rs = Nothing

    OpenJet = True
    Exit Function

OpenJetError:
    MsgBox "Error making Jet connection. Ending test.", _
        vbCritical, "Connect Error"
    OpenJet = False

End Function
```

13. The OpenRDO function serves essentially the same purpose as OpenJet, retrieving environment and connection handles from ODBC, and then creating a resultset.

```
Private Function OpenRDO(sConn As String) As Boolean
Dim rdoEnv As rdoEnvironment
Dim rdoConn As rdoConnection
Dim rdoRS As rdoResultset
Dim vValue As Variant

    On Error GoTo OpenRDOError

    'Allocate an ODBC environment handle
    Set rdoEnv = rdoEnvironments(0)
    Set rdoConn = rdoEnv.OpenConnection("", _
        rdDriverNoPrompt, False, sConn)
    Set rdoRS = rdoConn.OpenResultset(txtQuery.Text, _
        rdOpenKeyset, rdConcurRowVer, 0)

    rdoRS.MoveLast
    vValue = rdoRS(0)
    rdoRS.MoveFirst
    vValue = rdoRS(0)
    rdoRS.MoveLast
    vValue = rdoRS(0)

    rdoConn.Close
```

continued on next page

continued from previous page

```
                    Set rdoEnv = Nothing
                    Set rdoConn = Nothing
                    Set rdoRS = Nothing

                    OpenRDO = True
                    Exit Function

                OpenRDOError:
                    frmRDOErrors.ErrorColl = rdoErrors
                    'MsgBox "Error making RDO connection. Ending test.", _
                    '    vbCritical, "Connect Error"
                    OpenRDO = False

                End Function
```

14. If an error occurs when making a database connection, the **Benchmark** procedure ends the test. **ClearResults** simply clears the results text boxes so that no confusing intermediate results are displayed to the end user.

```
                Private Sub ClearResults()
                Dim i As Integer

                    txtRDOResult(0).Text = ""
                    txtJetResult(0).Text = ""

                    For i = 0 To 3
                        txtRDOResult(i).Text = ""
                        txtJetResult(i).Text = ""
                    Next
                End Sub
```

15. Add the following code to the **Click** event procedure of the **cmdClose** command button. This code ends the program by unloading the form from memory.

```
                Private Sub cmdClose_Click()
                    Unload Me
                End Sub
```

16. In the Project, [Project Name] Options menu item, set the startup form to **frmPerformance**. You can also set an application description, but that is not required for the operation of this application.

Comments

Benchmarking a database connection is at best an art form, at worst misleading and confusing. You have two big strikes against you before you even start:

✔ Windows is a multitasking operating system, and both Windows 95 and NT are preemptively multitasking. This means that if Windows decides it should devote some processor time to other applications or services, the benchmarking times are skewed. In older versions of Windows you could usually minimize this effect by closing all other applications, but modern versions have so many services and OLE functions happening that it is hard to eliminate all influences.

✔ Database connections, particularly over a network, are subject to traffic and errors that could be caused at any point on the network.

✔ Windows NT complicates matters further because it allows Windows Services, programs that run outside a user's permissions, even when no one is logged on to the workstation or server. As these services proliferate to include fax and email servers, backup servers, and on and on, a machine can become bogged down in threads that have nothing to do with database connections.

These conditions are complicated further because different types of database connections can be affected by the type of data returned and the form of the resultsets if any. Several discussions can be seen online with one person claiming that one type of connection is clearly superior to another, while another person swears the opposite, and both have the data to prove their argument. The point is that you must test how you access your databases using real data under real conditions to discover what works best for your data with your network under your system demands.

The code in this How-To includes some strategically placed `DoEvents` statements. Even in Win32 programming, `DoEvents` is a necessary evil that releases control from the application and tells Windows that it can go off and do other tasks and then return to continue running the application. Without these statements, the form would not be able to update itself, giving the user the impression that nothing is happening. All the `DoEvents` in this code, however, are outside the timing loops so that the benchmarks are not affected by anything that might be pending in Windows and hogging the processor.

CHAPTER 3
DATA OBJECTS

3

DATA OBJECTS

by George Szabo

How do I...

RDO was arguably the single most important inclusion of Visual Basic 4 with regards to serious enterprise client/server development. RDO is a thin wrapper that uses the ODBC API directly, bypassing the Jet database engine, while maintaining the simplicity and ease of use found in Jet's data access objects. Figure 3.1 shows the RDO object model that simplifies use of the ODBC API. But what truly makes RDO compelling is its capability to easily provide access and control over aspects of the server that previously could be done only by using the ODBC API directly. These features include support for stored procedures with input and output variables, multiple resultsets, setting of engine isolation levels, creation and control of cursors, management of connections, and speed. RDO was clearly making major strides in Enterprise development as Microsoft leveraged it through DAO in what it referred to as ODBC direct. ODBC direct allowed DAO programming to tap into the RDO model with DAO syntax.

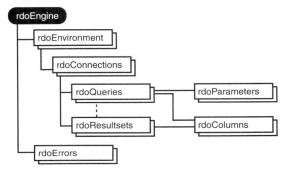

Figure 3.1 The remote database object model

Visual Basic 6 brings with it a new and improved version of RDO, but more important, it brings a new direction with ActiveX Data Objects (ADO).

ADO's primary benefits are high speed, ease of use, low memory overhead, and a small disk footprint. ADO is a departure from the model followed with data access objects (DAO) or remote data objects (RDO) where you must navigate through a hierarchy to create objects, as shown in Figure 3.2. Instead, with ADO most objects can be independently created. This results in an easier to use syntax. ADO also supports many features available in RDO such as support for stored procedures with parameters and return values, a variety of cursor types, and the capability to control the number of rows returned by a recordset. Two features that make ADO more appealing than either of its counterparts are its capability to cache changes to data locally and batch update the server, thus reducing network traffic. This is critical when developing for the Internet. The second feature is support for free-threaded objects, which is essential when being deployed as part of a Web application. ADO has limitations in this early stage of the game, and although it handles much of the functionality that RDO provides, it does not handle all of it. For example, ADO does not provide a way to create ODBC data sources. In the future, these limitations will be addressed.

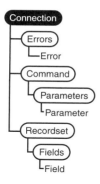

Figure 3.2 The active database object model

In this chapter, you explore basic RDO and ADO methods along with more advanced topics such as stored procedures, resultset management, and asynchronous queries. The How-To's in this chapter have been developed with SQL Server and a data source name of PUBS_DSN. It is recommended that you create this data source name on your system prior to running the examples. For information on connecting to a data source refer to Chapter 2, "Getting Connected." Note that all projects use the PUBS sample database that comes with Microsoft SQL Server. For your convenience, an **.MDB** file containing the PUBS tables and data has been included on the CD-ROM that accompanies this book. Note, however, that How-To's, 3.4, 3.6, 3.8, and 3.10 will not work with an Access database file because it does not provide support for stored procedures or server-side cursors. For an explanation of server-side cursors, refer to How-To 3.5.

3.1 Create and Run an SQL Query with RDO

The process of client/server development is based on the capability of a client to submit a request to a server. In the world of database engines, this takes the form of Structured Query Language (SQL). This How-To walks you through the steps needed to submit an SQL query using RDO to an ODBC-compliant data source.

3.2 Use RDO to Insert, Update, and Delete Records

A fundamental aspect of SQL is the capability to insert, update, and delete records from a data source. This How-To guides you through the creation of a simple data entry form complete with your own navigation buttons all linked to your ODBC source through the RDO's powerful **rdoResultset** object.

3.3 Use rdoQuery to Parameterize a Query

The benefit of parameterizing queries is similar to the benefit of creating parameterized functions. A single SQL statement or stored procedure can be used multiple times and can modify its execution based on parameters you pass to it, allowing you to centralize logic in your application and make it more maintainable. This How-To creates a query form that allows you to enter search criteria and retrieve authors and their information from the PUBS database.

3.4 Control the Number of Rows Returned in a Resultset by RDO

The concept of load balancing is central to the client/server development question. If you have a client and a server, how do you balance the processing work so that the client and the server perform optimally? RDO provides control over data access load balancing through the rdoQuery object. This How-To creates a form where you can explore each option and combination with immediate feedback from your choices.

3.5 Retrieve Multiple Resultsets with RDO

Business activities can be grouped into a unit of work. These work units are better modeled by the submission of multiple requests and the receipt of multiple resultsets within a single call. This How-To walks you through the mechanics of submitting multiple requests simultaneously and handling the resultsets that are returned.

3.6 Perform an Asynchronous Query with RDO

Have you ever executed a query that took more than a few seconds to execute? If you submitted the query using a synchronous method, then you know that your application is unavailable until the request is filled. This How-To shows you how to submit asynchronous queries. After the request is submitted, control is returned to your application. Additionally, you learn how to cancel a request that is processing.

3.7 Submit an SQL Query Using ADO

Active data objects provides a new way of submitting and accessing data. Object models such as DAO and RDO require that you create and use objects in a particular order. To use a resultset object, you must first create an environment object, then a connection object, and finally a resultset object. ADO does not rely on this type of hierarchy. By removing this requirement in ADO, you are given a new flexibility that makes code easier to write and maintain. This How-To introduces you to the basics of submitting SQL statements using ADO.

3.8 Create a Prepared Statement Using ADO

Many queries are reused throughout an application—for example, an Update statement for customer information or a search query that retrieves a list of names. Whenever a query is used repeatedly, it is a good idea to use a prepared statement. This How-To walks you through the steps for using ADO to create prepared statements as well as demonstrates the benefit of this practice.

3.9 Parameterize a Query with ADO

Have you ever created a query by concatenating a string from a series of text boxes and option buttons? There is a better way, one that will make your code more legible and maintainable. ADO provides strong support for the creation of queries with parameters. This How-To helps you explore the use of parameters with ADO queries.

3.10 Use Transactions with ADO

When an application is dealing with a unit of work, transactions are a critical part of defining what that unit is. Unit implies that all parts of that job must be completed successfully for any of the actions to be valid. Withdrawing cash from your ATM is an example of a transaction. You request money, your account balance is checked and the amount debited, and then you are given cash. If no cash comes out, the entire transaction needs to be rolled back. This How-To demonstrates the use of transaction syntax with ADO commands.

COMPLEXITY
BEGINNING

3.1 How do I...
Create and run an SQL query with RDO?

COMPATIBILITY: VISUAL BASIC 5 AND 6

Problem

I understand how to write SQL statements, but how do I use RDO to submit a statement to my database server?

Technique

The client/server process is comprised of requests and answers. SQL queries are an intricate part of this client/server process. There are two standard ways you can submit queries using RDO. Both methods require you to establish a connection to your data source. After a connection is made, you can submit an SQL query by using an **rdoQuery** object or the **rdoConnection** object directly. In this How-To, you use the **OpenResultset** method directly on your open connection object. For information on using the **rdoQuery** object see How-To 3.3.

Steps

Open and run project SUBMIT.VBP. The running program appears as shown in Figure 3.3. As the application loads, you are prompted for a data source name. Select a data source name (DSN) that connects to the PUBS database, and the form appears.

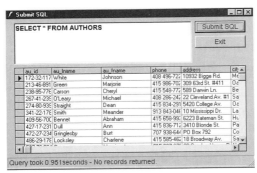

Figure 3.3 The form as it appears at runtime

Enter an SQL Select statement in the text box and click the Submit SQL button to send it to the back-end database engine. If the Select statement returns records, they are displayed in the dbGrid control. If no results are found, the status bar is updated to reflect the execution time of the query and states that no records were returned. To create this project, complete the following steps:

1. Create a new project called SUBMIT.VBP. Select Form1, and add objects and set properties as shown in Table 3.1.

Table 3.1 SUBMIT.FRM form and control properties

OBJECT	PROPERTY	SETTING
Form	Name	frmSubmitSQL
	Caption	"Submit SQL"
TextBox	Name	txtSQL
	MultiLine	True
CommandButton	Name	cmdSubmitSQL
	Caption	"Submit SQL"
CommandButton	Name	cmdExit
	Caption	"Exit"
MSRDC	Name	rdcDisplay

OBJECT	PROPERTY	SETTING
DBGrid	Name	DBGrid1
	DataSource	rdcDisplay
StatusBar	Name	StatusBar1
	Align	Align Bottom
	Style	sbrSimple
	SimpleText	" "

2. The first thing you need to do is to dimension object variables for the environment and the connection. Add the following code to the General Declarations section of the form:

```
Option Explicit
Dim Env As rdoEnvironment
Dim Cn As rdoConnection
```

3. The form uses the environment and connection variables dimensioned in the General section of the form. Add the following code to the **Form_Load** event. In this example, you use the **OpenConnection** method to prompt the user to select a DSN at runtime.

```
Private Sub Form_Load()
    '
    'first you need to set up the RDO environment
    Set Env = rdoEnvironments(0)
    '
    'open a connection to a data source.
    Set Cn = Env.OpenConnection("", rdDriverPrompt, True, "")
End Sub
```

4. Enter the following code for the Submit SQL button **Click** event. This code performs the action of submitting the SQL query from the text box to the selected data source. This code also takes advantage of the **rdoErrors** collection and **rdoError** objects to view errors generated during the RDO process. Notice that a **Timing** object is used to time the execution of the SQL statement. The **Timing** class is described later in this How-To.

```
Private Sub cmdSubmitSQL_Click()
    StatusBar1.SimpleText = "Processing Request ..."
    StatusBar1.Refresh
    On Error GoTo cmdSubmitSQL_error
    'you will use the timing object to time the whole
    'process including connect time.
    Dim oTiming As Timing
    Set oTiming = New Timing
    Call oTiming.Start
    '
    'the following routine is everything that must
```

continued on next page

continued from previous page

```
                    'be done to submit an SQL statement using
                    'RDO.
                    Dim Rst As rdoResultset
                    '
                    'submit the SQL statement and get the results
                    Set Rst = Cn.OpenResultset(txtSQL.Text, rdUseClientBatch)
                    '
                    'finish timing of submission
                    oTiming.Finish

                    '
                    'Check rowcount property to see if any records
                    'were returned.
                    If Rst.RowCount > 0 Then
                        StatusBar1.SimpleText = "Your SQL query has
                        ➥returned records"
                                & " in just " & oTiming.ElapsedTime & " seconds!"
                        Set rdcDisplay.Resultset = Rst
                    Else
                        StatusBar1.SimpleText = "Query took "
                                ➥& oTiming.ElapsedTime
                                & "seconds - No records returned."
                    End If

                cmdSubmitSQL_Exit:
                    Set oTiming = Nothing
                    Exit Sub

                cmdSubmitSQL_error:
                    'if error occurs check the RDO Collection for errors.
                    Dim i As Integer
                    For i = 0 To rdoErrors.Count - 1
                    MsgBox rdoErrors(i).Description
                    Next i
                    'when done close all objects
                    GoTo cmdSubmitSQL_Exit
                End Sub
```

5. Enter the following code for the Exit button **Click** event. At the
conclusion of your application, it is important to release the connection to
your data source as well as the ODBC environment variable. This is done
with the following **Close** method:

```
Private Sub cmdExit_Click()
    '
    'close out all objects in reverse order.
    Cn.Close
    Env.Close
    End
End Sub
```

6. Choose Insert, Class Module from Visual Basic's menu to add a class
module to this project. The class appears in the project window. Open the

class module and press the F4 key to view the class's properties. Set the `Name` property to `Timing`.

7. Add the following code to the General Declarations section of the `Timing` class module. You need to declare the `timeGetTime` API function to have access to a method that returns timing values with a millisecond resolution. The standard `Time()` function in Visual Basic only provides for seconds.

```
Option Explicit
'
'dimension readonly variables for timing events
Dim mStartTime As Long
Dim mFinishTime As Long
Dim mElapsedTime As Long
'
'declare API to get time in milliseconds.
Private Declare Function timeGetTime Lib "winmm.dll" () As Long
```

8. Add the following methods and properties to the `Timing` class. These methods and properties allow you to time execution of SQL queries and have access to the elapsed time values in milliseconds.

```
'method to store start time
Public Sub Start()
    mStartTime = timeGetTime
End Sub

'method to store finish time and calculate
'elapsed time in milliseconds
Public Sub Finish()
    mFinishTime = timeGetTime
    mElapsedTime = mFinishTime - mStartTime
End Sub

'read-only property to access elapsed time.
Public Property Get ElapsedTime()
    ElapsedTime = mElapsedTime / 1000
End Property
```

How It Works

The RDO model is followed to allow execution of an SQL query. First, an environment variable is set and a connection opened to a data source using the `OpenConnection` method. After a connection is made, any SQL statements entered in the text box control are submitted to the data source using the `OpenResultset` method, which returns the results into an `rdoResultset` object variable labeled `Rst` for this project. The project uses a class module called `Timing` to actually time the execution of SQL queries in milliseconds. The resultset and elapsed time of the query are presented to the user via a remote data control and bound DBGrid control. This is accomplished by binding the

DBGrid control to the Remote Data Control (RDC) and setting the RDC's resultset property to the resultset generated by the `OpenResultset` method that is coded behind the Execute SQL button. Figure 3.4 shows the path that your SQL statement must travel using the RDO model.

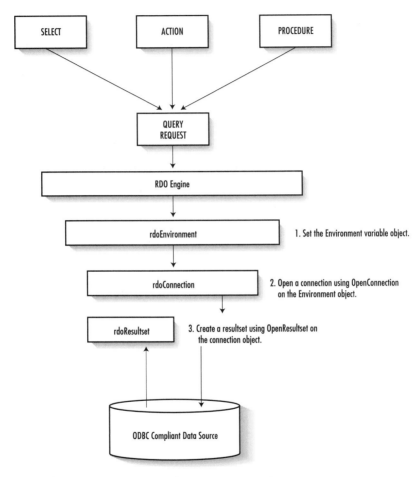

Figure 3.4 SQL query path to an ODBC data source

Comments

This project used the default values of many RDOs to demonstrate the fundamental steps required to execute SQL queries using RDO. Many options can be set for each object and method used in this How-To. Try submitting a variety of SQL statements including `Insert`, `Update`, and `Delete` statements and see how this implementation handles these statements. Try submitting procedures such as Use Master to change the current database in use by the connection. Finally, you might want to try modifying this project to connect without prompting you for a DSN. This can be done by specifying either a DSN or a connection string in the `OpenConnection` method and then changing `rdDriverPrompt` to `rdDriverNoPrompt`. Give it a try.

COMPLEXITY
INTERMEDIATE

3.2 How do I...
Use RDO to insert, update, and delete records?

COMPATIBILITY: VISUAL BASIC 4, 5, AND 6

Problem

I am familiar with standard SQL statements such as `Insert`, `Update`, and `Delete`. Is there an easier way to perform these functions using RDO?

Technique

RDO provides a special object called the `resultset` object. It provides functionality that can make simple data manipulation easier. Microsoft has gone to great lengths to mirror the object interface exposed by Jet and Database Access Objects (DAO). The RDO contains methods such as `AddNew`, `Update`, `Delete`, `MoveNext`, `MovePrevious`, `MoveFirst`, and `MoveLast`. All these methods should look familiar to you if you have used DAO at all. This How-To uses an RDO resultset object to directly manipulate and view records in the Authors table of the PUBS database. Additionally, you create your own navigation buttons and display and collect information, all without using bound controls.

Steps

Open and run the project `AUTHINFO.VBP`. The running program appears as shown in Figure 3.5. Click the navigation buttons on the form to move from record to record. Try changing a record and moving to another record without clicking the Update button. Now move back to the record you changed. Your changes are gone. Now make changes and select Update before moving to another record. If you revisit the changed records, you see that your changes were stored. All this is done without the use of bound controls.

Complete the following steps to create this project:

1. Create a new project called `AUTHINFO.VBP`. Select `Form1`, and add objects and set properties as shown in Table 3.2.

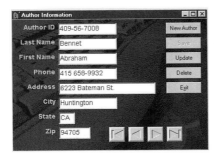

Figure 3.5 The form as it appears at runtime

Table 3.2 AUTHINFO.FRM form and control properties

OBJECT	PROPERTY	SETTING
Form	Name	frmAuthorInf
	Caption	"Author Information"
	Icon	"books04.ico"
	Picture	"setup.bmp"
CommandButton	Name	cmdNewAuthor
	Caption	"New Author"
CommandButton	cmdExit	
	Caption	"E&xit"
CommandButton	cmdDelete	
	Caption	"Delete"
CommandButton	cmdUpdate	
	Caption	"Update"
CommandButton	cmdSave	
	Caption	"Save"
	Enabled	False
TextBox	Name	txtAuthorID
TextBox	Name	txtLastName
TextBox	Name	txtFirstName
TextBox	Name	txtPhone
TextBox	Name	txtAddress
TextBox	Name	txtCity
TextBox	Name	txtState
TextBox	Name	txtZip
CommandButton	Name	cmdMoveLast

OBJECT	PROPERTY	SETTING
	Picture	"Arw02rt.ico"
	Down Picture	"Arw02rtb.ico"
	Style	1 - Graphical
CommandButton	Name	cmdMoveNext
	Picture	"Arw01rt.ico"
	Down Picture	
	Style	1 - Graphical
CommandButton	Name	cmdMovePrevious
	Picture	"Arw01lt.ico"
	Down Picture	"Arw01ltb.ico"
	Style	1 - Graphical
CommandButton	Name	cmdMoveFirst
	Picture	"Arw02lt.ico"
	Down Picture	"Arw02ltb.ico"
	Style	1 - Graphical
Label	Name	Label8
	Alignment	Right Justify
	BackStyle	Transparent
	Caption	"Zip"
	ForeColor	&H00C0C0C0&
Label	Name	Label7
	Alignment	Right Justify
	BackStyle	Transparent
	Caption	"State"
	ForeColor	&H00C0C0C0&
Label	Name	Label6
	Alignment	Right Justify
	BackStyle	Transparent
	Caption	"City"
	ForeColor	&H00C0C0C0&
Label	Name	Label5
	Alignment	Right Justify
	BackStyle	Transparent
	Caption	"Address"
	ForeColor	&H00C0C0C0&
Label	Name	Label4
	Alignment	Right Justify

continued on next page

Table 3.2 continued

OBJECT	PROPERTY	SETTING
	BackStyle	Transparent
	Caption	"Phone"
	ForeColor	&H00C0C0C0&
Label	Name	Label3
	Alignment	Right Justify
	BackStyle	Transparent
	Caption	"First Name"
	ForeColor	&H00C0C0C0&
Label	Name	Label2
	Alignment	Right Justify
	BackStyle	Transparent
	Caption	"Last Name"
	ForeColor	&H00C0C0C0&
Label	Name	Label1
	Alignment	Right Justify
	BackStyle	Transparent
	Caption	"Author ID"
	ForeColor	&H00C0C0C0&

2. The first thing you need to do is to dimension object variables for the environment, connection, and resultset. This is done by adding the following code to the General Declarations section of the form:

```
Option Explicit
'dimension your environment, connection and result
'object variables here. this will make them shareable
'within the form.
Dim Env As rdoEnvironment
Dim Cn As rdoConnection
Dim rstAuthor As rdoResultset
```

3. The form uses the environment and connection variables dimensioned in the General Declarations section of the form. Add the following code to the Form_Load event. In this example, you use the OpenConnection method to prompt the user to select a DSN at runtime.

```
Private Sub Form_Load()
    'set the environment variable to the default
    'environment
    Set Env = rdoEnvironments(0)
    '
    'since the application may potentially run against an
```

```
'MDB file which is not a true database server and does
'not support server-side cursors, here you will specify
'that the connection use ODBC cursors. This will work
'with SQL Server as well.
Env.CursorDriver = rdUseOdbc
'
'Open a connection. Since the DSN and Connection
'strings are empty, the ODBC Driver Selection Window
' will prompt you at runtime for a DSN etc.
Set Cn = Env.OpenConnection(dsname:="", _
                            Prompt:=rdDriverPrompt, _
                            ReadOnly:=False, _
                            Connect:="")
'
'with the connection complete you will now load
'the author information into the application
Call LoadAuthorInfo
End Sub
```

4. Create the following subroutine that retrieves all authors' information from the Authors tables located in the PUBS database. This subroutine is called during the **Form_Load** event.

```
Private Sub LoadAuthorInfo()
    Dim sSQL As String
    sSQL = "SELECT * FROM Authors ORDER BY au_lname"
    'using the connection opened earlier you will now
    'create an updateable resultset.
    Set rstAuthor = Cn.OpenResultset(Name:=sSQL, _
                                     Type:=rdOpenDynamic, _
                                     LockType:=rdConcurRowver)
    'Check to see if any records were returned
    If rstAuthor.EOF <> True Then
        'display the records to the form
        Call DisplayRecord
    Else
        MsgBox "No records found"
    End If
End Sub
```

5. Enter the following routines to handle the **MoveNext** and **MovePrevious** navigation of records handled by the **rstAuthor** resultset. These routines are used in the next step to prevent navigation beyond the first or last records of the resultset.

```
Private Sub aniMoveFirst_Click()
    rstAuthor.MoveFirst
    Call DisplayRecord
End Sub

Private Sub aniMoveLast_Click()
    rstAuthor.MoveLast
    Call DisplayRecord
End Sub
```

6. Handling the event of moving past the current resultset can be a bit tricky. Here you use **MoveNext** and check whether you have moved too far. If this is the case, then you use **MoveLast**. Trying to use **MovePrevious** will not work because previous and next have no meaning when you are beyond the resultset at End Of File (EOF). **MoveLast** and **MoveFirst** both work because you are moving to a specific record.

```
Private Sub aniMoveNext_Click()
    If rstAuthor.EOF <> True Then
        rstAuthor.MoveNext
        If rstAuthor.EOF = True Then
            rstAuthor.MoveLast
            Beep
        Else
            Call DisplayRecord
        End If
    End If
End Sub


'same as the movenext routine.
Private Sub aniMovePrevious_Click()
    If rstAuthor.BOF <> True Then
        rstAuthor.MovePrevious
        If rstAuthor.BOF = True Then
            rstAuthor.MoveFirst
            Beep
        Else
            Call DisplayRecord
        End If
    End If
End Sub
```

7. Add the following code for each of the buttons that appear on the form:

```
'the New Author button and the Save button work in
'unison. First you clear the form and let the user
'enter new information. The Save button stores the
'informationi to the database.
Private Sub cmdNewAuthor_Click()
    Call ClearRecord
    Call DisableButtons
End Sub

'Once user selects save you will optimistically use
'the AddNew method of the resultset. Set the resultset
'to the new values and update (save).
Private Sub cmdSave_Click()
    rstAuthor.AddNew
    Call SetAuthorInfo
    rstAuthor.Update
    Call EnableButtons
End Sub

'this update routine is used to save changes to a
'currently present record. remember that you must call
```

```
'Edit before you set values and call Update.
Private Sub cmdUpdate_Click()
    rstAuthor.Edit
    Call SetAuthorInfo
    rstAuthor.Update
End Sub

'Deleting a record does not move you to the previous
'or next record. Your location simply becomes invalid
'Here you requery to adjust the set size. this also
'eliminates the need to move off the record you are
'deleting.
Private Sub cmdDelete_Click()
    rstAuthor.Delete
    rstAuthor.Requery
    Call DisplayRecord
End Sub

'As you exit you will need to close all of the object
'variables. Actually closing the form should take care
'of it for you just like closing the environment object
'automatically closes all objects within it.
Private Sub cmdExit_Click()
    rstAuthor.Close
    Cn.Close
    Env.Close
    End
End Sub
```

8. Add the following routines to the form. These routines provide methods for displaying and retrieving information from the text boxes on the form.

```
'routine to display current row of resultset on form.
Private Sub DisplayRecord()
    txtAuthorID.Text = rstAuthor("au_id")
    txtLastName.Text = rstAuthor("au_lname")
    txtFirstName.Text = rstAuthor("au_fname")
    txtPhone.Text = rstAuthor("phone")
    txtAddress.Text = rstAuthor("address")
    txtCity.Text = rstAuthor("city")
    txtState.Text = rstAuthor("state")
    txtZip.Text = rstAuthor("zip")
End Sub


Private Sub ClearRecord()
    'this is a good place to set up default values
    txtAuthorID.Text = ""
    txtLastName.Text = ""
    txtFirstName.Text = ""
    txtPhone.Text = ""
    txtAddress.Text = ""
    txtCity.Text = ""
    txtState.Text = "WA"
    txtZip.Text = ""
End Sub
```

continued on next page

continued from previous page

```
'routine to set resultset to current values on form.
'This is a good place for validations.
Private Sub SetAuthorInfo()
    rstAuthor("au_id") = txtAuthorID.Text
    rstAuthor("au_lname") = txtLastName.Text
    rstAuthor("au_fname") = txtFirstName.Text
    rstAuthor("phone") = txtPhone.Text
    rstAuthor("address") = txtAddress.Text
    rstAuthor("city") = txtCity.Text
    rstAuthor("state") = txtState.Text
    rstAuthor("zip") = txtZip.Text
    rstAuthor("contract") = 0
End Sub
```

9. Add these routines to the form to enable and disable the navigation buttons. These routines are used to synchronize the navigation buttons with the corresponding navigation available for the underlying resultset.

```
'routine to disable the buttons on form.
Private Sub DisableButtons()
    cmdSave.Enabled = True

    cmdNewAuthor.Enabled = False
    cmdUpdate.Enabled = False
    cmdMoveFirst.Enabled = False
    cmdMovePrevious.Enabled = False
    cmdMoveNext.Enabled = False
    cmdMoveLast.Enabled = False
End Sub

'routine to enable the buttons on form.
Private Sub EnableButtons()
    cmdSave.Enabled = False

    cmdNewAuthor.Enabled = True
    cmdUpdate.Enabled = True
    cmdMoveFirst.Enabled = True
    cmdMovePrevious.Enabled = True
    cmdMoveNext.Enabled = True
    cmdMoveLast.Enabled = True
End Sub
```

How It Works

The `rdoResultset` object provides all the functionality to make this project work. First, you step through the process of creating an `rdoResultset` by dimensioning and using both an environment and a connection. After the connection to a data source is established, the `OpenResultset` method is used on the connection to create a dynamic resultset. To understand what a dynamic resultset refers to, you must first understand what a cursor is. A cursor in a resultset is similar in concept to a cursor in your word processing program. The cursor simply marks the current record you are on within a resultset. A dynamic cursor refers to cursors where the membership, order, and values in the resultset can constantly change. As rows are updated, deleted, or inserted, these changes are detected by the cursor as data is accessed.

Cursors can be created and maintained by either the server database engine or the client ODBC driver manager. Be aware that, though dynamic cursors provide a great deal of functionality, they require a great deal of overhead from whoever is maintaining them. Finally, with an **rdoResultset** object populated, you can take advantage of the DAO-like methods of **MoveFirst**, **MovePrevious**, **MoveNext**, and **MoveLast** to easily navigate the records contained in the resultset. Additionally, the application uses the **AddNew**, **Update**, and **Delete** methods to automate those activities as well.

Comments

Although the methods used in this How-To resemble those found in the DAO syntax, their implementation is significantly different. The DAO implementations automate the process with little flexibility, whereas RDO provides the capability to control all aspects from the cursor type to the record-locking method. Take this application and try running it on two or more machines at the same time. Make changes to the Authors table using this project to see how changes made by one user can be seen by other users. This How-To works with an **.MDB** file, but to truly see what implication cursor selection has on performance, you need to use a true database server engine like Microsoft SQL Server. Now that you have a basic understanding of how to manipulate records using RDO, try enhancing the form by adding a button to cancel when you are in the middle of adding a new record.

COMPLEXITY
BEGINNING

3.3 How do I...
Use rdoQuery **to parameterize a query?**

COMPATIBILITY: VISUAL BASIC 5 AND 6

Problem

I need to include a parameterized query (one that can accept variable information) in my application. I have been generating the SQL myself by concatenating strings based on options the user selects. The code is very ugly, and, additionally, this does not allow me to create a prepared statement or bind parameters to get better performance. Is there a way to do this using RDO?

Technique

The rdoQuery object is similar to the RDO 1.0 method rdoPreparedStatement, which it replaces. The difference is that the rdoQuery object not only has the capability to be persisted into a Visual Basic project, but you have the option of specifying whether the query and its parameters are prepared. So using the rdoQuery object, you can create parameterized queries and use a great deal of the power built into the RDO model.

A powerful feature of any language is the capability to use parameters that can be set at the time of execution. SQL is no exception. Couple the capability to pass parameters with the capability to precompile a request, as with a prepared statement, and you can imagine the benefits with regard to execution time. In this How-To, you create a simple form that accepts three parameters used to retrieve book information by an author from the PUBS database. You cannot use this project with an .MDB database file because the Microsoft Access database engine does not support prepared statements.

Steps

Open and run project PARAM.VBP. When the application starts, you are prompted to select a data source name. Specify a DSN that points to the PUBS database, which comes with Microsoft SQL Server. As you run this project, you see a message box showing the prepared statement that has been created (see Figure 3.6).

Figure 3.6 The form that shows the prepared statement that is being created

After the application is running, you can select a Social Security number from the combo box and specify a start date and end date that are used to retrieve the author's book sales information. The running program appears as shown in Figure 3.7.

Complete the following steps to create this project:

1. Create a new project called PARAM.VBP. Select Form1, and add objects and set properties as shown in Table 3.3.

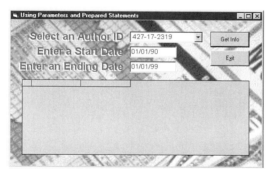

Figure 3.7 The form that allows runtime parameter input

Table 3.3 PARAMAPP.FRM form and control properties

OBJECT	PROPERTY	SETTING
Form	Name	frmParamApp
	Caption	"Using Parameters and Prepared Statements"
	ForeColor	&H000000FF&
TextBox	Name	txtEndDate
TextBox	Name	txtStartDate
ComboBox	Name	cmbAuthorId
CommandButton	Name	cmdExit
	Caption	"E&xit"
CommandButton	Name	cmdGetInfo
	Caption	"Get Info"
DBGrid	Name	DBGrid1
	DataSource	rdcDisplay
Label	Name	Label6
	Alignment	Right Justify
	BackStyle	Transparent
	Caption	"Enter an Ending Date"
	ForeColor	&H00008000&
Label	Name	Label5
	Alignment	Right Justify
	BackStyle	Transparent
	Caption	"Enter a Start Date"
	ForeColor	&H00008000&

continued on next page

Table 3.3 continued

OBJECT	PROPERTY	SETTING
Label	Name	Label4
	Alignment	Right Justify
	BackStyle	Transparent
	Caption	"Select an Author ID"
	ForeColor	&H00008000&
Label	Name	Label3
	Alignment	Right Justify
	BackStyle	Transparent
	Caption	"Enter an Ending Date"
	ForeColor	&H00FFFFFF&
Label	Name	Label2
	Alignment	Right Justify
	BackStyle	Transparent
	Caption	"Enter a Start Date"
	ForeColor	&H00FFFFFF&
Label	Name	Label1
	Alignment	Right Justify
	BackStyle	Transparent
	Caption	"Select an Author ID"
	ForeColor	&H00FFFFFF&
RemoteDataControl	Name	rdcDisplay
	DataSourceName	" "
	RecordSource	" "
	Connect	" "

2. The first thing you need to do is to dimension object variables for the environment, connection, prepared statement, and resultset. Add the following code to the General Declarations section of the form:

```
Option Explicit
'dimension your environment and connection variables
Dim Env As rdoEnvironment
Dim Cn As rdoConnection
Dim Ps As rdoQuery
Dim Rst As rdoResultset
```

3. On loading the form, you will set up the environment and require the user to specify a data source name to open a connection. This is accomplished by adding the following code to the **Form_load** event. This code also calls

two procedures to load the authors' Social Security numbers from the
Authors table into a combo box and initialize the rdoQuery that will be
used to return a resultset.

```
Private Sub Form_load()
    '
    'set the environment and connection objects
    Set Env = rdoEnvironments(0)
    Set cn = Env.OpenConnection("", rdDriverPrompt, True, "")
    '
    'Load the authors' social security number into the
    'combo box
    LoadAuthorIds
    '
    'initialize the rdo prepared statement
    InitializeStatement
    '
    'set default values
    txtStartDate = "01/01/90"
    txtEndDate = "01/01/99"
End Sub
```

4. Enter the following code into your form. The LoadAuthorIds procedure
creates a resultset of all available author Social Security numbers, which
are stored in the au_id field of the Authors table found in the PUBS
database. The values are then added to the combo box list.

```
Private Sub LoadAuthorIds()
    Dim rstAuthorIds As rdoResultset
    Dim sSQL As String
    Dim i As Integer

    sSQL = "SELECT au_id FROM authors ORDER BY au_id"
    Set rstAuthorIds = cn.OpenResultset(sSQL)

    'Check rowcount property to see if any records were
    'returned.
    If rstAuthorIds.RowCount <> 0 Then
        'load list
        cmbAuthorId.Clear
        While Not rstAuthorIds.EOF = True
            cmbAuthorId.AddItem rstAuthorIds("au_id")
            rstAuthorIds.MoveNext
        Wend
    Else
        MsgBox "Unable to load Author Ids"
    End If

    rstAuthorIds.Close
    '
    'that's all there is to it
End Sub
```

5. Add the following subroutine to your form. This code creates the
rdoQuery so that it is ready for use. This makes the most sense because
the purpose of using a prepared statement is to have it precompiled by the
database engine and ready for execution after parameters are set.

```
Private Sub InitializeStatement()
    'dimension variables for
    Dim sSQL As String
    '
    'construct SQL statement. Question marks are used as
    'placeholders for parameters.
    sSQL = "SELECT T1.au_lname, T3.title, T2.royaltyper,
        ➥T3.price, T4.qty"
        & " FROM authors T1, titleauthor T2, titles T3,
        ➥sales T4"
        & " WHERE T1.au_id = T2.au_id AND T2.title_id =
        ➥T3.title_id"
        & " AND T3.title_id = T4.title_id"
        ➥& " AND T1.au_id = ? AND T4.ord_date
        ➥BETWEEN ? and ?"
    '
    'display the select statement so you can see what
    'you are creating.
    MsgBox sSQL
    'set the SQL statement for the rdoQuery object
    Ps.SQL = sSQL
    'prepare the statement
    Ps.Prepared = True
    ' set the active connection for this query
    Ps.ActiveConnection = Cn

End Sub
```

6. Add the following code to your form. This procedure handles the setting
of parameters and creation of the resultset. This code includes the setting
of various rdoParameter properties that you can adjust. They are included
here to illustrate their use although they are actually set to default values.

```
Private Sub cmdGetInfo_Click()
    'After an rdoQuery object has been set you must
    'provide values for each of the ? placeholders that
    'is assigned as an input value. All placeholders are
    'input by default. Here you will set all values of
    'each parameter although it is not necessary if
    'the default settings are appropriate.
    'Set the parameters direction
    Ps.rdoParameters(0).Direction = rdoParamInput
    Ps.rdoParameters(1).Direction = rdoParamInput
    Ps.rdoParameters(2).Direction = rdoParamInput
    '
    'You could use these statements to check the
    'datatype of each parameter.
    'Ps.rdoParameters(0).Type    'rdTypeCHAR
    'Ps.rdoParameters(1).Type    'rdTypeDATE
    'Ps.rdoParameters(2).Type    'rdTypeDATE
```

```
        '
        'You could use these statements to
        'check the parameter name.
        '"Paramn" where "n" is the ordinal number.
        'Ps.rdoParameters(0).Name   'Param0
        'Ps.rdoParameters(1).Name   'Param1
        'Ps.rdoParameters(2).Name   'Param2
        '
        'Set the parameters value
        Ps.rdoParameters(0).Value = cmbAuthorId.Text
        Ps.rdoParameters(1).Value = txtStartDate.Text
        Ps.rdoParameters(2).Value = txtEndDate.Text
        '
        'In order to use resultset with the RDC you CANNOT
        'use a cursor type of rdOpenForwardOnly,
        'so here we set it to rdOpenKeyset
        Ps.CursorType = rdOpenKeyset
        Set Rst = Ps.OpenResultset
        Set rdcDisplay.Resultset = Rst
End Sub
```

7. As you exit, it is a good practice to close all the object variables. Actually, closing the form should take care of it for you just like closing the environment object automatically closes all objects within it.

```
Private Sub cmdExit_Click()
    Ps.Close
    Cn.Close
    Env.Close
    End
End Sub
```

How It Works

After the application is connected to a data source, the real work is performed by the **rdoQuery**. In this How-To, the **rdoQuery** is created and set as a prepared statement as the form loads so that it is ready to be used immediately. The SQL used to create the **rdoQuery** includes three parameters:

✔ Social Security number of the author in question

✔ Earliest date for sales

✔ Latest date for sales

The following query is used:

```
SELECT  T1.au_lname, T3.title, T2.royaltyper, T3.price, T4.qty
FROM    authors T1, titleauthor T2, titles T3, sales T4
WHERE   T1.au_id = T2.au_id
    AND T2.title_id = T3.title_id
    AND T3.title_id = T4.title_id
    AND T1.au_id = ?
    AND T4.ord_date BETWEEN ? and ?
```

A question mark is used to hold the place of parameters that will be provided prior to executing the statement. The syntax used for parameter placeholders in the prepared statement is identical to the syntax used when performing an ODBC `SQLPrepare` function. After the statement is prepared and compiled on the server, parameters can be set and executed repeatedly.

This How-To introduces the use of the `rdoParameters` collection and the `rdoParameter` properties of `Name`, `Type`, `Direction`, and `Value`. If you are using default settings for these properties, you only need to set the `Value` property. It is very important that you do not create a resultset with a cursor type of `rdoOpenForwardOnly`. This will cause an error when you try to pass it to the remote data control and data grid. The remote data control will only accept a resultset that contains a keyset. So in this example we use `rdoOpenKeyset`. When the prepared statement is executed, the resultset is passed to a remote data control with a bound DBGrid control to display the results to the user.

Comments

Parameterizing your queries is a powerful feature. Using the `rdoQuery` object simplifies the process by allowing you to set values for parameters using the `rdoParameters` collection. The syntax is easier to read and also to debug. The `rdoQuery` object has the added benefit of speed of execution, which accompanies any precompiled statement, but you must remember to specify that you want it prepared.

COMPLEXITY
INTERMEDIATE

3.4 How do I...
Control the number of rows returned in a resultset by RDO?

COMPATIBILITY: VISUAL BASIC 5 AND 6

Problem

The client machines that will run my applications have limited resources. I want to optimize the performance of the client machines by controlling the number of rows buffered on the client machine. Additionally, I need a way to control how much the clients can request from the server. Is there a way to limit a resultset other than the `where` clause of the actual SQL?

Technique

The `rdoQuery` object provides several properties to give you control over the load balance of a request. Load balancing used in this context refers to the division of labor between the client and the server to process and handle a request. The properties that provide this control are `RowsetSize`, `KeysetSize`, and `MaxRows`. All these properties work directly with a cursor. A *cursor* is a collection of logical rows managed by the ODBC cursor library or the database engine.

The `RowsetSize` property determines how many rows of the keyset are returned to the application. `KeysetSize` controls the number of rows in the keyset buffer. The keyset buffer contains a set of only the key values used to retrieve rows of data contained within a server or ODBC cursor library. `MaxRows` does exactly that. It limits the maximum number of rows returned by any query executed using its `rdoPreparedStatement` object.

In this How-To, you create an application that accepts an SQL statement in a text box and processes it with the previously mentioned property settings. You can interactively adjust the `RowsetSize`, `KeysetSize`, and `MaxRows` as well as set the cursor driver, cursor type, and lock type. This allows you to experiment with various combinations to see how different combinations affect execution of a query.

Steps

Open and run project `RETSET.VBP`. The running program appears as shown in Figure 3.8. Enter a `SELECT` statement such as `SELECT * FROM Authors` and click Execute. The query displays the execution time in the form's caption, and the results appear in the text box below the query.

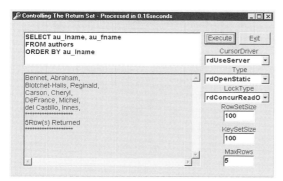

Figure 3.8 The form as it appears at runtime with a limited resultset

Notice that the query only returned 5 rows of a possible 24 rows that exist in the Authors table. This is controlled by the `MaxRows` property setting. Set `MaxRows` to `10` and again click Execute. Ten rows are returned. Experiment with different cursor combinations to see how different combinations affect execution of the query. To create this project, complete the following steps:

1. Create a new project called RETSET.VBP. Select Form1, and add objects and set properties as shown in Table 3.4.

Table 3.4 RETSET.FRM form and control properties

OBJECT	PROPERTY	SETTING
Form	Name	frmReturnSet
	Caption	"Controlling The Return Set"
	Icon	"wrench.ico"
ComboBox	Name	cmbLockType
	Style	Dropdown List
ComboBox	Name	cmbType
	Style	Dropdown List
ComboBox	Name	cmbCursorDriver
	Style	Dropdown List
TextBox	Name	txtDisplay
	BackColor	&H00C0C0C0&
	Locked	True
	MultiLine	True
	ScrollBars	Both
TextBox	Name	txtKeySetSize
	Text	"100"
TextBox	Name	txtRowSetSize
	Text	"100"
TextBox	Name	txtMaxRows
	Text	"5"
TextBox	Name	txtSQL
	MultiLine	True
CommandButton	Name	cmdExit
	Caption	"E&xit"
CommandButton	Name	cmdExecute
	Caption	"Execute"
Label	Name	Label6
	Alignment	Center
	Caption	"LockType"
Label	Name	Label5
	Alignment	Center
	Caption	"Type"

OBJECT	PROPERTY	SETTING
Label	Name	Label4
	Alignment	Center
	Caption	"CursorDriver"
Label	Name	Label3
	Alignment	Center
	Caption	"KeySetSize"
Label	Name	Label2
	Alignment	Center
	Caption	"MaxRows"
Label	Name	Label1
	Alignment	Center
	Caption	"RowSetSize"

2. You first must dimension object variables for the environment, connection, prepared statement, and resultset. This is done by adding the following code to the General Declarations section of the form:

```
Option Explicit
'
'dimension environment and connection variables
Dim Env As rdoEnvironment
Dim Cn As rdoConnection
'
'dimension object variables for a prepared
'statement and resultset
Dim Ps As rdoQuery
Dim Rst As rdoResultset
'
'holds the connect string created during initial
'startup.
Dim sConnect As String
```

3. On loading the form, you will set up the environment and require the user to specify a data source name to open a connection. Add the following code to the **Form_Load** event. This code also stores the connection string in **sConnect** so that you can use it later when a new connection is needed.

```
Private Sub Form_Load()
    'set the environment variable and open a connection
    'by prompting user for DSN. This is done by leaving
    'the source parameter empty and the connect parameter
    'empty and specifying rdDriverPrompt.
    Set Env = rdoEnvironments(0)
    Env.CursorDriver = rdUseServer
    Set Cn = Env.OpenConnection(dsName:="", _
                            Prompt:=rdDriverPrompt, _
                            ReadOnly:=True, _
```

continued on next page

continued from previous page

```
                                          Connect:="")
      '
      'store the connection string for later use
      sConnect = Cn.Connect
      '
      'populate the combo boxes
      LoadComboBoxes
End Sub
```

4. Add the following subroutine to load default values into the combo boxes that correspond with the constants available for each of the properties you will be adjusting. You can review the listed constants in the Visual Basic Enterprise help file.

```
Private Sub LoadComboBoxes()
      '
      'load cmbCursorDriver with cursor driver options
      cmbcursordriver.List(0) = "rdUseIfNeeded"
      cmbcursordriver.ItemData(0) = 0
      cmbcursordriver.List(1) = "rdUseOdbc"
      cmbcursordriver.ItemData(1) = 1
      cmbcursordriver.List(2) = "rdUseServer"
      cmbcursordriver.ItemData(2) = 2
      '
      'set default
      cmbcursordriver.ListIndex = 2
      '
      'load cmbType with cursor type options
      cmbtype.List(0) = "rdOpenForwardOnly"
      cmbtype.ItemData(0) = 0
      cmbtype.List(1) = "rdOpenStatic"
      cmbtype.ItemData(1) = 3
      cmbtype.List(2) = "rdOpenKeyset"
      cmbtype.ItemData(2) = 1
      cmbtype.List(3) = "rdOpenDynamic"
      cmbtype.ItemData(3) = 2
      '
      'set default
      cmbtype.ListIndex = 1
      '
      'load cmbLockType with cursor locktype options
      cmbLockType.List(0) = "rdConcurLock"
      cmbLockType.ItemData(0) = 2
      cmbLockType.List(1) = "rdConcurReadOnly"
      cmbLockType.ItemData(1) = 1
      cmbLockType.List(2) = "rdConcurRowver"
      cmbLockType.ItemData(2) = 3
      cmbLockType.List(3) = "rdConcurValues"
      cmbLockType.ItemData(3) = 4
      '
      'set default
      cmbLockType.ListIndex = 1
End Sub
```

5. Add the following code for the cursor driver combo box. If the choice in the cursor driver combo box changes, then the connection is closed, the cursor driver changed, and the connection reopened.

```
Private Sub cmbcursordriver_Click()
    '
    'check to see if anything has really changed.
    If cmbcursordriver.ItemData(cmbcursordriver.ListIndex) = _
        Env.CursorDriver Then
            Exit Sub
    End If
    '
    'close connection and reopen with new cursor driver
    Cn.Close
    '
    'reset the environment cursor to your selection
    Env.CursorDriver = cmbcursordriver.ItemData
    ➥(cmbcursordriver.ListIndex)
    '
    'reuse connection string from initial prompt.
    Set Cn = Env.OpenConnection(dsName:="", _
                                Prompt:=rdDriverNoPrompt, _
                                ReadOnly:=True, _
                                Connect:=sConnect)
End Sub
```

6. Add the following code to your form for the Execute button's **Click** event. This code applies all the property settings selected on the form to the **rdoPreparedStatement** object and the **rdoResultset** object before execution. Note that this subroutine creates an instance of the **Timing** class. You need to include this class with this project.

```
Private Sub cmdExecute_Click()
    On Error GoTo cmdExecute_Error
    Dim oTiming As Timing
    Set oTiming = New Timing
    '
    'clear the text box that displays results
    txtDisplay.Text = ""
    txtDisplay.Refresh
    '
    'now you will create the prepared statement.
    Ps.SQL = txtSQL.Text
    Ps.Prepared = True
    Ps.ActiveConnection = Cn
    '
    'Here you will set the various options for number
    'of rows returned.rdOpenStatic, rdOpenKeyset,
    'rdOpenForwardOnly
    'rdOpenDynamic
    Ps.RowsetSize = txtRowSetSize.Text
    Ps.KeysetSize = CLng(txtKeySetSize.Text)
    Ps.MaxRows = CLng(txtMaxRows.Text)
    '
    'start timing the request.
```

continued on next page

continued from previous page

```
            oTiming.Start
            '
            'Resultset is opened using options from comboboxes.
            Set Rst = Ps.OpenResultset( _
                        Type:=cmbtype.ItemData(cmbtype.ListIndex), _
                        ➥LockType:=cmbLockType.ItemData
                        ➥(cmbLockType.ListIndex))
            '
            'stop timing of request.
            oTiming.Finish
            '
            'Display the rows returned by the open resultset
            'method
            Call DisplayResults

            Me.Caption = "Controlling The Return Set - Processed in " _
                        & oTiming.ElapsedTime & "seconds"
            '
            'it is important to close the resultset since
            'reusing it without closing it simply appends results
            'and DOES NOT automatically reinitialize it.
            Rst.Close
            Ps.Close
            Exit Sub
        cmdExecute_Error:
        Dim oRDOError As rdoError
        Dim sErr As String
            For Each oRDOError In rdoErrors
            sErr = sErr & vbCrLf & oRDOError.Description
            Next
            MsgBox sErr
            Exit Sub
        End Sub
```

7. After the resultset has been returned, the following code takes care of displaying it in the display text box:

```
Private Sub DisplayResults()
    Dim myCol As rdoColumn
    Dim sRst As String
    Dim iRstCount As Integer

    iRstCount = 0
    sRst = ""
    txtDisplay.Text = ""
    Do
        Do Until Rst.EOF = True
            'display results
            For Each myCol In Rst.rdoColumns
                sRst = sRst & myCol.Value & ", "
            Next
            sRst = sRst & vbCrLf
            iRstCount = iRstCount + 1
            Rst.MoveNext
        Loop
```

```
                sRst = sRst & "********************" & vbCrLf _
                            & iRstCount & "Row(s) Returned " & vbCrLf _
                            & "********************" & vbCrLf & vbCrLf

        Loop Until Rst.MoreResults = False
        txtDisplay.Text = txtDisplay.Text & sRst
        'Me.Caption = iRstCount & " Resultsets Returned!"
    End Sub
```

8. As you exit, it is a good practice to close all the object variables. Actually, closing the form should take care of it for you just like closing the environment object automatically closes all objects within it.

```
Private Sub cmdExit_Click()
    Cn.Close
    Env.Close
    End
End Sub
```

9. Choose Insert, Class Module from Visual Basic's menu to add a class module to this project. The class appears in the project window. Open the class module and press F4 to view the class's properties. Set the `Name` property to `Timing`.

10. Add the following code to the General Declarations section of the `Timing` class module. You must declare the `timeGetTime` API function to have access to a method that returns timing values with a millisecond resolution. The standard `Time()` function in Visual Basic only provides for seconds.

```
Option Explicit
'
'dimension readonly variables for timing events
Dim mStartTime As Long
Dim mFinishTime As Long
Dim mElapsedTime As Long
'
'declare API to get time in milliseconds.
Private Declare Function timeGetTime Lib "winmm.dll" () As Long
```

11. Add the following methods and properties to the `Timing` class. These methods and properties allow you to time execution of SQL queries and have access to the elapsed time values in milliseconds.

```
'method to store start time
Public Sub Start()
    mStartTime = timeGetTime
End Sub

'method to store finish time and calculate elapsed
'time in milliseconds
Public Sub Finish()
```

continued on next page

continued from previous page

```
            mFinishTime = timeGetTime
            mElapsedTime = mFinishTime - mStartTime
        End Sub

        'read-only property to access elapsed time.
        Public Property Get ElapsedTime()
            ElapsedTime = mElapsedTime / 1000
        End Property
```

How It Works

This How-To allows you to explore the variety of options that affect performance when working with `rdoQueries`. Figure 3.9 shows how `KeysetSize`, `RowsetSize`, and `MaxRows` affect the client and the server's portion of the load in processing a request.

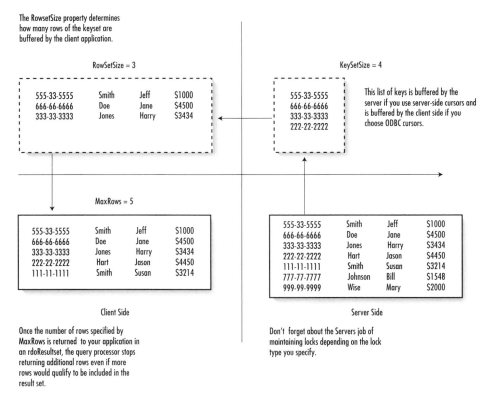

Figure 3.9 Illustrating the implications of RowSetSize, KeySetSize, and MaxRows

It is worth noting that although the `KeysetSize` is depicted in the figure as affecting processing on the server, this is, in fact, determined by the choice in cursor drivers. If the cursor driver is ODBC, then the keyset is actually maintained by the client machine, versus the use of the server's cursor driver, which would then manage the keyset with the server's resources. Please note that using a cursor type of `rdUseServer`, along with a cursor type of `rdOpenStatic` and a lock type of `rdConcurRowver`, will result in an error. This How-To allows you to see which combinations work and which do not.

> **NOTE**
>
> Although cursor driver and record locking options can apply to a resultset generated either with or without a prepared statement, limiting the number of rows returned by a query can be done only by using an `rdoQuery` and setting the `MaxRows` property.

On the server side of this project, the `KeysetSize` property controls the number of keysets buffered on the server if server-side cursors are set for the environment at the time the connection is established. On the client side, the `RowsetSize` property determines how many rows of the keyset are buffered by the application. This property must be set before creating an `rdoResultset` object. Tuning the size of `RowsetSize` can affect performance and the amount of memory required to maintain the keyset buffer.

An additional aspect of RDO used in this How-To is that the `rdoQuery` object's `MaxRows` property is mapped to the ODBC statement option `SQL_MAX_ROWS`. When `MaxRows` is set to a value greater than 0, the maximum number of rows processed by Microsoft SQL Server is limited to the value of `MaxRows`. After you change `MaxRows` for an `rdoQuery`, it stays set until you change it in code or close the object. If you insert, update, or delete an action query using an `rdoQuery` with a `MaxRows` setting that is not set to the default, the number of rows that get processed will be limited to the number set in `MaxRows`.

Comments

Creating scalable applications requires the capability to control the balance of the load. As an application's usage demands grow, adjustments must be made to optimize each configuration. You might consider setting these properties based on an external configuration file or Registry entry either on a workstation or, better yet, at the business server where your RDO code will reside and provide communication between the business services and data services objects.

COMPLEXITY
INTERMEDIATE

3.5 How do I...
Retrieve multiple resultsets with RDO?

COMPATIBILITY: VISUAL BASIC 4, 5, AND 6

Problem

An SQL statement can contain any number of **SELECT** statements or stored procedures. Each **SELECT** statement returns a resultset. How can I handle multiple resultsets using RDO?

Technique

RDO provides a special method that can be used with the **rdoResultset** object. This method is called **MoreResults**. As you navigate forward through a resultset and finally hit the end of file (EOF), you can use the **MoreResults** method to find out whether any additional results are pending. If **MoreResults** returns **True**, then you can proceed to retrieve additional results until no more exist.

Steps

Open and run project **MULTIRS.VBP**. The running program appears as shown in Figure 3.10. Enter multiple **SELECT** statements into the text box provided at the top. Make sure that you separate each SQL statement with a semicolon. Click the Retrieve Results button. The form's caption changes to display how many resultsets were returned. The resultsets are displayed in the lower text box.

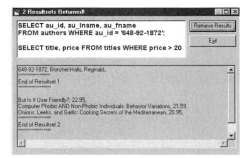

Figure 3.10 The form as it appears at runtime containing multiple result-sets

Complete the following steps to create this project:

1. Create a new project called MULTIRS.VBP. Select Form1, and add objects and set properties as shown in Table 3.5.

Table 3.5 MULTIRS.FRM form and control properties

OBJECT	PROPERTY	SETTING
Form	Name	frmMultiRS
	BorderStyle	Fixed Single
	Caption	"Multiple Result Sets"
	Icon	"note03.ico"
CommandButton	Name	cmdExit
	Caption	"E&xit"
TextBox	Name	txtDisplay
	BackColor	&H00C0C0C0&
	Locked	True
	MultiLine	True
	ScrollBars	Both
TextBox	Name	txtSQL
	MultiLine	True
CommandButton	Name	cmdRetrieveResults
	Caption	"Retrieve Results"

2. The first thing you need to do is to dimension object variables for the environment, connection, prepared statement, and resultset. Add the following code to the General Declarations section of the form:

```
Option Explicit
Dim Env As rdoEnvironment
Dim Cn As rdoConnection
Dim Ps As rdoQuery
Dim Rst As rdoResultset
```

3. On loading the form, you will set up the environment and require the user to specify a data source name to open a connection. Add the following code to the Form_load event:

```
Private Sub Form_Load()
    Set Env = rdoEnvironments(0)
    'Env.CursorDriver = rdUseOdbc
    Set Cn = Env.OpenConnection("", rdDriverPrompt, True, "")
End Sub
```

4. Add the following code for the Retrieve Results command button `Click` event. This code deactivates the use of cursors, thus allowing the receipt of multiple resultsets by creating an `rdoQuery` object and setting its `RowsetSize = 1`.

```
Private Sub cmdRetrieveResults_Click()
    Dim sSQL As String
    Dim iHowMany As Integer
    On Error GoTo cmdRetrieveResults_Error
    '
    'clear any results that are displayed within the
    'lower text box.
    txtDisplay.Text = ""
    '
  'create a prepared statement
    sSQL = txtSQL.Text
    Ps.SQL = sSQL
    Ps.Prepared = True
    Ps.ActiveConnection = Cn
    '
    'set the rowsetsize to 1 in order to deactivate
    'the use of cursors.
    Ps.RowsetSize = 1
    '
    'Process the SQL statements from the forms text box.
    Set Rst = Ps.OpenResultset(Type:=rdOpenForwardOnly, _
                        LockType:=rdConcurReadOnly)
    If Rst.EOF Then
        MsgBox "No results"
        GoTo cmdRetrieveResults_Exit
    Else
        DisplayResults
    End If

cmdRetrieveResults_Exit:
    Rst.Close
    Ps.Close
    Exit Sub
cmdRetrieveResults_Error:
    MsgBox rdoErrors(0).Description
End Sub
```

5. After the SQL statement is processed and the results are available, you can gain access to each resultset with the following code, which you should add to your project:

```
Private Sub DisplayResults()
    Dim myCol As rdoColumn
    Dim sRst As String
    Dim iRstCount As Integer

    iRstCount = 0
    sRst = ""

    Do
```

```
        Do Until Rst.EOF = True
            'display results
            For Each myCol In Rst.rdoColumns
                sRst = sRst & myCol.Value & ", "
            Next
            sRst = sRst & vbCrLf
            Rst.MoveNext
        Loop
        iRstCount = iRstCount + 1
        sRst = sRst & "*****************" & vbCrLf _
                    & "End of Resultset " & iRstCount & vbCrLf _
                    & "*****************" & vbCrLf & vbCrLf

    Loop Until Rst.MoreResults = False
    txtDisplay.Text = txtDisplay.Text & sRst
    Me.Caption = iRstCount & " Resultsets Returned!"
End Sub
```

6. As you exit, it is a good practice to close all the object variables. Actually, closing the form should take care of it for you just like closing the environment object automatically closes all objects within it.

```
Private Sub cmdExit_Click()
Cn.Close
Env.Close
End
End Sub
```

How It Works

A simple form is created that allows you to enter an SQL statement. This statement is used to create an **rdoResultset**. If the SQL statement contains multiple **SELECT** statements, then it returns more than one resultset. A forward-only resultset is created with **RowsetSize** set to 1 to prevent the use of cursors on the back end. As the application moves through the resultset using the **MoveNext** method, the program tests to see whether the resultset is at end of file (EOF). When **EOF** is true, then the project uses the **MoreResults** method to begin processing the following set of results, if they exist.

It is important to note that calling **MoreResults** at any point during the retrieval of results automatically discards the remaining rows in that resultset. When no additional resultsets remain to be processed, the **MoreResults** method returns **False**, and both the **BOF** and **EOF** properties of the **rdoResultset** object are set to **True**.

Comments

Business applications are centered on the concept of a unit of work. Whether that unit consists of loading a screen full of list boxes or processing a complex financial transaction, each would benefit from the capability to bundle multiple statements into a single call. There are some restrictions on the RDO implementation of handling multiple resultsets. One restriction is that you cannot use a server-side cursor to handle the resultset. A second restriction is that you must process the resultsets sequentially. Limitations aside, the capability of RDO to handle multiple resultsets is a powerful feature.

COMPLEXITY
ADVANCED

3.6 How do I...
Perform an asynchronous query with RDO?

COMPATIBILITY: VISUAL BASIC 4, 5, AND 6

Problem

Many times queries are submitted that require more than a second or two to be processed. When these queries are submitted, the client application enters a frozen state, and no more work can be done within the client application until the query is complete and a resultset is generated. How can I submit SQL statements asynchronously?

Technique

RDO provides the capability to submit an SQL statement asynchronously to an ODBC source if the ODBC driver supports this functionality. This is accomplished by creating a resultset with **rdAsyncEnable** passed as a parameter. RDO uses a method of polling to see whether a submitted request is complete. RDO polls the data source repeatedly to determine whether the query has completed. The **AsyncCheckInterval** property allows you to change the duration of time between checks.

Each time you check on the status of an asynchronous query, the server must respond. This response costs in processing time. Adjusting check times allows you to fine-tune performance by checking on a query's status only when necessary. This How-To walks you through an exploration of asynchronous query submission.

Steps

Open and run project **FETCHIT.VBP**. The running program appears as shown in Figure 3.11. You are prompted to select a data source name from a list. When the form is up, choose File, New Fetch Form from the menu. This presents you with an SQL submission form. Enter an SQL statement in the text box.

Figure 3.11 The form as it appears at runtime with a single Fetch form open

After you have entered an SQL statement, click the Fetch button. The form changes in size, and a spinning bone appears. The spinning bone is meant to demonstrate at what point the client application regains control and how long it takes to actually get results (see Figure 3.12).

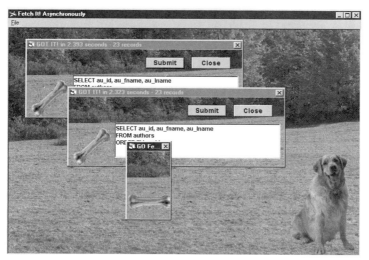

Figure 3.12 The form as it appears with several requests pending

When the query is complete, the bone stops spinning, and the Fetch form is returned to its original size. Additionally, the execution time of the query is posted in the title bar of the child form (see Figure 3.13).

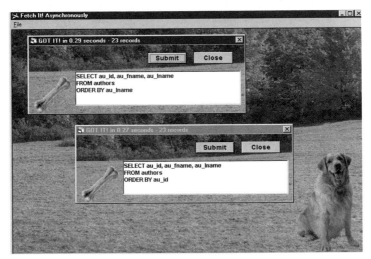

Figure 3.13 The form as it appears after results are available

To create this project, complete the following steps:

1. Create a new project called FETCHIT.VBP.

2. Select Form1, and add objects and set properties as shown in Table 3.6.

Table 3.6   CFETCHIT.FRM form and control properties

OBJECT	PROPERTY	SETTING
Form	Name	cfrmFetchI
	BorderStyle	Fixed Single
	Caption	"GO Fetch It!"
	MaxButton	False
	MDIChild	True
	Picture	"meadow2.bmp"
CommandButton	Name	cmdClose
	Caption	"Close"
Timer	Name	Timer1
	Enabled	False
	Interval	250

OBJECT	PROPERTY	SETTING
CommandButton	Name	cmdSubmit
	Caption	"Submit"
TextBox	Name	txtSQL
	BackColor	&H00FFFFFF&
	MultiLine	True
Label	Name	lblMessage
	Alignment	Center
	BackStyle	Transparent
	Caption	"Click Bone to Cancel"
	ForeColor	&H000000FF&
Image	Name	imgBone
PictureClip	Name	picBones
	Picture	"boneicons.bmp"

3. You first must dimension object variables for the environment, connection, and resultset. Add the following code to the General Declarations section of the form. Additionally, an object variable is dimensioned to use the Timing class, which provides the capability to time execution speed of SQL submissions.

```
Option Explicit
Private Env As rdoEnvironment
Private Cn As rdoConnection
Private Rst As rdoResultset
Private oTiming As Timing
Private mFrmOrigWidth As Long
```

4. On loading the form, you will set up the environment and require the user to specify a data source name to open a connection. Add the following code to the Form_load event:

```
Private Sub Form_Load()
    'set up the environment
    Set Env = rdoCreateEnvironment(Str$(gEnvCount),
    ➥rdoDefaultUser, rdoDefaultPassword)
    gEnvCount = gEnvCount + 1
    'use odbc cursors
    Env.CursorDriver = rdUseOdbc

    'Since you want asynchronous handling of a query
    'you will need a separate connection per request.
    'This line simply prompts for a
    'Data Source Name (DSN).
    Set Cn = Env.OpenConnection("", rdDriverPrompt, True, "")
    Cn.AsyncCheckInterval = 5000
    '
End Sub
```

5. Add the following code to your form for the Submit button's **Click** event to handle the details of displaying the bone graphic and resizing the form during the time that the form waits for the submission to be completed:

```
Private Sub cmdSubmit_Click()
    Dim rc As Integer

    If txtSQL.Text = "" Then
        MsgBox "You must enter a SQL Statement to process"
        Exit Sub
    End If
    Set oTiming = New Timing
    oTiming.Start
    '
    'submit sql request
    rc = SubmitRequest
    If rc 0> True Then
        Me.Caption = "Unable to process request..."
        Exit Sub
    End If
    '
    'set GUI stuff to demonstrate the ability to
    'do other processes while SQL request is being
    'processed asynchronously.
    Timer1.Enabled = True
    mFrmOrigWidth = Me.Width
    Me.Width = txtSQL.Left
    lblMessage.Visible = True
End Sub
```

6. Add the following code to the image control's **Click** event. This code allows the user to handle the asynchronous query process at will. This is done by using the **Cancel** method against the connection variable object.

```
Private Sub imgBone_Click()
    'cancel submitted query.
    Cn.Cancel
    Timer1.Enabled = False
    Me.Width = mFrmOrigWidth
    lblMessage.Visible = False
    Me.Caption = "Last Request Cancelled..."
    Set oTiming = Nothing
    Rst.Close
End Sub
```

7. Add the following code to the **Timer1** control's **Timer** event. This code is responsible for cycling through the pictures of the bone causing it to appear to rotate. Additionally, this routine checks the **StillExecuting** property of the resultset to see whether the query has completed yet.

```
Private Sub Timer1_Timer()
    Static i As Integer
    If i = 8 Then
        If Rst.StillExecuting = False Then
```

```
            Timer1.Enabled = False
            oTiming.Finish
            DisplayResults
            Exit Sub
        End If
        i = 0
    End If
    imgBone.Picture = Me.picBones.GraphicCell(i)
    i = i + 1
End Sub
```

8. Add the following code to your form. This code actually submits the query taken from the form's text box and submits it to the back-end engine.

```
Private Function SubmitRequest() As Integer
    Dim i As Integer
    On Error GoTo SubmitRequest_Error
    '
    'Open resultset static so you can get a rowcount,
    'note that rdAsyncEnable is passed as the fourth
    'argument when opening a resultset directly
    'against the connection.
    Set Rst = Cn.OpenResultset(txtSQL.Text, _
                          rdOpenStatic, _
                          rdConcurReadOnly, _
                          rdAsyncEnable)
    SubmitRequest = True

SubmitRequest_exit:
    Exit Function

SubmitRequest_Error:
    Dim Er As rdoError
    Dim sErrText As String
    For Each Er In rdoErrors
        sErrText = sErrText & Er.Description & vbCrLf
    Next
    MsgBox sErrText
    SubmitRequest = False
End Function
```

9. Add the following code to your form to display the timing results and row count of the asynchronous query results:

```
Private Sub DisplayResults()
    Me.Caption = "GOT IT! in " & oTiming.ElapsedTime
    ➥& " seconds"
    Me.Width = mFrmOrigWidth
    lblMessage.Visible = False
    Set oTiming = Nothing
    If Rst.StillExecuting = False Then
        Me.Caption = Me.Caption & " - " & Rst.RowCount
        ➥& " records"
        Rst.Close
    End If
End Sub
```

10. As you exit, it is a good practice to close all the object variables. Actually, closing the form should take care of it for you just like closing the environment object automatically closes all objects within it.

```
Private Sub cmdClose_Click()
    Cn.Close
    Env.Close
    Unload Me
End Sub
```

11. Insert an MDI form, and add objects and set properties as shown in Table 3.7.

Table 3.7 FETCHIT.FRM form and control properties

OBJECT	PROPERTY	SETTING
MDIForm	Name	mfrmFetchIt
	BackColor	&H8000000C&
	Caption	"Fetch It! Asynchronously"
	Picture	"meadow.bmp"
mFile	Caption	"&File"
mFNewFetchForm	Caption	"&New Fetch Form"
mFExit	Caption	"E&xit"

12. Dimension an object variable for the MDI child form.

```
Option Explicit
Dim ocfrmFetchForm As cfrmFetchIt
```

13. Enter the following code for the New Fetch Form menu Click event. This code creates a new instance of the MDI child form.

```
Private Sub mFNewFetchForm_Click()
    Set ocfrmFetchForm = New cfrmFetchIt
    ocfrmFetchForm.Show
End Sub

Private Sub mFExit_Click()
    End
End Sub
```

14. Insert a new standard module and set the name to General.

15. Each child form will have its own environment, connection, and resultset. Enter the following code into the standard module called GENERAL.BAS. The genvCount variable is used to generate a unique name for each child form created.

```
Option Explicit
Global gEnvCount As Integer

Public Sub Main()
    'show main form
    mfrmFetchIt.Show
End Sub
```

16. Choose Insert, Class Module from the Visual Basic menu to add a class module to this project. The class appears in the project window. Open the class module and press F4 to view the class's properties. Set these properties as shown in Table 3.8.

Table 3.8 TIMING.CLS class module property settings

OBJECT	PROPERTY	SETTING
Class Module	Name	"Timing"
	Creatable	False
	Public	False

17. Add the following code to the General Declarations section of the `Timing` class module. You need to declare the `timeGetTime` API function to have access to a method that returns timing values with a millisecond resolution. The standard `Time()` function in Visual Basic only provides for seconds.

```
Option Explicit
'
'dimension readonly variables for timing events
Dim mStartTime As Long
Dim mFinishTime As Long
Dim mElapsedTime As Long
'
'declare API to get time in milliseconds.
Private Declare Function timeGetTime Lib "winmm.dll" () As Long
```

18. Add the following methods and properties to the `Timing` class. These methods and properties allow you to time execution of SQL queries and have access to the elapsed time values in milliseconds.

```
'method to store start time
Public Sub Start()
    mStartTime = timeGetTime
End Sub

'method to store finish time and calculate elapsed
'time in milliseconds
Public Sub Finish()
    mFinishTime = timeGetTime
    mElapsedTime = mFinishTime - mStartTime
```

continued on next page

continued from previous page

```
End Sub

'read-only property to access elapsed time.
Public Property Get ElapsedTime()
    ElapsedTime = mElapsedTime / 1000
End Property
```

How It Works

The project consists of two forms, a parent MDI form and a child MDI form. The parent form serves as a container for any number of child forms that can be instantiated by way of the menu bar option New Fetch Form. After a Fetch form has been created, a data source selected, and an SQL statement entered into the text box, the asynchronous query submission can be made by clicking the Submit button. There are two main pieces to the asynchronous puzzle. First, you need to submit the SQL statement using the `CreateResultset` method and set the `rdAsyncEnable` option. This works only if your ODBC driver supports this functionality (Microsoft Access ODBC drivers do not support this functionality).

The second step takes place after a query has been submitted. This step involves methods for notifying the user when the request is done. The two styles available for this type of notification are server-side callbacks and polling. Server-side callbacks involve the server receiving a handle to a client application object, which is used to notify the client when the request is complete. Polling is a method in which the client checks back with the server periodically to see what the status is on the request. This How-To used the polling method by checking the status on the request using the `StillExecuting` property of the resultset object. Additionally, polling intervals can be fine-tuned using the `AsyncCheckInterval` property of the `rdoConnection` object.

Comments

It is important to note that polling too often can negatively affect your server as well as workstation performance. If, on the other hand, you choose to poll less frequently, you get better performance, but affect the speed of getting results. Asynchronous queries make a lot of sense for any request that takes more than a few seconds to process.

It is important to consider the question of asynchronous processing within the three-tier client/server architecture. In this model, RDO is providing connectivity between the Business services layer and the Data services layer. Within these layers, some processes make sense to be executed asynchronously, especially decision support queries or batch processing queries. Examine the task at hand and decide which tool in your toolbox to use.

COMPLEXITY
BEGINNING

3.7 How do I...
Submit an SQL query using ADO?

COMPATIBILITY: VISUAL BASIC 6

Problem

I understand how to write SQL statements, but how do I submit a statement to my database server with ADO?

Technique

The bread and butter of client/server development is comprised of processing requests and answers in the form of SQL queries and resultsets. ADO provides a simplified method for submitting SQL queries to a database. Unlike remote data objects where a strict hierarchy is needed to create objects, ADO allows you more flexibility by creating **Recordset** objects without forcing you to build it tied to a single connection object. In this How-To, you use an ADO recordset to submit queries on the active connection.

Steps

Open and run project **SUBMIT_ADO.VBP**. The running program appears as shown in Figure 3.14. The application requires the creation of a Data Source Name **PUBS_DSN** that points to the PUBS sample database in SQL Server.

Figure 3.14 The ADO query form as it appears at runtime with a list of all titles from the PUBS database

Enter an SQL `Select` statement in the text box and click the Submit SQL button to send it to the back-end database engine. If the `Select` statement returns records, they are displayed in the DataGrid control. If no results are found, then the status bar is updated to reflect the execution time of the query and states that no records were returned. Complete the following steps to create the project:

1. Create a new project called `SUBMIT_ADO.VBP`. Select `Form1`, and add objects and set properties as shown in Table 3.9.

Table 3.9 `SUBMIT_ADO..FRM` form and controls properties

OBJECT	PROPERTY	SETTING
Form	Name	frmSubmitSQL
	Caption	"Submit SQL using ADO"
TextBox	Name	txtSQL
	MultiLine	True
CommandButton	Name	cmdSubmitSQL
	Caption	"Submit SQL"
CommandButton	Name	cmdExit
	Caption	"Exit"
ADODC	Name	adoDisplay
DataGrid	Name	DataGrid1
	DataSource	adoDisplay
StatusBar	Name	StatusBar1
	Align	Align Bottom
	Style	single panel
	SimpleText	""

2. The first thing you need to do is to dimension object variables for the connection. Add the following code to the General Declarations section of the form:

```
Option Explicit
Dim Cn As ADODB.Connection
```

3. The form uses the connection variable dimensioned in the General section of the form. Add the following code to the `Form_Load` event. In this example, you use the `Open` method to connect to the data source.

```
Private Sub Form_Load()
    'open a connection to a data source
    Set Cn = New ADODB.Connection
    Cn.ConnectionString = "driver={SQL Server};" & _
        "server=BIGBOY;uid=sa;pwd=;database=pubs"
```

```
    Cn.ConnectionTimeout = 30
    Cn.Open

End Sub
```

4. Enter the following code for the Submit SQL button `Click` event. This code performs the action of submitting the SQL query from the text box to the selected data source. This code also takes advantage of ADO's `Errors` collection and `Error` objects to view errors generated during the ADO process. Notice that a `Timing` object is used to time the execution of the SQL statement. The `Timing` class is described later in this How-To.

```
Private Sub cmdSubmitSQL_Click()
    StatusBar1.SimpleText = "Processing Request ..."
    StatusBar1.Refresh
    On Error GoTo cmdSubmitSQL_error
    'you will use the timing object to time the whole
    'process including connect time.
    Dim oTiming As Timing
    Set oTiming = New Timing
    Call oTiming.Start
    '
    'the following routine is everything that must
    'be done to submit an SQL statement using ADO.
    Dim Rst As New ADODB.Recordset
    '
    'submit the SQL statement and get the results.
    Rst.Open txtSQL.Text, Cn, adOpenStatic, adLockReadOnly
    '
    'finish timing of submission
    oTiming.Finish
    '
    'Check rowcount property to see if any records
    'were returned.

    If Rst.RecordCount > 0 Then
        StatusBar1.SimpleText = "Your SQL query
        ➥has returned records" _
                & " in just " & oTiming.ElapsedTime
                ➥& " seconds!"
        Set Adodc1.Recordset = Rst
    Else
        StatusBar1.SimpleText = "Query took "
        ➥& oTiming.ElapsedTime _
                & "seconds - No records returned."
        Set Adodc1.Recordset = Rst
    End If
    '
    'that's all there is to it
    '
cmdSubmitSQL_Exit:
    Set oTiming = Nothing
    Exit Sub
```

continued on next page

continued from previous page

```
cmdSubmitSQL_error:
    'if error occurs check the ADO Collection for errors.
    'It is nested under the connection object
    Dim i As Integer
    For i = 0 To Cn.Errors.Count - 1
    MsgBox Cn.Errors(i).Description
    Next i
    'make sure and manually clear the errors collection
    'when you are done.
    Cn.Errors.Clear
    'when done close all objects
    GoTo cmdSubmitSQL_Exit
End Sub
```

5. Enter the following code for the Exit button `Click` event. At the conclusion of your application, it is an important practice to release the connection to your data source. This is done with the `Close` method that follows.

```
Private Sub cmdExit_Click()
    '
    'close out all objects.
    Cn.Close
End
End Sub
```

6. Choose Insert, Class Module from Visual Basic's menu to add a class module to this project. The class appears in the project window. Open the class module and press the F4 key to view the class's properties. Set the `Name` property to `Timing`.

7. Add the following code to the General Declarations section of the `Timing` class module. You need to declare the `timeGetTime` API function to have access to a method that returns timing values with a millisecond resolution. The standard `Time()` function in Visual Basic only provides for seconds.

```
Option Explicit
'
'dimension readonly variables for timing events
Dim mStartTime As Long
Dim mFinishTime As Long
Dim mElapsedTime As Long
'
'declare API to get time in milliseconds.
Private Declare Function timeGetTime Lib "winmm.dll" () As Long
```

8. Add the following methods and properties to the `Timing` class. These methods and properties allow you to time execution of SQL queries and have access to the elapsed time values in milliseconds.

```
'method to store start time
Public Sub Start()
    mStartTime = timeGetTime
End Sub

'method to store finish time and calculate elapsed
'time in milliseconds
Public Sub Finish()
    mFinishTime = timeGetTime
    mElapsedTime = mFinishTime - mStartTime
End Sub

'read-only property to access elapsed time.
Public Property Get ElapsedTime()
    ElapsedTime = mElapsedTime / 1000
End Property
```

How It Works

The ADO objects `Connection` and `Recordset` are used to submit a query. First, a connection is opened to a data source using the `Open` method of the `Connection` object. After a connection is made, any SQL statements entered in the text box control are submitted to the data source using the `Open` method of the `Recordset` object, which returns the results into the ADO recordset object variable labeled `Rst` for this project.

The project uses a class module called `Timing` to actually time the execution of SQL queries in milliseconds. The resultset and elapsed time of the query are presented to the user via the active data control and bound `DataGrid` control. This is accomplished by binding the `DataGrid` control to the ADO Data control and setting the Data control's recordset property to the recordset generated by the `Open` method that is coded behind the Execute SQL button.

Comments

ADO simplifies the process of submitting SQL queries by allowing you to create recordset objects and connection objects separately. Models such as DAO and RDO require that you create objects in a specific order and within a specific hierarchy. Because ADO frees you from this, the process is simplified. This demonstrates the fundamental steps required in executing SQL queries using ADO.

Many options can be set for each object and method used in this How-To. Try submitting a variety of SQL statements including `Insert`, `Update`, and `Delete` statements and see how this implementation handles these statements. Try changing the current database with procedures such as Use Master. This How-To relies on a Data Source Name of `PUBS_DSN`. Try creating a DSN-less connection by including a connection string in the `Open` method of the `ADODB.Connection` object. Go ahead and give it a whirl.

COMPLEXITY
ADVANCED

3.8 How do I...
Create a prepared statement using ADO?

COMPATIBILITY: VISUAL BASIC 6

Problem

I need to optimize my SQL queries so that they are more efficient. I know that the actual SQL is written well, but I also want to create a prepared statement to get better performance. Is there a way to do this using ADO?

Technique

ADO's **Command** object provides support for the ODBC **SQLPrepare** function. The command object allows you to select whether you want the command executed as a prepared statement. Applications are often built on a set of queries that are used repeatedly. Each time they are submitted to the server, the request must be compiled and executed. Preparing the statement provides the capability to precompile a request, thus reducing compile time.

In this How-To you create a simple form that allows you to specify an SQL statement and the number of times you want it executed. The program will run it prepared and unprepared and then present the execution time for each. You cannot use this project with an **.MDB** database file because the Microsoft Access database engine does not support prepared statements.

Steps

Open and run project **PREPAREADO.VBP**. The application assumes that you have a Data Source Name of **PUBS_DSN** that points to the PUBS database, which comes with Microsoft SQL Server. Note that you should try a new SQL statement for each test because the SQL database is designed to optimize performance by caching results of recent queries. If you click the button more than once, you can see the effect of server caching.

After the application is running, you can enter a **Select** statement in the text box and specify the number of submission times for the test. The running program appears as shown in Figure 3.15.

To create this project, complete the following steps:

1. Create a new project called **PEPAREADO.VBP**. Select **Form1**, and add objects and set properties as shown in Table 3.10.

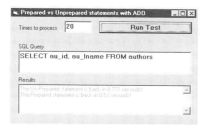

Figure 3.15 The form that allows runtime parameter input for an ADO query

Table 3.10 PREPAREADO.FRM form and control properties

OBJECT	PROPERTY	SETTING
Form	Name	frmPrepareADO
	Caption	"Using Parameters and Prepared Statements with ADO"
	ForeColor	&H000000FF&
TextBox	Name	txtEndDate
TextBox	Name	txtStartDate
ComboBox	Name	cmbAuthorId
CommandButton	Name	cmdExit
	Caption	"E&xit"
CommandButton	Name	cmdGetInfo
	Caption	"Get Info"
DataGrid	Name	DataGrid1
	DataSource	adoDisplay
Label	Name	Label3
	Alignment	Right Justify
	BackStyle	Transparent
	Caption	"Enter an Ending Date"
	ForeColor	&H00FFFFFF&
Label	Name	Label2
	Alignment	Right Justify
	BackStyle	Transparent
	Caption	"Enter a Start Date"
	ForeColor	&H00FFFFFF&
Label	Name	Label1
	Alignment	Right Justify

continued on next page

Table 3.10 continued

OBJECT	PROPERTY	SETTING
	BackStyle	Transparent
	Caption	"Select an Author ID"
	ForeColor	&H00FFFFFF&
ActiveDataControl	Name	adoDisplay
	DataSourceName	" "
	RecordSource	" "
	Connect	" "

2. The first thing you need to do is to dimension object variables for two connections and two command objects. Add the following code to the General Declarations section of the form:

```
Option Explicit
    Dim Cn As ADODB.Connection
    Dim Cn2 As ADODB.Connection
    Dim cmdPrepared As ADODB.Command
    Dim cmdNotPrepared As ADODB.Command
```

3. On loading the form, you will open two connections. Add the following code to the **Form_load** event. Note that the words *YOURSERVERNAME* should be replaced by the name of your actual server.

```
Private Sub Form_Load()
    Dim strCn As String

    'Open a connection.. Replace the Server Name
    'with the name of your own server
    strCn = "driver={SQL Server};" & _
            "server=YOURSERVERNAME;" & _
            "uid=sa;pwd=;" & _
            "database=pubs"

    ' Open first connection
    Set Cn = New ADODB.Connection
    Cn.Open strCn

    ' Open second connection
    Set Cn 2= New ADODB.Connection
    Cn2.Open strCn

End Sub
```

4. The Run Test button **Click** event runs the prepared versus unprepared statement test. Add the following code to the **cmdRunTest_click** event:

```
Private Sub cmdRunTest_Click()
    Dim i As Integer
```

```
Dim strCommand As String

' Create two command objects for the same
' command — one prepared and one not prepared.
strCommand = txtSQL.Text

Set cmdPrepared = New ADODB.Command
Set cmdPrepared.ActiveConnection = Cn
cmdPrepared.CommandText = strCommand
cmdPrepared.Prepared = True

Set cmdNotPrepared = New ADODB.Command
Set cmdNotPrepared.ActiveConnection = Cn2
cmdNotPrepared.CommandText = strCommand

txtResults.Text = "The Gauntlet is down!"
txtResults.Refresh

'Execute Test
'you will use the timing object to time the
'whole process.

Dim oTiming As Timing
Set oTiming = New Timing
Call oTiming.Start

'execute the command that has NOT been prepared
For i = 1 To txtCount.Text
    cmdNotPrepared.Execute
Next i

'finish timing of submission
oTiming.Finish
'
'Display the results
txtResults.Text = "The Un-Prepared statement is back" _
            & " in " & oTiming.ElapsedTime & " seconds!"
txtResults.Refresh

Dim oTiming2 As Timing
Set oTiming2 = New Timing
Call oTiming2.Start

'execute the command that HAS been prepared
For i = 1 To txtCount.Text
    cmdPrepared.Execute
Next i

'finish timing of submission
oTiming2.Finish
'
'Display the results
txtResults.Text = txtResults.Text & vbCrLf & _
                "The Prepared statement is back" _
            & " in " & oTiming2.ElapsedTime & " seconds!"
```

continued on next page

continued from previous page

```
'clean up
Set oTiming = Nothing
Set oTiming2 = Nothing

End Sub
```

5. Enter the following code for the Exit button `Click` event. At the conclusion of your application, it is an important practice to release the connection to your data source. This is done with the following `Close` method:

```
Private Sub Form_Unload(Cancel As Integer)
'clean up by closing connection
Cn.Close
Cn2.Close
End Sub
```

How It Works

When the form loads, two connection objects are used to make two separate connections to the database. When the Run Test button is clicked, two command objects are created. Both are set to contain the SQL statement entered in the text box. One of the command objects is flagged to create a prepared statement by setting its `Prepare` property to true, where the other command object is not prepared. Each command is then executed over a separate connection. When the number of times specified on the form is executed, the results are presented in the result text box. Note that setting the `Prepare` property to true does not prepare the statement until it is executed against an active connection.

Comments

Optimizing the operation of queries is always a high priority, especially when a user is waiting. It is amazing how many times users can push Ctrl+Alt+Del in 30 seconds. Preparing your statements can help to minimize the wait. The ease of choosing whether to prepare the statement is one strength of the ADO syntax. There is, however, another lesson that is shown by this example. Connections and commands are not linked by a hierarchy. This means that you can create them independently as we did in this How-To. Additionally, it means that you can mix and match your commands and connections. Imagine having a query that searches multiple databases for information. A single query could be stored in a command object and executed against multiple connections. Try connecting the unprepared statement to an `.MDB` file and running the example. This will show you the flexibility of this new model.

COMPLEXITY
BEGINNING

3.9 How do I...
Parameterize a query with ADO?

COMPATIBILITY: VISUAL BASIC 6

Problem

I need to include a parameterized query (one that can accept variable information) in my application. I have been generating the SQL myself by concatenating strings based on options the user selects. The code is very ugly and, additionally, this does not allow me to create a prepared statement or bind parameters to get better performance. Is there a way to do this using ADO?

Technique

The ADO `command` object provides support for the ODBC `SQLPrepare` function. A powerful feature of any language is the capability to use parameters, which can be set at the time of execution. SQL is no exception. Couple the capability to pass parameters with the capability to precompile a request, as with a prepared statement, and you can imagine the benefits with regard to execution time. Using the ADO `command` object, you can specify whether the statement be precompiled on the server. Additionally, ADO provides support for input and output variables.

In this How-To, you create a simple form that accepts three parameters used to retrieve book information by author from the PUBS database. You cannot use this project with an `.MDB` database file because the Microsoft Access database engine does not support prepared statements. If you want to use an `.MDB`, you will need to set the prepare property of the `command` object to false.

Steps

Open the project `PARAM_ADO.VBP`. Set the connection string for your server in the `form_load` area. This example works with the PUBS database, which comes with Microsoft SQL Server. As you run this project, you see a message box showing the prepared statement that has been created.

When the application is running, you can select a Social Security number from the combo box and specify a start date and end date that are used to retrieve the author's book sales information. The running program appears as shown in Figure 3.16. Complete the following steps to create this project:

1. Create a new project called `PARAM_ADO.VBP`. Select `Form1`, and add objects and set properties as shown in Table 3.11.

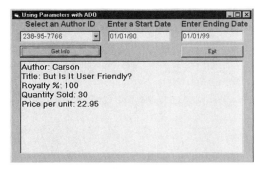

Figure 3.16 The form uses the Authors ID to return information about the Authors books and sales

Table 3.11   PARAMADO.FRM form and control properties

OBJECT	PROPERTY	SETTING
Form	Name	frmPARAMADO
	Caption	"Using Parameters
		and Prepared Statements with ADO"
	ForeColor	&H000000FF&
TextBox	Name	txtEndDate
TextBox	Name	txtStartDate
ComboBox	Name	cmbAuthorId
CommandButton	Name	cmdExit
	Caption	"E&xit"
CommandButton	Name	cmdGetInfo
	Caption	"Get Info"
Label	Name	Label3
	Alignment	Left Justify
	BackStyle	Transparent
	Caption	"Enter an Ending Date"
Label	Name	Label2
	Alignment	Left Justify
	BackStyle	Transparent
	Caption	"Enter a Start Date"
Label	Name	Label1
	Alignment	Left Justify
	BackStyle	Transparent
	Caption	"Select an Author ID"

OBJECT	PROPERTY	SETTING
Textbox	Name	adoDisplay
	Multiline	True

2. The first thing you need to do is to dimension object variables for the connection, command, and resultset. Add the following code to the General Declarations section of the form:

```
Option Explicit
'dimension your environment and connection variables
    Dim Cn As ADODB.Connection
    Dim Ps As ADODB.Command
    Dim Rst As ADODB.Recordset
```

3. On loading the form, you will open a connection. Add the following code to the **Form_load** event. This code also calls two procedures to load the authors' Social Security numbers from the Authors table into a combo box and initialize the ADO **command** object that will be used to return a recordset. Make sure to change the server name in the connection string in the following code from *YOURSERVERNAME* to the actual name of your server.

```
Private Sub Form_Load()
    Dim strCn As String

    ' Open a connection.
    strCn = "driver={SQL Server};" & _
            "server=YOURSERVERNAME;" & _
            "uid=sa;pwd=;" & _
            "database=pubs"

    Set Cn = New ADODB.Connection
    Cn.Open strCn

    'call routine to initialize the SQL statement that
    'will take the parameters
    InitializeStatement

    'call routine to load the combo box with author ssn's
    LoadAuthorIds

    'set default values
    txtStartDate = "01/01/90"
    txtEndDate = "01/01/99"
End Sub
```

4. Enter the following code into your form. The **LoadAuthorIds** procedure creates a recordset of all available author Social Security numbers that are stored in the **au_id** field of the Authors table found in the PUBS database. The values are then added to the combo box list.

```
Private Sub LoadAuthorIds()
    ' dimension all needed variables
    Dim rstAuthorIds As New ADODB.Recordset
    Dim sSQL As String
    Dim i As Integer

    sSQL = "SELECT au_id FROM authors ORDER BY au_id"
    Set rstAuthorIds = New ADODB.Recordset
    rstAuthorIds.Open sSQL, Cn, adOpenStatic

    'Check rowcount property to see if any records
    'where returned.
    If rstAuthorIds.RecordCount > 0 Then
        'load list
        cmbAuthorId.Clear
        While Not rstAuthorIds.EOF = True
            cmbAuthorId.AddItem rstAuthorIds("au_id")
            rstAuthorIds.MoveNext
        Wend
    Else
        MsgBox "Unable to load Author Ids"
    End If

    rstAuthorIds.Close
    '
    'that's all there is to it
End Sub
```

5. Add the following subroutine to your form. This code creates the ADO command so that it is ready for use. This makes the most sense because the purpose of using a prepared statement is to have it precompiled by the database engine and ready for execution after parameters are set.

```
Private Sub InitializeStatement()
    'dimension variables
    Dim sSQL As String
    '
    'construct SQL statement. Question marks are used
    'as placeholders for parameters.
    sSQL = "SELECT T1.au_lname, T3.title, T2.royaltyper,
➠T3.price, T4.qty" _
        & " FROM authors T1, titleauthor T2, titles T3, sales T4" _
        & " WHERE T1.au_id = T2.au_id AND T2.title_id =
➠T3.title_id" _
        & " AND T3.title_id = T4.title_id" _
        & " AND T1.au_id = ? AND T4.ord_date BETWEEN ? and ?"

    'display the sql statement in a message box
    MsgBox sSQL

    'create command object to store the sql to prepare
    Set Ps = New ADODB.Command
    Ps.CommandText = sSQL
    Ps.Prepared = True
    Ps.ActiveConnection = Cn

End Sub
```

6. Add the following code to your form. This procedure handles the setting of parameters and creation of the recordset. This code includes the setting of various ADO **Parameter** properties that you can adjust. They are included here to illustrate their use although they are actually set to default values.

```
Private Sub cmdGetInfo_Click()

    'After a Command object has been set you must
    'provide values for each of the ? placeholders that
    'is assigned as an input value. All placeholders are
    'input by default. Here you will set all values of
    'each parameter although it is not necessary if the
    'default settings are appropriate.
    'SET THE PARAMETERS DIRECTION
    Ps.Parameters(0).Direction = adParamInput
    Ps.Parameters(1).Direction = adParamInput
    Ps.Parameters(2).Direction = adParamInput

    'You could use these statements to check the
    'datatype of each parameter
    'Ps.Parameters(0).Type      'adTypeCHAR
    'Ps.Parameters(1).Type      'adTypeDATE
    'Ps.Parameters(2).Type      'adTypeDATE
    '
    'You could use these statements to check the
    'parameter name.
    'Ps.Parameters(0).Name      'Param0
    'Ps.Parameters(1).Name      'Param1
    'Ps.Parameters(2).Name      'Param2

    'Set the parameters value
    Ps.Parameters(0).Value = cmbAuthorId.Text
    Ps.Parameters(1).Value = txtStartDate.Text
    Ps.Parameters(2).Value = txtEndDate.Text

    'you must initialize the object
    Dim Rst As New ADODB.Recordset

    'you must set the cursor type so the recordset
    'will work with the ado data control and grid.
    Rst.CursorType = adOpenKeyset
    'now execute the statement
    Set Rst = Ps.Execute

    'display results
    If Rst.RecordCount = True Then
        AdoDisplay.Text = ""
        Do While Rst.EOF = False
            AdoDisplay.Text = "Author: " & Rst("au_lname")
        ➡& vbCrLf & _
                "Title: " & Rst("Title") & vbCrLf & _
                "Royalty %: " & Rst("Royaltyper") & vbCrLf & _
                "Quantity sold: " & Rst("qty") & vbCrLf & _
                "Price per Unit: " & Rst("price") & vbCrLf & _
```

continued on next page

continued from previous page

```
                    Rst.MoveNext
              Loop

         Else
              MsgBox "no records returned. Try again"

         End If
    End Sub
```

7. As you exit, it is a good practice to close all the object variables. Actually, closing the form should take care of it for you.

```
Private Sub cmdExit_Click()
    'clean up
    Cn.Close
    End
End Sub
```

How It Works

After the application is connected to a data source, the real work is performed by the ADO **command** object. In this How-To, the **command** object is created as the form loads so that it is ready to be used immediately. The **command** object has several properties. In this How-To, we set the prepare property to true so that a prepared statement is created and the parameters are bound to the **command** object. The SQL used to set the **commandtext** property includes three parameters:

✔ Social Security number of the author in question

✔ Earliest date for sales

✔ Latest date for sales

```
SELECT  T1.au_lname, T3.title, T2.royaltyper, T3.price, T4.qty
FROM    authors T1, titleauthor T2, titles T3, sales T4
WHERE   T1.au_id = T2.au_id
   AND T2.title_id = T3.title_id
   AND T3.title_id = T4.title_id
   AND T1.au_id = ?
   AND T4.ord_date BETWEEN ? and ?
```

A question mark is used to hold the place of parameters that will be provided prior to executing the statement. The syntax used for parameter placeholders in the prepared statement is identical to the syntax used when performing an ODBC **SQLPrepare** function. After the statement is prepared and compiled on the server, parameters can be set and executed repeatedly.

This How-To introduces the use of the ADO **Parameters** collection and the **Parameter** properties of **Name**, **Type**, **Direction**, and **Value**. If you are using default settings for these properties, you only need to set the **Value** property.

After the prepared statement is executed, the resultset is displayed in a text box to the user.

Comments

This How-To demonstrates the use of the **Parameters** collection as it pertains to ADO. Parameters are referenced by index number. The command object is a pivotal piece in ADO's arsenal. The command object allows you to prepare SQL statements for execution and choose easily where and how you want it to run. Because the command object is independent of connections or recordsets, you can reuse it in a variety of scenarios. Perhaps you need to update customer information on multiple systems. A single command object could collect all the customer's information from an input screen using parameters and then be executed against multiple connections. In the end, you have cleaner, more maintainable code and serious power for your applications.

COMPLEXITY
BEGINNING

3.10 How do I...
Use transactions with ADO?

COMPATIBILITY: VISUAL BASIC 6

Problem

The programs I write deal with a unit of work. People make changes to a set of records and then want the option to put everything back the way it was. The problem is that after I leave a record, I have to update it. The logic I have to write to track every change users make and then reverse it if needed is impossible to maintain. How can I let people make changes to multiple records and then have the choice to either accept all changes or put everything back as it was?

Technique

Being able to define a unit of work and make decisions about committing all of it or rolling back all changes is critical to any serious application. This type of transaction is a staple in our industry. ADO provides three methods to support transactions: **BeginTrans**, **CommitTrans**, and **RollbackTrans**. By wrapping our changes to the database with this syntax, this How-To allows the user to selectively commit changes on a record-by-record basis and then choose to roll back or commit all changes when all rows have been processed.

Steps

Open the project TRANS_ADO.VBP. In the form_load method change the connection string to point to your server by replacing *YOURSERVERNAME* with the real name of the server running the SQL Server PUBS sample database. Now start the application. When the application starts, click the Start Transaction button.

As you run this project, you see a message box that prompts you with the name of an author and the state the author is from. Select Yes to change the state to "ZZ" or No to leave it alone. Only authors from CA will appear. At the end of this process you are prompted to either commit or roll back changes. Select a choice, and the result of your changes appear in the results text box, as shown in Figure 3.17. Please be aware that the code in this How-to will reset the ZZ to CA after you are done so that you can run the application multiple times and start fresh. If you wish to prevent the reset, you can remove the code that resets these values.

Figure 3.17 The Transaction form as it appears at runtime

Complete the following steps to create this project:

1. Create a new project called TRANS_ADO.VBP. Select Form1, and add objects and set properties as shown in Table 3.12.

Table 3.12 TRANSADO.FRM form and control properties

OBJECT	PROPERTY	SETTING
Form	Name	frmTRANSADO
	Caption	"Use Transactions with ADO"
	ForeColor	&H000000FF&

OBJECT	PROPERTY	SETTING
TextBox	Name	txtResults
	Multiline	true
CommandButton	Name	cmdRunTrans
	Caption	"Run Transaction"

2. The first thing you need to do is to dimension object variables for the connection and recordset. This is done by adding the following code to the General Declarations section of the form:

```
Option Explicit
' this example allows you to change Author State
' information in the Authors table found in the
' Pubs database. State is changed from CA to ZZ.
' At the end you are given a choice to rollback
' all changes or commit. By default this example
' returns data to its original state.

    Dim Cn As ADODB.Connection
    Dim rstAuthors As ADODB.Recordset
```

3. On loading the form, you will open a connection to the PUBS sample database. Prior to running the example you must change the server specified from *YOURSERVERNAME* to the actual name of your server.

```
Private Sub Form_Load()
    ' Open connection.
    Dim strCn As String

    strCn = "driver={SQL Server}; & _
        "server=YOURSERVERNAME;" & _
        "uid=sa;pwd=; & _
        "database=pubs"

    Set Cn = New ADODB.Connection
    Cn.Open strCn

End Sub
```

4. Add the following code to the Run Transaction button:

```
Private Sub cmdRunTrans_Click()
    Dim strAuthor As String
    Dim strMessage As String

    ' Open Authors table.
    Set rstAuthors = New ADODB.Recordset
    With rstAuthors
        .CursorType = adOpenDynamic
        .LockType = adLockPessimistic
        .Activeconnection = Cn
```

continued on next page

continued from previous page

```
        .Open "authors", , , , adCmdTable
        .MoveFirst
End With

'begin the transaction. this is done on
'the connection object
Cn.BeginTrans

' Loop through recordset and ask user if the person
' want to change the state for a specified author.
Do Until rstAuthors.EOF
    If Trim(rstAuthors!State) = "CA" Then
        strAuthor = rstAuthors!au_fname & " "
        ➡& rstAuthors!au_lname
        strMessage = "Author: " & strAuthor & vbCr & _
        "Change state to ZZ?"

        ' Change the title for the specified
        ' employee.
        If MsgBox(strMessage, vbYesNo) = vbYes Then
            rstAuthors!State = "ZZ"
            rstAuthors.Update
        End If
    End If

        rstAuthors.MoveNext
Loop

' Ask if the user wants to commit to all the
' changes made above.
If MsgBox("Save all changes?", vbYesNo) = vbYes Then
    Cn.CommitTrans
Else
    Cn.RollbackTrans
End If

' Print current data in recordset.
rstAuthors.Requery
rstAuthors.MoveFirst
txtResults.Text = ""
Do While Not rstAuthors.EOF
    txtResults.Text = txtResults.Text & _
        rstAuthors!au_fname & " " & _
        rstAuthors!au_lname & _
        " - " & rstAuthors!State & vbCrLf
    rstAuthors.MoveNext
Loop

' For this demo all data is returned to its
' orignial state.
rstAuthors.MoveFirst
Do Until rstAuthors.EOF
    If Trim(rstAuthors!State) = "ZZ" Then
        rstAuthors!State = "CA"
        rstAuthors.Update
    End If
```

```
        rstAuthors.MoveNext
    Loop

End Sub
```

5. Enter the following code for the Forms `Unload` event. At the conclusion of your application, it is an important practice to release the connection to your data source. This is done with the following `Close` method:

```
Private Sub Form_Unload(Cancel As Integer)
'clean up by closing connection
rstAuthors.Close
Cn.Close
End Sub
```

How It Works

The ADO connection object has three methods designed to implement transactions: `BeginTrans`, `CommitTrans`, and `RollbackTrans`. This How-To begins by making a connection to the database using the ADO `Connection` object. When the Run Transaction button is clicked, `BeginTrans` is issued to the database. At this point, a transaction has been started. A `Recordset` object is used to open the Authors table, which is part of the PUBS sample database in SQL Server. The `adcmdTable` option is set for the `Recordset` because it will be opening a table directly.

All authors with a state of CA are presented to the user one by one. The option is to change the state from CA to ZZ. For each record, the user can choose to make the change or leave it alone. When the recordset reaches the last record, the user is presented with an option to commit the complete transaction or cancel it. After the user makes a choice, the changes are either written or rolled back using the `CommitTrans` and `RollbackTrans` syntax. Results are displayed in the results text box. Because this is a demo, the final step is to return all data back to its original condition so that an update is performed to change any ZZs back to CAs.

Comments

Every time you withdraw money from an ATM machine, you are involved in a transaction. The ATM transaction involves debiting your account as one step. The second step is to give you the cash. What if your account was debited, but you received no cash? That is what transactions are all about. Either both things happen, or neither does. The ATM example is a good way to explain a unit of work.

Transactions allow us to delineate a unit of work and say that all tasks in this unit of work must be completed successfully or none will be completed. The simplicity of this syntax allows you to take advantage of this concept when modeling your business rules and creating applications. It does not, however, guarantee that the rules you write and the transactions you design will work for the business. That is up to you. Hopefully, this How-To will get you started on the path to integrating transactions into your applications.

CHAPTER 4

USER INTERFACE DESIGN

4

USER INTERFACE DESIGN

by David Jung

How do I...

The user component of a three-tier design can determine the difference between a program that is readily accepted and produces a productive end user and a program that is difficult to use and produces a frustrated end user. The graphical user interface of the Windows operating systems (Windows 95 and above and Windows NT 4.0 and above), as with most 32-bit Windows applications such as Office 97, provides for a common set of elements that help make an application familiar and useful.

In a three-tier development environment, the separation of data access and business logic from the user interface is critical. In a distributed model, the business components can still be embedded in either user components or database components, but the proper deployment of business components should be completely separate from the other two layers. When designing business components, they will either physically reside on the database server or user's system, or they can reside on a separate application server such as the Microsoft Transaction Server. By having the components separate from either layer, any change to business rules need to be applied only to the business component, and the change needs to be applied only once and in one location. If the business logic is embedded within each application, each application would need to be updated and redeployed throughout the enterprise. You can probably envision the deployment schedule nightmare ahead with the latter method.

As a practical example of the value of modularizing business components, consider the question of managing data display. The rate at which data is displayed to the user, especially large amounts of data, is an important factor in developing most client/server applications. A traditional way to retrieve information is to get all the information you've requested, no matter how many rows are returned, store it in arrays or controls, and synchronize the information through the use of primary and foreign keys. With large amounts of data, this can slow down your application considerably. Through the use of business components, optimizing your applications can become much easier. Working the business components separate from your application gives you the freedom to experiment with different methods of retrieving and manipulating data without affecting your production applications. Your front-end application does not need to be concerned with how the data is retrieved, just as long as it is retrieved.

The first five How-To's in this chapter demonstrate standard user interface design for your client-tier applications. Each How-To builds on the last to produce a fully integrated and feature-rich application interface. The sample application used throughout this chapter is a simple image-tracking database. This program allows you to categorize and track all bitmap (.BMP) and icon (.ICO) format files on your system. This chapter does not adhere strictly to the three-tier client/server structure. For simplicity's sake, the Microsoft Remote Data Control (MSRDC) is used to connect to a Microsoft Access 8.0 or SQL Server (6.5) database through an ODBC connection. You will need to have an Image

Database ODBC data source connected to either the Access Data **Idata.mdb** or similar database that can be easily replicated on any database platform.

How-To 4.1 demonstrates how to build multiple document interface (MDI) applications. It demonstrates techniques such as tiling and cascading MDI child windows and menu negotiation. But what client application would be complete without the familiar toolbar for accessing the features of the application? How-To 4.2 adds a toolbar to the program to provide this familiar application interface. Another important context-rich feature provided in Windows is the use of the right mouse click. How-To 4.3 demonstrates how adding right mouse-click support to your applications can provide quick and simple access to common features.

How-To 4.4 demonstrates how drag-and-drop support for an application from the Windows Explorer provides easy and common-sense integration of your application with the Windows environment. Support for dragging image files from the Windows Explorer to the application is demonstrated through some simple API calls and an add-on OCX control (**MSGHOOK.OCX**). Also, drag-and-drop inside an application can be implemented for moving controls and data between objects. How-To 4.5 uses the tab control to provide a simple and easy method for organizing and presenting information to the user.

An interesting comparison can be made between How-To 4.1 and How-To 4.5. Each implements the same basic image-tracking application, but the interface of the first pales in comparison to that of the last. A rich user interface can truly make the difference between a mediocre application and an intuitive one.

The next six How-To's in this chapter demonstrate different methods for displaying the data for a fictitious hotel chain. The tables for the hotel database are stored in **Hotels7.MDB** located on the CD under Chapter 4, or if you run the SQL script under this chapter on SQL Server, the hotel database is **db_HotelSystem**. Because you are using ODBC, you do not need to be concerned with whether you are using an MDB or an SQL Server database. Refer to Chapter 2, "Getting Connected," to create an ODBC Data Source Name (DSN). The How-To's use the DSN **dsnWaiteSQL**. The business rules in the class modules are used as part of the actual program. In a real distributed component environment, they would not be part of the application but would be implemented as out-of-process ActiveX servers. Refer to Chapter 6, "Business Objects," for more information on business objects and out-of-process ActiveX servers.

The last three How-To's of this chapter demonstrate how you build a user interface that can be used over the World Wide Web. A lot of organizations are making their applications Web-enabled, which means their applications are available over the Internet, to extend their reach to more customers. This is known as e-business or e-commerce. The e- stands for electronic.

NOTE

The data model used throughout this chapter is the Remote Data Object (RDO) model and the Remote Data Control (RDC) because this chapter deals more with display with the user interface in general and displaying data to the user interface not accessing the data. The examples can easily be modified to use the ActiveX Data Object (ADO) and ActiveX Data Control (ADC) because the object models are similar.

4.1 Create a Simple MDI Application

Windows 95 multiple document interface (MDI) applications are common and include just about any standard word processor or spreadsheet program. Providing many different child windows within a parent window is the key to providing support for working on different documents within an application. In this How-To, an image viewer and a data entry screen are provided for the image database.

4.2 Build an Active Toolbar to Simplify Access to Menu Functions

The simple image inventory program built in How-To 4.1 provides for many different menu options for navigating through the program. To make these menu features easier to navigate, a toolbar with appropriate icons is added to the interface to simplify use of the program.

4.3 Implement Right Mouse Button Context Menus

Context-sensitive, right mouse clicks can be useful for providing access to application features within the context of where the click took place. In this How-To, menu features pop up within the context of the right mouse click and, in one example, with the left mouse click also.

4.4 Make an Application Drag-and-Drop Capable

The image view application developed in the previous How-To's benefit greatly from a little drag-and-drop magic. Being able to drag several bitmap image files from a directory listed in (for example) the Windows Explorer to the program, and automatically have them added to the database, immeasurably speeds up the categorization of images on a system. And, being able to preview an image before it is placed into the database also is a powerful tool. A preview window is added that previews a dropped image and then allows that image to be dragged to the database.

4.5 Organize Form Contents Using the Tab Control

Our image inventory program is missing a couple of key features that are provided together with a nice interface via the tab control. The user must have a simple way to select sort options and view several images at once. With the tab control, these features can be added to different tabs on the control.

4.6 Load a List or Combo Box with the Results of a Query

Visual Basic 6 provides list controls that bind to a database table. In a distributed component architecture, you want to avoid using these controls. Bound controls do not allow you to manage data on a transaction basis. They are linked to a database field, and when you update the field, the database is updated. By developing business objects, the business components rather than the data layer handle the way the data is retrieved and how it is placed in a control. This How-To shows you how to create a class module that uses the remote data object (RDO) to retrieve information from a database table and populate a combo box control.

4.7 Populate an Unbound Grid

Visual Basic 6 provides a grid control that binds to a database table. In a distributed component architecture, you want to avoid using this control for the reasons given previously. This How-To shows you how to create a class module that uses the remote data object to retrieve information from a database table and populate an unbound grid control.

4.8 Display Calculated Fields in an Unbound Grid

As part of some decision support systems, you want to be able to show the result of calculations in a spreadsheet-style format. In a distributed component architecture, retrieving data from a database table and making calculations are considered part of the business objects; they should be defined into two different class modules. This How-To shows you how to create a class that uses the remote data object to retrieve information from a database table and populate an unbound grid control. Also, it shows you how to create a class module used to handle mathematical calculations.

4.9 Control the Number of Rows Displayed

When retrieving large amounts of data, displaying a small subset of information and controlling the amount the user sees at a given time can increase your application's performance and reduce network traffic. This How-To shows you how to use the remote data object's `GetRows` method to limit the amount of rows retrieved from the table and placed in the resultset.

4.10 Create a Master/Detail Form

Many times you have information in one table that drives information from another table. By retrieving only the information requested, you speed up the user's perception of how fast the application operates. In this How-To, you create a class module that uses the remote data object to retrieve information from database tables and display the information in the respective unbound grids. The information retrieved is based on what the user selects in a combo box.

4.11 Create a Query by Example

Many times your users want to look up information in the system. Instead of taking the time to educate them on how the database is designed, how the tables relate to one another, and how to create queries to retrieve the information they want, you can develop a query form to help users perform their own lookups. In this How-To, you create an interface so that by using a series of check boxes, radio buttons, and some user input, users can visually select the type of information they want with minimal knowledge of the database tables.

4.12 Build an HTML Application Interface

As more organizations become Internet aware, they want to establish a "Web presence." A Web presence can be as simple as putting up a Web site on the Internet to electronic commerce to allowing users to connect to corporate data through an Internet connection. One of the most popular trends is to create traditional applications using Internet technology. Visual Basic can be used to create Web-based applications, but this How-To uses a more traditional Internet approach and HTML (hypertext markup language) to create a user interface for an application.

4.13 Add ActiveX Controls to the Interface

With the capability to create ActiveX controls in Visual Basic, you might want to use them on your Web applications. This How-To shows how ActiveX controls can be used on an HTML application interface. This How-To illustrates how ActiveX scripting can be used to extend the functionality of the HTML document.

4.14 Place Data on the Web Page

What good is any system if you can put information into a database, but you can't extract it? This How-to shows how you get information out of a database and put it onto a Web page. The method you use is known as Active Server Pages (ASP). To use ASP technology, you must have the Internet Information Server (IIS) installed on your system. Note: For Windows 95/98 users, it's called Personal Web Services. For Windows NT Workstation users, it's called Peer Web Services.

COMPLEXITY
BEGINNING

4.1 How do I...
Create a simple MDI application?

COMPATIBILITY: VISUAL BASIC 5 AND 6

Problem

Multiple document interfaces (MDIs) are a standard for the Windows 95 user interface. How do I build a Windows MDI application that provides support for multiple menus based on the current child form and that provides features such as window tiles and cascades?

Technique

Multiple document interfaces consist of a parent window, which typically shows the menus of the program and contains child windows. The child windows cannot be moved outside the frame of the parent window. Visual Basic provides a simple way to create MDI parent and child forms. A standard object that can be added to a project is an MDI form. The standard Visual Basic form can become the child of an MDI form simply by setting its MDIChild property to True. Visual Basic then automatically handles showing the menus for the child window in the MDI form. The Arrange method of the MDI form is used to arrange the child windows.

Steps

Open and run 4-1.VBP. The running program appears as shown in Figure 4.1. This figure shows the MDI form without the child windows being shown. Note that there are only two primary menu groups to choose from. Choose File, Open Database from the Visual Basic menu to open the image database.

After the image database is opened, two child windows are shown. The first window shows the standard image file information for the current image, including an editable field for adding comments to the image. The second shows a view of the image currently being edited. To browse the database, select the record menu for the various options as shown in Figure 4.2.

Try out the options on the View menu to see the image in different sizes. You can use the Windows menu to tile the windows and see how the form's appearance changes. You can also cascade the child windows.

Figure 4.1 The MDI form at runtime

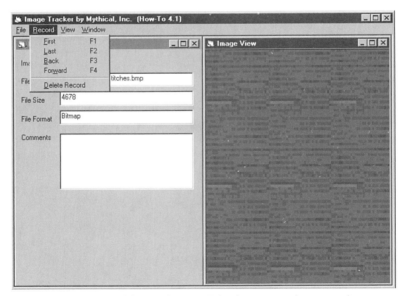

Figure 4.2 The child windows with the Record menu shown

Complete the following steps to create this project:

1. Create a new project called 4-1.VBP. Add the objects and properties listed in Table 4.1 to the MDI form, ImageTracker.

Table 4.1 The form's objects and properties

OBJECT	PROPERTY	SETTING
MDIForm	Name	ImageTracker
	AutoShowChildren	0 'False
	Caption	"Image Tracker by Mythical, Inc."
		(How-To 4.1)"

2. Add the menus shown in Table 4.2 to the ImageTracker MDI form.

Table 4.2 The ImageTracker form's menus

CONTROL NAME	CAPTION
mFile	"&File"
mOpenImage	"&Open Image Database"
mBar	"-"
mExit	"E&xit"
mWindow	"&Window"
mImageData	"Image &Data"
mImageView	"Image &View"

3. Insert a new form into the project and save it as IView.frm. Add the objects and properties listed in Table 4.3 to the ImageView form.

Table 4.3 The ImageView form's objects and properties

OBJECT	PROPERTY	SETTING
Form	Name	ImageView
	Caption	"Image View"
	MDIChild	-1 'True
PictureBox	Name	DispPict
	Appearance	0 'Flat
	AutoSize	-1 'True
	BackColor	&H00FF0000&
	ForeColor	&H80000008&

continued on next page

Table 4.3 continued

OBJECT	PROPERTY	SETTING
	Picture	"pastel.bmp"
	ScaleMode	3 'Pixel
PictureBox	Name	BackPict
	AutoRedraw	-1 'True
	AutoSize	-1 'True
	BackColor	&H000000FF&
	BorderStyle	0 'None
	ScaleMode	3 'Pixel
	Visible	0 'False

4. Add the menus from Table 4.4 to the `ImageView` form.

Table 4.4 The `ImageView` form's menus

CONTROL NAME	CAPTION	INDEX	CHECKED	SHORTCUT KEY
mFile	"&File"			
mNewImage	"&New Image"			
mBar	"-"			
mExit	"E&xit"			
mRecord	"&Record"			
mBrowse	"&First"	0		F1
mBrowse	"&Last"	1		F2
mBrowse	"&Back"	2		F3
mBrowse	"For&ward"	3		F4
mBar2	"-"			
mDelete	"&Delete Record"			
mView	"&View"			
mSize	"&Fit in Window"	0		
mSize	"&Actual Size"	1	-1 'True	
mSize	"&50 Percent"	2		
mSize	"&200 Percent"	3		
mWindow	"&Window"			
mTile	"&Tile"			
mCascade	"&Cascade"			
mBar1	"-"			
mShowWindow	"Image &Data"	0		
mShowWindow	"Image &View"	1		

5. Insert a new form into the project and save it as **IData.frm**. Add the objects and properties listed in Table 4.5 to the **ImageData** form.

Table 4.5 The **ImageData** form's objects and properties

OBJECT	PROPERTY	SETTING
Form	Name	ImageData
	Caption	"Image Data"
	MDIChild	-1 'True
	Visible	0 'False
TextBox	Name	ImageInfo
	DataField	"Comments"
	DataSource	"MSRDC1"
	Index	4
	MultiLine	-1 'True
TextBox	Name	ImageInfo
	DataField	"FileFormat"
	DataSource	"MSRDC1"
	Index	3
TextBox	Name	ImageInfo
	DataField	"FileSize"
	DataSource	"MSRDC1"
	Index	2
	Locked	-1 'True
TextBox	Name	ImageInfo
	DataField	"FileName"
	DataSource	"MSRDC1"
	Index	1
TextBox	Name	ImageInf
	DataField	"ImageID"
	DataSource	"MSRDC1"
	Index	0
	Locked	-1 'True
CommonDialog	Name	CommonDialog1
	DefaultExt	".bmp"
	DialogTitle	"Find Image File"
	Filter	"*.bmp; *.wmf"
	FilterIndex	1
	InitDir	"c:\windows"

continued on next page

Table 4.5 continued

OBJECT	PROPERTY	SETTING
MSRDC	Name	MSRDC1
	Visible	0 'False
	DataSourceName	"Image Database"
	RecordSource	"select * from ImageData order by ImageID"
	RecordsetType	1
	KeysetSize	0
	ReadOnly	0 'False
	UserName	" "
	Password	" "
	CursorDriver	2
	EOFAction	1
	BOFAction	1
	Caption	"MSRDC1"
	Prompt	3
	LockType	3
	Appearance	1
Label	Name	Comment
	AutoSize	-1 'True
	Caption	"Comments"
Label	Name	FileFormat
	AutoSize	-1 'True
	Caption	"File Format"
Label	Name	FileSize
	AutoSize	-1 'True
	Caption	"File Size"
Label	Name	FileName
	AutoSize	-1 'True
	Caption	"File Name"
Label	Name	ImageID
	AutoSize	-1 'True
	Caption	"Image ID"

6. Add the menus from Table 4.6 to the ImageData form.

Table 4.6 The ImageData form's menus

CONTROL NAME	CAPTION	INDEX	CHECKED	SHORTCUT KEY
mFile	"&File"			
mNewImage	"&New Image"			
mBar	"-"			
mExit	"E&xit"			
mRecord	"&Record"			
mBrowse	"&First"	0		F1
mBrowse	"&Last"	1		F2
mBrowse	"&Back"	2		F3
mBrowse	"For&ward"	3		F4
mBar2	"-"			
mDelete	"&Delete Record"			
mView	"&View"			
mSize	"&Fit in Window"	0		
mSize	"&Actual Size"	1	-1 'True	
mSize	"&50 Percent"	2		
mSize	"&200 Percent"	3		
mWindow	"&Window"			
mTile	"&Tile"			
mCascade	"&Cascade"			
mBar1	"-"			
mShowWindow	"Image &Data"	0		
mShowWindow	"Image &View"	1		

7. Add the following code to the MDI form. When the MDI form is loaded, the ImageData form is hidden to ensure that only the MDI form is visible. This provides the user with the option of whether to open the database.

```
Private Sub MDIForm_Load()

'   Hide the ImageData form when
'   the MDI form is first loaded
ImageData.Hide

End Sub
```

8. When the MDI form is unloaded or the Exit menu is selected, the program needs to be ended by calling the **MenuExit** method.

```
Private Sub MDIForm_QueryUnload(Cancel As Integer,
➥UnloadMode As Integer)

'   Call the MenuExit program to
'   end the program
MenuExit

End Sub

Private Sub MDIForm_Unload(Cancel As Integer)

'   Call the MenuExit Yes, procedure> to
'   end the program
MenuExit

End Sub

Private Sub mExit_Click()

'   Call the MenuExit program to
'   end the program
MenuExit

End Sub
```

9. When the Image Data menu option is selected, the **MenuOpenData** method is called to open the image database. Note the next two steps are additional ways of opening the database from the program.

```
Private Sub mImageData_Click()

'   Call the MenuOpenData method to open the
'   Image database
MenuOpenData

End Sub
```

10. When the Image View menu option is selected, the **MenuOpenData** method is called to open the image database.

```
Private Sub mImageView_Click()

'   Call the MenuOpenData method to open the
'   Image database
MenuOpenData

End Sub
```

11. When the Open Image Database menu option is selected, the MenuOpenData method is called to open the image database.

```
Private Sub mOpenImage_Click()

'   Call the MenuOpenData method to open the
'   Image database
MenuOpenData

End Sub
```

12. Add the following code to the **ImageView** form. Insert the following **SizeViewPict** routine into the general declarations section of the form. This routine handles moving and sizing the display picture to fit on the viewable area of the form. It also calls the **SetView** routine to show the appropriate image from the database with the selected viewer options.

```
Public Sub SizeViewPict()

'   Allow for a small border
'   around the display picture
DispPict.Top = 5
DispPict.Left = 5
DispPict.Width = Me.Width - 5
DispPict.Height = Me.Height - 5

'   Set the view to the current
'   view option
SetView IView

End Sub
```

13. When the form is loaded, the view is set to Actual Size (1). Also, the **MenuBrowse** function is called to set the database to the first record.

```
Private Sub Form_Load()

'   Initially set IView to 1.
IView = 1

'   Call the MenuBrowse function
'   to show the first record
MenuBrowse 1

End Sub
```

14. When the display picture is painted, the size of the picture is set, and the image is redrawn using the **SizeViewPict** method. Note that this also handles updating the image when the form is resized because the resized event triggers the **Paint** event.

```
Private Sub DispPict_Paint()

'  Size the view picture
SizeViewPict

End Sub
```

15. When the form would otherwise be unloaded by this procedure, the unload is canceled, and the window is minimized. This ensures that the form cannot be unloaded while the application is still running. There is no need to unload the form except when the program is ended.

```
Private Sub Form_Unload(Cancel As Integer)

'  Cancel the unload.  We don't want the
'  form to be unloaded while the program is
'  running so that it does not have to be
'  re-initialized.  Instead, the form will be
'  minimized.
Cancel = -1
Me.WindowState = 1

End Sub
```

16. When one of the browse options for the database is selected from the menu (or through shortcut keys such as F1), the MenuBrowse routine is called to manipulate the database appropriately. Note that the index of the menu option selected is passed into the MenuBrowse routine to indicate the action to take.

```
Private Sub mBrowse_Click(Index As Integer)

'  Browse the record set depending on the
'  menu option chosen.
MenuBrowse Index

End Sub
```

17. When the user selects the Cascade menu option, the MenuCascade routine is called. Also, the SizeViewPict function is called to ensure that the displayed image is updated.

```
Private Sub mCascade_Click()

'  Cascade the windows
MenuCascade

'  Size the view picture after the cascade
SizeViewPict

End Sub
```

18. The user can delete a record in the database by selecting the Delete menu option. When this happens, the `MenuDelete` routine is called to delete the current record.

```
Private Sub mDelete_Click()

'   Call the MenuDelete function to
'   delete the selected record.
MenuDelete

End Sub
```

19. When the Exit menu option is selected, the `MenuExit` routine is called.

```
Private Sub mExit_Click()

'   Call the MenuExit function to
'   exit the program.
MenuExit

End Sub
```

20. The New Image menu option initiates the addition of a new image to the database by calling the `MenuNewImage` routine.

```
Private Sub mNewImage_Click()

'   Call the MenuNewImage function to get
'   a new image
MenuNewImage

End Sub
```

21. The `mShowWindow` control array of menu options allows for either the `ImageData` or `ImageView` child windows to be shown by calling the `MenuShowWindow` routine.

```
Private Sub mShowWindow_Click(Index As Integer)

'   Call the MenuShowWindow function to show
'   the selected window.
MenuShowWindow Index

End Sub
```

22. The Tile menu option calls the `MenuTile` function to tile the MDI child windows.

```
Private Sub mTile_Click()

'   Call the menu tile function to
'   tile the windows
MenuTile

End Sub
```

23. The mSize menu options allow for the view to be sized as either fit in window - 0 index, actual size - 1 index, 50% - 2 index, or 200% - 3 index. Note that the index indicates which value will be passed in to set the view appropriately.

```
Private Sub mSize_Click(Index As Integer)

'   Set the view depending on the menu option
'   selected
SetView Index

End Sub
```

24. Add the following code to IData.frm. The form's resize event ensures that the data-entry fields are resized to fit on the form.

```
Private Sub Form_Resize()

Dim N As Integer

'   Resize the Image Info controls to
'   fit on the form when it is resized
For N = 1 To 4
    ImageData.ImageInfo(N).Width = ImageData.Width -
ImageData.ImageInfo(N).Left - 300
Next N

End Sub
```

25. When the form is unloaded by the user, the unload event is canceled, and the form is minimized. You do not want the form to be unloaded while the primary MDI application is still running; you simply want the form to be minimized. In some MDI applications, you might indeed want to have the form (that is, a document) closed.

```
Private Sub Form_Unload(Cancel As Integer)

'   We don't want the form to be unloaded so that
'   it will not have to be re-initialized
Cancel = -1

'   Instead minimize the form
Me.WindowState = 1
End Sub
```

26. When one of the browse options for the database is selected from the menu (or through hot keys such as F1), the MenuBrowse routine is called to manipulate the database appropriately. Note that the index of the menu option selected is passed into the MenuBrowse routine to indicate the action to take.

```
Private Sub mBrowse_Click(Index As Integer)

'   Browse the result set depending
'   on the menu selected
MenuBrowse Index

End Sub
```

27. The Cascade menu calls the **MenuCascade** routine to cascade the child windows.

```
Private Sub mCascade_Click()

'   Cascade the windows
MenuCascade

End Sub
```

28. The Delete menu option calls the **MenuDelete** routine to delete the current record of the resultset.

```
Private Sub mDelete_Click()

'   Delete the current record
'   of the resultset
MenuDelete

End Sub
```

29. The Exit menu option calls the **MenuExit** routine to exit the application.

```
Private Sub mExit_Click()

'   Call the MenuExit method to
'   exit the program
MenuExit

End Sub
```

30. The New Image menu option calls the **MenuNewImage** routine to open the common file dialog box to find a new image to add to the database.

```
Private Sub mNewImage_Click()

'   Call the MenuNewImage function to allow
'   the user to select a new image to add to the
'   database
MenuNewImage

End Sub
```

31. The Image Data and Image View menu options invoke the **MenuShowWindow** routine to show the specified window indicated by the index.

```
Private Sub mShowWindow_Click(Index As Integer)

'   Call the MenuShowWindow function to show
'   the window selected
MenuShowWindow Index

End Sub
```

32. The View menu provides several size options for the image view. The index indicates the view option.

```
Private Sub mSize_Click(Index As Integer)

'   Set the view based on the menu
'   selection
SetView Index

End Sub
```

33. The Tile menu option calls the **MenuTile** routine to tile the child windows.

```
Private Sub mTile_Click()

'   Tile the windows
MenuTile

End Sub
```

34. Insert a new module into the project and save it as **MenLogic.bas**. This module holds the primary routines for performing the various menu tasks. The module consolidates the logic needed to perform the menu options for both the **ImageData** and **ImageView** forms. Add the **StretchBlt** API function to the global declarations section of the module. This function is used for stretching the viewed image.

```
'   StretchBlt will be used for the Image Viewer
Private Declare Function StretchBlt Lib "gdi32"
➡(ByVal hdc As Long, ByVal x As Long, ByVal y As Long,
➡ByVal nWidth As Long, ByVal nHeight As Long,
➡ByVal hSrcDC As Long, ByVal xSrc As Long,
➡ByVal ySrc As Long, ByVal nSrcWidth As Long,
➡ByVal nSrcHeight As Long, ByVal dwRop As Long)
As Long

Const SRCCOPY = &HCC0020

'   IView globally stores the current view for
'   the image  I.E.  Fit in Window, 50%

Public IView As Integer
```

35. The MenuExit routine ends the program.

```
'   Handles ending the program when
'   users select exit from the menu
Public Sub MenuExit()
    End
End Sub
```

36. The MenuTile routine handles calling the **Arrange** method of the MDI form. The **VBTileVertical** constant is used to tile the child forms.

```
'   Handles tiling the windows
'   on the MDI form
Public Sub MenuTile()

'   Do a vertical tile
ImageTracker.Arrange vbTileVertical

End Sub
```

37. The MenuCascade routine handles calling the **Arrange** method of the MDI form. The **VBTileVertical** constant is used to cascade the child forms.

```
Public Sub MenuCascade()

'   Cascade the child forms
ImageTracker.Arrange vbCascade

End Sub
```

38. The SetView routine handles setting the view indicated by the index. First, the menu option for the last view is unchecked, and the current index is checked. The current picture is cleared, and depending on the index, the image is copied from the **BackPict** picture box to the **DispPict** picture box. **StretchBlt** is used to perform the image stretching. Finally, the palette from the **BackPict** is copied to the display picture to ensure that the displayed image colors are correct.

```
Public Sub SetView(Index)

'   When a new image view is selected,
'   the original menu selection is
'   unchecked
ImageView.mSize(IView).Checked = False
ImageData.mSize(IView).Checked = False

'   Set the new view to the index
'   parameter
IView = Index

'   Check the new menu option for the
'   selected view.
```

continued on next page

continued from previous page

```
                ImageData.mSize(IView).Checked = True
                ImageView.mSize(IView).Checked = True

                '  Clear the displayed picture
                ImageView.DispPict.Cls

                '  Depending on the view selected, the
                '  original image will be copied to the
                '  display picture appropriately
                Select Case IView

                    Case 0   'Fit in the Window
                        Call StretchBlt(ImageView.DispPict.hdc, 0, 0,
                ➥ImageView.DispPict.ScaleWidth,
                ➥ImageView.DispPict.ScaleHeight,
                ➥ImageView.BackPict.hdc, 0, 0,
                ➥ImageView.BackPict.ScaleWidth,
                ➥ImageView.BackPict.ScaleHeight, SRCCOPY)

                    Case 1   'Actual Size
                        Call StretchBlt(ImageView.DispPict.hdc, 0, 0,
                ➥ImageView.BackPict.ScaleWidth,
                ➥ImageView.BackPict.ScaleHeight,
                ➥ImageView.BackPict.hdc, 0, 0, ImageView.BackPict.
                ➥ScaleWidth, ImageView.BackPict.ScaleHeight, SRCCOPY)

                    Case 2 '50%
                        Call StretchBlt(ImageView.DispPict.hdc, 0, 0,
                ➥ImageView.BackPict.ScaleWidth * 0.5,
                ➥ImageView.BackPict.ScaleHeight * 0.5,
                ➥ImageView.BackPict.hdc, 0, 0, ImageView.BackPict.ScaleWidth,
                ➥ImageView.BackPict.ScaleHeight, SRCCOPY)

                    Case 3 '200%
                        Call StretchBlt(ImageView.DispPict.hdc, 0, 0,
                ➥ImageView.BackPict.ScaleWidth * 2,
                ➥ImageView.BackPict.ScaleHeight * 2,
                ➥ImageView.BackPict.hdc, 0, 0,
                ➥ImageView.BackPict.ScaleWidth,
                ➥ImageView.BackPict.ScaleHeight, SRCCOPY)

                End Select

                '  Copy the palette from the holding picture
                '  to the displayed picture.  This ensures that
                '  the image's colors are displayed correctly.
                ImageView.DispPict.Picture.hPal =
                ➥ImageView.BackPict.Picture.hPal

                End Sub
```

39. The MenuShowWindow function handles showing the appropriate form.

```
Public Sub MenuShowWindow(Index)

'   Check to see which Windows (Form)
'   is to be displayed.
Select Case Index

    Case 0  'Show ImageData
        ImageData.Show
        ImageData.WindowState = 0

    Case 1  'Show ImageView
        ImageView.Show
        ImageView.WindowState = 0

End Select

End Sub
```

40. The MenuOpenData routine queries users whether they want to open the database. If so, the **ImageData** and **ImageView** forms are shown.

```
Public Sub MenuOpenData()

Dim Msg As String
Dim Style As Integer
Dim Title As String
Dim Response As Integer

'   Set the Message, Style, and Title
'   of the message box
Msg = "Do you want to open the Image Database ?"
Style = vbYesNo + vbQuestion + vbDefaultButton1
Title = "Open Image Database"

'   Retrieve the user's response
Response = MsgBox(Msg, Style, Title)

'   If it was a yes, then show the ImageData
'   and ImageView forms.  Also start the view
'   in Tiled mode.
If Response = vbYes Then
    ImageView.Show
    ImageData.Show
    MenuTile
End If

End Sub
```

41. The MenuBrowse routine handles browsing through the database by manipulating the remote data control. First, a check is done to ensure that there are available records to browse. If not, the New Image dialog box is shown. Otherwise, the appropriate move method of the resultset is called. After the move has been made, a check is done to see whether the database is at the end of file (**eof**) or beginning of file (**bof**), and, if so, the **MoveLast** and **MoveFirst** methods are called to ensure there is a current record. Then the image is loaded into the **BackPict** picture, and the new view is set with the **SetView** method.

```
Public Sub MenuBrowse(MoveType)

Dim ImageName As String

'   Check the RowCount.  If it is 0
'   then there are no images in the
'   database.  We then need to show the New Image
'   dialog to add the first image.
If ImageData.MSRDC1.Resultset.RowCount = 0 Then MenuNewImage
    Exit Sub
End If

'   Depending on the type of move
'   selected by the user, the resultset
'   is manipulated appropriately.
Select Case MoveType

    Case 0   'Move to First Record
        ImageData.MSRDC1.Resultset.MoveFirst

    Case 1   'Move to Last Record
        ImageData.MSRDC1.Resultset.MoveLast

    Case 2   'Move to Previous Record
        ImageData.MSRDC1.Resultset.MovePrevious

    Case 3   'Move to Next Record
        ImageData.MSRDC1.Resultset.MoveNext

End Select

'   Check to see if the End of File or
'   Beginning of File has been reached in
'   the result set.  If so, then move first or
'   last to ensure that a current record is
'   always visible
If ImageData.MSRDC1.Resultset.EOF = True Then
    ImageData.MSRDC1.Resultset.MoveLast
End If
```

```
If ImageData.MSRDC1.Resultset.BOF = True Then
  ➡ImageData.MSRDC1.Resultset.MoveFirst
End If

' Get the Image name from the database
ImageName = ImageData.MSRDC1.Resultset("FileName")

' Depending on whether or not the image file
' name is set, the picture display is
' set appropriately.
If ImageName <> "" Then
    ImageView.BackPict.Picture = LoadPicture(ImageName)
    SetView IView
Else
    ImageView.BackPict.Picture = LoadPicture("")
    SetView IView
End If

End Sub
```

42. The `MenuNewImage` function handles setting up the common file dialog box to help the user find `.BMP` or `.ICO` files to track. When a `.BMP` or `.ICO` file is selected, a new record is added to the database, and the appropriate data for the image file is stored.

```
Public Sub MenuNewImage()

Dim ImageID As Integer
Dim ImageType As String

' Ensure an Update is done
ImageData.MSRDC1.Resultset.MoveNext

' Set the filter type of the dialog
' box
ImageData.commondialog1.Filter = "Bitmaps (*.bmp)¦*.bmp¦Icons
➡(*.ico)¦*.ico All Files (*.*)¦*.*"


' Set the title of the dialog
ImageData.commondialog1.DialogTitle = "New Image File"

' Set the filter index to that of the
' bitmap
ImageData.commondialog1.FilterIndex = 1

' Set the flags to ensure that the
' file must exist
ImageData.commondialog1.Flags = cdlOFNFileMustExist

' Show the dialog box
ImageData.commondialog1.ShowOpen
```

continued on next page

continued from previous page

```
    ' Check to see if the filename was set
If ImageData.commondialog1.filename <> "" Then

    ' Add a new record
    ImageData.MSRDC1.Resultset.AddNew

    ' Set the file name
    ImageData.MSRDC1.Resultset("FileName") =
    ImageData.commondialog1.filename

    ' Set the file size
    ImageData.MSRDC1.Resultset("FileSize") =
    FileLen(ImageData.commondialog1.filename)

    ' Get the extension of the image
    ImageType = Right$(ImageData.commondialog1.filename, 3)

    ' Set the file format depending on
    ' the extension
    Select Case UCase$(ImageType)

        Case "BMP"   'Standard bitmap
            ImageData.MSRDC1.Resultset("FileFormat") = "Bitmap"

        Case "ICO"   'Standard Icon
            ImageData.MSRDC1.Resultset("FileType") = "Icon"

    End Select

    ' Update the result set
    ImageData.MSRDC1.Resultset.Update

    ' Select SQL statement to get the
    ' new result set
    ImageData.MSRDC1.SQL = "select * from ImageData
➥order by ImageID"

    ' Refresh the result set
    ImageData.MSRDC1.Refresh

    ' Move to the last record which was
    ' just added.
    MenuBrowse 1

End If

End Sub
```

43. The MenuDelete routine deletes the current record and moves to the next record.

```
Public Sub MenuDelete()

' Delete the current record
ImageData.MSRDC1.Resultset.Delete
```

```
'  Move to the next record.
MenuBrowse 3

End Sub
```

How It Works

The multiple document interface provides a framework for working with multiple windows of information. The fundamentals of making the application successful fall into these three areas:

✔ *Menu setup*—The menu setup is the key to interfacing with the application. Note that the MDI menu is different from the menus for the `ImageData` and `ImageView` forms. When the `ImageData` or `ImageView` forms are loaded, their menus take over the menus for the MDI form. To make sure that the code for the similar menu options works the same and is easily maintainable, a BAS module is added with routines for each menu option.

✔ *Control and image resizing*—Part of the key to ensuring that child windows appear correctly when they are resized, tiled, or cascaded is ensuring that the controls on those forms are also resized. In the `ImageData form resize` event, the controls on the form are sized to fit on the form. For the Image View `DispPict` picture that shows the image, its resize event handles call the `SizeViewPict` routine to ensure that the image is updated and fits in the window.

✔ *Database interface*—The database interface in this How-To is provided more for basic functionality than for demonstrating sophisticated database manipulation. The Microsoft remote data control is used with a 32-bit ODBC connection, Image Database. In this case, the database, `IData.MDB`, is provided in Microsoft Access 8.0 format, and the ODBC driver is for Access 8.0. The database has one table and the fields it contains are shown in Table 4.7.

Table 4.7 The `IData` database's `ImageData` table format

FIELD	FORMAT	DESCRIPTION
ImageID	AutoNumber	Auto count field
FileName	Text	The name of the file including the path
FileSize	Number	The size of the image file
FileFormat	Text	The image format of the file
Comments	Text	Image comments

Note that the database does not have to be in Access and can reside on any ODBC-compatible database such as Microsoft SQL Server.

The image is stretched and sized using the standard Windows API `StretchBlt` function with the `SRCCOPY` raster operation to copy the image source. To ensure that the image appears correctly, the palette from the back picture where the actual image is stored is copied to the display picture. The palette can be retrieved from the picture object (`picture.hpal`) of the picture box.

Comments

This How-To adds a few extra touches that would not be necessary in a real application. For example, there is no need to ask users whether they want to open the database, and, in fact, the database could open automatically when the application starts up. But the method used serves to show the different menu options for the MDI form versus the child windows. In this case, the child windows' menus are the same, but later How-To's in the chapter show how the menus can diverge.

COMPLEXITY
INTERMEDIATE

4.2 How do I...
Build an active toolbar to simplify access to menu functions?

COMPATIBILITY: VISUAL BASIC 5 AND 6

Problem

Most popular Windows 95 user interfaces implement the use of a toolbar. How can I add an integrated toolbar to the MDI `ImageTracking` database application? The toolbar should facilitate easy use of all the program features.

Technique

The toolbar control, combined with the `ImageList` control, provides an effective method for adding toolbars to an MDI application. The `ImageList` holds a list of the icons for the buttons on the toolbar. The toolbar also provides for the use of ToolTips for the various button options.

Steps

Open and run `4-2.VBP`. The running program appears as shown in Figure 4.3.

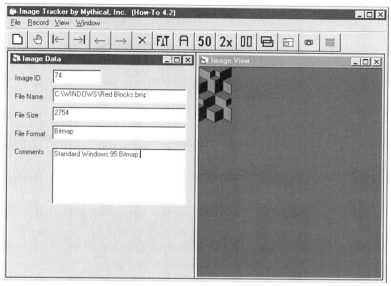

Figure 4.3 The form as it appears at runtime

Figure 4.4 shows the MDI child forms cascaded after selecting the Cascade toolbar button. Also note that the menu for the MDI form is hidden. This is done by selecting the Hide Menu option, which is the last tool button.

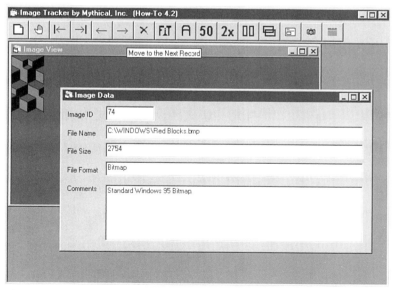

Figure 4.4 The MDI form without the menu visible

Complete the following steps to create this project:

1. Create a new project called 4-2.VBP. Add the objects and properties listed in Table 4.8 to Form1 and save the form as 4-2.FRM.

Table 4.8 The MDI form's objects and properties

OBJECT	PROPERTY	SETTING
MDIForm	Name	ImageTracker
	AutoShowChildren	0 'False
	BackColor	&H8000000C&
	Caption	"Image Tracker by Mythical, Inc. (How-To 4.2)"
Toolbar	Name	ImageTool
	Align	1 'Align Top
	Negotiate	-1 'True
	ImageList	"MDIButtons"
	ButtonWidth	926
	ButtonHeight	847
	AllowCustomize	0 'False
	NumButtons	17 (See ImageList for image icons)
	AlignSet	-1 'True
	Wrappable	0 'False
ImageList	Name	MDIButtons
	ImageWidth	28
	ImageHeight	26
	MaskColor	12632256
	NumImages	17
	i1	open.bmp
	i2	new.bmp
	i3	hand.bmp
	i4	first.bmp
	i5	last.bmp
	i6	prev.bmp
	i7	next.bmp
	i8	delete.bmp
	i9	fit.bmp
	i10	actual.bmp
	i11	50.bmp
	i12	2x.bmp

OBJECT	PROPERTY	SETTING
	i13	tile.bmp
	i14	cascade.bmp
	i15	data.bmp
	i16	camera.bmp
	i17	menu.bmp

2. Add the menus shown in Table 4.9 to the `ImageTracker` MDI form.

Table 4.9 The form's menus

CONTROL NAME	CAPTION	INDEX	CHECKED	SHORTCUT KEY
mFile	"&File"			
mOpenImage	"&Open Image Database"			
mBar	"-"			
mExit	"E&xit"			
mWindow	"&Window"			
mImageData	"Image &Data"			
mImageView	"Image &View"			
mBar3	"-"			
mShowTool	"Show Toolbar"		-1 'True	
mShowMenu	"Show Menu"		-1 'True	

3. Insert a new form into the project and save it as `IView.frm`. Add the objects and properties listed in Table 4.10 to the form.

Table 4.10 The form's objects and properties

OBJECT	PROPERTY	SETTING
Form	Name	ImageView
	Caption	"Image View"
	MDIChild	-1 'True
PictureBox	Name	DispPict
	Appearance	0 'Flat
	AutoSize	-1 'True
	BackColor	&H00FF0000&
	ForeColor	&H80000008&
	Picture	"pastel.bmp"
	ScaleMode	3 'Pixel

continued on next page

Table 4.10 continued

OBJECT	PROPERTY	SETTING	
PictureBox	Name	BackPict	
	AutoRedraw	-1	'True
	AutoSize	-1	'True
	BackColor	&H000000FF&	
	BorderStyle	0	'None
	ScaleMode	3	'Pixel
	Visible	0	'False

4. Add the menus in Table 4.11 to the ImageView form.

Table 4.11 The form's objects and properties

CONTROL NAME	CAPTION	INDEX	CHECKED		SHORTCUT KEY
mFile	"&File"				
mNewImage	"&New Image"				
mBar	"-"				
mExit	"E&xit"				
mRecord	"&Record"				
mBrowse	"&First"	0			F1
mBrowse	"&Last"	1			F2
mBrowse	"&Back"	2			F3
mBrowse	"For&ward"	3			F4
mBar2	"-"				
mDelete	"&Delete Record"				
mView	"&View"				
mSize	"&Fit in Window"	0			
mSize	"&Actual Size"	1	-1	'True	
mSize	"&50 Percent"	2			
mSize	"&200 Percent"	3			
mWindow	"&Window"				
mTile	"&Tile"				
mCascade	"&Cascade"				
mBar1	"-"				
mShowWindow	"Image &Data"	0			
mShowWindow	"Image &View"	1			
mBar3	"-"				
mShowTool	"Show Toolbar"		-1	'True	
mShowMenu	"Show Menu"		-1	'True	

5. Insert a new form into the project and save it as `IData.frm`. Add the objects and properties listed in Table 4.12 to the form.

Table 4.12 The form's objects and properties

OBJECT	PROPERTY	SETTING
Form	Name	ImageData
	Caption	"Image Data"
	MDIChild	-1 'True
	Visible	0 'False
TextBox	Name	ImageInfo
	DataField	"Comments"
	DataSource	"MSRDC1"
	Index	4
	MultiLine	-1 'True
TextBox	Name	ImageInfo
	DataField	"FileFormat"
	DataSource	"MSRDC1"
	Index	3
TextBox	Name	ImageInfo
	DataField	"FileSize"
	DataSource	"MSRDC1"
	Index	2
	Locked	-1 'True
TextBox	Name	ImageInfo
	DataField	"FileName"
	DataSource	"MSRDC1"
	Index	1
TextBox	Name	ImageInfo
	DataField	"ImageID"
	DataSource	"MSRDC1"
	Index	0
	Locked	-1 'True
CommonDialog	Name	CommonDialog1
	DefaultExt	".bmp"
	DialogTitle	"Find Image File"
	Filter	"*.bmp; *.wmf"
	FilterIndex	1
	InitDir	"c:\windows"

continued on next page

Table 4.12 continued

OBJECT	PROPERTY	SETTING
MSRDC	Name	MSRDC1
	Visible	0 'False
	DataSourceName	"Image Database"
	RecordSource	"select * from ImageData
		order byImageID"
	RecordsetType	1
	KeysetSize	0
	ReadOnly	0 'False
	UserName	" "
	Password	" "
	CursorDriver	2
	EOFAction	1
	BOFAction	1
	Caption	"MSRDC1"
	Prompt	3
	LockType	3
Label	Name	Comments
	AutoSize	-1 'True
	Caption	"Comments"
Label	Name	FileFormat
	AutoSize	-1 'True
	Caption	"File Format"
Label	Name	FileSize
	AutoSize	-1 'True
	Caption	"File Size"
Label	Name	FileName
	AutoSize	-1 'True
	Caption	"File Name"
Label	Name	ImageID
	AutoSize	-1 'True
	Caption	"Image ID"

6. Add the menus in Table 4.13 to the ImageView form.

Table 4.13 The form's objects and properties

CONTROL NAME	CAPTION	INDEX	CHECKED		SHORTCUT KEY
mFile	"&File"				
mNewImage	"&New Image"				
mBar	"-"				
mExit	"E&xit"				
mRecord	"&Record"				
mBrowse	"&First"	0			F1
mBrowse	"&Last"	1			F2
mBrowse	"&Back"	2			F3
mBrowse	"For&ward"	3			F4
mBar2	"-"				
mDelete	"&Delete Record"				
mView	"&View"				
mSize	"&Fit in Window"	0			
mSize	"&Actual Size"	1	-1	'True	
mSize	"&50 Percent"	2			
mSize	"&200 Percent"	3			
mWindow	"&Window"				
mTile	"&Tile"				
mCascade	"&Cascade"				
mBar1	"-"				
mShowWindow	"Image &Data"	0			
mShowWindow	"Image &View"	1			
mBar3	"-"				
mShowTool	"Show Toolbar"		-1	'True	
mShowMenu	"Show Menu"		-1	'True	

NOTE

Only code that is different from or added to the last How-To will be described. If you need additional information regarding the other code, see How-To 4.1 for a complete explanation.

7. Add the following code to the **ImageTracker** form. The toolbar has a button collection that defines the buttons for the toolbar. By referencing the index of the button, you can determine which button was selected and call the appropriate function. Note that the toolbar buttons each reference a corresponding menu option. Thus, the original code for each menu option can be called. For the Image Data and Image View buttons, when only the MDI form is loaded, the database is opened; otherwise, the corresponding form is shown.

```
Private Sub ImageTool_ButtonClick(ByVal Button As Button)

Select Case Button.Index

    Case 1
        '   Open the Image Database
        MenuOpenData

    Case 2

        '   Call the MenuNewImage function to get
        '   a new image
        MenuNewImage

    Case 3
        '   Exit the program
        MenuExit

    Case 4
        '   Move to the first record
        MenuBrowse 0

    Case 5
        '   Move to the last record
        MenuBrowse 1

    Case 6
        '   Move back a record
        MenuBrowse 2

    Case 7
        '   Move forward a record
        MenuBrowse 3

    Case 8
        '   Delete the current record
        '   of the result set
        MenuDelete

    Case 9
        '   Set the View to fit in the Window
        SetView 0
```

```
    Case 10
        '   Set the View to actual size
        SetView 1

    Case 11
        '   Set the View to 50 %
        SetView 2

    Case 12
        '   Set the View to 200 %
        SetView 3

    Case 13
        '   Tile the windows
        MenuTile

    Case 14
        '   Cascade the Windows
        MenuCascade

    Case 15
        '   If the ImageData form is not
        '   visible then call the
        '   MenuOpenData function to open
        '   the database.  Otherwise, show
        '   the ImageData Window (0)
        If ImageData.Visible = False Then
            MenuOpenData
        Else
            MenuShowWindow 0
        End If

    Case 16
        '   If the ImageData form is not
        '   visible then call the
        '   MenuOpenData function to open
        '   the database.  Otherwise, show
        '   the ImageView Window (1)
        If ImageData.Visible = False Then
            MenuOpenData
        Else
            MenuShowWindow 1
        End If

    Case 17
        '   Show or hide the Menu depending
        '   on the current setting.
        MenuShowMenu

End Select

End Sub
```

8. When the `ImageTool` toolbar is double-clicked, the toolbar becomes invisible. But it is important to ensure that the MDI forms menu is visible. If it is not, then the toolbar should not be hidden.

```
Private Sub ImageTool_DblClick()

'   If the menu or ImageTracker is
'   visible then hide the toolbar.
'   Note we can not hide the toolbar
'   if the menu is also hidden.  the
'   user would be lost at that point.
If Me.mWindow.Visible = True Then
    MenuShowTool
End If

End Sub


Private Sub MDIForm_Load()

'  Hide the ImageData form when
'   the MDI form is first loaded
ImageData.Hide

End Sub

Private Sub MDIForm_QueryUnload(Cancel As Integer,
➥UnloadMode As Integer)

'   Call the MenuExit program to
'   end the program
MenuExit

End Sub

Private Sub MDIForm_Unload(Cancel As Integer)

'   Call the MenuExit program to
'   end the program
MenuExit

End Sub

Private Sub mExit_Click()

'   Call the MenuExit program to
'   end the program
MenuExit

End Sub


Private Sub mImageData_Click()
```

```
'   Call the MenuOpenData method to open the
'   Image database
MenuOpenData

End Sub

Private Sub mImageView_Click()

'   Call the MenuOpenData method to open the
'   Image database
MenuOpenData

End Sub

Private Sub mOpenImage_Click()

'   Call the MenuOpenData method to open the
'   Image database
MenuOpenData

End Sub
```

9. When the Show Menu option is selected, the `MenuShowMenu` routine is called to handle either showing or hiding the form's menus.

```
Private Sub mShowMenu_Click()

'   Show or hide the Menu
MenuShowMenu

End Sub
```

10. The Show ToolBar menu option calls the `MenuShowTool` routine to handle showing and hiding the toolbar.

```
Private Sub mShowTool_Click()

'   Show or hide the Toolbar
MenuShowTool

End Sub
```

11. Add the following code to the `ImageView` form:

```
Public Sub SizeViewPict()

'   Allow for a small border
'   around the display picture
DispPict.Top = 5
DispPict.Left = 5
DispPict.Width = Me.Width - 5
DispPict.Height = Me.Height - 5
```

continued on next page

continued from previous page

```
'  Set the view to the current
'  view option
SetView IView

End Sub

Private Sub DispPict_Paint()

'  Size the view picture
SizeViewPict

End Sub

Private Sub Form_Load()

'  Initially set IView to 1.
IView = 1

'  Call the MenuBrowse function
'  to show the first record
MenuBrowse 1

End Sub

Private Sub Form_Unload(Cancel As Integer)

'  Cancel the unload.  We don't want the
'  form to be unloaded while the program is
'  running so that it does not have to be
'  re-initialized.  Instead, the form will be
'  minimized.
Cancel = -1
Me.WindowState = 1

End Sub


Private Sub mBrowse_Click(Index As Integer)

'  Browse the record set depending on the
'  menu option chosen.
MenuBrowse Index

End Sub


Private Sub mCascade_Click()

'  Cascade the windows
MenuCascade

'  Size the view picture after the cascade
SizeViewPict

End Sub
```

```
Private Sub mDelete_Click()

'   Call the MenuDelete function to
'   delete the selected record.
MenuDelete

End Sub


Private Sub mExit_Click()

'   Call the MenuExit function to
'   exit the program.
MenuExit

End Sub


Private Sub mNewImage_Click()

'   Call the MenuNewImage function to get
'   a new image
MenuNewImage

End Sub
```

12. The Show Menu option calls the **MenuShowWindow** routine to show and hide the form's menu.

```
Private Sub mShowMenu_Click()

'   Show or hide the Menu
MenuShowMenu

End Sub
```

13. The Show Tool option calls the **MenuShowTool** routine to show and hide the toolbar.

```
Private Sub mShowTool_Click()

'   Show or hide the toolbar
MenuShowTool

End Sub

Private Sub mShowWindow_Click(Index As Integer)

'   Call the MenuShowWindow function to show
'   the selected window.
MenuShowWindow Index

End Sub
```

continued on next page

continued from previous page

```
Private Sub mTile_Click()

'   Call the menu tile function to
'   tile the windows
MenuTile

End Sub

Private Sub mSize_Click(Index As Integer)

'   Set the view depending on the menu option
'   selected
SetView Index

End Sub
```

14. Add the following code to the **ImageData** form:

```
Private Sub Form_Resize()

Dim N As Integer

'   Resize the Image Info controls to
'   fit on the form when it is resized
For N = 1 To 4
    ImageData.ImageInfo(N).Width = ImageData.Width -
....ImageData.ImageInfo(N).Left - 300
Next N

End Sub

Private Sub Form_Unload(Cancel As Integer)

'   We don't want the form to be unloaded so that
'   it will not have to be re-initialized
Cancel = -1

'   Instead minimize the form
Me.WindowState = 1
End Sub

Private Sub mBrowse_Click(Index As Integer)

'   Browse the result set depending
'   on the menu selected
MenuBrowse Index

End Sub

Private Sub mCascade_Click()

'   Cascade the windows
MenuCascade

End Sub
```

```
Private Sub mDelete_Click()

'   Delete the current record
'   of the result set
MenuDelete

End Sub

Private Sub mExit_Click()

'   Call the MenuExit method to
'   exit the program
MenuExit

End Sub

Private Sub mNewImage_Click()

'   Call the MenuNewImage function to allow
'   the user to select a new image to add to the
'   database
MenuNewImage

End Sub
```

15. The Show Menu option handles calling the **MenuShowMenu** routine to show and hide the form's menus.

```
Private Sub mShowMenu_Click()

'   Show or hide the Menu
MenuShowMenu

End Sub
```

16. The Show ToolBar menu option handles calling the **MenuShowTool** routine to show and hide the toolbar.

```
Private Sub mShowTool_Click()

'   Show or hide the toolbar
MenuShowTool

End Sub

Private Sub mShowWindow_Click(Index As Integer)

'   Call the MenuShowWindow function to show
'   the window selected
MenuShowWindow Index

End Sub

Private Sub mSize_Click(Index As Integer)
```

continued on next page

continued from previous page

```
'  Set the View based on the menu
'  selection
SetView Index

End Sub

Private Sub mTile_Click()

'  Tile the windows
MenuTile

End Sub
```

17. Insert a new module into the project and save it as `MenLogic.bas`. Add the following code to the General Declarations section of the module:

```
'  StretchBlt will be used for the Image Viewer
Private Declare Function StretchBlt Lib "gdi32"
➡(ByVal hdc As Long, ByVal x As Long, ByVal y As Long,
➡ByVal nWidth As Long, ByVal nHeight As Long,
➡ByVal hSrcDC As Long, ByVal xSrc As Long,
➡ByVal ySrc As Long, ByVal nSrcWidth As Long,
➡ByVal nSrcHeight As Long, ByVal dwRop As Long)
As Long

Const SRCCOPY = &HCC0020


'  IView globally stores the current view for
'  the image  I.E.  Fit in Window, 50%
Public IView As Integer


'  Handles ending the program when
'  users select exit from the menu
Public Sub MenuExit()
    End
End Sub


'  Handles tiling the windows
'  on the MDI form
Public Sub MenuTile()

'  Do a vertical tile
ImageTracker.Arrange vbTileVertical

End Sub


Public Sub MenuCascade()
```

```
'  Cascade the child forms
ImageTracker.Arrange vbCascade

End Sub


Public Sub SetView(Index)

'  When a new image view is selected,
'  the original menu selection is
'  unchecked
ImageView.mSize(IView).Checked = False
ImageData.mSize(IView).Checked = False

'  Set the new view to the index
'  parameter
IView = Index

'  Check the new menu option for the
'  selected view.
ImageData.mSize(IView).Checked = True
ImageView.mSize(IView).Checked = True

'  Clear the displayed picture
ImageView.DispPict.Cls

'  Depending on the view selected, the
'  original image will be copied to the
'  display picture appropriately
Select Case IView

    Case 0   'Fit in the Window
        Call StretchBlt(ImageView.DispPict.hdc, 0, 0,
        ➥ImageView.DispPict.ScaleWidth,
        ➥ImageView.DispPict.ScaleHeight,
        ➥ImageView.BackPict.hdc, 0, 0,
        ➥ImageView.BackPict.ScaleWidth,
        ➥ImageView.BackPict.ScaleHeight, SRCCOPY)

    Case 1   'Actual Size
        Call StretchBlt(ImageView.DispPict.hdc, 0, 0,
        ➥ImageView.BackPict.ScaleWidth,
        ➥ImageView.BackPict.ScaleHeight,
        ➥ImageView.BackPict.hdc, 0, 0,
        ➥ImageView.BackPict.ScaleWidth,
        ➥ImageView.BackPict.ScaleHeight, SRCCOPY)

    Case 2 '50%
        Call StretchBlt(ImageView.DispPict.hdc, 0, 0,
        ➥ImageView.BackPict.ScaleWidth * 0.5,
        ➥ImageView.BackPict.ScaleHeight * 0.5,
        ➥ImageView.BackPict.hdc, 0, 0,
        ➥ImageView.BackPict.ScaleWidth,
        ➥ImageView.BackPict.ScaleHeight, SRCCOPY)
```

continued on next page

continued from previous page

```
            Case 3 '200%
                Call StretchBlt(ImageView.DispPict.hdc, 0, 0,
                ➥ImageView.BackPict.ScaleWidth * 2,
                ➥ImageView.BackPict.ScaleHeight * 2,
                ➥ImageView.BackPict.hdc, 0, 0,
                ➥ImageView.BackPict.ScaleWidth,
                ➥ImageView.BackPict.ScaleHeight, SRCCOPY)

        End Select

        '  Copy the palette from the holding picture
        '  to the displayed picture.  This ensures that
        '  the image's colors are displayed correctly.
        ImageView.DispPict.Picture.hPal =
        ➥ImageView.BackPict.Picture.hPal

        End Sub

        Public Sub MenuShowWindow(Index)

        '  Check to see which Windows (Form)
        '  is to be displayed.
        Select Case Index

            Case 0   'Show ImageData
                ImageData.Show
                ImageData.WindowState = 0

            Case 1   'Show ImageView
                ImageView.Show
                ImageView.WindowState = 0

        End Select

        End Sub

        Public Sub MenuOpenData()

        Dim Msg As String
        Dim Style As Integer
        Dim Title As String
        Dim Response As Integer
        Dim N As Integer

        '  Set the Message, Style and Title
        '  of the message box
        Msg = "Do you want to open the Image Database ?"
        Style = vbYesNo + vbQuestion + vbDefaultButton1
        Title = "Open Image Database"

        '  Retrieve the user's response
        Response = MsgBox(Msg, Style, Title)

        '  If it was a yes, then show the ImageData
        '  and ImageView forms.  Also start the view
        '  in Tiled mode.
        If Response = vbYes Then
```

```
    ImageView.Show
    ImageData.Show
    MenuTile

    ImageTracker.ImageTool.Buttons(1).Visible = False

    For N = 2 To ImageTracker.ImageTool.Buttons.Count

        ImageTracker.ImageTool.Buttons(N).Visible = True

    Next N

    '  Ensure that the menu item's the same
    '  for the ImageData and ImageView forms
    ImageView.mShowMenu.Checked = ImageTracker.mShowMenu.Checked
    ImageData.mShowMenu.Checked = ImageTracker.mShowMenu.Checked
    ImageView.mShowTool.Checked = ImageTracker.mShowTool.Checked
    ImageData.mShowTool.Checked = ImageTracker.mShowTool.Checked

End If

End Sub


Public Sub MenuBrowse(MoveType)

Dim ImageName As String

'  Check the RowCount.  If it is 0
'  then there are no images in the
'  database.  We then need to show the New Image
'  dialog to add the first image.
If ImageData.MSRDC1.Resultset.RowCount = 0 Then
    MenuNewImage
    Exit Sub
End If

'  Depending on the type of move
'  selected by the user, the result set
'  is manipulated appropriately.
Select Case MoveType

    Case 0  'Move to First Record
        ImageData.MSRDC1.Resultset.MoveFirst

    Case 1  'Move to Last Record
        ImageData.MSRDC1.Resultset.MoveLast

    Case 2  'Move to Previous Record
        ImageData.MSRDC1.Resultset.MovePrevious

    Case 3  'Move to Next Record
        ImageData.MSRDC1.Resultset.MoveNext

End Select
```

continued on next page

continued from previous page

```
'   Check to see if the End of File or
'   Beginning of File has been reached in
'   the result set.  If so, then move first or
'   last to ensure that a current record is
'   always visible
If ImageData.MSRDC1.Resultset.EOF = True Then
ImageData.MSRDC1.Resultset.MoveLast

If ImageData.MSRDC1.Resultset.BOF = True Then
ImageData.MSRDC1.Resultset.MoveFirst

'   Get the Image name from the database
ImageName = ImageData.MSRDC1.Resultset("FileName")

'   Depending on whether or not the image file
'   name is set, the picture display is
'   set appropriately.
If ImageName <> "" Then
    ImageView.BackPict.Picture = LoadPicture(ImageName)
    SetView IView
Else
    ImageView.BackPict.Picture = LoadPicture("")
    SetView IView
End If

End Sub

Public Sub MenuNewImage()

Dim ImageID As Integer
Dim ImageType As String

'   Ensure an Update is done
ImageData.MSRDC1.Resultset.MoveNext

'   Set the filter type of the dialog
'   box
ImageData.commondialog1.Filter = "Bitmaps (*.bmp)¦*.bmp¦Icons
➥(*.ico)¦*.ico¦ All Files (*.*)¦*.*"

'   Set the title of the dialog
ImageData.commondialog1.DialogTitle = "New Image File"

'   Set the filter index to that of the
'   bitmap
ImageData.commondialog1.FilterIndex = 1

'   Set the flags to ensure that the
'   file must exist
ImageData.commondialog1.Flags = cdlOFNFileMustExist

'   Show the dialog box
ImageData.commondialog1.ShowOpen

'   Check to see if the filename was set
If ImageData.commondialog1.filename <> "" Then
```

```
     '   Add a new record
     ImageData.MSRDC1.Resultset.AddNew

     '   Set the file name
     ImageData.MSRDC1.Resultset("FileName") =
     ImageData.commondialog1.filename

     '   Set the file size
     ImageData.MSRDC1.Resultset("FileSize") =
       FileLen(ImageData.commondialog1.filename)

     '   Get the extension of the image
     ImageType = Right$(ImageData.commondialog1.filename, 3)

     '   Set the file format depending on
     '   the the extension
     Select Case UCase$(ImageType)

         Case "BMP"   'Standard bitmap
             ImageData.MSRDC1.Resultset("FileFormat") = "Bitmap"

         Case "ICO"   'Standard Icon
             ImageData.MSRDC1.Resultset("FileType") = "Icon"

     End Select

     '   Update the result set
     ImageData.MSRDC1.Resultset.Update

     '   Select SQL statement to get the
     '   new result set
     ImageData.MSRDC1.SQL = "select * from ImageData
     ➥order by ImageID"

     '   Refresh the result set
     ImageData.MSRDC1.Refresh

     '   Move to the last record which was
     '   just added.
     MenuBrowse 1

End If

End Sub

Public Sub MenuDelete()

'   Delete the current record
ImageData.MSRDC1.Resultset.Delete

'   Move to the next record.
MenuBrowse 3

End Sub
```

18. The MenuShowTool routine handles showing and hiding the toolbar. The current status is set by the check status of the mShowTool menu option. If the menu is checked, then the toolbar is to be hidden, and all the Show ToolBar menu options are unchecked. If the menu is unchecked, then the Show ToolBar menu items are checked and the toolbar shown.

```
Public Sub MenuShowTool()

'  If the toolbar is checked then
'  do the logic to hide the toolbar
If ImageTracker.mShowTool.Checked = True Then

    '  Hide the toolbar
    ImageTracker.ImageTool.Visible = False

    '  Change the menu check
    ImageTracker.mShowTool.Checked = False

    '  If the ImageData and ImageView forms
    '  are visible then handle setting their
    '  menu check marks.  If they are not
    '  visible, they are not loaded.
    If ImageData.Visible = True Then
        ImageData.mShowTool.Checked = False
        ImageView.mShowTool.Checked = False
    End If

Else

    '  Make the toolbar visible
    ImageTracker.ImageTool.Visible = True

    '  Change the menu check
    ImageTracker.mShowTool.Checked = True

    '  If the ImageData and ImageView forms
    '  are visible then handle setting their
    '  menu check marks.  If they are not
    '  visible, they are not loaded.
    If ImageData.Visible = True Then
        ImageData.mShowTool.Checked = True
        ImageView.mShowTool.Checked = True
    End If

End If

End Sub
```

19. The MenuShowMenu routine handles showing and hiding the menus for the forms. If the Show Menu menu item is checked, then the menus are hidden; otherwise, the menus are shown. It is important to make sure that the toolbar is visible if the menu is to be hidden. If both the menu and toolbar were hidden, the user would be stuck.

```
Public Sub MenuShowMenu()

'  Check to see If the menu is already visible
If ImageTracker.mShowMenu.Checked = True Then

    '  If the tool bar is not visible,
    '  we do not want to also make the
    '  menu invisible
    If ImageTracker.ImageTool.Visible = False Then Exit Sub

    '  Make the ImageTracker menus
    '  invisible and set the menu
    '  check mark appropriately
    ImageTracker.mFile.Visible = False
    ImageTracker.mShowMenu.Checked = False
    ImageTracker.mWindow.Visible = False

    '  If the ImageData and ImageView forms
    '  are visible then handle setting their
    '  menu check marks and visible properties.
    '  If they are not visible, they are not
    '  loaded.
    If ImageData.Visible = True Then
        ImageData.mShowMenu.Checked = False
        ImageView.mShowMenu.Checked = False
        ImageView.mFile.Visible = False
        ImageData.mFile.Visible = False
        ImageData.mWindow.Visible = False
        ImageView.mWindow.Visible = False
        ImageData.mRecord.Visible = False
        ImageView.mRecord.Visible = False
        ImageData.mView.Visible = False
        ImageView.mView.Visible = False
    End If

Else

    '  Make the ImageTracker menus
    '  visible and set the menu
    '  check mark appropriately
    ImageTracker.mFile.Visible = True
    ImageTracker.mShowMenu.Checked = True
    ImageTracker.mWindow.Visible = True

    '  If the ImageData and ImageView forms
    '  are visible then handle setting their
    '  menu check marks and visible properties.
    '  If they are not visible, they are not
    '  loaded.
    If ImageData.Visible = True Then
        ImageData.mShowMenu.Checked = True
        ImageView.mShowMenu.Checked = True
        ImageData.mFile.Visible = True
        ImageView.mFile.Visible = True
        ImageData.mWindow.Visible = True
```

continued on next page

continued from previous page

```
              ImageView.mWindow.Visible = True
              ImageData.mRecord.Visible = True
              ImageView.mRecord.Visible = True
              ImageView.mView.Visible = True
              ImageData.mView.Visible = True
         End If

    End If

    End Sub
```

How It Works

If you compare the basic MDI application developed in How-To 4.1, you can easily see the benefits the toolbar interface provides to the user. Database browsing becomes obvious and easy to access through the toolbar buttons. Quickly switching between the different image views also becomes obvious as well as browsing the database.

Part of what makes the implementation of the toolbar possible is the use of the **ImageList** control. An **ImageList** simply holds a list of images. In this case, the images are the bitmap button icons. The **ToolBar** control references the image list for defining the icon to be placed on the buttons. Note that the button icons are provided in the application directory.

The routines called to implement the different menu functions also implement the toolbar functionality. An added feature to help customize the interface to the user's liking is to allow either the menu or the toolbar to be hidden. It is important to ensure that at least one is visible.

Comments

The **ToolBar** control allows for a customize feature to organize the buttons on the toolbar. In this How-To, the property is set to **False**. To allow your user to customize the interface to your application, you might want to consider providing this functionality.

New to Version 6.0 is a control called the CoolBar, which is a toolbar control that resembles the toolbar in products like Microsoft Internet Explorer 4.0 and Office 97. This example didn't use that control in order for the code to be compatible with VB 5 as well as VB 6.

COMPLEXITY
INTERMEDIATE

4.3 How do I...
Implement right mouse button context menus?

COMPATIBILITY: VISUAL BASIC 5 AND 6

Problem

The Windows interface provides a rich set of features with the use of the context-sensitive button. How can I provide context-sensitive menu support to help the user navigate the interfaces of my programs?

Technique

Visual Basic, starting with version 4, provides the PopupMenu method for providing instant pop-up menus based on the form's menus. With pop-up menus, based on the context of the mouse click, the appropriate menu can be shown with the most likely selection in bold. This How-To adds context-rich pop-up menus to the MDI application developed in the previous How-To's.

Steps

Open and run 4-3.VBP. Figure 4.5 shows the toolbar pop-up menu for setting the toolbar, menu, and window options. Figure 4.6 shows the running program and the right-click option for the Image View window. You can also perform a left-click to show the menu options to flip the image horizontally and vertically.

Figure 4.7 shows the right-click option for the Image Data window. This provides for quick selection of the database browse functions of the program.

Complete the following steps to create this project:

1. Create a new project called 4-3.VBP. Add the objects and properties listed in Table 4.14 to the form and save the form as 4-3.FRM.

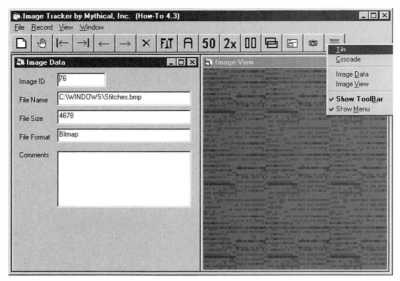

Figure 4.5 The form with the right-click pop-up menu for the toolbar

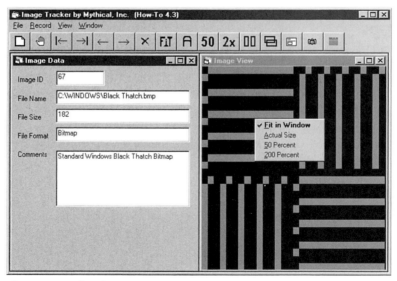

Figure 4.6 The form with the right-click pop-up menu for the Image View window

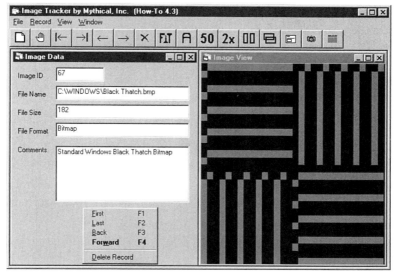

Figure 4.7 The form with the right-click pop-up menu for the Image Data window

Table 4.14 The MDI form's objects and properties

OBJECT	PROPERTY	SETTING
MDIForm	Name	ImageTracker
	AutoShowChildren	0 'False
	Caption	"Image Tracker by Mythical, Inc. (How-To 4.3)"
Toolbar	Name	ImageTool
	Align	1 'Align Top
	Negotiate	-1 'True
	ImageList	"MDIButtons"
	ButtonWidth	926
	ButtonHeight	847
	AllowCustomize	0 'False
	NumButtons	17 (See ImageList for button icons)
	AlignSet	-1 'True
	Wrappable	0 'False

continued on next page

Table 4.14 continued

OBJECT	PROPERTY	SETTING
ImageList	Name	MDIButtons
	ImageWidth	28
	ImageHeight	26
	MaskColor	12632256
	NumImages	17
	i1	open.bmp
	i2	new.bmp
	i3	hand.bmp
	i4	first.bmp
	i5	last.bmp
	i6	prev.bmp
	i7	next.bmp
	i8	delete.bmp
	i9	fit.bmp
	i10	actual.bmp
	i11	50.bmp
	i12	2x.bmp
	i13	tile.bmp
	i14	cascade.bmp
	i15	data.bmp
	i16	camera.bmp
	i17	menu.bmp

2. Add the menus shown in Table 4.15 to the ImageTracker form.

Table 4.15 The ImageTracker form's menus

CONTROL NAME	CAPTION	INDEX	CHECKED	SHORTCUT KEY
mFile	"&File"			
mOpenImage	"&Open Image Database"			
mBar	"-"			
mExit	"E&xit"			
mWindow	"&Window"			
mImageData	"Image &Data"			
mImageView	"Image &View"			
mBar3	"-"			
mShowTool	"Show Toolbar"		-1	'True
mShowMenu	"Show Menu"		-1	'True

3. Insert a new form into the project and save it as `IView.frm`. Add the objects and properties listed in Table 4.16 to the form.

Table 4.16 The `ImageView` form's objects and properties

OBJECT	PROPERTY	SETTING
Form	Name	ImageView
	Caption	"Image View"
	MDIChild	-1 'True
PictureBox	Name	DispPict
	BackColor	&H00C00000&
	BorderStyle	0 'None
	Picture	"pastel.bmp"
	ScaleMode	3 'Pixel
PictureBox	Name	BackPict
	AutoRedraw	-1 'True
	AutoSize	-1 'True
	BackColor	&H000000FF&
	BorderStyle	0 'None
	Picture	"pastel.bmp"
	ScaleMode	3 'Pixel
	Visible	0 'False

4. Add the menus shown in Table 4.17 to the `ImageView` form.

Table 4.17 The `ImageView` form's menus

CONTROL NAME	CAPTION	INDEX	CHECKED	SHORTCUT KEY
mFile	"&File"			
mNewImage	"&New Image"			
mBar	"-"			
mExit	"E&xit"			
mRecord	"&Record"			
mBrowse	"&First"	0		F1
mBrowse	"&Last"	1		F2
mBrowse	"&Back"	2		F3
mBrowse	"For&ward"	3		F4
mBar2	"-"			
mDelete	"&Delete Record"			

continued on next page

Table 4.17 continued

CONTROL NAME	CAPTION	INDEX	CHECKED	SHORTCUT KEY
mView	"&View"			
mSize	"&Fit in Window"	0		
mSize	"&Actual Size"	1	-1 'True	
mSize	"&50 Percent"	2		
mSize	"&200 Percent"	3		
mViewSet	"Viewer Settings"			
Flip	"Flip &Horizontal"	0		
Flip	"Flip &Vertical"	1		
mWindow	"&Window"			
mTile	"&Tile"			
mCascade	"&Cascade"			
mBar1	"-"			
mShowWindow	"Image &Data"	0		
mShowWindow	"Image &View"	1		
mBar3	"-"			
mShowTool	"Show Tool&Bar"			
mShowMenu	"Show &Menu"		-1 'True	

5. Insert a new form into the project and save it as `IData.frm`. Add the objects and properties listed in Table 4.18 to the form.

Table 4.18 The ImageData form's objects and properties

OBJECT	PROPERTY	SETTING
Form	Name	ImageData
	Caption	"Image Data"
	MDIChild	-1 'True
	Visible	0 'False
TextBox	Name	ImageInfo
	DataField	"Comments"
	DataSource	"MSRDC1"
	Index	4
	MultiLine	-1 'True
TextBox	Name	ImageInfo
	DataField	"FileFormat"
	DataSource	"MSRDC1"
	Index	3

OBJECT	PROPERTY	SETTING
TextBox	Name	ImageInfo
	DataField	"FileSize"
	DataSource	"MSRDC1"
	Index	2
	Locked	-1 'True
TextBox	Name	ImageInfo
	DataField	"FileName"
	DataSource	"MSRDC1"
	Index	1
TextBox	Name	ImageInfo
	DataField	"ImageID"
	DataSource	"MSRDC1"
	Index	0
	Locked	-1 'True
CommonDialog	Name	CommonDialog1
	DefaultExt	".bmp"
	DialogTitle	"Find Image File"
	Filter	"*.bmp; *.wmf"
	FilterIndex	1
	InitDir	"c:\windows"
MSRDC	Name	MSRDC1
	Visible	0 'False
	DataSourceName	"Image Database"
	RecordSource	"select * from ImageData order by ImageID"
	RecordsetType	1
	KeysetSize	0
	ReadOnly	0 'False
	UserName	""
	Password	""
	CursorDriver	2
	EOFAction	1
	BOFAction	1
	Prompt	3
	LockType	3

continued on next page

Table 4.18 continued

OBJECT	PROPERTY	SETTING
Label	Name	Comments
	AutoSize	-1 'True
	Caption	"Comments"
Label	Name	FileFormat
	AutoSize	-1 'True
	Caption	"File Format"
Label	Name	FileSize
	AutoSize	-1 'True
	Caption	"File Size"
Label	Name	FileName
	AutoSize	-1 'True
	Caption	"File Name"
Label	Name	ImageID
	AutoSize	-1 'True
	Caption	"Image ID"

6. Add the menus shown in Table 4.19 to the `ImageData` form.

Table 4.19 The `ImageData` form's menus

CONTROL NAME	CAPTION	INDEX	CHECKED	SHORTCUT KEY
mFile	"&File"			
mNewImage	"&New Image"			
mBar	"-"			
mExit	"E&xit"			
mRecord	"&Record"			
mBrowse	"&First"	0		F1
mBrowse	"&Last"	1		F2
mBrowse	"&Back"	2		F3
mBrowse	"For&ward"	3		F4
mBar2	"-"			
mDelete	"&Delete Record"			
mView	"&View"			
mSize	"&Fit in Window"	0		
mSize	"&Actual Size"	1	-1 'True	
mSize	"&50 Percent"	2		
mSize	"&200 Percent"	3		

CONTROL NAME	CAPTION	INDEX	CHECKED	SHORTCUT KEY
mWindow	"&Window"			
mTile	"&Tile"			
mCascade	"&Cascade"			
mBar1	"-"			
mShowWindow	"Image &Data"	0		
mShowWindow	"Image &View"	1		
mBar3	"-"			
mShowTool	"Show Tool&Bar"		-1 'True	
mShowMenu	"Show &Menu"		-1 'True	

NOTE

Only the new code added to the project will be commented. If you need additional information regarding the other code, see How-To's 4.1 and 4.2 for a complete explanation.

7. Add the following code to the ImageTracker form:

```
Private Sub ImageTool_ButtonClick(ByVal Button As Button)

Select Case Button.Index

    Case 1
        '   Open the Image Database
        MenuOpenData

    Case 2

        '   Call the MenuNewImage function to get
        '   a new image
        MenuNewImage

    Case 3
        '   Exit the program
        MenuExit

    Case 4
        '   Move to the first record
        MenuBrowse 0

    Case 5
        '   Move to the last record
        MenuBrowse 1
```

continued on next page

continued from previous page

```
Case 6
    '  Move back a record
    MenuBrowse 2

Case 7
    '  Move forward a record
    MenuBrowse 3

Case 8
    '  Delete the current record
    '  of the result set
    MenuDelete

Case 9
    '  Set the View to fit in the Window
    SetView 0

Case 10
    '  Set the View to actual size
    SetView 1

Case 11
    '  Set the View to 50 %
    SetView 2

Case 12
    '  Set the View to 200 %
    SetView 3

Case 13
    '  Tile the windows
    MenuTile

Case 14
    '  Cascade the Windows
    MenuCascade

Case 15
    '  If the ImageData form is not
    '  visible then call the
    '  MenuOpenData function to open
    '  the database.  Otherwise, show
    '  the ImageData Window (0)
    If ImageData.Visible = False Then
        MenuOpenData
    Else
        MenuShowWindow 0
    End If

Case 16
    '  If the ImageData form is not
    '  visible then call the
    '  MenuOpenData function to open
    '  the database.  Otherwise, show
    '  the ImageView Window (1)
    If ImageData.Visible = False Then
        MenuOpenData
```

```
         Else
              MenuShowWindow 1
         End If

     Case 17
          '   Show or hide the Menu depending
          '   on the current setting.
          MenuShowMenu

   End Select

   End Sub
```

8. The following code checks to see whether the right mouse click was performed on the toolbar. If so, then the `mWindow` menu is shown over the toolbar. Note that this menu provides the option to hide the toolbar.

```
Private Sub ImageTool_MouseDown(Button As Integer,
➡Shift As Integer, X As Single, Y As Single)

'   Check for the right mouse
'   button click
If Button = vbPopupMenuRightButton Then

     '   If the ImageData form is not visible then
     '   show the popup menu for ImageTracker form.
     '   Otherwise show the pop up menu for the
     '   ImageData form.
     If ImageData.Visible = False Then
         Me.PopupMenu mWindow, vbPopupMenuCenterAlign, , ,
         ➡mShowTool
     Else
         ImageData.PopupMenu ImageData.mWindow,
         ➡vbPopupMenuCenterAlign, ,, ImageData.mShowTool
     End If

End If

End Sub

Private Sub MDIForm_Load()

'   Hide the ImageData form when
'   the MDI form is first loaded
ImageData.Hide

End Sub
```

9. The following code checks to see whether a right mouse click was performed on the MDI form. The context of the click in this case is important. If the image database has not yet been opened, then the `mFile` menu is shown to give the user the option of opening the database or exiting the program. Otherwise, the `mWindow` menu is shown to provide the user with the standard window menu options.

```
Private Sub MDIForm_MouseDown(Button As Integer,
➥Shift As Integer, X As Single, Y As Single)

'   If the ImageData form is not visible,
'   then show the File menu from the
'   ImageTracker form
If (Button = vbPopupMenuRightButton) And
➥(ImageData.Visible <> True) Then
    Me.PopupMenu mFile, vbPopupMenuCenterAlign, , , mOpenImage
    Exit Sub
End If

'   If the ImageData form is visible,
'   then show the Window menu from the
'   ImageData form
If (Button = vbPopupMenuRightButton) And
➥(ImageData.Visible = True) Then
    ImageData.PopupMenu ImageData.mWindow,
        ➥vbPopupMenuCenterAlign ', ,
        ➥, ImageData.mImageData
End If

End Sub


Private Sub MDIForm_QueryUnload(Cancel As Integer,
➥UnloadMode As Integer)

'   Call the MenuExit program to
'   end the program
MenuExit

End Sub

Private Sub MDIForm_Unload(Cancel As Integer)

'   Call the MenuExit program to
'   end the program
MenuExit

End Sub

Private Sub mExit_Click()

'   Call the MenuExit program to
'   end the program
MenuExit

End Sub

Private Sub mImageData_Click()

'   Call the MenuOpenData method to open the
'   Image database
MenuOpenData
```

```
End Sub

Private Sub mImageView_Click()

'   Call the MenuOpenData method to open the
'   Image database
MenuOpenData

End Sub

Private Sub mOpenImage_Click()

'   Call the MenuOpenData method to open the
'   Image database
MenuOpenData

End Sub

Private Sub mShowMenu_Click()

'   Show or hide the Menu
MenuShowMenu

End Sub

Private Sub mShowTool_Click()

'   Show or hide the Toolbar
MenuShowTool

End Sub
```

10. Add the following code to the **ImageView** form:

```
Public Sub SizeViewPict()

'   Allow for a small border
'   around the display picture
disppict.Top = 5
disppict.Left = 5
disppict.Width = Me.Width - 5
disppict.Height = Me.Height - 5

'   Set the view to the current
'   view option
SetView IView

End Sub

Private Sub DispPict_Paint()

'   Size the view picture
SizeViewPict

End Sub
```

11. The following code checks to see which mouse button was clicked on the display picture. If it was the right mouse button, then the `mView` menu is shown to provide the different viewing options for the image. If the left mouse button was clicked, then the `mViewSet` menu is shown to provide the user with the options of flipping the image horizontally or vertically.

```
Private Sub DispPict_MouseDown(Button As Integer,
➥Shift As Integer, X As Single, Y As Single)

'   If the right mouse button is selected, then
'   the different image size options are shown.  If
'   it is a left mouse click then the flip options
'   are shown
If Button = vbPopupMenuRightButton Then
    Me.PopupMenu mView, vbPopupMenuCenterAlign, , , mSize(0)
Else
    Me.PopupMenu mViewSet, vbPopupMenuCenterAlign
End If

End Sub
```

12. The flip menu options provide the user with the option of flipping the displayed image either horizontally or vertically. A check is done to ensure that only one of the flip options can be selected at any one point. The `SizeViewPict` routine is called to display the image in the new state.

```
Private Sub Flip_Click(Index As Integer)

'   When the flip menu is clicked, the
'   check on the menu is set appropriately
If flip(Index).Checked = False Then
    flip(Index).Checked = True
Else
    flip(Index).Checked = False
End If

'   It is important to ensure that only
'   a vertical or horizotal flip can be
'   performed.  Thus, the menu item that
'   was not clicked is unchecked.
If Index = 1 Then
    flip(0).Checked = False
Else
    flip(1).Checked = False
End If

'   Based on the selection,
'   the image is redisplayed.
SizeViewPict

End Sub

Private Sub Form_Load()
```

```
'  Initially set IView to 0.
IView = 1

'  Call the MenuBrowse function
'  to show the first record
MenuBrowse 1

End Sub

Private Sub Form_Unload(Cancel As Integer)

'  Cancel the unload.  We don't want the
'  form to be unloaded while the program is
'  running so that it does not have to be
'  re-initialized.  Instead, the form will be
'  minimized.
Cancel = -1
Me.WindowState = 1

End Sub

Private Sub mBrowse_Click(Index As Integer)

'  Browse the record set depending on the
'  menu option chosen.
MenuBrowse Index

End Sub

Private Sub mCascade_Click()

'  Cascade the windows
MenuCascade

'  Size the view picture after the cascade
SizeViewPict

End Sub

Private Sub mDelete_Click()

'  Call the MenuDelete function to
'  delete the selected record.
MenuDelete

End Sub

Private Sub mExit_Click()

'  Call the MenuExit function to
'  exit the program.
MenuExit

End Sub
```

continued on next page

continued from previous page

```
Private Sub mNewImage_Click()

'   Call the MenuNewImage function to get
'   a new image
MenuNewImage

End Sub

Private Sub mShowMenu_Click()

'   Show or hide the Menu
MenuShowMenu

End Sub

Private Sub mShowTool_Click()

'   Show or hide the toolbar
MenuShowTool

End Sub

Private Sub mShowWindow_Click(Index As Integer)

'   Call the MenuShowWindow function to show
'   the selected window.
MenuShowWindow Index

End Sub

Private Sub mTile_Click()

'   Call the menu tile function to
'   tile the windows
MenuTile

End Sub

Private Sub mSize_Click(Index As Integer)

'   Set the view depending on the menu option
'   selected
SetView Index

End Sub
```

13. Add the following code to the **ImageData** form. The **MouseDown** event of the form checks to see whether a right mouse click was performed on the form. If so, then the **mRecord** menu is shown to provide the user with options for browsing the records of the database.

```
Private Sub Form_MouseDown(Button As Integer, Shift As Integer,
➥X As Single, Y As Single)

If Button = vbPopupMenuRightButton Then
    '   Show the Record menu for moving
    '   through the image records in the
    '   database
    Me.PopupMenu mRecord, vbPopupMenuCenterAlign, , , mBrowse(3)

End If

End Sub

Private Sub Form_Resize()

Dim N As Integer

'   Resize the Image Info controls to
'   fit on the form when it is resized
For N = 1 To 4
    ImageData.ImageInfo(N).Width = ImageData.Width -
    ImageData.ImageInfo(N).Left - 300
Next N

End Sub

Private Sub Form_Unload(Cancel As Integer)

'   We don't want the form to be unloaded so that
'   it will not have to be re-initialized
Cancel = -1

'   Instead minimize the form
Me.WindowState = 1
End Sub

Private Sub mBrowse_Click(Index As Integer)

'   Browse the result set depending
'   on the menu selected
MenuBrowse Index

End Sub

Private Sub mCascade_Click()

'   Cascade the windows
MenuCascade

End Sub

Private Sub mDelete_Click()
```

continued on next page

continued from previous page

```
'   Delete the current record
'   of the result set
MenuDelete

End Sub

Private Sub mExit_Click()

'   Call the MenuExit method to
'   exit the program
MenuExit

End Sub

Private Sub mNewImage_Click()

'   Cal the MenuNewImage function to allow
'   the user to select a new image to add to the
'   database
MenuNewImage

End Sub

Private Sub mShowMenu_Click()

'   Show or hide the Menu
MenuShowMenu

End Sub

Private Sub mShowTool_Click()

'   Show or hide the toolbar
MenuShowTool

End Sub

Private Sub mShowWindow_Click(Index As Integer)

'   Call the MenuShowWindow function to show
'   the window selected
MenuShowWindow Index

End Sub

Private Sub mSize_Click(Index As Integer)

'   Set the View based on the menu
'   selection
SetView Index

End Sub

Private Sub mTile_Click()
```

```
'   Tile the windows
MenuTile

End Sub
```

14. Insert a new module into the program and save it as `MenLogic.bas`. Add the following code to the General Declarations section of the form:

```
'   StretchBlt will be used for the Image Viewer Private Declare
➡Function StretchBlt Lib "gdi32" (ByVal hdc As Long,
➡ByVal X As Long, ByVal Y As Long, ByVal nWidth As Long,
➡ByVal nHeight As Long, ByVal hSrcDC As Long,
➡ByVal xSrc As Long, ByVal ySrc As Long,
➡ByVal nSrcWidth As Long, ByValnSrcHeight As Long,
➡ByVal dwRop As Long) As Long

Const SRCCOPY = &HCC0020

'   IView globally stores the current view for
'   the image  I.E.  Fit in Window, 50%
Public IView As Integer

'   Handles ending the program when
'   users select exit from the menu
Public Sub MenuExit()
     End
End Sub

'   Handles tiling the windows
'   on the MDI form
Public Sub MenuTile()

'   Do a vertical tile
ImageTracker.Arrange vbTileVertical

End Sub

Public Sub MenuCascade()

'   Cascade the child forms
ImageTracker.Arrange vbCascade

End Sub
```

15. The `SetView` routine handles setting the view indicated by the index. Note that the menu option for the last view is unchecked, and the current index is checked. The current picture is cleared, and depending on the index, the image is copied from the `BackPict` picture box to the `DispPict` picture box. `StretchBlt` is used to perform the image stretching, or the `PaintPicture` method of the `Picture` object is used to perform the horizontal and vertical flips of the image. Finally, the palette from `BackPict` is copied to the display picture to ensure that the image colors are correct.

```
Public Sub SetView(Index)

'  When a new image view is selected,
'  the original menu selection is
'  unchecked
ImageView.mSize(IView).Checked = False
ImageData.mSize(IView).Checked = False

'  Set the new view to the index
'  parameter
IView = Index

'  Check the new menu option for the
'  selected view.
ImageData.mSize(IView).Checked = True
ImageView.mSize(IView).Checked = True

'  Clear the displayed picture
ImageView.disppict.Cls

'  Depending on the view selected, the
'  original image will be copied to the
'  display picture appropriately
Select Case IView

'  Note that for the vertical and
'  horizontal flips, the height or
'  width is set to a negative value
'  and the starting point is set to
'  the height or width for the image
'  to be displayed.

    Case 0   'Fit in the Window
        If ImageView.flip(0).Checked = True Then
            '   Flip Horizontal
            ImageView.disppict.PaintPicture
            ➥ImageView.backpict.Picture,
            ➥ImageView.disppict.ScaleWidth, 0, -1 *
            ➥ImageView.disppict.ScaleWidth,
            ImageView.disppict.ScaleHeight,
0, 0, ImageView.backpict.ScaleWidth,
 ImageView.backpict.ScaleHeight
        Else

            If ImageView.flip(1).Checked = True Then
                '   Flip Vertical
                ImageView.disppict.PaintPicture
                ➥ImageView.backpict.Picture,
                0, ImageView.disppict.ScaleHeight,
                ➥ImageView.disppict.ScaleWidth, -1 *
                ➥ImageView.disppict.ScaleHeight, 0, 0,
                ImageView.backpict.ScaleWidth,
                ImageView.backpict.ScaleHeight
            Else
```

```
                 '  Normal Display
                 Call StretchBlt(ImageView.disppict.hdc, 0, 0,
                 ➥ImageView.disppict.ScaleWidth,
                 ➥ImageView.disppict.ScaleHeight,
                 ➥ImageView.backpict.hdc, 0,
                 ➥ImageView.backpict.ScaleHeight, SRCCOPY)
             End If
         End If

    Case 1    'Actual Size
        If ImageView.flip(0).Checked = True Then
             '  Flip Horizontal
             ImageView.disppict.PaintPicture
             ➥ImageView.backpict.Picture,
             ➥ImageView.backpict.ScaleWidth, 0, -1 *
             ➥ImageView.backpict.ScaleWidth,
             ➥ImageView.backpict.ScaleHeight,
             ➥0, 0, ImageView.backpict.ScaleWidth,
             ➥ImageView.backpict.ScaleHeight
         Else
             If ImageView.flip(1).Checked = True Then
                  '  Flip Vertical
                  ImageView.disppict.PaintPicture
                  ➥ImageView.backpict.Picture,
                  ➥ImageView.backpict.ScaleWidth, -1 *
                  ➥ImageView.backpict.ScaleHeight, 0, 0,
                  ➥ImageView.backpict.ScaleWidth, _
                  ➥ImageView.backpict.ScaleHeight
             Else
                  '  Normal Display
                  Call StretchBlt(ImageView.disppict.hdc, 0, 0,
                     ➥ImageView.backpict.ScaleWidth * 0.5, _
                     ➥ImageView.backpict.ScaleHeight * 0.5, _
                     ➥ImageView.backpict.hdc, _
                     ➥0, 0, ImageView.backpict.ScaleWidth, _
                     ➥ImageView.backpict.ScaleHeight, SRCCOPY)
             End If
         End If

    Case 2 '50%
        If ImageView.flip(0).Checked = True Then
             '  Flip Horizontal
             ImageView.disppict.PaintPicture
             ➥ImageView.backpict.Picture,
               ImageView.backpict.ScaleWidth * 0.5, 0,
               ➥-1 * ImageView.backpict.ScaleWidth * 0.5,
               ➥ImageView.backpict.ScaleHeight * 0.5, 0, 0,
               ➥ImageView.backpict.ScaleWidth,
               ➥ImageView.backpict.ScaleHeight
         Else
             If ImageView.flip(1).Checked = True Then
                  '  Flip Vertical
```

continued on next page

continued from previous page

```
                    ImageView.disppict.PaintPicture
                    ➡ImageView.backpict.Picture,
                    ➡0, ImageView.backpict.ScaleHeight * 0.5,
                    ➡ImageView.backpict.ScaleHeight * 0.5, 0, 0,
                    ➡ImageView.backpict.ScaleWidth,
                    ➡ImageView.backpict.ScaleHeight
                Else
                    ' Normal Display
                    Call StretchBlt(ImageView.disppict.hdc, 0, 0,
                    ➡ImageView.backpict.ScaleWidth * 0.5,
                    ➡ImageView.backpict.ScaleHeight * 0.5,
                    ImageView.backpict.hdc,
                    ➡0, 0, ImageView.backpict.ScaleWidth,
                    ➡ImageView.backpict.ScaleHeight, SRCCOPY)
                End If
            End If

        Case 3 '200%
            If ImageView.flip(0).Checked = True Then
                ' Flip Horizontal
                ImageView.disppict.PaintPicture
                ➡ImageView.backpict.Picture,
                ➡ImageView.backpict.ScaleWidth * 2, 0,
                ➡-1 * ImageView.backpict.ScaleWidth * 2,
                ➡ImageView.backpict.ScaleHeight * 2, 0, 0,
                ➡ImageView.backpict.ScaleWidth,
                ➡ImageView.backpict.ScaleHeight
            Else
                If ImageView.flip(1).Checked = True Then
                    ' Flip Vertical
                    ImageView.disppict.PaintPicture
                    ➡ImageView.backpict.Picture,
                    ➡0, ImageView.backpict.ScaleHeight * 2,
                    ➡ImageView.backpict.ScaleWidth * 2, _
                    -1 * ImageView.backpict.ScaleHeight * 2, 0, 0,
                    ➡ImageView.backpict.ScaleWidth,
                    ➡ImageView.backpict.ScaleHeight
                Else
                    ' Normal Display
                    Call StretchBlt(ImageView.disppict.hdc, 0, 0,
                    ➡ImageView.backpict.ScaleWidth * 2,
                    ➡ImageView.backpict.ScaleHeight * 2,
                    ➡ImageView.backpict.hdc,
                    ➡0, 0, ImageView.backpict.ScaleWidth,
                    ➡ImageView.backpict.ScaleHeight, SRCCOPY)
                End If
            End If

    End Select

    ' Copy the palette from the holding picture
    ' to the displayed picture.  This ensures that
```

```vb
'   the image's colors are displayed correctly.
ImageView.disppict.Picture.hPal = ImageView.backpict.Picture.hPal

End Sub

Public Sub MenuShowWindow(Index)

'   Check to see which Windows (Form)
'   is to be displayed.
Select Case Index

    Case 0   'Show ImageData
        ImageData.Show
        ImageData.WindowState = 0

    Case 1   'Show ImageView
        ImageView.Show
        ImageView.WindowState = 0

End Select

End Sub

Public Sub MenuOpenData()

Dim Msg As String
Dim Style As Integer
Dim Title As String
Dim Response As Integer
Dim N As Integer

'   Set the Message, Style and Title
'   of the message box
Msg = "Do you want to open the Image Database ?"
Style = vbYesNo + vbQuestion + vbDefaultButton1
Title = "Open Image Database"

'   Retrieve the user's response
Response = MsgBox(Msg, Style, Title)

'   If it was a yes, then show the ImageData
'   and ImageView forms.  Also start the view
'   in Tiled mode.
If Response = vbYes Then
    ImageView.Show
    ImageData.Show
    MenuTile

    ImageTracker.ImageTool.Buttons(1).Visible = False

    For N = 2 To ImageTracker.ImageTool.Buttons.Count

        ImageTracker.ImageTool.Buttons(N).Visible = True
```

continued on next page

continued from previous page

```
        Next N

        '  Ensure that the menu item's the same
        '  for the ImageData and ImageView forms
        ImageView.mShowMenu.Checked = ImageTracker.mShowMenu.Checked
        ImageData.mShowMenu.Checked = ImageTracker.mShowMenu.Checked
        ImageView.mShowTool.Checked = ImageTracker.mShowTool.Checked
        ImageData.mShowTool.Checked = ImageTracker.mShowTool.Checked

    End If

    End Sub

    Public Sub MenuBrowse(MoveType)

    Dim ImageName As String

    '  Check the RowCount.  If it is 0
    '  then there are no images in the
    '  database.  We then need to show the New Image
    '  dialog to add the first image.
    If ImageData.MSRDC1.Resultset.RowCount = 0 Then
        MenuNewImage
        Exit Sub
    End If

    '  Depending on the type of move
    '  selected by the user, the result set
    '  is manipulated appropriately.
    Select Case MoveType

        Case 0  'Move to First Record
            ImageData.MSRDC1.Resultset.MoveFirst

        Case 1  'Move to Last Record
            ImageData.MSRDC1.Resultset.MoveLast

        Case 2  'Move to Previous Record
            ImageData.MSRDC1.Resultset.MovePrevious

        Case 3  'Move to Next Record
            ImageData.MSRDC1.Resultset.MoveNext

    End Select

    '  Check to see if the End of File or
    '  Beginning of File has been reached in
    '  the result set.  If so, then move first or
    '  last to ensure that a current record is
    '  always visible
    If ImageData.MSRDC1.Resultset.EOF = True Then
        ImageData.MSRDC1.Resultset.MoveLast
    End If
    If ImageData.MSRDC1.Resultset.BOF = True Then
```

```
        ImageData.MSRDC1.Resultset.MoveFirst
End If

'  Get the Image name from the database
ImageName = ImageData.MSRDC1.Resultset("FileName")

'  Depending on whether or not the image file
'  name is set, the picture display is
'  set appropriately.
If ImageName <> "" Then
    ImageView.backpict.Picture = LoadPicture(ImageName)
    SetView IView
Else
    ImageView.backpict.Picture = LoadPicture("")
    SetView IView
End If

End Sub

Public Sub MenuNewImage()

Dim ImageID As Integer
Dim ImageType As String

'  Ensure an Update is done
If ImageData.MSRDC1.Resultset.RowCount <> 0 Then
    ImageData.MSRDC1.Resultset.MoveNext
End If

'  Set the filter type of the dialog
'  box
ImageData.commondialog1.Filter = "Bitmaps (*.bmp)¦*.bmp¦Icons
➡(*.ico)¦*.ico¦ All Files (*.*)¦*.*"

'  Set the title of the dialog
ImageData.commondialog1.DialogTitle = "New Image File"

'  Set the filter index to that of the
'  bitmap
ImageData.commondialog1.FilterIndex = 1

'  Set the flags to ensure that the
'  file must exist
ImageData.commondialog1.Flags = cdlOFNFileMustExist

'  Show the dialog box
ImageData.commondialog1.ShowOpen

'  Check to see if the filename was set
If ImageData.commondialog1.filename <> "" Then

    '  Add a new record
    ImageData.MSRDC1.Resultset.AddNew
```

continued on next page

continued from previous page

```
'   Set the file name
ImageData.MSRDC1.Resultset("FileName") =
➡ImageData.commondialog1.filename

'   Set the file size
ImageData.MSRDC1.Resultset("FileSize") =
➡FileLen(ImageData.commondialog1.filename)

'   Get the extension of the image
ImageType = Right$(ImageData.commondialog1.filename, 3)

'   Set the file format depending on
'   the extension
Select Case UCase$(ImageType)

    Case "BMP"  'Standard bitmap
        ImageData.MSRDC1.Resultset("FileFormat") = "Bitmap"

    Case "ICO"  'Standard Icon
        ImageData.MSRDC1.Resultset("FileType") = "Icon"

End Select

'   Update the result set
ImageData.MSRDC1.Resultset.Update

'   Select SQL statement to get the
'   new result set
ImageData.MSRDC1.SQL = "select * from ImageData
➡order by ImageID"

'   Refresh the result set
ImageData.MSRDC1.Refresh

'   Move to the last record which was
'   just added.
MenuBrowse 1

End If

End Sub

Public Sub MenuDelete()

'   Delete the current record
ImageData.MSRDC1.Resultset.Delete

'   Move to the next record.
MenuBrowse 3

End Sub

Public Sub MenuShowTool()
```

```
'  If the toolbar is checked then
'  do the logic to hide the toolbar
If ImageTracker.mShowTool.Checked = True Then

    If ImageTracker.mShowMenu.Checked = False Then Exit Sub

    '  Hide the toolbar
    ImageTracker.ImageTool.Visible = False

    '  Change the menu check
    ImageTracker.mShowTool.Checked = False

    '  If the ImageData and ImageView forms
    '  are visible then handle setting their
    '  menu check marks.  If they are not
    '  visible, they are not loaded.
    If ImageData.Visible = True Then
        ImageData.mShowTool.Checked = False
        ImageView.mShowTool.Checked = False
    End If

Else

    '  Make the toolbar visible
    ImageTracker.ImageTool.Visible = True

    '  Change the menu check
    ImageTracker.mShowTool.Checked = True

    '  If the ImageData and ImageView forms
    '  are visible then handle setting their
    '  menu check marks.  If they are not
    '  visible, they are not loaded.
    If ImageData.Visible = True Then
        ImageData.mShowTool.Checked = True
        ImageView.mShowTool.Checked = True
    End If

End If

End Sub

Public Sub MenuShowMenu()

'  Check to see If the menu is already visible
If ImageTracker.mShowMenu.Checked = True Then

    '  If the tool bar is not visible,
    '  we do not want to also make the
    '  menu invisible
    If ImageTracker.ImageTool.Visible = False Then Exit Sub

    '  Make the ImageTracker menus
    '  invisible and set the menu
```

continued on next page

continued from previous page

```
                     '  check mark appropriately
                     ImageTracker.mFile.Visible = False
                     ImageTracker.mShowMenu.Checked = False
                     ImageTracker.mWindow.Visible = False

                     '  If the ImageData and ImageView forms
                     '  are visible then handle setting their
                     '  menu check marks and visible properties.
                     '  If they are not visible, they are not
                     '  loaded.
                     If ImageData.Visible = True Then
                         ImageData.mShowMenu.Checked = False
                         ImageView.mShowMenu.Checked = False
                         ImageView.mFile.Visible = False
                         ImageData.mFile.Visible = False
                         ImageData.mWindow.Visible = False
                         ImageView.mWindow.Visible = False
                         ImageData.mRecord.Visible = False
                         ImageView.mRecord.Visible = False
                         ImageData.mView.Visible = False
                         ImageView.mView.Visible = False
                         ImageView.mViewSet.Visible = False
                     End If

                 Else

                     '  Make the ImageTracker menus
                     '  visible and set the menu
                     '  check mark appropriately
                     ImageTracker.mFile.Visible = True
                     ImageTracker.mShowMenu.Checked = True
                     ImageTracker.mWindow.Visible = True

                     '  If the ImageData and ImageView forms
                     '  are visible then handle setting their
                     '  menu check marks and visible properties.
                     '  If they are not visible, they are not
                     '  loaded.
                     If ImageData.Visible = True Then
                         ImageData.mShowMenu.Checked = True
                         ImageView.mShowMenu.Checked = True
                         ImageData.mFile.Visible = True
                         ImageView.mFile.Visible = True
                         ImageData.mWindow.Visible = True
                         ImageView.mWindow.Visible = True
                         ImageData.mRecord.Visible = True
                         ImageView.mRecord.Visible = True
                         ImageView.mView.Visible = True
                         ImageData.mView.Visible = True
                         ImageView.mViewSet.Visible = True
                     End If

                 End If

                 End Sub
```

How It Works

The key to making pop-up menus useful to the user is providing an intuitive use for already provided menus. It should become a natural habit for the user to attempt a right mouse click to bring up menu options applicable to the context of where the click was performed. In this How-To, each major user interface element of the program is supported through right-click pop-up menus.

The `ImageView` form can be easily manipulated through both the left and right mouse buttons, which provide quick access to the different methods available to manipulate the images. Because there is no specific use for the left mouse click on the `ImageView` form, it is logical to provide additional pop-up menu access to the provided manipulation methods.

The `ImageData` form pop-up menu is intuitive. The options for manipulating the records in the database are displayed. But one additional right-click feature automatically is provided by the text controls on the form. You can right-click on the text boxes, and the control automatically provides the standard edit, copy, and paste menu options for manipulating the text in the control.

The How-To also provides the toolbar with a right-click pop-up menu, which shows the window menu options. This is useful for easily accessing all the user interface options of the program such as showing and hiding the toolbar and menus.

Comments

In this How-To, users might become so comfortable with the use of the toolbar and the pop-up menu support that they no longer want to see the menus of the forms at all, perhaps to maximize screen work space, for example. It would be a nice feature to allow users to turn on and off the interface features.

COMPLEXITY
ADVANCED

4.4 How do I...
Make an application drag-and-drop capable?

COMPATIBILITY: VISUAL BASIC 5 AND 6

Problem

So far my MDI application supports toolbars and pop-up menus. My users also want to be able to manipulate images directly by dragging them to appropriate locations. How do I support drag and drop both in the program interface and for outside objects dropped onto the application?

Technique

Providing drag-and-drop support for an application can be implemented in two ways. The first is the simple concept of dragging and dropping the user interface elements of an application around within the application. For example, you can drag and drop the MDI child windows of an MDI application. Or, as this How-To shows, you can drag and drop the toolbar to either the top or the bottom of the MDI window. The other type of drag and drop is support for dragging objects from outside the application onto your program. In this How-To, it would be logical to drop image files onto the program and have them automatically added to the database. Visual Basic does not provide explicit support for this kind of drag and drop. But with a few API calls and a special custom control, Msghook, this can be readily accomplished.

Steps

Open and run 4-4.VBP. Select the drag button on the toolbar to initiate the dragging of the toolbar. The toolbar can be dragged from the top to the bottom of the form or vice versa. Figure 4.8 shows the Windows Explorer with a file that has been dragged from the Explorer to the Image View window and added to the database.

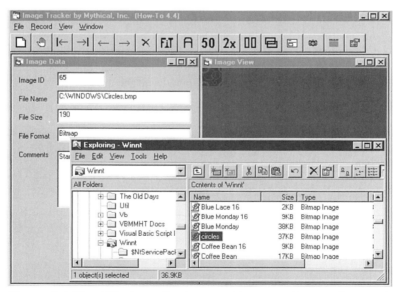

Figure 4.8 The Windows Explorer with a new image dragged and added to the database

Note that in this project, as shown in Figure 4.8, multiple images can be dragged to the Image View window, and all will be added to the database. However, users might want to look at a group of images without committing themselves to adding them to the database. You are going to add an Image Preview window for this purpose. Figure 4.9 shows the Preview window of the program, which supports images being dragged to it and displayed but not added to the database. Note that the image from the Preview window can be dragged to the Image View window and added to the database.

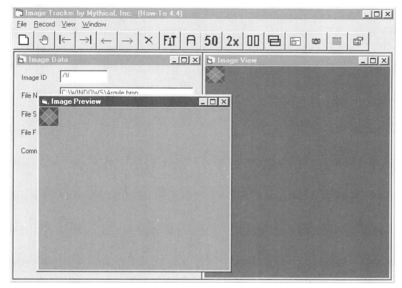

Figure 4.9 The Image Preview window

Complete the following steps to create this project:

1. Create a new project called 4-4.VBP. Add the objects and properties listed in Table 4.20 to the form and save the form as 4-4.FRM.

Table 4.20 The MDI form's objects and properties

OBJECT	PROPERTY	SETTING
MDIForm	Name	ImageTracker
	AutoShowChildren	0 'False
	BackColor	&H8000000C&
	Caption	"Image Tracker by Mythical, Inc. (How-To 4.4)"

continued on next page

Table 4.20 continued

OBJECT	PROPERTY	SETTING
Toolbar	Name	ImageTool
	Align	1 'Align Top
	Negotiate	-1 'True
	ImageList	"MDIButtons"
	ButtonWidth	926
	ButtonHeight	847
	AllowCustomize	0 'False
	NumButtons	18 (See ImageList for Button Icons)
	AlignSet	-1 'True
	Wrappable	0 'False
ImageList	Name	MDIButtons
	ImageWidth	28
	ImageHeight	26
	MaskColor	12632256
	NumImages	18
	i1	open.bmp
	i2	new.bmp
	i3	hand.bmp
	i4	first.bmp
	i5	last.bmp
	i6	prev.bmp
	i7	next.bmp
	i8	delete.bmp
	i9	fit.bmp
	i10	actual.bmp
	i11	50.bmp
	i12	2x.bmp
	i13	tile.bmp
	i14	cascade.bmp
	i15	data.bmp
	i16	camera.bmp
	i17	menu.bmp
	i18	prop.bmp

2. Add the menus shown in Table 4.21 to the ImageTracker form.

Table 4.21 The `ImageTracker` form's menus

CONTROL NAME	CAPTION	INDEX	CHECKED	SHORTCUT KEY
mFile	"&File"			
mOpenImage	"&Open Image Database"			
mBar	"-"			
mExit	"E&xit"			
mWindow	"&Window"			
mImageData	"Image &Data"			
mImageView	"Image &View"			
mBar3	"-"			
mShowTool	"Show Toolbar"		-1 'True	
mShowMenu	"Show Menu"		-1 'True	

3. Insert a new form into the project and save it as `IView.frm`. Add the objects and properties listed in Table 4.22 to the form.

Table 4.22 The image view form's objects and properties

OBJECT	PROPERTY	SETTING
Form	Name	ImageView
	Caption	"Image View"
	MDIChild	-1 'True
PictureBox	Name	DispPict
	BackColor	&H00C00000&
	BorderStyle	0 'None
	Picture	"pastel.bmp"
	ScaleMode	3 'Pixel
PictureBox	Name	BackPict
	AutoRedraw	-1 'True
	AutoSize	-1 'True
	BackColor	&H000000FF&
	BorderStyle	0 'None
	Picture	"pastel.bmp"
	ScaleMode	3 'Pixel
	Visible	0 'False
Msghook	Name	Msghook

4. Add the menus shown in Table 4.23 to the `ImageView` form.

Table 4.23 The `ImageView` form's menus

CONTROL NAME	CAPTION	INDEX	CHECKED		SHORTCUT KEY
mFile	"&File"				
mNewImage	"&New Image"				
mBar	"-"				
mExit	"E&xit"				
mRecord	"&Record"				
mBrowse	"&First"	0			F1
mBrowse	"&Last"	1			F2
mBrowse	"&Back"	2			F3
mBrowse	"For&ward"	3			F4
mBar2	"-"				
mDelete	"&Delete Record"				
mView	"&View"				
mSize	"&Fit in Window"	0			
mSize	"&Actual Size"	1	-1	'True	
mSize	"&50 Percent"	2			
mSize	"&200 Percent"	3			
mViewSet	"Viewer Settings"				
Flip	"Flip &Horizontal"	0			
Flip	"Flip &Vertical"	1			
mWindow	"&Window"				
mTile	"&Tile"				
mCascade	"&Cascade"				
mBar1	"-"				
mShowWindow	"Image &Data"	0			
mShowWindow	"Image &View"	1			
mPreview	"Image &Preview"				
mBar3	"-"				
mShowTool	"Show Tool&Bar"		-1	'True	
mShowMenu	"Show &Menu"		-1	'True	

5. Insert a new form into the project and save it as `IData.frm`. Add the objects and properties listed in Table 4.24 to the form.

Table 4.24 The `ImageData` form's objects and properties

OBJECT	PROPERTY	SETTING
Form	Name	ImageData
	Caption	"Image Data"
	MDIChild	-1 'True
	Visible	0 'False
TextBox	Name	ImageInfo
	DataField	"Comments"
	DataSource	"MSRDC1"
	Index	4
	MultiLine	-1 'True
TextBox	Name	ImageInfo
	DataField	"FileFormat"
	DataSource	"MSRDC1"
	Index	3
TextBox	Name	ImageInfo
	DataField	"FileSize"
	DataSource	"MSRDC1"
	Index	2
	Locked	-1 'True
TextBox	Name	ImageInfo
	DataField	"FileName"
	DataSource	"MSRDC1"
	Index	1
TextBox	Name	ImageInfo
	DataField	"ImageID"
	DataSource	"MSRDC1"
	Index	0
	Locked	-1 'True
CommonDialog	Name	CommonDialog1
	DefaultExt	".bmp"
	DialogTitle	"Find Image File"
	Filter	"*.bmp; *.wmf"
	FilterIndex	1
	InitDir	"c:\windows"

continued on next page

Table 4.24 continued

OBJECT	PROPERTY	SETTING
MSRDC	Name	MSRDC1
	Visible	0 'False
	DataSourceName	"Image Database"
	RecordSource	"select * from ImageData order by ImageID"
	RecordsetType	1
	KeysetSize	0
	ReadOnly	0 'False
	UserName	""
	Password	""
	CursorDriver	2
	EOFAction	1
	BOFAction	1
	Prompt	3
	LockType	3
Label	Name	ImageLabel
	AutoSize	-1 'True
	Caption	"Comments"
	DataSource	"MSRDC1"
	Index	4
Label	Name	ImageLabel
	AutoSize	-1 'True
	Caption	"File Format"
	DataSource	"MSRDC1"
	Index	3
Label	Name	ImageLabel
	AutoSize	-1 'True
	Caption	"File Size"
	DataSource	"MSRDC1"
	Index	2
Label	Name	ImageLabel
	AutoSize	-1 'True
	Caption	"File Name"
	DataSource	"MSRDC1"
	Index	1

OBJECT	PROPERTY	SETTING
Label	Name	ImageLabel
	AutoSize	-1 'True
	Caption	"Image ID"
	DataSource	"MSRDC1"
	Index	0

6. Add the menus shown in Table 4.25 to the ImageData form.

Table 4.25 The ImageData form's menus

CONTROL NAME	CAPTION	INDEX	CHECKED	SHORTCUT KEY
mFile	"&File"			
mNewImage	"&New Image"			
mBar	"-"			
mExit	"E&xit"			
mRecord	"&Record"			
mBrowse	"&First"	0		F1
mBrowse	"&Last"	1		F2
mBrowse	"&Back"	2		F3
mBrowse	"For&ward"	3		F4
mBar2	"-"			
mDelete	"&Delete Record"			
mView	"&View"			
mSize	"&Fit in Window"	0		
mSize	"&Actual Size"	1	-1 'True	
mSize	"&50 Percent"	2		
mSize	"&200 Percent"	3		
mWindow	"&Window"			
mTile	"&Tile"			
mCascade	"&Cascade"			
mBar1	"-"			
mShowWindow	"Image &Data"	0		
mShowWindow	"Image &View"	1		
mPreview	"Image &Preview"			
mBar3	"-"			
mShowTool	"Show Tool&Bar"		-1 'True	
mShowMenu	"Show &Menu"		-1 'True	

7. Insert a new form into the project and save it as `Preview.frm`. This form will become the Image Preview window. Add the objects and properties listed in Table 4.26 to the form.

Table 4.26 The `Preview` form's objects and properties

OBJECT	PROPERTY	SETTING
Form	Name	Preview
	Caption	"Image Preview"
PictureBox	Name	PrevPict
	Appearance	0 'Flat
	BackColor	&H00808080&
	BorderStyle	0 'None
	DragIcon	"pastel.bmp"
	DragMode	1 'Automatic
	ForeColor	&H80000008&
Msghook	Name	Msghook

NOTE

Only the new code added to the project will be commented. If you need additional information regarding the other code, see the previous How-To's for a complete explanation.

8. Add the following code to the `ImageTracker` form. The `ButtonClick` event of the toolbar handles calling the appropriate routines for each toolbar button. Note that the last button initiates the drag process for the toolbar control.

```
Private Sub ImageTool_ButtonClick(ByVal Button As Button)

Select Case Button.Index

    Case 1
        '   Open the Image Database
        MenuOpenData

    Case 2

        '   Call the MenuNewImage function to get
        '   a new image
        MenuNewImage
```

```
Case 3
    '  Exit the program
    MenuExit

Case 4
    '  Move to the first record
    MenuBrowse 0

Case 5
    '  Move to the last record
    MenuBrowse 1

Case 6
    '  Move back a record
    MenuBrowse 2

Case 7
    '  Move forward a record
    MenuBrowse 3

Case 8
    '  Delete the current record
    '  of the result set
    MenuDelete

Case 9
    '  Set the View to fit in the Window
    SetView 0

Case 10
    '  Set the View to actual size
    SetView 1

Case 11
    '  Set the View to 50 %
    SetView 2

Case 12
    '  Set the View to 200 %
    SetView 3

Case 13
    '  Tile the windows
    MenuTile

Case 14
    '  Cascade the Windows
    MenuCascade

Case 15
    '  If the ImageData form is not
    '  visible then call the
    '  MenuOpenData function to open
    '  the database.  Otherwise, show
```

continued on next page

continued from previous page

```
                        '  the ImageData Window (0)
                        If ImageData.Visible = False Then
                            MenuOpenData
                        Else
                            MenuShowWindow 0
                        End If

                Case 16
                        '  If the ImageData form is not
                        '  visible then call the
                        '  MenuOpenData function to open
                        '  the database.  Otherwise, show
                        '  the ImageView Window (1)
                        If ImageData.Visible = False Then
                            MenuOpenData
                        Else
                            MenuShowWindow 1
                        End If

                Case 17
                        '  Show or hide the Menu depending
                        '  on the current setting.
                        MenuShowMenu

                Case 18
                        '  Start the drag process for the
                        '  toolbar.
                        ImageTool.Drag

        End Select

        End Sub

        Private Sub ImageTool_MouseDown(Button As Integer,
        ➥Shift As Integer, X
        As Single, Y As Single)

        '  Check for the right mouse
        '  button click
        If Button = vbPopupMenuRightButton Then

                '  If the ImageData form is not visible then
                '  show the popup menu for ImageTracker form.
                '  Otherwise show the pop up menu for the
                '  ImageData form.
                If ImageData.Visible = False Then
                    Me.PopupMenu mWindow, vbPopupMenuCenterAlign, , ,
                    ➥mShowTool
                Else
                    ImageData.PopupMenu ImageData.mWindow,
                    ➥vbPopupMenuCenterAlign, ,
                      , ImageData.mShowTool
                End If

        End If

        End Sub
```

9. When the MDI form has a control dropped on it, which in this case is the toolbar, a check is done to see whether the toolbar is dropped on the top half or the bottom half of the MDI form. Depending on which half, the alignment of the toolbar is changed.

```
Private Sub MDIForm_DragDrop(Source As Control, X As Single,
➥Y As Single)

'   Check to see if the drop was on
'   the top or bottom half of the
'   MDI form
If (Y - (ImageTool.Height / 2)) > (ImageTracker.Height / 2) Then
    ImageTool.Align = 2
Else
    ImageTool.Align = 1
End If

End Sub


Private Sub MDIForm_Load()

'   Hide the ImageData form when
'   the MDI form is first loaded
ImageData.Hide

End Sub


Private Sub MDIForm_MouseDown(Button As Integer,
➥Shift As Integer, X As Single, Y As Single)

'   If the ImageData form is not visible,
'   then show the File menu from the
'   ImageTracker form
If (Button = vbPopupMenuRightButton) And
➥(ImageData.Visible <> True) Then
    Me.PopupMenu mFile, vbPopupMenuCenterAlign, , , mOpenImage
    Exit Sub
End If

'   If the ImageData form is visible,
'   then show the Window menu from the
'   ImageData form
If (Button = vbPopupMenuRightButton) And
➥(ImageData.Visible = True) Then
    ImageData.PopupMenu ImageData.mWindow,
        ➥vbPopupMenuCenterAlign ', ,
        , ImageData.mImageData
End If

End Sub


Private Sub MDIForm_QueryUnload(Cancel As Integer,
➥UnloadMode As Integer)
```

continued on next page

continued from previous page

```
'  Call the MenuExit program to
'  end the program
MenuExit

End Sub

Private Sub MDIForm_Unload(Cancel As Integer)

'  Call the MenuExit program to
'  end the program
MenuExit

End Sub

Private Sub mExit_Click()

'  Call the MenuExit program to
'  end the program
MenuExit

End Sub

Private Sub mImageData_Click()

'  Call the MenuOpenData method to open the
'  Image database
MenuOpenData

End Sub

Private Sub mImageView_Click()

'  Call the MenuOpenData method to open the
'  Image database
MenuOpenData

End Sub

Private Sub mOpenImage_Click()

'  Call the MenuOpenData method to open the
'  Image database
MenuOpenData

End Sub

Private Sub mShowMenu_Click()

'  Show or hide the Menu
MenuShowMenu

End Sub

Private Sub mShowTool_Click()
```

```
'   Show or hide the Toolbar
MenuShowTool

End Sub
```

10. Add the following code to the **ImageView** form. The **DragDrop** event of the **DispPict** control handles the drag and drop of the toolbar as well as the drop of a picture control from the preview picture. For the toolbar, a check is done to see which half of the display picture the toolbar has been dropped on, and the toolbar is aligned appropriately. If the toolbar is not the dropped object, then the only other object that can be dropped onto the picture is the preview image. In that case, the **PreviewFileName** public property of the **Preview** form is checked to see whether there is a current image loaded into the Preview window. If so, then the **DropNewImage** function is called.

```
Private Sub DispPict_DragDrop(Source As Control, X As Single,
➥Y As Single)

'   If the dropped control is the
'   toolbar then we need to do the
'   necessary checking to see if the
'   toolbar should be re-aligned
If Source.Name = "ImageTool" Then

        '   Check to see if the toolbar drop
        '   was on the top or bottom half of the
        '   picture box.  Note that the picture
        '   box is in pixel mode so we need to
        '   convert the coordinates to twips.
        If ((Y * Screen.TwipsPerPixelY) -
        ➥(ImageTracker.ImageTool.Height / 2))

            > (ImageTracker.Height / 2) Then
            ImageTracker.ImageTool.Align = 2
        Else
            ImageTracker.ImageTool.Align = 1
        End If

        Exit Sub

End If

'   Otherwise a new file should have
'   been dropped on the picture box
'   from the preview window.  We need
'   to check to ensure that there is
'   a picture file associated with the
'   preview.  If so then add the image to
'   the database.
If Preview.PreviewFileName <> "" Then
    DropNewImage Preview.PreviewFileName
End If

End Sub
```

11. The Show Preview menu option shows the Preview window.

```
Private Sub mPreview_Click()

'  Show the preview window
Preview.Show

End Sub
```

12. The Msghook control handles processing messages to the control's parent window. In this case, you will be checking for the WM_DROPFILES message, which indicates that a file has been dropped from the Windows Explorer. The DragQueryFile API function is first used to retrieve the number of files dragged from the Explorer. DragQueryFile is also used to return the filename of the specified dropped file. It is then checked to see whether it is a bitmap or an icon. If it is an image file, then the DropNewImage routine is called to add the image to the database.

```
Private Sub Msghook_Message(ByVal msg As Long,
➡ByVal wp As Long, ByVal lp As Long, result As Long)

Dim NumFiles As Integer
Dim Buffer As String 'Byte
Dim N As Integer
Dim NameLen As Integer

'  Set the buffer up to recieve the
'  filename
Buffer = Space$(256)

'  See if the drop file message was
'  sent
If msg = WM_DROPFILES Then

     '  Retrieve the number of files
     '  dropped.
     NumFiles = DragQueryFile(wp, -1&, Buffer, Len(Buffer))

     '  Loop through the files and add them to
     '  the image database.
     For N = 0 To (NumFiles - 1)

          '  Get the filename of the file and
          '  retrieve the length of the
          '  filename
          NameLen = DragQueryFile(wp, N, Buffer, 128)

          '  Check to see if the file is a
          '  bitmap or icon.
          If (UCase(Right((Left(Buffer, NameLen)), 3)) = "BMP")
          Or (UCase(Right((Left(Buffer, NameLen)), 3)) = "ICO") Then
```

```
                    '  Add the image to the database
                    DropNewImage Left(Buffer, NameLen)

            End If

        Next N

        ' Tell the system the drag is done
        Call DragFinish(wp)

        '  Set the result
        result = 0

    End If

End Sub

Public Sub SizeViewPict()

'   Allow for a small border
'   around the display picture
disppict.Top = 5
disppict.Left = 5
disppict.Width = Me.Width - 5
disppict.Height = Me.Height - 5

'  Set the view to the current
'  view option
SetView IView

End Sub

Private Sub DispPict_Paint()

'  Size the view picture
SizeViewPict

End Sub

Private Sub DispPict_MouseDown(Button As Integer,
➥Shift As Integer, X As Single, Y As Single)

'  If the right mouse button is selected, then
'  the different image size options are shown.  If
'  it is a left mouse click then the flip options
'  are shown
If Button = vbPopupMenuRightButton Then
    Me.PopupMenu mView, vbPopupMenuCenterAlign, , , mSize(0)
Else
    Me.PopupMenu mViewSet, vbPopupMenuCenterAlign
End If

End Sub
```

continued on next page

continued from previous page

```
Private Sub Flip_Click(Index As Integer)

'   When the flip menu is clicked, the
'   check on the menu is set appropriately
If flip(Index).Checked = False Then
    flip(Index).Checked = True
Else
    flip(Index).Checked = False
End If

'   It is important to ensure that only
'   a vertical or horizontal flip can be
'   performed.  Thus, the menu item that
'   was not clicked is unchecked.
If Index = 1 Then
    flip(0).Checked = False
Else
    flip(1).Checked = False
End If

'   Based on the selection,
'   the image is redisplayed.
SizeViewPict

End Sub
```

13. When the form is loaded, the `EnableFileDrop` routine is called to enable the form to accept the drop files message from the system. Also, the `Msghook` control is set up to handle the messages for the form and sets the control to receive the `WM_DROPFILES` message.

```
Private Sub Form_Load()

'   Enable the form to accept
'   file drops
EnableFileDrop Me.hwnd

'   Setup MsgHook control
Msghook.HwndHook = Me.hwnd
Msghook.Message(WM_DROPFILES) = True

'   Initially set IView to 0.
IView = 1

'   Call the MenuBrowse function
'   to show the first record
MenuBrowse 1

End Sub

Private Sub Form_Unload(Cancel As Integer)

'   Cancel the unload.  We don't want the
'   form to be unloaded while the program is
```

```vb
'   running so that it does not have to be
'   re-initialized.  Instead, the form will be
'   minimized.
Cancel = -1
Me.WindowState = 1

End Sub

Private Sub mBrowse_Click(Index As Integer)

'   Browse the record set depending on the
'   menu option chosen.
MenuBrowse Index

End Sub

Private Sub mCascade_Click()

'   Cascade the windows
MenuCascade

'   Size the view picture after the cascade
SizeViewPict

End Sub

Private Sub mDelete_Click()

'   Call the MenuDelete function to
'   delete the selected record.
MenuDelete

End Sub

Private Sub mExit_Click()

'   Call the MenuExit function to
'   exit the program.
MenuExit

End Sub

Private Sub mNewImage_Click()

'   Call the MenuNewImage function to get
'   a new image
MenuNewImage

End Sub

Private Sub mShowMenu_Click()

'   Show or hide the Menu
MenuShowMenu
```

continued on next page

continued from previous page

```
End Sub

Private Sub mShowTool_Click()

'   Show or hide the toolbar
MenuShowTool

End Sub

Private Sub mShowWindow_Click(Index As Integer)

'   Call the MenuShowWindow function to show
'   the selected window.
MenuShowWindow Index

End Sub

Private Sub mTile_Click()

'   Call the menu tile function to
'   tile the windows
MenuTile

End Sub

Private Sub mSize_Click(Index As Integer)

'   Set the view depending on the menu option
'   selected
SetView Index

End Sub
```

14. Add the following code to the **ImageData** form:

```
Private Sub Form_MouseDown(Button As Integer,
➥Shift As Integer, X As Single, Y As Single)

If Button = vbPopupMenuRightButton Then
    '   Show the Record menu for moving
    '   through the image records in the
    '   database
    Me.PopupMenu mRecord, vbPopupMenuCenterAlign, , , mBrowse(3)

End If

End Sub

Private Sub Form_Resize()

Dim n As Integer

'   Resize the Image Info controls to
'   fit on the form when it is resized
For n = 1 To 4
    ImageData.ImageInfo(n).Width = ImageData.Width -
```

```
        ImageData.ImageInfo(n).Left - 300
    Next n

End Sub

Private Sub Form_Unload(Cancel As Integer)

'   We don't want the form to be unloaded so that
'   it will not have to be re-initialized

Cancel = -1

'   Instead minimize the form
Me.WindowState = 1

End Sub

Private Sub mBrowse_Click(Index As Integer)

'   Browse the result set depending
'   on the menu selected
MenuBrowse Index

End Sub

Private Sub mCascade_Click()

'   Cascade the windows
MenuCascade

End Sub

Private Sub mDelete_Click()

'   Delete the current record
'   of the result set
MenuDelete

End Sub

Private Sub mExit_Click()

'   Call the MenuExit method to
'   exit the program
MenuExit

End Sub

Private Sub mNewImage_Click()

'   Cal the MenuNewImage function to allow
'   the user to select a new image to add to the
'   database
MenuNewImage

End Sub
```

15. The Show Preview menu option handles showing the Preview window.

```
Private Sub mPreview_Click()

'   Show the Preview form
Preview.Show

End Sub

Private Sub mShowMenu_Click()

'   Show or hide the Menu
MenuShowMenu

End Sub

Private Sub mShowTool_Click()

'   Show or hide the toolbar
MenuShowTool

End Sub

Private Sub mShowWindow_Click(Index As Integer)

'   Call the MenuShowWindow function to show
'   the window selected
MenuShowWindow Index

End Sub

Private Sub mSize_Click(Index As Integer)

'   Set the View based on the menu
'   selection
SetView Index

End Sub

Private Sub mTile_Click()

'   Tile the windows
MenuTile

End Sub
```

16. Add the following code to the **Preview** form. The **PreviewFileName** public variable holds the name of the dropped image onto the Preview window. This is used when the preview picture is dropped onto the database viewer. The filename in the variable is used as a reference to the image to be tracked.

```
'   Public property that will indicate
'   what filename is associated with
'   the preview

Public PreviewFileName As String
```

17. When the form is loaded, the `EnableFileDrop` routine is called to enable the form to accept the drop files message from the system. Also, the `Msghook` control is set up to handle the messages for the `Preview` form and set the control to receive the `WM_DROPFILES` message.

```
Private Sub Form_Load()

'   Enable the preview to accept
'   file drag and drop
EnableFileDrop Me.hwnd

'   Setup the MsgHook control
Msghook.HwndHook = Me.hwnd
Msghook.Message(WM_DROPFILES) = True

'   Move the preview picture to the
'   top left
PrevPict.Top = 0
PrevPict.Left = 0

'   Set the preview picture width
'   and height
PrevPict.Width = Preview.Width
PrevPict.Height = Preview.Height

End Sub

Private Sub Form_Resize()

'   When the form is resized,
'   resize the picture
PrevPict.Width = Preview.Width
PrevPict.Height = Preview.Height

End Sub

Private Sub Form_Unload(Cancel As Integer)

'   When the preview is unloaded,
'   make sure the ImageTracker form
'   is visible
ImageTracker.Show

End Sub
```

18. The `Msghook` control handles processing messages to the control's parent window. In this case, you are checking for the `WM_DROPFILES` message, which indicates that a file has been dropped from the Windows Explorer. The `DragQueryFile` API function is first used to retrieve the number of files dragged from the Explorer. `DragQueryFile` is also used to return the filename of the specified dropped file. It is then checked to see whether it is a bitmap or an icon. If it is an image file, then the `DropNewImage` routine is called to add the image to the database.

```
Private Sub Msghook_Message(ByVal msg As Long,
➡ByVal wp As Long, ByVal lp As Long, result As Long)

Dim NumFiles As Integer
Dim Buffer As String 'Byte
Dim N As Integer
Dim NameLen As Integer

'   Set the buffer up to receive the
'   filename
Buffer = Space$(256)

'   See if the drop file message was
'   sent
If msg = WM_DROPFILES Then

    '   Retrieve the number of files
    '   dropped.
    NumFiles = DragQueryFile(wp, -1&, Buffer, Len(Buffer))

    '   Get the filename of the file and
    '   retrieve the length of the
    '   filename
    NameLen = DragQueryFile(wp, N, Buffer, 128)

    '   Check to see if the file is a
    '   bitmap or icon.
    If (UCase(Right((Left(Buffer, NameLen)), 3)) = "BMP") Or
    (UCase(Right((Left(Buffer, NameLen)), 3)) = "ICO") Then

        '   Load the picture into the preview
        PrevPict.Picture = LoadPicture(Left(Buffer, NameLen))

        '   Set the filename of the form
        PreviewFileName = Left(Buffer, NameLen)

    End If

    ' Tell the system the drag is done.
    Call DragFinish(wp)

    '   Set the result
    result = 0

End If

End Sub
```

19. Insert a new module into the project and save it as MenLogic.bas. This
code handles most of the menu logic for the ImageData and ImageView
forms.

```
'   StretchBlt will be used for the Image Viewer
Private Declare Function StretchBlt Lib "gdi32"
➡(ByVal hdc As Long, ByVal X As Long, ByVal Y As Long,
➡ByVal nWidth As Long, ByVal nHeight As Long,
```

```
➥ByVal hSrcDC As Long, ByVal xSrc As Long,
➥ByVal ySrc As Long,
ByVal nSrcWidth As Long, ByVal nSrcHeight As Long,
➥ByVal dwRop As Long)
As Long

Const SRCCOPY = &HCC0020

'    IView globally stores the current view for
'    the image  I.E.  Fit in Window, 50%
Public IView As Integer

'    Handles ending the program when
'    users select exit from the menu
Public Sub MenuExit()
    End
End Sub

'    Handles tiling the windows
'    on the MDI form
Public Sub MenuTile()

'    Do a vertical tile
ImageTracker.Arrange vbTileVertical

End Sub

Public Sub MenuCascade()

'    Cascade the child forms
ImageTracker.Arrange vbCascade

End Sub

Public Sub SetView(Index)

'    When a new image view is selected,
'    the original menu selection is
'    unchecked
ImageView.mSize(IView).Checked = False
ImageData.mSize(IView).Checked = False

'    Set the new view to the index
'    parameter
IView = Index

'    Check the new menu option for the
'    selected view.
ImageData.mSize(IView).Checked = True
ImageView.mSize(IView).Checked = True

'    Clear the displayed picture
ImageView.disppict.Cls

ImageView.disppict.Picture.hPal =
➥ImageView.backpict.Picture.hPal
```

continued on next page

continued from previous page

```
'   Depending on the view selected, the
'   original image will be copied to the
'   display picture appropriately
Select Case IView

'   Note that for the vertical and
'   horizontal flips, the height or
'   width is set to a negative value
'   and the starting point is set to
'   the height or width for the image
'   to be displayed.

    Case 0   'Fit in the Window
        If ImageView.flip(0).Checked = True Then
            '   Flip Horizontal
            ImageView.disppict.PaintPicture
            ➥ImageView.backpict.Picture,
            ➥ImageView.disppict.ScaleWidth, 0, -1 *
            ➥ImageView.disppict.ScaleWidth,
            ➥ImageView.disppict.ScaleHeight,
          0, 0, ImageView.backpict.ScaleWidth,
            ImageView.backpict.ScaleHeight
        Else

            If ImageView.flip(1).Checked = True Then
                '   Flip Vertical
                ImageView.disppict.PaintPicture
                  ➥ImageView.backpict.Picture,
                  ➥0, ImageView.disppict.ScaleHeight,
                  ➥ImageView.disppict.ScaleWidth, -1 *
                  ➥ImageView.disppict.ScaleHeight, 0, 0,
                  ➥ImageView.backpict.ScaleWidth,
                  ➥ImageView.backpict.ScaleHeight
            Else
                '   Normal Display
                Call StretchBlt(ImageView.disppict.hdc, 0, 0,
                  ➥ImageView.disppict.ScaleWidth,
                  ➥ImageView.disppict.ScaleHeight,
                  ➥ImageView.backpict.hdc, 0, 0,
                  ➥ImageView.backpict.ScaleWidth,
                  ➥ImageView.backpict.ScaleHeight, SRCCOPY)
            End If
        End If

    Case 1   'Actual Size
        If ImageView.flip(0).Checked = True Then
            '   Flip Horizontal
            ImageView.disppict.PaintPicture
            ➥ImageView.backpict.Picture,
            ➥ImageView.backpict.ScaleWidth, 0,
            ➥-1 * ImageView.backpict.ScaleWidth,
            ➥ImageView.backpict.ScaleHeight, 0, 0,
            ➥ImageView.backpict.ScaleWidth,
            ➥ImageView.backpict.ScaleHeight
        Else
            If ImageView.flip(1).Checked = True Then
                '   Flip Vertical
```

```
            ImageView.disppict.PaintPicture
                ➥ImageView.backpict.Picture, 0,
                ➥ImageView.backpict.ScaleHeight,
                ➥ImageView.backpict.ScaleWidth, -1 *
                ➥ImageView.backpict.ScaleHeight, 0, 0,
                ➥ImageView.backpict.ScaleWidth,
                ➥ImageView.backpict.ScaleHeight
        Else
            '  Normal Display
            Call StretchBlt(ImageView.disppict.hdc, 0, 0,
                ➥ImageView.backpict.ScaleWidth,
                ➥ImageView.backpict.ScaleHeight,
                ➥ImageView.backpict.hdc, 0, 0,
                ➥ImageView.backpict.ScaleWidth,
                ➥ImageView.backpict.ScaleHeight, SRCCOPY)
        End If
    End If

Case 2 '50%
    If ImageView.flip(0).Checked = True Then
        '  Flip Horizontal
        ImageView.disppict.PaintPicture
        ➥ImageView.backpict.Picture,
          ImageView.backpict.ScaleWidth * 0.5, 0,
            ➥-1 * ImageView.backpict.ScaleWidth *0.5,
        ➥ImageView.backpict.ScaleHeight * 0.5, 0, 0,
        ➥ImageView.backpict.ScaleWidth,
        ➥ImageView.backpict.ScaleHeight
    Else
        If ImageView.flip(1).Checked = True Then
            '  Flip Vertical
            ImageView.disppict.PaintPicture
            ➥ImageView.backpict.Picture, 0,
            ➥ImageView.backpict.ScaleHeight * 0.5,
              ImageView.backpict.ScaleWidth * 0.5,
                ➥-1 * ImageView.backpict.ScaleHeight *
                ➥0.5, 0, 0,
                ➥ImageView.backpict.ScaleWidth,
                ➥ImageView.backpict.ScaleHeight
        Else
            '  Normal Display
            Call StretchBlt(ImageView.disppict.hdc, 0, 0,
                ➥ImageView.backpict.ScaleWidth * 0.5,
                ➥ImageView.backpict.ScaleHeight * 0.5,
                ➥ImageView.backpict.hdc, 0, 0,
                ➥ImageView.backpict.ScaleWidth,
                ➥ImageView.backpict.ScaleHeight, SRCCOPY)
        End If
    End If

Case 3 '200%
    If ImageView.flip(0).Checked = True Then
        '  Flip Horizontal
        ImageView.disppict.PaintPicture
        ➥ImageView.backpict.Picture,
          ➥ImageView.backpict.ScaleWidth * 2, 0,
```

continued on next page

continued from previous page

```
                                    ➥-1 * ImageView.backpict.ScaleWidth * 2,
                                    ➥ImageView.backpict.ScaleHeight * 2, 0, 0,
                                    ➥ImageView.backpict.ScaleWidth,
                                    ➥ImageView.backpict.ScaleHeight
                    Else
                        If ImageView.flip(1).Checked = True Then
                            '  Flip Vertical
                            ImageView.disppict.PaintPicture
                              ImageView.backpict.Picture, 0,
                              ➥ImageView.backpict.ScaleHeight * 2,
                              ➥ImageView.backpict.ScaleWidth * 2,
                              ➥-1 * ImageView.backpict.ScaleHeight *
                              ➥2, 0, 0,
                              ➥ImageView.backpict.ScaleWidth,
                              ➥ImageView.backpict.ScaleHeight
                        Else
                            '  Normal Display
                            Call StretchBlt(ImageView.disppict.hdc, 0, 0,
                              ImageView.backpict.ScaleWidth * 2,
                              ➥ImageView.backpict.ScaleHeight * 2,
                              ➥ImageView.backpict.hdc,
                              ➥0, 0, ImageView.backpict.ScaleWidth,
                              ➥ImageView.backpict.ScaleHeight, SRCCOPY)
                        End If
                    End If

            End Select

            '  Copy the palette from the holding picture
            '  to the displayed picture.  This ensures that
            '  the images colors are displayed correctly.
            ImageView.disppict.Picture.hPal =
            ➥ImageView.backpict.Picture.hPal

            End Sub

            Public Sub MenuShowWindow(Index)

            '  Check to see which Windows (Form)
            '  is to be displayed.
            Select Case Index

                Case 0   'Show ImageData
                    ImageData.Show
                    ImageData.WindowState = 0

                Case 1   'Show ImageView
                    ImageView.Show
                    ImageView.WindowState = 0

            End Select

            End Sub

            Public Sub MenuOpenData()

            Dim msg As String
```

```
Dim Style As Integer
Dim Title As String
Dim Response As Integer
Dim N As Integer

'  Set the Message, Style and Title
'  of the message box
msg = "Do you want to open the Image Database ?"
Style = vbYesNo + vbQuestion + vbDefaultButton1
Title = "Open Image Database"

'  Retrieve the users response
Response = MsgBox(msg, Style, Title)

'  If it was a yes, then show the ImageData
'  and ImageView forms.  Also start the view
'  in Tiled mode.
If Response = vbYes Then
    ImageView.Show
    ImageData.Show
    MenuTile

    ImageTracker.ImageTool.Buttons(1).Visible = False

    For N = 2 To ImageTracker.ImageTool.Buttons.Count

        ImageTracker.ImageTool.Buttons(N).Visible = True

    Next N

    '  Ensure that the menu item's the same
    '   for the ImageData and ImageView forms
    ImageView.mShowMenu.Checked = ImageTracker.mShowMenu.Checked
    ImageData.mShowMenu.Checked = ImageTracker.mShowMenu.Checked
    ImageView.mShowTool.Checked = ImageTracker.mShowTool.Checked
    ImageData.mShowTool.Checked = ImageTracker.mShowTool.Checked

End If

End Sub

Public Sub MenuBrowse(MoveType)

Dim ImageName As String

'  Check the RowCount.  If it is 0
'  then there are no images in the
'  database.  We then need to show the New Image
'  dialog to add the first image.
If ImageData.MSRDC1.Resultset.RowCount = 0 Then
    MenuNewImage
    Exit Sub
End If

'  Depending on the type of move
'  selected by the user, the result set
```

continued on next page

continued from previous page

```
'  is manipulated appropriately.
Select Case MoveType

    Case 0  'Move to First Record
        ImageData.MSRDC1.Resultset.MoveFirst

    Case 1  'Move to Last Record
        ImageData.MSRDC1.Resultset.MoveLast

    Case 2  'Move to Previous Record
        ImageData.MSRDC1.Resultset.MovePrevious

    Case 3  'Move to Next Record
        ImageData.MSRDC1.Resultset.MoveNext

End Select

'  Check to see if the End of File or
'  Beginning of File has been reached in
'  the result set.  If so, then move first or
'  last to ensure that a current record is
'  always visible
If ImageData.MSRDC1.Resultset.EOF = True Then
    ImageData.MSRDC1.Resultset.MoveLast
End If

If ImageData.MSRDC1.Resultset.BOF = True Then
    ImageData.MSRDC1.Resultset.MoveFirst
End If

'  Get the Image name from the database
ImageName = ImageData.MSRDC1.Resultset("FileName")

'  Depending on whether or not the image file
'  name is set, the picture display is
'  set appropriately.
If ImageName <> "" Then
    ImageView.backpict.Picture = LoadPicture(ImageName)
    SetView IView
Else
    ImageView.backpict.Picture = LoadPicture("")
    SetView IView
End If

End Sub

Public Sub MenuNewImage()

Dim ImageID As Integer
Dim ImageType As String

'  Ensure an Update is done
If ImageData.MSRDC1.Resultset.RowCount <> 0 Then
```

```
      ImageData.MSRDC1.Resultset.MoveNext
End If

'  Set the filter type of the dialog
'  box
ImageData.commondialog1.Filter = _
  "Bitmaps (*.bmp)¦*.bmp¦Icons
  ➥(*.ico)¦*.ico¦All Files (*.*)¦*.*"

'  Set the title of the dialog
ImageData.commondialog1.DialogTitle = "New Image File"

'  Set the filter index to that of the
'  bitmap
ImageData.commondialog1.FilterIndex = 1

'  Set the flags to ensure that the
'  file must exist
ImageData.commondialog1.Flags = cdlOFNFileMustExist

'  Show the dialog box
ImageData.commondialog1.ShowOpen

'  Check to see if the filename was set
If ImageData.commondialog1.FileName <> "" Then

    '  Add a new record
    ImageData.MSRDC1.Resultset.AddNew

    '  Set the file name
    ImageData.MSRDC1.Resultset("FileName") =
    ImageData.commondialog1.FileName

    '  Set the file size
    ImageData.MSRDC1.Resultset("FileSize") =
      FileLen(ImageData.commondialog1.FileName)

    '  Get the extension of the image
    ImageType = Right$(ImageData.commondialog1.FileName, 3)

    '  Set the file format depending on
    '  the the extension
    Select Case UCase$(ImageType)

        Case "BMP"  'Standard bitmap
            ImageData.MSRDC1.Resultset("FileFormat") = "Bitmap"

        Case "ICO"  'Standard Icon
            ImageData.MSRDC1.Resultset("FileType") = "Icon"

    End Select

    '  Update the result set
    ImageData.MSRDC1.Resultset.Update
```

continued on next page

continued from previous page

```
              '  Select SQL statement to get the
              '  new result set
              ImageData.MSRDC1.SQL = "select * from ImageData
              ➥order by ImageID"

              '  Refresh the result set
              ImageData.MSRDC1.Refresh

              '  Move to the last record which was
              '  just added.
              MenuBrowse 1

      End If

      End Sub

      Public Sub MenuDelete()

      '  Delete the current record
      ImageData.MSRDC1.Resultset.Delete

      '  Move to the next record.
      MenuBrowse 3

      End Sub

      Public Sub MenuShowTool()

      '  If the toolbar is checked then
      '  do the logic to hide the toolbar
      If ImageTracker.mShowTool.Checked = True Then

          If ImageTracker.mShowMenu.Checked = False Then Exit Sub

          '  Hide the toolbar
          ImageTracker.ImageTool.Visible = False

          '  Change the menu check
          ImageTracker.mShowTool.Checked = False

          '  If the ImageData and ImageView forms
          '  are visible then handle setting their
          '  menu check marks.  If they are not
          '  visible, they are not loaded.
          If ImageData.Visible = True Then
             ImageData.mShowTool.Checked = False
             ImageView.mShowTool.Checked = False
          End If

      Else

          '  Make the toolbar visible
          ImageTracker.ImageTool.Visible = True
```

```
        '  Change the menu check
        ImageTracker.mShowTool.Checked = True

        '  If the ImageData and ImageView forms
        '  are visible then handle setting their
        '  menu check marks.  If they are not
        '  visible, they are not loaded.
        If ImageData.Visible = True Then
            ImageData.mShowTool.Checked = True
            ImageView.mShowTool.Checked = True
        End If

    End If

End Sub

Public Sub MenuShowMenu()

'  Check to see If the menu is already visible
If ImageTracker.mShowMenu.Checked = True Then

    '  If the tool bar is not visible,
    '  we do not want to also make the
    '  menu invisible
    If ImageTracker.ImageTool.Visible = False Then Exit Sub

    '  Make the ImageTracker menus
    '  invisible and set the menu
    '  check mark appropriately
    ImageTracker.mFile.Visible = False
    ImageTracker.mShowMenu.Checked = False
    ImageTracker.mWindow.Visible = False

    '  If the ImageData and ImageView forms
    '  are visible then handle setting their
    '  menu check marks and visible properties.
    '  If they are not visible, they are not
    '  loaded.
    If ImageData.Visible = True Then
        ImageData.mShowMenu.Checked = False
        ImageView.mShowMenu.Checked = False
        ImageView.mFile.Visible = False
        ImageData.mFile.Visible = False
        ImageData.mWindow.Visible = False
        ImageView.mWindow.Visible = False
        ImageData.mRecord.Visible = False
        ImageView.mRecord.Visible = False
        ImageData.mView.Visible = False
        ImageView.mView.Visible = False
        ImageView.mViewSet.Visible = False
    End If

Else

    '  Make the ImageTracker menus
    '  visible and set the menu
```

continued on next page

continued from previous page

```
'  check mark appropriately
   ImageTracker.mFile.Visible = True
   ImageTracker.mShowMenu.Checked = True
   ImageTracker.mWindow.Visible = True

'  If the ImageData and ImageView forms
'  are visible then handle setting their
'  menu check marks and visible properties.
'  If they are not visible, they are not
'  loaded.
   If ImageData.Visible = True Then
      ImageData.mShowMenu.Checked = True
      ImageView.mShowMenu.Checked = True
      ImageData.mFile.Visible = True
      ImageView.mFile.Visible = True
      ImageData.mWindow.Visible = True
      ImageView.mWindow.Visible = True
      ImageData.mRecord.Visible = True
      ImageView.mRecord.Visible = True
      ImageView.mView.Visible = True
      ImageData.mView.Visible = True
      ImageView.mViewSet.Visible = True
   End If

End If

End Sub
```

20. The `DropNewImage` routine handles adding the newly dropped image to the database. First, the record pointer in the database is moved to the next record, which ensures that the update is done for the current record. Then a new record is added to the database and the different fields set to the Image file information.

```
Public Sub DropNewImage(FileName)

Dim ImageID As Integer
Dim ImageType As String

'  Ensure an Update is done
ImageData.MSRDC1.Resultset.MoveNext

'  Add a new record
ImageData.MSRDC1.Resultset.AddNew

'  Set the file name
ImageData.MSRDC1.Resultset("FileName") = FileName

'  Set the file size
ImageData.MSRDC1.Resultset("FileSize") = FileLen(FileName)

'  Get the extension of the image
ImageType = Right$(FileName, 3)
```

```
'  Set the file format depending on
'  the extension
Select Case UCase$(ImageType)

    Case "BMP"  'Standard bitmap
        ImageData.MSRDC1.Resultset("FileFormat") = "Bitmap"

    Case "ICO"  'Standard Icon
        ImageData.MSRDC1.Resultset("FileType") = "Icon"

End Select

'  Update the result set
ImageData.MSRDC1.Resultset.Update

'  Select SQL statement to get the
'  new result set
ImageData.MSRDC1.SQL = "select *
➡from ImageData order by ImageID"

'  Refresh the result set
ImageData.MSRDC1.Refresh

'  Move to the last record which was
'  just added.
MenuBrowse 1

End Sub
```

21. Insert a new module into the project and save it as **Dropfile.bas**. The appropriate API functions are declared for enabling the Visual Basic forms to accept the file drag messages from the system. See the "How It Works" section for further details.

```
'  Declare the API file functions
'  and constants for the file drag
'  and drop
Declare Function GetWindowLong Lib "user32" Alias
➡"GetWindowLongA" (ByVal hwnd As Long,
➡ByVal nIndex As Long) As Long

Declare Function SetWindowLong Lib "user32" Alias
➡"SetWindowLongA" (ByVal hwnd As Long,
➡ByVal nIndex As Long, ByVal dwNewLong As Long) As Long

Declare Sub DragAcceptFiles Lib "shell32.dll"
➡(ByVal hwnd As Long, ByVal
fAccept As Long)

Declare Sub DragFinish Lib "shell32.dll" (ByVal HDROP As Long)

Declare Function DragQueryFile Lib "shell32.dll" Alias
➡"DragQueryFileA" (ByVal HDROP As Long,
```

continued on next page

continued from previous page

```
➥ByVal UINT As Long, ByVal lpStr As String,
➥ByVal ch As Long) As Long

Public Const GWL_EXSTYLE = (-20)
Public Const WS_EX_ACCEPTFILES = &H10&
Public Const WM_DROPFILES = &H233
```

22. The `EnableFileDrop` routine handles enabling the Visual Basic forms to accept the drag file messages from the system. First, the window style for the form is retrieved. Then the style is changed to accept dropped files by using the `SetWindowLong` API. The `DragAcceptFiles` API function is used to indicate to the system that the form can handle dropped files.

```
Sub EnableFileDrop(hwnd As Long)

Dim Style As Long

'  Get the Window style
Style = GetWindowLong(hwnd, GWL_EXSTYLE)

'  Set to the form to accept
'  dropped files
Style = SetWindowLong(hwnd, GWL_EXSTYLE,
➥Style Or WS_EX_ACCEPTFILES)

'  Indicate to the system that
'  dragged files will be accepted
'  by the form
DragAcceptFiles hwnd, True

End Sub
```

How It Works

The drag-and-drop user interface feature provides an intuitive method for the user to both preview and add images to the database. The Windows Explorer is a natural and familiar interface for the user to browse the file system. If the user has many images to add to the database, simply using the New Image menu option for adding files would be cumbersome. With the Windows Explorer, multiple files can be dragged to the `ImageView` form and added to the database. In fact, with the implementation in this How-To, all the files from a directory can be dragged to the viewer, and only the `.BMP` and `.ICO` files will be added to the database.

The Preview window also provides a simple way of viewing image files without first adding them to the database. If the user wants to add the image to the database, then the user can drag the picture control on the Preview window to the Image View window, which then adds the image to the database. The Image View `DispPict` picture control's `DragDrop` event handles checking to see whether a file should be added to the database.

Visual Basic does not directly support file drag-and-drop features from the Windows Explorer. To make the file drag-and-drop features work, you have to use a special control, `Msghook`, and dip into the Windows API. Table 4.27 outlines the different API functions used to implement the drag and drop.

Table 4.27 The drag-and-drop APIs

FUNCTION	DESCRIPTION
GetWindowLong	Retrieves information about the specified window
ByVal hwnd As Long	Handle of the window
ByVal nIndex As Long	Offset of the value to retrieve
SetWindowLong	Changes an attribute of the specified window
ByVal hwnd As Long	Handle of the window
ByVal nIndex As Long	Offset of the value to set
ByVal dwNewLong As Long	The new value
DragAcceptFiles	Registers whether a window accepts dropped files
ByVal hwnd As Long	Handle of the window
ByVal fAccept As Long	True or False
DragFinish	Finishes drag by releasing allocated transfer memory
ByVal HDROP As Long	Handle to the dropped memory
DragQueryFile	Retrieves the names of the dropped files (returns the number dropped)
ByVal HDROP As Long	Handle of the structure for the dropped files
ByVal UINT As Long	Index of the file to query
ByVal lpStr As String	Buffer to receive the filename
ByVal ch As Long	Size of the buffer

The `EnableFileDrop` routine in the `DropFile` module handles setting the form style to accept drop files. But the system also needs to be notified to send the drop file message to the form. This is done with the `DragAcceptFiles` API. After the form is prepared to accept files, the `WM_DROPFILES` message is sent from the system. When this happens, the `Msghook` control, which has been set to monitor for the `WM_DROPFILES` message, fires its message event. When the event fires, check the message to ensure the `WM_DROPFILES` message was sent to the form. If so, then the `DragQueryFile` API is used to determine the number of files dropped and then each filename can be retrieved. If it is an image, then it is added to the database.

Visual Basic supports drag-and-drop methods for various custom controls. This is demonstrated in the How-To by dragging the preview picture to the Image View picture as well as dragging the toolbar to change its alignment. The toolbar and picture controls have a drag method that can be initiated to drag an outline of the control using the mouse. When the control is dropped, the `DragDrop` method of the object the control was dropped on is initiated. The

DragDrop method provides the name of the object dropped as well as X and Y drop locations. The coordinates allow you to determine how to change the alignment of the toolbar. For the DispPict control, you can determine whether the preview picture or the toolbar was dropped onto it by checking the name of the dropped object.

Comments

The drag-and-drop methods Visual Basic provides can be used to customize the interface of a program. For example, if the user wants to have the Comments field as the first field on the data entry form, then the drag-and-drop method could be used to change the order of the data-entry controls.

COMPLEXITY
INTERMEDIATE

4.5 How Do I...
Organize form contents using the tab control?

COMPATIBILITY: VISUAL BASIC 5 AND 6

Problem

The capability to provide the user with quick and simple views of different information in limited screen space can be invaluable to a program's interface. Windows 95 makes ample use of tabs for presenting information to the user. How can I utilize the tab control in my programs?

Technique

Visual Basic provides the SSTab control for implementing tabbed information in your Visual Basic programs. The image database program implemented in the chapter is missing a few critical features to make the interface complete. These include database sort options and the capability to view several images selected from a list without searching through the database. The tab control provides an effective method for accomplishing this.

Steps

Open and run 4-5.VBP. Figure 4.10 shows the ImageData form and the tab control.

The ImageData form now has a tab control, which provides the standard data entry fields for the displayed image but also provides a tab for sort options and three views of different images in the database. Figure 4.11 shows the different sort options for the images in the database. Select one of the options to sort the data.

The three View tabs provide a list box that contains all the images in the database and a picture control for viewing images selected in the list box. Select an image from the list to view it. Figure 4.12 shows an image selected on the View 1 tab.

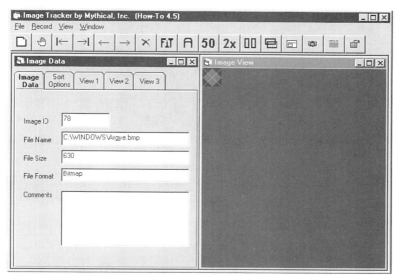

Figure 4.10 The form at runtime with the Image Data tab control

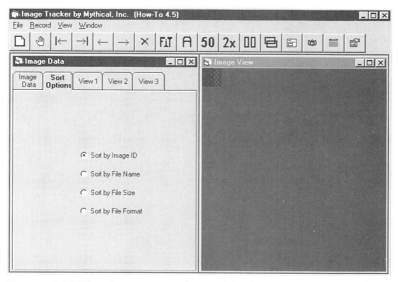

Figure 4.11 The form at runtime with the Sort Options tab control

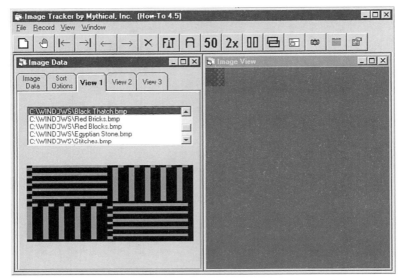

Figure 4.12 The form at runtime with the View 1 tab

Complete the following steps to create this project:

1. Create a new project called 4-5.VBP. Add the objects and properties listed in Table 4.28 to the form and save the form as 4-5.FRM.

Table 4.28 The MDI form's objects and properties

OBJECT	PROPERTY	SETTING
MDIForm	Name	ImageTracker
	AutoShowChildren	0 'False
	Caption	"Image Tracker by Mythical, Inc. (How-To 4.5)"
Toolbar	Name	ImageTool
	Align	1 'Align Top
	Negotiate	-1 'True
	ImageList	"MDIButtons"
	ButtonWidth	926
	ButtonHeight	847
	AllowCustomize	0 'False
	NumButtons	18
	AlignSet	-1 'True
	Wrappable	0 'False

OBJECT	PROPERTY	SETTING
ImageList	Name	MDIButtons
	ImageWidth	28
	ImageHeight	26
	MaskColor	12632256
	NumImages	18
	i1	open.bmp
	i2	new.bmp
	i3	hand.bmp
	i4	first.bmp
	i5	last.bmp
	i6	prev.bmp
	i7	next.bmp
	i8	delete.bmp
	i9	fit.bmp
	i10	actual.bmp
	i11	50.bmp
	i12	2x.bmp
	i13	tile.bmp
	i14	cascade.bmp
	i15	data.bmp
	i16	camera.bmp
	i17	menu.bmp
	i18	prop.bmp

2. Add the menus shown in Table 4.29 to the `ImageTracker` form.

Table 4.29 The `ImageTracker` form's menus

CONTROL NAME	CAPTION	INDEX	CHECKED	SHORTCUT KEY
mFile	"&File"			
mOpenImage	"&Open Image Database"			
mBar	"-"			
mExit	"E&xit"			
mWindow	"&Window"			
mImageData	"Image &Data"			
mImageView	"Image &View"			
mBar3	"-"			
mShowTool	"Show Toolbar"	-1	'True	
mShowMenu	"Show Menu"	-1	'True	

3. Insert a new form into the project and save it as `IView.frm`. Add the objects and properties shown in Table 4.30 to the form.

Table 4.30 The `ImageView` form's objects and properties

OBJECT	PROPERTY	SETTING
Form	Name	ImageView
	Caption	Image View"
	MDIChild	1 'True
PictureBox	Name	DispPict
	BackColor	H00C00000&
	BorderStyle	'None
	Picture	"pastel.bm"î
	ScaleMode	'Pixel
PictureBox	Name	BackPict
	AutoRedraw	1 'True
	AutoSize	1 'True
	BackColor	H000000FF&
	BorderStyle	0 'None
	Picture	"pastel.bmp"
	ScaleMode	'Pixel
	Visible	'False
Msghook	Name	Msghook

4. Add the menus shown in Table 4.31 to the `ImageView` form.

Table 4.31 The `ImageView` form's menus

CONTROL NAME	CAPTION	INDEX	CHECKED	SHORTCUT KEY
mFile	"&File"			
mNewImage	&New Image"			
mBar	"-"			
mExit	"E&xit"			
mRecord	"&Record"			
mBrowse	"&First"	0		F1
mBrowse	"&Last"	1		F2
mBrowse	"&Back"	2		F3
mBrowse	"For&ward"	3		F4
mBar2	"-"			

CONTROL NAME	CAPTION	INDEX	CHECKED	SHORTCUT KEY
mDelete	"&Delete Record"			
mView	"&View"			
mSize	"&Fit in Window"	0		
mSize	"&Actual Size"	1	-1 'True	
mSize	"&50 Percent"	2		
mSize	"&200 Percent"	3		
mViewSet	"Viewer Settings"			
Flip	"Flip &Horizontal"	0		
Flip	"Flip &Vertical"	1		
mWindow	"&Window"			
mTile	"&Tile"			
mCascade	"&Cascade"			
mBar1	"-"			
mShowWindow	"Image &Data"	0		
mShowWindow	"Image &View"	1		
mPreview	"Image &Preview"			
mBar3	"-"			
mShowTool	"Show Tool&Bar"		-1 'True	
mShowMenu	"Show &Menu"		-1 'True	

5. Insert a new form into the project and save it as `IData.frm`. This implements the image data form as a tab control. Add the objects and properties shown in Table 4.32 to the form.

Table 4.32 The ImageData form's objects and properties

OBJECT	PROPERTY	SETTING
Form	Name	ImageData
	Caption	"Image Data"
	MDIChild	-1 'True
	Visible	0 'False
SSTab	Name	SSTab1
	Caption	"View 3"
	TabsPerRow	5
	Tab	4
	TabOrientation	0
	Tabs	5

continued on next page

Table 4.32 continued

OBJECT	PROPERTY	SETTING
	Style	0
	TabMaxWidth	1323
	TabHeight	794
	TabCaption(0)	"Image Data"
	Tab(0).ControlCount	10
	Tab(0).ControlEnabled	0 'False
	Tab(0).Control(0)	"ImageInfo(0)"
	Tab(0).Control(1)	"ImageInfo(1)"
	Tab(0).Control(2)	"ImageInfo(2)"
	Tab(0).Control(3)	"ImageInfo(3)"
	Tab(0).Control(4)	"ImageInfo(4)"
	Tab(0).Control(5)	"ImageLabel(0)"
	Tab(0).Control(6)	"ImageLabel(1)"
	Tab(0).Control(7)	"ImageLabel(2)"
	Tab(0).Control(8)	"ImageLabel(3)"
	Tab(0).Control(9)	"ImageLabel(4)"
	TabCaption(1)	"Sort Options"
	Tab(1).ControlCount	4
	Tab(1).ControlEnabled	0 'False
	Tab(1).Control(0)	"Option1(0)"
	Tab(1).Control(1)	"Option1(1)"
	Tab(1).Control(2)	"Option1(2)"
	Tab(1).Control(3)	"Option1(3)"
	TabCaption(2)	"View 1"
	Tab(2).ControlCount	2
	Tab(2).ControlEnabled	0 'False
	Tab(2).Control(0)	"View(0)"
	Tab(2).Control(1)	"Thumb(0)"
	TabCaption(3)	"View 2"
	Tab(3).ControlCount	2
	Tab(3).ControlEnabled	0 'False
	Tab(3).Control(0)	"View(1)"
	Tab(3).Control(1)	"Thumb(1)"
	TabCaption(4)	"View 3"
	Tab(4).ControlCount	2
	Tab(4).ControlEnabled	-1 'True

OBJECT	PROPERTY	SETTING
	Tab(4).Control(0)	"View(2)"
	Tab(4).Control(1)	"Thumb(2)"
ListBox	Name	Thumb
	Index	2
ListBox	Name	Thumb
	Index	1
ListBox	Name	Thumb
	Index	0
OptionButton	Name	SortOpts
	Caption	"Sort by Image ID"
	Index	0
OptionButton	Name	SortOpts
	Caption	"Sort by File Name"
	Index	1
OptionButton	Name	SortOpts
	Caption	"Sort by File Size"
	Index	2
OptionButton	Name	SortOpts
	Caption	"Sort by File Format"
	Index	3
TextBox	Name	ImageInfo
	DataField	"ImageID"
	DataSource	"MSRDC1"
	Index	0
	Locked	-1 'True
TextBox	Name	ImageInfo
	DataField	"FileName"
	DataSource	"MSRDC1"
	Index	1
TextBox	Name	ImageInfo
	DataField	"FileSize"
	DataSource	"MSRDC1"
	Index	2
	Locked	-1 'True

continued on next page

Table 4.32 continued

OBJECT	PROPERTY	SETTING
TextBox	Name	ImageInfo
	DataField	"FileFormat"
	DataSource	"MSRDC1"
	Index	3
TextBox	Name	ImageInfo
	DataField	"Comments"
	DataSource	"MSRDC1"
	Index	4
	MultiLine	-1 'True
Image	Name	View
	Index	
	Stretch	1 'True
Image	Name	View
	Index	1
	Stretch	-1 'True
Image	Name	View
	Index	0
	Stretch	-1 'True
Label	Name	ImageLabel
	AutoSize	-1 'True
	Caption	"Image ID"
	Index	0
Label	Name	ImageLabel
	AutoSize	-1 'True
	Caption	"File Name"
	Index	1
Label	Name	ImageLabel
	AutoSize	-1 'True
	Caption	"File Size"
	Index	2
Label	Name	ImageLabel
	AutoSize	-1 'True
	Caption	"File Format"
	Index	3

OBJECT	PROPERTY	SETTING
Label	Name	ImageLabel
	AutoSize	-1 'True
	Caption	"Comments"
	Index	4
CommonDialog	Name	CommonDialog1
	DefaultExt	".bmp"
	DialogTitle	"Find Image File"
	Filter	"*.bmp; *.wmf"
	FilterIndex	1
	InitDir	"c:\windows"
MSRDC	Name	MSRDC1
	Visible	0 'False
	DataSourceName	"Image Database"
	RecordSource	"select * from ImageData order by ImageID"
	RecordsetType	1
	KeysetSize	0
	ReadOnly	0 'False
	UserName	""
	Password	""
	CursorDriver	2
	EOFAction	1
	BOFAction	1
	Prompt	3
	LockType	3

6. Add the menus shown in Table 4.33 to the `ImageData` form.

Table 4.33 The `ImageData` form's menus

CONTROL NAME	CAPTION	INDEX	CHECKED	SHORTCUT KEY
mFile	"&File"			
mNewImage	"&New Image"			
mBar	"-"			
mExit	"E&xit"			
mRecord	"&Record"			

continued on next page

Table 4.33 continued

CONTROL NAME	CAPTION	INDEX	CHECKED	SHORTCUT KEY
mBrowse	"&First"	0		F1
mBrowse	"&Last"	1		F2
mBrowse	"&Back"	2		F3
mBrowse	"For&ward"	3		F4
mBar2	"-"			
mDelete	"&Delete Record"			
mView	"&View"			
mSize	"&Fit in Window"	0		
mSize	"&Actual Size"	1	-1 'True	
mSize	"&50 Percent"	2		
mSize	"&200 Percent"	3		
mWindow	"&Window"			
mTile	"&Tile"			
mCascade	"&Cascade"			
mBar1	"-"			
mShowWindow	"Image &Data"	0		
mShowWindow	"Image &View"	1		
mPreview	"Image &Preview"			
mBar3	"-"			
mShowTool	"Show Tool&Bar"		-1 'True	
mShowMenu	"Show &Menu"		-1 'True	

7. Insert a new form into the project and save it as `Preview.frm`. Add the objects and properties shown in Table 4.34 to the form.

Table 4.34 The `Preview` form's objects and properties

OBJECT	PROPERTY	SETTING
Form	Name	Preview
	Caption	"Image Preview"
PictureBox	Name	PrevPict
	Appearance	0 'Flat
	BackColor	&H00808080&
	BorderStyle	0 'None
	DragIcon	"pastel.bmp"
	DragMode	1 'Automatic
	ForeColor	H80000008&
Msghook	Name	Msghook

NOTE

Only the new code added to the project will be commented. If you need additional information regarding the other code, see the previous How-To's for a complete explanation.

8. Add the following code to the `ImageTracker` form:

```
Private Sub ImageTool_ButtonClick(ByVal Button As Button)

Select Case Button.Index

    Case 1
        '   Open the Image Database
        MenuOpenData

    Case 2

        '   Call the MenuNewImage function to get
        '   a new image
        MenuNewImage

    Case 3
        '   Exit the program
        MenuExit

    Case 4
        '   Move to the first record
        MenuBrowse 0

    Case 5
        '   Move to the last record
        MenuBrowse 1

    Case 6
        '   Move back a record
        MenuBrowse 2

    Case 7
        '   Move forward a record
        MenuBrowse 3

    Case 8
        '   Delete the current record
        '   of the result set
        MenuDelete

    Case 9
        '   Set the View to fit in the Window
        SetView 0

    Case 10
        '   Set the View to actual size
        SetView 1
```

continued on next page

continued from previous page

```
            Case 11
                ' Set the View to 50 %
                SetView 2

            Case 12
                ' Set the View to 200 %
                SetView 3

            Case 13
                ' Tile the windows
                MenuTile

            Case 14
                ' Cascade the Windows
                MenuCascade

            Case 15
                ' If the ImageData form is not
                ' visible then call the
                ' MenuOpenData function to open
                ' the database.  Otherwise, show
                ' the ImageData Window (0)
                If ImageData.Visible = False Then
                    MenuOpenData
                Else
                    MenuShowWindow 0
                End If

            Case 16
                ' If the ImageData form is not
                ' visible then call the
                ' MenuOpenData function to open
                ' the database.  Otherwise, show
                ' the ImageView Window (1)
                If ImageData.Visible = False Then
                    MenuOpenData
                Else
                    MenuShowWindow 1
                End If

            Case 17
                ' Show or hide the Menu depending
                ' on the current setting.
                MenuShowMenu

            Case 18
                ' Start the drag process for the
                ' toolbar.
                ImageTool.Drag

        End Select

    End Sub
```

```
Private Sub ImageTool_MouseDown(Button As Integer,
➡Shift As Integer, X
As Single, Y As Single)

'  Check for the right mouse
'  button click
If Button = vbPopupMenuRightButton Then

    '   If the ImageData form is not visible then
    '   show the popup menu for ImageTracker form.
    '   Otherwise show the pop up menu for the
    '   ImageData form.
    If ImageData.Visible = False Then
        Me.PopupMenu mWindow, vbPopupMenuCenterAlign, , ,
        ➡mShowTool
    Else
        ImageData.PopupMenu ImageData.mWindow,
        ➡vbPopupMenuCenterAlign, ,
        , ImageData.mShowTool
    End If

End If

End Sub

Private Sub MDIForm_DragDrop(Source As Control,
➡X As Single, Y As Single)

'  Check to see if the drop was on
'  the top or bottom half of the
'  MDI form
If (Y - (ImageTool.Height / 2)) > (ImageTracker.Height / 2) Then
    ImageTool.Align = 2
Else
    ImageTool.Align = 1
End If

End Sub

Private Sub MDIForm_Load()

'  Hide the ImageData form when
'  the MDI form is first loaded
ImageData.Hide

End Sub

Private Sub MDIForm_MouseDown(Button As Integer,
➡Shift As Integer, X As Single, Y As Single)

'  If the ImageData form is not visible,
'  then show the File menu from the
'  ImageTracker form
If (Button = vbPopupMenuRightButton) And
➡(ImageData.Visible <> True) Then
```

continued on next page

continued from previous page

```
            Me.PopupMenu mFile, vbPopupMenuCenterAlign, , , mOpenImage
            Exit Sub
    End If

    '  If the ImageData form is visible,
    '  then show the Window menu from the
    '  ImageData form
    If (Button = vbPopupMenuRightButton) And
    ➥(ImageData.Visible = True) Then
        ImageData.PopupMenu ImageData.mWindow,
        ➥vbPopupMenuCenterAlign , , , ImageData.mImageData
    End If

    End Sub

    Private Sub MDIForm_QueryUnload(Cancel As Integer,
    ➥UnloadMode As Integer)

    '  Call the MenuExit program to
    '  end the program
    MenuExit

    End Sub

    Private Sub MDIForm_Unload(Cancel As Integer)

    '  Call the MenuExit program to
    '  end the program
    MenuExit

    End Sub

    Private Sub mExit_Click()

    '  Call the MenuExit program to
    '  end the program
    MenuExit

    End Sub

    Private Sub mImageData_Click()

    '  Call the MenuOpenData method to open the
    '  Image database
    MenuOpenData

    End Sub

    Private Sub mImageView_Click()

    '  Call the MenuOpenData method to open the
    '  Image database
    MenuOpenData

    End Sub

    Private Sub mOpenImage_Click()
```

```
'   Call the MenuOpenData method to open the
'   Image database
MenuOpenData

End Sub

Private Sub mShowMenu_Click()

'   Show or hide the Menu
MenuShowMenu

End Sub

Private Sub mShowTool_Click()

'   Show or hide the Toolbar
MenuShowTool

End Sub
```

9. Add the following code to the Image Data form. Add the `PopulateLists` routine to the General Declarations section of the form. The `PopulateLists` routine is a public method of the form that populates the three view list boxes with a set of files in the database. Note that the images are sorted by the current sort options selection.

```
Public Sub PopulateLists()

Dim N As Integer
Dim RS As rdoResultset

'   Get a copy of the record set
Set RS = MSRDC1.Resultset

'   Move to the first record.
RS.MoveFirst

'   Clear the list boxes.
For N = 0 To 2
    Thumb(N).Clear
Next

'   Move through the recordset and fill the
'   image list boxes for the thumb nails
Do Until RS.EOF

    '   Loop through and add the image names
    For N = 0 To 2
        Thumb(N).AddItem RS("Filename")
    Next

    '   Move to the next record
    RS.MoveNext

Loop

End Sub
```

10. When the form is loaded, the view list boxes are filled by calling the
PopulateLists routine.

```
Private Sub Form_Load()

'   Populate the list boxes
PopulateLists

End Sub

Private Sub Form_MouseDown(Button As Integer,
➥Shift As Integer, X As Single, Y As Single)

If Button = vbPopupMenuRightButton Then
    '   Show the Record menu for moving
    '   through the image records in the
    '   database
    Me.PopupMenu mRecord, vbPopupMenuCenterAlign, , , mBrowse(3)

End If

End Sub

Private Sub Form_Resize()

Dim N As Integer

'   Size the tab control to fit in
'   the form.
SSTab1.Width = ImageData.Width - 110
SSTab1.Height = ImageData.Height - 500

'   Resize the other controls on the tab
For N = 1 To 4
    '   Resize the image info text
    '   boxes
    ImageData.ImageInfo(N).Width = SSTab1.Width - 1400

    '   Resize the thumb nail lists
    '   and the view image controls
    If N < 4 Then
        Thumb(N - 1).Width = SSTab1.Width - 450
        View(N - 1).Width = SSTab1.Width - 450
        View(N - 1).Height = SSTab1.Height -
        View(N - 1).Top - 750
    End If
Next N

End Sub

Private Sub Form_Unload(Cancel As Integer)

'   We don't want the form to be unloaded so that
'   it will not have to be re-initialized
Cancel = -1
```

```
'  Instead minimize the form
Me.WindowState = 1

End Sub

Private Sub mBrowse_Click(Index As Integer)

'  Browse the result set depending
'  on the menu selected
MenuBrowse Index

End Sub

Private Sub mCascade_Click()

'  Cascade the windows
MenuCascade

End Sub

Private Sub mDelete_Click()

'  Delete the current record
'  of the result set
MenuDelete

End Sub

Private Sub mExit_Click()

'  Call the MenuExit method to
'  exit the program
MenuExit

End Sub

Private Sub mNewImage_Click()

'  Call the MenuNewImage function to allow
'  the user to select a new image to add to the
'  database
MenuNewImage

End Sub

Private Sub mPreview_Click()

'  Show the Preview form
Preview.Show

End Sub

Private Sub mShowMenu_Click()

'  Show or hide the Menu
MenuShowMenu
```

continued on next page

continued from previous page

```
End Sub

Private Sub mShowTool_Click()

'   Show or hide the toolbar
MenuShowTool

End Sub

Private Sub mShowWindow_Click(Index As Integer)

'   Call the MenuShowWindow function to show
'   the window selected
MenuShowWindow Index

End Sub

Private Sub mSize_Click(Index As Integer)

'   Set the View based on the menu
'   selection
SetView Index

End Sub

Private Sub mTile_Click()

'   Tile the windows
MenuTile

End Sub
```

11. The Sort options show up on the second tab of the tab control. Several
different methods are provided for sorting the database. The SQL property
of the remote data control is set to the appropriate SQL select statement
for the sort. Then the remote data control is refreshed, and the view lists
are repopulated.

```
Private Sub SortOpts_Click(Index As Integer)

Select Case Index

    Case 0
        MSRDC1.SQL = "select * from ImageData order by ImageID"

    Case 1
        MSRDC1.SQL = "select * from ImageData order by FileName"

    Case 2
        MSRDC1.SQL = "select * from ImageData order by FileSize"
```

```
        Case 3
            MSRDC1.SQL = "select * from ImageData order
            ➥by FileFormat"

    End Select

    MSRDC1.Refresh
    PopulateLists

    '  Move to the last record which was
    '  just added.
    MenuBrowse 1

    End Sub
```

12. When the thumbnail list of images on the image data form is clicked, the name of the image to be viewed is retrieved from the list, and the image is displayed in the image box. Note that the image box **stretch** property is set to **True** to stretch the image to fit in the box.

```
Private Sub Thumb_Click(Index As Integer)

    '  When the lists are clicked on
    '  load the files into the image
    '  controls
    View(Index).Picture =
    ➥LoadPicture(Thumb(Index).List(Thumb(Index).ListIndex))

    End Sub
```

13. Add the following code to the **ImageView** form:

```
Private Sub DispPict_DragDrop(Source As Control,
➥X As Single, Y As Single)

'  If the dropped control is the
'  toolbar then we need to do the
'  necessary checking to see if the
'  tool bar should be re-aligned
If Source.Name = "ImageTool" Then

    '  Check to see if the toolbar drop
    '  was on the top or bottom half of the
    '  picture box.  Note that the picture
    '  box is in pixel mode so we need to
    '  convert the coordinates to twips.
    If ((Y * Screen.TwipsPerPixelY) -
    ➥(ImageTracker.ImageTool.Height / 2))
        > (ImageTracker.Height / 2) Then
            ImageTracker.ImageTool.Align = 2
    Else
```

continued on next page

continued from previous page

```
                         ImageTracker.ImageTool.Align = 1
            End If

            Exit Sub

    End If

    '  Otherwise a new file should have
    '  been dropped on the picture box
    '  from the preview window.  We need
    '  to check to ensure that there is
    '  a picture file associated with the
    '  preview.  If so, then add the image to
    '  the database.
    If Preview.PreviewFileName <> "" Then
        DropNewImage Preview.PreviewFileName
    End If

    End Sub

    Private Sub mPreview_Click()

    '  Show the preview window
    Preview.Show

    End Sub

    Private Sub Msghook_Message(ByVal msg As Long,
    ➥ByVal wp As Long, ByVal lp As Long, result As Long)

    Dim NumFiles As Integer
    Dim Buffer As String 'Byte
    Dim N As Integer
    Dim NameLen As Integer

    '  Set up the buffer to receive the
    '  filename
    Buffer = Space$(256)

    '  See if the drop file message was
    '  sent
    If msg = WM_DROPFILES Then

        '  Retrieve the number of files
        '  dropped.
        NumFiles = DragQueryFile(wp, -1&, Buffer, Len(Buffer))

        '  Loop through the files and add them to
        '  the image database.
        For N = 0 To (NumFiles - 1)

            '  Get the filename of the file and
            '  retrieve the length of the
```

```
                         '  filename
                         NameLen = DragQueryFile(wp, N, Buffer, 128)

                         '  Check to see if the file is a
                         '  bitmap or icon.
                         If (UCase(Right((Left(Buffer, NameLen)), 3)) = "BMP") Or
                          (UCase(Right((Left(Buffer, NameLen)), 3)) = "ICO") Then

                             '  Add the image to the database
                             DropNewImage Left(Buffer, NameLen)

                         End If

                 Next N

                 '  Tell the system the drag is done
                 Call DragFinish(wp)

                 '  Set the result
                 result = 0

         End If

         End Sub

         Public Sub SizeViewPict()

         '  Allow for a small border
         '  around the display picture
         disppict.Top = 5
         disppict.Left = 5
         disppict.Width = Me.Width - 5
         disppict.Height = Me.Height - 5

         '  Set the view to the current
         '  view option
         SetView IView

         End Sub

         Private Sub DispPict_Paint()

         '  Size the view picture
         SizeViewPict

         End Sub

         Private Sub DispPict_MouseDown(Button As Integer,
         ➥Shift As Integer, X As Single, Y As Single)

         '  If the right mouse button is selected, then
         '  the different image size options are shown.  If
         '  it is a left mouse click then the flip options
         '  are shown
         If Button = vbPopupMenuRightButton Then
```

continued on next page

continued from previous page

```
          Me.PopupMenu mView, vbPopupMenuCenterAlign, , , mSize(0)
Else
    Me.PopupMenu mViewSet, vbPopupMenuCenterAlign
End If

End Sub

Private Sub Flip_Click(Index As Integer)

'  When the flip menu is clicked, the
'  check on the menu is set appropriately
If flip(Index).Checked = False Then
    flip(Index).Checked = True
Else
    flip(Index).Checked = False
End If

'  It is important to ensure that only
'  a vertical or horizotal flip can be
'  performed.  Thus, the menu item that
'  was not clicked is unchecked.
If Index = 1 Then
    flip(0).Checked = False
Else
    flip(1).Checked = False
End If

'  Based on the selection,
'  the image is redisplayed.
SizeViewPict

End Sub

Private Sub Form_Load()

'  Enable the form to accept
'  file drops
EnableFileDrop Me.hwnd

'  Setup MsgHook control
Msghook.HwndHook = Me.hwnd
Msghook.Message(WM_DROPFILES) = True

'  Initially set IView to 0.
IView = 1

'  Call the MenuBrowse function
'  to show the first record
MenuBrowse 1

End Sub


Private Sub Form_Unload(Cancel As Integer)
```

```
'   Cancel the unload.  We don't want the
'   form to be unloaded while the program is
'   running so that it does not have to be
'   re-initialized.  Instead, the form will be
'   minimized.
Cancel = -1
Me.WindowState = 1

End Sub

Private Sub mBrowse_Click(Index As Integer)

'   Browse the record set depending on the
'   menu option chosen.
MenuBrowse Index

End Sub

Private Sub mCascade_Click()

'   Cascade the windows
MenuCascade

'   Size the view picture after the cascade
SizeViewPict

End Sub

Private Sub mDelete_Click()

'   Call the MenuDelete function to
'   delete the selected record.
MenuDelete

End Sub

Private Sub mExit_Click()

'   Call the MenuExit function to
'   exit the program.
MenuExit

End Sub

Private Sub mNewImage_Click()

'   Call the MenuNewImage function to get
'   a new image
MenuNewImage

End Sub

Private Sub mShowMenu_Click()
```

continued on next page

continued from previous page

```
'   Show or hide the Menu
MenuShowMenu

End Sub

Private Sub mShowTool_Click()

'   Show or hide the toolbar
MenuShowTool

End Sub

Private Sub mShowWindow_Click(Index As Integer)

'   Call the MenuShowWindow function to show
'   the selected window.
MenuShowWindow Index

End Sub

Private Sub mTile_Click()

'   Call the menu tile function to
'   tile the windows
MenuTile

End Sub

Private Sub mSize_Click(Index As Integer)

'   Set the view depending on the menu option
'   selected
SetView Index

End Sub
```

14. Add the following code to the **Preview** form:

```
'   Public property that will indicate
'   what filename is associated with
'   the preview
Public PreviewFileName As String

Private Sub Form_Load()

'   Enable the preview to accept
'   file drag and drop
EnableFileDrop Me.hwnd

'   Setup the MsgHook control
Msghook.HwndHook = Me.hwnd
Msghook.Message(WM_DROPFILES) = True

'   Move the preview picture to the
'   top left
```

```
PrevPict.Top = 0
PrevPict.Left = 0

'  Set the preview picture width
'  and height
PrevPict.Width = Preview.Width
PrevPict.Height = Preview.Height

End Sub

Private Sub Form_Resize()

'  When the form is resized,
'  resize the picture
PrevPict.Width = Preview.Width
PrevPict.Height = Preview.Height

End Sub

Private Sub Form_Unload(Cancel As Integer)

'  When the preview is unloaded,
'  make sure the ImageTracker form
'  is visible
ImageTracker.Show

End Sub

Private Sub Msghook_Message(ByVal msg As Long,
➥ByVal wp As Long, ByVal lp As Long, result As Long)

Dim NumFiles As Integer
Dim Buffer As String 'Byte
Dim N As Integer
Dim NameLen As Integer

'  Set up the buffer to receive the
'  filename
Buffer = Space$(256)

'  See if the drop file message was
'  sent
If msg = WM_DROPFILES Then

    '  Retrieve the number of files
    '  dropped.
    NumFiles = DragQueryFile(wp, -1&, Buffer, Len(Buffer))

    '  Get the filename of the file and
    '  retrieve the length of the
    '  filename
    NameLen = DragQueryFile(wp, N, Buffer, 128)

    '  Check to see if the file is a
    '  bitmap or icon.
```

continued on next page

continued from previous page

```
                        If (UCase(Right((Left(Buffer, NameLen)), 3)) = "BMP") Or
                        (UCase(Right((Left(Buffer, NameLen)), 3)) = "ICO") Then

                            '  Load the picture into the preview
                            PrevPict.Picture = LoadPicture(Left(Buffer, NameLen))

                            '  Set the filename of the form
                            PreviewFileName = Left(Buffer, NameLen)

                        End If

                        ' Tell the system the drag done.
                        Call DragFinish(wp)

                        '  Set the result
                        result = 0

                    End If

                End Sub
```

15. Insert a new module into the project and save it as MenuLogic.bas.

```
'   StretchBlt will be used for the Image Viewer
Public Declare Function StretchBlt Lib "gdi32"
➥(ByVal hdc As Long, ByVal X As Long, ByVal Y As Long,
➥ByVal nWidth As Long, ByVal nHeight As Long,
➥ByVal hSrcDC As Long, ByVal xSrc As Long,
➥ByVal ySrc As Long, ByVal nSrcWidth As Long,
➥ByVal nSrcHeight As Long, ByVal dwRop As Long)
As Long

Global Const SRCCOPY = &HCC0020

'   IView globally stores the current view for
'   the image  I.E.  Fit in Window, 50%
Public IView As Integer

'   Handles ending the program when
'   users select exit from the menu
Public Sub MenuExit()
    End
End Sub

'   Handles tiling the windows
'   on the MDI form
Public Sub MenuTile()

'   Do a vertical tile
ImageTracker.Arrange vbTileVertical

End Sub

Public Sub MenuCascade()
```

```
'  Cascade the child forms
ImageTracker.Arrange vbCascade

End Sub

Public Sub SetView(Index)

'  When a new image view is selected,
'  the original menu selection is
'  unchecked
ImageView.mSize(IView).Checked = False
ImageData.mSize(IView).Checked = False

'  Set the new view to the index
'  parameter
IView = Index

'  Check the new menu option for the
'  selected view.
ImageData.mSize(IView).Checked = True
ImageView.mSize(IView).Checked = True

'  Clear the displayed picture
ImageView.disppict.Cls

ImageView.disppict.Picture.hPal =
➡ImageView.backpict.Picture.hPal

'  Depending on the view selected, the
'  original image will be copied to the
'  display picture appropriately
Select Case IView

'  Note that for the vertical and
'  horizontal flips, the height or
'  width is set to a negative value
'  and the starting point is set to
'  the height or width for the image
'  to be displayed.

    Case 0   'Fit in the Window
        If ImageView.flip(0).Checked = True Then
            '  Flip Horizontal
            ➡ImageView.disppict.PaintPicture
            ➡ImageView.backpict.Picture,
            ➡ImageView.disppict.ScaleWidth, 0, -1 *
            ➡ImageView.disppict.ScaleWidth,
            ➡ImageView.disppict.ScaleHeight,
            ➡0, 0, ImageView.backpict.ScaleWidth,
            ➡ImageView.backpict.ScaleHeight
        Else

            If ImageView.flip(1).Checked = True Then
                '  Flip Vertical
                ImageView.disppict.PaintPicture
```

continued on next page

continued from previous page

```
                              ImageView.backpict.Picture,
                                0, ImageView.disppict.ScaleHeight,
                                ➥ImageView.disppict.ScaleWidth, -1 *
                                ➥ImageView.disppict.ScaleHeight, 0, 0,
                                ➥ImageView.backpict.ScaleWidth,
                                ➥ImageView.backpict.ScaleHeight
                    Else
                         ' Normal Display
                         Call StretchBlt(ImageView.disppict.hdc, 0, 0,
                                ➥ImageView.disppict.ScaleWidth,
                                ➥ImageView.disppict.ScaleHeight,
                                ➥ImageView.backpict.hdc, 0, 0,
                                ➥ImageView.backpict.ScaleWidth,
                                ➥ImageView.backpict.ScaleHeight, SRCCOPY)
                    End If
                End If

            Case 1  'Actual Size
                If ImageView.flip(0).Checked = True Then
                     ' Flip Horizontal
                     ➥ImageView.disppict.PaintPicture
                     ➥ImageView.backpict.Picture,
                     ➥ImageView.backpict.ScaleWidth, 0, -1 *
                     ➥ImageView.backpict.ScaleWidth,
                     ➥ImageView.backpict.ScaleHeight,
                     ➥0, 0, ImageView.backpict.ScaleWidth,
                     ➥ImageView.backpict.ScaleHeight
                Else
                    If ImageView.flip(1).Checked = True Then
                         ' Flip Vertical
                         ImageView.disppict.PaintPicture
                         ImageView.backpict.Picture,
                         0, ImageView.backpict.ScaleHeight,
                         ImageView.backpict.ScaleWidth, -1 *
                         ImageView.backpict.ScaleHeight, 0, 0,
                         ImageView.backpict.ScaleWidth,
                         ImageView.backpict.ScaleHeight
                    Else
                         ' Normal Display
                         Call StretchBlt(ImageView.disppict.hdc, 0, 0,
                                ➥ImageView.backpict.ScaleWidth,
                                ➥ImageView.backpict.ScaleHeight,
                                ➥ImageView.backpict.hdc, 0,
                                ➥0, ImageView.backpict.ScaleWidth,
                                ➥ImageView.backpict.ScaleHeight, SRCCOPY)
                    End If
                End If

            Case 2  '50%
                If ImageView.flip(0).Checked = True Then
                     ' Flip Horizontal
                     ImageView.disppict.PaintPicture
                     ➥ImageView.backpict.Picture,
                     ➥ImageView.backpict.ScaleWidth * 0.5, 0,
                     ➥-1 * ImageView.backpict.ScaleWidth * 0.5,
                     ➥ImageView.backpict.ScaleHeight * 0.5, 0, 0,
```

```
                    ➥ImageView.backpict.ScaleWidth,
                    ➥ImageView.backpict.ScaleHeight
            Else
                If ImageView.flip(1).Checked = True Then
                    '   Flip Vertical
                    ImageView.disppict.PaintPicture
                    ➥ImageView.backpict.Picture,
                    ➥0, ImageView.backpict.ScaleHeight * 0.5,
                    ➥ImageView.backpict.ScaleWidth * 0.5,
                    ➥-1 * ImageView.backpict.ScaleHeight *
                    ➥0.5, 0, 0,
                    ➥ImageView.backpict.ScaleWidth,
                    ➥ImageView.backpict.ScaleHeight
                Else
                    '   Normal Display
                    Call StretchBlt(ImageView.disppict.hdc, 0, 0,
                      ➥ImageView.backpict.ScaleWidth * 0.5,
                      ➥ImageView.backpict.ScaleHeight * 0.5,
                      ➥ImageView.backpict.hdc,
                      ➥0, 0, ImageView.backpict.ScaleWidth,
                      ➥ImageView.backpict.ScaleHeight, SRCCOPY)
                End If
            End If

        Case 3 '200%
            If ImageView.flip(0).Checked = True Then
                '   Flip Horizontal
                ImageView.disppict.PaintPicture
                ➥ImageView.backpict.Picture,
                ➥ImageView.backpict.ScaleWidth * 2, 0,
                ➥-1 * ImageView.backpict.ScaleWidth * 2,
                ➥ImageView.backpict.ScaleHeight
                ➥2, 0, 0,
                ➥ImageView.backpict.ScaleWidth,
                ➥ImageView.backpict.ScaleHeight
            Else
                If ImageView.flip(1).Checked = True Then
                    '   Flip Vertical
                    ImageView.disppict.PaintPicture
                      ➥ImageView.backpict.Picture,
                      ➥0, ImageView.backpict.ScaleHeight * 2,
                      ➥ImageView.backpict.ScaleWidth * 2,
                      ➥-1 * ImageView.backpict.ScaleHeight *
                      ➥2, 0, 0,
                      ➥ImageView.backpict.ScaleWidth,
                      ➥ImageView.backpict.ScaleHeight
                Else
                    '   Normal Display
                    Call StretchBlt(ImageView.disppict.hdc, 0, 0,
                      ➥ImageView.backpict.ScaleWidth * 2,
                      ➥ImageView.backpict.ScaleHeight * 2,
                      ➥ImageView.backpict.hdc,
                      ➥0, 0, ImageView.backpict.ScaleWidth,
                      ➥ImageView.backpict.ScaleHeight, SRCCOPY)
```

continued on next page

continued from previous page

```
                          End If
                    End If

         End Select

         ' Copy the palette from the holding picture
         ' to the displayed picture.  This ensures that
         ' the image's colors are displayed correctly.
         ImageView.disppict.Picture.hPal =
       ➥ImageView.backpict.Picture.hPal

         End Sub

         Public Sub MenuShowWindow(Index)

         ' Check to see which Windows (Form)
         ' is to be displayed.
         Select Case Index

             Case 0   'Show ImageData
                 ImageData.Show
                 ImageData.WindowState = 0

             Case 1   'Show ImageView
                 ImageView.Show
                 ImageView.WindowState = 0

         End Select

         End Sub

         Public Sub MenuOpenData()

         Dim msg As String
         Dim Style As Integer
         Dim Title As String
         Dim Response As Integer
         Dim N As Integer

         ' Set the Message, Style, and Title
         ' of the message box
         msg = "Do you want to open the Image Database ?"
         Style = vbYesNo + vbQuestion + vbDefaultButton1
         Title = "Open Image Database"

         ' Retrieve the user's response
         Response = MsgBox(msg, Style, Title)

         ' If it was a yes, then show the ImageData
         ' and ImageView forms.  Also start the view
         ' in Tiled mode.
         If Response = vbYes Then
             ImageView.Show
             ImageData.Show
             MenuTile
```

```
ImageTracker.ImageTool.Buttons(1).Visible = False

For N = 2 To ImageTracker.ImageTool.Buttons.Count

    ImageTracker.ImageTool.Buttons(N).Visible = True

Next N

'   Ensure that the menu item is the same
'   for the ImageData and ImageView forms
ImageView.mShowMenu.Checked = ImageTracker.mShowMenu.Checked
ImageData.mShowMenu.Checked = ImageTracker.mShowMenu.Checked
ImageView.mShowTool.Checked = ImageTracker.mShowTool.Checked
ImageData.mShowTool.Checked = ImageTracker.mShowTool.Checked

End If

End Sub

Public Sub MenuBrowse(MoveType)

Dim ImageName As String

'   Check the RowCount.  If it is 0,
'   then there are no images in the
'   database.  We then need to show the New Image
'   dialog to add the first image.
If ImageData.MSRDC1.Resultset.RowCount =
➥0 Then MenuNewImage: Exit Sub

'   Depending on the type of move
'   selected by the user, the result set
'   is manipulated appropriately.
Select Case MoveType

    Case 0   'Move to First Record
        ImageData.MSRDC1.Resultset.MoveFirst

    Case 1   'Move to Last Record
        ImageData.MSRDC1.Resultset.MoveLast

    Case 2   'Move to Previous Record
        ImageData.MSRDC1.Resultset.MovePrevious

    Case 3   'Move to Next Record
        ImageData.MSRDC1.Resultset.MoveNext

End Select

'   Check to see if the End of File or
'   Beginning of File has been reached in
'   the result set.  If so, then move first or
'   last to ensure that a current record is
'   always visible
If ImageData.MSRDC1.Resultset.EOF = True Then
ImageData.MSRDC1.Resultset.MoveLast
```

continued on next page

continued from previous page

```
If ImageData.MSRDC1.Resultset.BOF = True Then
ImageData.MSRDC1.Resultset.MoveFirst

'   Get the Image name from the database
ImageName = ImageData.MSRDC1.Resultset("FileName")

'   Depending on whether or not the image file
'   name is set, the picture display is
'   set appropriately.
If ImageName <> "" Then
    ImageView.backpict.Picture = LoadPicture(ImageName):
    ➥SetView IView
Else
    ImageView.backpict.Picture = LoadPicture(""):
    ➥SetView IView
End If

End Sub

Public Sub MenuNewImage()

Dim ImageID As Integer
Dim ImageType As String

'   Ensure an Update is done
If ImageData.MSRDC1.Resultset.RowCount <> 0 Then
➥ImageData.MSRDC1.Resultset.MoveNext
End If

'   Set the filter type of the dialog
'   box
ImageData.commondialog1.Filter = "Bitmaps (*.bmp)¦*.bmp¦Icons
(*.ico)¦*.ico¦ All Files (*.*)¦*.*"

'   Set the title of the dialog
ImageData.commondialog1.DialogTitle = "New Image File"

'   Set the filter index to that of the
'   bitmap
ImageData.commondialog1.FilterIndex = 1

'   Set the flags to ensure that the
'   file must exist
ImageData.commondialog1.Flags = cdlOFNFileMustExist

'   Show the dialog box
ImageData.commondialog1.ShowOpen

'   Check to see if the filename was set
If ImageData.commondialog1.FileName <> "" Then

    '   Add a new record
    ImageData.MSRDC1.Resultset.AddNew

    '   Set the file name
    ImageData.MSRDC1.Resultset("FileName") =
    ➥ImageData.commondialog1.FileName
```

```
     '  Set the file size
     ImageData.MSRDC1.Resultset("FileSize") =
       FileLen(ImageData.commondialog1.FileName)

     '  Get the extension of the image
     ImageType = Right$(ImageData.commondialog1.FileName, 3)

     '  Set the file format depending on
the extension
     Select Case UCase$(ImageType)

         Case "BMP"  'Standard bitmap
             ImageData.MSRDC1.Resultset("FileFormat") = "Bitmap"

         Case "ICO"  'Standard Icon
             ImageData.MSRDC1.Resultset("FileType") = "Icon"

     End Select

     '  Update the result set
     ImageData.MSRDC1.Resultset.Update

     '  Select SQL statement to get the
     '  new result set
     ImageData.MSRDC1.SQL = "select * from ImageData
     ➡order by ImageID"

     '  Refresh the result set
     ImageData.MSRDC1.Refresh

     '  Since we have changed the record set
     '  the image lists need to be updated
     ImageData.PopulateLists

     '  Move to the last record which was
     '  just added.
     MenuBrowse 1

End If

End Sub

Public Sub MenuDelete()

'  Delete the current record
ImageData.MSRDC1.Resultset.Delete

'  Since we have changed the record set
'  the image lists need to be updated
ImageData.PopulateLists

'  Move to the next record.
MenuBrowse 1
```

continued on next page

continued from previous page

```
        End Sub

        Public Sub MenuShowTool()

        '  If the toolbar is checked then
        '  do the logic to hide the toolbar
        If ImageTracker.mShowTool.Checked = True Then

                '  If the menu is not shown, then don't
                '  hide the tool bar.
                If ImageTracker.mShowMenu.Checked = False Then Exit Sub

                '  Hide the toolbar
                ImageTracker.ImageTool.Visible = False

                '  Change the menu check
                ImageTracker.mShowTool.Checked = False

                '  If the ImageData and ImageView forms
                '  are visible then handle setting their
                '  menu check marks.  If they are not
                '  visible, they are not loaded.
                If ImageData.Visible = True Then
                    ImageData.mShowTool.Checked = False
                    ImageView.mShowTool.Checked = False
                End If

        Else

                '  Make the toolbar visible
                ImageTracker.ImageTool.Visible = True

                '  Change the menu check
                ImageTracker.mShowTool.Checked = True

                '  If the ImageData and ImageView forms
                '  are visible then handle setting their
                '  menu check marks.  If they are not
                '  visible, they are not loaded.
                If ImageData.Visible = True Then
                    ImageData.mShowTool.Checked = True
                    ImageView.mShowTool.Checked = True
                End If

        End If

        End Sub

        Public Sub MenuShowMenu()

        '  Check to see If the menu is already visible
        If ImageTracker.mShowMenu.Checked = True Then

                '  If the toolbar is not visible,
                '  we do not want to also make the
```

```
'  menu invisible
If ImageTracker.ImageTool.Visible = False Then Exit Sub

    '  Make the ImageTracker menus
    '  invisible and set the menu
    '  check mark appropriately
    ImageTracker.mFile.Visible = False
    ImageTracker.mShowMenu.Checked = False
    ImageTracker.mWindow.Visible = False

    '  If the ImageData and ImageView forms
    '  are visible then handle setting their
    '  menu check marks and visible properties.
    '  If they are not visible, they are not
    '  loaded.
    If ImageData.Visible = True Then
        ImageData.mShowMenu.Checked = False
        ImageView.mShowMenu.Checked = False
        ImageView.mFile.Visible = False
        ImageData.mFile.Visible = False
        ImageData.mWindow.Visible = False
        ImageView.mWindow.Visible = False
        ImageData.mRecord.Visible = False
        ImageView.mRecord.Visible = False
        ImageData.mView.Visible = False
        ImageView.mView.Visible = False
        ImageView.mViewSet.Visible = False
    End If

Else

    '  Make the ImageTracker menus
    '  visible and set the menu
    '  check mark appropriately
    ImageTracker.mFile.Visible = True
    ImageTracker.mShowMenu.Checked = True
    ImageTracker.mWindow.Visible = True

    '  If the ImageData and ImageView forms
    '  are visible then handle setting their
    '  menu check marks and visible properties.
    '  If they are not visible, they are not
    '  loaded.
    If ImageData.Visible = True Then
        ImageData.mShowMenu.Checked = True
        ImageView.mShowMenu.Checked = True
        ImageData.mFile.Visible = True
        ImageView.mFile.Visible = True
        ImageData.mWindow.Visible = True
        ImageView.mWindow.Visible = True
        ImageData.mRecord.Visible = True
        ImageView.mRecord.Visible = True
        ImageView.mView.Visible = True
        ImageData.mView.Visible = True
```

continued on next page

continued from previous page

```
            ImageView.mViewSet.Visible = True
        End If

    End If

End Sub

Public Sub DropNewImage(FileName)

Dim ImageID As Integer
Dim ImageType As String

'   Ensure an Update is done
ImageData.MSRDC1.Resultset.MoveNext

'   Add a new record
ImageData.MSRDC1.Resultset.AddNew

'   Set the file name
ImageData.MSRDC1.Resultset("FileName") = FileName

'   Set the file size
ImageData.MSRDC1.Resultset("FileSize") = FileLen(FileName)

'   Get the extension of the image
ImageType = Right$(FileName, 3)

'   Set the file format depending on
'   the extension
Select Case UCase$(ImageType)

    Case "BMP"  'Standard bitmap
        ImageData.MSRDC1.Resultset("FileFormat") = "Bitmap"

    Case "ICO"  'Standard Icon
        ImageData.MSRDC1.Resultset("FileType") = "Icon"

End Select

'   Update the result set
ImageData.MSRDC1.Resultset.Update

'   Select SQL statement to get the
'   new result set
ImageData.MSRDC1.SQL = "select *
➥from ImageData order by ImageID"

'   Refresh the result set
ImageData.MSRDC1.Refresh

'   Move to the last record which was
'   just added.
MenuBrowse 1

End Sub
```

16. Insert a new module into the project and save it as `DropFile.bas`.

```
'  Declare the API file functions
'  and constants for the file drag
'  and drop
Declare Function GetWindowLong Lib "user32" Alias
➡"GetWindowLongA" (ByVal hwnd As Long,
➡ByVal nIndex As Long) As Long

Declare Function SetWindowLong Lib "user32" Alias
➡"SetWindowLongA" (ByVal hwnd As Long,
➡ByVal nIndex As Long, ByVal dwNewLong As Long) As Long

Declare Sub DragAcceptFiles Lib "shell32.dll"
➡(ByVal hwnd As Long, ByVal fAccept As Long)

Declare Sub DragFinish Lib "shell32.dll" (ByVal HDROP As Long)

Declare Function DragQueryFile Lib "shell32.dll" Alias
➡"DragQueryFileA" (ByVal HDROP As Long,
➡ByVal UINT As Long, ByVal lpStr As String,
➡ByVal ch As Long) As Long

Public Const GWL_EXSTYLE = (-20)
Public Const WS_EX_ACCEPTFILES = &H10&
Public Const WM_DROPFILES = &H233

Sub EnableFileDrop(hwnd As Long)

Dim Style As Long

'  Get the Window style
Style = GetWindowLong(hwnd, GWL_EXSTYLE)

'  Set to the form to accept
'  dropped files
Style = SetWindowLong(hwnd, GWL_EXSTYLE,
➡Style Or WS_EX_ACCEPTFILES)

'  Indicate to the system that
'  dragged files will be accepted
'  by the form
DragAcceptFiles hwnd, True

End Sub
```

How It Works

The tab control is a relatively easy tool to use in your applications. In this How-To, it provides a straightforward way to add different sort options for the application. Also the user might need to quickly view several images at once. The three View tabs provide thumbnail views of different images in the database. The list boxes provide a list of all the images in the database. The user can quickly flip between the images by clicking the tabs. The tab control can be useful for adding to your program those features that don't work well in a limited menu format but don't need to be seen at all times.

Comments

Another tab could be provided to give the user options for searching the image database for particular recordsets. Or another View tab could be provided to show all three of the thumbnails on a single tab. This type of multiview flexibility makes the tab control an invaluable tool.

COMPLEXITY
BEGINNING

4.6 How do I...
Load a list or combo box with the results of a query?

COMPATIBILITY: VISUAL BASIC 5 AND 6

Problem

I have a small amount of data I want to retrieve and use to populate a list box or combo box. I want to have a generic routine so that I can use it throughout my application.

Technique

In Visual Basic version 3 and earlier versions, you would have placed the code for this routine in a standard module. With version 5 and above, the routine should be placed in a class module. Class modules should be used to define procedures for all objects in your applications. Standard modules should contain procedures that do not pertain to any object. They should be used to contain any references to API functions.

The routine you are about to design is a simple one, designed to display information in a list-based control, such as a list box or combo box. Essentially, this becomes a data access object (not to be confused with Microsoft's Data Access Object) that you can reuse in other applications or that can become part of a business object that is an OLE automation server, which can be used by applications throughout your enterprise.

Steps

Open and run CNTLFILL.VBP. The form shown in Figure 4.13 appears. When the combo box receives focus, it is filled with the names of the hotels from the Hotels table in the Hotel database. Every time the combo box receives focus, either by clicking it with the mouse or tabbing to it, the Hotels table is required, and the combo box is populated with the list of hotel names. To exit the program, click OK.

This How-To uses a class that represents the physical database access and custom control manipulation used by this application.

Figure 4.13 The combo box control filled via a class module

To create this project, complete the following steps:

1. Start Visual Basic and create a new project. Save the project as CNTLFILL.VBP. Select the default form, Form1, name it frmHotelListing, and save it as CNTLFILL.FRM. Assign the objects and properties for this form as listed in Table 4.35.

Table 4.35 Objects and properties of CNTLFILL.FRM

OBJECT	PROPERTY	SETTING
Form	Name	frmHotelListing
	Appearance	1 - 3D
	Caption	"Hotel Listing"
Label	Name	lblHotelListing
	Caption	"&Hotels:"
Combo Box	Name	cboHotels
	Style	2 - Dropdown List
Command Button	Name	cmdOK
	Caption	"OK"

2. Insert the following code into the General Declarations section of the frmHotelListing. This creates a new object of **CDataObjects** when the object variable is declared.

```
Option Explicit

' Assign the Hotel Name Member to Data Object
Private m_Hotels As CDataObjects
```

3. Insert the following code into the **Form_Load** event. As the form loads, this event creates the instance of the object, **CDataObject**. The object will be developed later in this How-To. If an error occurs, the error is trapped and displayed through the **Error** subroutine.

```
Private Sub Form_Load()

On Error GoTo Err_Form_Load

    ' Create the instance
    Set m_Hotels = New CDataObjects

Exit_Form_Load:
    Exit Sub

Err_Form_Load:
    Call afx_GenericError("Form_Load: ", Err)
    Resume Exit_Form_Load

End Sub
```

4. Insert the following code in the **Form_Unload** event. As the form gets unloaded, the reference to the object created in the **Form_Load**, **CDataObjects**, is terminated, and the application is ended. If an error occurs, the error is displayed through the **Error** procedure.

```
Private Sub Form_Unload(cancel As Integer)

    On Error GoTo Err_Form_Unload

    ' Clear the references
    Set m_Hotels = Nothing

Exit_Form_Unload:
    Exit Sub

Err_Form_Unload:
    Call afx_GenericError("Form_Unload:", Err)
    Resume Exit_Form_Unload
End Sub
```

5. Insert the following code in the **cboHotels_GotFocus** event. When the focus of the application is on the combo box, the **FillControl** method defined in **CDataObject** is performed using the **Select** SQL statement, and the combo box is populated with the names of the hotels.

```
Private Sub cboHotels_GotFocus()

Dim sSQL As String

    sSQL = "Select Hotel, Name from tbl_Hotels"

    ' Fill the combo box with the information from the database
    m_Hotels.FillControl cboHotels, sSQL, "hotel", "name"
End Sub
```

6. Insert the following code in the cmdOK_Click event. This causes the Form_Unload event to be performed.

```
Private Sub cmdOK_Click()
    Unload Me
End Sub
```

7. Choose Insert, Class Module from the Visual Basic menu to add a new class module. Name it CDataObjects and save it as CDATAOBJ.CLS.

8. Add the following code to the General Declarations section of the CDataObjects class module. The first constant defines your database member. The next defines your connection member.

```
Option Explicit

' Database
Private m_env As rdoEnvironment

' Connection
Private m_con As rdoConnection
```

9. Insert the following code in the Class_Initialize event of CDataObject. When this class is initialized, a logical connection to ODBC is made. If an error occurs during any process of opening the database or establishing the resultset, the generic error handling routine is called.

```
Private Sub Class_Initialize()

    Dim sSql As String

    On Error GoTo Err_Class_Initialize

    ' use the default environment
    Set m_env = rdoEnvironments(0)
    ' Open the connection
    Set m_con = m_env.OpenConnection(dsName:="dsnWaiteSQL", _
        Connect:="uid=sa;pwd=")

Exit_Class_Initialize:
    Exit Sub

Err_Class_Initialize:
    Call afx_GenericError("Class_Initialize:", Err)
    Resume Exit_Class_Initialize
End Sub
```

10. Add the following code to the Class_Terminate event of the CDataObject class module. This event closes the RDO environment to the object variables opened in the Class_Initialize procedure. By closing the RDO environment, all connections and resultsets related to it are also closed.

```
Private Sub Class_Terminate()

    On Error GoTo Err_Class_Terminate

    ' Close the RDO Environment
    If Not (m_env Is Nothing) Then
        m_env.Close
    End If

    ' Clear the references
    Set m_env = Nothing

Exit_Class_Terminate:
    Exit Sub

Err_Class_Terminate:
    Call afx_GenericError("Class_Terminate:", Err)
    Resume Exit_Class_Terminate
End Sub
```

11. Add the following public method to the **CDataObjects** class module. This method is used to fill the desired list-based control with the requested information. The control is first cleared before any information is added to it. The **rdoResultset** is created based on the SQL query passed to this procedure. As the resultset is processed, the selected control is populated. When it is completed, the control's **ListIndex** property is set to the first record. Note that this method passes through the use of the **ParamArray** argument. The use of this allows you to provide an arbitrary number of arguments. The information passed in the **ParamArray** consists of the names of the columns that you want to display in the control.

```
' Fill any list type control with the data
'
' Parameters:
'   cntl        list type control to fill
'   sSQL        SQL Statement
'   sIDColumn   name of the column containing the record ID
'   sColumns    name of the columns of data to display
Public Sub FillControl(cntl As Control, rs As rdoResultset, _
    sIDColumn As String, ParamArray sColumns() As Variant)

    Dim sData As String
    Dim i As Integer
    Dim rs as rdoResultset

    On Error GoTo Err_FillControl

    ' Clear the list
    cntl.Clear

    ' open the resultset
    Set rs = m_con.OpenResultset(sSQL)

    ' Add each record to control
    ' until the end of the file
```

```
            If (Not rs.BOF) Then
                Do Until rs.EOF
                    ' Concatenate each desired column
                    sData = ""
                    For i = 0 To UBound(sColumns)
                        sData = sData & " " & rs(cstr(sColumns(i)))
                    Next
                    ' Add the item to the list
                    cntl.AddItem sData
                    cntl.ItemData(cntl.NewIndex) = rs(sIDColumn)

                    ' Move to the next row
                    rs.MoveNext
                Loop
            End If
            ' Set control to highlight the first record
            ' in the list
            cntl.ListIndex = 0

    Exit_FillControl:
        Exit Sub

    Err_FillControl:
        Call afx_GenericError("FillControl:", Err)
        Resume Exit_FillControl
    End Sub
```

12. Choose Insert, Module from the Visual Basic menu to add a standard module to the project. This module is used for error handling. Go to the module's property list by pressing F4, name it **bError**, and save the file as **ERROR.BAS**. Add the following code to a public subprocedure. Two values are going to be passed to this procedure. One is a string value, the name of the procedure in which the remote data object error occurred. The other is a long value, which is the error number that occurred. When an error occurs in any of the modules, this procedure is executed. The system beeps to notify the user that an error has occurred. The procedure the error occurred in, a description of the error, and the error number are displayed in a message box.

```
' Generic Error routine
Public Sub afx_GenericError(sProcedure As String, lErr As Long)
    On Error GoTo Err_afx_GenericError

    Beep
    MsgBox sProcedure & " " & Error$(lErr) & ". " & vbCrLf _
        & "Error Nbr: " & CStr(lErr)
Exit_afx_GenericError:
    Exit Sub
Err_afx_GenericError:
    Call afx_GenericError("afx_GenericError:", Err)
    End
End Sub
```

How It Works

As the form loads, the m_Hotels member instantiates itself to the class module, CDataObjects. In that process, the connection to ODBC and the SQL Server database is made. Two controls can have focus—the combo box and command button. Focus refers to a control or window that can receive a mouse click or keyboard input at any one time. When the combo box receives focus, the SQL statement is executed through the procedure, FillControl.

In the FillControl procedure, the control you want to be filled is cleared, and the SQL statement is executed. The SQL statement is designed to retrieve the identification (ID) number and name of all the hotels in the Hotels table. The If statement checks to make sure that data is returned by the OpenResultset statement. If data is returned, the EOF (End Of File) flag will be set to False and the Do...Loop fills the control with the hotel names until no more data is in the resultset. As the hotel names are being added to the control, the index value of each added item is set to the hotel's ID number. Normally when you add an item to a list box or combo box, VB controls the index value. By using the NewIndex property, you are assigning the index equal to the value of the hotel's ID number. When a user selects a hotel name for the list, the index value will be that of the hotel ID number; this value can be used with other tables that use the hotel's ID number as part of a key.

When you click OK, the m_Hotels member is set to nothing, which causes the Class_Terminate event to be processed. This closes all your connections to the database.

Comments

The class that you just built, CDataObjects, can also populate a list box. Simply change the name of the combo box to the name of the list box.

COMPLEXITY
BEGINNING

4.7 How do I...
Populate an unbound grid?

COMPATIBILITY: VISUAL BASIC 5 AND 6

Problem

In my reservation system, I want to display the reservation information of our guests in a grid format. I don't want it to be bound to a data control because I don't want the overhead that comes with using it. Also, I don't want to use a bound data control because there is no easy way to control the database transaction. How do I accomplish this?

Technique

The `DBGrid` control is a good control for displaying information in a spreadsheet format, but you would have to bind it to a database through the use of the data control or remote data control. Because you don't want to bind the grid to a database like that, you are going to use the Microsoft `MSFlexGrid` control.

The Microsoft `MSFlexGrid` control is a more sophisticated grid control than the previous Microsoft grid control. It allows you to display your information in rows and columns just like any other original grid control, or you can have it bound to a database. When the grid is bound to a database, the data is displayed as read-only. The first thing you have to do is create an `rdoResultset` containing the rows and columns of interest. An `rdoResultset` is an object that contains the rows and columns of data that result from the query that was executed.

After the `rdoResultset` is created, you use the `rdoResultset` method, `MoveNext`, to access the data. At any given time, a pointer will be looking at only one row of data within the `rdoResultset`. The `MoveNext` method is used to iterate over the records in the `rdoResultset`. Loop through the `rdoResultset` until you reach the `rdoResultset` property, `EOF`, which stands for End Of File.

As you pass through each row, you process each column of the `rdoResultset` through the `rdoColumns` collection. The `rdoColumns` collection contains `rdoResultset`'s column data based on which row you are pointing to. The two `rdoColumns` properties you use to get the column information are `Name` and `Value`. When you move to an active row as described earlier, you access the column `Value` by referencing the `Name` property of the `rdoColumns` column. For a more in-depth explanation of RDO, see Chapter 3, "Data Objects."

The information you will use is from the Reservations table from the Hotels database. You are interested only in a few of the columns in the table; therefore, your `SQL` statement selects only the columns you want to display.

Steps

Open and run `CUSTRESV.VBP`. The form shown in Figure 4.14 appears. When the form loads, the grid is filled with the reservation number, the guest's first and last name (last name first), and his phone number. To exit the program, click OK.

Figure 4.14 The unbound grid control
filled with data from an `rdoResultset`

This How-To uses a class module similar to the one developed in How-To
4.6. A class module is used to perform the physical database access and custom
control.

Complete the following steps to create this project:

1. Create a new project and save it as **CUSTRESV.VBP**. Select the default form,
`Form1`, name it `frmResvInfo`, and save it as `RESVINFO.FRM`. Assign the
object and properties for this form as listed in Table 4.36.

Table 4.36 Objects and properties for RESVINFO.FRM

OBJECT	PROPERTY	SETTING
Form	Name	frmResvInfo
	Appearance	1 - 3D
	Caption	"Reservation Information"
Label	Name	lblCurResv
	Caption	"Current Reservations"
MSFlexGrid	Name	grdResvInfo
Command Button	Name	cmdOK
	Caption	"OK"

2. Insert the following code into the General Declarations section of
`frmResvInfo`. This creates a new object of **CDataObjects** when the object
variable, `m_Resv`, is declared.

```
Option Explicit

' Assign the Reservation Name Member to Data Object Class
Private m_Resv As CDataObjects
```

3. Insert the following code into the `Form_Load` event. As the form loads, the `Set` statement creates the instance of the object. The `With` statement executes a series of statements to set up the grid object's column widths and headers. The last statement performs the `FillGrid` method defined in `CDataObjects`, which populates the grid.

```
Private Sub Form_Load()

    Dim sSql as String

    On Error GoTo Err_Form_Load

    ' Create the instance
    Set m_Resvs = New CDataObjects

    ' Initialize Grid settings
    With grdResvInfo
        .ColWidth(0) = 720
        .ColWidth(1) = 1440
        .ColWidth(2) = 1440
        .ColWidth(3) = 1440
        .Row = 0
        .Col = 0
        .Text = "Res. No."
        .Col = 1
        .Text = "Guest Last Name"
        .Col = 2
        .Text = "First Name"
        .Col = 3
        .Text = "Phone No."
    End With

    sSql = "Select ResNo, LastName, FirstName, "
    sSql = sSql & "Phone from tbl_Reservations"

    m_Resv.FillGrid grdResvInfo, sSql, "ResNo", "LastName",
    ➥"FirstName", "Phone"
Exit_Form_Load:
    Exit Sub

Err_Form_Load:
    Call afx_GenericError("Form_Load:", Err)
    Resume Exit_Form_Load

End Sub
```

4. Insert the following code in the `Form_Unload` event. As the form gets unloaded, the reference to the object created in the `Form_Load`, `m_Resv`, is terminated, and the application ends. If an error occurs, the error is displayed through the `Error` procedure.

```
Private Sub Form_Unload(Cancel As Integer)

    On Error GoTo Err_Form_Unload

    Set m_Resv = Nothing

Exit_Form_Unload:
    Exit Sub

Err_Form_Unload:
    Call afx_GenericError("Form_Unload:", Err)
    Resume Exit_Form_Unload
End Sub
```

5. Insert the following code in the **cmdOK_Click** event. This causes the **Form_Unload** event to be performed.

```
Private Sub cmdOK_Click()

    On Error GoTo Err_cmdOK_Click

    Unload Me

Exit_cmdOK_Click:
    Exit Sub

Err_cmdOK_Click:
    Call afx_GenericError("cmdOK_Click:", Err)
    Resume Exit_cmdOK_Click
End Sub
```

6. Choose Insert, Class Module from the Visual Basic menu to add a new class module. Name it **CDataObjects** and save it as **CDATAOBJ.CLS**.

7. Add the following code to the General Declarations section of **CDataObjects**. The first constant defines your environment member. The last constant defines the database connection member.

```
Option Explicit

' Environment
Private m_env As rdoEnvironment

' Connection
Private m_con As rdoConnection
```

8. Insert the following code in the **Class_Initialize** event of the **CDataObject** class module. When this class is initialized, the environment and connection to the ODBC data source name is opened. If an error occurs during any process of opening the database or establishing the resultset, the error handling routine is called. The SQL statement is going to return every record in the table to the resultset member.

```
Private Sub Class_Initialize()

    Dim sSql As String

    On Error GoTo Err_Class_Initialize

    ' use the default environment
    Set m_env = rdoEnvironments(0)
    ' Open the connection
    Set m_con = m_env.OpenConnection(dsn:="dsnWaiteSQL", _
        connect:="UID=sa;pwd=")

Exit_Class_Initialize:
    Exit Sub

Err_Class_Initialize:
    Call afx_GenericError("Class_Initialize:", Err)
    Resume Exit_Class_Initialize
End Sub
```

9. Add the following code to the **Class_Terminate** event of the **CDataObject** class module. This event closes the RDO environment to the object variables that were opened in the **Class_Initialize** procedure. By closing the RDO environment, all connections and resultsets related to it are also closed.

```
Private Sub Class_Terminate()
    On Error GoTo Err_Class_Terminate

' Close the resultset and database
    If Not (m_env Is Nothing) Then
        m_env.Close
    End If

    ' Clear the references
    Set m_env = Nothing

Exit_Class_Terminate:
    Exit Sub

Err_Class_Terminate:
    Call afx_GenericError("Class_Terminate:", Err)
    Resume Exit_Class_Terminate
End Sub
```

10. Add the following **Public** method to the **CDataObjects** class module to fill the desired grid control with the requested information. The **OpenResultset** executes the SQL statement that gets all the information contained in the **tbl_Reservations** table. The **If** statement checks to make sure that data is returned to the resultset. If there is data, the **Do...Loop** processes each row of information, and the **For...Next** loop inserts information into each column in the grid.

```
' Fill an unbound grid control with the data
'
' Parameters:
'   cntl        list type control to fill
'   sSQL        SQL statement to process
'   sColumns    name of the columns of data to display
Public Sub FillGrid(cntl As Control, sSql As String,
➥ParamArray sColumns() As Variant)

    Dim sData As String
    Dim i As Integer
    Dim j As Long
    Dim lMaxRows As Long
    Dim rs As rdoResultset

    On Error GoTo Err_FillGrid

    ' Open the resultset
    Set rs = m_con.OpenResultset(sSql)

    ' Add each record until the end of the file
    j = 1
    If (Not rs.BOF) Then
        Do Until rs.EOF
            cntl.Row = j
            For i = 0 To UBound(sColumns)
                With cntl
                    .Col = i
                    .Text = rs(sColumns(i))
                End With
            Next
            ' Get next row and add another row
            ' to the grid
            rs.MoveNext
            j = j + 1
            cntl.Rows = j + 1
        Loop
    End If

Exit_FillGrid:
    Exit Sub

Err_FillGrid:
    Call afx_GenericError("FillGrid:", Err)
    Resume Exit_FillGrid

End Sub
```

11. Choose Insert, Module from the Visual Basic menu to add a standard module to the project. This module is used for error handling. Go to the module's property list by pressing F4, name it **bError**, and save the file as **ERROR.BAS**. Add the following code to a **Public Sub** procedure. Two values are going to be passed to this procedure. One is a string value and is the name of the procedure in which the remote data object error occurred. The other is a long value and is the error number that occurred. When an error occurs in any of the modules, this procedure is executed. The system beeps to notify the user that an error has occurred. The procedure the error occurred in, a description of the error, and the error number are displayed in a message box.

```
' Generic Error routine
Public Sub afx_GenericError(sProcedure As String, lErr As Long)
    On Error GoTo Err_afx_GenericError

    Beep
    MsgBox sProcedure & " " & Error$(lErr) & ". " & CStr(lErr)
Exit_afx_GenericError:
    Exit Sub
Err_afx_GenericError:

    Call afx_GenericError("afx_GenericError:", Err)
    Stop
End Sub
```

How It Works

As the form loads, the **m_Resv** member instantiates itself to the class module, **CDataObjects**. In this process, the connection to ODBC and the SQL Server database is made. Then the grid settings are established with the number of columns, their width, and column headers. The form then calls **FillGrid** and passes the name of the grid, the SQL statement to be processed, and which columns are to be used in the grid to the procedure. The **FillGrid** procedure is based on the **FillControl** procedure used in How-To 4.6. Based on the arguments passed to it, a nested loop is used to fill in the grid with the appropriate information.

In the **FillGrid** procedure, the **rdoResultset** is opened based on the SQL statement passed to it. In this example, the SQL statement is designed to retrieve the reservation number, first and last name of a guest, and their phone number from the **tbl_Reservations** table. The **If** statement checks to make sure that data was returned by the **OpenResultset** statement. If data is returned the **EOF** flag will be set to **false** and the **For...Next** loop is used to insert information into the grid's columns, while the **Do...Loop** points the insertion to the correct row on the grid. The **MoveNext** method moves the data pointer to the next row in the resultset. Because it is not known how many rows are going to be returned by the resultset, a counter is used to add a row to the grid each time a data pointer moves to the next row.

When you click OK, the **m_Resv** member is set to nothing, which causes the **Class_Terminate** event to be processed. This closes all your connections to the database.

Comments

This problem could have been solved using the DBGrid that also ships with Visual Basic 6; however, the MsFlexGrid control was designed with either bound or unbound data in mind. This means that MsFlexGrid is much easier to use in an unbound manner.

COMPLEXITY
BEGINNING

4.8 How do I...
Display calculated fields in an unbound grid?

COMPATIBILITY: VISUAL BASIC 5 AND 6

Problem

I want to show marketing the percentage of how much people are paying to stay at any one of our hotels versus what the rooms actually cost. How can I show calculated information in a spreadsheetlike manner without using a bound control? I do not want to use a bound control because I do not want the overhead of binding my database connection to a data control and then linking that to a control.

Technique

As with any business function, certain sets of formulas and rules apply to applications across the enterprise. By encapsulating these business rules in a class module outside the application, this function could be used in many other applications as well.

This How-To builds on what you learned in How-To 4.7. The same FillGrid procedure in CDataObjects is used to fill the grid with the calculated information. Because calculations are different from data access, the process of calculating numbers is going to be placed in a separate class module. The MsFlexGrid control is going to be used as in How-To 4.7 because it works well with unbound data.

Steps

Open and run CALCGRID.VBP. The form shown in Figure 4.15 appears. The grid is filled with the hotel number, reservation number, last and first name of the guest, the amount the guest paid for the reservation, the actual cost of the room, and the percentage of markup (or down) the guest paid. To exit the program, click OK.

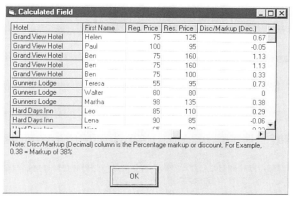

Figure 4.15 Payment markup or discount displayed in the grid

Complete the following steps to create this project:

1. Create a new project and save it as CALCGRID.VBP. Select the default form, Form1, name it frmMain, and save it as FMAIN.FRM. Assign the objects and properties for this form as listed in Table 4.37.

Table 4.37 Objects and properties of FMAIN.FRM

OBJECT	PROPERTY	SETTING
Form	Name	frmMain
	Appearance	1 - 3D
	Caption	"Calculated Field"
MsFlexGrid	Name	grdRoomRes
Command Button	Name	cmdOK
	Caption	"OK"
Label	Name	lblLegend
	Caption	"Note: Disc/Markup (Decimal) column is the Percentage markup or discount. For Example, 0.38 = Markup of 38%"

2. Insert the following code into the General Declarations section of the frmMain. This creates a new object of CDataObjects when the object variable, m_RoomResv, is declared.

```
Option Explicit

' Assign the member to the Data Object
Private m_RoomResv As CDataObjects
```

3. Insert the following code into the **Form_Load** event. As the form loads, the **Set** statement creates the instance of **CDataObject** to the member variable, **m_RoomResv**. The **With** statement prepares the grid with the appropriate number of columns and sets up their width. Then the **FillGrid** procedure is called and fills the grid, **grdRoomRes**.

```
Private Sub Form_Load()

    On Error GoTo Err_Form_Load

    ' Create the instance
    Set m_RoomResv = New CDataObjects

    ' Initialize Grid Settings
    With grdRoomRes
        .Cols = 6
        .ColWidth(0) = 1800
        .ColWidth(1) = 720
        .ColWidth(2) = 1440
        .ColWidth(3) = 1080
        .ColWidth(4) = 900
        .ColWidth(5) = 900
        .Row = 0
        .Col = 0
        .Text = "Hotel"
        .Col = 1
        .Text = "Res. No"
        .Col = 2
        .Text = "Guest's Last Name"
        .Col = 3
        .Text = "First Name"
        .Col = 4
        .Text = "Reg. Price"
        .Col = 5
        .Text = "Res. Price"
    End With

    sSQL = "SELECT c.Name, b.ResNo, b.LastName, "
    sSQL = sSQL & "b.FirstName, b.Amount, a.Price "
    sSQL = sSQL & "From tbl_Rooms a, tbl_Reservations b "
    sSQL = sSQL & ", tbl_Hotels c "
    sSQL = sSQL & "Where a.Room = b.Room "
    sSQL = sSQL & "And a.Hotel = b.Hotel "
    sSQL = sSQL & "And b.Hotel = c.Hotel "
    sSQL = sSQL & "Order by c.Name"

    m_RoomResv.FillGrid grdRoomRes, sSQL, "Hotel", _
        "ResNo", "LastName", "FirstName", "Amount", "Price"
    m_RoomResv.CalcPercent grdRoomRes      ' Fill the control

Exit_Form_Load:
    Exit Sub

Err_Form_Load:
    Call afx_GenericError("Form_Load:", Err)
    Resume Exit_Form_Load
End Sub
```

4. Insert the following code in the **Form_Unload** event. As the form gets unloaded, the reference to the member created in the **Form_Load**, m_RoomResv, is terminated, and the application ends.

```
Private Sub Form_Unload(Cancel As Integer)

    Set m_RoomResv = Nothing

End Sub
```

5. Enter the following code in the **cmdOK** command button's **Click** event. This procedure invokes the **Form_Unload** event to end the sample program.

```
Private Sub cmdOK_Click()

    On Error GoTo Err_cmdOK_Click

    Unload Me

Exit_cmdOK_Click:
    Exit Sub

Err_cmdOK_Click:
    Call afx_GenericError("cmdOK_Click:", Err)
    Resume Exit_cmdOK_Click
End Sub
```

6. Choose Insert, Class Module from the Visual Basic menu to add a new class module. Name it **CDataObjects** and save it as **CDATAOBJ.CLS**.

7. Add the following code to the General Declarations section of the **CDataObjects** class module. The first constant defines your environment member. The next constant defines your database connection.

```
Option Explicit

' Environment
Private m_env As rdoEnvironment

' Connect
Private m_con As rdoConnection
```

8. Insert the following code in the **Class_Initialize** event of the **CDataObject** class module. When this class is initialized, the **Set** statement assigns the m_Calcs member to the **CCalculations** object. Then the RDO environment and connection to your ODBC data source name is opened. If an error occurs during any process of opening, the error handling routine is called.

```
Private Sub Class_Initialize()

    Dim sSql As String

    On Error GoTo Err_Class_Initialize

    Set m_Calcs = New CCalculations

    ' use the default workspace and database
    Set m_env = rdoEnvironments(0)
    Set m_con = m_env.OpenConnection("dsnWaiteSQL", , ,
    ➥"UID=sa;PWD= ")

Exit_Class_Initialize:
    Exit Sub

Err_Class_Initialize:
    Call afx_GenericError("Class_Initialize:", Err)
    Resume Exit_Class_Initialize
End Sub
```

9. Add the following code to the **Class_Terminate** event of the **CDataObject** class module. This event closes all the connections to the object variables opened in the **Class_Initialize** procedure. By closing the RDO environment, all connections and resultsets related to it are also closed.

```
Private Sub Class_Terminate()

    On Error GoTo Err_Class_Terminate

' Close the RDO environment
    If Not (m_env Is Nothing) Then
        m_env.Close
    End If

    ' Clear the references
    Set m_env = Nothing
Exit_Class_Terminate:
    Exit Sub

Err_Class_Terminate:
    Call afx_GenericError("Class_Terminate:", Err)
    Resume Exit_Class_Terminate

End Sub
```

10. Add the following **Public** method to the **CDataObject** class module to fill the desired grid control with the requested information. The **OpenResultset** performs the SQL statement passed to it. The **If** statement checks to make sure that data was returned to the resultset. If there is data, the **Do...Loop** processes each row of information, and the **For...Next** loop inserts information into each column of the grid.

```
' Fill an unbound grid control with the data
'
' Parameters:
'   cntl        list type control to fill
'   sSQL        SQL statement
'   sColumns    name of the columns of data to display
Public Sub FillGrid(cntl As Control, sSQL As String, _
    ParamArray sColumns() As Variant)

    On Error GoTo Err_FillGrid

    Dim sData As String
    Dim x As Long
    Dim y As Long
    Dim nMaxRows As Long
    Dim rs As rdoResultset

    ' Open the resultset
    Set rs = m_con.OpenResultset(sSQL)

    ' Add each record until the end of the file
    y = 1
    If (Not rs.BOF) Then
        Do Until rs.EOF
            cntl.Row = y
            For x = 0 To UBound(sColumns)
                With cntl
                    .Col = x
                    .Text = rs(x)
                End With
            Next
            ' Get next row and add another row
            ' to the grid
            rs.MoveNext
            y = y + 1
            cntl.Rows = y + 1
        Loop
    End If

Exit_FillGrid:
    Exit Sub
Err_FillGrid:
    Call afx_GenericError("FillGrid:", Err)
    Resume Exit_FillGrid

End Sub
```

11. Add the following **Private** method to the **CDataObjects** class module. This method performs the calculation of the price variance of how much the guest paid for the reservation versus what the room actually cost. The grid to be used is passed to this method through the argument variable. The first process adds one more row to the gird control to contain the percentage value of the discount, and percentage is placed in the column's title. Next, to process the calculations, the fourth and fifth columns are looped through to get the dividend and divisor to calculate the percentage. The dividend and divisor are passed to the member, m_Calcs properties, Dividend and Divisor. The m_Calcs member has a method to calculate the percentage. The result of the calculation is placed in the percentage column by getting the m_Calcs property Percentage. If an error occurs during this method, the error-handling routine handles displaying the error to the user. The following steps explain how the m_Calcs handles the calculation of the percentage.

```
Private Sub CalcPercent(cntl As Control)

    Dim x As Long
    Dim y As Long

    On Error GoTo Err_CalcPercent

    ' Set up Discount/Markup column
    With cntl
        .Cols = .Cols + 1
        .Col = .Cols - 1
        .ColWidth(.Cols - 1) = 1740
        .Row = 0
        .Text = "Disc/Markup (Dec.)"
    End With
    ' Process the Discount/Markup
    For y = 1 To cntl.Rows - 1
        cntl.Row = y
        For x = 4 To 5
            cntl.Col = x
            If x = 5 Then
                m_Calcs.Divisor = CDbl(cntl.Text)
            Else
                m_Calcs.Dividend = CDbl(cntl.Text)
            End If
        Next x
        ' Add info to column
        With cntl
            .Col = 6
            .Text = m_Calcs.Percentage
        End With
    Next y

Exit_CalcPercent:
    Exit Sub

Err_CalcPercent:
    Call afx_GenericError("CalcPercent:", Err)
    Resume Exit_CalcPercent
End Sub
```

12. Choose Insert, Class Module from the Visual Basic menu to add a new class module. Name it CCalculations and save it as CCALC.CLS.

13. Add the following code to the General Declarations section of the **CCalculations** class module. The members defined here are variables that will be used for calculating the percentage of price variance.

```
Option Explicit

Private m_Divisor As Double
Private m_Dividend As Double
Private m_Percentage As Double
```

14. Add the following **Public Property** procedures to the **CCalculations** class module. The **Property Let** and **Get** are used to define the **Divisor** member. These procedures expose the properties to the other parts of the application.

```
Public Property Let Divisor(dDivisor As Double)
    m_Divisor = dDivisor
End Property

Public Property Get Divisor() As Double
    Divisor = m_Divisor
End Property
```

15. Add the following **Public Property** procedures to the **CCalculations** class module. The **Property Let** and **Get** are used to define the **Dividend** member. These procedures expose the properties to the other parts of the application.

```
Public Property Let Dividend(dDividend As Double)
    m_Dividend = dDividend
End Property

Public Property Get Dividend() As Double
    Dividend = m_Dividend
End Property
```

16. Add the following **Public Property** procedures to the **CCalculations** class module. The **Property Let** and **Get** are used to define the **Percentage** member. These procedures expose the properties to the other parts of the application. In the **Property Get** procedure, the calculation for the percentage is performed and formatted to display up to two decimal places.

```
Public Property Let Percentage(dPercentage As Double)
    m_Percentage = dPercentage
End Property

Public Property Get Percentage() As Double

    Percentage = Format(((m_Divisor / m_Dividend) /
    ➥m_Dividend), "#.00")

End Property
```

17. Choose Insert, Module from the Visual Basic menu to add a standard module to the project. This module is used for error handling. Go to the module's property list by pressing F4, name it **bError**, and save the file as **ERROR.BAS**. Add the following code to a **Public Sub** procedure. Two values are going to be passed to this procedure. One is a string value and is the name of the procedure in which the remote data object error occurred. The other is a long value and is the error number that occurred. When an error occurs in any of the modules, this procedure is executed. The system beeps to notify the user that an error has occurred. The procedure the error occurred in, a description of the error, and the error number are displayed in a message box.

```
' Generic Error routine
Public Sub afx_GenericError(sProcedure As String, lErr As Long)
    On Error GoTo Err_afx_GenericError

    Beep
    MsgBox sProcedure & " " & Error$(lErr) & ". " & CStr(lErr)

Exit_afx_GenericError:
    Exit Sub
Err_afx_GenericError:
    Call afx_GenericError("afx_GenericError:", Err)
    Stop
End Sub
```

How It Works

As the form loads, the **m_RoomResv** member variable is assigned the class module, **CDataObjects**. As **CDataObjects** gets initialized, the connection to ODBC and the SQL Server database is made. Then the grid control gets set up. The column headings and their widths are applied to the control. The **Form_Load** procedure then calls the **FillGrid** procedure. Based on the arguments passed to the procedure, a **For...Next** loop is used to fill the grid with the appropriate information.

In the **FillGrid** procedure, the **rdoResultset** is opened based on the SQL statement passed to it. The **If** statement checks to make sure that data was returned by the **OpenResultset** statement. If data is returned, the **For...Next** loop is used to insert information into the grid's columns, while the **Do...Loop** points the insertion to the correct row on the grid. The **MoveNext** method moves the data pointer to the next row in the resultset. Because it is not known how many rows are going to be returned by the resultset, a counter is used to add a row to the grid each time the data pointer moves to the next row.

After the **FillGrid** procedure is performed, the **CalcPercent** procedure is called. First, a new column is added to the grid, and its header information is set up. Then the nested **For...Next** loops are used to process each row in the grid. The column header row and the last row are not processed. The header row is not processed because it already has the value of the column title. The last row is not processed because there is no information to place in it. The first `For...Next` loop is used to process the rows, and the second `For...Next` loop is used to process the columns. When the discount or markup value is calculated, the `Percentage` procedure is performed, and the calculated value is added to the cell.

When you click OK, the `m_RoomResv` member is set to nothing, which causes the `Class_Terminate` event to be processed. This closes all your connections to the database.

Comments

If you plan to use the `CDataObject`'s procedures in more than one application, it would be a good idea to put them in an ActiveX DLL or ActiveX Server. By doing so, you separate the business function from the application, so if the business function needs to be changed, you can change it without affecting any application that uses it.

COMPLEXITY
BEGINNING

4.9 How do I...
Control the number of rows displayed?

COMPATIBILITY: VISUAL BASIC 5 AND 6

Problem

I have a large amount of data I want to retrieve and use to populate a list box or combo box. The problem I'm having is that the more information being retrieved into the resultset, the longer it takes to fill the control. I'm getting many complaints from my users about how long this process is taking. Rather than retrieving all the records from the database tables based on my query, how do I limit the number of records retrieved into my resultset? Also, how do I get the rest of the records when the users want to see them?

Technique

One factor many developers overlook when it comes to retrieving data is how much is actually needed at any one time. Using lookup controls such as a list box or combo box, there is a finite amount of space the user can see at one given time. For example, in a forecasting system, you might have more than 10,000 different organizations to look at. One method of displaying this information is to break the organizations down by cost groups and have the information split into two or more different list boxes.

Another way of retrieving a controlled amount of data is by using cursors, or row pointers, to allow for moving up and down in a resultset with both relative and absolute positioning. Relative positioning refers to moving through a list of data through the use of a plus or minus value. Absolute positioning refers to moving the record pointer to an exact record number. For example, you have 5,000 rows of information, and your record pointer is pointing at record 2,500. On your form, command buttons allow the user to move to the next or previous 100 rows. This is an example of relative positioning. Also on your form, command buttons allow the user to go to a specific record number. When you click the button, you enter the value 3,500 and press Enter. The record pointer now goes directly to record 3,500, and you display the record information for that record's row. This is an example of absolute positioning.

When retrieving a large amount of data for example—more than 1,000 rows—rather than display all the rows at once, fetch only the first 100 rows and display them in the list box. As the user scrolls through the data, when he reaches the 100th row, then he can fetch the next 100, and so on.

This How-To uses the `rdoResultset` method `GetRows`. The `GetRows` method uses relative positioning. It retrieves the number of rows from an `rdoResultset` based on the argument you pass to it and puts the resulting information in a variant array.

Steps

Open and run `CURSORS.VBP`. The form shown in Figure 4.16 appears. When the form loads, an `rdoResultset` is created. The list box is filled with the list of the guests of the hotel. Instead of displaying all the guests at once, only the first five guests are displayed. To display more, press the command button, and the next five are displayed, and so on. When the list box has all the rows from the `rdoResultset` in it, a message box appears notifying you that you have retrieved all the records, and you will not be able to click the button again.

Figure 4.16 The first five records of registered guests

Complete the following steps to create this project:

1. Create a new project called **CURSORS.VBP**. Open **Form1** and name it **fMain**. Save it as **FMAIN.FRM**. Add the objects and assign the properties to the form as listed in Table 4.38.

Table 4.38 Objects and properties of FMAIN.FRM

OBJECT	PROPERTY	SETTING
Form	Name	frmMain
	Caption	"Registered Guests"
List Box	Name	lstGuests
Command Button	Name	cmdGetMoreNames
	Caption	"Display More Guests"
Command Button	Name	cmdClose
	Caption	Close

2. Add the following code to the General Declarations section of **fMain**. The first variable is used to make the number of columns from the SQL statement available throughout the form. The next variable is used to build a two-dimensional array that contains the names of the guests. The last variable is for the **rdoResultset**.

```
Option Explicit

Dim nColumns As Integer
Dim vGuests As Variant
Dim rs As rdoResultset
```

3. Insert the following code in the **Form_Load** event. As the form loads, the **rdoResultset** is created. The SQL statement is not being built in the normal fashion but through a function. This is explained in a later step. After the **rdoResultset** is created, the first set of rows is retrieved and is displayed by calling the **FetchRows** subroutine.

```
Private Sub Form_Load()

    Dim env As rdoEnvironment
    Dim con As rdoConnection
    Dim sSQL As String

    On Error GoTo Err_Form_Load

    ' Use the default environment
    Set env = rdoEnvironments(0)
    ' Open the connection
```

continued on next page

continued from previous page

```
Set con = env.OpenConnection(dsName:="dsnWaiteSQL",
➡Connect:="UID=sa;pwd=")

' Create the result set
sSQL = "Select " & BuildSQL("FirstName", "LastName")
sSQL = sSQL & " from tbl_Reservations Order by FirstName"
Set rs = con.OpenResultset(sSQL)

' Get the first set of rows
Call FetchRows

Exit_Form_Load:
    Exit Sub

Err_Form_Load:
    Call afx_GenericError("Form_Load:", Err)
    Resume Exit_Form_Load
End Sub
```

4. Insert the following code in the **Form_Unload** event. As the form gets unloaded, the reference to the RDO resultset created in the **Form_Load** is closed and set to **Nothing**.

```
Private Sub Form_Unload(Cancel as Integer)

    On Error GoTo Err_Form_Unload

    rs.Close
    Set rs = Nothing

Exit_Form_Unload
    Exit Sub

Err_Form_Unload
    Call afx_GenericError(("Form_Unload:", Err)
    Resume Exit_Form_Unload
```

5. Insert the following function, **BuildSQL**, to the form module. The function returns a string value, and because you do not know how many select items the query is going to have, the function accepts arguments via the **ParamArray**. This function has three purposes. First, it establishes how many select items are going to be used in the SQL statement. It stores that number in the module variable **nColumns**. Second, it puts the passed arguments into a contiguous string used in the SQL statement. And because the SQL statement is dynamically built, it removes the last comma from the SQL statement. If the last comma were left in the statement, an error would result.

```
Function BuildSQL(ParamArray sSql() As Variant) As String

    Dim x As Integer
    Dim sSelect As String

    On Error GoTo Err_BuildSQL

    ' Get the Number of columns
    nColumns = UBound(sSql())
    ' Build the Select criteria
    For x = 0 To nColumns
        sSelect = sSelect & sSql(x) & ","
    Next
    ' Remove the last comma
    sSelect = Left(sSelect, Len(sSelect) - 1)

    BuildSQL = sSelect

Exit_BuildSQL:
    Exit Function

Err_BuildSQL:
    Call afx_GenericError("BuildSQL:", Err)
    Resume Exit_BuildSQL
End Function
```

6. Insert the following procedure code, `FetchRows`, to the form module. When an `rdoResultset` is first created, its `BOF` and `EOF` properties are set to `False`. If the `rdoResultset` is `True`, then there are no more rows to receive, and you exit the procedure. Otherwise, the `rdoResultset` method, `GetRows`, is called and retrieves the specified number of rows. Then use the number for columns from the `nColumns` variable and the `UBound` function to get how many rows were actually retrieved using the `GetRows` method. The argument you assign the method is the number of rows returned; in this How-To, you set it to 5. The nested `For...Next` loop is used to populate the list box.

```
Private Sub FetchRows()

    Dim y As Integer
    Dim x As Integer
    Dim sGuest As String

    On Error GoTo Err_FetchRows

    ' Check resultset for guests
    If rs.BOF Then
        MsgBox prompt:="No Guests found", Title:="Guest List"
        cmdGetMoreRows.Enabled = False
        Exit Sub
    ElseIf rs.EOF Then
```

continued on next page

continued from previous page

```
        MsgBox prompt:="No more guests found", Title:="Guest List"
            cmdGetMoreRows.Enabled = False
            Exit Sub
    End If
    ' Get the next set of rows
    vGuests = rs.GetRows(5)

        ' Add the guest names to the list box
    For y = 0 To UBound(vGuests, 2)
        sGuest = ""
        For x = 0 To nColumns
            sGuest = sGuest & " " & vGuests(x, y)
        Next x
        lstGuests.AddItem sGuest
    Next y

Exit_FetchRows:
    Exit Sub
Err_FetchRows:
    Call afx_GenericError("FetchRows:", Err)
    Resume Exit_FetchRows
End Sub
```

7. Insert the following code in the **Click** event of the command button, **cmdClose**. This unloads the form, which triggers the **Form_Unload** event.

```
Private Sub cmdClose_Click()

    Unload Me

End Sub
```

8. Insert the following code in the **Click** event of the command button **cmdGetMoreRows**. This calls the **FetchRows** subprocedure.

```
Private Sub cmdGetMoreRows_Click()

    On Error GoTo Err_cmdGetMoreRows_Click

    Call FetchRows

Exit_cmdGetMoreRows_Click:
    Exit Sub

Err_cmdGetMoreRows_Click:
    Call afx_GenericError("cmdGetMoreRows_Click:", Err)
    Resume Exit_cmdGetMoreRows_Click
End Sub
```

9. Choose Insert, Module from the Visual Basic menu to add a standard module to the project. This module is used for error handling. Go to the module's property list by pressing F4, name it **bError**, and save the file as **ERROR.BAS**. Add the following code to a **Public Sub** procedure. Two values are going to be passed to this procedure. One is a string value and is the name of the procedure in which the remote data object error occurred. The other is a long value and is the error number that occurred. When an error occurs in any of the modules, this procedure is executed. The system beeps to notify the user that an error has occurred. The procedure the error occurred in, a description of the error, and the error number are displayed in a message box.

```
' Generic Error routine
Public Sub afx_GenericError(sProcedure As String, lErr As Long)
    On Error GoTo Err_afx_GenericError

    Beep
    MsgBox sProcedure & " " & Error$(lErr) & ". " & CStr(lErr)

Exit_afx_GenericError:
    Exit Sub

Err_afx_GenericError:
    Call afx_GenericError("afx_GenericError:", Err)
    Resume Exit_afx_GenericError
End Sub
```

How It Works

When the form loads, connections to ODBC and the database are made. Then the **Load** event creates the **rdoResultset** based on the SQL query and retrieves the first five rows in the resultset. If the query was successful in retrieving information, the **FetchRows** procedure continues. If no data was retrieved, the **rs.BOF** flag is true, and a message box notifies the user. If no more information is in the resultset, the **rs.EOF** flag is true, and a message box notifies the user. To retrieve a group of rows at one time, the **GetRows** method is used. It retrieves the number of rows specified and places them into the array, **vGuests**. It then places a record pointer on the next row of information in the resultset. When the command button to get more guest names is clicked, the **FetchRows** procedure retrieves the next five rows based on where the record pointer lies. If only three rows are left when the **GetRows** method is called, then only three rows are retrieved, and the **rdoResultset's EOF** property is set to **True**.

When you click Close, the RDO resultset is closed and is set to **Nothing**. Then the application ends.

Comments

There is a caveat you should to be aware of when using the **GetRows** method. If the **rdoResultset** contains a binary large object (BLOB) or the **rdoColumn** object has a data type of **rdTypeLONGVARBINARY** or **rdTypeLONGVARCHAR**, you must use the **GetChunk** method. If you use the **GetRows** method against such a resultset, you receive the error message **Error 40036 - Unbound Column - use GetChunk**.

COMPLEXITY
INTERMEDIATE

4.10 How do I...
Create a Master/Detail form?

COMPATIBILITY: VISUAL BASIC 5 AND 6

Problem

In Microsoft Access, I can design a form with an embedded child form. The main form would contain primary information, such as customer information, and the embedded child form would contain detail information, such as customer order information. This method uses bound controls so that when I change the primary information, the child information is updated because they are linked by a common key, typically the customer's account number. How would I implement something like this in Visual Basic?

Technique

Visual Basic, unlike Microsoft Access, does not allow you to embed a form within another form. You must design all the form's components onto one form. Rather than using bound controls to link different database tables together, you use the remote data object to create resultsets with the necessary information based on criteria that the user selects from a combo box.

Steps

Open and run HOTEL.VBP, and you see the form shown in Figure 4.17. The combo box labeled Hotel is filled with the names of the hotels from the database table, tbl_Hotels. The grid to the right of the combo box displays all the rooms available at the hotel selected in the Hotel combo box. The bottom grid displays all the reservations made at the hotel selected in the Hotel combo box.

Complete the following steps to create this project:

1. Select Form1, which was created when you first created this project. Name it frmReservations and save it as HOTELRES.FRM. Assign the objects and properties for this form as listed in Table 4.39. The form should look and be laid out similarly to Figure 4.17.

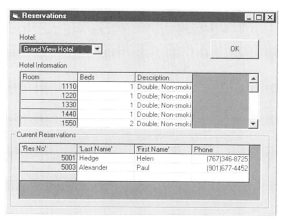

Figure 4.17 Hotel room and reservation
information displayed in two grids

Table 4.39 Objects and properties of HOTELRES.FRM

OBJECT	PROPERTY	SETTING
Form	Name	frmReservations
	Appearance	1 - 3D
	Caption	"Reservations"
Label	Name	lblHotel
	Caption	"&Hotel"
Label	Name	lblHotelInfo
	Caption	"Hotel &Info"
Combo Box	Name	cboHotels
	Style	2 - Dropdown List
Frame	Name	fraCurrentReservations
	Caption	"Current Reservations"
MsFlexGrid	Name	grdRoomInfo
MsFlexGrid	Name	grdResv
Command Button	Name	cmdOK
	Caption	"OK"

2. Insert the following code in the General Declarations section of
frmReservations. This creates a new object member for CDataObjects
when the object variable, m_Resv, is declared.

```
Option Explicit

' Assign the Resv member to the Data Object
Private m_Resv As CDataObjects
```

3. Insert the following code in the Form_Load event. As the form loads, this
event creates the instance of the data access object for the m_Resv member
variable. The FillControl method performs the SQL statement, and the
cboHotel combo box is populated with the name of the hotels.

```
Private Sub Form_Load()

    On Error GoTo Err_Form_Load

    ' Set the SQL Statment for Hotels
    sSQL = "Select Hotel, Name from tbl_Hotels"

    m_Resv.FillControl cboHotel, sSQL, "hotel", "name"

Exit_Form_Load:
    Exit Sub

Err_Form_Load:
    Call afx_GenericError("Form_Load:", Err)
    Resume Exit_Form_Load
End Sub
```

4. Insert the following code in the Form_Unload event. As the form gets
unloaded, the reference to the members created in the Form_Load, m_Resv,
is terminated, and the application ends.

```
Private Sub Form_Unload(Cancel As Integer)

    On Error GoTo Err_Form_Unload

    ' Clear the reference
    Set m_Resv = Nothing

Exit_Form_Unload:
    Exit Sub

Err_Form_Unload:
    Call afx_GenericError("Form_Unload:", Err)
    Resume Exit_Form_Unload
End Sub
```

5. Enter the following code in the **cboHotel** combo box's **Click** event. This subroutine changes the pointer to an hourglass to provide feedback to the user that something is happening. Based on the hotel selected in the **cboHotel** combo box, the room and reservation information about the desired hotel is displayed in its respective grid. Then the mouse pointer changes back to its default setting.

```
Private Sub cboHotel_Click()

    Dim sSQL As String

    On Error GoTo Err_cboHotel_Click

    Screen.MousePointer = vbHourglass

    sSQL = "Select Room, Beds, Description "
    sSQL = sSQL & "From tbl_Rooms a, tbl_Roomtypes b "
    sSQL = sSQL & "Where a.roomtype = b.roomtype "
    sSQL = sSQL & "And Hotel = " & cboHotel.ListIndex + 1
    m_Resv.FillGrid grdRoomInfo, sSQL, "Room", "Beds",
    ➥"Description"

    ' Set the SQL Statement for Reservations
    sSQL = "Select ResNo as 'Res No', LastName as 'Last Name', "
    sSQL = sSQL & "FirstName as 'First Name', Phone "
    sSQL = sSQL & "From tbl_Reservations "
    sSQL = sSQL & "Where hotel = " & cboHotel.ListIndex + 1
    m_Resv.FillGrid grdResv, sSQL, "Res. No", "Last Name",
    ➥"First Name", "Phone"

    Screen.MousePointer = vbDefault

Exit_cboHotel_Click:
    Exit Sub
Err_cboHotel_Click:
    Call afx_GenericError("cboHotel_Click:", Err)
    Resume Exit_cboHotel_Click
End Sub
```

6. Add the following code to the form for the OK command button's **Click** event. This subroutine causes the **Form_Unload** event to be triggered to end the program.

```
Private Sub cmdOK_Click()

    On Error GoTo Err_cmdOK_Click

    Unload Me

Exit_cmdOK_Click:
    Exit Sub

Err_cmdOK_Click:
    Call afx_GenericError("cmdOK_Click:", Err)
    Resume Exit_cmdOK_Click
End Sub
```

7. Choose Insert, Class Module from the Visual Basic menu to add a new class module. Name it **CDataObjects** and save it as **CDATAOBJ.CLS**.

8. Add the following code to the General Declarations section of **CDataObjects**. The first variable defines your RDO environment member. The next defines your RDO connection member.

```
Option Explicit

' Database
Private m_env As rdoEnvironment

' Connection
Private m_con As rdoConnection
```

9. Insert the following code in the **Class_Initialize** event of **CDataObject**. When this class is initialized, the RDO environment and connection are opened. If an error occurs during any process of opening, the error-handling routine is called.

```
Private Sub Class_Initialize()

    Dim sSql As String

    On Error GoTo Err_Class_Initialize

    ' use the default environment
    Set m_env = rdoEnvironments(0)
    ' Open the connection
    Set m_con = m_env.OpenConnection(dsName:="dsnWaiteSQL",
    ➥Connect:="UID=sa;pwd=")

Exit_Class_Initialize:
    Exit Sub

Err_Class_Initialize:
    Call afx_GenericError("Class_Initialize:", Err)
    Resume Exit_Class_Initialize
End Sub
```

10. Add the following code to the **Class_Terminate** event of the **CDataObject**. This event closes the RDO environment to the object variables opened in the **Class_Initialize** procedure. By closing the RDO environment, all connections and resultsets related to it are also closed. If an error occurs during any process, the error-handling routine is called.

```
Private Sub Class_Terminate()

    On Error GoTo Err_Class_Terminate

    ' Close the resultset and database
    If Not (m_env Is Nothing) Then
```

```
        m_env.Close
    End If

    ' Clear the references
    Set m_env = Nothing
Exit_Class_Terminate:
    Exit Sub

Err_Class_Terminate:
    Call afx_GenericError("Class_Terminate:", Err)
    Resume Exit_Class_Terminate
End Sub
```

11. Add the following **Public** method to the **CDataObjects** class to fill the desired control, either a list box or combo box, with the requested information. The **ParamArray** argument allows for an optional number of arbitrary arguments to be passed to this method. The control is cleared before any information is added to it. The **rdoResultset** is created based on the SQL statement that is passed to this procedure. As the resultset is processed, the selected control is populated. When the pointer has processed every record in the resultset, the control's **ListIndex** property is set to the first record.

```
' Fill any list type control with the data
'
' Parameters:
'   cntl        list type control to fill
'   sSQL        SQL Statement
'   sIDColumn   name of the column containing the record ID
'   sColumns    name of the columns of data to display
Private Sub FillControl(cntl As Control, sSQL as string, _
    sIDColumn As String, ParamArray sColumns() As Variant)

    Dim sData As String
    Dim i As Integer
    Dim rs as rdoResultset

    On Error GoTo Err_FillControl

    ' Clear the list
    cntl.Clear

    ' open the resultset
    Set rs = m_con.OpenResultset(sSQL)


    ' Add each record until the end of the file
    If (Not rs.BOF) Then
        Do Until rs.EOF
            ' Concatenate each desired column
            sData = ""
            For i = 0 To UBound(sColumns)
                sData = sData & " " & rs(cstr(sColumns(i)))
```

continued on next page

continued from previous page

```
                Next
                ' Add the item to the list
                cntl.AddItem sData
                cntl.ItemData(cntl.NewIndex) = rs(sIDColumn)

                ' Move to the next row
                rs.MoveNext
            Loop
        End If

        ' Set control to highlight the first record
        ' in the list
        cntl.ListIndex = 0

Exit_FillControl:
    Exit Sub

Err_FillControl:
    Call afx_GenericError("FillControl:", Err)
    Resume Exit_FillControl
End Sub
```

12. Add the following **Public** method to fill the desired grid control with the requested information. First, the procedure determines how many rows must be added to the grid and adds one to the count to include the column headers. Using the **UBound** function against the **sColumns'** **ParamArray**, the number of columns for the grid is determined, and the grid's row and column counts are adjusted accordingly. The width of the columns is set to one inch. The **rdoResultset** object has a collection called **rdoColumns**, which represents the column information of the **rdoResultset**. By using the **Name** property of the **rdoColumns**, the database column name is returned and placed in the column heading of the grid. The record pointer is then reset to the beginning of the **rdoResultset** and is processed into the grid.

```
' Fill an unbound grid control with the data
'
' Parameters:
'   cntl        list type control to fill
'   sSQL        SQL statement
'   sColumns    name of the columns of data to display
Pbulic Sub FillGrid(cntl As Control, rs As rdoResultset, _
    ParamArray sColumns() As Variant)

    Dim sData As String
    Dim i As Integer
    Dim j As Long
    Dim lMaxRows As Long
    Dim rs As rdoResultset
    Dim sFieldName As String

    On Error GoTo Err_FillGrid
```

```
        ' Open the resultset
        Set rs = m_con.OpenResultset(sSQL)

' Set up the grid
      With cntl
          .Cols = UBound(sColumns) + 1
          .Rows = cntl.Rows
      End With
      For i = 0 To cntl.Cols - 1
          cntl.ColWidth(i) = 1440
      Next i

      ' Fill in the Column headers from the
      ' Database column names
      If (Not rs.BOF) Then
          cntl.Row = 0
          For i = 0 To cntl.Cols - 1
              cntl.Col = i
              sFieldName = rs.rdoColumns(i).Name
              cntl.Text = sFieldName
          Next


          ' Add each record until the end of the file
          j = 1
          Do Until rs.EOF
              cntl.Row = j
              For i = 0 To UBound(sColumns)
                  With cntl
                      .Col = i
                      .Text = rs(i)
                  End With
              Next
              ' Get next row
              rs.MoveNext
              j = j + 1
          Loop
      End If

Exit_FillGrid:
    Exit Sub
Err_FillGrid:
    Call afx_GenericError("FillGrid:", Err)
    Resume Exit_FillGrid
End Sub
```

13. Choose Insert, Module from the Visual Basic menu to add a standard module to the project. This module is used for error handling. Go to the module's property list by pressing F4, name it **bError**, and save the file as **ERROR.BAS**. Add the following code to a **Public Sub** procedure. Two values are going to be passed to this procedure. One is a string value and is the name of the procedure in which the remote data object error occurred. The other is a long value and is the error number that occurred. When an error occurs in any of the modules, this procedure is executed. The system beeps to notify the user that an error has occurred. The procedure the error occurred in, a description of the error, and the error number are displayed in a message box.

```
' Generic Error routine
Public Sub afx_GenericError(sProcedure As String, lErr As Long)
    On Error GoTo Err_afx_GenericError

    Beep
    MsgBox sProcedure & " " & Error$(lErr) & ". " & CStr(lErr)

Exit_afx_GenericError:
    Exit Sub

Err_afx_GenericError:
    Call afx_GenericError("afx_GenericError:", Err)
    Resume Exit_afx_GenericError
End Sub
```

How It Works

In this How-To, the detail form is the grid controls. When the form first loads, the m_Resv member is assigned to CDataObjects. CDataObjects gets initialized, and the OBDC and SQL Server database connections are made. Then the FillControl procedure is called, and it processes the SQL statement. The procedure fills the cboHotel combo box with a list of the hotel names. When the FillControl procedure sets the first item in the list as the selected item, the cboHotel_Click event is performed.

The cboHotel_Click event uses the combo box's selected items as part of the Where criteria of the SQL statement. This event calls the FillGrid procedure twice. Once is to fill the grdRoomInfo grid, and the other is to fill the grdResv grid.

When the OK button is clicked, the m_Resv member is set to Nothing, which causes the Class_Terminate event to be processed. This closes all your connections to the database.

Comments

Visual Basic is different from Microsoft Access when it comes to form design. One of the biggest paradigms Access programmers have to overcome is the fact that Visual Basic does not support the Form/Subform concept.

COMPLEXITY
INTERMEDIATE

4.11 How do I...
Create a query by example?

COMPATIBILITY: VISUAL BASIC 5 AND 6

Problem

Occasionally, my users must look up information using different search criteria. Often the resulting data from the query actually contains the same information, only the order in which the data is to be laid out or the date range on which to base the query is different. How can I accomplish this without rewriting the query each time they request this information?

Technique

This technique is often called Query by Example. It is not new; search engines within database programs have been using it for years. The technique is simple. Many times your users want to create their own reports based on layouts they have received in other reports, but they are unfamiliar with how the data items are related to one another. The users would, therefore, have trouble specifying the exact criteria they need to get the results they want. By knowing what information users want to retrieve and the possible variations of their requests, your application can use combo boxes, check boxes, radio buttons, and text boxes to have the users select and deselect items for their searches. The user basically builds a query from the components you provide.

Steps

Open and run **QBE.VBP**, and you see the form shown in Figure 4.18. The information in the Hotel combo box comes from the **tbl_Hotels** table from the Hotels database. The information in the Payment Type combo box comes from the **tbl_PaymentTypes** table from the Hotels database. First, select a hotel where you want to see whether there are any reservations. Then select a payment type to help narrow the search. If you want to look up all payment types, select the All item. The other items, Arrival Date, Departure Date, and Sort By, are optional parameters. Click the Find command button to perform the search. If any information is found, it will be put in the grid with the frame Results (see Figure 4.19). If no information is found, then a message box appears notifying you that no records were found. The Clear command button clears the results grid. The End command button exits the program.

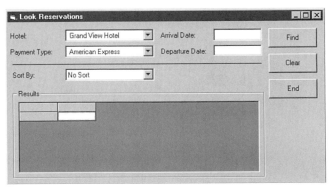

Figure 4.18 Reservation lookup form before a query

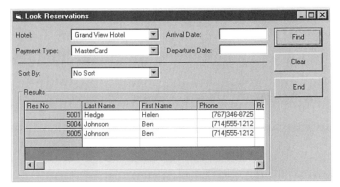

Figure 4.19 Results of a reservation lookup

Complete the following steps to create this project:

1. Create a new project and save it as **QBE.VBP**. Select the default form, **Form1**, name it **frmMain**, and save it as **FMAIN.FRM**. Assign the objects and properties for this form as listed in Table 4.40. The form should look similar to Figure 4.18 illustrated earlier. The **Line** object is not defined in the table because it is added just to show the separation of the **Where** criteria versus **Order By** criteria.

Table 4.40 Objects and properties of FMAIN.FRM

OBJECT	PROPERTY	SETTING
Form	Name	frmMain
	Appearance	1 - 3D
	Caption	"Lookup Reservations"
Command Button	Name	cmdFind
	Caption	"Find"
Command Button	Name	cmdClear
	Caption	"Clear"
Command Button	Name	cmdEnd
	Caption	"End"
Label	Name	lblHotel
	Caption	"&Hotel:"
Label	Name	lblPaymentType
	Caption	"&Payment Type:"
Label	Name	lblArrivalDate
	Caption	"&Arrival Date:"
Label	Name	lblDepartureDate
	Caption	"&Departure Date:"
Label	Name	lblSortBy
	Caption	"&Sort By:"
Combo Box	Name	cboHotels
	Style	2 - Dropdown List
Combo Box	Name	cboPaymentType
	Style	2 - Dropdown List
Combo Box	Name	cboSortBy
	Style	2 - Dropdown List
Line	Name	Line1
Text Box	Name	txtArrivalDate
	Text	""
Text Box	Name	txtDepartureDate
	Text	""
Frame	Name	fraResults
	Caption	"Results"
MsFlexGrid	Name	grdRes

2. Insert the following code into the General Declarations section of `frmMain`. This creates a new object of `CDataObjects` when the object variable, `m_Res`, is declared.

```
Option Explicit

' Assign the Res Name Member to the Data Object
Private m_Res As CDataObjects
```

3. Insert the following code in the `Form_Load` event. As the form loads, this event creates the instance of the data access object for the `m_Res` member variable. The Hotel combo box and Payment Type combo box are filled with data from their respective tables. The Sort By combo box is populated through the `AddItem` method, and the control is set to display the first record in its list.

```
Private Sub Form_Load()

    Dim sSQL As String

    On Error GoTo Err_Form_Load

    ' Create the instance
    Set m_Res = New CDataObjects

    ' Fill the combo box with the information from the database
    sSQL = "Select Hotel, Name from tbl_Hotels"
    m_Res.FillControl cboHotels, sSQL, "Hotel", "Name"

    sSQL = "Select payment, descrip from tbl_PaymentTypes "
    sSQL = sSQL & "Order By descrip"
    m_Res.FillControl cboPaymentType, sSQL, "payment", "descrip"

    ' Fill the Sort By combo box
    cboSortBy.AddItem "No Sort"
    cboSortBy.AddItem "Last Name"
    cboSortBy.AddItem "First Name"
    cboSortBy.AddItem "Arrival Date"
    cboSortBy.AddItem "Departure Date"
    cboSortBy.ListIndex = 0

Exit_Form_Load:
    Exit Sub

Err_Form_Load:
    Call afx_GenericError("Form_Load: ", Err)
    Resume Exit_Form_Load

End Sub
```

4. Insert the following code in the `Form_Unload` event. As the form gets unloaded, the reference to the object created in the `Form_Load`,

CDataObjects, is terminated, and the application ends. If an error occurs, the error is displayed through the **Error** procedure.

```
Private Sub Form_Unload(cancel As Integer)

    On Error GoTo Err_Form_Unload

    ' Clear the references
    Set m_Res = Nothing

Exit_Form_Unload:
    Exit Sub

Err_Form_Unload:
    Call afx_GenericError("Form_Unload:", Err)
    Resume Exit_Form_Unload
End Sub
```

5. Enter the following code in the form for the **Find** command button's **Click** event. This procedure first investigates the Sort By combo box to determine what type of sorting the query requires. Then the SQL statement is built by concatenating the **sSQL** variables so that part of the **Where** clause can be built dynamically. After it is built, the **FillGrid** procedure is executed to fill the **grdRes** grid. Note: In the Arrival and Departure dates section of the query, if you are using an Access database, replace the ticks (') with pound signs (#). Access uses these symbols when comparing date fields. All other database management systems use the tick marks.

```
Private Sub cmdFind_Click()

    Dim sSortBy As String

    On Error GoTo Err_cmdFind_Click

    ' Establish sort criteria
    Select Case cboSortBy.ListIndex
        Case 0
            sSortBy = "No Sort"
        Case 1
            sSortBy = "LastName"
        Case 2
            sSortBy = "FirstName"
        Case 3
            sSortBy = "DateIn"
        Case 4
            sSortBy = "DateOut"
    End Select

    ' Fill the grid
    sSQL = "select resno as 'Res No', lastname as 'Last Name', "
    sSQL = sSQL & "firstname as 'First Name', Phone, "
```

continued on next page

continued from previous page

```
                sSQL = sSQL & "room as 'Room Nbr', datein as 'Arrival', "
                sSQL = sSQL & "dateout as 'Depart' "
                sSQL = sSQL & "From tbl_reservations "
                sSQL = sSQL & "Where hotel = " &
            ➥cboHotels.ListIndex + 1 & " "
                If cboPaymentType.ListIndex <> 5 Then ' All Payment Types
                    sSQL = sSQL & "And Payment = "
                    sSQL = sSQL & cboPaymentType.ItemData
                ➥(cboPaymentType.ListIndex)
        & " "
                End If
                If txtArrivalDate <> "" Then
                    sSQL = sSQL & "and DateIn >= '" & txtArrivalDate & "' "
                End If
                If txtDepartureDate <> "" Then
                    sSQL = sSQL & "and DateOut <= '" &
                ➥txtDepartureDate & "' "
                End If
                If sSortBy <> "No Sort" Then
                    sSQL = sSQL & "Order by " & sSortBy
                End If

                m_Res.FillGrid grdRes, sSQL, "Res No", "Last Name",
            ➥"First Name", _
                    "Phone", "Room Nbr", "Arrival", "Depart"

        Exit_cmdFind_Click:
            Exit Sub

        Err_cmdFind_Click:
            Call afx_GenericError("cmdFind_Click:", Err)
            Resume Exit_cmdFind_Click
        End Sub
```

6. Add the following code to the form for the **End** command button's **Click** event. This subroutine causes the **Form_Unload** event to be triggered to end the program.

```
Private Sub cmdEnd_Click()

    On Error GoTo Err_cmdEnd_Click

    Unload Me

Exit_cmdEnd_Click:
    Exit Sub

Err_cmdEnd_Click:
    Call afx_GenericError("cmdEnd_Click:", Err)
    Resume Exit_cmdEnd_Click
End Sub
```

7. Add the following code to the form's **Clear** command button's **Click** event. This procedure clears all the data and leaves the column headers intact.

```
Private Sub cmdClear_Click()

    Dim x As Integer
    Dim y As Integer

    On Error GoTo Err_cmdClear_Click

    With grdRes

        .Rows = 2

        For y = 0 To .Cols - 1
            .Col = y
            For x = 1 To .Rows - 1

                .Row = x
                .Text = ""

            Next x
        Next y
    End With

Exit_cmdClear_Click:
    Exit Sub

Err_cmdClear_Click:
    Call afx_GenericError("cmdClear_Click:", Err)
    Resume Exit_cmdClear_Click
End Sub
```

8. Choose Insert, Class Module from the Visual Basic menu to add a new class module. Name it **CDataObjects** and save it as **CDATAOBJ.CLS**.

9. Add the following code to the General Declarations section of the **CDataObjects** class module. The first variable defines your **Environment** member. The next variable defines your database connection member.

```
Option Explicit

' Database
Private m_env As rdoEnvironment

' Connection
Private m_con As rdoConnection
```

10. Insert the following code in the **Class_Initialize** event of the **CDataObject** class module. When this class is initialized, the environment and connection to the ODBC data source name is opened. If an error occurs during any process of opening, the error-handling routine is called.

```
Private Sub Class_Initialize()

    On Error GoTo Err_Class_Initialize

    ' use the default environment
    Set m_env = rdoEnvironments(0)
    ' Open the connection
    Set m_con = m_env.OpenConnection(dsName:="dsnWaiteSQL",
    ➥Connect:="UID=sa;pwd=")

Exit_Class_Initialize:
    Exit Sub

Err_Class_Initialize:
    Call afx_GenericError("Class_Initialize:", Err)
    Resume Exit_Class_Initialize
End Sub
```

11. Add the following code to the **Class_Terminate** event of the
CDataObject. This event closes the RDO environment object variables
opened in the **Class_Initialize** procedure. By closing the RDO
environment, all connections and resultsets related to it are also closed.

```
Private Sub Class_Terminate()

    On Error GoTo Err_Class_Terminate

    ' Close the resultset and database
    If Not (m_env Is Nothing) Then
        m_env.Close
    End If

    ' Clear the references
    Set m_env = Nothing


Exit_Class_Terminate:
    Exit Sub

Err_Class_Terminate:
    Call afx_GenericError("Class_Terminate:", Err)
    Resume Exit_Class_Terminate
End Sub
```

12. Add the following **Public** method to the **CDataObjects** class module to
fill the desired control, either a list box or combo box, with the requested
information. The **ParamArray** argument allows for an optional amount of
arbitrary arguments to be passed to this method. The control is cleared
before any information is added to it. The **rdoResultset** is created based
on the SQL statement passed to this procedure. After the resultset is
created, its information is populated into the selected control. After the
resultset is finished filling the control, the control's **ListIndex** property is
set to the first item so that it is displayed to the user.

```
' Fill any list type control with the data
'
' Parameters:
'   cntl         list-type control to fill
'   sSQL         SQL statement
'   sIDColumn    name of the column containing the record ID
'   sColumns     name of the columns of data to display
Public Sub FillControl(cntl As Control, sSQL as string, _
    sIDColumn As String, ParamArray sColumns() As Variant)

    Dim sData As String
    Dim i As Integer
    Dim rs as rdoResultset

    On Error GoTo Err_FillControl

    ' Clear the list
    cntl.Clear

    ' open the resultset
    Set rs = m_con.OpenResultset(sSQL)


    ' Add each record until the end of the file
    If (Not rs.BOF) Then
        Do Until rs.EOF
            ' Concatenate each desired column
            sData = ""
            For i = 0 To UBound(sColumns)
                sData = sData & " " & rs(CStr(sColumns(i)))
            Next
            ' Add the item to the list
            cntl.AddItem sData
            cntl.ItemData(cntl.NewIndex) = rs(sIDColumn)

            ' Move to the next row
            rs.MoveNext
        Loop
    End If

    ' Set control to highlight the first record
    ' in the list
    cntl.ListIndex = 0

Exit_FillControl:
    Exit Sub

Err_FillControl:
    Call afx_GenericError("FillControl:", Err)
    Resume Exit_FillControl
End Sub
```

13. Add the following `Public` method to the `CDataObjects` class module to fill the desired grid control with the requested information. The `OpenResultset` performs the SQL statement passed to it. The `If` statement checks to make sure that data was returned into the resultset. If there is data, the `Do...Loop` processes each row of information, and the `For...Next` loop inserts information into each column of the grid. If there is no information, a message box notifies the user.

```
' Fill an unbound grid control with the data
'
' Parameters:
'    cntl              list type control to fill
'    sSQL              SQL statement
'    sColumns          name of the columns of data to display
Private Sub FillGrid(cntl As Control, sSQL as String, _
    ParamArray sColumns() As Variant)

    Dim sData As String
    Dim i As Integer
    Dim j As Long
    Dim lMaxRows As Long
    Dim rs as rdoResultset
    Dim sFieldName As String

    On Error GoTo Err_FillGrid

    ' Open the resultset
    Set rs = m_con.OpenResultset(sSQL)
    ' Add each record until the end of file
    ' Set up the grid
    With cntl
        .Cols = UBound(sColumns) + 1
        .Rows =.Rows

        For i = 0 To cntl.Cols - 1
            cntl.ColWidth(i) = 1440
        Next i
        ' Clear the grid
        .Rows = 2
        .Row = 1
        For i = 0 To .Cols - 1
            .Col = i
            .Text = ""
        Next


        ' Fill in the Column headers from the
        ' Database column names

        If (Not rs.BOF) Then
            .Row = 0
            For i = 0 To .Cols - 1
                .Col = i
                sFieldName = rs.rdoColumns(i).Name
                .Text = sFieldName
```

```
                    Next
                    j = 1
                    Do Until rs.EOF
                        cntl.Row = j
                        For i = 0 To UBound(sColumns)

                            .Col = i
                            .Text = rs(sColumns(i))

                        Next
                        ' Get next row
                        rs.MoveNext
                    j = j + 1
                    Loop
                Else
                    MsgBox prompt:="No information available", _
                        Title:=App.Title
                End If
            End With

    Exit_FillGrid:
        Exit Sub
    Err_FillGrid:
        Call afx_GenericError("FillGrid:", Err)
        Resume Exit_FillGrid
    End Sub
```

14. Choose Insert, Module from the Visual Basic menu to add a standard
module to the project to be used for error handling. Go to the module's
property list by pressing F4, name it **bError**, and save the file as
ERROR.BAS. Add the following code to a **Public Sub** procedure. Two
values are going to be passed to this procedure. One is a string value and
is the name of the procedure in which the remote data object error
occurred. The other is a long value and is the error number that occurred.
When an error occurs in any of the modules, this procedure is executed.
The system beeps to notify the user that an error has occurred. The
procedure the error occurred in, a description of the error, and the error
number are displayed in a message box.

```
' Generic Error routine
Public Sub afx_GenericError(sProcedure As String, lErr As Long)
    On Error GoTo Err_afx_GenericError

    Beep
    MsgBox sProcedure & " " & Error$(lErr) & ". " & CStr(lErr)

Exit_afx_GenericError:
    Exit Sub

Err_afx_GenericError:
    Call afx_GenericError("afx_GenericError:", Err)
    Resume Exit_afx_GenericError
End Sub
```

How It Works

When the `frmMain` form loads, the Hotel and Payment Type combo boxes are populated with the information retrieved from the tables. Because there is no table for the `Sort By` options, they are added to the combo box hard-coded into the form.

The user must select a hotel, payment type, and method with which to sort by. The How-To defaults `Hotel` to `Grand View Hotel`, `Payment Type` to `American Express`, and the `Sort By` to `No Sort`, which stands for no sort order. The date ranges are optional parameters. When the Find button is clicked, the SQL query is built based on the provided information, and the results are displayed in the grid. If no data is available, the grid is cleared, and a message box notifies the user that no information is available, as illustrated in Figure 4.20.

When the Clear button is clicked, the grid is set back to two rows. All the rows are cleared except for the column headers. When you click the End button, the `m_Res` member is set to `Nothing`, which causes the `Class_Terminate` event to be processed. This closes all your connections to the database.

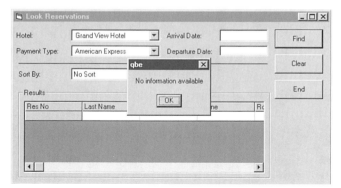

Figure 4.20 Reservation lookup notifies the user that no information is available

Comments

In this How-To, you hard-coded the Sort By combo box with values. This is not a good programming practice. If the Sort By criteria changes later, you would have to change the source code and redistribute the application. A better practice is to have the list come from a reference table, similar to the Hotel and Payment Type combo boxes. When information changes, all you must do is update the database table, and the application will reflect the changes.

Also, this example can be used as part of a report generator's interface. You can add another button labelled Print and write a routine to print the contents using VB's `Printer` object and `Printer` collection.

COMPLEXITY

INTERMEDIATE

4.12 How do I...
Build an HTML application interface?

COMPATIBILITY: VISUAL INTERDEV 1.X AND ABOVE

Problem

Several of our managers just came back from a marketing seminar, and they keep talking about *Web-enabled* applications. I've created HTML pages before to establish a Web presence for our organization, but what does it mean to make a Web-enabled application, and how do I accomplish this with Visual Basic?

Technique

When Microsoft became an Internet-aware company officially on December 7, 1995, the way we looked at data and applications was changed forever. At that point, every application that Microsoft made or had on the drawing board became Internet aware and was going to be Web-enabled.

If you ask a room full of developers what a Web-enabled application is, you'll likely get a room full of different answers, and many of them could be right. For the purpose of this How-To, a Web-enabled application simply means an application that runs over the Internet or a company's intranet.

The technology that enables the World Wide Web, more commonly referred to as the Web, makes a logical extension to the User Services layer in a client/server environment. Web technology refers to HTTP services, HTML, Perl/CGI (Common Gateway Interface) scripting, Java, JavaScript, and ActiveX Scripting, just to name a few. By writing HTML application interfaces, you can extend accessibility of your application to a greater number of users. HTML application interfaces are not like your standard HTML document that a company's "Webmaster" dishes out for the world to see. HTML application interfaces should be left to application developers or Web architects. A *Web architect*, a term not widely used, is a developer who creates applications using Web technology, as well as database access, COM/COM+/DCOM, and so on. In September 1997, Alan Cooper of Cooper Software, the "Father of Visual Basic," gave a keynote address at an Intranet Solutions conference. He referred to Webmasters as a bunch of lightweight developers who rely on the technology and components of others. Web architects are much more savvy developers because aside from using other people's technology, they know how to create their own to extend their applications, just like other developers.

To create an HTML application interface, you don't need the Visual Basic IDE. An HTML application interface can be created with any text editor, Microsoft Visual InterDev or Visual Studio, ActiveX Control Pad, Allaire's HomeSite, or WYSIWYG (What You See Is What You Get) editor such as Microsoft FrontPage 98 or Symantec Visual Page. In this How-To, you use Notepad, which comes with the Windows operating system, to create an HTML application interface. The application interface is going to be the main screen of a Web page for the Hotel Reservation system.

Steps

Open the `INDEX.HTM` file within Microsoft Internet Explorer (MSIE) browser. The file can be found on the CD in the `Source\Chap04\HT4-12` directory. This HTML document displays the main page for BoguSystems Hotel & Resorts home page. Figure 4.21 shows part of what the form looks like with MSIE. This HTML document uses the `<Table>` tags to help separate information into logical areas. Figure 4.22 illustrates the layout. The areas labeled `<Image>` and `<Table>` are covered in step 1. Three `<Table Data>` areas are surrounded by a `<Table Row>` section. `<Table Data 1>` is explained in step 2. `<Table Data 2>` and `3` are explained in step 3. The plain text area is covered in step 4.

Figure 4.21 BoguSystems' Hotels & Resorts home page displayed in MSIE

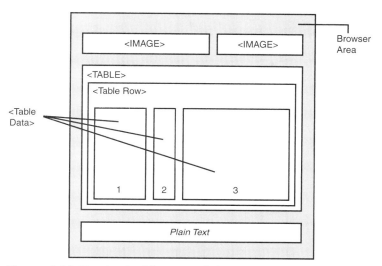

Figure 4.22 The logical layout of the `Index.htm` document

The steps in this How-To require that you have some knowledge of HTML. You are only going to create an HTML document, so you really don't need to be concerned with setting up a virtual directory with Microsoft Internet Information Server. (If you're running Windows NT Workstation, it's called *Peer Web Services*. If you're using Windows 95/98, it's called Personal Web Server.)

Complete the following steps to create this project:

1. Open Notepad, which comes with the Windows operating system. The shortcut to launch it is found in the Accessories menu from the Start button. There are many graphics associated with this exercise. Copy the `.GIF` files from `Chapter4\Ht12` directory on the CD to your project directory. Enter the following text and tags in the Notepad editor:

```
<HTML>
<HEAD>
  <TITLE>Welcome to the World of BoguSystems'
  ➥Hotels &amp; Resorts</TITLE>
</HEAD>

<BODY BGCOLOR="#FFFFFF" LINK="#000080" ALINK="#800000"
➥VLINK="#800000" TEXT="#000000">

<IMG SRC="boguslogo.GIF" WIDTH=380 HEIGHT=80 BORDER="0">
➥<IMG SRC="hotels.GIF" WIDTH=200 HEIGHT=80 BORDER="0">
<TABLE BORDER=0 CELLSPACING=0 CELLPADDING=0 WIDTH=600><TR>
  <TD><IMG ALT="" SRC="3.gif" WIDTH=76 HEIGHT=36></TD>
  <TD><IMG ALT="" SRC="5.gif" WIDTH=76 HEIGHT=36></TD>
  <TD><IMG ALT="" SRC="7.gif" WIDTH=76 HEIGHT=36></TD>
  <TD><IMG ALT="" SRC="8.gif" WIDTH=76 HEIGHT=36></TD></TR>
</TABLE>
<P>
```

2. Add the following HTML tags and text to the Notepad edit window. This sets up the main table, establishes a row within the table, and creates a list of graphic menus to be displayed along the left side of the document.

```
<TABLE WIDTH="600" BORDER="0" CELLSPACING="0" CELLPADDING="0">
<TR><TD WIDTH="175" VALIGN="TOP"><BR>
<A HREF="resv.html">
  <IMG NAME="reservations" SRC="reservation.gif"
  ➥WIDTH=172 HEIGHT=28 ALT="Reservations" BORDER=0
  ➥VSPACE=0 HSPACE=0></A><P>

<A HREF="directory.html">
  <IMG NAME="directory" SRC="directory.gif" WIDTH=172
  ➥HEIGHT=28 ALT="Hotel & Resort Directory" BORDER=0
  ➥VSPACE=0 HSPACE=0></A><P>

<A HREF="hotdeals.html">
  <IMG NAME="hotdeals" SRC="hotdeals.gif" WIDTH=172 HEIGHT=28
  ➥ALT="Hot Deals" BORDER=0 VSPACE=0 HSPACE=0></A><P>

<A HREF="meetings.html">
  <IMG NAME="meetings" SRC="meeting.gif" WIDTH=172 HEIGHT=28
  ➥ALT="Meeting Planning" BORDER=0 VSPACE=0 HSPACE=0></A><P>

<A HREF="sitemap.html">
  <IMG NAME="sitemap" SRC="sitemap.gif" WIDTH=172 HEIGHT=28
  ➥ALT="Sitemap" BORDER=0 VSPACE=0 HSPACE=0></A><P>

<A HREF="about.html">
  <IMG NAME="About BoguSystems" SRC="about.gif" WIDTH=172
  ➥HEIGHT=28 ALT="About BoguSystems" BORDER=0
  ➥VSPACE=0 HSPACE=0> </A></TD>
```

3. Add the following HTML tags and text to create the second and third Table Data columns. The first <TD> tag creates a gutter between the first and third column. The third Table Data column displays a welcome to every visitor. To make the page more personal, a JavaScript routine checks the time of day the Web visitor comes to the page and greets her with a "Good Morning," "Good Afternoon," or "Good Evening."

```
<TD WIDTH="25"> </TD>
<TD WIDTH="400" ALIGN="LEFT" VALIGN="TOP"><BR>
<FONT FACE="Arial, Helvetica" SIZE="+2"><B>
➥<SCRIPT LANGUAGE="JavaScript">
<!--
  var dt = new Date();
  var hr = dt.getHours();
  var msg = ((hr<12) ? "Morning" :"Evening");
  msg = ((hr>11)&&(hr<18) ? "Afternoon" : msg);
  msg=" Good "+msg+ " and ";
  document.write(msg);
<!-- end -->
</SCRIPT>
```

```
Welcome to<BR>
BoguSystems Hotels &amp; Resorts</B></FONT><P>
<CENTER><IMG SRC="flip-pic.gif" WIDTH=114 HEIGHT=110
➥BORDER="0"></CENTER></TD>
</TR>
```

4. Add the following HTML tags and text to the Notepad edit window. This is a text menu similar to the graphic menu you entered in step 2. This allows the user to continue to navigate to another HTML document without having to scroll back up the page if she is at the bottom of the document.

```
<TR><TD WIDTH="608" COLSPAN="3" ALIGN="CENTER" VALIGN="TOP">
➥<BR><BR>
<CENTER><FONT FACE="Arial, Helvetica" SIZE=2>
home ¦ <A HREF="resv.html">reservations</A> ¦
➥<A HREF="directory.asp">hotel directory</A>
 ¦ <A HREF="hotdeals.htm">hot deals</A>
 ➥ ¦ <A HREF="meeting.htm">meeting planner</A><BR>
<A HREF="sitemap.htm">sitemap</A>
➥¦ <A HREF="mailto:info@bogusystem.com ">
➥contact bogusystems</A>
 ¦ copyright notice</FONT></TD></TR></CENTER>
</FONT></TD></TR>
</TABLE><BR>
</BODY>
</HTML>
```

5. Save the file as Index.HTML in your project directory. You can now open up the file within your Internet browser to view the HTML document.

How It Works

INDEX.HTML is one of the four common root files that most Web servers look at as the default HTML file. The others are INDEX.HTM, DEFAULT.HTML, and DEFAULT.HTM. You can change the server to look for something else, of course, but it makes more sense to just use what is expected.

When a Web browser receives an HTML document, it interprets the contents of the document into a more presentable format, based on the HTML tags you use. Think of HTML as WordStar for the Internet. In case you're not familiar with WordStar, it was one of the most popular word processors for DOS-based and CP/M-based computers. The interface was all character based and in order to perform any formatting of your text, you needed to insert formatting codes before and after a word or phrase. Unlike the word processors of today where you highlight words or phrases and click on a format button, you never knew how your document was going to turn out until you printed it. The same holds true with HTML where you won't know how your document truly looks until you view it through a browser.

An HTML document consists of formatting tags and text and are broken into two sections, the head and the body. The head element resides between the `<HEAD>` and `</HEAD>` tags and contains metainformation about the information contained in the body element. This metafinformation usually does not have a direct visible effect within a browser's viewing window. The body element resides between the `<BODY>` and `</BODY>` tags and contains the "meat" of the HTML document.

As the browser opens the document, it figures out were all the text goes and this document uses the table tags, `<TABLE>`, `<TR>`, and `<TD>`, to display information in a logical manner. There is also a JavaScript routine that reads the system clock from the user's workstation to determine whether it is morning, afternoon, or evening to display the appropriate greeting.

Comments

As you might have guessed, it can be cumbersome to create Web files using an editor such as Notepad. If you have trouble visualizing how your document is going to lay out working strictly in the text like you do with Notepad, it might be worth spending the time to familiar yourself with a WYSIWYG editor. After you get more familiar with Web page layout, using a WYSIWYG editor to help with more difficult layouts and a sophisticated text editor such as Allaire's HomeSite or Microsoft's Visual InterDev will definitely help you be more productive. For more information about HTML in general, *HTML 4 How-To: The Definitive HTML 4 Problem Solver* by John Zakour (Waite Group Press) is a good reference.

COMPLEXITY
INTERMEDIATE

4.13 How do I...
Add ActiveX controls to the interface?

COMPATIBILITY: VISUAL STUDIO/VISUAL INTERDEV 1.X
AND ABOVE

Problem

I've created the Web interface for the application, but HTML `Forms` tags are really limited. Our organization has standardized on Microsoft Internet Explorer as its browser of choice. Can I use any of the ActiveX controls on my system, and what are design-time ActiveX controls?

Technique

The HTML Form tags are very limited. They were not designed with application development in mind. ActiveX controls with ActiveX scripting offer a great alternative because you will be working with controls you're familiar with and scripting code that you're already familiar with.

In case you're not familiar with the term ActiveX scripting, here's a quick overview. ActiveX scripting consists of a set of COM interfaces that define the specifications for ActiveX scripting hosts and ActiveX scripting engines. An example of an ActiveX scripting host is Microsoft Internet Explorer. VBScript and Microsoft's implementation of JavaScript, JScript, are examples of ActiveX scripting engines. Therefore, to take advantage of ActiveX scripting, you must be concerned with two COM parts, a host and an engine. You cannot effectively use one without the other. Currently, only versions of Microsoft Internet Explorer (MSIE) 3.0 and above support ActiveX scripting. An independent software vendor, NCompass Labs, offers a plug-in for Netscape Navigator/Communicator to make them ActiveX scripting enabled.

Design Time Controls (DTC) are standard ActiveX controls that can generate code for you. Like wizards, they create code in HTML pages or Active Server Pages (ASP). A design-time control has no binary runtime component. It's active only during design time and not at runtime. Only the text generated by the control is active during runtime. The design-time control persists as text with the METADATA and OBJECT tags. In ASP files, these tags appear within comments because they're used only by the authoring tools and not at runtime. At runtime, ASP strips off these tags before generating the HTML page. You can build design-time controls in Visual Basic and Visual C++.

To add ActiveX controls to your HTML application interface, you don't need the Visual Basic IDE. You can use the ActiveX Control Pad, Visual InterDev or Visual Studio, Allaire's HomeSite, or WYSIWYG (What You See Is What You Get) editor that supports ActiveX controls such as Microsoft FrontPage 98 or SoftQuad's HoTMetaL Pro. You can use a text editor or an HTML editor that doesn't support ActiveX controls, but it will be a miserable experience. In this How-To, you use the Design Time ActiveX Control Pad to add ActiveX controls to your application.

Steps

Open the INDEX.HTM file within Microsoft Internet Explorer (MSIE) browser. The file can be found on the CD in the Source\Chap04\HT13 directory. This HTML document uses the Frame tag to create two framed areas: one for the BoguSystem logo and the other for reservation information.

This Reservation HTML document displays what looks like an HTML form, but when you view the source file, you'll find that it doesn't use any HTML form at all. All the controls on the form are Microsoft Form ActiveX controls. Figure 4.23 shows part of what the form looks like with MSIE.

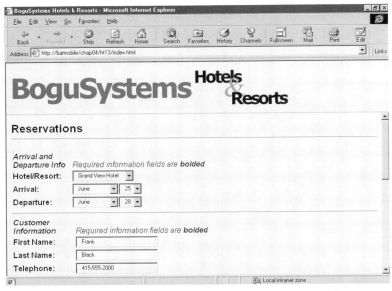

Figure 4.23 A reservation form displayed in MSIE with ActiveX controls

Complete the following steps to create this project:

1. Using the Design Time ActiveX Control Pad, enter the following HTML tags, VBScript procedures, and text. When finished, save the file as **INDEX.HTML** in your project directory.

```
<HTML>
<HEAD>
<TITLE>BoguSystems Hotels &amp; Resorts</TITLE>

<SCRIPT LANGUAGE="VBScript">
<!--
  Dim gHotel
  Dim gArrivalMonth
  Dim gArrivalDay
  Dim gDepartMonth
  Dim gDepartDay

  Dim gFirstName
  Dim gLastName
  Dim gTelephone
  Dim gEMail
  Dim gAddress
  Dim gSuite
  Dim gCity
```

```
      Dim gState
      Dim gZipCode

      Dim gSmoking
      Dim gComments

  Sub Window_onLoad()
      ' Clear Global variables
      gHotel = ""
      gArrivalMonth = ""
      gArrivalDay = ""
      gDepartMonth = ""
      gDepartDay = ""
      gFirstName = ""
      gLastName = ""
      gTelephone = ""
      gEMail = ""
      gAddress = ""
      gSuite = ""
      gCity = ""
      gState = ""
      gZipCode = ""
    gSmoking = False
      gComments = ""

      gConfirm = ""
  End Sub

  -->
  </SCRIPT>
  </HEAD>
  <!-- frames -->
  <FRAMESET  ROWS="110,*">
      <FRAME NAME="fraBanner" SRC="Banner.html" FRAMEBORDER="no">
      <FRAME NAME="fraMain" SRC="resv.htm" SCROLLING="auto"
  ➥FRAMEBORDER="no">
  </FRAMESET>
  </HTML>
```

2. Create a new HTML document and call it **RESV.HTML**. In this HTML document, you are going to enter some VBScript procedures and the ActiveX control on the form. First, enter the following text for the **Title** tag:

```
<TITLE>BoguSystems Hotels & Resorts - Reservations</TITLE>
```

3. Use the Script Wizard to enter the following code for the **Windows_OnLoad** event. Select the plus sign (+) next to Window item under the Select an Event list box. Then select the **OnLoad** event. Figure 4.24 shows the Script Wizard open on the **Windows_OnLoad** event. Select the Code View radio button so that you can enter the following code:

```
Sub Window_onLoad()

cboHotel.AddItem "Grand View Hotel"
cboHotel.AddItem "Mountain Side Resort"
cboHotel.AddItem "Hard Days Inn"
cboHotel.AddItem "Gunners Lodge"

cboArrivalMonth.AddItem "January"
cboArrivalMonth.AddItem "February"
cboArrivalMonth.AddItem "March"
cboArrivalMonth.AddItem "April"
cboArrivalMonth.AddItem "May"
cboArrivalMonth.AddItem "June"
cboArrivalMonth.AddItem "July"
cboArrivalMonth.AddItem "August"
cboArrivalMonth.AddItem "September"
cboArrivalMonth.AddItem "October"
cboArrivalMonth.AddItem "November"
cboArrivalMonth.AddItem "December"

cboDepartureMonth.AddItem "January"
cboDepartureMonth.AddItem "February"
cboDepartureMonth.AddItem "March"
cboDepartureMonth.AddItem "April"
cboDepartureMonth.AddItem "May"
cboDepartureMonth.AddItem "June"
cboDepartureMonth.AddItem "July"
cboDepartureMonth.AddItem "August"
cboDepartureMonth.AddItem "September"
cboDepartureMonth.AddItem "October"
cboDepartureMonth.AddItem "November"
cboDepartureMonth.AddItem "December"

nToday = now()
nMonth = month(now()) -1
cboArrivalMonth.ListIndex = nMonth
cboDepartureMonth.ListIndex = nMonth

Select Case nMonth
    Case 0,2,4,6,7,9,11
        For x = 1 to 31
            cboArrivalDay.AddItem x
            cboDepartureDay.AddItem x
        Next
    Case 1
        For x = 1 to 28
            cboArrivalDay.AddItem x
            cboDepartureDay.AddItem x
        Next
    Case Else
        For x = 1 to 30
            cboArrivalDay.AddItem x
            cboDepartureDay.AddItem x
        Next
End Select
```

```
cboArrivalDay.ListIndex = Day(Now()) -1
cboDepartureDay.ListIndex = Day(Now())

End Sub

-->
</SCRIPT>
</HEAD>
```

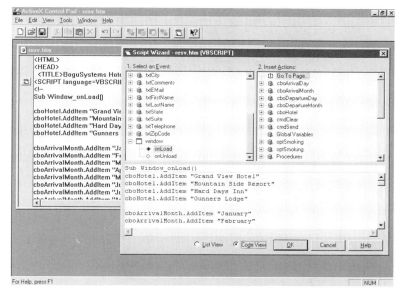

Figure 4.24 Design Time ActiveX Control Pad showing Script Wizard

4. This step is going to be a bit cumbersome because you integrate HTML tags and text with ActiveX controls. The following code uses a two-column table so that the text and ActiveX controls align properly. Enter the following HTML tags and text:

```
<BODY BGCOLOR="#FFFFFF" LINK="#000080" ALINK="#800000"
➥VLINK="#800000" TEXT="#000000">
<BASEFONT FACE="Arial, Helvetica">
<FONT SIZE="+2"><B>Reservations</B></FONT>
<HR>
<B><I></I></B><BR>
<TABLE>
<TR><TD WIDTH="120"><B><I>Arrival and Departure Info</I></B>
</TD>
<TD WIDTH="480" VALIGN="BOTTOM"><I>Required information fields
➥are <B>bolded</B></I></TD></TR>
<TR>
<TD><B>Hotel/Resort:</B></TD>
<TD>
```

5. Choose Edit, Insert ActiveX Control from the menu. From the Insert ActiveX Control dialog box, scroll down to select the Microsoft Forms 2.0 ComboBox. Two dialog boxes appear. One is titled Edit ActiveX Control, and the other is the Properties box. Not quite Visual Basic, but an incredible simulation. Assign the properties to the control as listed in Table 4.41. Figure 4.25 illustrates the Design Time ActiveX Control Pad with the Edit ActiveX Control and Properties windows open.

Table 4.41 Properties for the `cboHotel` combo box

OBJECT	PROPERTY	SETTING
Microsoft	ID	cboHotel
Forms 2.0	Width	128
Combo box	Height	24

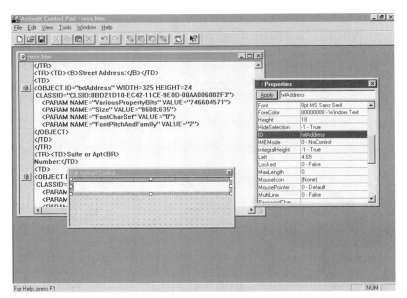

Figure 4.25 The Design Time ActiveX Control Pad displaying the Edit ActiveX Control and Properties dialog boxes

After you close the dialog boxes, your code should look similar to the following:

```
<OBJECT    ID="cboHotel"    WIDTH=128 HEIGHT=24
 CLASSID="CLSID:8BD21D30-EC42-11CE-9E0D-00AA006002F3">
    <PARAM NAME="VariousPropertyBits" VALUE="746604571">
    <PARAM NAME="DisplayStyle" VALUE="3">
    <PARAM NAME="Size" VALUE="2540;635">
```

```
    <PARAM NAME="MatchEntry" VALUE="1">
    <PARAM NAME="ShowDropButtonWhen" VALUE="2">
    <PARAM NAME="FontCharSet" VALUE="0">
    <PARAM NAME="FontPitchAndFamily" VALUE="2">
</OBJECT>
```

6. Add the following HTML tags and text to the HTML document. Then insert a set of Microsoft Forms 2.0 ComboBox controls to be used for Arrival Month and day information. Table 4.42 contains the properties for the controls.

```
</TD></TR>
<TR>
<TD><B>Arrival:</B></TD>
<TD>
```

Table 4.42 Properties for `ArrivalMonth` and `ArrivalDay` combo box

OBJECT	PROPERTY	SETTING
Microsoft Forms	ID	cboArrivalMonth
2.0 Combobox	Width	96
	Height	24
Microsoft Forms	ID	cboArrivalDay
2.0 Combobox	Width	49
	Height	24

After you close the dialog boxes, your code should look similar to the following:

```
<OBJECT ID="cboArrivalMonth" WIDTH=96 HEIGHT=24
 CLASSID="CLSID:8BD21D30-EC42-11CE-9E0D-00AA006002F3">
    <PARAM NAME="VariousPropertyBits" VALUE="746604571">
    <PARAM NAME="DisplayStyle" VALUE="3">
    <PARAM NAME="Size" VALUE="2540;635">
    <PARAM NAME="MatchEntry" VALUE="1">
    <PARAM NAME="ShowDropButtonWhen" VALUE="2">
    <PARAM NAME="FontCharSet" VALUE="0">
    <PARAM NAME="FontPitchAndFamily" VALUE="2">
</OBJECT>

<OBJECT ID="cboArrivalDay" WIDTH=49 HEIGHT=24
 CLASSID="CLSID:8BD21D30-EC42-11CE-9E0D-00AA006002F3">
    <PARAM NAME="VariousPropertyBits" VALUE="746604571">
    <PARAM NAME="DisplayStyle" VALUE="3">
    <PARAM NAME="Size" VALUE="1291;635">
    <PARAM NAME="MatchEntry" VALUE="1">
    <PARAM NAME="ShowDropButtonWhen" VALUE="2">
    <PARAM NAME="FontCharSet" VALUE="0">
    <PARAM NAME="FontPitchAndFamily" VALUE="2">
</OBJECT>
```

7. Add the following HTML tags and text to the HTML document. Then insert a set of Microsoft Forms 2.0 ComboBox controls for displaying the Departure Month and day information. Use Table 4.43 for the properties to define the controls.

```
</TD>
</TR>

<TR>
<TD><B>Departure: </B></TD>
<TD>
```

Table 4.43 Properties for DepartureMonth and DepartureDay combo box

OBJECT	PROPERTY	SETTING
Microsoft Forms 2.0 Combobox	ID	cboDepartureMonth
	Width	96
	Height	24
Microsoft Forms 2.0 Combobox	ID	cboDepartureDay
	Width	49
	Height	24

After you close the dialog boxes, your code should look similar to the following:

```
<OBJECT ID="cboDepartureMonth" WIDTH=96 HEIGHT=24
 CLASSID="CLSID:8BD21D30-EC42-11CE-9E0D-00AA006002F3">
    <PARAM NAME="VariousPropertyBits" VALUE="746604571">
    <PARAM NAME="DisplayStyle" VALUE="3">
    <PARAM NAME="Size" VALUE="2540;635">
    <PARAM NAME="MatchEntry" VALUE="1">
    <PARAM NAME="ShowDropButtonWhen" VALUE="2">
    <PARAM NAME="FontCharSet" VALUE="0">
    <PARAM NAME="FontPitchAndFamily" VALUE="2">
</OBJECT>

<OBJECT ID="cboDepartureDay" WIDTH=49 HEIGHT=24
 CLASSID="CLSID:8BD21D30-EC42-11CE-9E0D-00AA006002F3">
    <PARAM NAME="VariousPropertyBits" VALUE="746604571">
    <PARAM NAME="DisplayStyle" VALUE="3">
    <PARAM NAME="Size" VALUE="1291;635">
    <PARAM NAME="MatchEntry" VALUE="1">
    <PARAM NAME="ShowDropButtonWhen" VALUE="2">
    <PARAM NAME="FontCharSet" VALUE="0">
    <PARAM NAME="FontPitchAndFamily" VALUE="2">
</OBJECT>
```

8. Add the following HTML tags, text, and ActiveX controls to the rest of the HTML document:

```
</TD></TR></TABLE>
<HR>
<TABLE>
<TR><TD><B><I>Customer<BR>Information</I></B></TD>
<TD VALIGN="BOTTOM"><I>Required information fields are
➥<B>bolded</B></I></TD>
</TR>
<TR><TD><B>First Name:</B></TD>
<TD><OBJECT ID="txtFirstName" WIDTH=171 HEIGHT=24
 CLASSID="CLSID:8BD21D10-EC42-11CE-9E0D-00AA006002F3">
     <PARAM NAME="VariousPropertyBits" VALUE="746604571">
     <PARAM NAME="Size" VALUE="4493;635">
     <PARAM NAME="FontCharSet" VALUE="0">
     <PARAM NAME="FontPitchAndFamily" VALUE="2">
</OBJECT>
</TD>
</TR>
<TR><TD><B>Last Name:</B></TD>
<TD><OBJECT ID="txtLastName" WIDTH=171 HEIGHT=24
 CLASSID="CLSID:8BD21D10-EC42-11CE-9E0D-00AA006002F3">
     <PARAM NAME="VariousPropertyBits" VALUE="746604571">
     <PARAM NAME="Size" VALUE="4493;635">
     <PARAM NAME="FontCharSet" VALUE="0">
     <PARAM NAME="FontPitchAndFamily" VALUE="2">
</OBJECT>
</TD>
</TR>
<TR><TD><B>Telephone:</B></TD>
<TD>
<OBJECT ID="txtTelephone" WIDTH=171 HEIGHT=24
 CLASSID="CLSID:8BD21D10-EC42-11CE-9E0D-00AA006002F3">
     <PARAM NAME="VariousPropertyBits" VALUE="746604571">
     <PARAM NAME="Size" VALUE="4493;635">
     <PARAM NAME="FontCharSet" VALUE="0">
     <PARAM NAME="FontPitchAndFamily" VALUE="2">
</OBJECT>
</TD>
</TR>
<TR><TD><B>E-Mail Address:</B></TD>
<TD>
<OBJECT ID="txtEMail" WIDTH=171 HEIGHT=24
 CLASSID="CLSID:8BD21D10-EC42-11CE-9E0D-00AA006002F3">
     <PARAM NAME="VariousPropertyBits" VALUE="746604571">
     <PARAM NAME="Size" VALUE="4493;635">
     <PARAM NAME="FontCharSet" VALUE="0">
     <PARAM NAME="FontPitchAndFamily" VALUE="2">
</OBJECT>
</TD>
</TR>
<TR><TD></TD>
<TD>
```

continued on next page

continued from previous page

```
<I>A reservation confirmation will be sent to the e-mail
➥address provided.</I></TD>
</TR>
<TR><TD><B>Street Address:</B></TD>
<TD>
<OBJECT ID="txtAddress" WIDTH=325 HEIGHT=24
 CLASSID="CLSID:8BD21D10-EC42-11CE-9E0D-00AA006002F3">
    <PARAM NAME="VariousPropertyBits" VALUE="746604571">
    <PARAM NAME="Size" VALUE="4493;635">
    <PARAM NAME="FontCharSet" VALUE="0">
    <PARAM NAME="FontPitchAndFamily" VALUE="2">
</OBJECT>
</TD>
</TR>
<TR><TD>Suite or Apt<BR>
Number:</TD>
<TD>
<OBJECT ID="txtSuite" WIDTH=325 HEIGHT=24
 CLASSID="CLSID:8BD21D10-EC42-11CE-9E0D-00AA006002F3">
    <PARAM NAME="VariousPropertyBits" VALUE="746604571">
    <PARAM NAME="Size" VALUE="4493;635">
    <PARAM NAME="FontCharSet" VALUE="0">
    <PARAM NAME="FontPitchAndFamily" VALUE="2">
</OBJECT>
</TD>
</TR>
<TR><TD><B>City:</B></TD>
<TD>
<OBJECT ID="txtCity" WIDTH=325 HEIGHT=24
 CLASSID="CLSID:8BD21D10-EC42-11CE-9E0D-00AA006002F3">
    <PARAM NAME="VariousPropertyBits" VALUE="746604571">
    <PARAM NAME="Size" VALUE="4493;635">
    <PARAM NAME="FontCharSet" VALUE="0">
    <PARAM NAME="FontPitchAndFamily" VALUE="2">
</OBJECT>
</TD>
</TR>
<TR><TD><B>State:</B></TD>
<TD>
<OBJECT ID="txtState" WIDTH=50 HEIGHT=24
 CLASSID="CLSID:8BD21D10-EC42-11CE-9E0D-00AA006002F3">
    <PARAM NAME="VariousPropertyBits" VALUE="746604571">
    <PARAM NAME="Size" VALUE="1291;635">
    <PARAM NAME="FontCharSet" VALUE="0">
    <PARAM NAME="FontPitchAndFamily" VALUE="2">
</OBJECT>
</TD>
</TR>
<TR><TD><B>Zip/Postal Code:</B></TD>
<TD>
<OBJECT ID="txtZipCode" WIDTH=150 HEIGHT=24
 CLASSID="CLSID:8BD21D10-EC42-11CE-9E0D-00AA006002F3">
    <PARAM NAME="VariousPropertyBits" VALUE="746604571">
    <PARAM NAME="Size" VALUE="4493;635">
    <PARAM NAME="FontCharSet" VALUE="0">
```

```
            <PARAM NAME="FontPitchAndFamily" VALUE="2">
</OBJECT>
</TD>
</TR>
</TABLE>
<HR>
<TABLE>
<TR><TD><B><I>Special Request<BR>
Information:</I></B></TD>
<TD>
</TD>
</TR>
<TR><TD>Smoking<BR>Preferences:</TD>
<TD>

<OBJECT ID="optSmoking" WIDTH=144 HEIGHT=24
 CLASSID="CLSID:8BD21D50-EC42-11CE-9E0D-00AA006002F3">
    <PARAM NAME="VariousPropertyBits" VALUE="746588179">
    <PARAM NAME="BackColor" VALUE="2147483663">
    <PARAM NAME="ForeColor" VALUE="2147483666">
    <PARAM NAME="DisplayStyle" VALUE="5">
    <PARAM NAME="Size" VALUE="3810;635">
    <PARAM NAME="Value" VALUE="0">
    <PARAM NAME="Caption" VALUE="Non-Smoking Room">
    <PARAM NAME="FontName" VALUE="Arial">
    <PARAM NAME="FontHeight" VALUE="220">
    <PARAM NAME="FontCharSet" VALUE="0">
    <PARAM NAME="FontPitchAndFamily" VALUE="2">
</OBJECT>

<OBJECT ID="optSmoking" WIDTH=144 HEIGHT=24
 CLASSID="CLSID:8BD21D50-EC42-11CE-9E0D-00AA006002F3">
    <PARAM NAME="VariousPropertyBits" VALUE="746588179">
    <PARAM NAME="BackColor" VALUE="2147483663">
    <PARAM NAME="ForeColor" VALUE="2147483666">
    <PARAM NAME="DisplayStyle" VALUE="5">
    <PARAM NAME="Size" VALUE="3810;635">
    <PARAM NAME="Value" VALUE="0">
    <PARAM NAME="Caption" VALUE="Smoking Room">
    <PARAM NAME="FontName" VALUE="Arial">
    <PARAM NAME="FontHeight" VALUE="220">
    <PARAM NAME="FontCharSet" VALUE="0">
    <PARAM NAME="FontPitchAndFamily" VALUE="2">
</OBJECT>
</TD>
</TR>
<TR><TD VALIGN="TOP">Comments:</TD>
<TD>

<OBJECT ID="txtComments" WIDTH=407 HEIGHT=87
 CLASSID="CLSID:8BD21D10-EC42-11CE-9E0D-00AA006002F3">
    <PARAM NAME="VariousPropertyBits" VALUE="2894088219">
    <PARAM NAME="Size" VALUE="10747;2275">
    <PARAM NAME="FontCharSet" VALUE="0">
    <PARAM NAME="FontPitchAndFamily" VALUE="2">
```

continued on next page

continued from previous page

```
</OBJECT>
</TD>
</TR>
</TABLE>
<CENTER>

<OBJECT ID="cmdSend" WIDTH=96 HEIGHT=32
 CLASSID="CLSID:D7053240-CE69-11CD-A777-00DD01143C57">
    <PARAM NAME="Caption" VALUE="Send Form">
    <PARAM NAME="Size" VALUE="2540;846">
    <PARAM NAME="FontCharSet" VALUE="0">
    <PARAM NAME="FontPitchAndFamily" VALUE="2">
    <PARAM NAME="ParagraphAlign" VALUE="3">
</OBJECT>
    
<OBJECT ID="cmdClear" WIDTH=96 HEIGHT=32
 CLASSID="CLSID:D7053240-CE69-11CD-A777-00DD01143C57">
    <PARAM NAME="Caption" VALUE="Clear Form">
    <PARAM NAME="Size" VALUE="2540;846">
    <PARAM NAME="FontCharSet" VALUE="0">
    <PARAM NAME="FontPitchAndFamily" VALUE="2">
    <PARAM NAME="ParagraphAlign" VALUE="3">
</OBJECT>


</CENTER>

<P>
<CENTER><FONT FACE="Arial, Helvetica" SIZE=2>home
➥¦ reservations
➥¦ hotel directory ¦ hot deals ¦ meeting planner<BR>
sitemap ¦ contact bogusystems ¦ copyright notice</FONT></TD>
</TR></CENTER>

</BODY>
</HTML>
```

9. Now that you've placed all the ActiveX controls on the form, add the following code for the `cmdSend_Click` event, just like you would if you were using Visual Basic. Using the Script Wizard again, select the plus (+) next to `cmdSend` object in the Select an Event list box. Then select the `Click` event that appears underneath it. Mark the Code View radio button and enter the following code:

```
Sub cmdSend_Click()
    If cboHotel.ListIndex = -1 or _
        txtFirstName.Text = "" or _
        txtLastName.Text = "" or _
        txtTelephone.Text = "" or _
        txtEMail.Text = "" or _
        txtAddress.Text = "" or _
        txtCity.Text = "" or _
        txtState.Text = "" or _
```

```
        txtZipCode.Text = "" Then
        MsgBox "A required field is not filled in.
        ➡Please recheck form."
        Exit Sub
    End If

    parent.gHotel = cstr(cboHotel.ListIndex)
    parent.gArrivalMonth = cboArrivalMonth.ListIndex
    parent.gArrivalDay = cboArrivalDay.ListIndex
    parent.gDepartMonth = cboDepartureMonth.ListIndex
    parent.gDepartDay = cboDepartureDay.ListIndex
    parent.gFirstName = txtFirstName.Text
    parent.gLastName = txtLastName.Text
    parent.gTelephone = txtTelephone.Text
    parent.gEMail = txtEMail.Text
    parent.gAddress = txtAddress.Text
    parent.gSuite = txtSuite.Text
    parent.gCity = txtCity.Text
    parent.gState = txtState.Text
    parent.gZipCode = txtZipCode.Text
    If optSmoking(0).Value = True Then
        parent.gSmoking = False
    Else
        parent.gSmoking = True
    End If
    parent.gComments = txtComments.Text

    parent.frames(1).location.href = "thanks.html"
End Sub
```

10. Select the `cmdClear` object and choose the `Click` event similar to how you did in the preceding step. Enter the following code in the Code View area:

```
Sub cmdClear_Click()
  ' Reset combo boxes
    cboHotel.ListIndex = -1
    cboArrivalMonth.ListIndex = month(now()) -1
    cboDepartureMonth.ListIndex = month(now()) -1
    cboArrivalDay.ListIndex = Day(Now()) -1
    cboDepartureDay.ListIndex = Day(Now())

  ' Clear text boxes and option buttons
    txtFirstName.Text = ""
    txtLastName.Text = ""
    txtTelephone.Text = ""
    txtEMail.Text = ""
    txtAddress.Text = ""
    txtSuite.Text = ""
    txtCity.Text = ""
    txtState.Text = ""
    txtZipCode.Text = ""
    optNonSmoking.Value = 0
    optSmoking.Value = 0
    txtComments.Text = ""
```

continued on next page

continued from previous page

```
' Clear Global variables
  gHotel = ""
  gArrivalMonth = ""
  gArrivalDay = ""
  gDepartMonth = ""
  gDepartDay = ""
  gFirstName = ""
  gLastName = ""
  gTelephone = ""
  gEMail = ""
  gAddress = ""
  gSuite = ""
  gCity = ""
  gState = ""
  gZipCode = ""
gSmoking = False
  gComments = ""

End Sub
```

11. After all this is done, close the **Body** tag and the **HTML** tag. Then save the document as RESV.HTML.

```
<P>
<CENTER><FONT FACE="Arial, Helvetica" SIZE=2>
➥home ¦ reservations ¦ hotel directory ¦ hot deals
➥¦ meeting planner<BR>
sitemap ¦ contact bogusystems ¦ copyright notice</FONT></TD>
➥</TR></CENTER>
</BODY>
</HTML>
```

12. Create a new HTML document. This is going to be used to display a reservation confirmation notice to the user that his request is going to be processed. Save the document as THANKS.HTML.

```
<HTML>
<HEAD>
    <TITLE>Untitled</TITLE>
</HEAD>

<BODY><BASEFONT FACE="Arial, Helvetica" SIZE="2">
<FONT SIZE="+2"><B>Thank You!</B></FONT>
<HR>
Your Reservation has been received and will<BR>
be processed in the order in which it was received.
<P>
A confirmation number will be e-mailed to you<BR>
as soon as your order is processed. If you don't<BR>
receive a confirmation number within 24-hours,<BR>
please call our Customer Support <B>Toll-Free</B> Number<BR>
at <B>888-555-1212</B>.
<P>
```

```
Thank you for choosing to stay with<BR>
<B>BoguSystems Hotels & Resorts</B> where our<BR>
motto is <I>"No room is too big, no rate is too big!"</I>

<P>
<CENTER><FONT FACE="Arial, Helvetica" SIZE=2>home ¦ reservations
➥¦ hotel directory ¦ hot deals ¦ meeting planner<BR>
sitemap ¦ contact bogusystems ¦ copyright notice</FONT></TD>
➥</TR></CENTER>

</BODY>
</HTML>
```

How It Works

The first HTML document, INDEX.HTML, sets up the browser to contain two frames, one for the graphics banner, and the other to display all other pages. Just like in a Visual Basic application, the first VBScript code sets up a global variable used within this How-To. Because HTML cannot store data directly into memory like programming languages, we are using the browser to hold the information in variables as long as the INDEX.HTML form is loaded.

Just like a Visual Basic project's Form_Load event, the Window_OnLoad event performs the similar function. In this process, it initializes all the global variables being used. Then the two frames are initialized, and the two HTML documents are loaded: BANNER.HTML and RESV.HTML.

As the RESV.HTML document is loaded, it also contains a Window_OnLoad event. Because you are using ActiveX controls on this HTML document, many Visual Basic methods and properties are available for you to use. The first part of the ActiveX script is loading the combo boxes, cboArrivalMonth and cboDepartureMonth, with the months' names using the AddItem method. As in a Visual Basic program, you want the interface to appear to be user-friendly. The procedure determines the current month and then sets the ListIndex properties to the current month.

The Select Case statement is used to determine how many days must be added to the combo boxes, cboArrivalDay and cboDepartureDay. The For...Next loop is used to help reduce typing in a long series of numbers. Just like finding the current month, the current day is found and is filled in in the Arrival Day combo box. The day is incremented, and that value is placed in the Departure Day combo box.

The two command button events, cmdSend_Click and cmdClear_Click, should also look familiar. In the cmdSend_Click, you're checking to make sure that all the necessary fields are filled in. If not, you return a message to use; otherwise, you pass all the values to their respective global variables and then load the THANKS.HTML.

If this had been an actual application, as part of calling the THANKS.HTML document you would call a procedure that would write the information to a database, but that is out of the scope of this exercise.

Comments

Unless your organization standardizes on MSIE, you must make sure that your users have the NCompass Lab's plug-in installed on their systems. Otherwise, you will get a lot of calls from your users saying that they can't use your application. NCompass Lab's Web site is at http://www.ncompasslabs.com.

If you do plan to use ActiveX controls or DTCs, it's best that you use an editor that supports the insertion of them. Your development experience will be just that much more pleasant.

COMPLEXITY
INTERMEDIATE

4.14 How do I...
Place data on the Web page?

COMPATIBILITY: VISUAL INTERDEV/VISUAL STUDIO 1.X
AND ABOVE

Problem

Now that we have a Web presence, we want to allow our customers to get more information about our hotels, how many rooms are available, and our rates. This way, they can determine what a great value our hotel is for them if they decide to stay with us. How can we display information from our database regarding hotel and room information on our Web pages without having to type everything in ourselves?

Technique

Since the incarnation of the World Wide Web, the traditional method of accessing data from a database was through the use of CGI (Common Gateway Interface) scripts or Perl scripts. Since Microsoft entered the Internet fray, it has come up with two methods of its own. One method, which was really short lived, was known as the Internet Database Connector, or IDC. Some Web sites still use this technique, but the rest of the world has embraced Microsoft's latest scripting model known as Active Server Pages (ASP).

Active Server Pages was introduced as part of the Internet Information Server (IIS) 3.0 and has been greatly enhanced in the 4.0 release. ASP is a server-side scripting model that greatly simplifies server-side programming so that you can easily create dynamic content and powerful Web-based applications.

To access data from the database, within your Active Server Page you use the Microsoft Data Access Components (MDAC). MDAC 1.5, which ships with Windows NT 4.0 Option Pack, includes the latest versions of ActiveX Data Objects (ADO); Remote Data Services (RDS); the OLE DB Provider for ODBC; the ODBC driver manager; and updated Microsoft ODBC drivers for Microsoft SQL Server, Oracle, and Microsoft Access. Without going into too much detail about all these models because all that information could fill another book, this How-To focuses on ADO for database access.

ADO was designed to provide a universal high-level data access method and is a collection of OLE Automation objects that can retrieve, update, and create records using any OLE DB service component. If there is an OLE DB provider for it, the data is accessible through the object model of ADO. OLE DB will eventually replace ODBC as the native connectivity layer between data sources. Similar to how DAO (data access object) and RDO (remote data object) are "wrapper" object models for ODBC, ADO is a "wrapper" object model for OLE DB. So does that mean that DAO and RDO are going away? Not right away; but if you're planning to do any new development on both traditional client/server applications or Web-based client/server applications, ADO is the data access object model you should use. ADO is not just for Web database access. Because ADO is a COM object, any development environment that supports COM can use it. Figure 4.26 illustrates the hierarchy of how ADO fits into the scheme of data access. If you're concerned that it took you a while to figure out the difference between DAO and RDO, do not worry. Microsoft decided not to throw a new object model at you because ADO's model is based on DAO's model.

NOTE

Although a lot of the properties, methods, and objects in the ADO model are similar to DAO and RDO, there are some major differences. The main one is that you don't have to go through the heirarchy of the objects to use the method or property you want. Instead, you can create an object directly, even if it is low in the object hierarchy. For example, if you want to create an ADO recordset, you don't need to create a connection first then reference the `RecordSet` object. Simply create `RecordSet` and you can access its methods and properties directly.

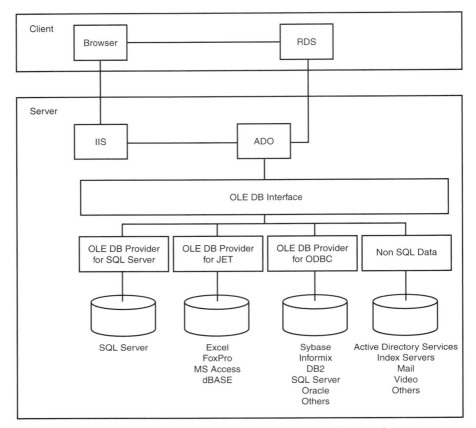

Figure 4.26 The Microsoft Data Access Components hierarchy

The HTML tag that denotes an ASP script is <% %>. Anything between these two tags gets executed on the server side. So how do ASP pages work? Figure 4.27 illustrates the request flow process of an ASP page. First, there is an HTTP request for an ASP to the Web server. Because the page that is requested has the extension .ASP, the server processes the request against ISAPI (Internet Server Application Programming Interface) components. When all the processing is done, the server sends the resulting HTML page back to the client in the form of an HTTP response. When the client receives the response, it processes the resulting HTML page just like any other HTML document. Because all the data processing is performed on the server, and the result is an HTML document, when you select View Source from your browser, you only see the resulting HTML—no server-side scripting code is viewable at all.

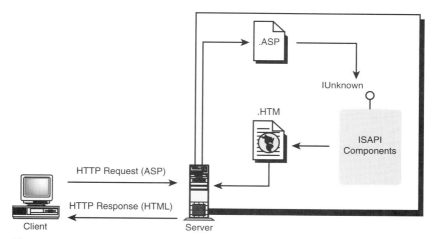

Figure 4.27 Request process flow for an ASP page with the Web server

Steps

The steps in this How-To show you how to create a virtual directory with the Internet Information Server (IIS) 4.0. Visual Studio 6.0 is used to create the Active Server Page that will retrieve data from an ODBC data source. Complete the following steps to create this project in IIS:

1. Create a virtual directory for this How-To. If you've already set up a virtual directory, you can skip to step 6. Assuming that you're using Microsoft Internet Information Server 4.0 for your Web server, open the Internet Service Manager.

2. Select the Default Web Site with a right mouse click. From the pop-up menu, choose New, Virtual Directory.

3. In the first New Virtual Directory Wizard dialog box, enter the virtual directory name `VBC_How413` and click the Next button.

4. In the next New Virtual Directory Wizard dialog box, enter the location name of the project directory you want the Web server to point to and click Next. You might choose something like `c:\projects\vbc_howto413`. If you don't remember the directory name, you can click the Browse button. If you want to create a new directory, you must use a command prompt or the Windows Explorer.

5. In the next New Virtual Directory Wizard dialog box, make sure that the first three check boxes are marked and click the Finish button. This allows you to read and execute files from the directory you specified in step 4. Because you are using Active Server Pages, which are similar to CGI/Perl scripts, they must be executed on the server. It is a good practice to keep your HTML documents and executable scripts in different directories. This is mainly done for partitioning your files, but it is also for security reasons. It's not a good idea to have your Internet directories set with both read and execute permissions.

6. For this How-To, you can use any HTML editor you want. Figure 4.28 illustrates the HTML code using Visual InterDev 6.0. The advantage of using an editor such as Visual InterDev is that the edit window displays different values in different colors, as in Visual Basic. This helps make editing your code easier because you can distinguish tags from scripts and constants. Also, version 6.0 of Visual InterDev has a built-in debugging routine to allow developers using ASP to set breakpoints, watch variables, and more, just like Visual Basic. It also provides a great interface that makes designing ASP files extremely easy, shielding the difficulty of dealing with an assorted mix of VBScript, JavaScript, CGI/Perl, HTML, and ActiveX controls.

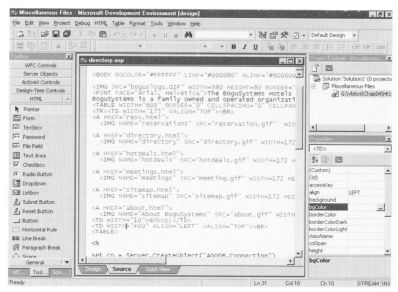

Figure 4.28 Visual InterDev 6.0 editor displaying an ASP document

7. This How-To uses the same **INDEX.HTML** file that you created in How-To 4.12. Either copy it from your How-To 4.12 working directory, the **Chap04\HT12** directory from the CD, or enter it yourself by entering the following HTML tags and text. You also must get the graphic images from the **Chap04\HT12** directory.

```
<HTML>
<HEAD>
  <TITLE>Welcome to the World of BoguSystems' Hotels &amp;
➡Resorts</TITLE>
</HEAD>
<BODY BGCOLOR="#FFFFFF" LINK="#000080" ALINK="#800000"
 VLINK="#800000" TEXT="#000000">

<IMG SRC="boguslogo.GIF" WIDTH=380 HEIGHT=80 BORDER="0">
<IMG SRC="hotels.GIF" WIDTH=200 HEIGHT=80 BORDER="0">
<TABLE BORDER=0 CELLSPACING=0 CELLPADDING=0 WIDTH=600><TR>
  <TD><IMG ALT="" SRC="3.gif" WIDTH=76 HEIGHT=36></TD>
  <TD><IMG ALT="" SRC="5.gif" WIDTH=76 HEIGHT=36></TD>
  <TD><IMG ALT="" SRC="7.gif" WIDTH=76 HEIGHT=36></TD>
  <TD><IMG ALT="" SRC="8.gif" WIDTH=76 HEIGHT=36></TD></TR>
</TABLE>
<P><TABLE WIDTH="600" BORDER="0" CELLSPACING="0"
➡CELLPADDING="0">
<TR><TD WIDTH="175" VALIGN="TOP"><BR>
```

continued on next page

continued from previous page

```
<A HREF="resv.html">
  <IMG NAME="reservations" SRC="reservation.gif" WIDTH=172
  HEIGHT=28 ALT="Reservations" BORDER=0 VSPACE=0
HSPACE=0></A><P>

<A HREF="directory.asp">
  <IMG NAME="directory" SRC="directory.gif" WIDTH=172
  HEIGHT=28 ALT="Hotel & Resort Directory" BORDER=0 VSPACE=0
  ➥HSPACE=0>
</A><P>

<A HREF="hotdeals.html">
  <IMG NAME="hotdeals" SRC="hotdeals.gif" WIDTH=172 HEIGHT=28
  ALT="Hot Deals" BORDER=0 VSPACE=0 HSPACE=0></A><P>

<A HREF="meetings.html">
  <IMG NAME="meetings" SRC="meeting.gif" WIDTH=172 HEIGHT=28
  ALT="Meeting Planning" BORDER=0 VSPACE=0 HSPACE=0></A><P>

<A HREF="sitemap.html">
  <IMG NAME="sitemap" SRC="sitemap.gif" WIDTH=172 HEIGHT=28
  ALT="Sitemap" BORDER=0 VSPACE=0 HSPACE=0></A><P>

<A HREF="about.html">
  <IMG NAME="About BoguSystems" SRC="about.gif" WIDTH=172
  ➥HEIGHT=28 ALT="About BoguSystems" BORDER=0
  ➥VSPACE=0 HSPACE=0></A></TD>
<TD WIDTH="25"> </TD>
<TD WIDTH="400" ALIGN="LEFT" VALIGN="TOP"><BR>
<FONT FACE="Arial, Helvetica" SIZE="+2"><B>
<SCRIPT LANGUAGE="JavaScript">
<!--
  var dt = new Date();
  var hr = dt.getHours();
  var msg = ((hr<12) ? "Morning" :"Evening");
  msg = ((hr>11)&&(hr<18) ? "Afternoon" : msg);
  msg=" Good "+msg+ " and ";
  document.write(msg);
<!-- end -->
</SCRIPT>
Welcome to<BR>
BoguSystems Hotels &amp; Resorts</B></FONT><P>
<CENTER><IMG SRC="flip-pic.gif" WIDTH=114 HEIGHT=110 BORDER="0">
</CENTER></TD>
</TR>
<TR><TD WIDTH="608" COLSPAN="3" ALIGN="CENTER" VALIGN="TOP">
➥<BR><BR>
<CENTER><FONT FACE="Arial, Helvetica" SIZE=2>
home ¦ reservations ¦ hotel directory ¦ hot deals
➥¦ meeting planner<BR>
sitemap ¦ contact bogusystems ¦ copyright notice
</FONT></TD></TR></CENTER>
</FONT></TD></TR>
</TABLE><BR>
</BODY>
</HTML>
```

8. Create a new HTML document and call it **DIRECTORY.ASP**. The file extension **.ASP** tells IIS that this file needs to be executed on the server and to send the resulting HTML page back to the client in the form of an HTTP response. Enter the following code in the HTML edit window:

```
<HTML>
<HEAD>
  <TITLE>BoguSystems Hotels &amp; Resorts -
  ➥Hotel Directory</TITLE>
</HEAD>

<BODY BGCOLOR="#FFFFFF" LINK="#000080" ALINK="#800000"
➥VLINK="#800000"
 TEXT="#000000">

<IMG SRC="boguslogo.GIF" WIDTH=380 HEIGHT=80 BORDER="0">
<IMG SRC="hotels.GIF" WIDTH=200 HEIGHT=80 BORDER="0"><BR>
<FONT FACE="Arial, Helvetica">
The BoguSystems Hotels &amp; Resorts have a reputation for
elegance, excitement, and entertainment. BoguSystems is a family
owned and operated organization.</FONT>
<TABLE WIDTH="600" BORDER="0" CELLSPACING="0" CELLPADDING="0">
<TR><TD WIDTH="175" VALIGN="TOP"><BR>
<A HREF="resv.html">
  <IMG NAME="reservations" SRC="reservation.gif" WIDTH=172
  ➥HEIGHT=28 ALT="Reservations" BORDER=0
  ➥VSPACE=0 HSPACE=0></A><P>

<A HREF="directory.html">
  <IMG NAME="directory" SRC="directory.gif" WIDTH=172 HEIGHT=28
  ALT="Hotel & Resort Directory" BORDER=0 VSPACE=0
  ➥HSPACE=0></A><P>

<A HREF="hotdeals.html">
  <IMG NAME="hotdeals" SRC="hotdeals.gif" WIDTH=172 HEIGHT=28
  ALT="Hot Deals" BORDER=0 VSPACE=0 HSPACE=0></A><P>

<A HREF="meetings.html">
  <IMG NAME="meetings" SRC="meeting.gif" WIDTH=172 HEIGHT=28
  ALT="Meeting Planning" BORDER=0 VSPACE=0 HSPACE=0></A><P>

<A HREF="sitemap.html">
  <IMG NAME="sitemap" SRC="sitemap.gif" WIDTH=172 HEIGHT=28
  ALT="Sitemap" BORDER=0 VSPACE=0 HSPACE=0></A><P>

<A HREF="about.html">
  <IMG NAME="About BoguSystems" SRC="about.gif" WIDTH=172
  HEIGHT=28 ALT="About BoguSystems" BORDER=0 VSPACE=0 HSPACE=0>
</A></TD>
<TD WIDTH="10"> </TD>
<TD WIDTH="400" ALIGN="LEFT" VALIGN="TOP"><BR>
<TABLE>
```

9. Enter the following server-side scripting that will complete the ASP page started in step 8. Notice that the ADO connectivity model is similar to DAO in that you need to create a connection to the data access object model, create a recordset, and process through the recordset. Also notice that you can have HTML tags and text within the server-side scripting.

```
<%
set cn = Server.CreateObject("ADODB.Connection")
'cn.open "data source=dsnHotelSQL;user id=sa;password=;"
cn.open "data source=dsnHotels8;user id=Admin;password=;"

sSQL = "SELECT Name, Desc "
sSQL = sSQL & "FROM tbl_Hotels "
set rs = cn.execute(sSQL)

Do While Not RS.EOF
HotelNbr = HotelNbr + 1
%>

<tr><TD><FONT FACE="Arial, Helvetica">
<B><%=rs(0)%></B><% =rs(1)%></font></TD>
<TD ALIGN="CENTER" BGCOLOR="#FFFFAE">
<FONT FACE="Arial, Helvetica"><%
Select Case HotelNbr
  Case 1
%>
<A HREF="roominfo.asp?HotelNbr=1">Room Info</A>
<%
  Case 2
%>
<A HREF="roominfo.asp?HotelNbr=2">Room Info</A>
<%
  Case 3
%>
<A HREF="roominfo.asp?HotelNbr=3">Room Info</A>
<%
  Case 4
%>
<A HREF="roominfo.asp?HotelNbr=3">Room Info</A>
<%
End Select
%></FONT>
</TD></tr>
<%
  RS.MoveNext
Loop

RS.Close
cn.close
%>
<P></FONT>
</TD>
</TR></TABLE><P>
<CENTER><FONT FACE="Arial, Helvetica" SIZE=2>
```

```
home ¦ reservations ¦ hotel directory ¦ hot deals ¦
➥meeting planner<BR>
sitemap ¦ contact bogusystems ¦ copyright notice</FONT></TD>
➥</TR></CENTER></table>
</BODY>
</HTML>
```

10. Create a new HTML document and call it ROOMINFO.ASP. Enter the following code in the HTML edit window. The first part of the ASP page processes the data that passed from the HTTP request. Based on the parameter passed, the title of the resulting HTML page varies accordingly.

```
<%
sHotelNbr = Request.QueryString("HotelNbr")
SELECT CASE sHotelNbr
CASE 1
  PageTitle = "Grand View Hotel - Room Info"
CASE 2
  PageTitle = "Mountain Side Resort - Room Info"
CASE 3
  PageTitle = "Hard Days Inn - Room Info"
CASE 4
  PageTitle = "Gunners Lodge - Room Info"
END SELECT
%>
<HTML>
<HEAD>
    <TITLE><%=PageTitle%></TITLE>
</HEAD>

<BODY BGCOLOR="#FFFFFF" TEXT="#000000" LINK="#0000FF"
➥ALINK="#FFFFFF" VLINK="#800080" LEFTMARGIN=0 TOPMARGIN=0>
<IMG SRC="boguslogo.GIF" WIDTH=380 HEIGHT=80 BORDER="0">
<IMG SRC="hotels.GIF" WIDTH=200 HEIGHT=80 BORDER="0"><BR>
<FONT FACE="Arial, Helvetica">
The BoguSystems Hotels &amp; Resorts have a reputation for
➥elegance, excitement, and entertainment.
➥BoguSystems is a family owned and operated organization.
➥</FONT>
<TABLE WIDTH="600" BORDER="0" CELLSPACING="0" CELLPADDING="0">
<TR><TD WIDTH="175" VALIGN="TOP"><BR>
<A HREF="resv.html">
  <IMG NAME="reservations" SRC="reservation.gif" WIDTH=172
➥HEIGHT=28 ALT="Reservations" BORDER=0 VSPACE=0
➥HSPACE=0></A><P>

<A HREF="directory.asp">
  <IMG NAME="directory" SRC="directory.gif" WIDTH=172 HEIGHT=28
  ALT="Hotel & Resort Directory" BORDER=0 VSPACE=0 HSPACE=0>
  </A><P>

<A HREF="hotdeals.html">
  <IMG NAME="hotdeals" SRC="hotdeals.gif" WIDTH=172 HEIGHT=28
  ALT="Hot Deals" BORDER=0 VSPACE=0 HSPACE=0></A><P>
```

continued on next page

continued from previous page

```
<A HREF="meetings.html">
  <IMG NAME="meetings" SRC="meeting.gif" WIDTH=172 HEIGHT=28
  ALT="Meeting Planning" BORDER=0 VSPACE=0 HSPACE=0></A><P>

<A HREF="sitemap.html">
  <IMG NAME="sitemap" SRC="sitemap.gif" WIDTH=172 HEIGHT=28
  ALT="Sitemap" BORDER=0 VSPACE=0 HSPACE=0></A><P>

<A HREF="about.html">
  <IMG NAME="About BoguSystems" SRC="about.gif" WIDTH=172
  ➡HEIGHT=28 ALT="About BoguSystems" BORDER=0
  ➡VSPACE=0 HSPACE=0></A></TD>
<TD WIDTH="425" ALIGN="LEFT" VALIGN="TOP"><BR>
<FONT FACE="Arial, Helvetica">
```

11. Enter the following server-side scripting that will complete the ASP page
started in step 10. The first recordset gets the hotel description again based
on the user's selection. The second recordset retrieves information
regarding the hotel's rooms, description, rates, and the number of rooms
the hotel has based on its description and rates.

```
<%

set cn = Server.CreateObject("ADODB.Connection")
'cn.open "data source=dsnHotelSQL;user id=sa;password=;"
cn.open "data source=dsnHotels8;user id=Admin;password=;"

  sSQL = "SELECT Name, Desc "
  sSQL = sSQL & "FROM tbl_Hotels "
  sSQL = sSQL & "WHERE Hotel = " & sHotelNbr
  set rsHotelInfo = cn.execute(sSQL)

  Do While Not rsHotelInfo.EOF
%>
    <B><%=rsHotelInfo(0)%></B><% =rsHotelInfo(1)%>
<P>
<%
    rsHotelInfo.MoveNext
  Loop

rsHotelInfo.Close

sSQL = "SELECT a.Description As [Room Description],
➡a.Beds As [Nbr of Beds], "
sSQL = sSQL & "b.Price As [Rate ($)], Count(*) AS
➡[Available Rooms] "
sSQL = sSQL & "FROM tbl_RoomTypes a, tbl_Rooms b "
sSQL = sSQL & "WHERE a.RoomType = b.RoomType "
sSQL = sSQL & "AND b.Hotel = " & sHotelNbr & " "
sSQL = sSQL & "Group by a.description, a.beds, b.price"
set rsRoomInfo = cn.execute(sSQL)

if not rsRoomInfo.EOF then
%>
```

```
<TABLE WIDTH="425" BORDER="1">
<TR>
<%
  for i = 0 to rsRoomInfo.Fields.Count - 1
%>
<TH>
<%
  response.write rsRoomInfo(i).name
%>
</TH>
<%
  next
  Do While Not rsRoomInfo.EOF
%>
</TR>
<tr>
<%
    For i = 0 to rsRoomInfo.Fields.Count - 1
%>
<td>
<%
      response.write rsRoomInfo(i)
%>
</td>
<%
    Next
    rsRoomInfo.MoveNext
%>
</tr>
<%
  Loop
end if
rsRoomInfo.Close
cn.close
%>
</TD>
</TR></TABLE><P>
<CENTER><FONT FACE="Arial, Helvetica" SIZE=2>
home ¦ reservations ¦ hotel directory ¦ hot deals
➡¦ meeting planner<BR>
sitemap ¦ contact bogusystems ¦ copyright notice</FONT>
</TD></TR></CENTER></table>
</BODY>
</HTML>
```

How It Works

To run the Web application, open your Internet browser. Because ASP pages execute on the server, they are browser independent. Unless the resulting HTML page contains items such as ActiveX controls specific to MSIE, you can use any Internet browser.

To access the Web application, enter the name of your Web server and the name of the virtual directory you created at the beginning of this How-To with `INDEX.HTML`. For example, to run this Web application, type `http://localhost/VBC_How413/index.html` on the address line. If you're running Personal Web Server, Peer Web Server or IIS on your system, localhost will work for the server name, otherwise use the name of the Web server in place of localhost. `VBC_How413` is the name of the virtual directory in which the `INDEX.HTML` file resides. Click the Hotel Directory button, and your browser should look similar to Figure 4.29. If you view the source of this document, you will notice that it looks like a standard HTML document. There is no reference to the ASP scripting at all.

When you click the Room Info link to the right of any of the hotel descriptions, the `ROOMINFO.ASP` file is processed by the server, and what is returned should look similar to Figure 4.30.

Figure 4.29 The result of the `DIRECTORY.ASP` page shown in MSIE

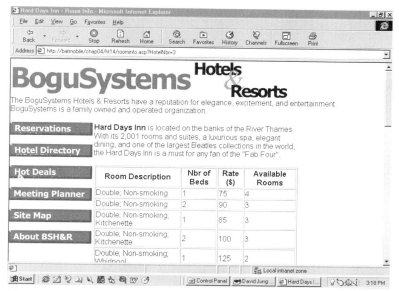

Figure 4.30 The result of the `ROOMINFO.ASP` page displaying the room information for the Hard Days Inn

Comments

When displaying any information on a Web page, ASP provides more than just data access. Because ASP files are executed on the server versus on the client's workstation, you can do calculations, date retrievals, display random pictures, and more without having to work if the client's browser supports the scripting you're using.

If you're using SQL Server, an alternative method of displaying data on an HTML page is by using SQL Server Web Assistant. This method uses triggers and stored procedures to format data output to HTML pages. How-To 7.11 in Chapter 7, "Basic SQL Server Management," provides an example of how to use SQL Server to create Web pages with data on them.

CHAPTER 5

OBJECT-ORIENTED APPLICATION DEVELOPMENT

5

OBJECT-ORIENTED APPLICATION DEVELOPMENT

by Noel Jerke

How do I...

You cannot begin client/server development with Visual Basic 6 without thinking about objects. Microsoft is beginning to embrace the idea of object-oriented analysis and design throughout all its development products. Visual C++ and Visual J++ are based on the object-oriented methodology. Microsoft's important component-integration strategy, ActiveX, is based on the concept of a world of objects working together.

449

This chapter provides an introduction to the basic fundamentals of object-oriented analysis and design and, most importantly, explains how to apply these techniques to your client/server programs. How-To 5.1 is a simple example of using Visual Basic's fundamental object-oriented building tool: the class. How-To 5.2 discusses the uses of a very flexible data type called the collection and how it relates to working with classes.

The last two How-To's provide two examples of implementing an object model and building a simple three-tier application that uses ActiveX components. Chapter 6, "Business Objects," provides a detailed explanation of designing, building, and implementing business objects using ActiveX components.

5.1 Utilize the Basics of Object-Oriented Programming

There are a few fundamental concepts to understand before doing object-oriented analysis and design. Certainly, this How-To cannot begin to discuss all the facets of good object-oriented programming. But it introduces the core concepts you need to move forward with Visual Basic 6.

5.2 Implement a Basic Class Module

The *class module* is the key tool used to implement object techniques in your applications. This How-To builds a simple class that encapsulates a set of properties and methods for working with disk files.

5.3 Use a Collection of Classes

The *collection object* provides a method for referring to a related group of items as a single unit or object. A collection of classes is a convenient method for dealing with a large set of instances of your class in a simple fashion. This section demonstrates how to use a collection of `Bitmap` classes.

5.4 Implement an Object Model

This section implements a simple object model for browsing a set of bitmaps and performing features such as image fades. Two new classes are added to the `DiskFile` and `Bitmap` classes created earlier. This How-To demonstrates how the classes work together to provide the functionality of the program.

5.5 Build ActiveX Components

The object model developed in How-To 5.3 can be extended to provide even greater encapsulation based on out-of-process ActiveX executables and in-process ActiveX DLLs. In this section, a new class is added to this example that also stores the bitmap data in an image database.

5.6 Implement Interfaces

Polymorphism is a powerful concept in object-oriented programming. The capability to interact with different types of objects without knowing the type up front enables you to abstract away complexity in your applications. In this

How-To, you build an automobile value calculator that calls an automobile object that interacts with different auto model objects.

5.7 Build an ActiveX Control

One of the best ways to abstract away complexity with Visual Basic is to wrap it up into an ActiveX control that can be used within your Web pages and other Visual Basic programs. In this section, you take your image-manipulation classes and wrap them up into an ActiveX control. The control is demonstrated in both a Visual Basic form and an HTML Web page.

COMPLEXITY
BEGINNING

5.1 How do I...
Utilize the basics of object-oriented programming?

COMPATIBILITY: N/A

Problem

The class module appears to be Microsoft's primary building tool for implementing three-tiered client/server systems. How do I use the class module in my projects?

Technique

Object-oriented programming seeks to break down the complexity of software systems so that you will not be overwhelmed by all the different subsystems that go into building a small or large-scale software project. If you think for a moment about Visual Basic, Microsoft has abstracted away most of the tedium of Windows programming and has exposed only certain aspects of Windows programming to you, as the programmer, so that you don't have to worry about all the complexities of the Windows system. Abstracting away complexity makes a large system easier to handle. After all, even airplane pilots do not have to completely understand every detail of how an airplane works; they need to know primarily how to operate the plane. Engineers and mechanics are available to deal with the contents of the various components of the instrumentation, flight control systems, engines, and so on.

Abstraction is related closely to encapsulation. The best example of encapsulation is an ActiveX custom control. A control completely hides or encapsulates the underlying logic behind the functionality exposed by the control. Likewise, the class module gives the Visual Basic programmer the capability to encapsulate program code and exposes only the methods for using the class.

The Class Module

A *class* is any group of templates that can be created (instantiated) into objects that fit a certain profile. An example could include the airplane wing in the earlier example or an employee in a company. The class module in Visual Basic provides a way to define these classes and encapsulate their underlying functionality into a template. The class also exposes only the functionality needed by the user to handle the object effectively. With the airplane wing, the pilot has controls and settings that manipulate the wing.

A class module can have properties and methods. *Methods* define the functionality of the class. For example, the picture-box control is an object you use in your applications to display images. A method of the picture-box control is `Circle`. This draws a circle on the picture box. Your class objects can have their own methods that define the function of the object. With the picture-box control, you can set the background and foreground color properties of the picture box to change its appearance. Similarly, your class can have properties that define the attributes of the object. Note that these methods and properties do not have to be exposed to other objects. They can be either *public* or *private*. Private methods and properties are accessible only from within the class module. Public methods and properties are exposed to the rest of the program.

Relating Objects

Objects would be pretty boring and not very useful if you could not define relationships between them. For example, it would be pretty hard to model an airplane object if it could not be made up of many different objects that worked together to define the functionality of the plane. A control panel works with the mechanical parts of the plane to give feedback to the pilot. The engines work with the wings to provide flight for the plane.

Several types of relationships can define how objects relate to each other. The first is the *is-a* relationship. You could define a class wing that has all the basic properties and methods for any type of airplane wing, for example. However, the wing of the new Boeing 777 could have additional properties and methods beyond those of a standard wing, so the Boeing 777 wing would be a type of standard wing. It would have all the basic functionality of a wing but would add to that definition. Another good example is that of the airplane seat. Each seat has arms, cushions, and so on. The first-class seats would have additional properties that the coach-class seats would not, though.

The second type is the *has-a* relationship. In the airplane example, there are many has-a relationships. For example, the airplane has a set of wings, engines, and landing gear. Classes with a has-a relationship are composed of other classes to define their functionality.

The third type is the *uses* relationship. This is where two objects work together or collaborate to provide functionality. The airline uses the plane to transport passengers, for example. The passengers use the airline to get to their destinations. Each of these objects—the airline, plane, and passengers—collaborate.

Two object-oriented constructs enable you to define these relationships between classes. The first is *inheritance*. Inheritance was designed to remove redundancy in code between similar objects. In the airline example, you can have up to three types of passengers on the plane: first-class, business-class, and coach-class passengers. Each passenger has a set of common information and methods in the system, but each also has specific attributes and methods that uniquely define him or her. You could design three objects that all completely define each type of passenger, but you would certainly have redundancy with properties, such as name and address, and methods, such as bag check and check-in. Using inheritance, you would want to define a general passenger class and then define three classes for first-class, business-class, and coach-class passengers. These three classes would inherit the general passenger class and would add functionality specific to the specialized class. The first-class passenger might receive extra frequent-flyer miles or a special check-in procedure, for example.

The second idea is *polymorphism*. Suppose the airline decides that the check-in method for first-class passengers is going to differ from that of any of the other passenger types. In the airline example of a general passenger object, you would need a way to override the general check-in method. A programming language that supports polymorphism would allow you to do this. So, for the first, business, and coach passenger classes, you would call the check-in method, but for the first-class passenger, the functionality of the method would be different from that of the underlying passenger class.

Unfortunately, the class module in Visual Basic does not readily support inheritance or polymorphism. One class module can contain another class module, and certainly, different class modules can work together. But you cannot simply inherit all the attributes and methods from one class to another. Likewise, this makes polymorphism difficult to implement from direct class-to-class relationships. Visual Basic does support creating polymorphism through the addition of the `implements` keyword, though. By using class templates, which contain only an outline of all methods and properties, you can create polymorphism of methods and properties between classes. An example of this is demonstrated in How-To 5.6. Although Visual Basic is not completely object oriented, the primary ideas of abstraction and encapsulation make a great leap forward in the way you will build your programs, and you will be able to derive the primary benefits of object-oriented methodologies.

The rest of this chapter introduces the class module, collections of classes, a simple object model, and how to build ActiveX components.

COMPLEXITY
BEGINNING

5.2 How do I...
Implement a basic class module?

COMPATIBILITY: VISUAL BASIC 5 AND 6

Problem

The class module appears to be Microsoft's primary building tool for implementing three-tiered client/server systems. How do I utilize the class module in my projects?

Technique

To demonstrate, you will take the idea of an everyday disk file and encapsulate it in a class module. A disk file has many different properties such as directory location and file size. Also, you can perform many methods on a file such as copying and deleting the file.

Steps

Open and run 5-2.VBP. The running program appears as shown in Figure 5.1.

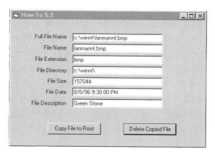

Figure 5.1 The form as it appears at runtime

The text boxes on the form show the different properties of the **DiskFile** class created to encapsulate a graphic such as the **lanmannt.bmp** file. You can perform two methods on the disk file. The first is to copy the file to a new location. Click Copy File to Root to copy the clouds bitmap to the root directory. To delete the copy of the file, click Delete Copied File, which uses the **Delete** method of the class.

Complete the following steps to create this project:

1. Create a new project called 5-2.VBP. Add the objects and properties listed in Table 5.1 to Form1, and save the form as 5-2.FRM.

Table 5.1 5-2.VBP's objects and properties

OBJECT	PROPERTY	SETTING
Form	Name	Form1
	Caption	"How-To 5.2"
CommandButton	Name	DelFile
	Caption	"Delete Copied File"
CommandButton	Name	Copy
	Caption	"Copy File to Root"
TextBox	Name	FileInfo
	Index	0 - 6
	Locked	-1 'True
Label	Name	FileLabels
	AutoSize	-1 'True
	Caption	"File Description"
	Index	6
Label	Name	FileLabels
	AutoSize	-1 'True
	Caption	"File Date"
	Index	5
Label	Name	FileLabels
	AutoSize	-1 'True
	Caption	"File Size"
	Index	4
Label	Name	FileLabels
	AutoSize	-1 'True
	Caption	"File Directory"
	Index	3
Label	Name	FileLabels
	AutoSize	-1 'True
	Caption	"File Extension"
	Index	2

continued on next page

Table 5.1 continued

OBJECT	PROPERTY	SETTING
Label	Name	FileLabels
	AutoSize	-1 'True
	Caption	"File Name"
	Index	1
Label	Name	FileLabels
	AutoSize	-1 'True
	Caption	"Full File Name"
	Index	0

2. Add the following set of code to the General Declarations section of the form. You will create two instances of the **DiskFile** class. One will be for the current clouds bitmap on the system; the second will be used for the copied file.

```
Option Explicit

'  Declare our two classes globally
Dim DF1 As DiskFile
Dim DF2 As DiskFile
```

3. After the Copy button is clicked, the **CopyFile** method of the first **DiskFile** class is called. The directory to copy the file to is passed in as an argument. In this case, the file is copied to the root of C.

```
Private Sub Copy_Click()

'  Copy the file to the root
DF1.CopyFile "c:\"

End Sub
```

4. After the **DelFile** button is clicked, the second **DiskFile** class is set up to be created with the copied clouds bitmap. Then the **DeleteFile** method of the class is called to delete the file.

```
Private Sub DelFile_Click()

'  Set the second class to the
'  copied file and then delete
'  it
DF2.FileName = "c:\clouds.bmp"
DF2.DeleteFile

End Sub
```

5. When the form is loaded, the two **DiskFile** classes are created. The first class is set up to point to the clouds bitmap in the Windows directory. The file-description property of the class is also set. Then each property of the **DiskFile** class is displayed in the text boxes on the form.

```
Private Sub Form_Load()

'  Create our two new classes
Set DF1 = New DiskFile
Set DF2 = New DiskFile

'  Set the class file name
DF1.FileName = "c:\windows\clouds.bmp"

'  Set the file name description
DF1.FileDesc = "Clouds Bitmap"

'  Show the full filename including
'  directory
FileInfo(0).Text = DF1.FileName

'  Show just the filename
FileInfo(1).Text = DF1.File

'  Show the file extension
FileInfo(2).Text = DF1.FileExt

'  Show the file directory
FileInfo(3).Text = DF1.Directory

'  Show the file size
FileInfo(4).Text = DF1.FileSize

'  Show the file date
FileInfo(5).Text = DF1.FileDate

'  Show the file description
FileInfo(6).Text = DF1.FileDesc

End Sub
```

6. Insert a new class module into the project by opening the Insert menu and choosing Class Module. Set the name property of the class to **DiskFile**, and save the class as **DiskFile.cls**. Add the following code to the General Declarations section of the class. These properties will help define the attributes of the disk file for the class.

```
Option Explicit

'  Member property of the class that
'  stores the filename
Private m_FileName As String

'  Member property of the class that
'  stores the file description
Private m_FileDesc As String
```

7. The following public properties allow other programs to set and retrieve the file description for the class. Note that the description is stored in a private variable, m_FileDesc.

```
'   The get and set properties of the class
'   for the file description
Public Property Let FileDesc(s As String)
    m_FileDesc = s
End Property

Public Property Get FileDesc() As String
    FileDesc = m_FileDesc
End Property
```

8. The File property handles just returning the filename without the directory location of the file. Note that you call the ParseFile routine to get the filename.

```
'   Get the file name by itself.
'   I.E. c:\windows\clouds.bmp is clouds.bmp
Public Property Get File() As String
    File = ParseFile()
End Property
```

9. The FileName property can be retrieved and set.

```
'   Set and get the filename property for
'   the class
Public Property Let FileName(s As String)
    m_FileName = s
End Property

Public Property Get FileName() As String
    FileName = m_FileName
End Property
```

10. The FileSize property returns the file size of the current file by calling the Visual Basic FileLen function.

```
'   Get the file size
Public Property Get FileSize() As Long
    FileSize = FileLen(m_FileName)
End Property
```

11. The FileExt property calls the ParseExt function, which returns the extension for the current file.

```
'   Get the file extension
Public Property Get FileExt() As String
    FileExt = ParseExt()
End Property
```

12. The `Directory` property returns just the directory location of the file by calling the `ParseDir` function.

```
'  Get the directory of the file
Public Property Get Directory() As String
    Directory = ParseDir()
End Property
```

13. The `FileDate` property returns the file date by calling Visual Basic's `FileDateTime` function.

```
'  Get the date of the file
Public Property Get FileDate() As Date
    FileDate = FileDateTime(m_FileName)
End Property
```

14. The `ParseFile` function is a private method of the class. The `m_FileName` private property is searched to find just the filename and excludes the directory location.

```
'  Parse out the file name. Note that this is
'  a private method. It is only utilized in the
'  File property
Private Function ParseFile() As String

Dim N As Integer

ParseFile = ""

'  Start from the end of the file name
'  and look for the '\' character. Thus the
'  file part of the file name will be known
For N = Len(m_FileName) To 1 Step -1

    If Mid(m_FileName, N, 1) = "\" Then
        ParseFile = Right(m_FileName, Len(m_FileName) - N)
        N = -1
    End If

Next N

End Function
```

15. The `ParseDir` function is a private method of the class. The `m_FileName` private property is searched to find just the directory location of the file and excludes the filename.

```
'  Parse out the file directory. Note that
'  this is a private class method and is only
'  utilized by the Directory property
Private Function ParseDir() As String
```

continued on next page

continued from previous page

```
Dim N As Integer

ParseDir = ""

'   Start from the end of the file name
'   and look for the first '\' character. Thus
'   the location of the file name will be known
'   and the rest is the directory location
For N = Len(m_FileName) To 1 Step -1

    If Mid(m_FileName, N, 1) = "\" Then
        ParseDir = Left(m_FileName, N)
        N = -1
    End If

Next N

End Function
```

16. The `ParseExt` function is a private method of the class. The `m_FileName` private property is searched to find just the file extension and to exclude the directory location and filename.

```
'   GetExt retrieves the file extension if
'   there is one. This is only used by the
'   FileExt property
Private Function ParseExt() As String

Dim N As Integer

ParseExt = "(N/A)"

'   Start from the end of the file name
'   and look for the '.' character. Thus
'   the location of the extension will be known
'   in the file name string
For N = Len(m_FileName) To 1 Step -1

    If Mid(m_FileName, N, 1) = "." Then
        ParseExt = Right(m_FileName, Len(m_FileName) - N)
        N = -1
    End If

Next N

End Function
```

17. The `CopyFile` method of the class copies the current disk file to the specified location. Note that the `ParseFile` private method of the class is called to get just the filename for use in Visual Basic's `FileCopy` procedure.

```
'   Public method of the class to
'   copy the file to a new location
Public Sub CopyFile(NewLocation)
    FileCopy m_FileName, NewLocation + ParseFile
End Sub
```

18. The DeleteFile method deletes the current file.

```
'   Public method of the class to
'   delete the file
Public Sub DeleteFile()
    Kill m_FileName
End Sub
```

19. When the class is initialized, the filename and description are set to the appropriate defaults.

```
'   When the class is initialized
'   the filename, description and
'   extension will be set to
'   N/A.
Private Sub Class_Initialize()
m_FileName = "Uninitialized"
m_FileDesc = "N/A"
End Sub
```

How It Works

A simple class, DiskFile, is set up here to help encapsulate the use of disk files. By setting the FileName property of the class from the form, all the various properties of the file are just a simple class reference away. And the class provides two methods, CopyFile and DeleteFile, which make working with the file simple.

Now examine the class in more detail. The properties are set up using the Property construct of Visual Basic. Using the Property construct, you can check the value sent in by the user, or you can execute other logic. Note that the property can be read, written, or both read and written, depending on whether you use both the Let and Get properties. The Let property sets the value. The Get property retrieves the value. Note that if you are setting a property to an object, you use the Set keyword instead of Let. Also, the property can be set to public or private. The following example shows setting and retrieving the FileName property of the class:

```
'   Set and get the filename property for
'   the class
Public Property Let FileName(s As String)
    m_FileName = s
End Property

Public Property Get FileName() As String
    FileName = m_FileName
End Property
```

The following code demonstrates how to return just the directory location of the file. When the class property is called, the return value is actually the return value of the private **ParseDir** method. If you wanted to, you could check to manipulate the **Directory**, such as setting it all to uppercase, checking to ensure that it is not null, and so on.

```
'  Get the directory of the file
Public Property Get Directory() As String
    Directory = ParseDir()
End Property
```

Methods of the class are identical in meaning to the familiar subroutines and functions of Visual Basic. The key is setting the method to be either public or private to indicate whether the method is visible to the rest of the program. You want to expose only those methods that you want other parts of your application to access.

Finally, note that the class module has two standard routines built in: **Initialize** and **Terminate**. The **Initialize** routine is called when the class is created, and the **Terminate** routine is called when the class is destroyed. You can add appropriate code to these routines to handle class initialization and termination events such as setting default properties and deleting any objects created by the class.

In the form module, the class is easy to use. Note that the class is declared globally in the General Declarations section of the form. But the class actually is created by setting the global variable to a new instance of the class object when the form is loaded, or in subsequent processing. The following code demonstrates this:

```
Set DF1 = New DiskFile
Set DF2 = New DiskFile
```

Note that multiple instances of the class can be created. After you create the class, you can use the various properties and methods. The class module provides an invaluable tool for taking complex objects and encapsulating their functionality into an object that is easy to implement and reuse.

You might have noticed the m naming convention for the private variables of the class module. The m stands for *member.* These private properties of the class are member properties for the class that represents the properties or attributes.

Comments

This introductory example can be easily expanded to allow the user to select any file from the system and display its properties. However, the code does not clean up the created objects when unloading the form. It is very important in object-oriented programming to clean up the "garbage" by destroying the objects instantiated from the classes after you are finished with them.

The class module is the fundamental building block for constructing the functionality of your applications. The capability to abstract away and encapsulate complex segments of your code will become a powerful tool in your programming arsenal. Plus, you will be able to develop powerful business objects to implement the second tier of three-tier client/server architecture.

COMPLEXITY
INTERMEDIATE

5.3 How do I...
Use a collection of classes?

COMPATIBILITY: VISUAL BASIC 5 AND 6

Problem

Microsoft has provided another powerful tool beside the class module: the collection object. How can I use this collection object to extend the use of classes?

Technique

Here, you will reuse the `DiskFile` class from the last How-To and add a new class module, `Bitmap`, to the project. The `Bitmap` class will be a special type of disk file. Although you cannot have the `Bitmap` class directly inherit the `DiskFile` class, the `Bitmap` class will be composed of a `DiskFile` class that will have the basic information about the bitmap file. You will add to the `Bitmap` class properties and methods specific to image files.

Steps

Open and run **5-3.VBP**. The running program appears, as shown in Figure 5.2.

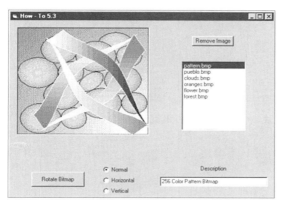

Figure 5.2 The form at runtime

The form shows a picture box that will display the various images when they are selected in the list box. Select the Oranges bitmap in the list box, and select the Vertical option. Then click Rotate Bitmap. The image now is flipped vertically, as shown in Figure 5.3.

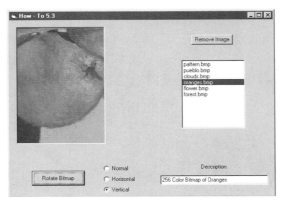

Figure 5.3 The Oranges bitmap flipped vertically

To remove images from the bitmap list, click Remove Image. This removes the selected images from the **Bitmaps** collection, as shown in Figure 5.4.

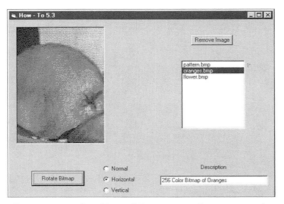

Figure 5.4 The list of images after several have been removed

To create this project, complete the following steps. These How-To's build on the code from the previous How-To's. Only new code is commented in each How-To. For further explanation of code that is covered in a different How-To, refer to that How-To.

1. Create a new standard EXE project called **5-3.VBP**. Add the objects and properties listed in Table 5.2 to the form, and save the form as **5-3.FRM**.

Table 5.2 5-3.VBP's objects and properties

OBJECT	PROPERTY	SETTING
Form	Name	Form1
	Caption	"How-To 5.3"
CommandButton	Name	Remove
	Caption	"Remove Image"
CommandButton	Name	Display
	Caption	"Rotate Bitmap"
TextBox	Name	FileDesc
ListBox	Name	ImageList
OptionButton	Name	DisplayOpt
	Caption	"Vertical"
	Index	2
OptionButton	Name	DisplayOpt
	Caption	"Horizontal"
	Index	1
OptionButton	Name	DisplayOpt
	Caption	"Normal"
	Index	0
	Value	-1 'True
PictureBox	Name	DispPict
	AutoSize	-1 'True
	Picture	"pueblo.bmp"
PictureBox	Name	BackPict
	AutoSize	-1 'True
	Visible	0 'False
Label	Name	Label1
	AutoSize	-1 'True
	Caption	"Description"

2. Add the following code to the General Declarations section of the form. A collection is created that will hold your series of bitmaps for the program.

```
Option Explicit

'   Bitmaps will be our collection of
'   bitmaps for viewing
Dim Bitmaps As Collection
```

3. Depending on the `Display` option, call the appropriate method of the `Bitmap` class to either flip the image or show it in the normal orientation.

```
Private Sub Display_Click()

'   Depending on the display option
'   show the bitmap appropriately
If DisplayOpt(0).Value = True Then
➥Bitmaps.Item(ImageList.ListIndex + 1).Load
If DisplayOpt(1).Value = True Then
➥Bitmaps.Item(ImageList.ListIndex + 1).Flip 1
If DisplayOpt(2).Value = True Then
➥Bitmaps.Item(ImageList.ListIndex + 1).Flip 2

End Sub
```

4. When the form is loaded, a `Bitmap` class is created and the `Bitmaps` collection is created. Then, all the bitmap images are set up and added to the collection. The key for each collection member will be a simple counter.

```
Private Sub Form_Load()

Dim N As Integer
Dim BMP As Bitmap

'   Create the new collection of bitmaps
Set Bitmaps = New Collection

'   Create the bitmap object and add
'   it to the collection
For N = 1 To 6

    '   Create an instance of the bitmap
    Set BMP = New Bitmap

    '   Set the display picture
    '   properties
    Set BMP.BackPict = BackPict
    Set BMP.DispPict = DispPict

    '   Depending on the count, add the
    '   appropriate image and set the
```

```
      '  description
      Select Case N

          Case 1
              BMP.FileInfo.FileName = App.Path + "\pattern.bmp"
              BMP.FileInfo.FileDesc = "256 Color Pattern Bitmap"

          Case 2
              BMP.FileInfo.FileName = App.Path + "\pueblo.bmp"
              BMP.FileInfo.FileDesc =
              ➥"Bitmap of an Pueblo Adobe Dwelling"

          Case 3
              BMP.FileInfo.FileName = App.Path + "\clouds.bmp"
              BMP.FileInfo.FileDesc = "Microsoft Clouds Bitmap"

          Case 4
              BMP.FileInfo.FileName = App.Path + "\oranges.bmp"
              BMP.FileInfo.FileDesc = "256 Color Bitmap of Oranges"

          Case 5
              BMP.FileInfo.FileName = App.Path + "\flower.bmp"
              BMP.FileInfo.FileDesc =
              ➥"256 Color Bitmap of a Blossoming Flower"

          Case 6
              BMP.FileInfo.FileName = App.Path + "\forest.bmp"
              BMP.FileInfo.FileDesc =
              ➥"Standard Windows 95 Forest Bitmap"

      End Select

      '  Add the Bitmap class to the
      '  collection of bitmaps and set
      '  the key as the count
      Bitmaps.Add Item:=BMP, Key:=CStr(N)

      '  Add just the name of the image file
      '  to the list box
      ImageList.AddItem (BMP.FileInfo.File)

      '  Destroy the instance of the bitmap class
      Set BMP = Nothing

Next N

'  Set the image list to the first
'  selection
ImageList.ListIndex = 0

End Sub
```

5. When the form is unloaded, the members of the collection are removed. Note that the **For...Each...Next** construct is used to move through each object in the **Bitmaps** collection.

```
Private Sub Form_Unload(Cancel As Integer)

Dim N As Integer
Dim Obj as object

'   Destroy all of the bitmap instances
'   when the form is unloaded
For Each Obj In Bitmaps
    Bitmaps.Remove 1
Next

End Sub
```

6. When the **ImageList** box is clicked, the new image is loaded by calling the **load** function of the appropriate **Bitmap** class. Then, the file description is shown by retrieving the file-description property of the **FileInfo** class that is part of the **Bitmap** class.

```
Private Sub ImageList_Click()

'   When an image in the list is
'   clicked on, load the image
Bitmaps.Item(ImageList.ListIndex + 1).Load

'   Set the file description in the
'   text box
FileDesc.Text = Bitmaps.Item(ImageList.ListIndex
➥+ 1).FileInfo.FileDesc
End Sub
```

7. After the Remove button is clicked, the currently selected image from the **Bitmap** class is removed.

```
Private Sub Remove_Click()

'   Always ensure there is at least
'   one entry in the list box
If ImageList.ListCount > 1 Then

    '   Remove the specified image from
    '   the collection and the list box
    Bitmaps.Remove ImageList.ListIndex + 1
    ImageList.RemoveItem ImageList.ListIndex
End If

'   Set the selection to the
'   first image
ImageList.ListIndex = 0

End Sub
```

8. Insert a new class module into the project and save it as **Bitmap.cls**. Add the following code to the General Declarations section of the class. Note that the **DiskFile** class is declared as a public property of the class. Thus, its methods and properties are exposed to any of your code that uses the **Bitmap** class.

```
Option Explicit

'   A Bitmap is a type of DiskFile
'   So, the Bitmap class will use
'   the properties and methods of
'   the DiskFile class for its
'   functionality
Public FileInfo As DiskFile

'   Declare the global properties of the
'   class. m_DispPict is the standard
'   display picture. m_BackPict is the
'   background picture that will be used
'   for the image flipping.
Private m_DispPict As Control
Private m_BackPict As Control
```

9. The **DispPict** property of the class handles taking in a picture-box control for displaying the bitmap. Note that the **Set** keyword is used because an object—in this case, a control—is being passed into the property.

```
'   Get the Display picture control
Public Property Set DispPict(AControl As Control)
    Set m_DispPict = AControl
End Property
```

10. To do the image flips, you will need a working picture box that will not be visible to the user. So, when the property is set the **AutoRedraw** property of the picture is set to **True**, and the picture box is set to be **Invisible**. This creates a working memory device context that will store the image in memory.

```
'   Get the Background picture control.
'   It is important to ensure that this
'   picture is invisible and that the
'   AutoRedraw property is true so that it
'   will act as a memory device context and
'   hold its image for later work
Public Property Set BackPict(AControl As Control)
    Set m_BackPict = AControl
    m_BackPict.AutoRedraw = True
    m_BackPict.Visible = False
End Property
```

11. The Load method of the class handles loading the bitmap into both the BackPict and DispPict picture boxes.

```
'   The load method of the class loads
'   the image into the two display pictures
Public Sub Load()
    m_BackPict.Picture = LoadPicture(FileInfo.FileName)
    m_DispPict.Picture = LoadPicture(FileInfo.FileName)
End Sub
```

12. The Flip method of the class flips the image based on the passed parameter. To rotate the image, use the PaintPicture method of the picture box.

```
'   The Flip method of the class will rotate
'   the picture accordingly
Public Sub Flip(Rotate)

'   Depending on the rotation selected, the
'   original image will be copied to the
'   display picture appropriately
Select Case Rotate

'   Note that for the vertical and
'   horizontal flips, the height or
'   width is set to a negative value
'   and the starting point is set to
'   the height or width for the image
'   to be displayed. The PaintPicture
'   method of the picture box is used
'   to do the rotation
    Case 1  'Actual Size
            '  Flip Horizontal
            m_DispPict.PaintPicture m_BackPict.Picture,
        m_BackPict.ScaleWidth,   0, -1 * m_BackPict.ScaleWidth,
        m_BackPict.ScaleHeight, 0, 0, m_BackPict.ScaleWidth,
        m_BackPict.ScaleHeight

    Case 2
            '  Flip Vertical
            m_DispPict.PaintPicture m_BackPict.Picture, 0,
            m_BackPict.ScaleHeight, m_BackPict.ScaleWidth, -1 *
        m_BackPict.ScaleHeight, 0, 0, m_BackPict.ScaleWidth,
            m_BackPict.ScaleHeight

End Select

End Sub
```

13. When the class is initialized, the DiskFile class is created.

```
Private Sub Class_Initialize()
        '  When the class is initialized,
        '  the DiskFile class is created
        Set FileInfo = New DiskFile
End Sub
```

14. When the class is terminated, the `DiskFile` class is destroyed.

```
Private Sub Class_Terminate()
    '  When the class is terminated
    '   the DiskFile class is destroyed
    Set FileInfo = Nothing
End Sub
```

15. Insert a new class module into the project and save it as `DiskFile.cls`. Add the following code to `DiskFile.cls`:

```
Option Explicit

'  Member property of the class that
'  stores the filename
Private m_FileName As String

'  Member property of the class that
'  stores the file description
Private m_FileDesc As String

'  The get and set properties of the class
'  for the file description
Public Property Let FileDesc(s As String)
    m_FileDesc = s
End Property

Public Property Get FileDesc() As String
    FileDesc = m_FileDesc
End Property

'  Get the file name by itself.
'   I.E. c:\windows\clouds.bmp is clouds.bmp
Public Property Get File() As String
    File = ParseFile()
End Property

'  Set and get the filename property for
'  the class
Public Property Let FileName(s As String)
    m_FileName = s
End Property

Public Property Get FileName() As String
    FileName = m_FileName
End Property

'  Get the file size
Public Property Get FileSize() As Long
    FileSize = FileLen(m_FileName)
End Property

'  Get the file extension
Public Property Get FileExt() As String
```

continued on next page

continued from previous page

```
            FileExt = ParseExt()
        End Property

        '  Get the directory of the file
        Public Property Get Directory() As String
            Directory = ParseDir()
        End Property

        '  Get the date of the file
        Public Property Get FileDate() As Date
            FileDate = FileDateTime(m_FileName)
        End Property

        '  Parse out the file name. Note that this is
        '  a private method. It is only utilized in the
        '  File property
        Private Function ParseFile() As String

        Dim N As Integer

        ParseFile = ""

        '  Start from the end of the file name
        '  and look for the '\' character. Thus the
        '  file part of the file name will be known
        For N = Len(m_FileName) To 1 Step -1

            If Mid(m_FileName, N, 1) = "\" Then
                ParseFile = Right(m_FileName, Len(m_FileName) - N)
                N = -1
            End If

        Next N

        End Function

        '  Parse out the file directory. Note that
        '  this is a private class method and is only
        '  utilized by the Directory property
        Private Function ParseDir() As String

        Dim N As Integer

        ParseDir = ""

        '  Start from the end of the file name
        '  and look for the first '\' character. Thus
        '  the location of the file name will be known
        '  and the rest is the directory location
        For N = Len(m_FileName) To 1 Step -1

            If Mid(m_FileName, N, 1) = "\" Then
                ParseDir = Left(m_FileName, N)
```

```
            N = -1
        End If

    Next N

    End Function

    '  GetExt retrieves the file extension if
    '  there is one. This is only used by the
    '  FileExt property
    Private Function ParseExt() As String

    Dim N As Integer

    ParseExt = "(N/A)"

    '  Start from the end of the file name
    '  and look for the '.' character. Thus
    '  the location of the extension will be known
    '  in the file name string
    For N = Len(m_FileName) To 1 Step -1

        If Mid(m_FileName, N, 1) = "." Then
            ParseExt = Right(m_FileName, Len(m_FileName) - N)
            N = -1
        End If

    Next N

    End Function

    '  Public method of the class to
    '  copy the file to a new location
    Public Sub CopyFile(NewLocation)
        FileCopy m_FileName, NewLocation + ParseFile
    End Sub

    '  Public method of the class to
    '  delete the file
    Public Sub DeleteFile()
        Kill m_FileName
    End Sub

    '  When the class is initialized
    '  the filename, description and
    '  extension will be set to
    '  N/A.
    Private Sub Class_Initialize()

    m_FileName = "Uninitialized"
    m_FileDesc = "N/A"

    End Sub
```

How It Works

To demonstrate the collection object, a new class, `Bitmap`, has been added to the project for working with bitmaps. This class handles displaying bitmaps at different orientations and uses the `DiskFile` class created in the last How-To to provide a basic set of properties and methods for the bitmap file itself.

The collection object provides a method for referring to a related group of items as a single unit or object. A collection of classes is a convenient method for dealing with a large set of instances of your `Bitmap` class in a simple fashion. In this case, you have a collection of `Bitmap` classes. You will add each `Bitmap` class to the collection and then, in your image manipulation, you simply will reference the collection.

To add items to the bitmap, use the `Add` method of the `Bitmap` class. The `Item` property indicates the item to be added, and the `Key` property gives a name to the added item. In this case, the item to be added is a `Bitmap` class:

```
Bitmaps.Add Item:=BMP, Key:=CStr(N)
```

One of the ways to traverse the collection is to use the `For Each` syntax. The following code loops through each object in the collection and removes the bitmap object from the collection:

```
For Each Obj In Bitmaps
    Bitmaps.Remove 1
Next
```

The collection does not have to be of uniform objects. You can add many types of objects to the collection. Each object's properties can be accessed through the collection:

```
If DisplayOpt(0).Value = True Then Bitmaps.Item(ImageList.ListIndex + 1).Load
```

This code references the `Bitmap` class. First, the collection is referenced—`Bitmaps`. Then the `Item` property of the class is used to reference the appropriate item in the collection. Next, the method or property of the class is referenced directly, which in this case is the `Load` method of the `Bitmap` class.

Comments

The collection object provides one of the easiest ways to organize a collection of classes that are similarly related. Instead of trying to create arrays of classes, the collection object offers a dynamic and versatile way to work with groups of classes. You might be familiar with some built-in collections such as printers. Visual Basic will enumerate these types of objects in collections.

COMPLEXITY
ADVANCED

5.4 How do I...
Implement an object model?

COMPATIBILITY: VISUAL BASIC 5 AND 6

Problem

Now that I have seen how to a build a class and use a collection of classes, how do I put this all together to implement an object model?

Technique

An *object model* represents how different objects in a software system interact with each other. As you have seen, it is a relatively easy matter to define a couple of classes to add functionality to your application. Things can get a little more complicated when working with multiple classes, though. In this example, you will combine the previously built `DiskFile` and `Bitmap` classes with two new classes—`VertFade` and `PatBrush`. `VertFade` and `PatBrush` will add the capability to perform a vertical fade on the bitmap images. The `VertFade` class will use a collection of pattern brushes that are defined by the `PatBrush` class. The `Bitmap` class will have a new fade method that will collaborate with the `VertFade` class to perform a fade on the bitmap. The primary form generally does not need to know about the `DiskFile`, `VertFade`, and `PatBrush` classes; these will be abstracted away from the client implementation. All these classes working together define the object model for your project.

Steps

Open and run `5-4.VBP`. Figure 5.5 shows the form at runtime.

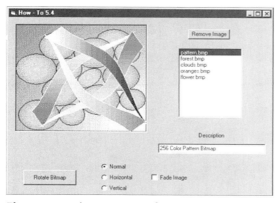

Figure 5.5 The running form

Figure 5.6 shows this application with the Oranges bitmap in a mid-fade pattern.

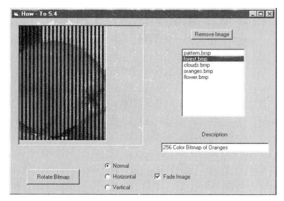

Figure 5.6 The Oranges bitmap in mid-fade pattern

To show the vertical fade, enable the Fade Image check box. Then switch to another image. Each image will exit with a vertical fade before the next image is shown. Complete the following steps to create this project:

1. Create a new standard EXE project called 5-4.VBP. Add the objects and properties listed in Table 5.3 to the form, and save the form as 5-4.FRM.

Table 5.3 5-4.VBP's objects and properties

OBJECT	PROPERTY	SETTING
Form	Name	Form1
	Caption	"How-To 5.4"
CheckBox	Name	FadeImage
	Caption	"Fade Image"
CommandButton	Name	Remove
	Caption	"Remove Image"
CommandButton	Name	Display
	Caption	"Rotate Bitmap"
TextBox	Name	FileDesc
ListBox	Name	ImageList
OptionButton	Name	DisplayOpt
	Caption	"Vertical"
	Index	2

OBJECT	PROPERTY	SETTING
OptionButton	Name	DisplayOpt
	Caption	"Horizontal"
	Index	1
OptionButton	Name	DisplayOpt
	Caption	"Normal"
	Index	0
	Value	-1 'True
PictureBox	Name	DispPict
	Picture	"pastel.bmp"
PictureBox	Name	BackPict
	AutoRedraw	-1 'True
	Picture	"pastel.bmp"
	Visible	0 'False
Label	Name	Label1
	AutoSize	-1 'True
	Caption	"Description"

2. Add the following code to the General Declarations section of the form. The **Bitmaps** collection is declared for holding the list of images to be used in the application.

```
Option Explicit

'   Bitmaps will be our collection of
'   bitmaps for viewing
Dim Bitmaps As Collection
```

3. When the bitmap classes are set up, note the reference to the **FileInfo** **DiskFile** class, which is contained in the **Bitmap** class. This is done because Visual Basic does not offer true inheritance. If it did, you would not have to reference **FileInfo** directly.

```
Private Sub Display_Click()

'   Depending on the display option
'   show the bitmap appropriately
If DisplayOpt(0).Value = True Then Bitmaps.Item
➥(ImageList.ListIndex + 1).Load
If DisplayOpt(1).Value = True Then Bitmaps.Item
➥(ImageList.ListIndex + 1).Flip 1
```

continued on next page

continued from previous page

```
            If DisplayOpt(2).Value = True Then Bitmaps.Item
        ➥(ImageList.ListIndex + 1).Flip 2

        End Sub

        Private Sub Form_Load()

        Dim N As Integer
        Dim BMP As Bitmap

        '  Create the new collection of bitmaps
        Set Bitmaps = New Collection

        '  Create the bitmap object and add
        '  it to the collection
        For N = 1 To 5

            '  Create an instance of the bitmap
            Set BMP = New Bitmap

            '  Set the display picture
            '  properties
            Set BMP.BackPict = BackPict
            Set BMP.DispPict = DispPict

            '  Depending on the count, add the
            '  appropriate image and set the
            '  description
            Select Case N

                Case 1
                    BMP.FileInfo.FileName = App.Path + "\pattern.bmp"
                    BMP.FileInfo.FileDesc = "256 Color Pattern Bitmap"

                Case 2
                    BMP.FileInfo.FileName = App.Path + "\forest.bmp"
                    BMP.FileInfo.FileDesc =
                    ➥"Standard Windows 95 Forest Bitmap"

                Case 3
                    BMP.FileInfo.FileName = App.Path + "\clouds.bmp"
                    BMP.FileInfo.FileDesc = "Microsoft Clouds Bitmap"

                Case 4
                    BMP.FileInfo.FileName = App.Path + "\oranges.bmp"
                    BMP.FileInfo.FileDesc ="256 Color Bitmap of Oranges"

                Case 5
                    BMP.FileInfo.FileName = App.Path + "\flower.bmp"
                    BMP.FileInfo.FileDesc =
                    ➥"256 Color Bitmap of a Blossoming Flower"

            End Select

            '  Add the Bitmap class to the
            '  collection of bitmaps and set
```

```
    '  the key as the count
    Bitmaps.Add Item:=BMP, Key:=CStr(N)

    '  Add just the name of the image file
    '  to the list box
    ImageList.AddItem (BMP.FileInfo.File)

    '  Destroy the instance of the bitmap class
    Set BMP = Nothing

Next N

'  Set the image list to the first
'  selection
ImageList.ListIndex = 0

End Sub

Private Sub Form_Unload(Cancel As Integer)

Dim N As Integer

'  Destroy all of the bitmap instances
'  when the form is unloaded
For N = 1 To Bitmaps.Count
    Bitmaps.Remove 1
Next N

End Sub
```

4. When an image is selected, the `Fade` method of the `Bitmap` class is called.

```
Private Sub imageList_Click()

'  Call the fade method of the class to
'  perform a vertical blind fade on the
'  image
If FadeImage.Value = 1 Then
➥Bitmaps.Item(ImageList.ListIndex + 1).Fade

'  When an image in the list is
'  clicked on, load the image
Bitmaps.Item(ImageList.ListIndex + 1).Load

'  Set the file description in the
'  text box
FileDesc.Text =
➥Bitmaps.Item(ImageList.ListIndex + 1).FileInfo.FileDesc

End Sub

Private Sub Remove_Click()
```

continued on next page

continued from previous page

```
'   Always ensure there is at least
'   one entry in the list box
If ImageList.ListCount > 1 Then

    '   Remove the specified image from
    '   the collection and the list box
    Bitmaps.Remove ImageList.ListIndex + 1
    ImageList.RemoveItem ImageList.ListIndex
End If

'   Set the selection to the
'   first image
ImageList.ListIndex = 0

End Sub
```

5. Insert a new class into the project and save it as **Bitmap.cls**. Add the following code to **Bitmap.cls**:

```
Option Explicit

'   A Bitmap is a type of DiskFile
'   So, the Bitmap class will use
'   the properties and methods of
'   the DiskFile class for its
'   functionality
Public FileInfo As DiskFile

'   Declare the global properties of the
'   class. m_DispPict is the standard
'   display picture. m_BackPict is the
'   background picture that will be used
'   for the image flipping.
Private m_DispPict As Control
Private m_BackPict As Control

'   Get the Display picture control
Public Property Set DispPict(AControl As Control)
    Set m_DispPict = AControl
    m_DispPict.AutoSize = True
End Property

'   Get the Background picture control
'   It is important to ensure that this
'   picture is invisible and that the
'   AutoRedraw property is true so that it
'   will act as a memory device context and
'   hold its image for later work
Public Property Set BackPict(AControl As Control)
    Set m_BackPict = AControl
    m_BackPict.AutoRedraw = True
    m_BackPict.Visible = False
    m_BackPict.AutoSize = True
End Property
```

6. The Fade method of the Bitmap class handles creating an instance of the VertFade class to perform the vertical fade. The class is set up to have the BackPict and DispPict picture boxes perform the fade. The Setup method of the class is called, and then the Fade method is run to perform the fade. Note that after the fade finishes, a slight pause allows the viewer to see the full black image before the picture box is hidden. Then the picture box is hidden, and a slight pause is performed when the picture box is hidden. These two pauses help provide visual cues to the user as to when the fade is done and before the next image is loaded.

```
Public Sub Fade()

Dim T As Variant
Dim VF As VertFade

'   Create the vertical fade class
Set VF = New VertFade

'   Set the pictures used to perform
'   the fade
Set VF.BackPict = m_BackPict
Set VF.DispPict = m_DispPict

'   Set up the fade
VF.Setup

'   Perform the fade
VF.Fade

'   Get the current time
T = Time

'   Let the black fade show for
'   a few seconds
Do Until Time > (T + 0.0000001)
Loop

'   Destroy the instance of the class
Set VF = Nothing

'   Make the displayed picture invisible
m_DispPict.Visible = False

'   For better effect, let the image
'   stay invisible for a few seconds
T = Time

Do Until Time > (T + 0.0000001)
Loop

End Sub

'   The load method of the class loads
'   the image into the two display pictures
```

continued on next page

continued from previous page

```
Public Sub Load()
    m_DispPict.Picture = LoadPicture(FileInfo.FileName)
    m_BackPict.Picture = LoadPicture(FileInfo.FileName)
    m_DispPict.Visible = True
End Sub

'   The Flip method of the class will rotate
'   the picture accordingly
Public Sub Flip(Rotate)

'   Depending on the rotation selected, the
'   original image will be copied to the
'   display picture appropriately
Select Case Rotate

'   Note that for the vertical and
'   horizontal flips, the height or
'   width is set to a negative value
'   and the starting point is set to
'   the height or width for the image
'   to be displayed. The PaintPicture
'   method of the picture box is used
'   to do the rotation
    Case 1  'Actual Size
            '   Flip Horizontal
            m_DispPict.PaintPicture m_BackPict.Picture,
    ➥m_BackPict.ScaleWidth, 0, -1 * m_BackPict.ScaleWidth,
    ➥m_BackPict.ScaleHeight, 0, 0, m_BackPict.ScaleWidth,
    ➥m_BackPict.ScaleHeight

    Case 2
            '   Flip Vertical
            m_DispPict.PaintPicture m_BackPict.Picture, 0,
    ➥m_BackPict.ScaleHeight, m_BackPict.ScaleWidth, -1 *
    ➥m_BackPict.ScaleHeight, 0, 0, m_BackPict.ScaleWidth,
    ➥m_BackPict.ScaleHeight

End Select
End Sub

Private Sub Class_Initialize()
    '   When the class is initialized,
    '   the DiskFile class is created
    Set FileInfo = New DiskFile
End Sub

Private Sub Class_Terminate()
    '   When the class is terminated
    '   the DiskFile class is destroyed
    Set FileInfo = Nothing
End Sub
```

7. Insert a new class into the project and save it as `DiskFile.cls`. Add the following code to `DiskFile.cls`:

```
Option Explicit

'  Member property of the class that
'  stores the filename
Private m_FileName As String

'  Member property of the class that
'  stores the file description
Private m_FileDesc As String

'  The get and set properties of the class
'  for the file description
Public Property Let FileDesc(s As String)
    m_FileDesc = s
End Property

Public Property Get FileDesc() As String
    FileDesc = m_FileDesc
End Property

'  Get the file name by itself.
'  I.E. c:\windows\clouds.bmp is clouds.bmp
Public Property Get File() As String
    File = ParseFile()
End Property

'  Set and get the filename property for
'  the class
Public Property Let FileName(s As String)
    m_FileName = s
End Property

Public Property Get FileName() As String
    FileName = m_FileName
End Property

'  Get the file size
Public Property Get FileSize() As Long
    FileSize = FileLen(m_FileName)
End Property

'  Get the file extension
Public Property Get FileExt() As String
    FileExt = ParseExt()
End Property

'  Get the directory of the file
Public Property Get Directory() As String
```

continued on next page

continued from previous page

```
        Directory = ParseDir()
    End Property

    '  Get the date of the file
    Public Property Get FileDate() As Date
        FileDate = FileDateTime(m_FileName)
    End Property

    '  Parse out the file name. Note that this is
    '  a private method. It is only utilized in the
    '  File property
    Private Function ParseFile() As String

    Dim N As Integer

    ParseFile = ""

    '  Start from the end of the file name
    '  and look for the '\' character. Thus the
    '  file part of the file name will be known
    For N = Len(m_FileName) To 1 Step -1

        If Mid(m_FileName, N, 1) = "\" Then
            ParseFile = Right(m_FileName, Len(m_FileName) - N)
            N = -1
        End If

    Next N

    End Function

    '  Parse out the file directory. Note that
    '  this is a private class method and is only
    '  utilized by the Directory property
    Private Function ParseDir() As String

    Dim N As Integer

    ParseDir = ""

    '  Start from the end of the file name
    '  and look for the first '\' character. Thus
    '  the location of the file name will be known
    '  and the rest is the directory location
    For N = Len(m_FileName) To 1 Step -1

        If Mid(m_FileName, N, 1) = "\" Then
            ParseDir = Left(m_FileName, N)
            N = -1
        End If

    Next N

    End Function
```

```
'  GetExt retrieves the file extension if
'  there is one. This is only used by the
'  FileExt property
Private Function ParseExt() As String

Dim N As Integer

ParseExt = "(N/A)"

'  Start from the end of the file name
'  and look for the '.' character. Thus
'  the location of the extension will be known
'  in the file name string
For N = Len(m_FileName) To 1 Step -1

    If Mid(m_FileName, N, 1) = "." Then
        ParseExt = Right(m_FileName, Len(m_FileName) - N)
        N = -1
    End If

Next N

End Function

'  Public method of the class to
'  copy the file to a new location
Public Sub CopyFile(NewLocation)
    FileCopy m_FileName, NewLocation + ParseFile
End Sub

'  Public method of the class to
'  delete the file
Public Sub DeleteFile()
    Kill m_FileName
End Sub

'  When the class is initialized
'  the filename, description and
'  extension will be set to
'  N/A.
Private Sub Class_Initialize()

m_FileName = "Uninitialized"
m_FileDesc = "N/A"

End Sub
```

8. Insert a new class into the project and save it as **PatBrush.cls**. Add the following code to the General Declarations section of the class. The appropriate Win32 API functions, types, and constants are declared for creating bitmap pattern brushes.

```
Option Explicit

'   The BITMAPINFOHEADER contains basic information
'   about the bitmap we will create
Private Type BITMAPINFOHEADER '40 bytes
        biSize As Long
        biWidth As Long
        biHeight As Long
        biPlanes As Integer
        biBitCount As Integer
        biCompression As Long
        biSizeImage As Long
        biXPelsPerMeter As Long
        biYPelsPerMeter As Long
        biClrUsed As Long
        biClrImportant As Long
End Type

'   This data structure holds the header info as
'   well as the color data
Private Type BITMAPINFO
    bmiHeader As BITMAPINFOHEADER
' Array length is arbitrary; may be changed
    bmiColors As String * 8
End Type

'   Selects an object into a device context
Private Declare Function SelectObject Lib "gdi32"
(ByVal hdc As Long, ByVal hObject As Long) As Long

'   Creates a DIB Bitmap
Private Declare Function CreateDIBitmap Lib "gdi32"
(ByVal hdc As Long, lpInfoHeader As BITMAPINFOHEADER, ByVal
dwUsage As Long, ByVallpInitBits$, lpInitInfo As BITMAPINFO,
ByVal wUsage As Long) As Long

'   Deletes a created object
Private Declare Function DeleteObject Lib "gdi32"
➡(ByVal hObject As Long)
As Long

'   Creates a pattern brush
Private Declare Function CreatePatternBrush Lib "gdi32"
➡(ByVal HBITMAP As
Long) As Long

'   Paints a picture with the specified pattern
Private Declare Function PatBlt Lib "gdi32" (ByVal hdc As Long,
➡ByVal x
As Long, ByVal y As Long, ByVal nWidth As Long,
➡ByVal nHeight As Long,
ByValdwRop As Long) As Long

Const DIB_RGB_COLORS = 0         '   color table in RGBs
Const CBM_INIT = &H4&            '   initialize bitmap
```

```
Const PATCOPY = &HF00021      '  Used for Pattern Copy
Const BI_RGB = 0&             '  RGB Bitmap

'  Declare m_BitInfoH as type BITMAPINFOHEADER
Dim m_BitInfoH As BITMAPINFOHEADER

'  Declare m_BitInfo as type BITMAPINFO
Dim m_BitInfo As BITMAPINFO

'  Holds the Screen data for building the bitmap
Dim m_Scrn As String * 32

'  Holds the handle to the brush
Dim m_Hbr As Long
Dim m_OrgHbr As Long

'  Declare our objects to be passed in
Private m_DispPict As Object
Private m_Array(8) As String * 8
```

9. The `SetupBitmap` method of the class will set up an 8×8 bitmap header with the two colors passed in as parameters. The bitmap header needs to be set up appropriately for creating a bitmap brush with two colors. More information about the type structures is provided in the "How It Works" section.

```
Public Sub SetupBitmap(r1, g1, b1, r2, g2, b2)

'  Standard 40 Byte Header
m_BitInfoH.biSize = 40

'  This will be an 8 by 8 bitmap
m_BitInfoH.biWidth = 8
m_BitInfoH.biHeight = 8

'  One Plane
m_BitInfoH.biPlanes = 1

'  Specifies the number of bits per pixel
m_BitInfoH.biBitCount = 1

'   No Compression
m_BitInfoH.biCompression = BI_RGB

'  These values are rarely used
m_BitInfoH.biSizeImage = 0
m_BitInfoH.biXPelsPerMeter = 0
m_BitInfoH.biYPelsPerMeter = 0

'  Two colors used
m_BitInfoH.biClrUsed = 2
```

continued on next page

continued from previous page

```
'   This ensures that all colors are important
m_BitInfoH.biClrImportant = 0

'   Sets the colors for the bits
'   and background
m_BitInfo.bmiColors = Chr$(r1) + Chr$(g1) + Chr$(b1) + "0" +
Chr$(r2) +  Chr$(g2) + Chr$(b2) + "0"

End Sub
```

10. The **BuildBitmap** function loops through the string array **m_array**. This array is a series of eight characters of either 1s or 0s. The 1s and 0s represent the bit pattern for the bitmap. The **m_Scrn** variable will have every fourth byte set to the calculated value, **V**. A string is created with the overall bit data with which to create the pattern. From the bitmap created, the pattern brush is created.

```
Public Sub BuildBitmap()

Dim Counter as Integer
Dim V as integer
Dim C As Integer
Dim CompBitmap As Long

'   We will loop through each element in the array
For Counter = 1 To 8

    '   v will hold the value of the bit pattern, we
    '   need to reset it for each row
    V = 0

    '   We will loop through each row and set the bit values
    For C = 0 To 7

        '   We check for a 1 in the array and if it is one we
        '   then calculate the decimal value of the binary position
        '   for example in 00000100, the 1 is = to 2^2 = 4
        If Mid$(m_Array(Counter), C + 1, 1) = "1" Then
    ➡V = V + 2 ^ C

    Next C

    Mid$(m_Scrn, (Counter - 1) * 4 + 1, 1) = Chr$(V)

Next Counter

'   Set the BitmapInfoHeader field of m_BitInfo
m_BitInfo.bmiHeader = m_BitInfoH
```

```
'  Create the 8x8 bitmap specified by m_scrn
CompBitmap = CreateDIBitmap(m_DispPict.hdc, m_BitInfoH,
➥CBM_INIT,  m_Scrn, m_BitInfo, DIB_RGB_COLORS)


'  Create the bitmap pattern from the screen
m_Hbr = CreatePatternBrush(CompBitmap)

End Sub
```

11. The `DeleteBrush` method deletes the current brush for the bitmap.

```
Public Sub DeleteBrush()

Dim Throw As Long

'  Select the original brush into the picture
Throw = SelectObject(m_DispPict.hdc, m_OrgHbr)

'  Delete the created brush
Throw = DeleteObject(m_Hbr)

End Sub
```

12. The `ShowPattern` method selects the brush into the display device context. The pattern then is copied into the device context using `PatBlt`.

```
Public Sub ShowPattern()

Dim m_OrgHbr, Throw As Long

'  Select the brush into the display
'  picture
m_OrgHbr = SelectObject(m_DispPict.hdc, m_Hbr)

'  Show the pattern screen
Throw = PatBlt(m_DispPict.hdc, 0, 0,
➥m_DispPict.ScaleWidth, m_DispPict.ScaleHeight, PATCOPY)

'  Select the original brush into the picture
Throw = SelectObject(m_DispPict.hdc, m_OrgHbr)

'  Delete the created brush
Throw = DeleteObject(m_Hbr)

End Sub
```

13. The `SetPattern` property sets and retrieves the string bit pattern for the pattern bitmap.

```
Public Sub SetPattern(s, index)
    '  Set the pattern sent in
    m_Array(index). = s
End Sub

'  Get the picture for display
Public Property Set DispPict(AControl As Object)
    Set m_DispPict = AControl
End Property
```

14. When the class is terminated, be sure to delete the brush.

```
Private Sub Class_Terminate()

'  Delete the brush if it exists
If m_Hbr <> 0 Then DeleteBrush

End Sub
```

15. Insert a new class into the project and save it as **VertFade.cls**. Add the following code to the General Declarations section of the class. A collection of pattern brushes is declared that will create the pattern bitmaps needed for the vertical fade. Also, the **BitBlt** API function is declared to copy the pattern bitmap to the display.

```
Option Explicit

'  PatBrushes is a collection of
'  bitmap brushes
Dim m_PatBrushes As Collection

'  BitBlt will be used for the image copies
Private Declare Function BitBlt Lib "gdi32"
➥(ByVal hDestDC As Long, ByVal
x As Long, ByVal y As Long, ByVal nWidth As Long,
ByVal nHeight As Long, ByVal hSrcDC As Long,
ByVal xSrc As Long, ByVal ySrc As Long, ByVal
dwRop As Long) As Long

'  Constants for the BitBlt copies
Const SRCCOPY = &HCC0020
Const SRCAND = &H8800C6

'  Globally declare the members of the class
Dim m_BackPict As Control
Dim m_DispPict As Control
```

16. The **BackPict** and **DispPict** picture-box controls will be set to perform the fade on the images.

```
'  BackPict and DispPict are the picture
'  controls for performing the fade
Public Property Set BackPict(AControl As Control)
```

```
    Set m_BackPict = AControl
End Property

Public Property Set DispPict(AControl As Control)
    Set m_DispPict = AControl
End Property
```

17. The CreateFade method handles setting up the bitmap brushes in the PatBrush classes that will be used to perform the vertical fade. Each PatBrush class in the PatBrushes collection is looped through to create the patterns. Note that the cnt variable is incremented only with each brush. Thus, the string in Pat$ for each brush is used eight times. Then the bitmap is set up for that brush, and you move to the next brush.

```
Public Sub CreateFade()

Dim Cnt As Long
Dim N As Long
Dim Pat As String
Dim Brush

Cnt = 0

'   Create 10 transition brushes
For Each Brush In m_PatBrushes

Cnt = Cnt + 1

    '   Set up the 8x8 pattern
    For N = 1 To 8

        '   Depending on Cnt and N the appropriate row of
        '   the bitmap pattern is set.
        If Cnt = 1 Then Pat$ = "00000000"

        If Cnt = 2 Then Pat$ = "10000000"

        If Cnt = 3 Then Pat$ = "11000000"

        If Cnt = 4 Then Pat$ = "11100000"

        If Cnt = 5 Then Pat$ = "11110000"

        If Cnt = 6 Then Pat$ = "11111000"

        If Cnt = 7 Then Pat$ = "11111100"

        If Cnt = 8 Then Pat$ = "11111110"

        If Cnt = 9 Then Pat$ = "11111111"

        If Cnt = 10 Then Pat$ = "11111111"
```

continued on next page

continued from previous page

```
            '  Set the row bits
            Brush.SetPattern Pat$, N

            Pat$ = ""

        Next N

    '  Call the setup bitmap function and
    '  pass in the colors
    Brush.SetupBitmap 255, 255, 255, 0, 0, 0

    '  Build the pattern bitmap
    Brush.BuildBitmap

Next Brush

End Sub
```

18. The `Fade` method of the class handles looping through the pattern brushes. First, the back picture is cleared. Then the next pattern bitmap is displayed in the back picture by calling the `ShowPattern` method of the `PatBrush` class. After the pattern is displayed in the hidden picture, the image is copied to the display picture. Note that the pattern is created out of the view of the user, so while the picture is cleared and the pattern is shown no flickers are seen in the process.

```
Public Sub Fade()

Dim Cnt As Integer
Dim Throw As Integer
Dim Brush As Object

    '  Create the Vertical Patterns
    CreateFade

    '  Loop through the patterns and
    '  display the pattern brush
    For Cnt = 1 To 10

        '  Clear the back picture
        m_BackPict.Cls

        '  Display the pattern
        m_PatBrushes.Item(Cnt).ShowPattern

        '  Copy the Pattern to the screen
        Throw = BitBlt(m_DispPict.hdc, 0, 0, m_DispPict.ScaleWidth,
        ➥m_DispPict.ScaleHeight, m_BackPict.hdc, 0, 0, SRCAND)

    Next Cnt

End Sub
```

19. The Setup method handles creating the PatBrushes collection. Each PatBrush class is set up and added to the collection of pattern brushes.

```
Public Sub Setup()

Dim N As Integer
Dim PB As PatBrush

'   Create the collection of vertical
'   pattern brushes
Set m_PatBrushes = New Collection

'   Set the picture widths
m_DispPict.Width = m_BackPict.Width
m_DispPict.Height = m_BackPict.Height

'   Set the picture autoredraw and visible
'   property
m_BackPict.AutoRedraw = True
m_BackPict.Visible = False

'   Set up the collection
For N = 1 To 10

    '   Create the pattern brush
    Set PB = New PatBrush

    '   Set the display picture for
    '   the pattern. In this case it
    '   will be the working back picture
    Set PB.DispPict = m_BackPict

    ' Add the class to the collection
    m_PatBrushes.Add Item:=PB, Key:=CStr(N)

Next N

End Sub
```

20. When the class is terminated, the pattern brushes are deleted and the collection is destroyed.

```
Private Sub Class_Terminate()

Dim Brush

'   Delete the brushes
For Each Brush In m_PatBrushes
    Brush.DeleteBrush
Next Brush

'   Delete the collection
Set m_PatBrushes = Nothing

End Sub
```

How It Works

There are two aspects of this How-To to explore. The first is the object-oriented model used to design the project. The second is the little bit of Windows API magic used to perform the vertical fade.

The object-oriented model used is based on exposing the **Bitmap** class to the form. The **Bitmap** class works with several other classes to build its functionality, though. The beauty of the project is that the primary program logic, that of browsing the bitmaps, is not filled with the underlying functionality of how the bitmaps are displayed or how the fade is performed.

The **Bitmap** class uses the **DiskFile** class and is, in fact, a type of disk file. The **Bitmap** class collaborates with the **VertFade** class to provide the fade functionality. The **VertFade** class uses a collection of pattern brushes created by the **PatFade** class to provide the vertical fade patterns. Each class encapsulates a set of functionality that hides its complexity from the rest of the program. For example, the **VertFade** class does not have to know much about how to create pattern brushes; it only needs to know how to work with the **PatBrush** class. The form does not need to understand any of the underlying intricacies of a bitmap; it just calls the methods of the **Bitmap** class. This simple object model demonstrates the power of object-oriented programming and techniques. One of the primary side benefits of this methodology is that you now have a set of four classes that can be reused by any future applications and can be easily added to your applications. This is very similar to the concepts that made VBXs and OCXs so popular.

In case you are wondering how the underlying bitmap logic works, take a look at the **VertFade** and **PatBrush** classes. Each class is creatable within the context of the program (not public). The **PatBrush** class handles creating a Windows bitmap brush from a specified pattern.

Bitmaps can be built bit by bit using the Windows API. For a bitmap brush, an 8×8 bitmap can be built and used as a brush. You must accomplish four primary steps to do this:

1. Set up the bit pattern—the **SetPattern** method of the class.

2. Set up the bitmap structure—the **SetupBitmap** method of the class.

3. Build the bitmap object—the **BuildBitmap** method of the class.

4. Show the bitmap brush—the **ShowPattern** method of the class.

The first step is to define the pattern of the 8×8 bitmap. This is done by passing in a string that defines the vertical pattern of the pattern bitmap (for example, `"11000000"`). This is a convenient way to define, bit by bit, the bitmap format. The **BuildBitmap** function handles converting the array into the data needed to build the bitmap. The following is one example of the vertical pattern array:

```
m_array(1) = "11110000"
m_array(2) = "11110000"
m_array(3) = "11110000"
m_array(4) = "11110000"
m_array(5) = "11110000"
m_array(6) = "11110000"
m_array(7) = "11110000"
m_array(8) = "11110000"
```

When the bitmap is set up, the Windows bitmap structures are initialized and the colors for the background and bits are determined. Table 5.4 details the BITMAPINFO API structure. Table 5.5 details the BITMAPINFOHEADER API structure.

Table 5.4 BITMAPINFO API-type structure

MEMBER	DESCRIPTION
biSize As Long	Specifies the number of bytes required by the structure
biWidth As Long	Specifies the width of the bitmap, in pixels
biHeight As Long	Specifies the height of the bitmap, in pixels
biPlanes As Integer	Specifies the number of planes for the target device (always 1)
biBitCount As Integer	Specifies the number of bits per pixel: 1, 4, 8, 16, 24, or 32
biCompression As Long	Specifies the type of compression for a compressed bottom-up bitmap
biSizeImage As Long	Specifies the size, in bytes, of the image (usually 0)
biXPelsPerMeter As Long	Specifies the horizontal resolution in pixels per meter (usually 0)
biYPelsPerMeter As Long	Specifies the vertical resolution in pixels per meter (usually 0)
biClrUsed As Long	Specifies the number of color indexes in the color table
biClrImportant As Long	Specifies the number of important color indexes (usually 0)

Table 5.5 BITMAPINFOHEADER API-type structure

MEMBER	DESCRIPTION
bmiHeader As BITMAPINFOHEADER	Points to a BITMAPINFOHEADER structure
bmiColors() As Byte	Specifies a byte array to indicate colors

Note that the bitmap colors are easily set as every four bytes for the bmiColors byte field. The first byte of the four is the red value, the second green, the third blue, and the last must be 0. The first set of four is color index 0 in the bitmap palette, the second set of four is color index 1, and so on.

The next step builds the bitmap and provides a handle for creating the brush. The key to building the bitmap is converting the m_array string into a format usable by the CreateDIBitmap function. The CreateDIBitmap function expects the bitmap data to be placed in 4-byte blocks, so every row in the bitmap image must end on a 4-byte boundary. Each element of m_array is converted into a binary number with the following loop:

```
For C = 0 To 7
If Mid$(m_Array(Counter), C + 1, 1) = "1" Then V = V + 2 ^ C
    Next C
```

The string array (m_Array) essentially represents a binary number that must be converted into a single decimal value, which in this code is represented by V. That decimal value then is placed in every fourth byte of a string that represents the bitmap data. The following code does this:

```
Mid$(m_Scrn, (Counter - 1) * 4 + 1, 1) = Chr$(V)
```

The m_Scrn variable will hold the bitmap values for each row of the pattern to be created (with each row being every four bytes). This then can be used in the CreateDIBitmap function as shown here:

```
'  Create the 8x8 bitmap specified by m_scrn
CompBitmap = CreateDIBitmap(m_DispPict.hdc, m_BitInfoH, CBM_INIT, m_Scrn,
m_BitInfo, DIB_RGB_COLORS)
```

The CreateDIBitmap function takes six parameters that will build the bitmap. Table 5.6 is a breakdown of each.

Table 5.6 CreateDIBitmap parameters

PARAMETER	DESCRIPTION
ByVal hDC As Long	The device context in which to build the bitmap
lpInfoHeader as BITMAPINFOHEADER	The bitmap format
ByVal dwUsage As Long	Defines whether or not the bitmap is initialized
ByVal lpInitBits$	Points to the bitmap bit data
lpInitInfo as BITMAPINFO	Contains the BITMAPHEADER and color information
ByVal wUsage As Long	Specifies whether the colors contain explicit red, green, blue (RGB) values or palette indexes

After the handle of the bitmap is created, the bitmap pattern brush is easily created with the CreatePatternBrush function, which only takes the handle to the bitmap as a parameter. The pattern is easily displayed using the PatBLT function. First, your new pattern brush must be selected into the device context by using the SelectObject API.

The VertFade class creates a series of pattern brushes. The BitBrush class builds the vertical patterns by building a set of pattern brushes based on a set of 10 strings sent into each consecutive pattern brush, with each string representing a step in the vertical fade. Each PatBrush class in the array will be set up to be a series of pattern bitmaps that get progressively black, with a vertical pattern.

After this series of bitmaps is created, the next step is to loop through them and build the next fade image. This is done in the `Fade` method. Then the pattern merely needs to be copied into your background picture box and then copied to the display image using `BitBlt`. This two-step process is done to reduce screen flickering during the fade process.

Comments

Additional functionality could be easily added to the program by adding new classes to give additional features, or the current classes could be easily extended. A method could be added to the `VertFade` class to do a type of reverse fade to let the images fade in, for example. In the next How-To, you will add an element of persistence to store the bitmap information in a database. Also, you will make this program into a simple three-tier application.

COMPLEXITY
INTERMEDIATE

5.5 How do I...
Build ActiveX components?

COMPATIBILITY: VISUAL BASIC 5 AND 6

Problem

The code from the last How-To implements a simple object model. How do I extend this application to store the image data in a database, and how do I break out some of the classes to be in-process DLLs and out-of-process ActiveX components?

Technique

An Access database, `IData.mdb`, is created to store basic image data including image ID, filename, filesize, file format, and comments. An ActiveX component will be created that handles retrieving and storing data in the `IData.mdb` file. This ActiveX component will be registered in the system and called from the sample tier client application. You will also encapsulate the `DiskFile` class into an ActiveX DLL that can be called from your application.

Steps

Open and run `5-5.VBP`. Figure 5.7 shows the form at runtime.

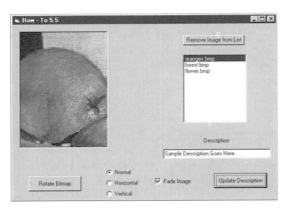

Figure 5.7 The form at runtime

The application has the same functionality as all the previous How-To's. The underlying implementation has changed significantly, though. The persistent data about the bitmap images is being pulled from the database. As the Description text box in Figure 5.8 shows, if you want to change and store the description of the images in the database, simply click Update Description.

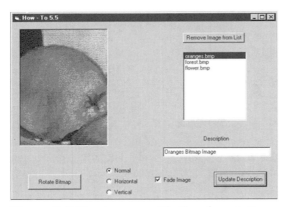

Figure 5.8 The image with the description updated

Complete the following steps to create this project:

1. Create a new project called **5-5.VBP**. Add the objects and properties listed in Table 5.7 to the form, and save the form as **5-5.FRM**.

Table 5.7 5-5.VBP's objects and properties

OBJECT	PROPERTY	SETTING
Form	Name	Form1
	Caption	"How-To 5.5"
CommandButton	Name	UpdateDesc
	Caption	"Update Description"
CheckBox	Name	FadeImage
	Caption	"Fade Image"
	Value	1 'Checked
CommandButton	Name	Remove
	Caption	"Remove Image from List"
CommandButton	Name	Display
	Caption	"Rotate Bitmap"
TextBox	Name	FileDesc
ListBox	Name	ImageList
OptionButton	Name	DisplayOpt
	Caption	"Vertical"
	Index	2
OptionButton	Name	DisplayOpt
	Caption	"Horizontal"
	Index	1
OptionButton	Name	DisplayOpt
	Caption	"Normal"
	Index	0
	Value	-1 'True
PictureBox	Name	DispPict
	Picture	"pastel.bmp"
PictureBox	Name	BackPict
	AutoRedraw	-1 'True
	Picture	"pastel.bmp"
	Visible	0 'False
Label	Name	Label1
	AutoSize	-1 'True
	Caption	"Description"

2. Add the following code to the General Declarations section of the form. The **IData** object is created. Note that a reference to the **ImageData** server is needed in the project references.

```
Option Explicit

'   Bitmaps will be our collection of
'   bitmaps for viewing
Dim Bitmaps As Collection

'   Globally declare the ImageData
'   class
Dim IData As ImageData
```

3. The **UpdateDesc** button handles updating the image comments in both the bitmap class and the database.

```
Private Sub UpdateDesc_Click()

'   Update the file description
Bitmaps.Item(ImageList.ListIndex + 1).FileInfo.FileDesc
➥= FileDesc.Text

'   Store the new file description in
'   the database by calling the remote
'   servers UpdateComments method
IData.UpdateComments FileDesc.Text, Bitmaps.Item
➥(ImageList.ListIndex + 1).ID

End Sub

Private Sub Display_Click()

'   Depending on the display option
'   show the bitmap appropriately
If DisplayOpt(0).Value = True Then Bitmaps.Item
➥(ImageList.ListIndex + 1).Load
If DisplayOpt(1).Value = True Then Bitmaps.Item
➥(ImageList.ListIndex + 1).Flip 1
If DisplayOpt(2).Value = True Then Bitmaps.Item
➥(ImageList.ListIndex + 1).Flip 2

End Sub
```

4. When the form is loaded, the **ImageData** class is created. When the **Bitmaps** collection is set up, the collection is based on the current set of images in the database. The **Bitmap** class is created with the specified image ID, filename, and comments/description.

```
Private Sub Form_Load()

Dim N As Integer
Dim BMP As Bitmap
Dim ID As Integer

'   Create an instance of the
'   ImageData object
Set IData = New ImageData

'   Open the connection in the
'   remote object
IData.InitConnect

'   Get the ID set
IData.GetIDSet

'   Initially set ID to true
ID = True

'   Create the new collection of bitmaps
Set Bitmaps = New Collection

'   Loop through the images in the
'   database until all are added to
'   our bitmaps collection
Do Until ID = False

    '   Create an instance of the bitmap
    Set BMP = New Bitmap

    '   Set the display picture
    '   properties
    Set BMP.BackPict = BackPict
    Set BMP.DispPict = DispPict

    '   Get the next image ID
    ID = IData.GetNextID

    '   Check to see if False was returned
    '   if so then end the loop
    If ID = False Then Exit Do

    '   Set the bitmap filename
    BMP.FileInfo.filename = IData.GetFileName(ID)

    '   Set the bitmap description
    BMP.FileInfo.FileDesc = IData.GetComments(ID)

    '   Set the bitmaps ID
    BMP.ID = ID

    '   Add the Bitmap class to the
    '   collection of bitmaps and set
```

continued on next page

continued from previous page

```
                        '  the key as the count
                        Bitmaps.Add Item:=BMP, Key:=CStr(ID)

                        '  Add just the name of the image file
                        '  to the list box
                        ImageList.AddItem (BMP.FileInfo.File)

                        '  Destroy the instance of the bitmap class
                        Set BMP = Nothing

                Loop

                '  Set the image list to the first
                '  selection
                ImageList.ListIndex = 0

                End Sub

                Private Sub Form_Unload(Cancel As Integer)

                Dim N As Integer

                '  Destroy all of the bitmap instances
                '  when the form is unloaded
                For N = 1 To Bitmaps.Count
                    Bitmaps.Remove 1
                Next N

                '  Kill the Idata instance
                Set IData = Nothing

                End Sub

                Private Sub imageList_Click()

                '  Call the fade method of the class to
                '  perform a vertical blind fade on the
                '  image
                If FadeImage.Value = 1 Then Bitmaps.Item
                ➡(ImageList.ListIndex + 1).Fade

                '  When an image in the list is
                '  clicked on, load the image
                Bitmaps.Item(ImageList.ListIndex + 1).Load

                '  Set the file description in the
                '  text box
                FileDesc.Text = Bitmaps.Item(ImageList.ListIndex + 1).
                ➡FileInfo.FileDesc

                End Sub

                Private Sub Remove_Click()
```

```
'  Always ensure there is at least
'  one entry in the list box
If ImageList.ListCount > 1 Then

     '  Remove the specified image from
     '  the collection and the list box
     Bitmaps.Remove ImageList.ListIndex + 1
     ImageList.RemoveItem ImageList.ListIndex
End If

'  Set the selection to the
'  first image
ImageList.ListIndex = 0

End Sub
```

5. Insert a new class into the project and save it as `Bitmap.cls`. Add the following code to `Bitmap.cls`:

```
Option Explicit

'  A Bitmap is a type of DiskFile
'  So, the Bitmap class will use
'  the properties and methods of
'  the DiskFile class for its
'  functionality
Public FileInfo As DiskFile

'  Declare the global properties of the
'  class. m_DispPict is the standard
'  display picture. m_BackPict is the
'  background picture that will be used
'  for the image flipping.
Private m_DispPict As Control
Private m_BackPict As Control
Private m_ID As Integer

'  Provide a unique ID to reference the bitmap
Public Property Let ID(I As Integer)
    m_ID = I
End Property

Public Property Get ID() As Integer
    ID = m_ID
End Property

'  Get the Display picture control
Public Property Set DispPict(AControl As Control)
    Set m_DispPict = AControl
    m_DispPict.AutoSize = True
End Property

'  Get the Background picture control
'  It is important to ensure that this
```

continued on next page

continued from previous page

```
'  picture is invisible and that the
'  AutoRedraw property is true so that it
'  will act as a memory device context and
'  hold its image for later work
Public Property Set BackPict(AControl As Control)
     Set m_BackPict = AControl
     m_BackPict.AutoRedraw = False
     m_BackPict.Visible = False
     m_BackPict.AutoSize = True
End Property

Public Sub Fade()

Dim T As Variant
Dim VF As VertFade

'  Create the vertical fade class
Set VF = New VertFade

'  Set the pictures used to perform
'  the fade
Set VF.BackPict = m_BackPict
Set VF.DispPict = m_DispPict

'  Set up the fade
VF.Setup

'  Perform the fade
VF.Fade

'  Get the current time
T = Time

'  Let the black fade show for
'  a few seconds
Do Until Time > (T + 0.0000001)
Loop

'  Destroy the instance of the class
Set VF = Nothing

'  Make the displayed picture invisible
m_DispPict.Visible = False

'  For better effect, let the image
'  stay invisible for a few seconds
T = Time

Do Until Time > (T + 0.0000001)
Loop

End Sub

'  The load method of the class loads
'  the image into the two display pictures
```

```
Public Sub Load()
    m_DispPict.Picture = LoadPicture(FileInfo.FileName)
    m_BackPict.Picture = LoadPicture(FileInfo.FileName)
    m_DispPict.Visible = True
End Sub

'   The Flip method of the class will rotate
'   the picture accordingly
Public Sub Flip(Rotate)

'   Depending on the rotation selected, the
'   original image will be copied to the
'   display picture appropriately
Select Case Rotate

'   Note that for the vertical and
'   horizontal flips, the height or
'   width is set to a negative value
'   and the starting point is set to
'   the height or width for the image
'   to be displayed. The PaintPicture
'   method of the picture box is used
'   to do the rotation
    Case 1  'Actual Size
            '  Flip Horizontal
            m_DispPict.PaintPicture m_BackPict.Picture,
        m_BackPict.ScaleWidth, 0, -1 * m_BackPict.ScaleWidth,
        m_BackPict.ScaleHeight, 0, 0, m_BackPict.ScaleWidth,
        m_BackPict.ScaleHeight

    Case 2
            '  Flip Vertical
            m_DispPict.PaintPicture m_BackPict.Picture, 0,
        m_BackPict.ScaleHeight, m_BackPict.ScaleWidth, -1 *
        m_BackPict.ScaleHeight, 0, 0, m_BackPict.ScaleWidth,
        m_BackPict.ScaleHeight

End Select

End Sub

Private Sub Class_Initialize()
    '  When the class is initialized,
    '  the DiskFile class is created
    Set FileInfo = New DiskFile
End Sub

Private Sub Class_Terminate()
    '  When the class is terminated
    '  the DiskFile class is destroyed
    Set FileInfo = Nothing
End Sub
```

6. The bitmap class uses the **DiskFile** object, which is an ActiveX DLL file. Add a reference to the project for the ActiveX DLL file.

7. Insert a new class into the project and save it as **PatBrush.cls**.

```
Option Explicit

'  The BITMAPINFOHEADER contains basic information
'  about the bitmap we will create
Private Type BITMAPINFOHEADER '40 bytes
        biSize As Long
        biWidth As Long
        biHeight As Long
        biPlanes As Integer
        biBitCount As Integer
        biCompression As Long
        biSizeImage As Long
        biXPelsPerMeter As Long
        biYPelsPerMeter As Long
        biClrUsed As Long
        biClrImportant As Long
End Type

'  This data structure holds the header info as
'  well as the color data
Private Type BITMAPINFO
    bmiHeader As BITMAPINFOHEADER
    bmiColors As String * 8 ' Array length is arbitrary;
    ➥may be changed
End Type

'  Selects an object into a device context
Private Declare Function SelectObject Lib "gdi32"
➥(ByVal hdc As Long,
ByVal hObject As Long) As Long

'  Creates a DIB Bitmap
Private Declare Function CreateDIBitmap Lib "gdi32"
➥(ByVal hdc As Long,
lpInfoHeader As BITMAPINFOHEADER, ByVal dwUsage As Long, ByVal
lpInitBits$,
lpInitInfo As BITMAPINFO, ByVal wUsage As Long) As Long

'  Destroy the class instance
Private Declare Function DeleteObject Lib "gdi32"
➥(ByVal hObject As Long)
As Long

'  Creates a pattern brush
Private Declare Function CreatePatternBrush Lib "gdi32"
➥(ByVal HBITMAP As
Long) As Long

'  Paints a picture with the specified pattern
Private Declare Function PatBlt Lib "gdi32" (ByVal hdc As Long,
➥ByVal x
```

```
As Long, ByVal y As Long, ByVal nWidth As Long,
➡ByVal nHeight As Long,
ByVal dwRop As Long) As Long

Const DIB_RGB_COLORS = 0        ' color table in RGBs
Const CBM_INIT = &H4&           ' initialize bitmap
Const PATCOPY = &HF00021        ' Used for Pattern Copy
Const BI_RGB = 0&               ' RGB Bitmap

' Declare m_BitInfoH as type BITMAPINFOHEADER
Dim m_BitInfoH As BITMAPINFOHEADER

' Declare m_BitInfo as type BITMAPINFO
Dim m_BitInfo As BITMAPINFO

' Holds the Screen data for building the bitmap
Dim m_Scrn As String * 32

' Holds the handle to the brush
Dim m_Hbr As Long
Dim m_OrgHbr As Long

' Declare our objects to be passed in
Private m_DispPict As Object
Private m_Array(8) As String * 8

Public Sub SetupBitmap(r1, g1, b1, r2, g2, b2)

' Standard 40 Byte Header
m_BitInfoH.biSize = 40

' This will be an 8 by 8 bitmap
m_BitInfoH.biWidth = 8
m_BitInfoH.biHeight = 8

' One Plane
m_BitInfoH.biPlanes = 1

' Specifies the number of bits per pixel
m_BitInfoH.biBitCount = 1

'  No Compression
m_BitInfoH.biCompression = BI_RGB

' These values are rarely used
m_BitInfoH.biSizeImage = 0
m_BitInfoH.biXPelsPerMeter = 0
m_BitInfoH.biYPelsPerMeter = 0

' Two colors used
m_BitInfoH.biClrUsed = 2

' This ensures that all colors are important
m_BitInfoH.biClrImportant = 0

' Sets the colors for the bits
' and background
```

continued on next page

continued from previous page

```
m_BitInfo.bmiColors = Chr$(r1) + Chr$(g1) + Chr$(b1) + "0" +
➥Chr$(r2) +
Chr$(g2) + Chr$(b2) + "0"

End Sub

Public Sub BuildBitmap()

Dim Counter as integer
dim V as integer
dim C As Integer
Dim CompBitmap As Long

'  We will loop through each element in the array
For Counter = 1 To 8

    '  v will hold the value of the bit pattern, we
    '  need to reset it for each row
    V = 0

    '  We will loop through each row and set the bit values
    For C = 0 To 7

    '  We check for a 1 in the array and if it is one we
    '  then calculate the decimal value of the binary position
    '  for example in 00000100, the 1 is = to 2^2 = 4
    If Mid$(m_Array(Counter), C + 1, 1) = "1" Then V = V + 2 ^ C
    Next C
    Mid$(m_Scrn, (Counter - 1) * 4 + 1, 1) = Chr$(V)

Next Counter

'  Set the BitmapInfoHeader field of m_BitInfo
m_BitInfo.bmiHeader = m_BitInfoH

'  Create the 8x8 bitmap specified by m_scrn
CompBitmap = CreateDIBitmap(m_DispPict.hdc, m_BitInfoH,
➥CBM_INIT, m_Scrn,
m_BitInfo, DIB_RGB_COLORS)

'  Create the bitmap pattern from the screen
m_Hbr = CreatePatternBrush(CompBitmap)

End Sub

Public Sub DeleteBrush()
Dim Throw As Long

'  Select the original brush into the picture
Throw = SelectObject(m_DispPict.hdc, m_OrgHbr)

'  Delete the created brush
Throw = DeleteObject(m_Hbr)

End Sub
```

```
Public Sub ShowPattern()

Dim m_OrgHbr, Throw As Long

'  Select the brush into the display
'  picture
m_OrgHbr = SelectObject(m_DispPict.hdc, m_Hbr)

'  Show the pattern screen
Throw = PatBlt(m_DispPict.hdc, 0, 0, m_DispPict.ScaleWidth,
m_DispPict.ScaleHeight, PATCOPY)

'  Select the original brush into the picture
Throw = SelectObject(m_DispPict.hdc, m_OrgHbr)

'  Delete the created brush
Throw = DeleteObject(m_Hbr)

End Sub

Public Sub SetPattern(s, index)
      '  Set the pattern sent in
     m_Array(index) = s
End Sub

'  Get the picture for display
Public Property Set DispPict(AControl As Object)
     Set m_DispPict = AControl
End Property

Private Sub Class_Terminate()

'  Delete the brush if it exists
If m_Hbr <> 0 Then DeleteBrush

End Sub
```

8. Insert a new class module into the project and save it as `VertFade.cls`.

```
Option Explicit

'  PatBrushes is a collection of
'  bitmap brushes
Dim m_PatBrushes As Collection

'  BitBlt will be used for the image copies
Private Declare Function BitBlt Lib "gdi32"
➥(ByVal hDestDC As Long, ByVal
x As Long, ByVal y As Long, ByVal nWidth As Long,
➥ByVal nHeight As Long,
ByVal hSrcDC As Long, ByVal xSrc As Long, ByVal ySrc As Long,
➥ByVal
```

continued on next page

continued from previous page

```
                        dwRop As Long)
                        As Long

                        '  Constants for the BitBlt copies
                        Const SRCCOPY = &HCC0020
                        Const SRCAND = &H8800C6

                        '  Globally declare the members of the class
                        Dim m_BackPict As Control
                        Dim m_DispPict As Control

                        '  BackPict and DispPict are the picture
                        '  controls for performing the fade
                        Public Property Set BackPict(AControl As Control)
                            Set m_BackPict = AControl
                        End Property

                        Public Property Set DispPict(AControl As Control)
                            Set m_DispPict = AControl
                        End Property

                        Public Sub CreateFade()

                        Dim Cnt As Long
                        Dim N As Long
                        Dim Pat As String
                        Dim Brush

                        Cnt = 0

                        '  Create 10 transition brushes
                        For Each Brush In m_PatBrushes

                        Cnt = Cnt + 1

                            '  Set up the 8x8 pattern
                            For N = 1 To 8

                                '  Depending on Cnt and N the appropriate row of
                                '  the bitmap pattern is set.
                                If Cnt = 1 Then Pat$ = "00000000"

                                If Cnt = 2 Then Pat$ = "10000000"

                                If Cnt = 3 Then Pat$ = "11000000"

                                If Cnt = 4 Then Pat$ = "11100000"

                                If Cnt = 5 Then Pat$ = "11110000"

                                If Cnt = 6 Then Pat$ = "11111000"

                                If Cnt = 7 Then Pat$ = "11111100"

                                If Cnt = 8 Then Pat$ = "11111110"
```

```
    If Cnt = 9 Then Pat$ = "11111111"

    If Cnt = 10 Then Pat$ = "11111111"

    ' Set the row bits
    Brush.SetPattern Pat$, N

    Pat$ = ""

  Next N

' Call the setup bitmap function and
' pass in the colors
Brush.SetupBitmap 255, 255, 255, 0, 0, 0

' Build the pattern bitmap
Brush.BuildBitmap

Next Brush

End Sub

Public Sub Fade()

Dim Cnt As Integer
Dim Throw As Integer
Dim Brush As Object

' Create the Vertical Patterns
CreateFade

' Loop through the patterns and
' display the pattern brush
For Cnt = 1 To 10

    ' Clear the back picture
    m_BackPict.Cls

    ' Display the pattern
    m_PatBrushes.Item(Cnt).ShowPattern

    ' Copy the Pattern to the screen
    Throw = BitBlt(m_DispPict.hdc, 0, 0, m_DispPict.ScaleWidth,
      m_DispPict.ScaleHeight, m_BackPict.hdc, 0, 0, SRCAND)

Next Cnt

End Sub

Public Sub Setup()

Dim N As Integer
Dim PB As PatBrush
```

continued on next page

continued from previous page

```
    '  Create the collection of vertical
    '  pattern brushes
    Set m_PatBrushes = New Collection

    '  Set the picture widths
    m_DispPict.Width = m_BackPict.Width
    m_DispPict.Height = m_BackPict.Height

    '  Set the picture autoredraw and visible
    '  property
    m_BackPict.AutoRedraw = True
    m_BackPict.Visible = False

    '  Set up the collection
    For N = 1 To 10

        '  Create the pattern brush
        Set PB = New PatBrush

        '  Set the display picture for
        '  the pattern. In this case it
        '  will be the working back picture
        Set PB.DispPict = m_BackPict

        ' Add the class to the collection
        m_PatBrushes.Add Item:=PB, Key:=CStr(N)

    Next N

End Sub

Private Sub Class_Terminate()

Dim Brush

    '  Delete the brushes
    For Each Brush In m_PatBrushes
        Brush.DeleteBrush
    Next Brush

    '  Delete the collection
    Set m_PatBrushes = Nothing

End Sub
```

9. Create a second project and save it as **5-4-DLL.VBP**. This project will be used to encapsulate the **DiskFile** class in an ActiveX DLL file. Insert a new BAS module into the project and save it as **module1.bas**. Add an empty **Sub Main** to the module.

```
Public Sub Main()

End Sub
```

10. Insert a new class into the project and save it as `DiskFile.cls`.

```
Option Explicit

'  Member property of the class that
'  stores the filename
Private m_FileName As String

'  Member property of the class that
'  stores the file description
Private m_FileDesc As String

'  The get and set properties of the class
'  for the file description
Public Property Let FileDesc(s As String)
    m_FileDesc = s
End Property

Public Property Get FileDesc() As String
    FileDesc = m_FileDesc
End Property

'  Get the file name by itself.
'  I.E. c:\windows\clouds.bmp is clouds.bmp
Public Property Get File() As String
    File = ParseFile()
End Property

'  Set and get the filename property for
'  the class
Public Property Let FileName(s As String)
    m_FileName = s
End Property

Public Property Get FileName() As String
    FileName = m_FileName
End Property

'  Get the file size
Public Property Get FileSize() As Long
    FileSize = FileLen(m_FileName)
End Property

'  Get the file extension
Public Property Get FileExt() As String
    FileExt = ParseExt()
End Property

'  Get the directory of the file
Public Property Get Directory() As String
    Directory = ParseDir()
End Property

'  Get the date of the file
Public Property Get FileDate() As Date
```

continued on next page

continued from previous page

```
            FileDate = FileDateTime(m_FileName)
    End Property


    '  Parse out the file name. Note that this is
    '  a private method. It is only utilized in the
    '  File property
    Private Function ParseFile() As String

    Dim N As Integer

    ParseFile = ""

    '  Start from the end of the file name
    '  and look for the '\' character. Thus the
    '  file part of the file name will be known
    For N = Len(m_FileName) To 1 Step -1

        If Mid(m_FileName, N, 1) = "\" Then
            ParseFile = Right(m_FileName, Len(m_FileName) - N)
            N = -1
        End If

    Next N

    End Function


    '  Parse out the file directory. Note that
    '  this is a private class method and is only
    '  utilized by the Directory property
    Private Function ParseDir() As String

    Dim N As Integer

    ParseDir = ""

    '  Start from the end of the file name
    '  and look for the first '\' character. Thus
    '  the location of the file name will be known
    '  and the rest is the directory location
    For N = Len(m_FileName) To 1 Step -1

        If Mid(m_FileName, N, 1) = "\" Then
            ParseDir = Left(m_FileName, N)
            N = -1
        End If

    Next N

    End Function


    '  GetExt retrieves the file extension if
    '  there is one. This is only used by the
```

```
'  FileExt property
Private Function ParseExt() As String

Dim N As Integer

ParseExt = "(N/A)"

'  Start from the end of the file name
'  and look for the '.' character. Thus
'  the location of the extension will be known
'  in the file name string
For N = Len(m_FileName) To 1 Step -1

    If Mid(m_FileName, N, 1) = "." Then
        ParseExt = Right(m_FileName, Len(m_FileName) - N)
        N = -1
    End If

Next N

End Function

'  Public method of the class to
'  copy the file to a new location
Public Sub CopyFile(NewLocation)
    FileCopy m_FileName, NewLocation + ParseFile
End Sub

'  Public method of the class to
'  delete the file
Public Sub DeleteFile()
    Kill m_FileName
End Sub

'  When the class is initialized
'  the filename, description and
'  extension will be set to
'  N/A.
Private Sub Class_Initialize()

m_FileName = "Uninitialized"
m_FileDesc = "N/A"

End Sub
```

11. Create a new project and save it as **5-4-SRV.VBP**. This will be an ActiveX executable that will provide the database connectivity to the third tier of data. Insert a new BAS module into the project and save it as **Module1.bas**.

```
Public Sub Main()

End Sub
```

12. Add the following code to the General Declarations section of the project. Note that a global RDO environment, connection, and resultset are declared.

```
Option Explicit

'   Declare a global result set which
'   can be used to retrieve all of
'   the image IDs in the database
Dim m_IDResultSet As rdoResultset

'   Dim a remote data environment
Dim Env As rdoEnvironment

'   Dim a remote data connection
Dim Con As rdoConnection

'   Declare a remote data record set
Dim RS As rdoResultset
```

13. The `InitConnect` method of the class handles opening the connection to the database. The global RDO environment variable, `Env`, is set to the first member of the `rdoEnvironments` collection. Then the RDO connection, `con`, is set to the ODBC `ImageDatabase` connection. You now have your connection to the database established. This method should be first used when the class is called.

```
Public Sub InitConnect()

'   Set the remote data environment
Set Env = rdoEnvironments(0)

'   Open the ODBC connection
Set Con = Env.OpenConnection(dsName:="Image Database",
Prompt:=rdDriverNoPrompt)

End Sub
```

14. The private `DBExec` method handles executing the specified SQL command on the database.

```
Private Sub DBExec(cmd$)

'   Execute the specified SQL Command
Con.Execute cmd$

End Sub
```

15. The `DBOpenRec` private method handles opening a resultset based on the specified SQL command.

```
Private Sub DBOpenRec(cmd$)

'   Open a resultset based on the
'   SQL query. rdOpenKeySet indicates
'   that the rows can be updated.
Set RS = Con.OpenResultset(cmd$, rdOpenKeyset, rdConcurRowver)

End Sub
```

16. The `GetComments` method retrieves the comments for a specified image in the database. It uses the `DBOpenRec` method to retrieve the resultset. It then returns the value of the `Comments` field of the database.

```
Public Function GetComments(ImageID As Integer) As String

'   Get the comments field for the specified
'   image
DBOpenRec "Select * from ImageData Where ImageID = " +
➥Trim(Str$(ImageID))

'   Return the value
GetComments = RS("Comments")

End Function
```

17. The `GetFileName` method retrieves the filename for a specified image in the database. It uses the `DBOpenRec` method to retrieve the resultset. It then returns the value of the `FileName` field of the database.

```
Public Function GetFileName(ImageID As Integer) As String

'   Get the file name for the specified
'   image
DBOpenRec "Select * from ImageData Where ImageID = " +
➥Trim(Str$(ImageID))

'   Return the file name
GetFileName = RS("FileName")

End Function
```

18. The `GetFileFormat` method retrieves the comments for a specified image in the database. It uses the `DBOpenRec` method to retrieve the resultset. It then returns the value of the `FileFormat` field of the database.

```
Public Function GetFileFormat(ImageID As Integer) As String

'   Get the file format for the specified
'   image
DBOpenRec "Select * from ImageData Where ImageID = " +
➥Trim(Str$(ImageID))

'   Return the file format
GetFileFormat = RS("FileFormat")

End Function
```

19. The `GetIDSet` method retrieves a resultset of all the images in the database. This is set to the private resultset, **m_IDResultSet** property.

```
Public Sub GetIDSet()

'  Select all of the images
'  in the database
DBOpenRec "Select * from ImageData"

'  Set the global IDResultSet class
'  member to have the list of images
Set m_IDResultSet = RS

End Sub
```

20. The `GetNextID` method retrieves the next ID in the resultset. This method allows a calling application to be able to move through the database and retrieve all the entries. When the last record is reached, **False** is returned from the function.

```
Public Function GetNextID() As Integer

'  Check to see if the end of the
'  result set has been reached
If m_IDResultSet.EOF <> True Then
    '  Get the next Image ID and
    '   return the value
    GetNextID = m_IDResultSet("ImageID")

    '  Move to the next record
    m_IDResultSet.MoveNext
Else
    '  Close the result set if the
    '   end of the result set was reached.
    m_IDResultSet.Close

    '  Return False as the value
    GetNextID = False
End If

End Function
```

21. The `UpdateComments` method handles updating the comments of the image. The new comments and the image ID are passed in as parameters.

```
Public Sub UpdateComments(NewComments As String, ID As Integer)

'  Update the comments for the
'   specified Image
DBExec "Update ImageData set Comments = '" + NewComments +
"' where ImageID = " + LTrim(Str$(ID))

End Sub
```

How It Works

This How-To demonstrates how to break an application up into a three-tier architecture using the various tools provided in Visual Basic. The first tier is the client application that provides the basic functionality of the program. This tier uses the `Bitmap`, `VertFade`, and `PatBrush` classes within the project. Two ActiveX components have been created that are easy to reuse and incorporate into the client application. The `DiskFile` ActiveX DLL and the `ImageData` ActiveX executable comprise the second tier. Finally, the third tier is the data tier, which consists of the database. With ODBC, the database in this example can reside in an Access MDB or on the SQL Server.

To create the ActiveX DLL and ActiveX executable, be sure to add the classes to separate projects from your client application. For the ActiveX DLL file, simply compile the project as an ActiveX DLL instead of an EXE. Set the project options to include an appropriate project and application name. This name will show up in the references dialog box in the client application.

For the ActiveX executable, open the Project menu and choose Disk Properties. Then select the Project tab. For the start mode, select the ActiveX executable option. Be sure to give the project a name and fill out the description. You will need to compile the program as an EXE file and then run the EXE to register the ActiveX executable. After it is registered, the client project will show the ActiveX executable in the references dialog box.

Note that in the client application, the References menu is under the Tool menu. Be sure the `Disk` and `IData` objects are selected. After you do this, press the F2 key to bring up the object browser. Select either the `Disk` or `IData` objects, and you can review the various properties and methods of each object. This will correspond directly to the public methods and properties in your ActiveX DLL and ActiveX executable projects.

Comments

The rest of the chapters in this book expand on using ActiveX components to build business objects, collections, and so on. After the How-To's in this chapter, you should have a strong feel for the object-oriented capabilities of Visual Basic and for the opportunities to rethink how your applications can be designed and built.

NOTE

If you are going to use the created DLL on another machine, you will have to register it using the regsv32 program. As for the EXE, if it is going to be used on another machine, then executing it on the new machine will register it appropriately.

5.6 How do I...
Implement interfaces?

COMPATIBILITY: VISUAL BASIC 5 AND 6

Problem

I have several objects that implement the same basic functions and properties in similar ways, but each object has its own logic and business rules for implementation. Is there any way I can combine these objects into one interface for easy execution without worrying about the underlying implementation?

Technique

Visual Basic provides an interface for implementing polymorphism. Polymorphism lets you manipulate many kinds of objects without worrying about what kind each one is. Multiple interfaces are a feature of the Component Object Model (COM); they allow you to evolve your programs over time, adding new functionality without breaking old code. *Polymorphism* means that many classes can provide the same property or method, and a caller doesn't have to know what class an object belongs to before calling the property or method.

This sample application will implement an auto value calculation program. The program will calculate the value of different models of cars based on basic information. Each model of automobile will have its own business rules for calculating value. By using interfaces, you can design classes for each model that know how to calculate their value. Each will have similar properties and methods but will function differently. An implementation class of `Automobile` will be used as the interface to the model classes.

Steps

Open and run `5-6.VBP`. Figure 5.9 shows the form at runtime. The program has inputs for the Model Year, Model, Mileage, Condition, and Upgrade Package. Based on those inputs, you can select the car model and then calculate the value.

Figure 5.10 shows a sample calculation for the GoGo model.

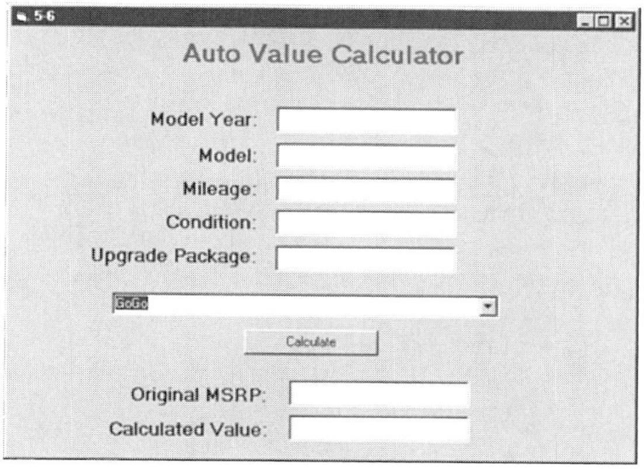

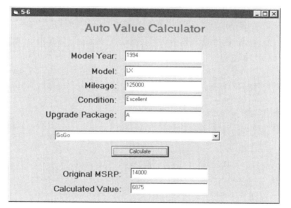

Figure 5.9 The form at runtime

Figure 5.10 A GoGo car model calculation

Figure 5.11 shows the calculation form filled out with new data. Note that the model for the SuperStar model is LX; this is not a valid model type. Note that the error shows up in the Calculated Value field. The `SuperStar` calculation class knows how to check to see whether valid data has been entered.

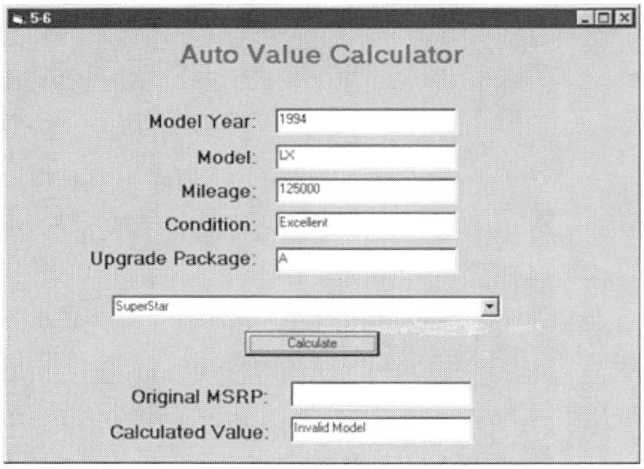

Figure 5.11 The SuperStar model with incorrect information entered

Finally, Figure 5.12 shows a special calculation for refurbished SuperStar models. Note that the calculated value is higher than the original Manufacturer Suggested Retail Price (MSRP). A similar setting is not possible for the GoGo model.

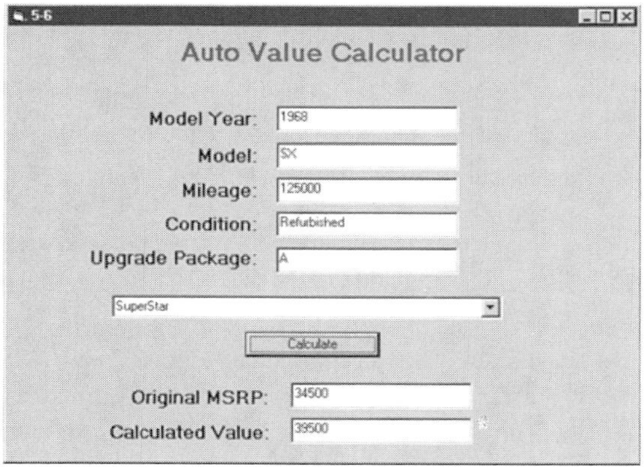

Figure 5.12 The SuperStar restored model calculation

To create this project, complete the following steps:

1. Create a new project called 5-6.VBP. Add the objects and properties listed in Table 5.8 to the form, and save the form as 5-6.FRM.

Table 5.8 5-5.VBP's objects and properties

OBJECT	PROPERTY	SETTING
Form	Name	Form1
	Caption	"5-6"
TextBox	Name	txtOriginalMSRP
CommandButton	Name	cmdCalculate
	Caption	"Calculate"
TextBox	Name	txtCalculatedValue
TextBox	Name	txtUpgradePackage
TextBox	Name	txtCondition
TextBox	Name	txtMileage
TextBox	Name	txtModel
TextBox	Name	txtModelYear
ComboBox	Name	cboAutoList
	Text	"Select Auto"
Label	Name	lblOriginalMSRP
	AutoSize	-1 'True
	Caption	"Original MSRP:"
	Font	
	Name	"MS Sans Serif"
	Size	12
Label	Name	lblTitle
	Alignment	2 'Center
	Caption	"Auto Value Calculator"
	Font	
	Name	"MS Sans Serif"
	Size	18
	ForeColor	&H00FF0000&

continued on next page

Table 5.8 continued

OBJECT	PROPERTY	SETTING
Label	Name	lblCalculatedValue
	AutoSize	-1 'True
	Caption	"Calculated Value:"
	Font	
	Name	"MS Sans Serif"
	Size	12
Label	Name	lblUpgradePackage
	AutoSize	-1 'True
	Caption	"Upgrade Package:"
	Font	
	Name	"MS Sans Serif"
	Size	12
Label	Name	lblCondition
	AutoSize	-1 'True
	Caption	"Condition:"
	Font	
	Name	"MS Sans Serif"
	Size	12
Label	Name	lblMileage
	AutoSize	-1 'True
	Caption	"Mileage:"
	Font	
	Name	"MS Sans Serif"
	Size	12
Label	Name	lblModel
	AutoSize	-1 'True
	Caption	"Model:"
	Font	
	Name	"MS Sans Serif"
	Size	12
Label	Name	lblModelYear
	AutoSize	-1 'True
	Caption	"Model Year:"
	Font	
	Name	"MS Sans Serif"
	Size	12

2. Add the following code to the General Declarations section of the form. A collection is created to store the different objects for the car models, and your car models and implementation class are globally declared.

```
'  Require all variables to be declared
Option Explicit

'  Create collection for storing the auto types
Dim AutoTypes As Collection

'  Declare our two model type classes
Dim GG As GoGo
Dim SS As SuperStar

'  Declare our implementing class
Dim Auto As Automobile
```

3. The Calculate button controls the calculation of the automobile's value. First, the selected model type is retrieved from the combo box. That object is set to the implementation class, **Auto**. Then, regardless of the underlying implementation, the properties are set and the value is calculated. Note that the properties and methods being used are that of the underlying class, not the auto-implementation template. After the value is calculated, a check is done to see whether any errors are returned. If so, the error is shown; if not, the original MSRP and the calculated value are displayed.

```
'  Fired off when the calculate button
'  is clicked
Private Sub cmdCalculate_Click()

'  An index into the list box
Dim AutoTypeIndex As Integer

'  Holds the calculated value of the auto
Dim dblCalculatedValue As Double

'  Get the selected auto
AutoTypeIndex = cboAutoList.ListIndex

'  Set our implements class to the proper
'  model type
Set Auto = AutoTypes(AutoTypeIndex + 1)

'  Set the condition
Auto.condition = txtCondition.Text

'  Set the mileage
Auto.mileage = Val(txtMileage.Text)

'  Set the model
Auto.model = txtModel.Text
```

continued on next page

continued from previous page

```
'  Set the model year
Auto.modelyear = Val(txtModelYear.Text)

'  Set the Upgrade Package
Auto.upgradepackage = txtUpgradePackage.Text

'  Get the calculated value
dblCalculatedValue = Auto.CalculateValue

'  Check to see if an error was returned
If dblCalculatedValue = -1 Then

    '  Set the MSRP text to blank
    txtOriginalMSRP.Text = ""

    '  Show the error
    txtCalculatedValue = Auto.Error

Else

    '  Display the MSRP
    txtOriginalMSRP.Text = Auto.MSRP

    '  Show the calculated value
    txtCalculatedValue.Text = Auto.CalculateValue

End If

'  Reset the class
Auto.reset

End Sub
```

4. When the form is loaded, your two classes, **GoGo** and **SuperStar**, are created for the two models. These two objects are stored in a collection. Finally, the models are added to the combo box, and the first one is selected.

```
Private Sub Form_Load()

'  Create the GG and SS instances of the model classes
Set GG = New GoGo
Set SS = New SuperStar

'  Create a collection to hold the model classes
Set AutoTypes = New Collection

'  Add the model classes to the collection and tag them
'  accordingly
AutoTypes.Add GG, "GG"
cboAutoList.AddItem "GoGo"
```

```
AutoTypes.Add SS, "SS"
cboAutoList.AddItem "SuperStar"

'  Select the first item in the list
cboAutoList.ListIndex = 0

End Sub
```

5. Next, you want to create your interface class for Automobile. This will define the events, methods, and properties that any class must have that is of type Automobile. Note the template properties, which are **read** and **write**. You also define read-only properties. Finally, two procedures, CalculateValue and Reset, are required.

```
Option Explicit

'  Template properties for the Automobile class
Public model As String
Public modelyear As Integer
Public condition As String
Public upgradepackage As String
Public mileage As Long

'  Template for the read only error property
Public Property Get Error() As String

End Property

'  Read only property on the MSRP
Public Property Get MSRP() As Long

End Property

'  Poylmorphic method to calculate the model's value
Public Function CalculateValue() As Double

End Function

'  Polymorphic method to reset the settings of the object
Public Sub reset()

End Sub
```

6. Next create a new class called GoGo.cls and add the following code to the General Declarations section. The GoGo class will define the properties, events, and methods of the GoGo car. Note that it implements the Automobile interface.

```
'  Require variable declaration
Option Explicit

'  Implements the automobile interface
Implements Automobile

'  Private properties of the class
Private m_Condition As String
Private m_Mileage As Long
Private m_Model As String
Private m_ModelYear As Integer
Private m_UpgradePackage As String
Private m_error As String
Private m_MSRP As Long
```

7. Next create the required **CalculateValue** function. Note that it has the **Automobile_** indicator in front to tell Visual Basic that this is the function required by the automobile class template. Note that the way this **GoGo** class calculates values is different from the way the **SuperStar** class calculates values.

```
'  The Calculate method of the class.
'  Required since it is implementing the
'  Automobile interface.
Private Function Automobile_CalculateValue() As Double

'  Car value - long integer
Dim lngValue As Long

'  Make sure there are no errors reported in the settings
If m_error <> "" Then
    Automobile_CalculateValue = -1
    Exit Function
End If

'  Check to see if any of the inputs are blank.
If m_Condition = "" Or m_Mileage = 0 Or _
    m_Model = "" Or _
    m_ModelYear = 0 Or _
    m_UpgradePackage = "" Then

    '  Set the error message for the class
    m_error = "Not all properties have been properly set."

    '  Return a negative result
    Automobile_CalculateValue = -1

    '  Exit the function
    Exit Function

End If

'  Take off a $1000 for each year the car has been owned
lngValue = m_MSRP - ((Year(Now) - m_ModelYear) * 1000)
```

```
'  Take off $250 for each 10,000 miles
lngValue = lngValue - (m_Mileage / 10000 * 250)

'  Check for the condition of the car
Select Case m_Condition

    '  Poor - take off $1,000
    Case "POOR"
        lngValue = lngValue - 1000

    '  Fair - Take off $500
    Case "FAIR"
        lngValue = lngValue - 500

End Select

'  Return the car value
Automobile_CalculateValue = Int(lngValue)

End Function
```

8. Next set the condition of the automobile, which is again another required property of the class. That is why the **Automobile_** indicator is in front of the property name.

```
'  Property to set the condition of the automobile
Private Property Let Automobile_condition(ByVal condition
➡As String)

'  Get the value - Set it as upper case
m_Condition = UCase(condition)

'  Check all cases.  If none are found then set the
'  error field
Select Case m_Condition

    Case "POOR"

    Case "FAIR"

    Case "EXCELLENT"

    Case Else
        m_error = "Invalid Condition Property"

End Select

End Property

'  Return the condition
Private Property Get Automobile_condition() As String

Automobile_condition = m_Condition

End Property
```

9. Continue setting the properties of the class. Note the model will calculate the original MSRP value. That data could be database driven.

```
'  Return the error message.  Note that this is a
'  read only property.
Private Property Get Automobile_Error() As String

Automobile_Error = m_error

End Property


'  Set the mileage for the automobile
Private Property Let Automobile_Mileage(ByVal mileage As Long)

m_Mileage = mileage

'  Make sure the mileage is not less than 0
If m_Mileage < 0 Then

    m_error = "Invalid Mileage"

End If

End Property

'  Get the mileage
Private Property Get Automobile_Mileage() As Long

Automobile_Mileage = m_Mileage

End Property

'  Set the model
Private Property Let Automobile_Model(ByVal model As String)

'  Note we convert to upper case for easy
'  comparison
m_Model = UCase(model)

'  Check the model and set the MSRP value
Select Case m_Model

    Case "L"
        m_MSRP = m_MSRP + 12000

    Case "LX"
        m_MSRP = m_MSRP + 13500

    Case "LXS"
        m_MSRP = m_MSRP + 15000

    '  Set the error string
    Case Else
        m_error = "Invalid Model"
```

```
End Select

End Property

'   Return the model value
Private Property Get Automobile_Model() As String

Automobile_Model = m_Model

End Property

'   Set the year of the car
Private Property Let Automobile_ModelYear
➡(ByVal modelyear As Integer)

m_ModelYear = modelyear

'   The GoGo model started in 1994.  And the model year cannot
'   be greater than the current year + 1
If m_ModelYear < 1994 Or m_ModelYear > (Year(Now) + 1) Then

    m_error = "Invalid Model Year"

End If

End Property

'   Return the automobile year
Private Property Get Automobile_ModelYear() As Integer

Automobile_ModelYear = m_ModelYear

End Property

'   Return the calculated MSRP
Private Property Get Automobile_MSRP() As Long

Automobile_MSRP = m_MSRP

End Property

'   Reset the properties of the class
Private Sub Automobile_reset()

m_Condition = ""
m_Mileage = 0
m_Model = ""
m_ModelYear = 0
m_UpgradePackage = ""
m_error = ""
m_MSRP = 0

End Sub
```

10. The `UpgradePackage` required property will add to the original MSRP based on the cost of the upgrades.

```
'  Set the upgrade packages for the automobile
Private Property Let Automobile_UpGradePackage
➡(ByVal upgradepackage As String)

'  Note we convert to upper case for easy
'  comparison
m_UpgradePackage = UCase(upgradepackage)

'  Depending on the upgrade package, we add an appropriate value
'  to the MSRP
Select Case m_UpgradePackage

    Case "A"
        m_MSRP = m_MSRP + 500

    Case "B"
        m_MSRP = m_MSRP + 750

    Case "C"
        m_MSRP = m_MSRP + 1000

    '  An invalid upgrade package was entered
    Case Else
        m_error = "Invalid Upgrade Package"

End Select

End Property

'  Return the upgrade package setting
Private Property Get Automobile_UpGradePackage() As String

Automobile_UpGradePackage = m_UpgradePackage

End Property

'  Executed when the class is initialized
Private Sub Class_Initialize()

'  Set mileage to 0
m_Mileage = 0

'  Set model year to 0
m_ModelYear = 0

'  Set MSRP to 0
m_MSRP = 0

End Sub
```

11. Next create a new class called **SuperStar.cls** and add the following code to the General Declarations section. The **SuperStar** class will define the properties, events, and methods of the SuperStar car. Note that it implements the **Automobile** interface.

```
'   Require variable declaration
Option Explicit

'   Implements the automobile interface
Implements Automobile

'   Private properties of the class
Private m_Condition As String
Private m_Mileage As Long
Private m_Model As String
Private m_ModelYear As Integer
Private m_UpgradePackage As String
Private m_error As String
Private m_MSRP As Long
```

12. To comply with the automobile interface, add the **CalculateValue** function to your class. Note that this **CalculateValue** function will value the **SuperStar** class differently than the **GoGo** car class. But the calling program does not need to differentiate between the two.

```
'   The Calculate method of the class. Required since it is
'   implementing the Automobile interface.
Private Function Automobile_CalculateValue() As Double

'   Car value - long integer
Dim lngValue As Long

'   Make sure there are no errors reported in the settings
If m_error <> "" Then
    Automobile_CalculateValue = -1
    Exit Function
End If

    '   Set the error message for the class
If m_Condition = "" Or _
    m_Mileage = 0 Or _
    m_Model = "" Or _
    m_ModelYear = 0 Or _
    m_UpgradePackage = "" Then

    '   Set the error message for the class
    m_error = "Not all properties have been properly set."

        '   Return a negative result
        Automobile_CalculateValue = -1
```

continued on next page

continued from previous page

```
                                ' Exit the function
                              Exit Function

                      End If

                      ' Take off $700 for each model year
                      lngValue = m_MSRP - ((Year(Now) - m_ModelYear) * 700)

                      ' Take off $200 for each 10,000 miles
                      lngValue = lngValue - (m_Mileage / 10000 * 200)

                      ' Check for the condition of the car
                      Select Case m_Condition

                              ' Take off $500
                              Case "POOR"
                                  lngValue = lngValue - 500

                              ' Take off $250
                              Case "FAIR"
                                  lngValue = lngValue - 250

                              ' Special case for the upper end car.  Older models can be
                              ' refurbished and gain value
                              Case "REFURBISHED"

                                  ' Check to see if the car is over 10
                                  ' years old
                                  If Year(Now) - m_ModelYear > 10 Then
                                      ' Add $5000 onto the MSRP
                                      lngValue = m_MSRP + 5000
                                  End If

                      End Select

                      ' Return the calculated value
                      Automobile_CalculateValue = Int(lngValue)

                      End Function
```

13. Next define several properties for the class including the car's condition, mileage, model, and year. Note that several properties will check the initial property value and then based on that will make adjustments to other variables. In the case of the model year and upgrade package the original MSRP is calculated.

```
' Set the condition of the automobile
Private Property Let Automobile_condition
➥(ByVal condition As String)

' Get the value - Set it as upper case
m_Condition = UCase(condition)

' Check all cases.  If none are found then set the
```

```
'  error field
Select Case m_Condition

    Case "POOR"

    Case "FAIR"

    Case "EXCELLENT"

    Case "REFURBISHED"

    Case Else
        m_error = "Invalid Condition Property"

End Select

End Property

'  Return the automobile condition
Private Property Get Automobile_condition() As String

Automobile_condition = m_Condition

End Property

'  Return the error message.  Note that this is a
'  read only property.
Private Property Get Automobile_Error() As String

Automobile_Error = m_error

End Property

'  Set the mileage
Private Property Let Automobile_Mileage(ByVal mileage As Long)

m_Mileage = mileage

'  Check to see if the mileage is less than 0.  If
'  so then set the error message.
If m_Mileage < 0 Then

    m_error = "Invalid Mileage"

End If

End Property

'  Return the mileage for the automobile
Private Property Get Automobile_Mileage() As Long

Automobile_Mileage = m_Mileage

End Property
```

continued on next page

continued from previous page

```vb
Private Property Let Automobile_Model(ByVal model As String)

'   Note we convert to upper case for easy
'   comparison
m_Model = UCase(model)

'   Check the model and set the MSRP value
Select Case m_Model

    Case "S"
        m_MSRP = m_MSRP + 30000

    Case "SX"
        m_MSRP = m_MSRP + 33000

    Case "SXS"
        m_MSRP = m_MSRP + 38000

    '   Set the error string
    Case Else
        m_error = "Invalid Model"

End Select

End Property


'   Return the model of the automobile
Private Property Get Automobile_Model() As String

Automobile_Model = m_Model

End Property

'   Set the year of the car
Private Property Let Automobile_ModelYear
➡(ByVal modelyear As Integer)

m_ModelYear = modelyear

'   The SuperStar model started in 1960. And the model year can't
'   be greater than the current year + 1
If m_ModelYear < 1960 Or m_ModelYear > (Year(Now) + 1) Then

    m_error = "Invalid Model Year"

End If

End Property

'   Return the automobile year
Private Property Get Automobile_ModelYear() As Integer

Automobile_ModelYear = m_ModelYear

End Property
```

```
'  Return the calculated MSRP
Private Property Get Automobile_MSRP() As Long

Automobile_MSRP = m_MSRP

End Property

'  Reset the properties of the class
Private Sub Automobile_reset()

m_Condition = ""
m_Mileage = 0
m_Model = ""
m_ModelYear = 0
m_UpgradePackage = ""
m_error = ""
m_MSRP = 0

End Sub

'  Set the upgrade package
Private Property Let Automobile_UpGradePackage
➥(ByVal upgradepackage As String)

'  Note we convert to upper case for easy
'  comparison
m_UpgradePackage = UCase(upgradepackage)

'  Depending on the upgrade package, we add an appropriate value
'  to the MSRP
Select Case m_UpgradePackage
    Case "A"
        m_MSRP = m_MSRP + 1500
    Case "B"
        m_MSRP = m_MSRP + 3000
    Case Else
        m_error = "Invalid Upgrade Package"
End Select

End Property

'  Return the upgrade package setting
Private Property Get Automobile_UpGradePackage() As String

Automobile_UpGradePackage = m_UpgradePackage

End Property

'  Executed when the class is initialized
Private Sub Class_Initialize()

'  set mileage to 0
m_Mileage = 0
```

continued on next page

continued from previous page

```
'   set model year to 0
m_ModelYear = 0

'   Set MSRP to 0
m_MSRP = 0

End Sub
```

How It Works

You have two subclasses that define different types of automobiles. Each subclass uses the `implements` keyword in the class to indicate that it will fully comply with the interface defined in the `automobile.cls`. The `GoGo` and `SuperStar` classes define properties and methods as defined in the `Automobile` template class.

The `UpgradePackage` property, `Model` property, `Condition` property, and `CalculateValue` method are different between the two different classes (`GoGo` and `SuperStar`). The GoGo model has only been around since 1992, has three different models, different MSRPs, and calculates the final value differently.

Building these types of tools in a client/server system can simplify the interface to your objects and provide flexibility in changing the underlying business rules. In this case, the numbers in the model classes could be encapsulated in a database, which in turn could be encapsulated in an interface class. That way, if the database structure changes or the method of calculation changes, the entire program will not need to be rewritten.

Comments

Consider adding models and extending the tools within the classes. You can compile these classes into a COM object that would have a property that sets the model type and returns the value. Down the road, if the calculation method changes for any model, you can change the underlying class without breaking any programs relying on the `Automobile` class. As long as the model class does not change its implementation, the system will perform properly.

COMPLEXITY
INTERMEDIATE

5.7 How do I...
Build an ActiveX control?

COMPATIBILITY: VISUAL BASIC 5 AND 6

Problem

I want to encapsulate a set of code in an ActiveX control that I can use in Visual Basic applications and Internet Explorer. I know that Visual Basic allows me to do this, but I am not sure what steps to take.

Technique

In truth, creating Visual Basic controls is almost as simple as creating Visual Basic applications. Instead of forms, there is a **UserControl** interface. You can include other controls on this interface, but keep in mind that those controls will need to be distributed with your ActiveX control. The Visual Basic runtime will also need to be distributed with the control.

Instead of starting a standard EXE project, you will start an ActiveX control. The form interface is similar to the standard form interface. Keep in mind that the size of the form representing the **UserControl** interface will determine the size of the control at runtime.

In this example, you will take the image-fade utilities you built in previous sections of this chapter and encapsulate them into an ActiveX control. The control will have a public method, **ShowNext**, and a public property, **ImageCount**. These will allow the control to be manipulated from the hosting containers.

Steps

Open and compile the **5-7-VBP** project into an ActiveX OCX control. After it is compiled, open and run **5-7-Container.VBP**. Figure 5.13 shows the form at runtime. The figure shows the form with your control on it.

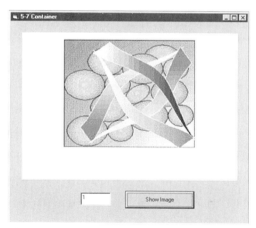

Figure 5.13 The form at runtime

Select a new image number between 1 and 5. Click Show Image to display the next image in your control. Figure 5.14 shows a figure as it has faded out.

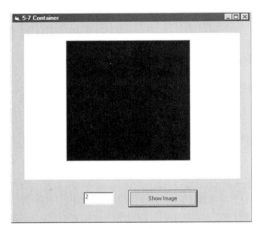

Figure 5.14 An image in transition

Next, run the `ImageFade.html` page to see the browser on the Web page. Figure 5.15 shows the same control in a Web page. You can also change the image number and see the images fading between each other.

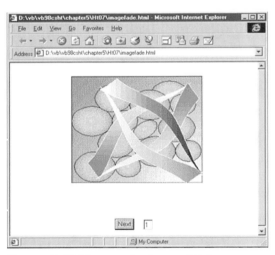

Figure 5.15 The control on a Web page

Complete the following steps to create this project:

1. Create a new ActiveX EXE project called **5-7.VBP**. Add the objects and properties listed in Table 5.9 to the user control, and save the control as **5-7.ctl**.

Table 5.9 5-7. VBP's objects and properties

OBJECT	PROPERTY	SETTING
UserControl	Name	ImageFade
	BackColor	&H00FFFFFF&
PictureBox	Name	BackPict
	AutoRedraw	-1 'True
	Visible	0 'False
PictureBox	Name	DispPict

2. Add the following code to the General Declarations section of the class. A Bitmaps collection is created to hold the bitmap values. The public ImageCount property will indicate the image to be displayed.

```
Option Explicit

'   Bitmaps will be our collection of
'   bitmaps for viewing
Dim Bitmaps As Collection

'   Indicates the image to be displayed.
Public ImageCount As Integer
```

3. The ShowNext method will call the Bitmap class and fade the image that is presently displayed. The Load function of the Bitmap class then will show the next image.

```
Public Sub ShowNext()

'   Ensure we don't try and display an image that does
'   not exist.
If ImageCount <= 5 Then

    '   Call the fade method of the class to
    '   perform a vertical blind fade on the
    '   image
    Bitmaps.Item(ImageCount).Fade

    '   When an image in the list is
    '   clicked on, load the image
    Bitmaps.Item(ImageCount).Load

End If

End Sub
```

4. The initialize event of the control is called when the control is instantiated. In this case, you create a **Bitmaps** collection to hold the instantiated bitmap objects. The initial image is set to 1 and then displayed.

```
Private Sub UserControl_Initialize()

Dim N As Integer
Dim BMP As Bitmap

'  Create the new collection of bitmaps
Set Bitmaps = New Collection

'  Create the bitmap object and add
'  them to the collection
For N = 1 To 5

    '  Create an instance of the bitmap
    Set BMP = New Bitmap

    '  Set the display picture
    '  properties
    Set BMP.BackPict = BackPict
    Set BMP.DispPict = DispPict

    '  Depending on the count, add the
    '  appropriate image and set the
    '  description
    Select Case N

        Case 1
            BMP.FileInfo.FileName = App.Path + "\pattern.bmp"
            BMP.FileInfo.FileDesc = "256 Color Pattern Bitmap"

        Case 2
            BMP.FileInfo.FileName = App.Path + "\forest.bmp"
            BMP.FileInfo.FileDesc =
            ➡"Standard Windows 95 Forest Bitmap"

        Case 3
            BMP.FileInfo.FileName = App.Path + "\clouds.bmp"
            BMP.FileInfo.FileDesc = "Microsoft Clouds Bitmap"

        Case 4
            BMP.FileInfo.FileName = App.Path + "\oranges.bmp"
            BMP.FileInfo.FileDesc = "256 Color Bitmap of Oranges"

        Case 5
            BMP.FileInfo.FileName = App.Path + "\flower.bmp"
            BMP.FileInfo.FileDesc =
            ➡"256 Color Bitmap of a Blossoming Flower"

    End Select

    '  Add the Bitmap class to the
    '  collection of bitmaps and set
```

```
                    '  the key as the count
                    Bitmaps.Add Item:=BMP, Key:=CStr(N)

                    '  Destroy the instance of the bitmap class
                    Set BMP = Nothing

                Next N

                ImageCount = 1

                '  Call the fade method of the class to
                '  perform a vertical blind fade on the
                '  image
                Bitmaps.Item(ImageCount).Fade

                '  When an image in the list is
                '  clicked on, load the image
                Bitmaps.Item(ImageCount).Load

                ImageCount = ImageCount + 1

                End Sub
```

5. When the control is terminated, the bitmap objects are destroyed.

```
Private Sub UserControl_Terminate()

Dim N As Integer

'  Destroy all of the bitmap instances
'  when the form is unloaded
For N = 1 To Bitmaps.Count
    Bitmaps.Remove 1
Next N

End Sub
```

6. In the container program, the **Click** event drives the **ImageFade** control. After the user clicks the command button, the **ImageCount** property of the control is set to the selected value. Then the **ShowNext** method of the class is fired off.

```
Private Sub cmdShowImage_Click()

'  Show the current image count
ImageFade.ImageCount = Val(txtImageValue.Text)

'  show the next image selected
ImageFade.ShowNext

End Sub
```

7. To utilize the control in a Web page, you will need to reference the object's class ID or GUID. This is determined when the object is created for deployment by the Package Wizard. The Web page will be automatically created. When the page is loaded, the Web page creates the control on the Web page. There are two items on the page: a command button and a text box input. The script on the page takes the user's input and then displays the proper image by calling the **ShowNext** method of the control.

```html
<HTML>

<BODY>

<center>

<!-- Create our object -->
<OBJECT classid="clsid:1D699B4C-B09C-11D1-B7C0-00AA00BC9278"
name="imagefade">
</OBJECT>

<BR><BR>

<!-- Next Image Button -->
<input type="button" value="Next" name="NextImage">

   

<!-- Input text box for the image number -->
<input type="text" value="1" name="ImageValue" size=1>

<!-- Script to control the control -->
<script language="vbscript">

    ' Click subroutine of the button
    Sub NextImage_OnClick

        ' Set the image count of the control
        ImageFade.ImageCount = ImageValue.Value

        ' Show the selected image
        ImageFade.ShowNext

    End Sub

</script>

</center>

</BODY>

</HTML>
```

8. Next add the **bitmap.cls**, **diskfile.cls**, **vertfade.cls**, and **patbrush.cls** classes developed in this chapter to your project.

How It Works

The image-fade code created throughout the chapter has been built into an object model. The power of ActiveX controls is to encapsulate code into easily reusable objects. The control then is easily used in different mediums, including Web pages and other Visual Basic programs.

Creating a control is not all that different than creating any other Visual Basic project. To test in a Web form, from the Project menu, choose the Properties option. On the Debugging tab, you can set a test Web page with appropriate script code or have the project immediately pop up in a Web page.

Note that the `UserControl` has both private and public properties and methods. The public properties and methods define the public interface for the control. You can define property pages for developers using your controls. The only downside with Visual Basic ActiveX controls is that they require the Visual Basic runtime DLL. For Web applications, this can require a long download if the end user does not have the control. For an intranet, though, this can be a minimal issue, with great rewards for controlling encapsulation and greater control on the client end.

Comments

Consider adding models and extending the tools in the classes. You can compile these classes into a COM object that would have a property that sets the model type and returns the value. Down the road, if the calculation method changes for any model, you can change the underlying class without breaking any programs relying on the `Automobile` class. As long as the model class does not change its implementation, the system will perform properly.

CHAPTER 6
BUSINESS OBJECTS

6

BUSINESS OBJECTS

by George Szabo

How do I...

A *business object* is a self-contained component of logic that encapsulates the business rules and processes of an organization's business model. In terms of Visual Basic 6, a business object is a class or classes used to encapsulate the business logic of your applications. This encapsulation of business logic can reside within the same executable as the user interface logic by being self contained within a class, or it can be partitioned away from the user interface code by separating it into ActiveX DLLs (in-process servers) or ActiveX EXEs (out-of-process servers) that can be called transparently from your user interfaces with no code changes.

Using Remote Automation, these business objects can then be deployed to different physical locations and still provide their encapsulated business logic to the client applications referencing them. All this can be done transparently to the client application and its code.

Design Principles

A variety of techniques can be used to create, design, and implement business objects today. This chapter provides the mechanical building blocks that enable you to assemble the business objects that you need. It is important to note that the quality of an object, and its value, is really based on the time and thought given to its design. There are several activities that you must do before you are ready to use these building blocks. You need to do the following:

✔ Define the objects that comprise the business you are dealing with.

✔ Clarify each object's characteristics and the relationship the objects have to each other.

✔ Group your objects into services (accounting, customers, sales).

✔ Define the interface that each of these objects will reveal.

These steps of requirements, analysis, and object modeling are commonly performed using tools like MS Visual Modeler or Rational Rose.

Persistent Objects

Additionally, you need to decide whether a business object should be designed as a *persistent object*—an object that remembers activities between requests—or as a *nonpersistent object* that does not retain any information from request to request. Each type of business object has its benefits. Persistent objects have the benefit of remembering the state of properties between requests so that you can execute multiple methods based on persistent properties. A request happens every time the object is instantiated and its methods and properties are called. This means that you don't have to set these properties every time, thus reducing the number of calls you must make.

Nonpersistent objects have the benefit of simplicity—much like using a black box function that contains no static variables. If your object provides financial calculations that will participate in a transaction within Microsoft Transaction Server (MTS), then you do not need to maintain state or context information; MTS does that for you. In fact, using persistent objects with MTS degrades performance. So in this case, a nonpersistent model is the way to go.

Where Should the Object Reside?

After you have defined your business objects, grouped them into services, and decided whether they are best implemented as persistent or nonpersistent objects, you are ready to enter into the discussion of physical partitioning of these objects. Prior to this point, all your work has been to define the logical design and implementation of your business object. Before you can move into designing the final object, you need to consider how it will be physically deployed because you need to code differently based on where the object will eventually reside. You can code your business logic and move it from being in the same executable as the client interface to being accessed on a remote server via the Internet (or more likely an intranet). But, as you partition your application's logic physically, execution time increases, requiring the use of special methods to bring execution speed back into acceptable parameters.

Making a thousand calls to an in-process server (ActiveX DLL) on your local machine might not be a big deal, but after you move to an out-of-process server (ActiveX EXE) and Remote Automation, you need to consider special methods to make your business objects usable. This can be done by reducing the number of calls by packaging data into a single call. Calling a remote out-of-process server can take up to 100 times as long as the same call to an in-process ActiveX DLL. This chapter contains How-To information that helps you compare the differences in execution speed as well as optimize communication between the client application and your business objects.

It is fair to say that centralized business services (business rules) are a goal for most developers. Over the past several years, stored procedures—precompiled instructions that your database engine can execute—have been marketed as the vehicle for encapsulating and centralizing business logic. Many a database administrator and SQL specialist have spent, and continue to spend, long days and nights trying to re-create business logic using the limited syntax available to stored procedures. The result of this experiment has been an inadequate capability to duplicate the business process. In the three-tier client/server model, by contrast, stored procedures are used for the execution of base level activities (SELECT, INSERTs, UPDATEs, DELETEs) in the data tier while the true business logic resides in your business objects in the business tier.

Why not place all this logic in the client where you have the greatest control and flexibility with logic, rather than in a remote server? This might be fine if you are writing business systems for 5 workstations. Obviously, though, when you have 50 or even 500 workstations, deploying new versions of an application every time the business rules change is expensive if not impossible. The alternative, described in this chapter, is to implement centralized business rules located in business objects (components) that can be accessed by all your client applications. If a rule changes, you can go to one place, change it, and redeploy without redeploying to a thousand workstations. There is a server hit, with regard to execution speed, that comes from dealing with a remotely deployed business object, but the benefits of maintainability and reuse provide enormous opportunities that competitive businesses must exploit.

Depending on your level of expertise, you might be able to use any of the How-To's in this chapter independently of the others. However, if you are new to the design of business objects, their use, and deployment, it is recommended that you work through these How-To's in order.

6.1 Set Up an ActiveX Business Object Project

The toughest part of building business objects is knowing where to start. Visual Basic has come a long way in simplifying the development of components, but it has also added so many options that it can be confusing. In this How-To, you walk through the creation of a template project that you can use as the starting point for understanding the internals of all your business objects.

6.2 Encapsulate Business Rules into a Class

This How-To uses the template created in How-To 6.1. You encapsulate logic to calculate an author's royalties for any given time period. You do this with classes and implement both standard and optimized methods for communication between the client interface and the business object interface.

6.3 Encapsulate Business Rules into an In-Process Server (ActiveX DLL)

A key to the Component Object Model is the capability to partition logic into discrete components. One place to put these components is in a server application that runs in a library (DLL) on the same machine as the primary application. Building on How-To 6.2, you see exactly what it takes to partition business logic out of a single executable into its own in-process server (ActiveX DLL).

6.4 Encapsulate Business Rules into an Out-of-Process Server (ActiveX EXE)

The other partitioning alternative is to use a server that runs as a remote executable on the network as an EXE file. Although in-process servers are faster than out-of-process servers, to deploy your business logic remotely the logic and its code must be contained in an ActiveX executable or out-of-process server. This How-To shows you what you need to do to create such a server.

6.5 Move My Business Object to a Remote Server

Centralized business services cannot be realized until business objects can be deployed remotely. In How-To's 6.3 and 6.4, both in-process DLL and out-of-process EXE servers are built. These servers are running on the local machine. This How-To walks you through both the automatic and manual process of deploying your business objects on a remote machine.

6.6 Pass Variant Arrays to and from a Business Object

It is often vital to optimize the execution speed of the implementation of a business object, particularly when it is deployed remotely. The use of variant arrays can give you a real speed advantage over conventional Visual Basic syntax. In this How-To, you use variant arrays to get and set information in a business object, resulting in execution times that are two to three times faster than standard dot operations. A *dot operation* is the syntax used to reference properties of an object using a dot between the two, for example, `MyList.Sortorder`.

You implement the use of a collection object within an ActiveX server. Collections are a powerful feature in Visual Basic, but implementing a collection within a business object is not a trivial matter. To maintain control over the object, you implement a wrapper for the collection object. A *wrapper* is a function whose purpose is to provide an interface to another function. This is done to safeguard how a client can use the collection within your business object. This How-To provides the scenario in which methods using variant arrays make sense.

6.7 Encapsulate Business Rules to Run in Microsoft Transaction Server (MTS)

Running components on a server provides many challenges; among these are speed, security, and transaction context. Prior to the existence of Microsoft Transaction Server, it was up to each development effort to deal with these issues through its own customized frameworks and infrastructure. The integration of MTS with NT has removed this burden with the capability to provide pooling of components for speed, integration with domain security, and support for transactions. This How-To walks you through the steps of running your components within Microsoft Transaction Server and gives you a brief introduction.

COMPLEXITY
INTERMEDIATE

6.1 How do I...

Set up an ActiveX business object project?

COMPATIBILITY: VB 4, 5, AND 6

Problem

I am about to begin developing business components. How do I set up my projects in Visual Basic? Where do I start?

Technique

There are a series of steps that you should take when starting a project that will result in either an in-process server or an out-of-process server. Even if you are going to keep the business logic in the same executable as the interface, using this template and understanding the issues will make partitioning your application later much easier.

Steps

Open **BUSOBJ.VBP**. The form for testing your business object's functionality appears in Figure 6.1.

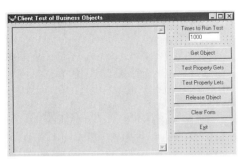

Figure 6.1 The internal test form for the business object template

Run the project. The form contains two text boxes and several buttons that exercise the methods and properties of the component object. As you click a button, a resulting message is displayed in the text box to the left of the buttons. The text box above the buttons is used to adjust the number of repetitions that a test executes. Although you can run this project, it does not contain any business logic or usefulness until you apply it to your own projects. This is done in How-To 6.2. The template project contains the following pieces:

✔ **SERVER.CLS**—This is the server class module that provides a secure entry point for your business component. This module also provides a reference to a second class module that will eventually hold the methods and properties that do the real work.

✔ **DEPOBJ.CLS**—This is a dependent class module that will eventually hold the methods and properties that will fill this business component. This class is not creatable by the public but must be created by the server class and passed to the requesting party.

✔ **GENERAL.BAS**—This is a standard code module that simply provides a subroutine called **MAIN**. Visual Basic projects must specify a startup form or procedure. Because a form cannot be specified for an ActiveX DLL or ActiveX EXE, you must use a subroutine called **MAIN**. This code module is included to hold the **MAIN** subroutine.

These three modules are all you need to create a business object, also referred to as a *component*. The template also includes a form to allow testing of the business object's methods and properties. The `TIMING.CLS` class module is included to provide support to the test form in timing execution speeds. The test form and timing class are included as key pieces to testing the functionality of your business object but are not required pieces. Complete the following steps to create this project:

1. Create a new standard EXE project called `BUSOBJ.VPB`.

2. Open the project property dialog box by choosing Project, Properties from the Visual Basic menu. You can see the Project Properties dialog box containing the primary options you need to set for an ActiveX server project in Figure 6.2.

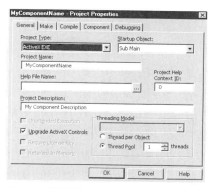

Figure 6.2 The General tab of the Visual Basic Project Properties dialog box

3. Set the properties listed in Table 6.1 for this project.

Table 6.1 The project's general settings

OBJECT	PROPERTY	SETTING
General tab	Project Type	ActiveX DLL
	Startup Object	Sub Main
	Project Name	MyComponentName
	Project Description	"My Component Description"
Component tab	Project Compatibility	checked

4. Create a new code module and save it as `GENERAL.BAS`.

5. Add the following code to the General Declarations section of the GENERAL.BAS code module. You declare a global remote data object (RDO) environment and connection object at this level so that when you open a connection, it remains open until you specifically close it. If you declared the RDO connection and environment inside a function, it would be closed each time the function completed and moved out of scope. This avoids the time-consuming task of having to connect repeatedly. If you want to use active data objects (ADO) rather than RDO to access data, you can replace the rdoEnvironment and rdoConnection objects with the ADODB.Connection object declaration. Note that if you do use RDO or ADO you must add a reference to the Microsoft Remote Data Objects library or the Microsoft Active Data Objects library within your project.

```
Option Explicit

    Global Env As rdoEnvironment
    Global Cn As rdoConnection

    'Use this Global constant to easily repoint this business
    'object towards a different data source.

    Global Const DB_TARGET = "ConfiguredDataSourceName'
```

6. Add the following procedure called MAIN to the GENERAL.BAS code module. The entry point was configured earlier by setting the startup form to SUB MAIN on the General tab. No code is required in the MAIN subprocedure. The code included here checks the start mode of the component. If the component has been compiled as an ActiveX EXE and is started by double-clicking on it or executing it from the command line, then the test form will be loaded. Here the evaluation code is commented out because you are going to be using the test form every time. When you compile your object as a ActiveX DLL or ActiveX EXE, you need to remove the comment marks in front of the If statement shown in the following code:

```
Sub MAIN()

    'If App.StartMode = vbSModeStandalone Then
        frmTestClient.Show vbModal
    'End If

End Sub
```

7. Create a new class module and save it as SERVER.CLS. Set the properties listed in Table 6.2 for this class. These settings are important. A project must have at least one class module that is public and creatable.

Table 6.2   Class option settings

OPTION	SETTING
Name	Server
DataBindingBehavior	0 - vbNone
DataSourceBehavior	0 - vbNone
Instancing	5 - MultiUse
MTSTransactionMode	1 - NoTransactions
Persistable	0 - NotPersistable

8. Add the following code to the General Declarations section of the **Server** class. The standard entry point into all business services objects is a creatable class module. All projects will use **Server** as this class's name. The following variables, properties, and methods are the starting point for all projects.

```
Option Explicit

'UserId is read-only by the client application. This will allow
'you to know who is using this object. This variable is set
'using the connect method.

Private m_UserId As String

'Password is neither read nor written by a client application.
'It is stored so that you can pass it on to other services or
'servers that may need a password supplied like a backend
'database server when you prepare a connection string.

Private m_Password As String

'Parent object is a reference to the object that instantiated
'this instance of this business object. It is neither read nor
'written by the client application. You will use this Object
'reference during termination to assure that this business
'object is properly released and replaced.

Private m_Parent As Object

'This declaration uses Early Binding to dimension an object
'variable that you will use to pass a reference to the client
'applications request. The reference to this member object
'variable is passed in the Load method of this class but could
'just as easily be passed as part of the Connect method.

Private m_DependentObject As DependentObject
```

9. The template you are now building is designed to provide a standard for the business objects you design and deploy. You have already taken the first step by creating a class module named **Server**. Now add the **Connect**

method to your **Server** class module. After your business object is instantiated, the client application or component must call the **Connect** method to gain access to the rest of the business object's properties and methods.

```
Sub Connect (UserId As String, _
             Password As String, _
             Optional Parent As Variant)

    Static Connected As Boolean

    'only allow this business object to be initialized once.

    If Connected Then Exit Sub

    'set the Connected flag to true.

    Connected = True

    'set all of the necessary variables declared earlier.

    m_UserId = UserId
    m_Password = Password

    'check for optional Parent parameter. This will be present
    'when the component is started by a pool manager.

    If IsMissing(Parent) Then
        Set m_Parent = Nothing
    Else
        Set m_Parent = Parent
    End If

    'You will use the User Id and Password to set up the
    'environment for Remote Data Objects

    rdoEngine.rdoDefaultUser = UserId
    rdoEngine.rdoDefaultPassword = Password

    'You will open a connection to the database. This
    'connection will then be used to issue SQL to the
    'Data Tier or to trigger Stored Procedures residing
    'within the database engine. Note that DB_TARGET is set in
    'the General.bas file. The DB_TARGET is the name of a valid
    'ODBC data source name (DSN).

    Set Env = rdoEngine.rdoEnvironments(0)
    Set Cn = Env.OpenConnection(dsname:=DB_TARGET, _
                                Prompt:=rdDriverNoPrompt, _
                                ReadOnly:=False, _
                                Connect:="")

End Sub
```

10. The UserId is a parameter provided to the Connect method, which was added to the Server class module earlier. To allow the client or pool manager to check the UserId, you need to create a property that can be read. This is done by adding the following code to the Server class module. Because there is no Let property for UserId in the Server class module, a client application cannot change the UserId. UserId is read-only.

```
Property Get UserId() As String

    'The UserId is read-only so you will only need to have this
    'routine to make it available to the client application.

    UserId = m_UserId

End Property
```

11. You need a method that allows the client to get a reference to dependent objects. Dependent classes are class modules set to public but not externally creatable. This is done by adding the following code to the Server class module. Note that this function could be part of the Connect method to reduce needed code.

```
Public Function Load() As DependentObject
'The Load Method of the Server Class creates a new instance
'of a dependent class and passes a reference to that class.'

    Set m_DependentObject = New DependentObject
    Set Load = m_DependentObject

End Function
```

TIP

Using mixed case when creating project names and other property names is done purposefully. Because Visual Basic checks your syntax as each line is completed, you can type these names all in lowercase when referencing them in later lines of code, and, as you leave the line, if the name is typed correctly, it will be properly formatted with uppercase and lowercase. If you have not typed the name correctly, it will remain all lowercase. This eliminates a great deal of aggravation that comes from debugging problems caused by mistyping object names and properties.

12. Create a new class module and save it as DEPOBJ.CLS. Set the properties listed in Table 6.3 for this class. This class is empty and contains no code. This will be the home of your business object's methods and properties. A client must call the Connect method of the Server class followed by the

Load method to gain access to this class. If you follow this process for all your business component objects, you will have a consistent process for controlling use of your components.

Table 6.3   Class option settings

OPTION	SETTING
Name	DependentObject
DataBindingBehavior	0 - vbNone
DataSourceBehavior	0 - vbNone
Instancing	2 - PublicNotCreatable
MTSTransactionMode	1 - NoTransactions
Persistable	0 - NotPersistable

13. As mentioned earlier, all you need to create your business object is the General.bas code module, the Server.cls class module, and the depobj.cls class module. These three files comprise the core of your business object. The following form and its code are used to test the functionality of the business object internally. Tools to test ActiveX components are in their infancy. This makes finding and fixing problems difficult. By testing your business object at every step of its development and deployment, you can catch problems early in the process, which will make life much easier later.

14. Select Form1, and add objects and set properties as shown in Table 6.4. Save the form as TESTFORM.FRM.

Table 6.4   The project's objects and properties

OBJECT	PROPERTY	SETTING
Form	Name	frmTestClient
	Caption	"Client Test of Business Objects"
	Icon	Handshak.ico
Label	Name	label1
	Caption	"Times to Run Test"
TextBox	Name	txtTestReps
	Text	"100"
TextBox	Name	txtDisplay
	Text	""
	MultiLine	True
	ScrollBars	2 - Vertical

OBJECT	PROPERTY	SETTING
CommandButton	Name	cmdGetObject
	Caption	"Get Object"
CommandButton	Name	cmdTestPropertyGets
	Caption	"Test Property Gets"
CommandButton	Name	cmdTestPropertyLets
	Caption	"Test Property Lets"
CommandButton	Name	cmdReleaseObject
	Caption	Release Object"
CommandButton	Name	cmdClear
	Caption	"Clear Form"
CommandButton	Name	cmdExit
	Caption	"E&xit"

15. The first thing you need to do with the test form to use the classes that you created is dimension object variables for the **Server** class as well as the **Dependent Object** class. Add the following code to the General Declarations section of the form:

```
Option Explicit
'dimension an object variable for the component
Dim oBusinessObject As MyComponentName.Server

'dimension an object variable for the main dependent object.
Dim oDependentObject As DependentObject

'Dimension a variable for the timing object
Dim oTiming As Timing
```

16. Add the following code to the test form **Load** event to make the timing class and its timing methods and properties available:

```
Private Sub Form_Load()

    'create an instance of the timing class so you can time
    'tests.
    Set oTiming = New Timing

End Sub
```

17. The first thing you need to do to test the methods and properties of the business component object is create an instance of the classes that you can test. Create an instance of the **Server** class module and any dependent classes you will be testing. Add the **GetObjectReference** and **GetDependentObjectReference** methods to the test form.

```
Private Sub GetObjectReference()

    'starting timing event
    oTiming.Start

    'Instantiate the Business Object
    Set oBusinessObject = New MyComponentName.Server

    'finish timing event.
    oTiming.Finish

    'Make sure that you successfully got the object
    If oBusinessObject Is Nothing Then
        txtDisplay.Text = txtDisplay.Text _
                            & "Bummer, couldn't get it.' _
                            & vbCrLf
    Else
        txtDisplay.Text = txtDisplay.Text _
                            & "Yahoo! Got the Business Object
                            ➥ in " _
                            & oTiming.ElapsedTime _
                            & " seconds' & vbCrLf
    End If

End Sub

Private Sub GetDependentObjectReference()

    'Dimension any variables that you need to pass when
    'getting a reference to the main dependent business
    'object. Place those here...
    Dim MyParameters As Variant

    'start timing event.
    oTiming.Start


    'now you allow the Business Object to pass a reference
    'to a newly created dependent object that represents the
    'main body of your business services for this object.
    Set oDependentObject = oBusinessObject.Load

    'finish timing event.
    oTiming.Finish

    'make sure you got a reference to the new dependent object.
    If oDependentObject Is Nothing Then
        txtDisplay.Text = txtDisplay.Text _
                            & "Bummer, couldn*t get Dependent
                            ➥Object.' _
                            & vbCrLf
    Else
        txtDisplay.Text = txtDisplay.Text _
                            & "Yahoo! Got the Dependent Object
                            ➥in " _
                            & oTiming.ElapsedTime _
                            & " seconds' & vbCrLf
```

```
      End If

  End Sub
```

18. After you have an instance of the classes you will be testing, you then need routines that exercise the properties and methods of those classes. The following `PropertyGet` and `PropertySet` procedures are provided as examples but need to be modified to work with your specific business component object. This is done in How-To 6.2.

```
Private Sub PropertyGet()

    'insert a routine that retrieves properties from
    'your business object using individual dot commands.
    '   txtDisplay.text = oDependentObject.PropertyName

End Sub

Private Sub PropertySet()

    'insert a routine that sets properties from the
    'business object using individual dot commands.
    '   oDependentObject.PropertyName = MyNewValue

End Sub
```

19. The test form allows the user to specify the number of times to run a test. A centralized routine is needed to run the property and method tests based on the number of repetitions specified on the form. Additionally, the tests must be timed and results displayed to the window. This is done by adding the following `RunTest` procedure to the test form:

```
Private Sub RunTest(sTestFunction As String, sDisplayText As
➥String)
    'this routine will run the tests on properties and methods
    'as many times as are specified in the txtTestReps textbox.
    'The default is 100

    Dim i As Integer
    Dim iReps As Integer

    'Make sure you have an object reference before you start
    If oDependentObject Is Nothing Then
        txtDisplay.Text = txtDisplay.Text _
                    & "No reference to Dependent Object
                    ➥found.' _
                    & vbCrLf

        Exit Sub
    Else

    End If

    'make sure that you have a valid value for number of
    'repetitions for the tests.
```

continued on next page

continued from previous page

```
            If txtTestReps.Text <> "" Then
                iReps = CInt(txtTestReps.Text)
            Else
                iReps = 1
            End If

            '************************
            'test interface of server
            '************************

            'start timing this event
            oTiming.Start

            'run test
            For i = 1 To iReps
                'Place the name of the functions you wish to test here
                Select Case sTestFunction
                Case "PropertyGet'
                    PropertyGet
                Case "PropertySet'
                    PropertySet
                End Select
            Next

            'stop timing event
            oTiming.Finish

            'display the time taken to retrieve the properties using
            'standard dot operation gets.
            txtDisplay.Text = txtDisplay.Text _
                            & Str(iReps) _
                            & " Rep(s) of " & sDisplayText & "
                            ➡in " _
                            & oTiming.ElapsedTime _
                            & " seconds' & vbCrLf

            'repeat this code for each function you wish to test.

    End Sub
```

20. The test form currently has two buttons designated to start the testing process. Add the following code to the **Click** events of those two buttons:

```
Private Sub cmdTestPropertyGets_Click()
    'call the RunTest procedure and provide it the name of the
    'test you wish to run as well as the text you want displayed
    'with timing results.

    Call RunTest("PropertyGet', "Standard Property Gets')

End Sub

Private Sub cmdTestPropertyLets_Click()
```

```
        Call RunTest("PropertySet', "Standard Property Lets')

    End Sub
```

21. You need a way to release your instances of the classes you are testing. This is done by setting your object variables equal to the keyword `Nothing`. Add the following method `ReleaseObjects`:

```
Private Sub ReleaseObjects()

    'start timing event
    oTiming.Start

    'de-reference ActiveX server objects that exist
    Set oDependentObject = Nothing
    Set oBusinessObject = Nothing

    'finish timing event.
    oTiming.Finish

    txtDisplay.Text = txtDisplay.Text _
                    & "Objects released in only " _
                    & oTiming.ElapsedTime _
                    & " seconds!' & vbCrLf

End Sub
```

22. Add the following code to the `Click` events of the GetObject, ReleaseObject, Exit, and Clear buttons on the test form. This code connects the buttons to the corresponding procedures you have already added to the test form.

```
Private Sub cmdGetObject_Click()

    'Get a reference to the royaltysvc component
    GetObjectReference

    'Get a reference to the Main Dependent Object
    'in this component.
    GetDependentObjectReference

End Sub

Private Sub cmdReleaseObject_Click()

    ReleaseObjects

End Sub

Private Sub cmdExit_Click()

    'you cannot use the END command in a DLL. During development
    'unload form and references to objects then manually stop
```

continued on next page

continued from previous page

```
            'the project with the VB toolbar stop button.
            Unload frmTestClient

    End Sub

    Private Sub cmdClear_Click()

            'use to clear the textbox.
            txtDisplay.Text = ""

    End Sub
```

23. Choose Insert, Class Module from Visual Basic's menu to add a class module to this project. The class appears in the project window. Open the class module and press the F4 key to view the class's properties. Set these properties as shown in Table 6.5.

Table 6.5 TIMING.CLS class module property settings

OBJECT	PROPERTY	SETTING
Class Module	Name	"Timing"
	Instancing	1 - Private

24. Add the following code to the General Declarations section of the `Timing` class module. You need to declare the `timeGetTime` API function to have access to a method that returns timing values with a millisecond resolution. The standard `Time()` function in Visual Basic only provides for seconds.

```
Option Explicit
'
'dimension readonly variables for timing events
Dim mStartTime As Long
Dim mFinishTime As Long
Dim mElapsedTime As Long
'
'declare API to get time in milliseconds.
Private Declare Function timeGetTime Lib "winmm.dll" () As Long
```

25. Add the following methods and properties to the `Timing` class. These methods and properties allow you to time execution of SQL queries and have access to the elapsed time values in milliseconds.

```
'method to store start time
Public Sub Start()
    mStartTime = timeGetTime
    mFinishTime = 0
    mElapsedTime = 0
End Sub

'method to store finish time and calculate elapsed time in
'milliseconds
```

```
Public Sub Finish()
    mFinishTime = timeGetTime
    mElapsedTime = mFinishTime - mStartTime
End Sub

'read-only property to access elapsed time.
Public Property Get ElapsedTime()
    ElapsedTime = mElapsedTime / 1000
End Property
```

How It Works

You must do two things to create an ActiveX server. First, you must set the startup form to **Sub Main**. Second, you must have a class module with its instancing property set to something other than private. If the ActiveX server project is going to be compiled as an ActiveX DLL, you additionally need to be sure that the **instancing** property is set to **5-MultiUse**.

It is important to note that ActiveX servers, especially those deployed remotely, often do not have forms that are used or visible. Additionally, all error messages should be handed back to the client and not displayed on the server. If the business object is running on a remote machine and pops up a message box, it will not return control to the client application until the message box is closed. There is no guarantee that anyone will be available to see or respond to it.

The form contained in the template is designed for use as a testing mechanism for the business logic contained in the project. As you develop your business objects, you will find that it is critical to use a phased approach to development and implementation. You need to test the project internally, then test on your local machine with a client calling your business object, and finally test remotely. If you skip one of these steps, it will come back to haunt you. Finding the cause of errors after you deploy remotely is not fun and can shorten anyone's life expectancy.

The **Server** class provides a standard entry point into all business objects. The entry point refers to the syntax used to reference your business object. Because your template project is called MyComponent and the single public class module is called **Server**, you would create the object by calling the **Server** class using the following syntax:

```
DIM ClientObject AS MyComponent.Server
SET ClientObject = NEW MyComponent.Server
ClientObject.Connect
```

To use any of the methods or access any of the properties, a client of the business object must instantiate the business object by dimensioning an object variable, setting the object variable to a new instance of the business object's **Server** class, and finally executing the **Connect** method. Standardizing on the use of a class module called **Server** allows you to control how people gain access to the methods and properties of your objects. The template uses a method called **Load** to allow public access to the dependent class found in the template. The dependent class is actually the future home of the properties and methods that will comprise the purpose of this component.

Comments

A template or boilerplate approach to starting a business object project is a good way to get over the hump. Of course, having written specifications and a plan helps, too. Take the template created in this How-To and copy it into a new directory. Using this template to create your business objects will get you up and running right away.

COMPLEXITY
ADVANCED

6.2 How do I...
Encapsulate business rules into a class?

COMPATIBILITY: VB 4, 5, AND 6

Problem

I want to keep all the business logic in my application for now but still be able to partition it out of the application easily if I need to in the future.

Technique

Significant architectural decisions can facilitate easy (or easier) partitioning of an application's services. Unless you understand what these are and develop with these restrictions in mind, you are headed for trouble. This How-To demonstrates how to encapsulate business rules into a class within your project. By applying the rules that will apply to an object destined for remote deployment, we will build a solid foundation for a maintainable and scalable application.

Steps

Open and run MYROYSVC.VBP. The running program appears as shown in Figure 6.3. The form that appears is the test form for the business rules encapsulated in this project. Click the Get Object button. The action and execution time are displayed on the form in a large text area. Click the Test Property Gets button. This tests the capability to get information from the business object. Click the Test Property Lets button to test writing information to the business object. Finally, click the Release Object button to release the business object and let it terminate.

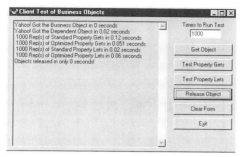

Figure 6.3 The Royalty Information Component's test form at runtime.

The first step is to determine what business question we need to answer. This component provides the royalty amounts for a given author during a time period specified by the client application. For information focusing on how to access data from a database server such as SQL Server, refer to Chapter 3, "Data Objects." For this How-To, we will hard code test data and a simple testing interface to allow us to focus on the mechanics of implementation and intercommunication between the client application and the services of the business object (component).

Although the encapsulation of business rules is often referred to as a business object, it is actually better referred to as a component because several objects (classes) exist within a single Visual Basic project. The project can actually be a wrapper around several objects that work together or are related by the services they provide. Figure 6.4 presents a diagram of the business object you will build in this How-To and the eventual role it plays in a three-tier client/server architecture.

To build the Royalty Service business object, complete the following steps:

1. Copy the template created with How-To 6.1 into a new directory.

2. Rename the VBP file from BUSOBJ.VPB to MYROYSVC.VPB.

3. Start the project.

4. Set the following options for the project by choosing Project, RoyaltySvc Properties from the menu. You can see the Project Properties tab containing the primary options you need to set for an ActiveX server project (refer to Figure 6.4). Set the properties listed in Table 6.6 for this project.

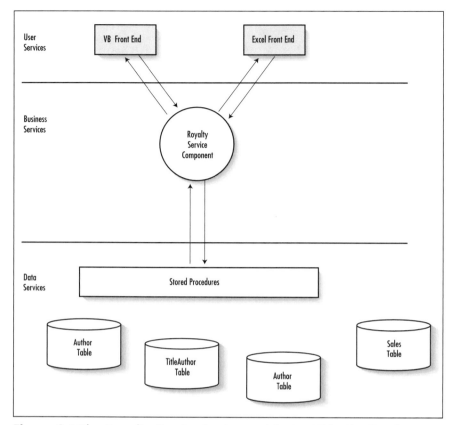

Figure 6.4 The Royalty Service business object within the Service Model diagram.

Table 6.6   The project's option settings

OBJECT	PROPERTY	SETTING
General Tab	Project Type	ActiveX EXE
	Startup Object	Sub Main
	Project Name	"Royaltysvc"
	Project Description	"Royalty Information"
Component Tab	Project Compatibility	Checked
	Start Mode	Standalone

5. When a project contains a class module with a `Public` property set to `True`, compiling the project generates a Registry entry. This is because setting a class module's `Public` property to `True` implies that you want to access it from another application through ActiveX, which requires that the object be entered in the Registry and assigned a class ID. Visual Basic automatically takes care of the registration for you—a great feature if that's what you really want to do. Because this project is not yet an ActiveX server, there is no need to generate a Registry entry for this project. How-To's 6.3 and 6.4 introduce the steps for converting this project into an ActiveX server. For now, tell Visual Basic to set the **Public** property of all class modules in this project to **False** to avoid the generation of a Registry entry. Steps 6 and 7 of this How-To take care of this for you.

6. Open **SERVER.CLS** from the project window in Visual Basic. While your cursor is in the class module, press the F4 key to display the property sheet. Set the following properties found in Table 6.7.

Table 6.7　Class option settings

OPTION	SETTING
Name	Server
DataBindingBehavior	0 - vbNone
DataSourceBehavior	0 - vbNone
Instancing	1 - Private

7. Add a new class module and save it as **AUTHOR.CLS**. Refer to Table 6.8 to configure settings for **AUTHOR.CLS**.

Table 6.8　Class option settings

OPTION	SETTING
Name	Author
DataBindingBehavior	0 - vbNone
DataSourceBehavior	0 - vbNone
Instancing	1 - Private

8. The purpose of this project is to construct a business object that provides an author's royalty information based on a data range. You need variables to store the author's information after it is retrieved. Add the following variables to the declarations section of **AUTHOR.CLS**. These variables are declared as private. This forces people to use the properties of the **Author** class to alter the private memory variables found in the declarations section of the **Author** class.

```
Option Explicit

'These are private variables for the author class.
```

continued on next page

continued from previous page

```
Private m_LastName As String
Private m_FirstName As String
Private m_AuthorId As String
Private m_StartDate As Date
Private m_EndDate As Date
Private m_TotalRoyalty As Currency
```

9. Add the following **Get** and **Let** properties to **AUTHOR.CLS** to provide controlled access to the private memory variables found in the declaration section of this class. A **Property Get** allows the client of your business object to read a property. A **Property Let** allows the client to write to a property. When the project is compiled, the client can use the object browser that comes with Visual Basic to see your object's public interface.

```
Public Property Get StartDate() As Date
    'Read
    StartDate = m_StartDate
End Property

Public Property Let StartDate(dtNewStartDate As Date)
    'Write
    m_StartDate = dtNewStartDate
End Property

Public Property Get EndDate() As Date
    'Read
    EndDate = m_EndDate
End Property

Public Property Let EndDate(dtNewEndDate As Date)
    'Write
    m_EndDate = dtNewEndDate
End Property

Public Property Get AuthorId() As String
    'Read
    AuthorId = m_AuthorId
End Property

Public Property Let AuthorId(sNewAuthorId As String)
    'Write
    m_AuthorId = sNewAuthorId
End Property

Public Property Get TotalRoyalty() As Currency
    'Read Only
    TotalRoyalty = m_TotalRoyalty
End Property

Public Property Get LastName() As String
    'Read
    LastName = m_LastName
End Property
```

```
Public Property Let LastName(sNewLastName As String)
    'Write
    m_LastName = sNewLastName
End Property

Public Property Get FirstName() As String
    'Read
    FirstName = m_FirstName
End Property

Public Property Let FirstName(sNewFirstName As String)
    'Write
    m_FirstName = sNewFirstName
End Property
```

10. The purpose of the **Author** class module is to provide an author's royalty
information for a specified time period. Add the following public **GetInfo**
method to the **Author** class module to accomplish the retrieval of the
author's royalty information. For now, you will provide hard coded values.
The next step would be to include code to access a data source for the
needed information. For examples on doing this, refer to Chapter 3, "Data
Objects." Note that whenever your procedure includes optional
parameters, you should check their existence in your code with the
IsMissing function.

```
Public Sub GetInfo(ByVal sAuthorId As String, _
                Optional ByVal dtStartDate As Variant, _
                Optional ByVal dtEndDate As Variant)
    '
    'use author*s id and date range to get royalty information
    'for this project you will hard code values for testing
    'purposes.
    m_AuthorId = sAuthorId
    '
    'because these parameters are optional you will need to
    'check whether they have been provided using the IsMissing
    'function.
    If IsMissing(m_StartDate) Then
        m_StartDate = "01/01/1900'
    Else
        m_StartDate = dtStartDate
    End If
    If IsMissing(m_EndDate) Then
        m_EndDate = "01/01/1999'
    Else
        m_EndDate = dtEndDate
    End If
    '
    'At this point the above information would be used with a
    'method like Remote Data Objects to retrieve the author*s
    'name and royalty information. For this example we will
    'hard code the return values.
    m_TotalRoyalty = 2500    'calculated value based on
                             'business logic
```

continued on next page

continued from previous page

```
                                        'qty * price
        m_LastName = "Shakespeare'
        m_FirstName = "William'


    End Sub
```

11. Add the `PropertyGetAll` and `PropertySetAll` methods to the `Author`
class module. These methods allow the client application to retrieve and
write multiple properties with a single call. This is an optimized method
that will become of greater importance as the user interface is separated
from the business object.

```
Public Sub PropertyGetAll(Optional ByVal StartDate As Variant,
                    Optional ByVal EndDate As Variant,
                    Optional ByVal FirstName As Variant,
                    Optional ByVal LastName As Variant,
                    Optional ByVal TotalRoyalty As Variant,
                    Optional ByVal AuthorId As Variant)


        If IsMissing(StartDate) Then
            'not requested
        Else
            StartDate = m_StartDate
        End If
        If IsMissing(EndDate) Then
            'not requested
        Else
            EndDate = m_EndDate
        End If
        If IsMissing(FirstName) Then
            'not requested
        Else
            FirstName = m_FirstName
        End If
        If IsMissing(LastName) Then
            'not requested
        Else
            LastName = m_LastName
        End If
        If IsMissing(TotalRoyalty) Then
            'not requested
        Else
            TotalRoyalty = m_TotalRoyalty
        End If
        If IsMissing(AuthorId) Then
            'not requested
        Else
            AuthorId = m_AuthorId
        End If


    End Sub


    Public Sub PropertySetAll(Optional ByVal StartDate As Variant,
                    Optional ByVal EndDate As Variant,
                    Optional ByVal FirstName As Variant,
```

```
                        Optional ByVal LastName As Variant,
                        Optional ByVal AuthorId As Variant)
        '
        'since parameters are optional, check to see if they exist
        'using the IsMissing function.
        If IsMissing(StartDate) Then
            'set a default here since it was not specified
        Else
            m_StartDate = StartDate
        End If
        If IsMissing(EndDate) Then
            'set a default here since it was not specified
        Else
            m_EndDate = EndDate
        End If
        If IsMissing(FirstName) Then
            'set a default here since it was not specified
        Else
            m_FirstName = FirstName
        End If
        If IsMissing(LastName) Then
            'set a default here since it was not specified
        Else
            m_LastName = LastName
        End If
        If IsMissing(AuthorId) Then
            'set a default here since it was not specified
        Else
            m_AuthorId = AuthorId
        End If

    End Sub
```

12. The template that you are using for this project needs to be updated to contain references to the newly added **Author** class module. Open the **SERVER.CLS** class module and change the following code in the General Declarations section:

```
Private m_DependentObject As DependentObject
```

```
should be changed to
```

```
Private m_DependentObject As Author
```

13. The **Load** method of the **Server** class module creates an instance of the **Author** class module and passes the object reference to the client application. The **Load** method from your template needs to be modified to work with the newly added **Author** class module. Modify the **Load** function of the **SERVER.CLS** class module to the following:

```
Public Function Load(AuthorId As Variant, _
                    Optional StartDate As Variant, _
                    Optional EndDate As Variant _
                    ) As Author
```

continued on next page

continued from previous page

```
                      '
                      'This method allows the client to get a reference
                      'to the dependent author object. The author class is set to
                      'public but is not externally creatable. Note that this
                      'function could be part of the initialize method to reduce
                      'code needed to get a reference to the author class.
                      '
                      Set m_DependentObject = New Author
                      '
                      'initialize the object with data
                      '
                      Call m_DependentObject.GetInfo(AuthorId, StartDate, EndDate)
                      '
                      'Pass the object reference back.
                      '
                      Set Load = m_DependentObject
                      '
              End Function
```

14. Highlight frmTestClient in the project window and click the View Code
button.

15. You need to change all references of MyComponentName to RoyaltySvc
because this is the project's new name. Choose Edit, Replace from the
Visual Basic menu. Set the Replace options to Current Module and Find
Whole Word Only. Enter MyComponentName in the Find What box and
enter RoyaltySvc in the Replace With box. Click Replace to complete the
changes. Clicking Replace rather than Replace All allows you to see what
exactly is being changed. Repeat this process to replace oDependentObject
with oAuthor and DependentObject with Author. This updates all generic
object references to the actual names being used by this project.

16. Now that the business object's class modules have been modified to
provide author royalty information based on a date range, it is time to
modify the test form. The test form included with the template provides
the framework for testing your business object. You need to modify the
form to specifically test the properties and methods that have been added.
The GetDependentObjectReference procedure must be modified to
support the three required parameters of the **Server** class module's **Load**
method, which are **Author ID**, **Start Date**, and **End Date**. This is done
by adding the following code to the test form:

```
Private Sub GetDependentObjectReference()

        'Dimension any variables that you need to pass when
        'getting a reference to the main dependent business
        'object. Place those here...
        Dim vAuthorId As Variant
        Dim vStartDate As Variant
        Dim vEndDate As Variant
```

```
'start timing event.
oTiming.Start

'Here you would set any parameters needed.
vAuthorId = "555-55-5555'
vStartDate = #1/1/97#
vEndDate = #6/30/97#

'now you allow the Business Object to pass a reference
'to a newly created dependent object that represents the
'main body of your business services for this object.
Set oAuthor = oBusinessObject.Load(vAuthorId, vStartDate,
➡vEndDate)

'finish timing event.
oTiming.Finish

'make sure you got a reference to the new dependent object.
If oAuthor Is Nothing Then
    txtDisplay.Text = txtDisplay.Text _
                      & "Bummer, couldn*t get Dependent
                      ➡Object.' _
                      & vbCrLf
Else
    txtDisplay.Text = txtDisplay.Text _
                      & "Yahoo! Got the Dependent
                      ➡Object in " _
                      & oTiming.ElapsedTime _
                      & " seconds' & vbCrLf
End If

End Sub
```

17. The following `PropertyGet` and `PropertySet` procedures read and write the author's properties. Add these procedures to the test form.

```
Private Sub PropertyGet()
'store property values in this variant
Dim vPropertyValues As Variant

'retrieve each property using a dot command
With oAuthor
    vPropertyValues = vPropertyValues & .AuthorId
    vPropertyValues = vPropertyValues & .LastName
    vPropertyValues = vPropertyValues & .FirstName
    vPropertyValues = vPropertyValues & .StartDate
    vPropertyValues = vPropertyValues & .EndDate
    vPropertyValues = vPropertyValues & .TotalRoyalty
End With

End Sub

Private Sub PropertySet()
'Hard code new values that will be set in the
'business object we are testing.
```

continued on next page

continued from previous page

```
With oAuthor
    .AuthorId = "333-333-3333'
    .LastName = "King'
    .FirstName = "Stephen'
    .StartDate = #1/1/97#
    .EndDate = #6/30/97#
End With

End Sub
```

18. The following `PropertyGetAll` and `PropertySetAll` procedures provide an optimized method for retrieving and writing property values to the `Author` class. This is done by passing multiple parameters to allow the reading or writing of property values with a single call. Add the following procedures to the test form:

```
Private Sub PropertyGetAll()
Dim vPropertyValues As Variant
Dim vStartDate As Variant
Dim vEndDate As Variant
Dim vFirstName As Variant
Dim vLastName As Variant
Dim vTotalRoyalty As Variant
Dim vAuthorId As Variant

'this routine uses a method of the Author class to
'retrieve all properties with a single call.
Call oAuthor.PropertyGetAll(vStartDate, vEndDate, vFirstName,
➥vLastName, _
                vTotalRoyalty, vAuthorId)

    vPropertyValues = vPropertyValues & vAuthorId
    vPropertyValues = vPropertyValues & vLastName
    vPropertyValues = vPropertyValues & vFirstName
    vPropertyValues = vPropertyValues & vStartDate
    vPropertyValues = vPropertyValues & vEndDate
    vPropertyValues = vPropertyValues & vTotalRoyalty

End Sub

Private Sub PropertySetAll()
'Dimension variables to pass to Business Object
Dim vStartDate As Variant
Dim vEndDate As Variant
Dim vFirstName As Variant
Dim vLastName As Variant
Dim vAuthorId As Variant

'Fill the variables with values for test
vStartDate = #1/1/97#
vEndDate = #6/30/97#
vFirstName = "Stephen'
vLastName = "King'
```

```
vAuthorId = "444-444-4444'

'this routine uses a method of the Author class to
'set all properties with a single call.
Call oAuthor.PropertySetAll(vStartDate, _
                            vEndDate, _
                            vFirstName, _
                            vLastName, _
                            vAuthorId)

End Sub
```

19. The `RunTest` procedure that you find in the template from How-To 6.1 must be modified to support the optimized methods, `PropertyGetAll` and `PropertySetAll`. Replace the template's `RunTest` procedure with this one.

```
Private Sub RunTest(sTestFunction As String, sDisplayText
➡As String)
    'this routine will run the tests on GETS as many times as
    'are specified in the txtTestReps textbox.
    'The default is 100

    Dim i As Integer
    Dim iReps As Integer

    'Make sure you have an object reference before you start
    If oAuthor Is Nothing Then
        txtDisplay.Text = txtDisplay.Text _
                        & "No reference to Dependent
                        ➡Object found.' _
                        & vbCrLf

        Exit Sub
    Else

    End If

    'make sure that you have a valid value for number of
    'repetitions for the tests.
    If txtTestReps.Text <> "" Then
        iReps = CInt(txtTestReps.Text)
    Else
        iReps = 1
    End If

    '**********************
    'test ability to get information from server   '
    '**********************

    'start timing this event
    oTiming.Start

    'run test
    For i = 1 To iReps
        'Place the name of the functions you wish to test here
```

continued on next page

continued from previous page

```
        Select Case sTestFunction
        Case "PropertyGet'
            PropertyGet
        Case "PropertySet'
            PropertySet
        Case "PropertyGetAll'
            PropertyGetAll
        Case "PropertySetAll'
            PropertySetAll

        End Select
    Next

    'stop timing event
    oTiming.Finish

    'display the time taken to retrieve the properties using
    'standard dot operation gets.
    txtDisplay.Text = txtDisplay.Text _
                    & Str(iReps) _
                    & " Rep(s) of " & sDisplayText
                ➡& " in " _
                    & oTiming.ElapsedTime _
                    & " seconds' & vbCrLf

    'repeat this code for each function you wish to test.

End Sub
```

20. The `Click` event for the `cmdTestPropertyGets` and
`cmdTestPropertyLets` buttons must be updated to include the execution
of tests for the optimized `PropertyGetAll` and `PropertySetAll` methods
added earlier. Change each button's `Click` event to the following:

```
Private Sub cmdTestPropertyGets_Click()

    Call RunTest("PropertyGet', "Standard Property Gets')
    Call RunTest("PropertyGetAll', "Optimized Property Gets')

End Sub

Private Sub cmdTestPropertyLets_Click()

    Call RunTest("PropertySet', "Standard Property Lets')
    Call RunTest("PropertySetAll', "Optimized Property Lets')

End Sub
```

How It Works

This project comprises the **Server** class module, the **Author** class module, and
the **GENERAL.BAS** code module on the business object side. The project also
contains a single test form and a class module that assists in timing the

execution of tests. The `Server` class module is the first class that must be created to work with this business object. The `Author` class contains all the author information that the client wants to access. The business object interface used in this project requires the use of the `Load` method (which is part of the `Server` class) to create an instance of the `Author` class and access its properties and methods. This allows you to put code in the `Load` method that weeds out who can and can't get to the `Author` class module, its properties, and methods.

The first step to creating this project is to use the template created in How-To 6.1. After the template is copied into a new directory, the `Public` property of all class modules is set to `False`, and the `Creatable` property is set to `not creatable`. This prevents Visual Basic from automatically placing entries in the Registry every time you compile the application. In later How-To's using this project, the `Public` and `creatable` properties of the `Server` and `Author` class modules will be changed, but this project attempts to show a self-contained implementation of a business object with an internal form to test the business object's interface.

The second step is to build the `Author` class, which encapsulates the functionality needed. For this project, you were trying to create an object that would provide an author's royalties based on a data range. This functionality is encapsulated into the `Author` class module with access to its functionality controlled by the `Server` class module's `Load` method. The `Author` class provides properties for the author's ID number, last name, first name, and total royalties as well as the date range being used to calculate the amount of royalties due to the author.

When the `Author` class is completed, the next step is to modify the test form to test the newly added functionality. A standardized name, `Server`, is used for the class module that grants access to the rest of the business objects' functionality. Next the project is assigned a permanent project name, `RoyaltySvc`. Whenever the business object is created by the test form, the project name is used to explicitly identify the `Server` class. This prevents the need for rewriting code when the test form is removed and compiled into its own executable. Internally, you could code the following:

```
dim myObject as Server
```

This works only when called internally to the project. Or you could code this:

```
dim myObject as RoyaltySvc.Server
```

This continues to work after the interface and business logic are separated into different components, as long as the business object retains the project name of `RoyaltySvc`.

Another important aspect of the way that this business object was implemented is the inclusion of two optimized methods for retrieving and setting information in the business object, `PropertyGetAll` and `PropertySetAll`. The key here is that the farther away you partition your business logic, the more costly dot operations become. A dot operation is the syntax used to reference properties of an object using a dot, as in the following:

```
myObject.LastName
myObject.FirstName
myObject.TotalRoyalty
```

The `PropertyGetAll` and `PropertyLetAll` methods of the `Author` class allow the passing of groups of variables utilizing one dot command rather than several. The `Timing` class that is part of the template used for this project displays the execution time for the reading and writing of properties. The execution times are displayed in the large text box that is part of the test form. The capability to view the execution times of various operations serves to familiarize you with the impact that partitioning and physical deployment have on the syntactical methods you can use when constructing your business object.

Comments

Business objects can implement a variety of interfaces. Figure 6.5 shows the object model for the `RoyaltySvc` business object as well as the public interface.

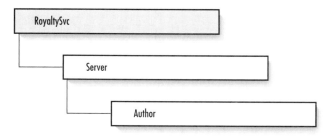

	Server	Author
Collections		
Member Objects	Author	
Properties	UserId Password Id Parent	LastName FirstName AuthorId StartDate EndDate RoyaltyTotal
Methods	Initialize Load	GetInfo
Optimized Methods		PropertyGetAll PropertySetAll

Figure 6.5 The `RoyaltySvc` object model and public interface

In general, there are two types of interface models: broad base and deep design. A broad-based interface implements all the properties and methods through a single object that can be referenced. This allows the client to create a single connection to the object and access a variety of properties, not necessarily all related or grouped. The Microsoft Word ActiveX interface is based on a broad design. The deep design is one that is explored in How-To 6.6. In a deep design, properties are grouped and tiered. To access features in a deeper layer, you need to gain a reference to that object or collection of objects. Each reference is another connection. For information on the cost of each connection during remote deployment, refer to How-To 6.5. The Excel ActiveX interface implements a deep design.

Many decisions must be made in designing a business object, but until you understand the mechanical implementations of this new technology, those decisions remain at bay. This project allows you to set the number of iterations for the testing of Get and Let properties and methods. Try the test form using a variety of settings from 1 to 1,000 repetitions. Review what impact volume has on the various techniques for accessing and setting business object values. When you have worked through this How-To, you will have a better understanding of just how all these variations can affect your project's performance. Understanding the strengths and limitations of this technology can only be to your advantage.

COMPLEXITY
BEGINNING

6.3   How do I...
Encapsulate business rules into an in-process server (ActiveX DLL)?

COMPATIBILITY: VB 5 AND 6

Problem

I have a Visual Basic project that contains code I want to share with other applications on the same machine. I want to use this project to create an ActiveX DLL that all the applications can use. How do I create an ActiveX DLL using this project?

Technique

Starting with Visual Basic 5, you can create ActiveX Dynamic Link Libraries (DLLs). This is an improvement over versions prior to Visual Basic 5. ActiveX objects provide an important component in the move to code reusability. As business rules are grouped into services and encapsulated into objects, these objects can be reused by various client applications, thus allowing you to write code that can truly be reused. Prior to Visual Basic 4, you needed to use a language such as C++ to create DLLs. In this How-To, you take an existing project and compile it as an ActiveX DLL. Because DLLs operate as in-process servers (using the same processing space as the application), speed should not be impacted significantly. You will include a speed check on execution.

Steps

Open and run `TESTDLL.VBP`. The running program appears as shown in Figure 6.6.

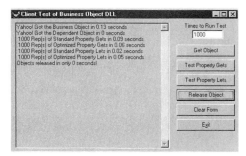

Figure 6.6 The TESTDLL project's test form at runtime

What you are seeing is a client application referencing the business object in `ROYDLL.DLL`. Because an ActiveX DLL is an in-process server, it operates within the memory space of the client. The execution speed is affected minimally by the fact that it is now fully contained within a DLL. Note that a client cannot access a DLL directly if it is on a remote machine. This is because a DLL does not create its own process but relies on operating within the process space of the client. To create an ActiveX DLL, perform the following steps:

1. Copy the template created in How-To 6.2 into a new directory.

2. Rename the `.VBP` file from `MYROYSVC.VBP` to `ROYDLL.VBP`. Rename the `.VBW` file from `MYROYSVC.VBW` to `ROYDLL.VBW`.

3. Open the project.

4. Make the following changes to the `GENERAL.BAS` file. Comment out the following code. Do not remove this code completely because you need to uncomment those lines that show the test form if you ever work on this object and want to test the functionality with the Visual Basic environment. You must remove this code to prevent the test form that is internal to the project from loading when the ActiveX DLL is used by a client.

```
'If App.StartMode = vbSModeStandalone Then
'    frmTestClient.Show vbModal
'End If.
```

5. Set the following options for the project by choosing Project, RoyaltySvc Properties from the menu option . You can see the Project Properties tab containing the primary options you need to set for an ActiveX server project. Set the properties listed in Table 6.9 for this project.

Table 6.9 The project's option settings

OBJECT	PROPERTY	SETTING
General Tab	Project Type	ActiveX DLL
	Startup Object	Sub Main
	Project Name	"Royaltysvc"
	Project Description	"Royalty Service Component DLL"
Component Tab	Project Compatibility	checked
	Start Mode	ActiveX Component

6. Set the following properties for the Server class and the Author class (see Tables 6.10 and 6.11, respectively).

Table 6.10 Class option settings for Server

OPTION	SETTING
Name	Server
DataBindingBehavior	0 - vbNone
DataSourceBehavior	0 - vbNone
Instancing	5 - MultiUse
MTSTransactionMode	1 - NoTransactions
Persistable	0 - NotPersistable

Table 6.11 Class option settings for Author

OPTION	SETTING
Name	Author
DataBindingBehavior	0 - vbNone
DataSourceBehavior	0 - vbNone
Instancing	2 - PublicNotCreatable
MTSTransactionMode	1 - NoTransactions
Persistable	0 - NotPersistable

7. Choose File, Make RoyDLL.DLL (see Figure 6.7). Set the filename to ROYDLL.DLL.

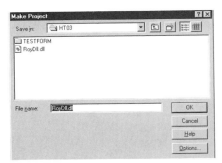

Figure 6.7 The Visual Basic Make Project dialog box preparing to make an ActiveX DLL

8. Click the Option button from the ActiveX DLL dialog box. Modify the Title field to Royalty Service DLL (see Figure 6.8).

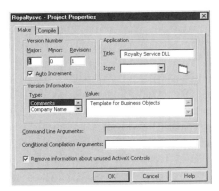

Figure 6.8 ActiveX DLL options are configured from the Projects Properties dialog box

9. Generate the DLL. This automatically creates an entry in the Registry. If you open a different project and then open your References list from the menu bar, you see the newly created DLL listed. Search the list for the description of the Royalty Service Component DLL.

10. Choose Project, RoyaltySvc Properties from the menu and then select the Component tab. Notice that the DLL you just compiled is already specified. This allows you to recompile the project without generating a new class ID in the Registry. Each time you compile this project, the DLL you specified is used as a guide to verify that the changes you have made are backward compatible. Now that you have that out of the way, you can separate out the test form.

11. Create a new subdirectory called `TestForm` and start a new project. Select Standard EXE. Remove the default `Form1` from the project.

12. Save the project as `TESTDLL.VBP`.

13. Copy the files `TESTFORM.FRM`, `TESTFORM.FRX`, and `TIMING.CLS` to the new directory for this project.

14. Choose Project, Add File from the Visual Basic menu. Add `TESTFORM.FRM` to the `TESTDLL` project.

15. Choose Project, Add File from the Visual Basic menu. Add `TIMING.CLS` to the `TESTDLL` project.

16. Open `TESTFORM.FRM` and change the `Caption` property to read Client Test of Business Object DLL.

17. Choose Project, Project1 Properties from the Visual Basic menu. Choose the General tab and specify the startup form as `frmTestClient`. Click OK.

18. Now you need to reference the business object. Choose Project, References. A dialog box appears that lists all the objects you can reference. Select Royalty Service Component DLL. Click OK.

19. Choose File, Make TestDLL.EXE from the Visual Basic menu.

20. Enter the filename, `TESTDLL.EXE`.

21. Click the Options button and set the `Title` property to `TESTDLL`. Click OK.

22. Generate an executable.

23. Run `TESTDLL.EXE`. This is the same test form used to test your project in How-To 6.2. Select each button on the form in order from top to bottom. Start with the Get Object button, which tells you whether your test form was able to create an instance of the `RoyaltySvc` business object. The Test Property Gets and Test Property Lets buttons run tests to exercise the capability to retrieve and write properties to the `RoyaltySvc` business object. The Release Object button releases the `RoyaltySvc` business object so that it unloads from memory. Each of these actions provides visible feedback within the test form's display text box.

How It Works

You could have simply tried to compile the application as an ActiveX DLL and responded to the error messages until it worked. The main change is that the test form is prevented from appearing when the ActiveX DLL is called by a client application. This is done by commenting out the form load action in the GENERAL.BAS file. Both class modules are set to public, and the server class module is set to Creatable MultiUse. At this point, an ActiveX DLL is generated by choosing File, Make ActiveX DLL from the menu.

Note that after you generate an ActiveX DLL or ActiveX EXE, entries are being made in the Registry. In this How-To, you are shown that Visual Basic sets the just generated DLL as the compatible ActiveX server. This prevents Visual Basic from creating a different identification entry in the Registry each time you compile.

When an ActiveX DLL is generated, a second application is created to test the capability to utilize this business object from a client application. The test form and time class module are copied into a new directory. A new Visual Basic project is started, and these files are added. The project, called TESTDLL.VBP, adds a reference to the new ActiveX DLL created earlier. This ActiveX DLL appears as Royalty Service Component DLL. When the test form's project references the ActiveX DLL, the project is compiled as TESTDLL.EXE. The test form allows you to create an instance of the business object, run tests on the capability to retrieve and store information in the business object, and release the business object. The Timing class module provides timing methods to measure the execution speed of all tests.

Comments

Visual Basic has done a great job of simplifying the process for creating usable ActiveX objects. This project has allowed you to take the first step toward partitioning logic out of an application by taking you step-by-step through the process of generating an ActiveX DLL. The second part of the process is creating a client application capable of using the RoyaltySvc ActiveX DLL.

Now that you have completed this project, you can run a test to see how different execution times are for retrieving and storing information within the RoyaltySvc business object. Compare these times to the execution time from How-To 6.2. If your tests are similar to those shown in this book, then you will find only a slight decrease in execution time when using a DLL. Considering the benefits of using libraries of reusable code, it is exciting to consider what aspects of your current projects you can first partition into DLLs. Please note that if you want to use the ActiveX DLL on a different machine you will need to register the ActiveX DLL on that machine with the Regsvr32.exe utility.

COMPLEXITY
BEGINNING

6.4   How do I...
Encapsulate business rules into an out-of-process server (ActiveX EXE)?

COMPATIBILITY: VB 5 AND 6

Problem

Many business functions change continuously. Each time they change, I must rewrite a portion of code in every application. I decided to move these functions to an ActiveX DLL, but I still must deploy the changes to every desktop. I want to centralize these functions on a server where every application could use them, but I can't use Microsoft Transaction Server. I know that I must create an out-of-process server (ActiveX EXE). How do I create an ActiveX EXE?

Technique

Code that changes on a regular basis is a good candidate for partitioning into an out-of-process server that can then be deployed on a remote machine. But before you can remotely deploy a business object, you must compile your business object as an ActiveX EXE. ActiveX DLLs are in-process servers, which means that they operate within the client application's process space. Because processes cannot span to a remote machine, a DLL could not be used on a remote machine; it must be on the local machine. This prevents it from being deployed centrally for all to use. Visual Basic allows you to take the same code that you used to generate an ActiveX DLL and recompile it as an ActiveX EXE without changing any code.

You can work around this problem by deploying the DLL on a server together with an ActiveX EXE that references it. In this case, the client machines will be calling the ActiveX EXE, which makes the calls on their behalf to the ActiveX DLL that would be running in its memory space on the server.

Steps

Open and run TESTEXE.VBP. The running program appears as shown in Figure 6.9.

Select the Get Object button first and then select the Test Property Gets and Test Property Lets buttons to retrieve and store information in the RoyaltySvc business object. Notice the difference in values between the normal dot operation methods and the parameterized methods that reduce calls between the client and server. The optimized methods provide significant savings in execution speed.

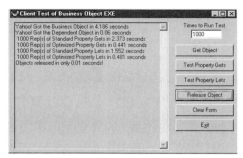

Figure 6.9 The client test form
running tests against the business
object ActiveX EXE

If you have worked through the earlier How-To's, you will see that the
timings on this out-of-process server are significantly slower than the same
operations against a DLL. The difference in execution time can range from 10
times slower to 100 times slower. This is important to understand when
deciding what will run locally and what should run on a centralized server. If
you don't have the luxury of using MTS, then read on. Crafting your business
objects to optimize performance for running remotely is critical if centralized
business services is your goal. The first step to deploying a business object you
create is to generate an out-of-process server that can run locally on the client
machine. To generate an ActiveX EXE, complete the following steps:

1. Create a new directory, copy in project **ROYDLL.VBP** from How-To 6.3, and
rename it **ROYEXE.VBP**. Rename the **.VBW** file **ROYEXE.VBW**.

2. After you compile this project as an ActiveX EXE, you can activate it using
two methods: standalone and ActiveX automation. Standalone means that
the out-of-process server is being started directly and not being called by
some other application. The following code checks the start mode of the
ActiveX EXE and displays the test form when the ActiveX EXE is started
directly by the user (standalone) and not by another application (ActiveX
server). This is very powerful. Consider that Excel and Word operate
similarly. To activate this feature, uncomment the following lines of code
that exist in the **GENERAL.BAS** file:

```
If App.StartMode = vbSModeStandalone Then

    frmTestClient.Show vbModal

End If
```

3. Choose Tools, Options from the menu and select the Project tab. Clear the
compatible ActiveX Server field and change the **Description** property to
Royalty Service Component EXE.

4. Select the Components tab and check the Remote Server Files check box. This tells Visual Basic to generate three files when you compile: EXE, VBR, and TLB. These files are needed for deploying the ActiveX EXE on a remote server.

5. Open the `Server` class module and press the F4 key to show the property sheet. Change instancing to `3-SingleUse`. This can be set as either Single Use or Multi-Use. Single Use means that each time a client requests this business object, a new instance and new process will be started on the machine where the ActiveX EXE resides. Multi-Use means that only one instance of the ActiveX EXE will run on the machine where it resides. Each request for services from this ActiveX EXE will be handled by the same instance of this business object. For multiple users of the same business object for this project, you want Single Use, which creates a new instance of the ActiveX EXE server for each client requesting services.

6. Choose File, Make ROYEXE File from the menu. When the Make EXE File dialog box appears, the filename should be set to `ROYEXE.EXE`. Change the application title to Royalty Service EXE. Check Auto Increment to activate version numbers. Click OK.

7. Generate the Executable. Notice that three files were generated (EXE, VBR, and TLB). These files are necessary for remote deployment of this object.

8. After the project has been compiled, choose Project, RoyaltySvc Properties from the menu and select the Component tab. Notice that the just-compiled EXE, `ROYEXE.EXE`, is in the Version Compatibility box. This is important because it safeguards backward compatibility of the project and also prevents Visual Basic from generating a different ID for this project each time it is compiled.

9. Create a new directory for the client test form. Copy files into the new directory from the TESTDLL Visual Basic project created in How-To 6.3. You should have five files: `TESTDLL.VBP`, `TESTDLL.VBW`, `TESTFORM.FRM`, `TESTFORM.FRX`, and `TIMING.CLS`.

10. Rename `TESTDLL.VBP` to `TESTEXE.VBP` and `TESTDLL.VBW` to `TESTEXE.VBW`. Open `TESTEXE.VBP`.

11. Choose Project, References from the menu and uncheck Royalty Service Component DLL. Page down through the reference list and place a check next to Royalty Service Component EXE. Click OK to save these changes to your project references.

12. Open `frmTestClient` form and change the caption property to read Client Test of RoyaltySvc EXE.

13. Choose File, Make EXE File. The name that appears is Make TestDLL.EXE. This will be changed.

14. Enter the filename, `TESTEXE.EXE`.

15. Select the Options button and set the `Title` property to `TESTEXE`. Click OK.

16. Generate an executable.

17. Run `TESTEXE.EXE`. This is the same test form used to test your project in How-To 6.2 and How-To 6.3. Select each button on the form in order from top to bottom. Start with the Get Object button, which tells you whether your test form was able to create an instance of the `RoyaltySvc` business object. Remember that this is an out-of-process server, which means that the `RoyaltySvc` business object must load in its own process space. This takes time. The test form displays just how much time it takes. The Test Property Gets and Test Property Lets buttons run tests to exercise the capability to retrieve and write properties to the `RoyaltySvc` business object. The Release Object button releases the `RoyaltySvc` business object so that it unloads from memory. Each of these actions provides visible feedback within the test form's display text box.

How It Works

Creating an out-of-process server (ActiveX EXE) requires that you have at least one class module with its `Public` property set to `True` and a `Creatable` property set to either `Multi-Use` or `Single Use`. Setting a class's `Public` property to `True` tells Visual Basic that you want other applications to be able to see and use the class's publicly declared properties and methods. Visual Basic takes the initiative and on compiling an ActiveX EXE, Visual Basic makes the appropriate Registry entries so that ActiveX-aware applications can use your newly compiled business object. The `Creatable` property of the class affects how the business object is loaded when a client needs to use the services provided by your business object. Multi-Use means that a single instance of the business object is loaded and multiple clients can use this single instance at one time. Setting a class to creatable `Single Use` means that each client needing the business object will have a separate copy loaded just for them. In this How-To, the `SERVER.CLS` has a `Public` property set to `True` and is configured as creatable `Single Use`.

After you have created `ROYEXE.EXE`, you can use it from any ActiveX aware application. In this How-To, the client test form used in How-To 6.3 is modified to reference the new out-of-process server (ActiveX EXE). This is done by opening the reference list for the test form in Visual Basic, deselecting Royalty Service Component DLL, and selecting Royalty Service Component EXE instead. All the code used by the test form to work with the `RoyaltySvc` business object remains untouched. Switching from a DLL to an EXE does not change how your client application refers to the business object. This is done transparently. This is an important point to understand. No changes to your client application's code need to be made to accommodate converting an ActiveX DLL to an ActiveX

EXE. How-To 6.5 explains how to move your out-of-process server to a remote machine.

One change was made to the **ROYEXE.VBP** project before it was compiled. The following code was added to the **GENERAL.BAS** file within the **Sub   MAIN** procedure:

```
If App.StartMode = vbSModeStandalone Then

    frmTestClient.Show vbModal

End If
```

This code checks the start mode of the ActiveX EXE and displays the test form when the ActiveX EXE is started directly by the user (standalone). The capability to know how the program was started, either by direct execution or an ActiveX call, allows you to respond differently to each scenario. This is exactly what you experience with applications such as Excel and Word. If you execute either of these applications, you are presented with the standard interface, but, if you control them through ActiveX, this is not the case. This code change was not required to create an ActiveX EXE but provides a powerful enhancement to the project.

Beware of the missing reference error. As you add and remove ActiveX servers from your Registry or recompile them with different class IDs, you might encounter a missing reference problem as shown in Figure 6.10.

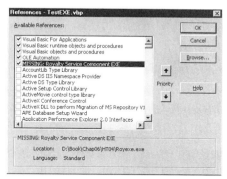

Figure 6.10 Missing reference in the
TESTEXE.VBP project

To fix this missing reference, you must deselect the reference that is missing and scan the reference list for the properly registered Royalty Service Component EXE and select it. Now your reference to the business object is repaired.

Comments

There simply is no easier way for creating out-of-process servers. This is not to say that making business objects is easy—it's not. Because the goal is reuse, it is critical that you allocate enough time to properly design these service objects. Fortunately, after you have taken all the time to design and code your business object, Visual Basic makes it a pleasure to compile and use.

Generating an out-of-process server is the first major step in deploying your business object remotely. How-To 6.5 takes you the rest of the way. Pay special attention to the performance of your object's every step made toward remote deployment. By running the client test applications, you can examine the execution times for both standard and optimized methods of retrieving and storing information in your business object. The more you understand what to expect, the more prepared you will be to handle the mechanics of coding for this new opportunity.

COMPLEXITY
BEGINNING

6.5 How do I...
Move my business object to a remote server?

COMPATIBILITY: VB 5 AND 6

Problem

I have a business object that needs to be used by many user workstations. How do I get it to run on its own server and allow everyone to use it?

Technique

Visual Basic automatically adds your ActiveX server application to the Registry of your machine each time you compile it. A new class ID is generated and references are placed in the Registry. The real question is what does it take to get your business server object to run on a remote machine as well as a client machine that has never used Visual Basic before. Visual Basic comes with an automated setup process to install your ActiveX business objects easily to any Windows NT, Windows 95, or Windows 98 system.

Steps

Open and run `TESTEXE.VBP`. The running program appears. Click the Get Object button first and then click the Test Property Gets and Test Property Lets buttons to retrieve and store information in the `RoyaltySvc` business object. Notice the difference in values between the normal dot operation methods and the bulk methods that reduce calls between the client and server. The optimized methods provide dramatic savings in execution speed. Compare the times generated using the remotely deployed business object with the times generated against a DLL. Notice that the optimized methods have a much greater impact when working with remotely deployed business objects.

The process of deploying a business object remotely can be a bit overwhelming if it doesn't work the first time. Therefore, this How-To outlines two methods for deploying your business objects. The first method uses the automated Package and Deployment Wizard that comes with Visual Basic. The second method is a manual method using step-by-step implementation techniques to catch and solve problems when they occur. First try the automatic process. If this doesn't work, then use the manual method.

Automatic Installation

1. Create a subdirectory. Name this directory **3-5Setup**.

2. Start the Visual Basic Package and Deployment Wizard, which you can find in your Visual Basic Program Group (see Figure 6.11).

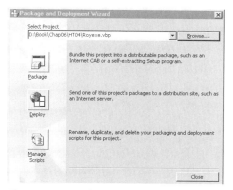

Figure 6.11 The Visual Basic Package and Deployment Wizard preparing to create a setup for the sample program

3. Specify the project file used to create the business object you are going to deploy. In this case, the business object is **ROYEXE.EXE** and was generated using **ROYEXE.VBP**. DO NOT select the Rebuild the Project's EXE File option unless you are sure that you have configured the project to reference the original ActiveX server for compatibility. To create an ActiveX server reference for your project, you need to open **ROYEXE.VBP** and choose Tools, Options from the menu; then select the Project tab and enter **ROYEXE.EXE** in the Compatible ActiveX Server field. Otherwise, a new class ID is generated each time the project is compiled.

4. The Package and Deployment Wizard processes the .VBP file and asks you where you want to place the setup files. Specify the new subdirectory you created earlier. If you have not created it yet, you can specify a new directory now, and it will create it for you. Select Directory and enter C:\Chapter7\4\Setup, for example; then click Next to continue.

5. The Package and Deployment Wizard attempts to find any ActiveX servers used by your application. Because this is the ActiveX server itself, none appear on the list. This server could very possibly reference other ActiveX servers or DLLs, in which case they would appear here. Click Next to continue.

6. You now have to select a deployment model. Select Install as ActiveX Automation Shared Component. You also need to check the box for Yes, Install Remote ActiveX Automation Server Components if this is the first time you are installing this on the remote machine. This refers to the Remote Automation Connection Manager and the Automation Manager, which provide support for Remote Automation. Refer to Chapter 1, "Client/Server Basics," for an overview of these tools.

7. At this point, you are presented with a list of the files that the Package and Deployment Wizard has determined are needed. You can save the template created by this process to reduce the time needed to create setup disks in the future. After you are done, click Finish to complete the process.

8. Now that the setup files are ready, copy them to a network server, if available, so that the setup can be executed from all workstations where you must install support for the remotely deployed business object.

9. To complete the deployment, go to each machine and run the setup program from the network location containing the setup files. Installation is automatic. You do, however, need to point the locally registered ActiveX server to the centralized remote location.

NOTE

The setup program generated by the wizard also provides a way to uninstall your component from the machine using ST5UNST.EXE. The uninstall command line refers to a log file created during setup.

Manual Installation

1. The following files are required on the server. Place them in a directory found in the path or place them in the System32 directory on an NT machine or the System directory of a Windows 95 machine. This is only required if you have never installed a Visual Basic application on the

machine or if you are preparing the machine as a home for remote
business objects (see Table 6.12).

Table 6.12 Files to install on your server to run a remote business
object

FILENAME	DESCRIPTION
CLIREG32.EXE	Registration program for Remote Automation on a client
AUTPRX32.DLL	Automation Proxy
AUTMGR32.EXE	Automation Manager
RACREG32.DLL	Support DLL for the Remote Automation Connection Manager
RACMGR32.EXE	Remote Automation Connection Manager

2. Unregister your server EXE from both the client and server machines so
that you have a clean start. Use the EXE name followed by /UNREGSERVER
to unregister it from the Registry. If you receive an error while trying to
unregister the business object, you might have a corrupt Registry. If this is
the case, you need to use regedit32.exe to find the problem. Try
searching for all Registry entries that contain the path to your business
object. In this case, it would be ROYEXE.EXE. After you find them, delete
the key that refers to your business object and start over. Do this on both
the local and remote machines. Remember, all machines must be able to
run VB applications.

3. Now register your business object again. From the command line execute
ROYEXE.EXE /REGSERVER. Test the component locally. Start up the
TESTEXE.EXE program and verify that it can reference the business object.
If you have a problem at this point, there is a problem with the test app's
capability to reference the object via the Registry. Try opening the test
application in Visual Basic and verifying that it contains a valid reference
to the ActiveX server you are trying to deploy. If the reference is missing,
then deselect it and find the current reference listing of the ROYEXE
business object. Select it and recompile your test application.

4. Start the Remote Automation Connection Manager (RACMGR32.EXE) on the
machine that will house the business object. RACMGR32.EXE can be found
in the VB/clisvr directory and needs to be installed along with
AUTMGR32.EXE and CMPMGR32.EXE in the directory, which is part of the
path on the server machine, to support Remote Automation and the
marshaling of requests to business objects. When you can start the Remote
Automation Connection Manager on the server, highlight the
RoyaltySvc.Server entry. Click the Client Access tab and select Allow All
Remote Creates. This eliminates security issues as a possible connection
problem. This setting should be changed after the components are

installed successfully. Start the Automation Manager (`AUTMGR32.EXE`). The server is now ready to receive requests.

5. You have successfully installed and tested the ActiveX server locally on both the client and server workstations. All that is left is to point the client machine object reference to the server machine's copy of the business object. Start the Remote Automation Connection Manager on the client machine (see Figure 6.12).

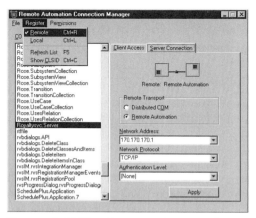

Figure 6.12 The Remote Automation Connection Manager configured to use a remote ActiveX server

6. Highlight the RoyaltySvc.Server ActiveX Class in the Remote Automation Connection Manager. Set the Network Address to the server machine's name. Set the Network Protocol to the appropriate protocol for your network. Set the Authentication Level to No Authentication for now. After the business object has been set up successfully, you can change this option to secure your system. For now, selecting No Authentication allows you to eliminate one possible reason why a remote automation server might not be accessible. Click the Apply button. Choose Register, Remote from the menu. After this is done, the remote symbol appears on the Server Connection tab associated with the `RoyaltySvc.Server` class.

7. Now that everything is configured properly, or so we hope, start the test application `TESTEXE.EXE`. Because you have verified that this test program worked successfully against the `ROYEXE.EXE` running on the local machine, it should now connect successfully to the `ROYEXE.EXE` located on the server workstation you specified in the Remote Automation Connection Manager. If you encounter an error, you are probably having a network connection problem. Verify that you have a good connection between the machines. Try to access a shared directory on the server machine from the client and then try to access the client from the server. If the problem persists, contact your network administrator for help.

How It Works

The key to deploying a business server object remotely is completely controlled by the Registry and the Automation Manager. The Registry provides the locally run client and server applications with a common address, whereas the Remote Automation Connection Manager is used to set overall security settings and modify entries in the Registry so that calls to an ActiveX server know where to go. The beauty of this is that a locally running application doesn't have any idea when it asks for an ActiveX object how it gets it. In Figure 6.13, you can see what the process path for a request looks like on both a single machine as well as with a remote machine involved.

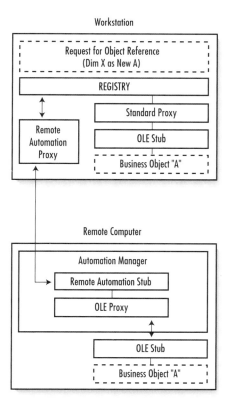

Figure 6.13 The remote automation communication process

The Automation Manager contains both a proxy and a stub that allow the Automation Manager to marshal requests and hand them to the regular ActiveX stub that unmarshals the information as it moves from the client to the server. A proxy is an object that packages parameters for a specific interface with the purpose of relaying a remote method call. The *proxy* is a DLL and runs in the process of the application sending a request. A stub operates in the process of the receiving application. The *stub* application is a DLL that unpackages the parameters from the proxy and actually makes the method call to the component on the remote machine. *Marshaling* refers to the process that allows the packaged parameters to be transmitted across process boundaries. The proxy/stub and marshaling process are all part of the DCOM architecture.

On the trip back from the remote component, the ActiveX stub hands the marshaled values back to the Automation Manager, which then transmits them to the Remote Automation proxy, which is responsible for unmarshaling the information to the ActiveX client. The bottom line here is that the Automation Manager, along with the Registry, seamlessly allows a client application to use your business object without changing a line of code in your application. It doesn't matter whether you are working with an ActiveX DLL on the local machine or an ActiveX EXE deployed on an NT Server across the network or Internet.

The Setup Wizard and the setup program it generates automate much of the task of installing the right pieces and making the right entries in the Registry of each machine. But when this goes awry, you can follow a manual process for stepping through the installation and deployment process. A manual installation might take a little longer initially, but should a problem occur, you are in a good position to identify what is going on.

Comments

Many factors are involved in the deployment of ActiveX servers to remote machines. Visual Basic's implementation is by far the easiest to use. Problems might occur but are resolvable if the process is taken in controlled steps.

COMPLEXITY
ADVANCED

6.6 How do I...
Pass variant arrays to and from a business object?

COMPATIBILITY: VB 5 AND 6

Problem

Deploying my business object as a Remote ActiveX object has killed performance. Things that took one second now take 10 to 100 times longer to execute. How can I improve the performance?

Technique

The problem is that remotely deploying a business object requires that you deal with the limitation of remote procedure call (RPC) access. Making an RPC requires a significant amount of overhead to establish and execute. The first step is to deal with the speed issues related to instantiating the object. The second step is to architect batch methods of setting and getting data to and from your object. The third step is to eliminate any values passed by reference.

Steps

Part of implementing this How-To is to create a situation that would take full advantage of the techniques that will be shown. You add a collection to the business object developed in earlier How-To's. The collection object creates a situation where a greater amount of data must be passed between the client and the server. This sets up a situation where passing variant arrays can be evaluated clearly against other standard methods.

Open and run project **COLLEXE.VBP**. The running program appears as shown in Figure 6.14.

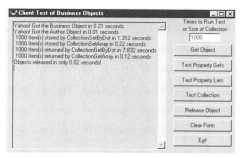

Figure 6.14 Client test of variant contained within a remotely deployed business object

First you need to click the Get Object button. Now click the Test Collection button. Four result lines are returned with timings. Two are for standard dot operation syntax methods; the other two are optimized methods that pass variant arrays to reduce the number of calls. Note that the text box now accepts a value to set how many objects to add to the collection. Try 50 and work your way up. See how size affects the difference in the various methods.

Now open and run the project **TESTCOLL.VBP**. The last project was operating against internal business objects. This project references the out-of-process server. Make sure that it is registered properly on your machine. Refer to How-To 6.5 if you need help. As you retry the Test Collection button, you see a dramatic difference. Now the variant array methods drastically outperform the standard dot operation methods. If you move the ActiveX server to a remote machine, this only serves to reinforce the value of the optimized methods. Complete the following steps to create this project:

1. Start by copying all files from How-To 6.4 into a new directory.

2. Rename the .VBP file from ROYEXE.VBP to COLLEXE.VBP. Rename the .VBW file from ROYEXE.VBW to COLLEXE.VBW.

3. Open the project.

4. Make the following changes to the GENERAL.BAS file. Comment out the following code. Do not remove this code completely because you will need to uncomment these lines that show the test form if you ever work on this object and want to test the functionality with the Visual Basic environment. You must remove this code to prevent the test form that is internal to the project from loading when the ActiveX DLL is used by a client.

```
'If App.StartMode = vbSModeStandalone Then
'    frmTestClient.Show vbModal
'End If.
```

5. Set the following options for the project by choosing Project, RoyaltySvc Properties from the menu. You can see the Project Properties tab containing the primary options you need to set for an ActiveX server project. Set the properties listed in Table 6.13 for this project.

Table 6.13   The project's property settings

OBJECT	PROPERTY	SETTING
General tab	Project Type	ActiveX DLL
	Startup Object	Sub Main
	Project Name	"Royaltysvc"
	Project Description	"Royalty Service Component DLL"
Component tab	Project Compatibility	checked
	Start Mode	ActiveX Component

6. Set the following properties for the Server class and the Author class (see Tables 6.14 and 6.15).

Table 6.14 Class option settings for Server

OPTION	SETTING
Name	Server
DataBindingBehavior	0 - vbNone
DataSourceBehavior	0 - vbNone
Instancing	5 - MultiUse
MTSTransactionMode	0 - NotAnMTSObject
Persistable	0 - NotPersistable

Table 6.15 Class option settings for Author

OPTION	SETTING
Name	Author
DataBindingBehavior	0 - vbNone
DataSourceBehavior	0 - vbNone
Instancing	2 - PublicNotCreatable
MTSTransactionMode	0 - NotAnMTSObject
Persistable	0 - NotPersistable

7. Choose Project, RoyaltySvc Properties from the menu and select the General tab settings. Change the property description field to Royalty Service Component EXE w/COLL.

8. Add these constants to the Declarations area of the GENERAL.BAS file. These are positional constants used for the CollectionGet and CollectionSet arrays. Because these constants are global, they can be seen by the client application that uses this component. This allows you to make changes to the array used to pass data and have the client piece automatically adjust.

```
Global Const royMaxColumns = 5
Global Const royTitlePosition = 1
Global Const royTitleIdPosition = 2
Global Const royRoyaltyPosition = 3
Global Const royBookPricePosition = 4
Global Const royQtySoldPosition = 5
```

9. Add the following method to the AUTHOR.CLS to provide a client with access to the Royalties class. The Royalties method creates a new instance of the Royalties class module and passes a reference back to the client.

```
Public Function Royalties() As Royalties

    Set Royalties = New Royalties

End Function
```

10. Add a new class module to the ROYCOLL.VBP project. Name the class ROYALTIES.CLS. Set the properties according to Table 6.16.

Table 6.16   Class option settings for Royalties

OPTION	SETTING
Name	Royalties
DataBindingBehavior	0 - vbNone
DataSourceBehavior	0 - vbNone
Instancing	2 - PublicNotCreatable
MTSTransactionMode	0 - NotAnMTSObject
Persistable	0 - NotPersistable

11. The Royalties class module provides a home for a collection object called m_Royalties. This collection holds detailed information on the authors' books and royalties. You could simply make the collection public to allow external applications to access the collection directly, but this would give you no control over how the collection is used. You would be unable to validate the type of information stored in the collection as well. By creating a class as a wrapper to the collection, you can create properties and methods to give controlled access to the collection. Add the following code to the General Declarations of the Royalties class module to dimension the private collection object that will hold the authors' detail information:

```
Option Explicit

'information about the author

'Declare the private collection that will hold royalty
'information.
Private m_Royalties As New Collection
```

12. Add the following four procedures to provide a public interface to the collection object that will contain author royalty information. Remember that a collection has four basic methods: Count, Item, Remove, and Add. The Count method provides you with the number of objects in the collection. The Item method allows you to access a particular object in the collection based on a key value. The Remove method allows you to remove an object from the collection, and the Add method allows you to add new objects (information) to the collection. You can provide a controlled public interface to the collection's four basic methods by adding the following methods to ROYALTIES.CLS:

```
Public Function Count() As Variant
    Count = m_Royalties.Count
End Function

Public Function Item(Key As Variant) As Royalty
    Set Item = m_Royalties.Item(Key)
End Function

Public Sub Remove(Key As Variant)
    m_Royalties.Remove Key
End Sub

Public Function Add(Optional Title As Variant, _
                Optional TitleId As Variant, _
                Optional Royalty As Variant, _
                Optional BookPrice As Variant, _
                Optional QtySold As Variant) As Object
    Dim NewRoyalty As Royalty
    Set NewRoyalty = New Royalty

    With NewRoyalty
            If IsMissing(Title) = False Then
            ➡.Title = Title
            If IsMissing(TitleId) = False Then
            ➡.TitleId = TitleId
            If IsMissing(Royalty) = False Then
            ➡.Royalty = Royalty
            If IsMissing(BookPrice) = False Then
            ➡.BookPrice = BookPrice
            If IsMissing(QtySold) = False Then
            ➡.QtySold = QtySold
    End With
    m_Royalties.Add NewRoyalty
    Set Add = NewRoyalty
End Function
```

13. Add the following CollectionSet method to ROYALTIES.CLS to set all values in a collection in a single pass. This method uses a variant array to pass information back and forth between the client and the ActiveX server. This method reduces the number of calls, thus accelerating the process of setting collection values.

```
Public Function CollectionSet(vRoyaltyArray As Variant)
    Dim ixRoyalty As Integer
    'erase old collection
    Do Until Me.Count = 0
        Me.Remove 1
    Loop
    'remember that me refers to the Royalties Class Object
    'therefore Me.Add executes the Add method contained in this
    'class to add values to the collection.
```

continued on next page

continued from previous page

```
    Do
        ixRoyalty = ixRoyalty + 1
        'The add method below is using named parameters
        'for greater flexibility.
        Me.Add Title:=(vRoyaltyArray(royTitlePosition, _
        ➥ixRoyalty)), _
            TitleId:=(vRoyaltyArray(royTitleIdPosition, _
            ➥ixRoyalty)), _
            Royalty:=(vRoyaltyArray(royRoyaltyPosition, _
            ➥ixRoyalty)), _
            BookPrice:=(vRoyaltyArray(royBookPricePosition, _
            ➥ixRoyalty)), _
            QtySold:=(vRoyaltyArray(royQtySoldPosition, _
            ➥ixRoyalty))
    Loop Until ixRoyalty >= UBound(vRoyaltyArray, 2)
End Function
```

14. Add the following `CollectionGet` method to `ROYALTIES.CLS` to get all
values in a collection in a single pass. This method uses a variant array to
pass information back and forth between the client and the ActiveX server.
This method reduces the number of calls, thus accelerating the process of
retrieving collection values.

```
Public Function CollectionGet() As Variant
    Dim vRoyaltyArray As Variant
    Dim ixRoyalty As Integer
    'Dimension variant variables to hold data that will be
    'returned using the PropertyGet method of the Royalty Class.
    Dim Title As Variant
    Dim TitleId As Variant
    Dim Royalty As Variant
    Dim BookPrice As Variant
    Dim QtySold As Variant
    'ReDimension the Variant as an Array. RoyMaxColumns
    ReDim vRoyaltyArray(1 To royMaxColumns, 1 To Me.Count)
    Do
        ixRoyalty = ixRoyalty + 1
        Me.Item(ixRoyalty).PropertyGet Title:=Title, _
                                        TitleId:=TitleId, _
                                        Royalty:=Royalty, _
                                        BookPrice:=BookPrice, _
                                        QtySold:=QtySold
        vRoyaltyArray(royTitlePosition, ixRoyalty) = Title
        vRoyaltyArray(royTitleIdPosition, ixRoyalty) = TitleId
        vRoyaltyArray(royRoyaltyPosition, ixRoyalty) = Royalty
        vRoyaltyArray(royBookPricePosition, ixRoyalty) =
        ➥BookPrice
        vRoyaltyArray(royQtySoldPosition, ixRoyalty) = QtySold
    Loop Until ixRoyalty >= Me.Count
    'Pass the variant array back to the client application.
    CollectionGet = vRoyaltyArray
End Function
```

15. Add a new class module to the ROYCOLL.VBP project. Name the class ROYALTY.CLS. Set the properties according to Table 6.17.

Table 6.17 Class option settings for Royalty

OPTION	SETTING
Name	Royalty
DataBindingBehavior	0 - vbNone
DataSourceBehavior	0 - vbNone
Instancing	2 - PublicNotCreatable
MTSTransactionMode	0 - NotAnMTSObject
Persistable	0 - NotPersistable

16. The Royalty class module provides the structure for the objects that will populate the private collection object that exists within the Royalties class module. The Royalty class resembles a database record. The Royalty class holds an author's Title (book name), Title ID (ISBN), royalty amount, book price, and quantity sold. Add the following code to the General Declarations of the Royalty class module to dimension the private variables needed to hold the author's detailed information:

```
Option Explicit
'dim the private variables that will hold royalty information.
Private m_Title As String
Private m_TitleId As Long
Private m_Royalty As Currency
Private m_BookPrice As Currency
Private m_QtySold As Long
```

17. To use this object to house an author's detailed information, you must be able to read and write the properties of the class. Add the following property Gets and Lets to ROYALTY.CLS to implement the capability to read and write values to this class:

```
Public Property Get Title() As String
    Title = m_Title
End Property

Public Property Let Title(NewTitle As String)
    m_Title = NewTitle
End Property

Public Property Get TitleId() As Long
    TitleId = m_TitleId
End Property

Public Property Let TitleId(NewTitleId As Long)
    m_TitleId = NewTitleId
End Property
```

continued on next page

continued from previous page

```
Public Property Get BookPrice() As Currency
    BookPrice = m_BookPrice
End Property

Public Property Let BookPrice(NewBookPrice As Currency)
    m_BookPrice = NewBookPrice
End Property

Public Property Get QtySold() As Long
    QtySold = m_QtySold
End Property

Public Property Let QtySold(NewQtySold As Long)
    m_QtySold = NewQtySold
End Property

Public Property Get Royalty() As Currency
    Royalty = m_Royalty
End Property

Public Property Let Royalty(NewRoyalty As Currency)
    m_Royalty = NewRoyalty
End Property
```

18. This project includes the use of variant arrays and bulk read and write
methods to improve the performance of remote ActiveX servers. The
`PropertyGet` method is a bulk read method that is used by the `Royalties`
class to populate a variant array sent back to the client application. This
method helps to reduce the number of calls being made and increases
execution speed for the remotely deployed business object.

```
Public Sub PropertyGet(Optional Title As Variant, _
                       Optional TitleId As Variant, _
                       Optional Royalty As Variant, _
                       Optional BookPrice As Variant, _
                       Optional QtySold As Variant)
    If IsMissing(Title) = False Then
        Title = m_Title
    End If
    If IsMissing(TitleId) = False Then
        TitleId = m_TitleId
    End If
    If IsMissing(Royalty) = False Then
        Royalty = m_Royalty
    End If
    If IsMissing(BookPrice) = False Then
        BookPrice = m_BookPrice
    End If
    If IsMissing(QtySold) = False Then
        QtySold = m_QtySold
    End If
End Sub
```

19. Compile `ROYCOLL.VBP` by choosing File, Make ROYCOLL.EXE from the menu. Generate an executable. This automatically installs the ActiveX server in your Registry. For information on deploying this ActiveX automation server remotely, refer to How-To 6.5.

20. After the project has been compiled, choose Project, RoyaltySvc Properties from the menu. Select the Component tab and select Project Compatibility. Then enter the just-compiled EXE, `ROYCOLL.EXE`, in the field provided for the Compatible ActiveX Server. This is important because it safeguards backward compatibility of the project and also prevents Visual Basic from generating a different ID for this project each time it is compiled.

21. Create a new directory for the client test form. Copy files into the new directory from the TESTEXE Visual Basic project created in How-To 6.4. You should have five files: `TESTEXE.VBP`, `TESTEXE.VBW`, `TESTFORM.FRM`, `TESTFORM.FRX`, and `TIMING.CLS`.

22. Rename `TESTEXE.VBP` as `TESTCOLL.VBP` and `TESTEXE.VBW` as `TESTCOLL.VBW`. Open `TESTCOLL.VBP`.

23. Choose Project, References from the menu and uncheck Royalty Service Component EXE. Page down through the reference list and place a check mark next to Royalty Service Component EXE w/COLL. Click OK to save these changes to your project references (see Figure 6.15).

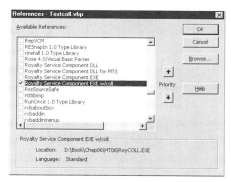

Figure 6.15 Setting references for the Client test form

24. Open the `frmTestClient` form and change the `Caption` property to read Client Test of RoyaltySvc EXE w/COLL.

25. You need to modify the Client test form to test the new collection and classes modules you have added to this project. Add the following controls and set the following properties found in Table 6.18. Refer to

Figure 6.14 earlier in this How-To for the placement of the Test Collection button and the new labels.

Table 6.18 `frmTestClient` form enhancements

OBJECT	PROPERTY	SETTING
CommandButton	Name	cmdTestCollection
	Caption	"Test Collection"
Label	Name	Label1
	Caption	"Times to Run Test"
Label	Name	Label2
	Caption	"or Size of Collection"

26. Dimension a variable for the new **Royalties** class module that is now part of the business object. You can do this by adding the following code to the General Declarations section of the **frmTestClient** form:

```
Dim oRoyalties As Royalties
```

27. Add the following code to the **cmdTestCollections Click** event to execute a test of the new **Royalties** class interface by reading and writing information to and from the **Royalties** class:

```
Private Sub cmdTestCollection_Click()
    Dim i As Integer
    Dim iReps As Integer

On Error GoTo cmdTestCollectionError
    'here you will get a reference to the royalties object
    Set oRoyalties = oAuthor.Royalties

    'Make sure you have an object reference before you start
    If oRoyalties Is Nothing Then
        txtDisplay.Text = txtDisplay.Text _
                    & "No reference to Royalties Collection
                    ➥Object found.' _
                    & vbCrLf
        Exit Sub
    End If

    '************************************************************
    'set collection data using dot operations               '
    '************************************************************
    'run test
        CollectionSetByDot

    '************************************************************
    'set collection data using variant array                '
    '************************************************************
    'run test
        CollectionSetArray
```

```
'***********************************************************
'get collection data using dot operations '
'***********************************************************
'run test
    CollectionGetByDot

'***********************************************************
'get collection data using variant array                 '
'***********************************************************
'run test
    CollectionGetArray

'release the royalties object
Set oRoyalties = Nothing

Exit Sub

'simple error handler to display error and proceed on
cmdTestCollectionError:
    MsgBox Err.Number & " " & Err.Description
    Resume Next

End Sub
```

28. Add the `CollectionGetByDot` procedure to the `frmTestClient` form. This procedure retrieves all the author's royalty information from the **Royalties** collection, which exists inside the **Royalties** class module, by fetching each line individually using an object reference and a dot command.

```
Private Sub CollectionGetByDot()
    Dim vTitle As Variant
    Dim lTitleId As Long
    Dim cRoyalty As Currency
    Dim cBookPrice As Currency
    Dim lQtySold As Long
    Dim ixRoyaltyCount As Variant

    'you are not using the repetitions field you are simply
    'retrieving the 'rows that are in the royalties collection.

    'start timing this event
    oTiming.Start

    'run test
    For ixRoyaltyCount = 1 To oRoyalties.Count

        'grab a reference to the royalty item you are going
        'to set. Retrieve the collection information one royalty
        'line at a time.
        With oRoyalties.Item(ixRoyaltyCount)
            vTitle = .Title
            lTitleId = .TitleId
            cRoyalty = .Royalty
```

continued on next page

continued from previous page

```
                              cBookPrice = .BookPrice
                              lQtySold = .QtySold
                      End With

              Next

              'stop timing event
              oTiming.Finish

              'display the time taken to retrieve the properties using
              'standard dot operation gets.
              txtDisplay.Text = txtDisplay.Text _
                          & Str(ixRoyaltyCount - 1) _
                          & " Item(s) returned by CollectionGetByDot
                          ➥in " _
                          & oTiming.ElapsedTime _
                          & " seconds' & vbCrLf

      End Sub
```

29. Add the `CollectionSetByDot` procedure to the `frmTestClient` form. This
fills the `Royalties` collection with author royalty objects (records) equal
to the number specified on the test form. This is done by setting each
object in the `Royalties` collection individually using an object reference
and a dot command.

```
Private Sub CollectionSetByDot()
    Dim vTitle As Variant
    Dim vTitleId As Variant
    Dim vRoyalty As Variant
    Dim vBookPrice As Variant
    Dim vQtySold As Variant
    Dim iReps As Long
    Dim i As Long

    'make sure that you have a valid value for number
    'of repetitions for the tests.
    If txtTestReps.Text <> "" Then
        iReps = CInt(txtTestReps.Text)
    Else
        iReps = 1
    End If

    'start timing this event
    oTiming.Start

    '***********************************
    ' RUN TEST                         '
    '***********************************
    'erase old collection
    Do Until oRoyalties.Count = 0
        oRoyalties.Remove 1
    Loop

    'populate the collection one royalty line at a time.
```

```
For i = 1 To iReps

    vTitle = "VB4 Client/Server How-To'
    vTitleId = 1234
    vRoyalty = 500
    vBookPrice = 50.5
    vQtySold = 5000

    oRoyalties.Add Title:=vTitle, _
            TitleId:=vTitleId, _
            Royalty:=vRoyalty, _
        BookPrice:=vBookPrice, _
            QtySold:=vQtySold

Next

'stop timing event
oTiming.Finish

'display the time taken to retrieve the properties using
'standard dot operation gets.
txtDisplay.Text = txtDisplay.Text _
            & Str(iReps) _
            & " Item(s) stored by CollectionSetByDot
            ➥in " _
            & oTiming.ElapsedTime _
            & " seconds' & vbCrLf

End Sub
```

30. Get all royalty records from the **Royalty** collection, which exists inside your business object, by fetching a variant array of data and parsing it on the client side. To use this optimized retrieval method, add the following **CollectionGetArray** to the **frmTestClient** form:

```
Private Sub CollectionGetArray()

    Dim sTitle As String
    Dim lTitleId As Long
    Dim cRoyalty As Currency
    Dim cBookPrice As Currency
    Dim lQtySold As Long
    Dim ixRoyaltyRow As Long
    Dim iRowsInArray As Long
    Dim vRoyaltyArray As Variant

'start timing this event
    oTiming.Start

    'retrieve a variant array of data with all collection
    'information
    vRoyaltyArray = oRoyalties.CollectionGet

    'get the array*s dimensions. You could use the count
    'property but that would require another call which you
```

continued on next page

continued from previous page

```
                          'don*t want to make in order to optimize speed.
                          'Remember that the ubound function needs to know the array
                          'and the second set of dimensions that represent the number
                          'of actual rows to which the variant array was
                          'redimensioned. That is why you enter the number 2.
              iRowsInArray = UBound(vRoyaltyArray, 2)

                          'parse the variant array
                          For ixRoyaltyRow = 1 To iRowsInArray

                              'populate the collection one royalty line at a time.
                              sTitle = vRoyaltyArray(royTitlePosition, ixRoyaltyRow)
                              lTitleId = vRoyaltyArray(royTitleIdPosition,
                              ➥ixRoyaltyRow)
                              cRoyalty = vRoyaltyArray(royRoyaltyPosition,
                              ➥ixRoyaltyRow)
                              cBookPrice = vRoyaltyArray(royBookPricePosition,
                              ➥ixRoyaltyRow)
                              lQtySold = vRoyaltyArray(royQtySoldPosition,
                              ➥ixRoyaltyRow)

                          Next

                          'stop timing event
                          oTiming.Finish

                          'display the time taken to retrieve the properties using
                          'standard dot operation gets.
                          txtDisplay.Text = txtDisplay.Text _
                                          & Str(iRowsInArray) _
                                          & " Item(s) returned by CollectionGetArray
                                          ➥in " _
                                          & oTiming.ElapsedTime _
                                          & " seconds' & vbCrLf

              End Sub
```

31. Set all royalty records from the **Royalty** collection, which exists inside
your business object, by sending a variant array of data to the business
object. The business object then parses the variant array and applies the
updates. This is done by adding the **CollectionSetArray** procedure to
the **frmClientTest** form.

```
Private Sub CollectionSetArray()

    Dim vRoyaltyArray As Variant
    Dim ixRoyalties As Long
    Dim iReps As Long

    'make sure that you have a valid value for number of
    'repetitions for the tests.
    If txtTestReps.Text <> "" Then
        iReps = CInt(txtTestReps.Text)
    Else
        iReps = 1
```

```
        End If

        'start timing this event
        oTiming.Start

        'set up your variant array dimensions
        ReDim vRoyaltyArray(royMaxColumns, iReps) 'add order

        'run test
        For ixRoyalties = 1 To iReps

            'stuff values into the array. The constants below that
            'have the word position in them are global constants
            'found in global bas file. This allows us to centralize
            'information about the position of each value within
            'the array.
            vRoyaltyArray(royTitlePosition, ixRoyalties) =
            ➥"VB How-To'
            vRoyaltyArray(royTitleIdPosition, ixRoyalties) = 55555
            vRoyaltyArray(royRoyaltyPosition, ixRoyalties) = 5000
            vRoyaltyArray(royBookPricePosition, ixRoyalties) = 55.5
            vRoyaltyArray(royQtySoldPosition, ixRoyalties) = 500

        Next

        'now that the array is full send it.
        oRoyalties.CollectionSet vRoyaltyArray

        'stop timing event
        oTiming.Finish

        'display the time taken to send a variant array and
        'set properties in the business object.
        txtDisplay.Text = txtDisplay.Text _
                        & Str(iReps) _
                        & " Item(s) stored by CollectionSetArray
                        ➥in " _
                        & oTiming.ElapsedTime _
                        & " seconds' & vbCrLf

    End Sub
```

How It Works

Two lessons are implemented by this How-To. First, a collection was added to the business object creating a much richer feature set and interface. Second, you implemented methods that passed variant arrays to optimize speed.

Adding a collection allows you to store and retrieve detail-level information about the authors' royalties. The business object can now store information about each title, its sales, and the book's price. Two class modules are added to the project, **Royalties** and **Royalty**, to handle the collection object that stores royalty information about the authors. Both of these classes are implemented as dependent classes. That means that external clients cannot simply create these objects at will. They can be created only by calling a method in the **Author** object. The **Royalty** class stores the actual royalty information and is added to a private collection that is part of the **Royalties** class. The **Royalties** class serves as a shell or wrapper for the collection and provides methods such as **Count** that mirror the standard **Count** property of the collection. Because the client cannot directly manipulate the collection except through the methods and properties of the **Royalties** class, you have created a much more secure and hopefully stable business object (see Figure 6.16).

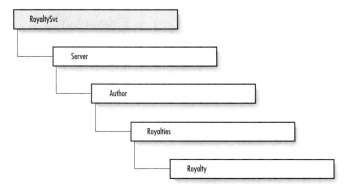

	Server	Author	Royalties	Royalty
Collections				
Member Objects	Author		Item	Parent
Properties	UserId	LastName	Count	TitleId
	Password	FirstName		Title
	Id	AuthorId		BookPrice
	Parent	StartDate		AuthorPerc
		EndDate		BookPerc
		RoyaltyTotal		QtySold
				BookRoyalty
Methods	Initialize	GetInfo	Add	
	Load		Remove	
Optimized Methods		PropertyGetAll	CollectinGetAll	PropertyGetAll
		PropertySetAll	CollectinSetAll	PropertySetAll

Figure 6.16 Properties and methods of the Royalty Service business object

In How-To 6.2, you saw how setting and getting properties in batches improves the performance of ActiveX server objects deployed as out-of-process servers. This was especially evident on remotely deployed ActiveX servers. The technique of passing individual parameters as part of a method, as demonstrated in **PropertyGetAll** and **PropertySetAll**, works in limited situations. When you start moving large amounts of data like those stored in a collection, you must use a new technique to pass information. The goal is still the same, to reduce the number of calls that need to be made. Note that you cannot pass user-defined types to remotely deployed business objects. This is a big limitation that cannot be circumvented without a great deal of effort. In this How-To you implemented the strategy of using a variant array to pass data to and from the server.

Although using variant arrays can be faster for remotely deployed business objects, it might not be better when working with ActiveX DLLs deployed locally. This is because the variant array is passed by value to the server. This passes a full copy of the data once to the server. Passing by reference, on the other hand, would have copied all the data to the server and then back again, thus doubling the work. This is not the case when passing values by reference locally. In a local scenario, passing a value by reference simply passes a pointer to the object. This is much faster than making a copy. So what does this mean? If you are working with a collection in an ActiveX DLL, you probably will want to pass values by reference, and you might not even want to implement an optimized method using variant arrays because the gains are minor until you deploy remotely. If you are deploying your business object remotely, these methods are critical to improving the usefulness of the business object.

To keep the focus clear, this How-To does not connect the data source to the business object. You can refer to Chapter 3, "Data Objects," for specifics on how to implement this aspect of the business object.

Comments

There are tricks to every situation. If you are creating in-process servers that run on the client's machine, then you will want to tailor your methods to optimize that situation. If, on the other hand, you are deploying your business object remotely, then you will want to include methods that pass parameters by value and package large amounts of data into variant arrays to **Set** and **Get** properties. You always need to include the standard **Get** and **Let** statements. After you have these done, you can proceed to add optimized methods as the situation dictates. Remember, ActiveX communication does not have to be slow. Methods like those demonstrated in this How-To dropped transfer times from numbers like 30 seconds to subsecond responses, depending on the situation. Try it out and see what you can eke out. This How-To has added a few more tricks to your remote bag.

COMPLEXITY
INTERMEDIATE

6.7 How do I...
Encapsulate business rules to run in Microsoft Transaction Server (MTS)?

COMPATIBILITY: VB 5 AND 6

Problem

I have created a number of components with functionality that the rest of my applications need access to. I have deployed them on a remote server, but they are slow and can't handle any serious load. I want to centralize these functions on a server where every application could use them, but the speed and security issues are killing me. I have access to Microsoft Transaction Server on an NT server. How do I create a component that can run in Microsoft Transaction Server?

Technique

Code that changes regularly is a good candidate for partitioning into components that can then be deployed on a remote machine. You have two options when you need to run a component remotely. You can compile your component as an ActiveX EXE and run it on a remote machine using OLE Automation, or you can compile it as an ActiveX DLL and deploy it on an NT machine using Microsoft Transaction Server. In this How-To, we will take the Business Object template and walk you through the steps to allow the component to run under MTS as well as tap into the other benefits MTS provides, such as transaction context.

Steps

Open and run TESTDLLMTS.VBP. The running program appears as shown in Figure 6.17.

You are seeing a client application referencing the business object in ROYDLLMTS.DLL running in MTS. Because an ActiveX DLL is an in-process server, it operates within the memory space of the client. In this case, the client is MTS running on a remote machine. The execution speed is affected minimally by the fact that it is now fully contained within a DLL. This is because MTS can create a pool of components and have them ready to go on request so that you do not get the performance hit caused by loading a component. Note that a client cannot access a DLL directly if it is on a remote machine unless it is running in MTS. This is because a DLL does not create its own process but relies on operating within the process space of the client. To create an ActiveX DLL that runs in MTS, perform the following steps:

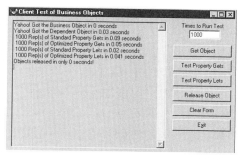

Figure 6.17 The client test form running tests against a component running within Microsoft Transaction Server

1. Copy the template created with How-To 6.2 into a new directory.

2. Rename the .VBP file from MYROYSVC.VBP to ROYDLLMTS.VBP. Rename the .VBW file from MYROYSVC.VBW to ROYDLLMTS.VBW.

3. Open the project.

4. Make the following changes to the GENERAL.BAS file. Comment out the following code. Do not remove this code completely because you will need to uncomment those lines that show the test form if you ever work on this object and want to test the functionality with the Visual Basic environment. You must remove this code to prevent the test form that is internal to the project from loading when the ActiveX DLL is used by a client.

```
'If App.StartMode = vbSModeStandalone Then
'    frmTestClient.Show vbModal
'End If.
```

5. Set the following options for the project by choosing Project, RoyaltySvc Properties from the menu. You can see the Project Properties tab containing the primary options you need to set for an ActiveX server project. Set the properties listed in Table 6.19 for this project.

Table 6.19 The project's property settings

OBJECT	PROPERTY	SETTING
General Tab	Project Type	ActiveX DLL
	Startup Object	Sub Main
	Project Name	"Royaltysvc"
	Project Description	"Royalty Service Component DLL for MTS"
Component Tab	Project Compatibility	checked
	Start Mode	ActiveX Component

6. Set the following properties for the `Server` class and the `Author` class (see Tables 6.20 and 6.21, respectively).

Table 6.20 Class option settings for `Server`

OPTION	SETTING
Name	Server
DataBindingBehavior	0 - vbNone
DataSourceBehavior	0 - vbNone
Instancing	5 - MultiUse
MTSTransactionMode	1 - NoTransactions
Persistable	0 - NotPersistable

Table 6.21 Class option settings for `Author`

OPTION	SETTING
Name	Author
DataBindingBehavior	0 - vbNone
DataSourceBehavior	0 - vbNone
Instancing	2 - PublicNotCreatable
MTSTransactionMode	1 - NoTransactions
Persistable	0 - NotPersistable

7. Open the Server class code and replace the `Connect` subroutine with the following:

```
Sub Connect (UserId As String, _
             Password As String)

'set all of the necessary variables declared earlier. This
'allows you to get the user ID and password and use them to
'gain access to data if needed.
```

```
              m_UserId = UserId
              m_Password = Password

              'You will use the User Id and Password to set up the
              'environment for Remote Data Objects

              rdoEngine.rdoDefaultUser = UserId
              rdoEngine.rdoDefaultPassword = Password

              'You will open a connection to the database. This
              'connection will then be used to issue SQL to the
              'Data Tier or to trigger Stored Procedures residing
              'within the database engine. Note that DB_TARGET is set in
              'the General.bas file. The DB_TARGET is the name of a valid
              'ODBC data source name (DSN).

              Set Env = rdoEngine.rdoEnvironments(0)
              Set Cn = Env.OpenConnection(dsname:=DB_TARGET, _
                                          Prompt:=rdDriverNoPrompt, _
                                          ReadOnly:=False, _
                                          Connect:='')

      End Sub
```

8. Choose File, Make RoyDLLMTS.DLL from the menu. Set the filename to ROYDLLMTS.DLL.

9. Click the Option button from the ActiveX DLL dialog box. Modify the Title field to Royalty Service DLL for MTS.

10. Generate the DLL. This automatically creates an entry in the Registry, but it does not automatically place it in MTS. If you open a different project and then open your References list from the menu bar, you will see the newly created DLL listed. Search the list for the description of the Royalty Service Component DLL.

11. Choose Project, RoyaltySvc Properties and select the Component tab. Notice that the DLL you just compiled is already specified. This allows you to recompile the project without generating a new class ID in the Registry. Each time you compile this project, the DLL you specified will be used as a guide to verify that the changes you have made are backward compatible. Now that you have that out of the way, you can separate out the test form.

12. Make the component DLL available in MTS. Make sure that the component is installed and available on the machine running Microsoft Transaction Server. Open the Microsoft Management Console (see Figure 6.18).

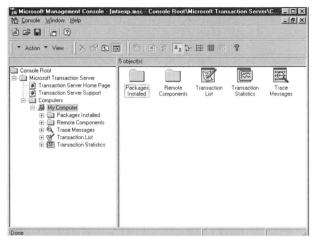

Figure 6.18 The Microsoft management Console
that allows administration of Microsoft
Transaction Services

13. Select the server on which you are going to install the component and
then select the Packages Installed folder. Right-click the Packages Installed
folder and select New and Package.

14. You are presented with the Package Wizard. Select Create an Empty
Package, specify the package name as Royalty Service, and click Next. You
now have a new folder called Royalty Service.

15. Click the new folder Royalty Service, and you see two new subfolders,
Components and Roles. We will not specify any roles for this How-To, so
select the Components folder. Right-click and select New and Component.

16. Select Install New Components. Click the Add Files button, navigate to
the `ROYDLLMTS.DLL` file, and select it.

17. Click Finish to complete the installation. The component is now available
in MTS (see Figure 6.19).

18. Create a new subdirectory called `TestForm` and start a new project. Select
Standard EXE. Remove the default Form1 from the project.

19. Save the project as `TESTDLLMTS.VBP`.

20. Copy the files `TESTFORM.FRM`, `TESTFORM.FRX`, and `TIMING.CLS` to the new
directory for this project.

21. Choose Project, Add File from the Visual Basic menu. Add `TESTFORM.FRM`
to the TESTDLL project.

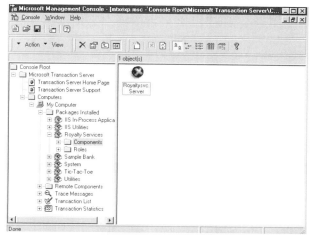

Figure 6.19 This is how the Royalty Service Component appears when running in Microsoft Transaction Server

22. Choose Project, Add File from the Visual Basic menu. Add **TIMING.CLS** to the TESTDLL project.

23. Open **TESTFORM.FRM** and change the **Caption** property to read Client Test of Business Object DLL in MTS.

24. Choose Project, Project1 Properties from the Visual Basic menu. Select the General tab and specify the startup form as **frmTestClient**. Click OK.

25. Now you need to reference the business object. Choose Project, References. A dialog box appears that lists all the objects you can reference. Select Royalty Service Component DLL for MTS. Click OK.

26. Choose File, Make TestDLLMTS.EXE from the Visual Basic menu.

27. Enter the filename, **TESTDLLMTS.EXE**.

28. Click the Options button and set the **Title** property to **TESTDLLMTS**. Click OK.

29. Generate an executable.

30. Run **TESTDLLMTS.EXE**. This is the same test form used to test your project in How-To 6.2. Select each button on the form in order from top to bottom. Start with the Get Object button, which tells you whether your test form was able to create an instance of the **RoyaltySvc** business object. The Test Property Gets and Test Property Lets buttons run tests to exercise the capability to retrieve and write properties to the **RoyaltySvc** business object. The Release Object button releases the `RoyaltySvc` business object so that it unloads from memory. Each of these actions provides visible feedback within the test form's display text box.

How It Works

The initial Business Object Template is used to jump start creating the component. The template is copied into a fresh directory, and the properties for the Server and Author classes are changed to prepare the component to run in MTS. At first glance, both the `Server` and `Author` classes do not have any special properties to allow them to run correctly under MTS. When you change their instancing property to anything other than `0-Private`, you are presented with additional properties to specify how the component works in MTS. The `Server` class is set to `MultiUse`, and the `Author` class is set to `PublicNotCreatable`. The MTS Transaction mode is set to `1- No Transactions` because the component will not be participating in a transaction. Finally, the component is compiled as an ActiveX DLL.

When an ActiveX DLL is generated, the Microsoft Management Console is used to add the component to Microsoft Transaction Server. This is done by navigating to the desired server, selecting the Installed Components folder, and adding the newly created component. Now that the component is available in MTS, a second application is created to test the capability to use this business object from a client application. The test form and time class module are copied into a new directory. A new Visual Basic project is started, and these files are added. The project, called `TESTDLLMTS.VBP`, adds a reference to the new ActiveX DLL created earlier. This ActiveX DLL appears as Royalty Service Component DLL for MTS. When the test form's project references the ActiveX DLL, the project is compiled as `TESTDLLMTS.EXE`. The test form allows you to create an instance of the business object, run tests on the capability to retrieve and store information in the business object, and release the business object. The `Timing` class module provides timing methods to measure the execution speed of all tests. With the test form and MTS management console running, you can click the Get Object button and see the `Royaltysvc.server` icon rotate. When the Release Object button is clicked, the icon stops rotating.

Comments

For a component to run in the MTS runtime environment, it must be a dynamic link library (DLL). If your components are implemented as executable files (.EXE files), they will not run in the MTS runtime environment. If you have developed a Remote Automation server executable component with Microsoft Visual Basic, you need to rebuild it as a DLL to use it with MTS.

MTS components are managed in the Microsoft Management Console. The console houses the MTS Explorer that assigns components to a package and controls the assignment of components to server processes. Additionally, the console allows you to control client access to components. Before a component can run with context in the MTS runtime environment, you have to use the Microsoft Management Console to define the component in the Microsoft Transaction Server catalog. The name of the implementation DLL as well as a set of MTS-specific information is tracked. MTS provides each component with a set of special attributes to provide capabilities beyond those available through COM. The transactional characteristics of a component are one of the features not available with basic COM components.

Some general rules of thumb for creating and running components in MTS ensure that references are safely passed between contexts. Whenever a component uses other components, you should run them all under Microsoft Transaction Server. Use the `CreateInstance` syntax when you need your components to create other components. If a component is going to be part of a transaction, always use the `SetComplete` or `SetAbort` methods to let the transaction know that the work the component is doing either succeeded or failed. Don't register components as "Requires a transaction" or "Requires a new transaction" unless they use `SetComplete` and `SetAbort` syntax.

Certain types of components really take advantage of the Microsoft Transaction Server concept. The granularity of a component directly affects its performance under MTS as well as its capability to be debugged and reused. Granularity is defined by the number of tasks performed by a single component. Fine-grained components perform a single task, like debiting an account. Fine-grained components consume and release resources quickly after a task is completed. Isolating a single business rule within a component can make it much easier to test. A coarse-grained component performs multiple tasks. Coarse-grained components are usually more difficult to debug and reuse. This is because a coarse-grained component does more "work" and thus limits MTS from having control over the optimal processing of the component.

Developing components to run under MTS control merits a complete book of its own. This How-To only introduces you to the idea of MTS and components. If you want to push your knowledge further, try taking the `Author` class and running it as its own component. Allow the `Server` component to create the `Author` component within MTS. This will whet your appetite for the power that Microsoft Transaction Server brings to the client/server development world.

CHAPTER 7

BASIC SQL SERVER MANAGEMENT

7

BASIC SQL SERVER MANAGEMENT

by David Jung

How do I...

In the process of building on the three-tiered client/server model, the last tier consists of the data and its services. Data services manage the information of your enterprise. Business objects interact with this tier directly to make decisions and enforce business rules.

The data services layer supports data definitions, data management, and transactions. *Data definitions* specify the logical design of your information and the data definition language (DDL) used to control the information. *Data management* is the use of the database manipulation language (DML) to perform operations on the data. *Transactions* are used to update the data and ensure referential integrity.

With the exception of the first How-To, this chapter focuses on the basics of building a database using Microsoft SQL Server 6.5 and optimizing tips and tricks. This chapter assumes that you already have installed SQL Server 6.5 on a system and that you have system administrator rights to the server, or equivalent privileges to create devices and database objects. If you plan to access SQL Server from a remote system, you must have the Microsoft SQL Server 6.5 Utilities installed on your client workstation. All the steps in this chapter's How-To's step through the graphical user interface portion of the SQL Enterprise Manager. In the "How It Works" sections, the DDL equivalents are discussed because the graphical user interface is providing an easier way to perform the DDL tasks. Microsoft refers to DDL and DML as *Transact-SQL.*

7.1 Use the SQL Editing Tools in Visual Basic

In previous versions of Visual Basic, you must use tools outside the Visual Basic integrated development environment (IDE) to work with your application's database. New to Visual Basic 6.0 is the capability to interact directly with every element of the database, from table manipulation to query building to stored procedure manipulation. You will find that this new interface is far superior to the Enterprise Manager. This How-To discusses using the Data view for all your database needs.

7.2 Create a Device

As you start designing your data services tier, you must define a disk file to store your databases and transaction logs. This How-To describes what those devices are and how to create them.

7.3 Create a Database

The *database* is an organized collection of data that is logically structured and maintained. This How-To offers some techniques for designing your databases and explains how to create them.

7.4 Create a Table

The most important function of a database is its tables, because that is where the information is stored. This How-To focuses on creating tables and fields using SQL Enterprise Manager.

7.5 Define Primary and Foreign Keys

A *relational database* implies the presence of relationships between the tables. To have a relationship, you first define a primary key. The elements that make up a table's primary key can be part of another table. These become foreign keys in the table, thus creating the primary key/foreign key relationship. This How-To explores this relationship further and shows you how to define the primary key/foreign key relationship.

7.6 Index a Table for Efficiency and Performance

The use of indexes is a way to increase performance when retrieving information from tables. This How-To shows you how to create indexes on your tables.

7.7 Create a Trigger to Control Data Integrity

Triggers are a special kind of stored procedure that is executed automatically when a user attempts data modification on a specific table. This How-To shows you how to create triggers.

7.8 Create a View

A *view* is a virtual table derived from one or more base tables in the database. Views provide a different look at the data in your tables, improve performance, and add another layer of security. This How-To shows you how to implement views.

7.9 Create and Execute a Stored Procedure

A *stored procedure* is a precompiled collection of DML statements that can accept and return one or more user-supplied parameters. This How-To shows you how to create and use stored procedures.

7.10 Create a Stored Procedure That Performs a Transaction

Stored procedures are often designed to handle a unit of work, such as inserting or updating data in a database table. This How-To focuses on creating a stored procedure that performs a transaction process and returns information to the calling procedure.

7.11 Create a Query Using SQL Server Web Assistant

This How-To discusses using the Web Assistant to create an HTML document, which will be generated every time a new reservation is made to an intranet.

7.12 Optimize My Server

There is no magic wand you can wave over SQL Server to make it run optimally. There are techniques and pitfalls to look out for that help tune your server. This How-To looks at some common things that go wrong when trying to tune your server.

WARNING

This chapter discusses version 6.5 of SQL Server only. Any version newer or older might not behave in the same manner depicted here.

COMPLEXITY
BEGINNING

7.1 How do I...
Use the SQL editing tools in Visual Basic?

COMPATIBILITY: VISUAL BASIC 6.0

Problem

When developing applications, I always have to use other tools to create stored procedures, edit tables, and test my queries. Is there a way I can do this within Visual Basic's IDE?

Technique

Since Visual Studio 5.0 (Service Pack 1) and Microsoft SQL Server 6.5 (Service Pack 2), users have been able to manipulate their data sources directly from within the Visual Studio IDE. Now that Visual Basic 6.0 is a bit more mature, it can interact with data sources just like the other Visual Studio counterparts. The component that allows you to do this is called the *Data View window*. The Data View window is the gateway to your database resources. You can find it on the toolbar or on the View menu. Figure 7.1 is an example of what the Data View window looks like with a query window open.

The Data View window enables you to view the elements of the database. To view a database, you must make a data link to a data source. A data link can be established to any database that has an OLE DB provider. OLE DB is the latest database connectivity COM object. If you don't have ODBC drivers, Visual Basic comes with an OLE DB provider for ODBC drivers.

After you make your connection, you see four groups below the data link you have established:

✔ Database diagrams—This group enables you to create simple relationship charts illustrating how your tables fit together. This group does not replace the higher-end data-modeling tools such as Logic Works ER/Win, but it enables you to create referential integrity between your tables more easily.

✔ Tables—This group gives you access to all the tables in your database. From here, you can add, update, and remove columns and attributes. You can add and remove tables from here, and you can also add and modify any triggers associated with a table.

✔ Views—The Views group enables you to add, update, and remove any view table you develop.

✔ Stored procedures—This group enables you to create, update, and remove any stored procedure you create in your database.

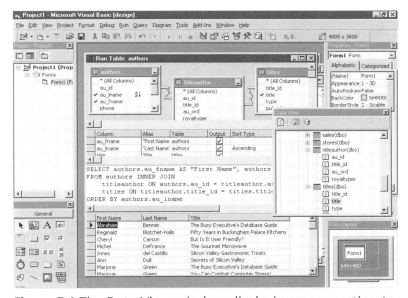

Figure 7.1 The Data View window displaying a connection to SQL Server's PUBS database and the Run Table window displaying a query output

Steps

This example illustrates how to create a data link to be used with the Data view using an Access 97 database and a SQL Server 6.5 database.

Creating a Data Link to Access 97

To create a data link to an Access 97 database from the Visual Basic IDE, complete the following steps:

1. Open Visual Basic using any type of project.

2. Choose Data View from the View menu.

3. Click the Add a New Data Link button found on the toolbar of the Data View window. It is the last button to the right. If you place the mouse over the button, the ToolTip description displays. When you press this button, it will invoke the Data Link Properties window, as shown in Figure 7.2.

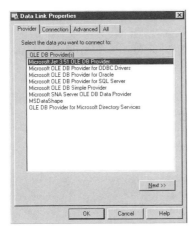

Figure 7.2 The first screen of the Create New Data Link Wizard

4. Select Microsoft Jet 3.51 OLE DB Provider on the Provider tab and click Next.

5. The tab Connection is for determining the name of the Access database you want to use. For this exercise, select one of the Access databases used in Chapter 4, "User Interface Design." You can either type the location and filename in the text field, or you can browse for it by clicking on the command button with the ellipse (...). The entry should look something like this:

```
e:\Chap04\idata.mdb
```

6. Because this database doesn't have a **SYSTEM.MDA** for security, leave the User name set to Admin. Click the Test Connection to test the connection to the specified data source. If it passes, you will get a message box that should resemble Figure 7.3.

7. You use the Advanced tab to set network server settings, connection timeout, and access permissions. Access databases are only concerned with access permissions. By default, the Share Deny None check box is marked. This setting allows other users to open the database while you're looking at it. For this example, this setting is adequate.

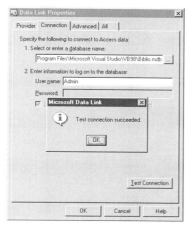

Figure 7.3 A successful test
of the data link

8. You use the All tab to view and edit all the Data Link properties for the
database connection you're trying to establish. For this exercise, the
default settings are adequate.

9. Click OK to active the data link you just created.

At this point, you can change the data link's name to something more
meaningful. By default, the Add a New Data Link generates the name
DataLink#. To rename the data link, select it, press the F2 button and change
the name. It's just like renaming a file in the Windows Explorer.

Creating a Data Link to SQL Server 6.5

Complete the following steps to create a data link to a SQL Server 6.5 database:

1. Choose Data View from the View menu.

2. Click the Add a New Data Link button on the toolbar of the Data View
window to add new data link (it is the last button to the right). If you
place the mouse over the button, the ToolTip description will display.
Press this button to invoke the Data Link Properties window.

3. Select Microsoft OLE DB Provider for SQL Server and click Next.

4. On the Connection tab, you must specify the server name of the SQL
Server you want to attach to. The drop-down list box displays all the
servers you connect to. For this exercise, use the system administrator's
user ID and password to connect to the server, assuming you know them.
Or you can use a user ID and password you know that will allow you onto

the database. If the password is blank, mark the Blank password check box. In the Select the database on the server, for this example, select the PUBS database that's installed with SQL Server. Figure 7.4 illustrates the data link window that is going to connect to the server and the database, pubs.

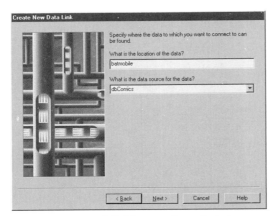

Figure 7.4 Establishing a data link to the server and database

5. For a data link that is using OLE DB Provider for SQL Server, the only setting you have available to set is the Connection timeout. This specifies the amount of time the OLE DB provider waits for initialization to the database to complete the connection. For this example, leaving it blank is fine.

6. The All tab is used to view and edit all the Data Link properties for the database connection you're trying to establish. For this exercise, the default settings are adequate.

7. Click OK and give the new data link a more meaningful name than DataLink2.

How It Works

The Data View window is a graphical user interface that allows you to view and work with the objects of the most databases, objects such as the tables, views, stored procedures, and more. It uses the OLE DB Provider drivers to provide connectivity to a particular database. Once a data link is created, a connection string is saved on your system with a .UDL extension. This file is known as a data link file.

For databases that use the Jet 3.51 OLE DB Provider for connectivity, you only view the table and view objects within the database. OLE DB Providers for ODBC, Oracle, and SQL Server display more database objects: tables, views, stored procedures, triggers, and so on.

Comments

This example showed only how to establish the data link. In the following How-To's that deal with database elements, you learn how to use the Data View window as well as SQL Server's Enterprise Manager to create database elements.

COMPLEXITY
BEGINNING

7.2 How do I...
Create a device?

COMPATIBILITY: SQL SERVER 6.5 ONLY

Problem

I've finished the database design that I'm going to use for my application. I've been told that I need to create a device for my database. What's a device and how do I create one?

Technique

A general definition of a *device* is a physical disk file where all SQL Server databases and transaction logs reside. A device consists of two names: a *logical* name and a *physical* name. The logical name is used by SQL Server to identify the device and is used in most SQL statements; it can be up to 30 characters in length. The physical name is an operating system file that specifies the full path where the device is physically located on the server's disk drive. The naming convention follows the rules for filenames in the operating system.

Two types of devices can be defined: the *database device* and the *backup device*. A database device stores databases and transaction logs. This device requires that you preallocate storage space on your server's disk drive; also, the device must reside on the server's local hard drive. A backup device stores backups of the database and transaction logs. Unlike a database device, a backup device can reside on both local and network storage media. If the backup device is on network media, it must be on a shared network directory. Table 7.1 shows an example of what logical and physical devices look like.

Table 7.1 Example of a logical and physical device

TYPE OF DEVICE	EXAMPLE
Logical	dv_Hotels
Physical database	C:\MSSQL\DATA\DVHOTELS.DAT
Physical backup device	C:\MSSQL\BACKUP\DVDHOTEL.DAT
Physical network backup device	\\SQLSERVR\BACKUP\DVDHOTEL.DAT

Steps

This example is in two parts. The first part illustrates how to create a database device, and the other part illustrates how to create a backup device.

Creating the Database Device

A database device is a file on the physical hard drive on the SQL Server that is used to allocate space to store a database and its transaction log. To create a database device, complete the following steps:

1. Open the SQL Enterprise Manager from your Microsoft SQL Server 6.5 Utilities group.

2. In the Server Manager window, select the server on which you want to create the device. In this example, the server GOTHAM_CITY is selected.

3. Click the Manage Database Devices button on the toolbar, or open the Manage menu and choose Database Devices. The Manage Database Devices window shown in Figure 7.5 appears.

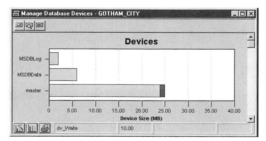

Figure 7.5 The Manage Database Devices window

4. To create a device on the Manage Database Devices window's toolbar, click the New Device button, which is the first button on the toolbar. ToolTip windows will appear for a lot of the toolbar-type buttons, so if it isn't obvious what the button is, bring the mouse close to the button to see whether a ToolTip message appears. The New Database Device window appears, which is similar to Figure 7.6, except that the text fields will be blank. The graph at the bottom of this window illustrates how much used and free space is available. By placing the mouse pointer over one of the bars in the graph, you can display in the status bar the amount of drive space available and used by that database device.

5. Assign the values listed in Table 7.2 to the New Database Device window. When you are finished, it should resemble Figure 7.6.

Table 7.2 Properties for the new database device

FIELD	PROPERTY	DESCRIPTION
Name	dv_Waite	Logical database device name
Drive	C:	Disk drive the database will reside on
Path	\MSSQL\DATA\dv_Waite.DAT	Physical database device name
Size (MB):	10	Size of the device in megabytes

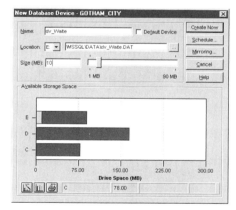

Figure 7.6 The New Database Device window

6. For this How-To, do not enable the Default Device check box. If you check this option on a device, it becomes part of the pool of default devices. If a database is designed without a device specified, a default device is used. Default devices are used in alphabetical order; when one device is filled up, SQL Server uses the next device. It is a good practice not to create default devices because databases and transaction logs are placed in database devices. If you build a database in a default device, you will not know which device it is placed in, which will make server maintenance more difficult.

7. To add the new device, click Create Now.

8. If the device is successfully added, a message box appears notifying you.

Creating the Backup Device

A backup device is used to back up and restore a database and transaction log. In previous versions of SQL Server, this was known as a *dump device*. A backup device is different from a database device in that a backup device does not have to reside solely on SQL Server's physical hard drive. It can be stored on storage media such as floppy drives, hard drives, tape, or other servers on the network. Complete the following steps to create a backup device:

1. In the Server Manager window, right-click the Backup Devices folder. Your screen will look like Figure 7.7.

Figure 7.7 Right-clicking the Backup Devices folder

2. Choose New Backup Device from the shortcut menu. The New Backup Device dialog box appears, which is similar to Figure 7.8.

Figure 7.8 The New Backup Device dialog box

3. In the Name text box, type the logical backup device name of `dmp_Waite`.

4. In this example, the backup device is stored on the same physical drive of SQL Server that contains the database device created earlier. If you want the backup device to be located on a network drive, you should type a value similar to this:

```
\\SQLSRVR\BACKUP\dmp_Waite
```

5. In the Type frame, the Disk Backup Device radio button is selected (which is the default). For this example, leave this radio button selected. If you want the backup device to be stored on a tape, select the Tape Backup Device radio button. If you select this radio button, you must mark or clear the Skip Headers check box. This check box is used to determine whether the ANSI tape labels are read. If the option is disabled, SQL Server recognizes any existing ANSI tape labels on the tape to which you are writing. This can be important because if there is any ANSI tape label on the tape you are writing to and the check box is disabled, SQL Server notifies you as to the contents of the ANSI label. If the check box is enabled, SQL Server ignores the ANSI label and performs its task of writing to the tape. The ANSI label could have been a notification that the information on the tape is still valid and that your write sequence just overwrote current data with your data.

6. Click Create to create the backup device.

7. If the device is successfully added, a message box appears notifying you.

How It Works

All the steps you are doing through the SQL Enterprise Manager graphical interface perform the DDL equivalents that you would issue through the Query Manager interface, which is also part of SQL Enterprise Manager. The Query Manager is an interface that enables you to enter DDL or DML calls directly against every database object you specify. In creating a database device through SQL Enterprise Manager, you are issuing the **DISK INIT** command. From Query Manager, you would issue the following command:

```
DISK INIT
NAME = dv_WaiteSQL
PHYSNAME = C:\MSSQL\DATA\dv_WaiteSQL.DAT
VDEVNO = 5
SIZE = 1024
```

The **VDEVNO** property is the number of the new device and is a number between 1 and 255. The number 0 is reserved for the *master device* and therefore cannot be used. The master device is a device that SQL Server creates when it is installed on the server. This device stores the master, model, and tempdb system databases and transaction logs. All SQL Server objects created are based on model database objects. After a device number is used, it cannot be used again until the device has been dropped. By using SQL Enterprise Manager, you do not have to know what device number to assign the device you are creating because the application figures it out for you.

The **SIZE** property at the command line is different from that used with SQL Enterprise Manager. Rather than megabytes, the **SIZE** property is in 2KB pages (2,048 bytes); therefore, 2MB is equal to 1,024 2KB pages.

Creating a backup device through SQL Enterprise Manager is the same as executing the system stored procedure **sp_addumpdevice** through ISQL. From the ISQL prompt, you would type the following:

```
sp_addumpdevice 'disk', 'dmp_Waite', 'C:\MSSQL\BACKUP\DMPWAITE.dat'
```

The first parameter after **sp_addumpdevice** indicates whether the device is going to be created on a disk or tape. The next parameter is the logical name of the backup device. The last parameter in the example is the physical name and path of the backup device. If the backup device is to be created on a tape, an additional parameter is included:

```
, @devstatus = noskip or skip
```

The **@devstatus** property is the equivalent of the Skip Header check box. If you set the property to **noskip**, SQL Server reads the ANSI label of the tape before performing a backup. If the ANSI label on the tape warns SQL Server that you do not have permission to write the tape, you (as the SQL administrator) are notified. If you set the property to **skip**, SQL Server does not read the ANSI label and therefore ignores such a warning.

Comments

When creating a backup device on a network, make sure that the account that SQL Server runs has the appropriate rights to the network server. There is a limit of 256 devices per SQL Server. Because device 0 is already used by SQL Server, you really have only 255 devices you can define.

COMPLEXITY
BEGINNING

7.3   How do I...
Create a database?

COMPATIBILITY: SQL SERVER 6.5 ONLY

Problem

Now that I've created my devices, I'm supposed to create a database. How do I do this?

Technique

A *database* is an organized, logical unit of storage and work within SQL Server. Each database defined is different and separate from other databases. A database can reside on one or more database devices that have been defined. Within a database are several associated database objects. These database objects consist of the following:

- ✔ Tables and indexes
- ✔ Derived tables (views)
- ✔ User-defined datatypes
- ✔ Defaults
- ✔ Rules
- ✔ Stored procedures
- ✔ Triggers

The use of tables, derived tables, stored procedures, and triggers is discussed in How-To's 7.4, 7.8, 7.9, and 7.7, respectively. For more information on user-defined datatypes, defaults, and rules, refer to *SQL Server Books Online*.

NOTE

SQL Server Books Online is the electronic version of the manual that is installed to the hard drive when you install SQL Server, unless you tell SQL Server to access it only from the CD-ROM. It is not available on the Internet.

Before you can create a database, you must first have created a database device for it. As stated earlier, a database can be located on one device or across multiple database devices (see Figure 7.9).

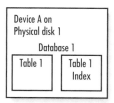

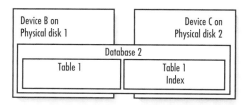

Figure 7.9 The devices and database structure

Each database has a *transaction log* associated with it. A transaction log is a storage area reserved by SQL Server that tracks all transactions—updates, inserts, and deletes—made to the database. By default, the transaction log is written to the same device to which you assign your database. When any change to the database is issued, the process is written to the transaction log before any physical changes are performed. As a general rule, your database device and transaction log should always be on separate devices. This helps improve your performance and allows you to keep a backup. Because the transaction log records every transaction, it competes for disk space and processing I/O with database data. By not having the transaction log on a separate device, you lose the capability to back up the transaction log. This can be important in an environment that has high transaction traffic, such as an order-entry system for a telemarketing company.

When allocating space for the transaction log, you should allocate roughly 10 to 30 percent of your database size. The size varies based on database use, so it is a good idea to monitor the size of the log to determine how much space you really need.

If you find that your database is running out of storage space or you want to reclaim unused storage space, you can resize the database. This is accomplished by using SQL Enterprise Manager or the **ALTER DATABASE** statement through the Query Analyzer. For information on the **ALTER DATABASE** syntax, refer to *SQL Server Books Online*. If you need to increase the size of the database's transaction log, you can use SQL Enterprise Manager or the **ALTER DATABASE** statement. The size of a transaction log can only be increased.

For data-recovery purposes, back up the transaction log on a regular basis. To dynamically back up your transaction log, you can write an ISQL file that performs the **DUMP TRANSACTION** statement or use SQL Enterprise Manager to schedule the backup. If the transaction log is located on the same device as the database, this cannot be done.

Steps

This example illustrates how to create a database and a separate transaction log. To do this, complete the following steps:

1. Open SQL Enterprise Manager from your Microsoft SQL Server 6.5 Utilities group.

2. In the Server Manager window, select the server on which you want to create the database. In this example, use the server GOTHAM_CITY.

3. Click the Manage Database button on the toolbar, or choose Databases from the Manage menu. The Manage Databases window shown in Figure 7.10 appears. The graph shows you a list of all the databases defined on the server and their storage usage. The light blue segment of the bar represents the used space that your database is occupying with actual information. The dark red signifies the available free space of the database.

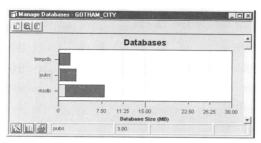

Figure 7.10 The Manage Databases window

4. To create a database in the Manage Databases window's toolbar, click the New Database button, which is the first button on the toolbar. The New Database window appears. The graph at the bottom of this window shows the devices on the server and their used and free space usage.

5. Assign the values listed in Table 7.3 in the New Database window.

Table 7.3 The first three properties for the new database

FIELD	PROPERTY	DESCRIPTION
Name	db_HotelSystem	Logical database name
Data Device	dv_Waite	Logical database device name
Size (MB)	5	Amount of space to allocate for the database

6. In the Log Device combo box, you are going to create a new device to store the transaction log. Select <new> from the list, and the New Database window appears, which is similar to Figure 7.11. Assign the values listed in Table 7.4 in the window to create the new device.

Table 7.4 Properties for the transaction log device

FIELD	PROPERTY	DESCRIPTION
Name	dvl_Waite	Logical database device name
Drive	C:	Disk drive the device will reside on
Path	\MSSQL\DATA\dvl_Waite.DAT	Physical database device name
Size (MB)	10	Size of device in megabytes

7. After the New Database window closes, assign 5MB to the log device.

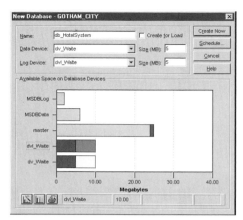

Figure 7.11 The New Database window

8. Click Create Now to add the database. Now that the database has been defined, you can start creating database objects such as tables and stored procedures.

How It Works

Each database is created in the image of the model database. The model database is created when SQL Server is first installed. If you do not specify a database device, the database is created on the default device (if it has space available). If no size is specified, the database is created with the size of the model database or the database size value in the system stored procedure **sp_configure**. The value that is larger is the value that is used.

All the steps you are doing through SQL Enterprise Manager perform the DDL equivalents you would issue through the Query Analyzer. In creating a database through SQL Enterprise Manager, you are issuing the **CREATE DATABASE** statement. From an ISQL prompt, you issue the following command to create this database:

```
CREATE DATABASE db_HotelSystem
ON dv_Waite = 5
LOG ON dvl_Waite = 5
```

The **CREATE DATABASE** statement creates the database named **db_HotelSystem** within the database device **dv_Waite** using 5MB of space within the device. The transaction log file uses a separate device **dvl_Waite** using 5MB of space within the log device.

When creating the database through SQL commands, you must make sure that the devices to which you are assigning the database already exist. If they don't, you must create them by using the **DISK INIT** command.

Comments

The maximum number of databases per SQL Server installation is 32,767.

COMPLEXITY
BEGINNING

7.4 How do I...
Create a table?

COMPATIBILITY: SQL SERVER 6.5 AND VISUAL BASIC 6.0

Problem

I've finished the database design that I'm going to use for my application. I've created the database, backup device, and the database object. How do I create a table to store the actual data?

Technique

A *table* is a database object that is a logical, two-dimensional data structure organized into rows and columns in which data is stored. You can create tables through SQL Enterprise Manager or by using DDL scripts (SQL statements).

Steps

In this example, you are going to use SQL Enterprise Manager to create the table in the database that you created in the preceding How-To. Then you are going to use the Data View window in Visual Basic to create the same table.

Creating a Table with SQL Enterprise Manager

To create a table using SQL Enterprise Manager, complete the following steps:

1. Open SQL Enterprise Manager from your Microsoft SQL Server 6.5 Utilities group.

2. To create a table, you must tell SQL Server to which database the table belongs. From the Server Manager window, select the server that contains the database in which you want to create the table. In How-To 7.2, you created the database on the server called GOTHAM_CITY, and the database was called **db_HotelSystem**. Click the plus sign (+) next to the database name, **db_HotelSystem**. Server Manager Explorer expands the database and shows the components of the database: Groups/Users and Objects.

3. Click the plus sign next to the Objects item. Server Manager Explorer expands the Objects item and shows all the database objects you can work with: Tables, Views, Stored Procedures, Rules, Defaults, and User Defined Datatypes.

4. Select the Tables object. Then choose Table from the Manage menu.

5. The Manage Tables window appears. For now, leave the Table combo box set to <new>. Assign the values listed in Table 7.5 to the Manage Tables window. When you are finished, the window should resemble Figure 7.12. Note that when defining an Integer datatype, you cannot assign the size. A size of 4 is automatically filled in.

Table 7.5   Properties for the hotels table

COLUMN NAME	DATATYPE	SIZE	NULLS
HotelID	int		No
HotelName	varchar	50	Yes

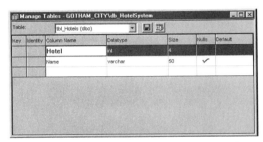

Figure 7.12 The Manage Tables window

6. This table is designed for basic hotel information: a hotel number and the name of the hotel. The Hotel column has been designed not to allow for nulls. Whenever a record in this table is inserted or updated, a non-null value must be provided in the Hotel column. If the user attempts to assign a null value to a field that does not have the Nulls column marked, an error occurs. You do not want a null value in the Hotel column because the Hotel column is required to have a legitimate row in the table.

7. To save the table, click the Save button, which is the icon with a disk on it on the Manage Tables toolbar. A dialog box appears. Enter the name of the table, **tbl_Hotels**, into the text box and click OK.

8. The table you have just created is empty. To populate it, run the SQL script **FILHOTEL.SQL** (located in this chapter's subdirectory on the CD-ROM) through ISQL or SQL Enterprise Manager's Query Analyzer.

9. Run the SQL script **HTL10A.SQL** (located in this chapter's subdirectory on the CD-ROM) to build the rest of the tables in this database and **HTL10B.SQL** to populate the tables.

Creating a Table Using Visual Basic's Data View Window

Complete the following steps to create a table using Visual Basic's Data View window:

1. Right-click the Tables folder and choose New Table from the shortcut menu.

2. Enter the table name `tblHotels` in the New Table dialog box.

3. Assign the values shown in Table 7.6 to the Design Table window. When you are finished, the window should resemble Figure 7.13.

Table 7.6 Properties for the Hotels table for the Design Table window

COLUMN NAME	DATATYPE	LENGTH	ALLOW NULLS
HotelID	int	4	unchecked
HotelName	varchar	50	checked

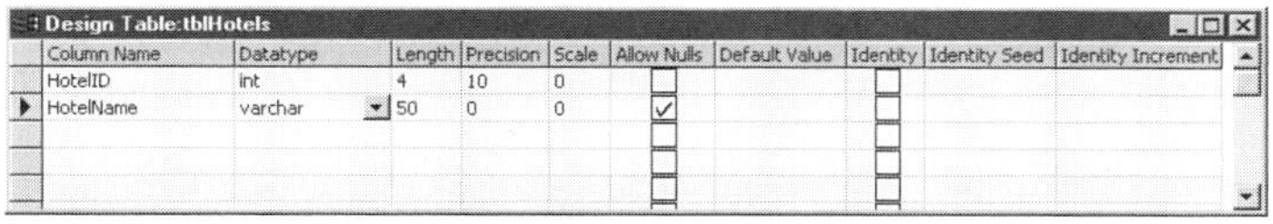

Figure 7.13 The Design Table window for the `tblHotels` table

4. To save the table, close the window by choosing Close from the control box or clicking the close window button.

5. A confirmation box asks whether you want to save the changes to the table. Choose Yes. The Save Change Script dialog box appears.

6. This dialog box displays a change script whenever a table change occurs and enables you to save the change script as a text file with a `.sql` extension in the `project` directory. If you don't want these changes to be saved each time there is a change to the table, disable the Automatically Generate Change Script on Every Save check box. In this example, choose No to continue.

How It Works

All the steps you are doing through the SQL Enterprise Manager graphics interface perform the DDL equivalents that you would issue through the Query Analyzer. In creating a table through SQL Enterprise Manager, you are issuing the **CREATE TABLE** command. From an ISQL prompt, you would issue the following command:

```
CREATE TABLE tbl_Hotels
    (Hotel      Int                NOT NULL,
    Name        VarChar(50)        NULL)
```

When creating a table, you should keep a few rules in mind. A table name can contain up to 30 characters. The maximum number of columns you can define for a table is 250 columns. Not including text and image fields, the number of bytes per row should not exceed 1,962 bytes.

Comments

Through SQL Enterprise Manager, you can change a column name or add more columns. You cannot modify the Datatype, Size, Nulls, and Default columns. If you must modify or remove a column, re-create the old table with the new attributes and types, move the data back to it, and then drop the temp table. You must do this because you might want to maintain the table name, especially if multiple production applications use it.

When using the Query Analyzer to add a column to a table that already exists, you use the **ALTER TABLE** statement. For further information on the **ALTER TABLE** syntax, refer to SQL Server Books Online.

Now that Visual Basic has the Data View window, your tasks of creating and modifying tables is much easier. In the past, you had to be familiar with the appropriate Transact-SQL commands. Now it's as easy as modifying a table in Microsoft Access.

COMPLEXITY
BEGINNING

7.5 How do I...
Define primary and foreign keys?

COMPATIBILITY: SQL SERVER 6.5 AND VISUAL BASIC 6.0

Problem

I've created my tables, but how do I ensure the integrity of my data? I've heard of referential integrity, but what does it mean and how does it apply to my tables?

Technique

Data integrity is an important part of database design. Data integrity schemes prevent users from entering incorrect or invalid data into the database tables. With the previous versions of SQL Server (versions 4.2 and 6.0), enforcing data integrity was not easily implemented. You had to use unique indexes and triggers to enforce integrity. SQL Server now supports data integrity with the use of primary key and foreign key relationships, also known as *referential integrity*.

Primary key and foreign key relationships are constraints placed on tables that define conditions the data must meet in order to be entered into a database table. A *primary key* is used to ensure that no duplicate values are entered into the table and that null values are not allowed; it also specifies whether a clustered or nonclustered index is created to enhance performance. It is a good practice to make a database table's primary key a nonclustered index. (Indexes are discussed in greater depth in the next section.) Only one primary key can be defined for a given table. The maximum number of columns that can make up a primary key is 16, with a total byte length of less than or equal to 254 bytes.

A *foreign key* is one or more columns that reference a primary key in a different table. A foreign key does not have to be unique. You can define an unlimited number of foreign keys for a table. As with the primary key, 16 columns is the maximum number of columns that can make up a foreign key, and its total byte length must be less than or equal to 254 bytes. The columns must match one for one the order of the columns and the datatype of the columns the primary key is referencing. When designing queries, you use primary and foreign keys to join two tables together. This also enforces referential integrity.

To create the primary key-to-foreign key relationships within SQL Server, you can use SQL Enterprise Manager or the DDL scripts (SQL statements) through the ISQL prompt. The steps that follow in the section "Creating Primary and Foreign Keys for the `tbl_Rooms` Table Using the Data View Window" describe how to create the primary key-to-foreign key relationships within Visual Basic's Data view.

Steps

This example uses SQL Enterprise Manager to create the primary and foreign key relationships between the `Hotels` and `Rooms` tables. If you did not go through How-To 7.4, run the SQL script `CMPLTHTL.SQL` (located in this chapter's subdirectory on the CD-ROM) in SQL Enterprise Manager's Query Analyzer or ISQL to build and populate the tables you use in this example.

The tables you will be working with are based on the `Hotel Reservation` tables used for part of Chapter 4, "User Interface Design." To understand the relationships of the tables, see the entity-relationship diagram in Figure 7.14. As a rule of thumb, you should create all the primary key information for the tables before creating the foreign key relations.

The following sections discuss particular tables within the database. To create the primary and foreign keys for these tables, complete the steps in each section.

Creating the Primary Key for the `tbl_Hotels` Table

To create the primary key for the `tbl_Hotels` table, follow these steps:

1. Open SQL Enterprise Manager from your Microsoft SQL Server 6.5 Utilities group.

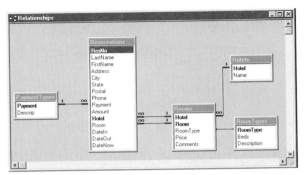

Figure 7.14 An entity-relationship diagram for
the Hotels database (db_HotelSystem)

2. In the Server Manager window, select the server that contains the database
in which you want to create the table. Using the information from How-To
7.2, use the server called GOTHAM_CITY and the database called
db_HotelSystem.

3. Click the plus sign (+) next to the database name. Server Manager
Explorer expands the database and shows the components of the database.

4. Click the plus sign next to the Objects item. Server Manager Explorer
expands the Objects item and shows all the database objects with which
you can work.

5. Click the plus sign next to the Tables folder. Right-click the table object
Hotels and choose Edit from the pop-up menu. The Manage Tables
window appears.

6. Click the Advanced Features button on the Manage Tables toolbar. This
brings up more detailed information about the table. If you cannot see all
the fields, maximize the Manage Tables window. Your screen should look
similar to Figure 7.15.

7. On the first tab, Primary Key/Identity, you will be setting up the primary
key for the Hotels table. Click the Column Names combo box in the
Primary Key frame. A list of column names that do not have the Null
column marked is displayed. Select the Hotel column name to be the
primary key.

8. The type of index should be defined as non-clustered. How-To 7.6
discusses clustered and non-clustered indexes.

9. Click the Add button to add the primary key information to the table. In
the Key column in the table grid, a key icon appears to illustrate that the
column has been designated as the primary key.

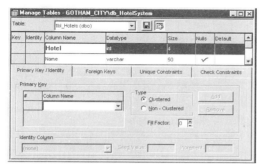

Figure 7.15 Manage Tables with the
Advanced Features selected

10. The Identity Column information is relevant only when you are creating a
table. An Identity column is an auto-incrementing column, similar to the
`Counter` field in Microsoft Access.

Creating Primary and Foreign Keys for the tbl_Rooms Table

1. Click on the Tables combo box and select the table, `tbl_Rooms`.

2. In the Primary Key frame, the column names that can be used for the
primary key are those columns that have the `Nulls` column not marked.
Select the values listed in Table 7.7 to define the primary key for the `Rooms`
table.

Table 7.7 Primary key columns for the Rooms table

COLUMN	SELECTION
1	Hotel
2	Room

3. The type of index should be defined as non-clustered; therefore, select the
non-clustered radio button. Non-clustered indexes are discussed in greater
detail in the next section.

4. Click the Add button to add the primary information to the table.

5. In order to create the foreign key relationship, you must click the Foreign
Keys tab. Your screen should look similar to Figure 7.16.

6. The `tbl_Rooms` table is dependent on the `tbl_Hotels` table; therefore,
select the `tbl_Hotels` table's primary key in the Referenced Table combo
box. The list item looks similar to this:

```
dbo.tbl_Hotels - PK_tbl_Hotels_2__10
```

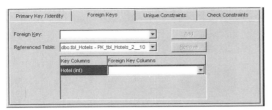

Figure 7.16 The Additional Features tab showing foreign key information

Because the primary key name is built by SQL Enterprise Manager, the exact primary key name might vary.

7. The foreign key of the **tbl_Rooms** table is **Hotel**. It relates to the primary key of the **tbl_Hotels** table, which is **Hotel**. In the Foreign Keys grid, select the Hotel column below the Foreign Key column. This means that a room record cannot exist in the **tbl_Rooms** table without a valid hotel number referenced in the **tbl_Hotels** table. Suppose you want to enter a new room number in the **tbl_Rooms** table. One of the requirements is that you enter a valid hotel number that resides in the **tbl_Hotels** table. This is important because it ensures that you don't end up with a room that does not exist in a hotel.

8. The Add button is enabled if the criteria selected are valid. Click Add, and SQL Enterprise Manager dynamically builds a foreign key name and displays it in the Foreign Keys combo box. The foreign key's name looks similar to this:

```
FK_tbl_Rooms_2__10
```

9. To save the information, click Save.

Creating the Primary Key for the tbl_Hotels Table Using Visual Basic's Data View

1. In the Data View window, right-click the Database Diagrams folder and choose New Diagram from the shortcut menu.

2. Open the **Tables** folder in the Data View window and drag the **tbl_Hotels** table to the New Database Diagram window.

3. In the New Database Diagram window, right-click the HotelID column and choose Set Primary Key from the shortcut menu. This places a key symbol next to the HotelID column and an asterisk (*) next to the table name. The asterisk denotes that a change has been made to the table but has not yet been saved (see Figure 7.17).

Figure 7.17 The New Database Diagram window depicting `tblHotels`' HotelID column as the primary key

4. To save the changes to the table, close the New Database Diagram window. If you have never saved the diagram before, it asks you to give the diagram a name. For this example, name the diagram `erdHotels` and click OK. You prefix the object with `erd` to notify any other developer that the file is an entity-relationship diagram file, just like prefixing an object with `tbl` signifies it as a table.

5. As in How-To 7.4, the Save Change Script window appears because the table has been altered. Choose No to continue.

Creating Primary and Foreign Keys for the `tbl_Rooms` Table Using the Data View Window

1. With the Data View and Database Diagram windows open, drag the table `tblRooms` to the Database Diagram window.

2. While pressing Ctrl, select the HotelID and Room columns.

3. Right-click on the `tblRooms` title bar. This brings up the table's context menu. Select Set Primary Key to set the two columns as concatenated keys.

4. Just like before, a key icon appears next to the column names, and an asterisk (*) appears next to the table's name.

5. To create the foreign key relationship between the **tblHotels** and **tblRooms** tables, select the column HotelID in the **tblRooms** table. Just like in Windows Explorer, where you click and drag a file to another folder, you're going to do the same with the HotelID column. Drag the column name to the **tblHotels** window within the Database Diagram window. Figure 7.18 illustrates what your screen should look like when dragging the HotelID column name from the **tblRooms** table to the **tblHotels** table.

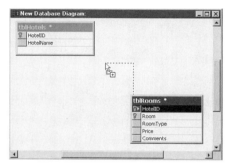

Figure 7.18 Dragging the HotelID column name from one table to another to create a foreign key relationship

When the mouse cursor is over the **tblHotels** window, release the mouse button. This displays the Create Relationship dialog box shown in Figure 7.19.

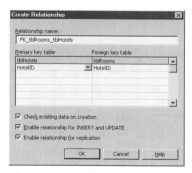

Figure 7.19 The Create Relationship dialog box between the tblHotels and tblRooms tables

6. As you can see, the dialog box generates a relationship name for you. It also displays the columns that relate the two tables. Enabling the Check Existing Data on Creation check box determines whether a violation in data integrity occurs when you create a relationship with tables that have data. The Enable Relationship check boxes are for referential integrity purposes. For this exercise, leave all these check boxes enabled and click OK. The New Database Diagram window now illustrates the relationship between the two tables, as shown in Figure 7.20.

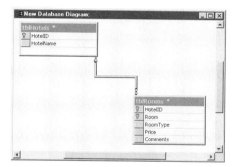

Figure 7.20 The New Database Diagram window illustrates the relationship between tblHotels and tblRooms

How It Works

All the steps performed through SQL Enterprise Manager perform the DDL equivalents via Transact-SQL, which you would issue through the ISQL prompt. When adding a primary and foreign key to a table, you are issuing the **ALTER TABLE** statement and adding constraints to the table. The **ALTER TABLE** statement for the **Hotels** table looks like this:

```
ALTER TABLE tbl_Hotels
    ADD
    CONSTRAINT PK_hotel PRIMARY KEY NONCLUSTERED
        (Hotel)
```

ALTER TABLE is used to add a new column or a data-integrity constraint to a database table. This **ALTER TABLE** statement adds a primary key constraint and nonclustered index to the **tbl_Hotels** database table using the Hotel column as the primary key. The nonclustered index is called **PK_hotel**.

Creating the primary and foreign keys of the **Rooms** table looks like this:

```
ALTER TABLE tbl_Rooms
    ADD
    CONSTRAINT PK_Rooms PRIMARY KEY NONCLUSTERED
        (Hotel, Room),
```

```
CONSTRAINT FK_Hotels FOREIGN KEY
    (Hotel)
    REFERENCES dbo.tbl_Hotels (Hotel)
```

The ALTER TABLE statement first adds a primary key constraint and nonclustered index to the tbl_Rooms database table using the Hotel and Room columns as the primary key. The second half of the ALTER TABLE statement adds a foreign key constraint to the tbl_Rooms database table using the tbl_Hotels database table as the reference table. The column used to list the reference is the Hotel column. The nonclustered index based on the Hotel and Room columns is called PK_Rooms. The foreign key constraint name is FK_Hotels.

Comments

You might have noticed that by using ISQL you need to supply the constraint names. Actually, if you do not provide a constraint name SQL Server generates a name and assigns it to the constraint.

COMPLEXITY
BEGINNING

7.6 How do I...
Index a table for efficiency and performance?

COMPATIBILITY: SQL SERVER 6.5 AND VISUAL BASIC 6.0

Problem

My tables have been created, and they all have their primary and foreign keys defined. I know that our developers are not going to write queries that solely go against the primary keys of a table. I have been told that I should have created indexes for my tables so that these auxiliary queries will run at a decent speed. How do I create indexes on my tables?

Technique

Indexes are used to speed access to data and to enforce uniqueness within a table. Indexes offer a good method for increasing data-storage performance because they keep track of key information and where it is located in the tables.

Before you start defining indexes on your tables, you should be aware that there are two types of indexes you can use: *clustered* and *nonclustered*. In a clustered index, the data is physically sorted and stored in the index order. For example, before a clustered index is applied to the customer database table, the physical order of the data in the database is in the order in which it was entered. For reporting purposes, you base a lot of reports on each customer's first and last name (last name first), so you create a clustered index on the database table based on the last and first name columns. The data is now physically sorted by each customer's last and first name. Now when you do a report, you do not need to add an `Order By` in your query because the data that is retrieved is alphabetized by each customer's last and first name.

A nonclustered index maintains an index file that contains pointers that reference where data is located in the table based on how the clustered index organized the data. When a query is performed and it uses a nonclustered index, a minimum of two disk reads is required. The first read scans the index for the indexed field, and the second read retrieves the actual data from the table.

Because the nonclustered index bases the location of the data on how the clustered index organizes it, it is a good practice to define your clustered index first, before you create a lot of nonclustered indexes. If you create a lot of nonclustered indexes, and then you create your clustered index, all the nonclustered indexes will be rebuilt because the locations of the data are going to be reorganized. If you have many nonclustered indexes when this happens, the rebuild can take a long time.

Using a clustered index instead of nonclustered indexes for data retrieval is almost always faster. When a query is performed that uses a clustered index, because the data is already in index order, another read is not required—you are already positioned on the rows you need. In Figure 7.21, the clustered index is based on the guest's last name. The guests' information has been rearranged based on the index, regardless of when the information was entered. When you need to retrieve information from this index, only one read from the index is necessary because the data is already in last-name order. In the nonclustered index, the index is also based on the guest's last name, but the guests' information stays in the order in which it was entered into the system. When you must retrieve information from this index, two processes must be performed: The first process reads the index to find out where the data is stored, and the second process retrieves the data.

When you create the primary key for your tables, you can create it as a clustered or nonclustered index to the table. It is not a good idea to create the clustered index against the primary key of the table because that is not how the information is always grouped or displayed in a report or customer lookup chart. For example, you rarely want to look up a chart by the customer number. The most common lookup is the customer's last name or company name. When you perform a lookup on a customer's number, you are usually interested in one record; therefore, you use the overhead of a clustered index just to find one record.

Steps

This example creates a clustered index in the **Reservations** database table using the guest's last and first name as the index.

Clustered Index

Index Key	Data Page
Adams	2
Jones	15
Smith	30
Zak	35

Non-Clustered Index

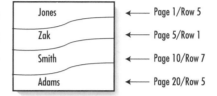

Index Key	Data Page/Row
Adams	20/5
Jones	1/10
Smith	10/7
Zak	5/1

Jones ← Page 1/Row 5
Zak ← Page 5/Row 1
Smith ← Page 10/Row 7
Adams ← Page 20/Row 5

Figure 7.21 Clustered versus nonclustered indexes

Creating a Clustered Index Using SQL Enterprise Manager

Complete the following steps to create a clustered index using SQL Enterprise Manager:

1. Open SQL Enterprise Manager from your Microsoft SQL Server 6.5 Utilities group.

2. In the Server Manager window, select the server that contains the database in which you want to create the table. Using the information from How-To 7.3, use the server called GOTHAM_CITY and the database called db_HotelSystem.

3. Choose Indexes from the Manage menu. The Manage Indexes dialog box appears.

4. In the Table combo box, select the tbl_Reservations table. Your Manage Indexes dialog box should look similar to Figure 7.22.

5. In the Index combo box, select <New> so that you can create a new index.

6. The text field of the combo box clears, and you can type the name of the new index, idx_LastFirst.

7. In the Available Columns in Table list box, select the LastName column and click Add. This moves the column name to the Columns in Index (Key) list box.

8. Select the FirstName column and click Add.

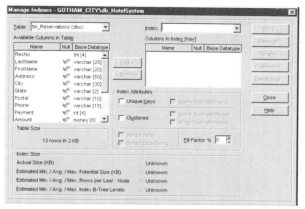

Figure 7.22 The index information for the
`tbl_Reservations` table

9. In the Index Attribute frame, enable the Clustered check box. A check mark appears.

10. The two radio buttons next to Clustered should become enabled so that you can modify them. Select the Allow Duplicate Rows radio button. You are allowing duplicate rows because a person with the same last name can make more than one reservation. Also, because this is not a primary key, duplicate rows do not matter as much.

11. Click Build to create the index.

12. A dialog box appears, giving you the option of executing this process now or at a scheduled time (see Figure 7.23). Because you don't have a lot of data or nonclustered indexes defined, click Execute Now.

Figure 7.23 The execute now
or schedule the task later
dialog box

The index is created, and a row is placed in the **sysindexes** database system table. **sysindexes** is a system table defined in each database that contains a record of all the clustered and nonclustered indexes. It also contains a record of all tables that have no indexes.

Creating a Clustered Index Using the Data View

To create a clustered index using the Data view, complete the following steps:

1. In the Data View window, open the Tables folder in the **dbHotel** database.

2. Open the **erdHotels** diagram in the Database Diagram folder.

3. If you have not added the **tblReservations** table to the diagram, select it from the Tables folder in the Data View window and drag it into the Database Diagram window.

4. Right-click the **tblReservations** table and choose Properties from the shortcut menu. The Properties dialog box appears, as shown in Figure 7.24.

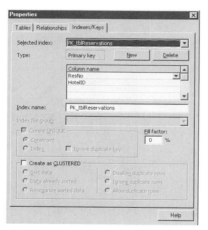

Figure 7.24 The Indexes/Keys tab in the Properties dialog box for tblReservations

5. Click New to create a new index. The system then generates an index name for the new index. Notice that the Type text box to the left of the New button changes from Primary Key to Index. This lets you know what type of index or key you're using.

6. In the Column Name list box, select the column names you want as part of this index. Each line is like a combo box where you can type the column name into the cell or use the drop-down list box. Select LastName on the first line and FirstName on the second line.

7. In the Index Name field, you can change the name of the index to anything you want. For this example, name it **IX_LastFirst**.

8. To make this a clustered index, enable the Create As CLUSTERED check box. This enables all the options within the frame. There are two sets of options: Sort Data options and Duplicate Row options. Leave the first option, Sort Data, alone. This is the default setting, and it organizes the data in ascending order. Because this index is not for the primary key, duplicate records don't concern you; therefore, select the Allow Duplicate Rows option.

9. To save this newly created index, simply close the dialog box.

How It Works

The DDL statement that SQL Enterprise Manager performed is the `CREATE INDEX` statement. The statement in ISQL looks something like this:

```
CREATE CLUSTERED INDEX idx_LastFirst
ON Reservations (LastName, FirstName)
WITH ALLOW_DUP_ROW
```

Comments

In an online transaction processing system, defining clustered indexes can slow down your system because of the data reorganization that occurs after each transaction—whether it is a single transaction or batch transactions. It is better to define clustered indexes on systems such as decision support systems or systems that have very little data input, or on tables used primarily for querying information.

When defining a clustered index, it is better to assign it before the tables get too much information or too many nonclustered indexes. When a clustered index is defined, all nonclustered indexes are rebuilt to reflect the clustered index. Depending on how much data or how many nonclustered indexes exist, this can be a very slow process.

COMPLEXITY
BEGINNING

7.7 How do I...
Create a trigger to control data integrity?

COMPATIBILITY: SQL SERVER 6.5 AND VISUAL BASIC 6.0

Problem

In previous versions of SQL Server, triggers are used to enforce complex business rules and the integrity of the data enforcing the primary and foreign key relationship. If I do not need triggers to enforce the primary and foreign key relationships anymore, what else can I use triggers for?

Technique

A *trigger* is a special kind of stored procedure of DML statements that is automatically executed when an **INSERT**, **DELETE**, or **UPDATE** is performed. The trigger is executed automatically whenever an application makes a specified change to the database table. Triggers get activated once per query and are treated as one transaction that can be rolled back if an error is detected during their execution. Each trigger can perform any number of functions and can call up to 16 stored procedures. The stored procedures can be system stored procedures or user-defined stored procedures, like the ones illustrated in How-To's 7.8 and 7.9. A trigger cannot be created against a view or temporary table, although it can reference them.

As mentioned earlier, SQL Server versions 4.2 and 6.0 relied on triggers to maintain data consistency. These triggers enforce business rules about the relationships between tables. In a traditional two-tier client/server model, enforcement of business rules can be handled on either tier. In a three-tier model, business rules are handled in the middle tier, the business services layer. Triggers should be used only to handle data operations. For further explanation of what makes up the business services layer, refer to Chapter 1, "Client/Server Basics," and Chapter 6, "Business Objects."

Steps

This example is applied to the **tbl_Rooms** database table. It is going to cascade a change throughout related tables in the database. Suppose you're changing all the room numbers for all the rooms in all the hotels in the system. Without the use of triggers, you could not update the room numbers without affecting the **tbl_Reservations** database table. The room numbers in the **tbl_Reservations** database table are related to the room numbers in the **tbl_Rooms** database table. The primary and foreign key relationship would not allow this to happen because the foreign key cannot exist without a primary key value. If you use an update trigger, the change of the room number in the **tbl_Rooms** database table will also update the room number in the **tbl_Reservations** database table, thus maintaining referential integrity.

Creating a Trigger for a Table Using SQL Enterprise Manager

Complete the following steps to create a trigger using SQL Enterprise Manager:

1. Open SQL Enterprise Manager from your Microsoft SQL Server 6.5 Utilities group.

2. In the Server Manager window, select the server that contains the database in which you want to create the table. Using the information from

How-To 7.3, use the server called GOTHAM_CITY and the database called db_HotelSystem.

3. Choose Triggers from the Manage menu. The Manage Triggers window appears, as shown in Figure 7.25.

```
Manage Triggers - GOTHAM_CITY\db_HotelSystem

Table:  tbl_Rooms (dbo)          Trigger:        <new>

CREATE TRIGGER trg_Update_Rooms ON dbo.tbl_Rooms
FOR UPDATE
AS
IF UPDATE(room)
BEGIN
    PRINT "Trigger trg_Update_Rooms was executed."
    UPDATE tbl_Reservations
        SET room = inserted.room
      FROM inserted, deleted
     WHERE room = deleted.room
       AND hotel = deleted.room
END
```

Figure 7.25 The Manage Triggers window with default information

4. Any triggers in the database are listed in the Trigger combo box.

5. Choose the database table for which you will design the trigger. In this example, you will use **tbl_Rooms (dbo)**. Because no triggers are defined for this table yet, choose <New> from the Trigger combo box to create a new trigger. The window displays what you need to start creating a trigger:

```
CREATE TRIGGER <TRIGGER NAME> ON dbo.tbl_Rooms
FOR INSERT,UPDATE,DELETE
AS
```

6. Enter the following code in the Manage Triggers window. Change <TRIGGER NAME> to **trg_Update_Rooms**. Remove the **INSERT** and **DELETE** options from the **FOR** definition because this trigger only applies to update actions against this table. The **IF UPDATE** keyword tests for an **INSERT** or **UPDATE** action against a specific column or columns in the database table. You did not leave **INSERT** in because SQL Server treats updates as **DELETE** and **INSERT** processes. In this example, you are checking to see whether the column room is being updated.

```
CREATE TRIGGER trg_Update_Rooms ON DBO.tbl_Rooms
FOR UPDATE

AS
IF UPDATE(room)
```

7. Continue to enter the following code in the Manage Trigger window. The **BEGIN** statement marks the beginning of the transaction. The **PRINT** statement prints a message to the test environment—the Query Analyzer or ISQL. The UPDATE statement will update the room value in the tbl_Reservations database table. The SET keyword specifies which column is going to be updated. In this example, the value the room is going to be updated to comes from the inserted table. The WHERE clause performs a search to find the row or rows that are going to be affected by the UPDATE. The values it is trying to match are the room and hotel values from the deleted table. The inserted and deleted tables are special system tables. They are temporary tables used by triggers to store information about the transaction. During a DELETE, SQL Server stores a copy of the deleted rows in the deleted table. During an INSERT, SQL Server stores a copy of the new rows being inserted in the inserted table. To SQL Server, an UPDATE is both a DELETE and an INSERT; therefore, the old rows being updated are copied in the deleted table, while the new, updated rows are copied in the inserted table. The END statement notifies SQL Server that the transaction is complete.

```
BEGIN
    PRINT "Trigger trg_Update_Rooms was executed."
    UPDATE tbl_Reservations
    SET tbl_Rooms.room = inserted.room
    FROM inserted, deleted
    WHERE tbl_Rooms_room = deleted.room
      AND tbl_Rooms.hotel = deleted.hotel

END
```

8. Click the Execute button next to the Trigger combo box. If the editor does not encounter any errors, the trigger is saved.

9. To test the trigger, load the Query Analyzer. On the Query tab, type the UPDATE statement. You are going to update the room number 2980 in hotel number 1 to 2780 in the tbl_Rooms database table. After you have typed this, click Execute.

```
UPDATE tbl_Rooms
SET Room = 2780
WHERE Room = 2980
AND Hotel = 1
```

Creating a Trigger for the tblRooms **Table Using Data View**

To create a trigger using the Data view, complete the following steps:

1. In the Data View window, right-click tblRooms, which is located in the Tables folder. Then choose New Trigger from the shortcut menu (see Figure 7.26).

2. A New Trigger window appears. Change tblRooms_Trigger1 to trg_Update_Rooms. Remove the /* Insert, Update, Delete */ comment from the FOR definition and replace it with the keyword UPDATE.

Figure 7.26 Choosing
New Trigger from the
context menu

Remove the /* If Update (column_name)... */ comment from the
window and replace it with the following code:

```
IF UPDATE(room)
BEGIN
    PRINT "Trigger trg_Update_Rooms was executed."
    UPDATE tblReservations
    SET tbl_Rooms.room = inserted.room
    FROM inserted, deleted
    WHERE tblRooms.room = deleted.room
    AND tblRooms.Hotel = deleted.hotel
END
```

3. Figure 7.27 shows the code in the New Trigger window. Click the cylinder
icon on the toolbar to save the new trigger to the table.

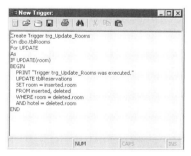

Figure 7.27 The New Trigger
window with the trigger
code for tblRooms

How It Works

When an update transaction is performed against the room column in the `tbl_Rooms` database table, this trigger is executed. Because the `tbl_Reservations` database table has a primary and foreign key relationship on the room column with the `tbl_Rooms` database table, the room value in `tbl_Reservations` must be updated as well. A reservation cannot exist without a valid room assigned to it. If you only update the room column in the `tbl_Rooms` database table without the corresponding room column in the `tbl_Reservations` database table, you violate this relationship rule. It is possible that the room you are updating does not have a reservation assigned to it, but you would never know that unless you had a report of all the rooms that did not have an assigned reservation.

As mentioned earlier, an **UPDATE** first performs a **DELETE** and then an **INSERT**. The **UPDATE** statement issued in step 9 of "Creating a Trigger for a Table Using SQL Enterprise Manager" deletes the row from the `tbl_Rooms` database table and copies the deleted row into the deleted table. Then it adds the new row with new information into the `tbl_Rooms` database table and copies the inserted row in the inserted table. The trigger is executed and performs an **UPDATE** on the `tbl_Reservations` database table. The criteria the **UPDATE** statement is going to use comes from the inserted and deleted table. The **UPDATE** statement is going to update the room value in the `tbl_Reservations` database table with a value of 2780 where the old room number used to be 2980 and the old hotel value was 1.

Comments

As you can see from this example, certain data integrity rules are handled through the use of the primary and foreign key constraints; therefore, there is little reason to use triggers to enforce that relationship as long as the table relationship is within the same database. As you saw here, triggers generally are used not to implement referential integrity but to keep tables in synch with one another. SQL Server still does not perform cross-database data integrity. Triggers would need to be used for this type of data integrity.

COMPLEXITY
BEGINNING

7.8 How do I...
Create a view?

COMPATIBILITY: SQL SERVER 6.5 AND VISUAL BASIC 6.0

Problem

This system is going to be available to a lot of people, and I'm afraid it is going to become a security nightmare. I've been told that I can create view tables and base my security on these tables rather than the actual database tables. What are view tables, and how can I implement them?

Technique

A good method for restricting access to information is using a *derived table* or *view*. A view is a virtual table that looks and feels like a real table. Views limit the amount of data a user can see and modify. Views can range from a single column of a table to the entire table, or even a combination of several tables. Views are not tables; therefore, they store no data, so any actual modifications to the real table will be under your control. But to the user or application developer, a view looks and acts like a table. You may use views to control user access to data and to simplify data presentation.

Because views are derived from tables, data access can be improved. Complex queries often join against a lot of tables; therefore, they take a long time to process. By defining views based on the query, the view has already arranged the information it is ultimately going to display or use. An example of a view is one based on an employee table. The base table contains the employee's salary, Social Security number, and other items of information that only someone in human resources should see. By using a view table, you can filter out all the private information and display only the public information. If you did not define a view table, you would have built some data security around the base table. Figure 7.28 shows how views interact with base tables.

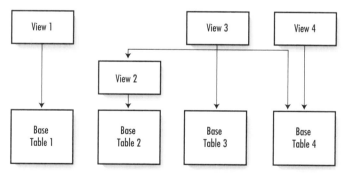

Figure 7.28 A view table schema against base tables

View table 1 is a derived table based on base table 1. The actual view table can be one column from base table 1, several columns, or a mirror of base table 1. View table 2 is derived from base table 2. In this instance, it probably consists of several columns from base table 2. View table 3 is derived from view table 2, base table 3, and base table 4. This type of view table probably derived from a query that needed to retrieve information from all three tables. Instead of having the query go against three physical database tables to make up the result set, the query goes after one virtual table that is based on the three tables. View table 4 is derived from base table 4.

Views can serve great purposes in a database-driven application. One benefit they provide is the capability to create status views of data that pull information from several tables and present a summary of it to the user. These views can then be the basis for management reports in the application.

Views provide an additional layer of security because they can limit the visible rows based on specified criteria without changing permission to the underlying table or tables. A view is created by using a standard SQL statement, so any selection that can be done with a DML statement can also be done from a view table.

Steps

This example creates a view table to show specific data from the `Reservations`, `Rooms`, `RoomTypes`, and `PaymentTypes` tables. This view table consists of the following:

✔ A guest's registration number

✔ A guest's last and first name

✔ The name of the hotel for which the reservation is made

✔ The room number in which the guest will be staying

✔ The number of beds in the room

✔ A description of the room

Without this view table, you would have to create a query that retrieves this information from four tables. By using the view, you must search only one table for the information. As a *database administrator* (DBA), without the view table you would need to define security access for the programmer to all four tables. With the view, you need to define security only for the view table.

Creating a View Using SQL Enterprise Manager

Complete the following steps to create a view using SQL Enterprise Manager:

1. Open SQL Enterprise Manager from your Microsoft SQL Server 6.5 Utilities group.

2. In the Server Manager window, select the server that contains the database in which you want to create the table. Using the information from How-To 7.3, use the server called GOTHAM_CITY and the database called `db_HotelSystem`.

3. Choose Views from the Manage menu. The Manage Views window appears, as shown in Figure 7.29. Any views in the database are listed in the View combo box.

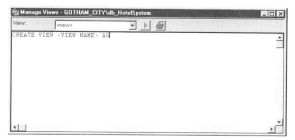

Figure 7.29 The Manage Views window

4. Choose <new> from the View combo box to create a new view. The window displays what you need to start creating a view:

```
CREATE VIEW <VIEW NAME> AS
```

5. Enter the following code in the Manage Views window to create the view to display certain aspects of a guest's reservation. The view table is called `vr_Reservations`. The column names that will make up this table are `ResNo`, `LastName`, `FirstName`, `PaymentDesc`, `Room`, `Beds`, and `RoomDesc`. As you can see, because a view is a virtual table, you can make column names a bit more meaningful than how they were originally designed. In this example, there are two description fields—one from the `tbl_PaymentTypes` table and the other from the `tbl_RoomTypes` table. Instead of having two columns with `Description` as their column name, you will name the columns `PaymentDesc` and `RoomDesc` to distinguish the differences. The `Select` statement defines the view table. The view is the set of rows and columns that result when the `Select` statement is executed. The `Select` statement is based on joining information from four tables with equal key values: `Payment` in `tbl_PaymentTypes` is equal to `Payment` in `tbl_Reservations`, `Room` in `tbl_Rooms` is equal to `Room` in `tbl_Reservations`, `Hotel` in `tbl_Rooms` is equal to `Hotel` in `tbl_Reservations`, and `RoomType` in `tbl_RoomTypes` is equal to `RoomType` in `tbl_Rooms`.

```
CREATE VIEW vr_Reservations
(ResNo, LastName, FirstName, PaymentDesc, Room, Beds, RoomDesc)
AS
SELECT a.ResNo, a.LastName, a.FirstName
     , b.Description
     , c.Room
     , d.Beds, d.Description
  FROM tbl_Reservations a, tbl_PaymentTypes b
     , tbl_Rooms c, tbl_RoomTypes d
 WHERE b.Payment = a.Payment
   AND c.Room = a.Room
   AND c.Hotel = a.Hotel
   AND d.RoomType = c.RoomType
```

> **TIP**
>
> Instead of typing the table name before each column name, you can use aliases to reduce your amount of typing when you must fully qualify each column. For example, if you had not used aliases, you would have had to type `Select tbl_Reservations.ResNo, tbl_Reservations.LastName`, and so on.

6. Click the Execute button to save the view. SQL Server scans the view for errors and if none are found, the view is saved.

7. To retrieve information for the newly created view table, start the Query Analyzer and enter the following statement:

```
select * from vr_Reservations
```

The resulting data should look similar to Figure 7.30.

Figure 7.30 Resulting data from querying the vr_Reservations view table

Creating the View Using the Data View

To create a view using the Data view, complete the following steps:

1. In the Data View window, right-click the Views folder. Then choose New View from the shortcut menu.

The New View window appears. It has four panes:

✔ Diagram—Allows for a graphical display of the tables you will use in your query and their relationships to one another.

✔ Grid—Enables you to specify query options, such as which column you want to display or how the result set should be sorted.

✔ SQL—Displays the SQL statement for the current view or query.

✔ Results—Displays the result of the query.

Because a view is a derived query, the Data View window treats it as such. To create the view for the reservation, you must expand the `tblReservations`, `tblPaymentTypes`, `tblRooms`, and `tblRoomTypes` tables.

2. Select the `ResNo` in the `tblReservations` table and drag it over to the Diagram pane. This places an input source window of all the columns in the `tblReservations` table in the Diagram pane.

3. Mark the other two columns, `LastName` and `FirstName`, in the `tblReservations` input source window. This adds the columns to the query.

4. Select the column name `Description` from the `tblPaymentTypes` table and drag it to the Diagram pane.

5. Select the column name `Room` from the `tblRooms` table and drag it to the Diagram pane.

6. Select the column name `Beds` from the `tblRoomTypes` table and drag it to the Diagram pane. In the input source window for the `tblRoomTypes` table, mark the column name `Description` to add the column to the query.

7. You might notice that two columns have the same name: `Description`. In the Grid pane, the second column, `Alias`, allows you to enter an alternative title for each column. For this exercise, change the `tblPaymentType`'s `Description` column to `PaymentDesc` and `tblRoomTypes`'s `Description` to `RoomDesc`.

8. To link all these tables together, see Table 7.8. Afterward, your New View window should look similar to Figure 7.31.

Table 7.8   Join criteria for the vr_Reservations view

INPUT SOURCE	SOURCE COLUMN	TARGET
tblReservations	Payment	tblPaymentType – PaymentID
tblReservations	HotelID	tblRooms – HotelID
tblRooms	RoomType	tblRoomTypes – tblRoomTypes

9. To test the view, choose Run from the Query menu in the Visual Basic IDE. Or you can choose Run from the New View window's context menu. The Results pane displays the result of the query.

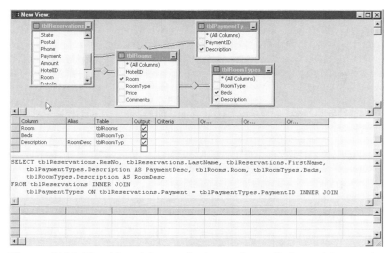

Figure 7.31 The New View window after all the tables and join criteria have been established

How It Works

This is a simple view statement. When this view table is queried against, the query performs as if it were going against the base tables. The difference is that the join will have already been preprocessed and simply executed. Had this join been written into your application, the engine would first check to see whether all the elements in the query exist, process the query, and then execute.

After you click Execute in step 6 of the "Creating a View Using SQL Enterprise Manager" procedure, the editor scans the view statement for errors. Also, SQL Server inserts the following lines before your procedure:

```
if exists (select * from sysobjects
        where id = object_id('dbo.vr_Reservations')
    and sysstat & 0xf = 2)
drop view dbo.vr_Reservations
GO
```

This statement checks to see whether there is a view procedure in your database with the same name. This statement is necessary when you make changes to the view procedure because you actually drop the original procedure and replace it with the new one.

Comments

When naming your views, you can use various naming strategies. Because views must be used for read-only access or controlled-update access, you might want to note that in your naming convention. If the view you just created was to be an update view, for example, you would have named it **vu_Reservations** rather than `vr_Reservations`. By no means is this a standard, but it does help developers and DBAs distinguish the types of views.

COMPLEXITY
INTERMEDIATE

7.9 How do I...
Create and execute a stored procedure?

COMPATIBILITY: SQL SERVER 6.5 AND VISUAL BASIC 6.0

Problem

In my Hotel system, I always need to look up standard room information that employees will use when scheduling a reservation. The query is fairly straightforward, but I don't want the query replicated across all my applications. This probably belongs in a business object, but I want it to be a stored procedure. What is a stored procedure, and how do I write one?

Technique

A *stored procedure* is a compiled SQL program. Within a stored procedure, you can perform conditional execution, declare variables, pass parameters, and perform other programming tasks. Stored procedures are reusable but not reentrant. If two users execute the same procedure simultaneously, two copies of the plan are loaded into memory. Because procedure query plans are built and optimized the first time they are read from disk, there's no guarantee that the plan is optimal every time the procedure is invoked. If your stored procedure accepts parameter lists that may require different forms of optimization, using `exec` with the `recompile` clause causes SQL Server not to cache the query plan. It rebuilds the plan each time the stored procedure is called.

The advantages of using stored procedures follow:

✔ Better performance and reduced server load because SQL is precompiled

✔ Easier change management

✔ Better control over database access because only approved SQL is permitted to run against the server

✔ Easier and tighter security administration because the only entry point to the database is through stored procedures

✔ Less network chat because fewer calls are made by the client and any required cursor processing takes place on the server exclusively

✔ More opportunity for asynchronous server processing because the client does not need to be involved in complicated transactions

✔ A solid foundation for migration to emerging three-tier client/server products

In a two-tiered model, business logic would be part of the stored procedure. In a distributed environment, stored procedures should be used to handle the basic data-manipulation tasks needed by the business layer.

Steps

This example illustrates how to create a stored procedure that will retrieve commonly sought out data. The stored procedure will require one parameter to be passed to it in order for it to qualify which hotel the procedure should query against.

Creating a Stored Procedure Using the SQL Enterprise Manager

Complete the following steps to create a stored procedure using SQL Enterprise Manager:

1. Open SQL Enterprise Manager from your Microsoft SQL Server 6.5 Utilities group.

2. In the Server Manager window, select the server that contains the database in which you want to create the stored procedure. Using the information from How-To 7.3, use the GOTHAM_CITY server and the db_HotelSystem database.

3. Choose Stored Procedures from the Manage menu. The Manage Stored Procedures window appears, as shown in Figure 7.32. The Procedure combo box lists any stored procedures in the database.

Figure 7.32 The Manage Stored Procedures window

4. Select <new> in the Procedure combo box to create a new stored procedure. The window displays what you need to start creating a stored procedure:

```
CREATE PROCEDURE <PROCEDURE NAME> AS
```

5. Replace <PROCEDURE NAME> with spp_RoomDesc.

6. Because you do not want all the rooms in all the hotels to be displayed, you are going to add the following argument variable to the first line of the procedure. This goes after the procedure name and before the AS:

```
@Hotel int
```

7. Your first line should look like this:

```
CREATE PROCEDURE spp_RoomDesc @Hotel int AS
```

The name of the stored procedure is spp_RoomDesc. The argument variable, @Hotel, is defined as an integer datatype to match the datatype of Hotel in the tbl_Rooms and tbl_RoomTypes tables. This means that the Visual Basic code that is using this stored procedure passes the Hotel number in as an integer value. This argument is used as part of the query's Where clause to retrieve only the rooms for a given hotel.

8. For readability, enter the following on the next line. At this point, you are simply entering a standard SQL query statement to retrieve the desired information.

```
SELECT a.room, b.beds, b.description, a.price
  FROM tbl_Rooms a, tbl_RoomTypes b
 WHERE a.hotel = @Hotel
   AND a.roomtype = b.roomtype
```

9. Click the Execute button next to the Procedure combo box. This scans the procedure for errors. If no errors are found, the procedure is stored in the database on the server. Contrary to popular belief, the Execute button does not really execute the stored procedure. It merely checks the system to see whether the stored procedure exists, makes sure there are no syntax errors, and then saves the procedure to the server.

10. To execute the procedure you must execute it from within SQL Query Manager or ISQL. Within SQL Query Manager or ISQL, type the following and press the Execute Query button:

```
EXEC spp_RoomDesc @hotel=3
```

Creating a Stored Procedure Using the Data View

To create a stored procedure using the Data view, complete the following steps:

1. Right-click the Stored Procedure folder and choose New Store Procedure from the context menu.

2. Replace StoredProcedure1 with spp_RoomDesc.

3. You need only one argument for this procedure. This argument limits the number of rooms you retrieve to one hotel versus all of them. Place the following argument and the datatype after the **spp_RoomDesc** name:

```
@HotelID int
```

4. Enter this code on the line following the **AS**:

```
SELECT a.room, b.beds, b.descriptions, a.price
  FROM tblRooms a, tblRoomTypes b
 WHERE a.HotelID = @HotelID
   AND a.RoomType = b.RoomType
```

Your procedure should resemble Figure 7.33.

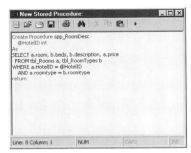

Figure 7.33 The Data View
New Stored Procedure
editor

5. Click the Debug button on the toolbar to execute and debug the procedure. This process invokes the T-SQL Debugger, which enables you to step through your procedure the way you step through your Visual Basic code.

How It Works

The syntax for creating a stored procedure follows:

```
CREATE PROCEDURE procedure_name [parameter1, ...]
AS SELECT select_criteria
FROM table_name
```

The **procedure_name** is the name of the stored procedure, which you called **sp_RoomDesc**. You used a parameter that is used as part of the **WHERE** criteria in your SQL query. A procedure can have up to 255 parameters defined. When placing a parameter in your stored procedure, the first character must be the at symbol (**@**) and the same datatype that it is requesting. In this example, the

`Hotel` datatype is an integer in the database; therefore, the parameter argument also must be an integer datatype. When this stored procedure is called, a parameter must be supplied; otherwise, an error occurs. If you would like the user to execute the stored procedure whether or not a parameter is supplied, you can provide a default value. For example, if you wanted the stored procedure to use hotel number 1 as the default value, the code in step 7 of the "Creating a Stored Procedure Using the SQL Enterprise Manager" section would look like this:

```
@Hotel int = 1
```

The `Select` statement returns the room number from the `Rooms` table and returns the beds, description, and price data from the `RoomTypes` table that have corresponding room numbers in the `Rooms` table.

The `Where` clause checks to make sure the room number returned from the `Rooms` table belongs to the hotel number that was requested.

After you click the Execute button in step 9 of the "Creating a Stored Procedure Using the SQL Enterprise Manager" section, the editor scans the procedure for errors. Also, SQL Server inserts the following lines before your procedure:

```
if exists (select * from sysobjects
          where id = object_id('dbo.proc_RoomDesc')
          and sysstat & 0xf = 4)
drop procedure dbo.proc_RoomDesc
GO
```

This statement checks to see whether there is a stored procedure in your database with the same name. This statement is necessary when you make changes to the stored procedure because you actually drop the original procedure and replace it with the new one.

When this procedure is called from your program or within ISQL, it performs the query and retrieves the information requested about the `Rooms` and `RoomTypes`.

Comments

When creating a stored procedure, almost everyone uses the editor that comes with SQL Enterprise Manager, as you did in this example. There is nothing wrong with working on the procedures this way, but you must be aware that by using this editor, you have no way to *version control* your changes to a procedure. In other words, after you make a change and click the Save Object button, there is no way for you to go back to a previous version of the procedure. After you create your stored procedures, it is a good practice to create SQL scripts for them and to store them on a drive that routinely gets backed up.

It also might be a good idea to use a tool such as Microsoft Visual SourceSafe to handle version control of the SQL scripts. Using a version control tool for your SQL scripts offers the same advantages of using it for your source code.

Refer to Chapter 1, "Client/Server Basics," for more information on using Visual SourceSafe.

Quite a few third-party tools are available to create, manage, and maintain stored procedures. For an idea of what is available, see Appendix B, "Client/Server Database Resources," for more information.

COMPLEXITY
INTERMEDIATE

7.10 How do I...
Create a stored procedure that performs a transaction?

COMPATIBILITY: SQL SERVER 6.5 AND VISUAL BASIC 6.0

Problem

Now that I know how to make simple stored procedures that replace my SQL queries in my code, I would like to know how to make more sophisticated stored procedures that perform the updating of a database table and contain error handling. What do I need for my stored procedure to do that?

Technique

A stored procedure that performs a unit of work that is more than just replacing SQL queries is often called a transactional stored procedure. This is because they perform several types of transactions, such as removing information from one table and inserting that information into another table. If you did this programmatically within your Visual Basic application, you would have to make sure you scope this unit of work properly. If any part of the transaction failed, you would have to program a way to ensure that the data is reset to the way it was before the transaction took place.

By having a stored procedure perform a transaction, the scope of work is limited to within the procedure itself. If something goes wrong within the transaction, the SQL that is executed is contained within the procedure, making it easy to back out any modifications made. Using the Microsoft Transaction Server (MTS) can also make rolling back a unit of work very easy. For more information on MTS, refer to Chapter 6, "Business Objects." For more information on how to call a stored procedure, refer to Chapter 3, "Data Objects."

Steps

Complete the following steps to create a stored procedure that performs a transaction:

1. Open SQL Enterprise Manager from your Microsoft SQL Server 6.5 Utilities group.

2. In the Server Manager window, select the server that contains the database in which you want to create the stored procedure. Using the information from How-To 7.3, use the GOTHAM_CITY server and the `db_HotelSystem` database.

3. Choose Stored Procedures from the Manage menu. The Manage Stored Procedures window appears.

4. Any stored procedures in the database are listed in the Procedure combo box.

5. Select <New> from the Procedure combo box to create a new stored procedure. The window displays what you need in order to start creating a stored procedure:

```
CREATE PROCEDURE <PROCEDURE NAME> AS
```

6. Replace <PROCEDURE NAME> with `proc_submit_resv`. The first line of the procedure should look like this:

```
CREATE PROCEDURE proc_submit_resv
```

7. This stored procedure will insert a reservation for a guest into the `tbl_Reservation` database table. To insert a guest, the `Insert` statement needs some information about the guest: the hotel at which the guest wants to stay, first and last name, address, phone number, method of payment, cost of the room, and date range of the guest's visit. Also, the type of room the guest would like to stay in is passed. Insert the following argument parameters into the stored procedure to define the argument parameters and their datatypes:

```
@Hotel          int,
@LastName       varchar (25),
@FirstName      varchar (20),
@Address        varchar (50),
@City           varchar (30),
@State          varchar (2),
@Postal         varchar (10),
@Phone          varchar (15),
@Payment        int,
@Amount         Money,
@DateIn         DateTime,
@DateOut        DateTime,
@RoomType       int,

AS
```

8. Insert the following code into the stored procedure to define some variables that are going to be used in this procedure. The `declare` statement defines the name and datatype of a local variable that can be used in the procedure. The text between /* and */ is comments. This text is not considered executable code—simply comments to help document the procedure.

```
/* Use this variable to hold our transaction return status */
declare @tran_status     int

/* Use this variable to hold the room number */
declare @RoomNbr         smallint

/* this will store the new reservation number after we create */
/* a reservation */
declare @resv_nbr         int
```

9. Insert the following code into the stored procedure to mark the starting point of a transaction:

```
BEGIN TRAN
```

10. Insert the following code into the stored procedure. Within the **If** statement, a query checks to make sure that the desired room type is available at the time this process was performed. It's a good practice to check this, because during the time you were on the phone with customers, you were only looking at an image of the data. Someone could have updated the room status after you performed your initial lookup. If a room exists, the process continues; otherwise, a negative value is moved to the **trans_status** local variable and the **abort_trans_exit** routine is performed.

```
/* make sure rooms are available */

if not exists(select * from tbl_Rooms where roomtype = @RoomType
and Hotel = @hotel and RoomStatus = "0")
begin
select @tran_status = -10000
        goto abort_trans_exit
end
```

11. Add the following code to the stored procedure. The last statement performs the insertion of the reservation into the **tbl_Reservations** database table. If an error occurs during the insertion transaction, a **-10001** is passed to the **@trans_error** local variable and the abort_trans_exit routine is performed.

```
/* create a reservation */

select @resv_nbr = max(resno) + 1 from tbl_Reservations
where hotel = @hotel

select @RoomNbr = min(room) from tbl_Rooms where Hotel = @hotel
    and roomtype = @RoomType
```

```
insert into tbl_Reservations
(ResNo, LastName, FirstName, Address, City, State, Postal,
 Phone, Payment, Amount, Hotel, Room, DateIn, DateOut, DateNow)
values(@resv_nbr, @lastname, @firstname, @address, @city,
 @state, @postal, @phone, @payment, @amount, @hotel, @roomnbr,
 @datein, @dateout, getdate())
if (@@error <> 0) /* something went wrong */
begin
select @tran_status = -10001
goto abort_trans_exit
end
```

12. Insert the following code into the stored procedure. This section handles the transaction when no errors occur. The **Commit Tran** statement completes the transaction. The **Print** statement is used only during the debugging process. When this stored procedure is compiled and executed through a program, SQL Server does not perform this statement. On successful processing, the return code of **0** is returned to the program that called this stored procedure, and the procedure terminates.

```
/* complete a normal transaction */
normal_exit:
commit tran
print 'tran completed'
return 0
```

13. Insert the following code into the stored procedure. This routine is performed whenever an error occurs during the course of this transaction. The **Rollback Tran** statement rolls you back to the beginning of the transaction and undoes everything up to that point. Any inserts, updates, or deletions to any table during the course of a transaction are cleared out as if the statements were never performed. A message of **Trans Abort** is displayed for debugging purposes. When this stored procedure is compiled and executed through a program, SQL Server does not perform this statement. The return code of whatever was passed to the local variable, **@trans_status**, is returned to the program that called this stored procedure, and the procedure terminates.

```
/* something went wrong and the transaction needs to be undone*/
abort_trans_exit:

rollback tran
print 'tran aborted'
return @tran_status
```

14. Click the Execute button. If no errors are found, the stored procedure is saved.

15. To test the stored procedure, open the Query Analyzer. On the Query tab, enter the following code and click Execute Query. The **Declare** statement defines **@ret_code** as a local variable within the Query Analyzer

environment. The `Exec` statement executes the stored procedure
`proc_submit_resv`. By assigning the stored procedure to the local variable
`@ret_code`, any return code sent by the procedure is passed to the
variable. The information after `proc_submit_resv` is the information the
procedure needs to complete the insert transactions. After the procedure
completes execution, the `select` statement displays the value the local
variable `@ret_code` contains. Your Query Analyzer should look similar to
Figure 7.34.

```
DECLARE @ret_code int
EXEC @ret_code = proc_submit_resv 1, "Smith", "Ben",
  "153 N. Main St.", "Irvine", "CA", "92714", "(714)555-1212",
  1, 75.00, "08/07/96", "08/08/96", 31
SELECT @ret_code
```

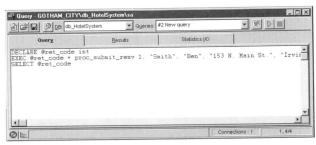

Figure 7.34 The Query Analyzer with the test SQL
statement

How It Works

When this stored procedure is executed, it must receive argument values from
the Visual Basic procedure that is calling it. In step 15, you are simulating a call
to the stored procedure. First, you define a variable, `@ret_code`, that will receive
a return code from the stored procedure when it finishes executing. Next, the
stored procedure is executed with all the necessary argument values. The
arguments get loaded into argument variables that are defined in step 7. The
local variables defined in step 8 are used in this procedure. The `Begin Tran`
statement marks the beginning of a transaction; this notifies SQL Server that a
unit of work is about to be performed. At this time, a transaction has been
recorded in the database's transaction log as an open transaction.

The first condition criterion, located in step 10, checks the `tbl_Rooms`
database table to ensure that the room the customer is requesting is still
available. If the query returns no information, it means that no rooms that match
the customer's request are available. If this happens, `-10000` is assigned to the
`@tran_status` variable and the `abort_trans_exit` subroutine is performed.

Why is this check so important? Before a reservation is actually processed, your users are looking at a snapshot, or static picture, of the data. When the user wants to modify the data, such as to make or update a reservation, you want to make sure that the picture has not been changed while you were looking at it. In this example, you want to make sure there are still rooms available to make a reservation.

In step 11, a query is performed to get a new reservation number to assign to this reservation. The query retrieves the largest reservation number found in the `tbl_Reservations` database table and increments that number by 1. Then the new number is assigned to the local variable `@resv_nbr`.

Next a room number is retrieved from the `tbl_Rooms` database table. The room number is assigned to the reservation. The query retrieves the first room number that is available based on the customer's request. The room number received from the query is assigned to the local variable `@roomnbr`.

Now that all the necessary components needed to make a reservation have been collected, an `INSERT` statement is issued to save the reservation information into the `tbl_Reservations` database table. The `@@error` variable is a global variable in SQL Server. Global variables are defined with the prefix of `@@`. The `@@error` variable is used to store the status of the last SQL statement performed. If it is equal to `0`, the SQL statement executed was successful. In this example, if the global variable does not equal `0`, `-10001` is assigned to the `@tran_status` variable and the `abort_trans_exit` subroutine is performed.

The procedure now passes the `normal_exit` label described in step 12. If there are no errors along the way, the `Commit Tran` statement is issued. This notifies SQL Server that the unit of work has been completed successfully, and the transaction record in the database's transaction log is marked as complete. On the Results tab of the Query Analyzer, the message `tran completed` is displayed. When this stored procedure is called from Visual Basic, a return code value of `0` is passed back to the calling procedure. In this example, the return code value of `0` is passed to the `@ret_code` variable defined on the Query Analyzer's Query tab.

Had any errors occurred, the procedure would have performed the subroutine `abort_trans_exit`. The `Rollback Tran` statement ends the transaction by updating any database tables. It is as if the transaction never took place. The database's transaction log is updated to show that the transaction was completed even though no data was written to any database table. In the Results tab of the Query Analyzer, the message `tran aborted` is displayed. When this stored procedure is called from a Visual Basic program, the value in the local variable `@tran_status` is passed back to the calling procedure. In this example, the value in the local variable `@tran_status` is passed to the `@ret_code` variable defined on the Query Analyzer's Query tab.

The `Select` statement's `@ret_code` is used to display the return code that is passed back from the stored procedure. Figure 7.35 shows a successful transaction. Except for a return code of `0`, the negative values do not mean anything unless you define them in your application.

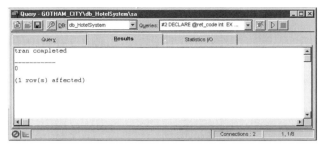

Figure 7.35 The Query Analyzer displays a successful transaction

Comments

As you might have noticed, the stored procedure has one entry point at the top, and then a standard exit and error exit subroutine, much like a Visual Basic function. It is recommended that you always try to handle the rollback of your transaction and exit of the stored procedure in one location, as described in steps 12 and 13.

COMPLEXITY
BEGINNING

7.11 How do I...

Create a query using SQL Server Web Assistant?

COMPATIBILITY: SQL SERVER 6.5 ONLY

Problem

I would like to post the most current reservation list on my company's intranet. How can I create an HTML document that updates every time a new reservation is made?

Technique

Client/server development has expanded because of the popularity of the Internet. Through the use of browser technology and *Hypertext Markup Language* (HTML), the Internet, which gives companies the freedom to communicate with their customers on an international scale, is being used to communicate with employees as well. An internal version of the Internet is called an *intranet*. HTML documents are created to contain internal information such as stock and financial reports, company announcements, and policy manuals. Employees are able to obtain more up-to-date information about their company without printing a lot of manuals, leaflets, and memorandums that get shelved, misplaced, or discarded.

SQL Server 6.5 introduced a new tool that makes it easy to generate an HTML document based on data from SQL Server. This tool is called the SQL Server Web Assistant and acts like any other wizard tool. It prompts you with a variety of questions and creates an HTML document. This document can be used once or set up to run as a scheduled SQL Server task. By setting up the document as a scheduled task, you can create it at designated times—for example, every hour—or whenever a table is updated.

Steps

To use the Web Assistant to create an HTML document that is generated every time the `tbl_Reservation` table is updated, complete the following steps:

1. In the SQL Server Utilities folder, double-click the SQL Server Web Assistant icon. This launches the wizard. Figure 7.36 shows the opening dialog box of the SQL Server Web Assistant.

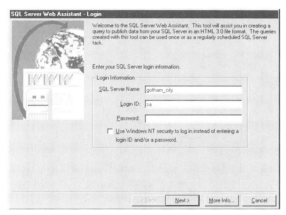

Figure 7.36 The SQL Server Web Assistant Login dialog box

2. The first dialog box that appears establishes the SQL Server login information. In the Login Information frame, enter the information shown in Table 7.9.

Table 7.9 Login information for the Web Assistant Login dialog box

TEXT BOX	VALUE	DESCRIPTION
SQL Server Name	GOTHAM_CITY	Name of the register server the data resides on
Login ID	sa	Login ID of the user who has the privilege to create procedures and access the tables being queried

3. The registered server is GOTHAM_CITY; make the appropriate changes for your system. Because this HTML document is the result of a query, it is a good idea to use a login ID that only has query access but privileges to issue the **CREATE PROCEDURE** command. If you enable the Use Windows NT Security to Log In Instead of Entering a Login ID and/or a Password check box, the trigger will rely on Windows NT's security to determine whether you have the appropriate database privileges.

4. Click the Next button to navigate to the next screen. Figure 7.37 shows the SQL Server Web Assistant Query screen.

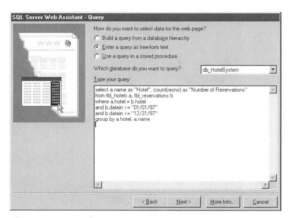

Figure 7.37 The SQL Server Web Assistant Query screen

5. This screen is used to build that query for the HTML document. Select the Enter a Query as Free-Form Text radio button. If you select this option, the form will change so that you can enter the Transact-SQL statement you will associate with this HTML document.

6. Select the **db_HotelSystem** database from the Which Database Do You Want to Query? combo box. This tells the Web Assistant which database you plan to use.

7. You want to generate an HTML document that displays the name of the hotel and the number of reservations that have been made in 1998. Enter the following Transact-SQL statement in the Type Your Query text box:

```
select a.name as "Hotel",
       count(resno) as "Number of Reservations"
from tbl_hotels a, tbl_reservations b
where a.hotel = b.hotel
and b.datein >= "01/01/98"
and b.datein <= "12/31/98"
group by a.name
```

8. Click Next to navigate to the next screen. Figure 7.38 shows the SQL Server Web Assistant Scheduling screen.

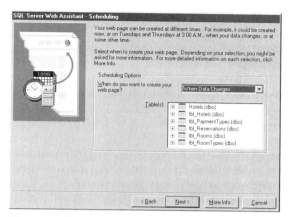

Figure 7.38 The SQL Server Web Assistant Scheduling screen

9. You use this screen to schedule when the query for the HTML document will be executed. In this example, you want the most up-to-date information. Select When Data Changes in the combo box. Table 7.10 lists the different scheduling options and their arguments.

Table 7.10 Scheduling time options

OPTION	ARGUMENT	DESCRIPTION
Now	None	Performs the query and creates the HTML document immediately
Later	Date and time	Performs the query and creates the HTML document at a selected time
When Data Changes	Table(s) and/or column(s)	Creates a trigger for a table base to perform the query and create the HTML document
On Certain Days of the Week	Days and time	Executes the query and creates the HTML document on a selected day and time of the week
On a Regular Basis	Every n hours, minutes days, or weeks	Executes the query and creates the HTML document at a recurring time

10. You are tracking data that is being entered into the `tbl_Reservations` table. Select that table in the Table(s) list box. A border appears around the table icon letting you know that the column has been selected.

11. Click Next to navigate to the next screen. Figure 7.39 shows the File Options screen of the SQL Server Web Assistant.

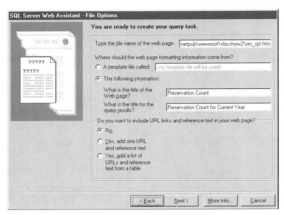

Figure 7.39 The SQL Server Web Assistant
File Options screen

12. You use this screen to set up file information about the HTML document that is to be generated. In the Type the File Name of the Web Page text box, enter the following information:

```
e:\InetPub\wwwroot\vbcshow2\resv_rpt.htm
```

You should place this document in whatever path is appropriate for your system.

13. Select the radio button The Following Information, if it isn't already marked.

14. In the What Is the Title of the Web Page? text box, enter **Reservation Count**. This will be the title that appears in the title bar of your HTML browser.

15. In the What Is the Title for the Query Results? text box, enter **Reservation Count for Current Year**. This will be the name of the report as it appears in the HTML document.

16. For this example, leave the No radio button selected. Because this HTML document is not going to be part of a larger Web page, you are not going to refer the viewers of the document to any other document or uniform resource locator (URL).

17. Click Next to navigate to the next screen. Figure 7.40 shows the SQL Server Web Assistant Formatting screen.

18. This screen is used to format the HTML document that is going to be generated. In the How Do You Want the Results Title to Look? combo box, leave HTML Header <H2> </H2> selected. HTML header tags 1 through 6 are allowed.

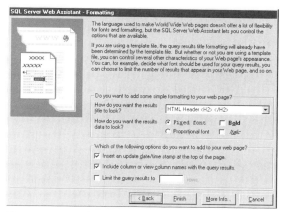

Figure 7.40 The SQL Server Web Assistant
Formatting screen

19. Use Fixed Font as the font format to display the query result in the HTML document.

20. In the second frame, enable the Insert an Update Date/Time Stamp at the Top of the Page check box. This lets viewers know the date and time of the document's last update by printing it on the report. Enable the Include Column or View Column Names with the Query Results check box to display the column name of each column within the query.

21. This is the last screen of the Web Assistant. Click Finish to continue. To go back and look over what you have entered, you can click Back to review any entry.

22. After the Web Assistant completes its task, a Done dialog box appears, as shown in Figure 7.41. Click Close to close the window and complete the process.

23. To test the trigger created by the Web Assistant, open the Query Analyzer. On the Query tab, enter the following Transact-SQL statement and click the Execute Query button. The `Declare` statement defines `@ret_code` as a local variable within the Query Analyzer environment. The `Exec` statement executes the stored procedure `proc_submit_resv`. By assigning the stored procedure to the local variable `@ret_code`, any return code returned by the procedure is passed to the variable. The information after `proc_submit_resv` is the information the procedure needs to complete the insert transactions. After the procedure completes execution, the `Select` statement displays the value the local variable `@ret_code` contains.

```
DECLARE @ret_code int
EXEC @ret_code = proc_submit_resv 1, "Dela Rental",
    "Oscar", "486 N. Ocean Place", "Atlanta", "GA",
```

```
"30339", "(703)853-1212", 1, 125.00, "9/23/97",
    "9/25/97", 31
SELECT @ret_code
```

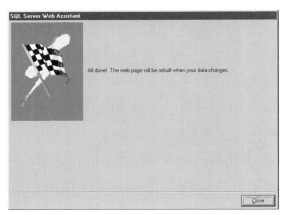

Figure 7.41 The final screen of the SQL Server Web Assistant displays the completion message

How It Works

Like all the other GUI components in SQL Server, the Web Assistant is an interface to Transact-SQL. The HTML document is generated based on your scheduling option. In step 3, you specify which registered server you want to log on to. After you enter the user ID and password, the Assistant logs you into SQL Server. By enabling the Use Windows NT Security to Log In Instead of Entering a Login ID and/or a Password check box, you tell SQL Server to use Windows NT security levels to determine whether you have access to SQL Server.

The Transact-SQL statement you entered in the Type Your Query text box in step 7 is the same as typing it into ISQL. This join query will retrieve information based on the contents of the **tbl_Hotels** and **tbl_Reservations** tables. The first part of the selection criteria retrieves the hotel names from the **Name** column of the **tbl_Hotel** table. The aggregate function **Count** will return the number of rows in the **tbl_Reservations** table. The **as** parameter and the following quoted text replace the default column name. In the **Where** clause, to avoid a *Cartesian* product, you match the hotel number from the **tbl_Hotels** table with the hotel number from the **tbl_Reservations** table. A Cartesian product is a result query that contains the number of rows in the first table times the number of rows in the second table. If you get a Cartesian result, the result of your query is meaningless because you have received all the possible combinations of the rows in every table in your query. Suppose that you have 4 hotels and 16 reservations. The result of the query will be 64 rows. Basically, multiply 4 by 16. If your tables had more information, a query like this could really slow down your server. Because you are interested only in the reservations made in 1998, you are checking the values in the **datein** column of the **tbl_Reservations** table. The **Group By** clause groups the output by the hotel names.

After you click Next in step 8, the Web Assistant checks to make sure you entered a valid Transact-SQL statement. However, it does not ensure that the query works. Therefore, it's best to try out your query within ISQL or the Query Analyzer before continuing to the next step.

In steps 9 and 10, you selected When Data Changes and the **tbl_Reservations** table. This means that when the data in the table changes, whether it is an update, insert, or delete, the Transact-SQL query and HTML document are generated by a trigger. Refer to How-To 7.7 for information on using triggers.

In step 12 you determine where the HTML document is created. It should be placed with other related HTML documents. The title, **Reservation Count**, is placed with the **<TITLE> </TITLE>** tags in the HTML document. The title will appear in the title bar of your browser. **Reservation Count for Current Year** appears in the body of the HTML document and will be the page header over the report columns. Because you specified No in step 16, no other URL address is added to the HTML document.

Steps 18 and 19 are for formatting the contents in the HTML document. In step 18 you tell the document to size the report title with the header 2 tags. In step 19, you specify that the actual contents of the report will be printed in a fixed font rather than a proportional font.

After you click Close in step 22, the **Insert**, **Update**, and **Delete** triggers are generated for the **tbl_Reservations** table based on the criteria you selected. The triggers use the stored procedure **sp_makewebtask** and all the data you input through the Web Assistant as arguments.

After you execute the query in step 23, a new reservation is added to **tbl_Reservation**, assuming that you created the stored procedure in How-To 7.9. To find out the results of the transaction and view the HTML document generated by the trigger, open your Internet browser. Then choose Open from the File menu. Go to the directory you specified in step 12, select the file, and click OK. The HTML document should look similar to Figure 7.42.

Comments

As the Internet and intranet continue to grow, the need for real-time data retrieval with a method to deliver the information quickly and easily continues to increase. The Web Assistant will become an invaluable tool.

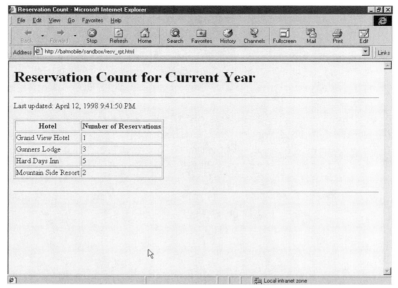

Figure 7.42 Microsoft Internet Explorer 4.0 displays the results of the HTML document

COMPLEXITY
INTERMEDIATE

7.12 How do I...
Optimize my server?

COMPATIBILITY: SQL SERVER 6.5 ONLY

Problem

I've installed a SQL Server based on what I've read in the manuals, but I know that a generic installation is not optimized for a production environment. What are some things I can do to increase performance?

Technique

You can use certain techniques to help the performance of your SQL Server.

Steps

Try one or more of the following suggestions to optimize the performance of your SQL Server installation:

Adding More Memory

With any Windows applications, the more physical memory available the better. The minimum memory requirement for an Intel-based SQL Server is 16MB. This does not include memory allocated to Windows NT Server. Configuring your system with this minimum install is considered a bare-bones system and should not be done unless you are the only person using the server and do not expect lightning-fast response times from SQL Server. Remember, Windows NT Server alone requires that you have at least 16MB to 24MB. In general, you should not configure a Windows NT Server with SQL Server with less than 32MB of physical memory. Regardless of the current price of memory these days, 64MB is a more realistic memory configuration.

You must be careful, though. Surprisingly, it is possible to allocate too much physical memory to SQL Server. If this happens, you can actually decrease performance by causing excessive paging. Be sure to use the Performance Monitor to watch the **PAGE FAULTS/SEC** counter. If page faults are being generated, your server has too much memory allocated to it.

Choosing a Fast Microprocessor

Because a lot of processing is done through the use of memory, it is a good idea to have a fast microprocessor in your server. Increasing your CPU power is considered one of the most effective ways to improve performance on the hardware level, next to increasing memory. Faster CPUs provide additional processing power to the operating system, SQL Server, and any other applications a server can use.

Windows NT Workstation 3.51 and Windows NT Server 3.51 support symmetric multiprocessing (SMP). Windows NT Workstation can handle up to two CPUs while Windows NT Server can handle up to four. Because SQL Server was designed using native Windows NT thread-level multiprocessing, it can take advantage of multiple CPUs—therefore taking advantage of SMP. *Native thread-level multiprocessing* means that tasks are processed at the thread level rather than the process level. This allows for preemptive operations and dynamic load balancing across multiple CPUs. A *thread* is a unit of execution in an application. A *process* is a running instance of an application. SQL Server is a process consisting of multiple threads.

Choosing a Fast Disk System

Not only are SQL Server transactions competing for processor and memory time, but they are competing for disk I/O as well. Data is constantly being read from and written to the disk drives. The components of a disk system are the drive controllers, I/O bus, and disk drives. All these components should be some of the latest and greatest technologies. For example, a dual-Pentium system with high-speed small computer small interface (SCSI) drives will have poor response time if the SCSI controller is based on a 16-bit Industry Standard

Architecture (ISA) technology. The power of the system CPU is also a crucial factor in effective I/O processing, of course. You might have the fastest drives money can buy, but if they are installed in a system that is running on an Intel-based 486DX/2 66 MHz CPU, you're going to have a processing bottleneck.

Treating the Transaction Log as a Separate Device

As mentioned earlier in this chapter, it is a good practice to leave the transaction log on a separate database device. In a heavy transaction-based system, the transaction log is going to be busy. If the transaction log is on the same device as the database, transactions will compete for disk I/O time. A transaction gets recorded as an open transaction in the transaction log first, then it is performed against the database tables, and then the transaction is closed in the transaction log. This might not sound so bad in a small environment, but what if the server is hit with more than 1,000 transactions an hour? By separating the transaction log and the database, as soon as the first transaction is recorded, the transaction is executed without delay, at which time the next transaction is recorded, and so on.

More important, you should make sure that the transaction log is also on a separate physical device (disk). This allows for faster writing (depending on the controller).

Disaster recovery is another important reason why you should have the transaction log on a separate device. In a heavy transaction-processing environment, such as an order-entry center, there can be more than 10,000 transactions an hour. To back up your data, you would have to take down the SQL Server to back up the database. This can take several hours to do, and many companies might not be able to afford that sort of downtime. This is why backups are usually performed at night and during nonpeak hours. Because the transaction log records every transaction that takes place, you have a picture of all the transactions taking place. Because transactions are smaller than database tables, it would be a good practice to back up the transaction log more frequently—every hour, every half-hour, or even every 15 minutes. If your SQL Server database crashes sometime during the day, you first recover the database from the preceding night's backup. Then you apply the transaction log by performing the restore on the transaction log to the database. The transaction log applies all the data insertions, deletions, and updates that are recorded in the log. For specifics on applying the transaction log to a restore, read the section "Restoring a Database or Applying a Transaction Log" in the SQL Server Books Online.

Increasing the Locks

A *lock* is a restriction on access to a resource in a multiuser environment. SQL Server installs with 5,000 maximum locks. In practice, this is never even close to what you will actually need. Try something more like 50,000.

Putting the `tempdb` in RAM

The `tempdb` is a database created by SQL Server to store temporary tables and other temporary working-storage information. If at all possible, you should put the `tempdb` in RAM by setting the configuration option to a positive number. Be careful not to allocate too large a `tempdb` for the physical memory on the machine. SQL Server behaves rather badly if it is trying to start with more memory than is actually available.

> **NOTE**
>
> Note that the `tempdb` configuration setting is in megabytes (for example, 30 means 30MB). Memory is in 2KB pages (for example, 30 means 60KB—not much memory at all). Don't get them mixed up.

Normally, a 30MB to 40MB `tempdb` is more than enough, unless you are doing some intense sorting or grouping. If you exceed the `tempdb` on a regular basis, first try to rethink the queries that are causing the problem before you increase the size of `tempdb`.

Examine SQL Queries and Use Stored Procedures

One of the most obvious tricks to help SQL Server performance (and it is the most overlooked) is to write good, clean queries. Try avoiding using the wildcard as the only element in your **SELECT** clause. Some people will argue that it makes dealing with recordsets or resultsets easier because if you add or remove a column from a table, you don't have to rewrite any SQL. That might work in some cases, but if you select only a wildcard and you only need five columns and there are eight, this doesn't really make sense because then you must programmatically find the five columns versus just getting the five you want right away.

The wildcard also makes SQL Server or any RDBMS work harder because it must figure out how many columns it has to return before it actually performs the query. By selecting only the columns you want, SQL Server doesn't have to do anything but retrieve your requested information.

As mentioned in How-To 7.9, a stored procedure is a precompiled SQL program. This means that the query or transaction instructions have already been examined by the server; therefore, the SQL doesn't have to be examined before it executes.

Using DBCC MEMUSAGE

The **DBCC MEMUSAGE** statement has been enhanced in Visual Basic 6.0; it displays more detailed output than can be used in tuning memory. This statement is used through ISQL or the Query Analyzer. It displays information on how memory is being used, provides a snapshot of the procedure and data caches, and enables you to accurately determine the size of the SQL Server executable code.

The information is broken down into three sections:

✔ How much of the server's memory is set aside at startup

✔ How much memory the largest 20 objects in the buffer cache used

✔ How much memory the largest 12 objects in the procedure cache used

The information the DBCC MEMUSAGE statement returns can assist you in your tuning process. DBCC MEMUSAGE is the only tool in SQL Server that can accurately determine the size of the SQL Server executable and how it is taking up resources on your server.

SQL Server reserves two areas for cache: *data* and *procedure*. These areas increase as the amount of memory increases. The procedure cache stores the most frequently used stored procedures. It is also used for compiling SQL for ad hoc queries. If SQL Server finds a procedure or a compilation already in the cache, SQL Server does not need to read it from the disk.

The data cache is used to store the most recently used data or index pages. If SQL Server finds a data or index page that has already been called by a user in the cache, SQL Server does not need to read it from the disk.

A fixed amount of space can be used by the procedure cache; therefore, it is possible to run out of space. A formula is documented in the SQL Server Books Online section "Sizing the Procedure Cache," which states that this is a good starting point for estimating the size of the procedure cache:

procedure cache = (maximum concurrent users) *
(size of largest plan) * 1.25

To determine the size of the largest page, use the DBCC MEMUSAGE statement. Remember that 1MB is equal to 512 pages.

How It Works

The two most common optimization methods are adding more memory to a dedicated SQL Server and tuning your SQL queries.

SQL Server is not just an application that resides on a server, it is a relational database system capable of performing thousands of transactions every minute. With adequate memory and setting the recommend server parameters, you will almost definitely increase your performance versus leaving the parameters set to their defaults, especially because the default memory configuration for SQL Server is 16MB no matter how much physical memory is installed on the system.

Bad queries are another common problem for any RDBMS. Types of queries that can slow down a server are too many joins among tables, passing too many parameters in the IN clause, not using indexes, or using indexes improperly, such as indexing a Yes/No field, which has 50 percent chance of being Yes or No. Be careful with union queries. If you are unioning only two resultsets, you'll probably be okay on performance. If you union any more resultsets, you might want to rethink what you're trying to retrieve. Queries with subselects can also degrade a server's performance because the subselect query must be executed before the main query, and each one must be processed by the server before they are executed. To query problems, recruit the help of your database administrator. The worst he can say is "What type of system do you think we have? A Cray?"

Comments

Keep in mind that you might turn all the right knobs and flip all the right switches and get only a minor increase in performance. Always remember that when tuning your SQL Server, your mileage might vary.

VISUAL BASIC AND ACTIVE SERVER PAGES ON THE WEB

8

VISUAL BASIC AND ACTIVE SERVER PAGES ON THE WEB

by Noel Jerke

How do I...

8.1 **Build a sample Web page using Active Server Pages?**

8.2 **Build a database-driven report with Active Server Pages?**

8.3 **Create an Active Server Pages component using Visual Basic?**

8.4 **Build a multipage tracking system?**

8.5 **Build reports based on ad-hoc query Web pages?**

8.6 **Build an Active Server Pages client/server messaging system?**

Internet technology is fast becoming a major aspect of corporate local-area networks (LANs) and wide-area networks (WANs). Microsoft has positioned the

Visual Basic language as a key part of Internet application development. In this chapter you will take a step away from the Visual Basic interface and work with Active Server Pages.

Active Server Pages with Microsoft's Internet Information Server 4.0 and Windows NT 4.0 provide the capability to build client/server browser–based applications with all the processing happening on the server. The beauty of the product is that you can easily do server-side programming to create custom Web pages that will work in any browser and give you easy access to your data.

With the release of Microsoft's Internet Information Server 3.0 and 4.0, the power to easily do server-side scripting was made simple. Typically a Web programmer doing server-side scripting was limited to Perl, CGI, or C/C++. If you were lucky, you might have been able to use Visual Basic. Now you can choose among several scripting programming languages, including VBScript. With these scripting tools, you can easily embed programming code into your Web pages that is executed on the server.

Active Server Pages (ASPs) with server-side scripting have the `.asp` extension. This indicates to Internet Information Server (IIS) that these pages should be reviewed to run any program code found in the pages.

NOTE

You must ensure that the directory where your ASP files are located has both read and execute rights in IIS.

The initial server-side script starts with the `<%` tag and ends with the `%>` tag. Within these tags in an HTML page you can use the Visual Basic, Scripting Edition (VBScript) language. This language is a subset of the full Visual Basic language. For example, VBScript variables are all of type **variant**. You cannot do a statement such as `Dim X as Integer`—only `Dim X`. This script language is similar to the client-side VBScript language (see Waite Group Press' *Visual Basic Script Interactive Course,* by Noel Jerke).

Active Server Pages are not limited to just server-side script code. A series of Component Object Model (COM) objects is built into IIS 4.0 that you can use to build your server-side applications. These will be used in this chapter. There is also tight integration with Visual Basic 5/6.0. With Visual Basic 5/6.0, you can develop COM objects that can be used from the Active Server Pages documents.

In this chapter you will explore how to build reports, components, and applications based on Active Server Pages. In the next chapter you will learn how to build IIS and Dynamic HTML applications with Visual Basic.

Note that in this chapter you must have installed Personal Web Server for Windows 95/98 or Internet Information Server for Windows NT. Also, you must create a virtual root for the chapter code. In this case, create a virtual root and point to the directory called **Chapter8**. From this mapping you will be able to process the pages through Active Server Pages. Also, it is assumed that you have a general working knowledge of HTML 3 or higher.

8.1 Build a Sample Web Page Using Active Server Pages

To get things started, this How-To focuses on building Active Server Pages and using some of the objects available in IIS.

8.2 Build a Database-Driven Report with Active Server Pages

The capability to build client/server applications in an Internet environment would not be complete without the capability to access a database. The Active Data Object (ADO) is also available via IIS and ASPs for accessing databases. Combined with Hypertext Markup Language (HTML) and the other IIS objects, dynamic Web browser–based and data-driven reports can be created.

8.3 Create an Active Server Pages Component Using Visual Basic

As mentioned earlier, COM objects can be created in Visual Basic, which can be accessed from ASPs. In this case the component developed will be a table generator. The COM object will be accessed from a Web page that will generate a multicolored table.

8.4 Build a Multipage Tracking System

It is possible to build applications that span multiple pages and keep state. Internet applications do not automatically remember what a user has done between pages. With ASPs it is possible to keep data across pages and to build extended interactive applications. This How-To also uses the table-building COM object built in How-To 8.3.

8.5 Build Reports Based on Ad-Hoc Query Web Pages

One of the powers of Internet technology is the capability to do quick and powerful reporting. This is in large part why intranets have become so powerful in the corporate world. Large databases can be developed in a central location, with each access via corporate Web servers. In this section you will explore how to build ad-hoc query reports.

8.6 Build an Active Server Pages Client/Server Messaging System

In this last How-To, a complete message system will be developed based on ASP technology. This example will combine your table-building COM object, a database, the client browser, and server-side code to build a complete client/server application.

8.1 How do I...
Build a sample Web page using Active Server Pages?

COMPATIBILITY: INTERNET INFORMATION SERVER 3.0 AND 4.0

Problem

I want to get started building applications based on Active Server Pages. How do I embed my server-side code into the HTML documents and access the IIS ASP object model?

Technique

To get started, you will design a simple Web page that shows the following information:

- ✔ Today's date

- ✔ The browser being used

- ✔ Whether today is Sunday

- ✔ The Hypertext Transfer Protocol (HTTP) header information sent between the browser and the server

You will do this with a combination of VBScript code and the COM objects provided.

Steps

Load IIS 4.0 and access your test Web site, replacing `localhost` with your Web server as appropriate:

```
http://localhost/Chapter8/ht01/default.asp
```

Figure 8.1 shows the Web page after it has been processed and delivered to the browser.

To create this project, complete the following steps:

1. Create a Web page called `default.asp` and add the following code to create the header:

```
<HTML>

<TITLE>Chapter 8, How-To 1</TITLE>

<BODY BGCOLOR=WHITE>
```

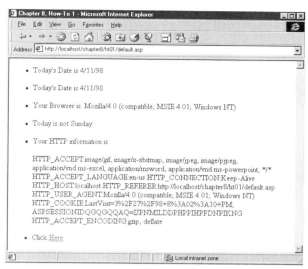

Figure 8.1 The Web page at runtime

2. Begin a list using the <UL> tag. The first item displayed in the list is the current date. You can display information from ASPs in two ways. The first way simply uses an equal (=) sign and then references the variable—all, of course, between <% %> brackets. The second way uses the **Response** object with the **Write** method. This writes data to the browser in the specified position within the HTML document.

```
<UL>


<!-- Display the date without using
     the write method of the response object
-->
<LI>Today's Date is <% = date %>

<BR><BR>

<!-- Display the date using the write
method of the response object
-->
<LI>Today's Date is <% response.write(date) %>

<BR><BR>
```

3. Use the **Request** object to retrieve the browser being used by the user. The **HTTP_USER_AGENT** key tells the **ServerVariables** method of the **Request** object to return the type of browser. This information then is displayed on the Web page.

```
<!-- Show the browser by accessing the
     server variables and displaying the
     HTTP_USER_AGENT
-->
<LI>Your Browser is: <% = Request.ServerVariables
➡("HTTP_USER_AGENT") %>

<BR><BR>
```

4. As with the full Visual Basic language, you can access standard functions, such as date and time, as well as many others. In this case you check to see what the current day is. If it is Sunday, the user is notified via HTML code that the day is Sunday. Otherwise the user is notified that the day is not Sunday.

```
<!-- If the day is Sunday then display
     the date.
-->
<% if day(date) = 1 then %>

<LI>Today is Sunday.


<!-- Note that the day is not Sunday
-->
<% else %>

<LI>Today is not Sunday.

<% end if %>

<BR><BR>
```

5. The browser type is not the only HTTP header information that can be displayed; the **ALL_HTTP** keyword tells the **Request** object to retrieve all HTTP information. Included in this information is the platform being used, where the user came from (the referrer), and so on.

```
<li>Your HTTP information is:<BR><BR>

<!-- Show all the HTTP header information with
     the server variables and the ALL_HTTP
     variable.
-->
<% = Request.ServerVariables("ALL_HTTP") %> <BR><BR>
```

6. Build a link to call **redirect.asp**.

```
<!-- Create an href -->
<li>Click <a href="redirect.asp"> Here </a>

</BODY>

</HTML>
```

7. Create a new Web page called `redirect.asp`. This page has no HTML code in it—only script. It uses the `Redirect` method of the `Response` object to send the user to back to the default page.

```
<%

'  Redirect back to the default page
Response.Redirect("default.asp")

%>
```

How It Works

Active Server Pages combine HTML code and script code into one page. Processing typically starts at the top of the page and continues down to the bottom of the page. The only exception is the use of subroutines and functions in the script.

Each time script will be used in the page, `<% %>` tags encapsulate the script code. The script code can be intermingled anywhere throughout the Web page. In fact, constructs such as `If Then Else` can be used to determine which HTML code will be visible. The following code fragment exhibits this:

```
<%  if flag = 1 then %>

    Show some HTML

<% else %>

    Show some other HTML

<% end if %>
```

If `flag` is `1`, the first HTML code is shown. If `flag` is not `1`, the second HTML code is displayed.

You also used some of the ASP object models to interact with the server and to display HTML code in the browser. Table 8.1 summarizes the different objects available.

Table 8.1 Active Server Page objects

OBJECT	DESCRIPTION
Application	You can use the `Application` object to share information among all users of a given application. An ASP-based application is defined as all the `.asp` files in a virtual directory and its subdirectories. Because the `Application` object can be shared by more than one user, you can use `Lock` and `Unlock` methods to ensure that multiple users do not try to alter a property simultaneously.
Response	You can use the `Response` object to send output to the client. This object controls writing HTML output, buffering content, expiring content, using cookies, and much more.

continued on next page

Table 8.1 continued

OBJECT	DESCRIPTION
Request	The Request object retrieves the values the client browser passed to the server during an HTTP request.
Server	The Server object provides access to methods and properties on the server. Most of these methods and properties serve as utility functions.
Session	You can use the Session object to store information needed for a particular user session. Variables stored in the Session object are not discarded when the user jumps between pages in the application; instead, these variables persist for the entire user session on the server. The Web server creates a Session object when a Web page from the application is requested by a user who does not already have a session. The server destroys the Session object when the session expires or is abandoned.

In addition to the objects in Table 8.1, you can use built-in components, including the Database Access Object (DAO), Ad Rotator, Content Rotator, Browser Capabilities, and File Access, among many others. In the next several How-To's, you will use the database-access component to build true ASP-based applications.

Comments

For further information on VBScript, review Microsoft's VBScript site at http://microsoft.com/vbscript. Keep in mind that the language was designed as a lightweight version of Visual Basic for scripting purposes only.

COMPLEXITY
BEGINNING

8.2 How do I...
Build a database-driven report with Active Server Pages?

COMPATIBILITY: INTERNET INFORMATION SERVER 3 AND 4

Problem

I have learned simple scripting techniques for my Active Server Pages, but I must be able to access my corporate data. How can I do this to build dynamic data-driven reports?

Technique

The Active Data Object (ADO) is available for accessing corporate databases. In this example you will design a database to list employees in a company. Then you will create a reporting ASP that will access the data and then display it in a table in your Web page.

Note that you will need to create an open database connectivity (ODBC) datasource name, `employee`, to access the employee database. The end of this section outlines the database structure you will create.

Steps

Open and run `report.asp`. Use this URL:

```
http://localhost/chapter8/ht02/report.asp
```

Figure 8.2 shows the Web page in the browser sorted by user ID.

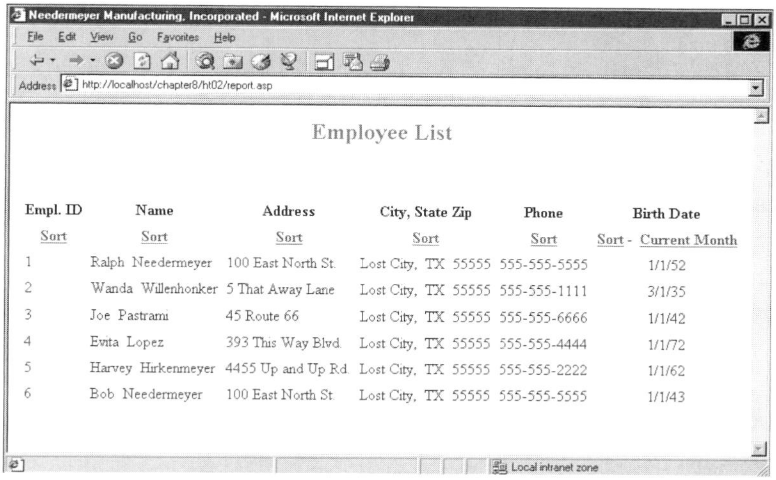

Figure 8.2 The default employee listing

You can sort any section of the report by clicking on the links above the column. For the birth date, you can select the `Current Month` link to show only the birthdays in the current month (see Figure 8.3).

Figure 8.4 shows the report listed by last name. Note the `sortid` parameter in the URL. This tells the `report.asp` page to sort by username.

Complete the following steps to create this project:

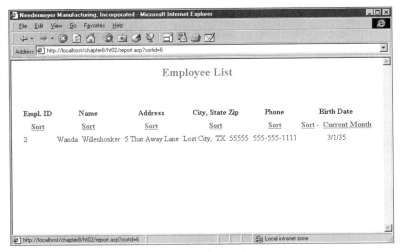

Figure 8.3 The current month's birthdays

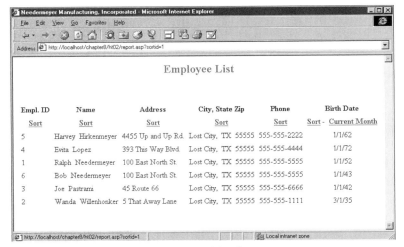

Figure 8.4 The employees sorted by last name

1. Start a new Active Server Page called `report.asp`. Add the following code to the top of the page:

```
<html>

<head>

<title>Needermeyer Manufacturing, Incorporated</title>
```

```
</head>

<body bgcolor=WHITE>

<center>

<!-- Display the header -->
<font size=5 color=RED>
  <strong>Employee List</strong>
</font>

<BR><BR><BR><BR>
```

2. To display the employee listing, the following code sets up the table and the table header. Each header shows the name of the column data.

```
<!-- Build a table to display the employees listing -->
<table cellpadding=3 cellspacing=3>

<!-- The first row -->
<TR>

  <!-- Build the header -->
  <TH>Employee ID</TH>
  <TH>Name</TH>
  <TH>Address</TH>
  <TH>City, State Zip</TH>
  <TH>Phone</TH>
  <TH align=center>Birth Date</TH>

</TR>
```

3. The next row builds the links for sorting the report. On each link, a **sortid** parameter tells the page how to sort the data. That ID parameter can then be read by the request and response objects.

```
<!-- Build the sort list.  Note that there is
     a parameter for each sort that will indicate
     the type of sort to be done.
-->
<TR>

  <!-- Show the sort columns -->
  <TH><a href="report.asp?sortid=0">Sort</a></TH>
  <TH><a href="report.asp?sortid=1">Sort</a></TH>
  <TH><a href="report.asp?sortid=2">Sort</a></TH>
  <TH><a href="report.asp?sortid=3">Sort</a></TH>
  <TH><a href="report.asp?sortid=4">Sort</a></TH>
  <TH><a href="report.asp?sortid=5">Sort</a> - 
      <a href="report.asp?sortid=6">Current Month</a>
  </TH>

</TR>
```

4. The script starts at this point. The first section of the script declares your variables.

```
<!-- Start the script -->
<%

'  Declare our variables
Dim dbEmployees
Dim rsEmployees
```

5. The first step in accessing the employee data is creating an Active Data Object. The **Server** object is used with the **CreateObject** method. A **Connection** object is first created. Next a connection is created by using the **Open** method of the **Connection** object. The datasource name is defined along with the username and password required to access the database.

```
'  Create an Active Data Object
set dbEmployees = Server.CreateObject("adodb.connection")

'  Open the database connection
dbEmployees.Open "dsn=Employee;uid=sa;pwd="
```

6. The SQL statement to query the database will be created based on the **sortid** parameter passed in the URL. The **sortid** value is retrieved using the **Request** parameter. A recordset is retrieved by calling the **Execute** method of the database connection. The result is stored in a resultset object, **rsEmployees**.

```
'  Build the sort query based on the sortid parameter
'  based on the QueryString parameter on the URL
select case Request.querystring("sortid")

    '  Order by employee id
    case 0
    set rsEmployees = dbEmployees.Execute("select * from
        employee order by idEmployee")

    '  Order by Last Name
    case 1
    set rsEmployees = dbEmployees.execute("select * from \
        employee order by chrLastName")

    '  Order by Address
    case 2
    set rsEmployees = dbEmployees.execute("select * from
        employee order by chrAddress")

    '  Order by City
    case 3
    set rsEmployees = dbEmployees.Execute("select * from
        employee order by chrCity")

    '  Order by Phone
```

```
            case 4
            set rsEmployees = dbEmployees.Execute("select * from
         ➥employee order by chrPhone")

            '  Order by birth date
            case 5
            set rsEmployees = dbEmployees.Execute("select * from
               employee order by dtBirthDate")

            '  Order by birth dates within this month
       case 6
            set rsEmployees = dbEmployees.execute("select * from
         ➥employee where
               datepart(mm, dtBirthDate) = " & month(now))


            '  Default order by employee id
            case else
            set rsEmployees = dbEmployees.Execute("select * from
               employee order by idEmployee")


     End Select

     %>

     <%
```

7. After the recordset has been retrieved, you can loop through the recordset until the last record is retrieved. Each record is written as a row. Each column accesses the **rsEmployees** recordset and gets the field value by name.

```
     '  Loop through the employee recordset
     do until rsEmployees.eof

     %>

     <!--  Build the row -->
     <TR>


     <!--  Show the employee id -->
     <TD><%=rsEmployees("idEmployee")%></td>

     <!--  Show the first name and last name -->
     <TD><%=rsEmployees("chrFirstName")%> 
         <%=rsEmployees("chrLastName")%>
     </td>

     <!-- Show the address -->
     <TD><%=rsEmployees("chraddress")%></td>

     <!--  Show the city, state and zip -->
     <TD><%=rsEmployees("chrCity")%>, 
         <%=rsEmployees("chrState")%> 
```

continued on next page

continued from previous page

```
            <%=rsEmployees("chrZip")%>
</td>

<!-- Show the phone -->
<TD><%=rsEmployees("chrPhone")%></td>

<!-- Show the Birth Date -->
<TD align=center><%=rsEmployees("dtBirthDate")%></td>

</tr>
```

8. After the record is written, the **MoveNext** method of the recordset is called to go to the next row. After all the records have been written, the database is closed.

```
<%

    ' Move to the next record in the recordset
rsEmployees.MoveNext

' Loop back
Loop


' Close the database connection
dbEmployees.Close

%>

</table>

</center>

</body>

</html>
```

9. The following SQL script creates the employee database. The **idEmployee** field is an identity column, a primary key, and cannot be null. Create a database device and corresponding database with which to run the script.

```
/****** Object:  Table dbo.employee
        Script Date: 3/8/98 8:23:32 PM ******/
CREATE TABLE dbo.employee (
    chrFirstName varchar (50) NULL ,
    chrLastName varchar (50) NULL ,
    chrAddress varchar (50) NULL ,
    chrCity varchar (50) NULL ,
    chrState varchar (50) NULL ,
    chrZip varchar (50) NULL ,
    chrPhone varchar (50) NULL ,
    dtBirthDate datetime NULL ,
    idEmployee int IDENTITY (1, 1) NOT NULL
)
GO
```

How It Works

In this example, the initial server-side script starts with the `<%` tag. Note that you have already started the table before the code. To build the listing table, you will blend together HTML code and Active Server Page script code.

Of course, to access data in your pages, you must have a database. The simplest way to get started is to build a Microsoft SQL database. Using the script and a DSN, you can have access to your data. The first thing you need in order to access your data is an ODBC datasource. For NT Server, you need a system DSN named `Employees`. Under Windows 95 peer Web services, you need a standard ODBC user Data Source Name (DSN) also named `Employees`.

Because the Active Data Object is an object, you must create an instance of the object to work with; you first do this in the code with the `CreateObject` method of the `Server` object. In this case you are creating an ADO connection. The `Connection` object relates to the SQL statement to carry out on the database, and the recordset will contain the set of records returned from the SQL statement.

In the code example, you first open the database connection using the `Open` method of the ADO `Connection` object. This establishes a connection with the database via the ODBC datasource indicated. In this case you will simply use the `Execute` method of the `Connection` object to retrieve all the clients in the database using a SQL `Select` statement. Note that the `Execute` method returns a recordset of all the employees. This recordset will be stored in the `rsEmployees` variable.

After you have the recordset, you simply loop through each record and add the code to the table columns. Note that in the loop, you have a mix of script code and HTML code divided by using the `<%` and `%>` tags. Thus with each iteration of the loop, you are building your table rows. Finally, it is important to close the database connection with the `Close` method of the `Connection` object.

You will find that the ADO syntax is not all that different than the syntax provided in standard Visual Basic code. The object model is certainly the same—only the method of coding the ADO changes.

Comments

In later sections of this chapter, you will explore database connectivity in greater detail as well as additional ASP objects and components. In this example, try to build different sort options to further sift through the data.

COMPLEXITY
INTERMEDIATE

8.3 How do I...
Create an Active Server Pages component using Visual Basic?

COMPATIBILITY: INTERNET INFORMATION SERVER 3 AND 4 AND
VISUAL BASIC 5 AND 6

Problem

Now that I have a taste of Active Server Pages programming, it was mentioned that I could create my own COM objects in Visual Basic 6 for access in my ASPs. How do I get started doing that?

Technique

One of the most common things done in any complex Web page is the building of tables. And in ASPs, tables are generated frequently to display database data. You will develop a class in Visual Basic 6 that will contain methods for creating the different structural parts of a table. You then will create and use this ActiveX DLL from your Active Server pages.

To support the interaction between the COM object and the calling Web page, the Microsoft Active Server Pages Object Library is referenced. When this is done, your Visual Basic COM object can interact with the calling Web page using the standard ASP objects.

Steps

Open and run **report.asp** using this URL:

```
http://localhost/chapter8/ht02/report.asp
```

Figure 8.5 shows the generated Web page with a multicolored table. The table is primarily generated through calls to the Visual Basic COM object.

To create this project, complete the following steps:

1. Create a new ActiveX DLL project in Visual Basic named **TableTools** and save it as **tabletools.vbp**.

2. Add a reference to the Microsoft Active Server Pages Object Library to the project.

3. Insert a class called **TableBuilder.cls**. Add the following set of code to the General Declarations section of the **TableBuilder** class. The *scripting context* is an object that allows you to access the current ASP calling your **TableTool** COM object. The other global variables enable you to indicate whether the row colors should rotate and what the current color is.

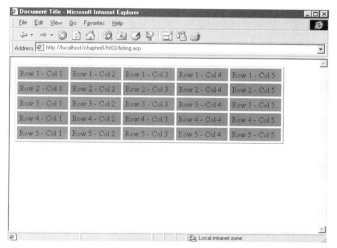

Figure 8.5 A dynamically generated table with row color variations

```
'   This is the scripting context object that
'   we will use to interface with the page that
'   this object will be used on.
Dim MyScriptingContext As ScriptingContext

'   Public properties of the COM object
Public RotateRowColors As Boolean
Public RowColor1 As String
Public rowcolor2 As String

'   Private properties of the project
Private CurrentColor As Integer
```

4. The `OnStartPage` event is called when the page creating the COM object is started. The scripting context for the page is passed into the method. The reference is stored globally for later use.

```
'   This function is called when the object is
'   created and the page is started.
Public Sub OnStartPage(ASP_Scripting_Context As
➡ScriptingContext)

'   We will need to store the scripting context
'   passed into the function globally for reference.
Set MyScriptingContext = ASP_Scripting_Context

End Sub
```

5. The `CreateTable` method will start a table with the specified parameters. You can specify the border size, cell padding, cell spacing, and width.

Note that the scripting context stored globally is used to write the HTML tagging to the Web page calling the COM object.

```
'  Create Table will create the table heading
'   tags.
Public Sub CreateTable(border As String, cellpadding As String,
➡cellspacing As String, width As String)

'  Create a variable that will hold the table header
Dim strTableTag As String

'Create a copy of the Response object
Set myresponse = MyScriptingContext.Response

'  Start the table tag
strTableTag = "<table "

'  Place in the border value for the table.
'  We need to check and ensure that the value
'  passed is a number, otherwise we write a
'  value of 0
If Val(border) > 0 Then
    strTableTag = strTableTag & "border=" & Chr(34) &
    ➡Val(border) & Chr(34)
Else
    strTableTag = strTableTag & "border=" & Chr(34) & "0"
    ➡& Chr(34)
End If

'  Place in the cellpadding value for the table.
'  We need to check and ensure that the value
'  passed is a number, otherwise we write a
'  value of 0
If Val(cellpadding) > 0 Then
    strTableTag = strTableTag & " cellpadding=" & Chr(34) &
    ➡Val(cellpadding) & Chr(34)
Else
    strTableTag = strTableTag & " cellpadding=" & Chr(34) & "0"
    ➡& Chr(34)
End If

'  Place in the cellspacing value for the table.
'  We need to check and ensure that the value
'  passed is a number, otherwise we write a
'  value of 0
If Val(cellspacing) > 0 Then
    strTableTag = strTableTag & " cellspacing=" & Chr(34) &
    ➡Val(cellspacing) & Chr(34)
Else
    strTableTag = strTableTag & " cellspacing=" & Chr(34) & "0"
    ➡& Chr(34)
End If

'  Place in the width value for the table.
'  We need to check and ensure that the value
'  passed is a number, otherwise we write a
'  value of 0
```

```
If Val(width) > 0 Then
    strTableTag = strTableTag & " width=" & Chr(34) &
    ➥Val(width) & Chr(34)
Else
    strTableTag = strTableTag & " width=" & Chr(34) & "0"
    ➥& Chr(34)
End If

'  End the table tag
strTableTag = strTableTag & ">" & Chr(10) & Chr(13)

'  Write out the opening table tag.  To make it
'  easy to read the generated code, we tack on a
'  line return.
myresponse.Write strTableTag

End Sub
```

6. The StartRow method uses the scripting context to write out the start of the table row to the calling page. Note that it references the global setting for row colors and sets the row color appropriately.

```
'  This function will start a new table row
Public Sub StartRow()

'  Create a Response object
Set myresponse = MyScriptingContext.Response

If RotateRowColors = False Then

    '  Write out the ending tag.  To make it easy to
    '  read the generated code, we tack on a line
    '  return.
    myresponse.Write ("<Tr>" & Chr(10) & Chr(13))

Else

    '  Check to see the current color
    If CurrentColor = 1 Then

        '  Create the table row with the row color
        myresponse.Write ("<tr bgcolor = """ & RowColor1 &
        ➥""" >" & Chr(10) & Chr(13))

        '  Set the current color to color 2
        CurrentColor = 2

    Else

        '  Create the row with the second color
        myresponse.Write ("<tr bgcolor = """ & rowcolor2 &
        ➥""" >" & Chr(10) & Chr(13))

        '  Set the current color to color 1
        CurrentColor = 1
```

continued on next page

continued from previous page

```
            End If

    End If


    End Sub
```

7. The `EndRow` method writes the ending tag for the row.

```
'   This function will write out the ending row tag
Public Sub EndRow()

'   Create a copy of the Response object
Set myresponse = MyScriptingContext.Response

'   Write out the ending table tag.  To make it easy
'   to read the generated code, we tack on a line
'   return.
myresponse.Write ("</Tr>" & Chr(10) & Chr(13))

End Sub
```

8. The `GenerateColumn` method generates a column with the specified value and aligns the column horizontally and vertically as specified.

```
'   This function generates a table column with
'   the specified value passed into the function.
Public Sub GenerateColumn(V As String, valign As String,
➥align As String)

'   Create a copy of the Response object
Set myresponse = MyScriptingContext.Response

'   Write out the column tags.  To make it easy to
'   read the generated code, we tack on a line
'   return.
myresponse.Write ("<TD valign=" & Chr(34) & valign & Chr(34) &
➥" align=" & Chr(34) & align & Chr(34) & ">" & V &
➥"</TD>" & Chr(10) & Chr(13))

End Sub
```

9. The `EndTable` method ends the table.

```
'   This function will write out the end
'   table tag.
Public Sub EndTable()

'   Create a variable that will hold the table header
Dim strTableTag As String

'   Create a Response object
Set myresponse = MyScriptingContext.Response

'   Build the ending table tag
```

```
strTableTag = "</table>" & Chr(10) & Chr(13)

'   Write out the closing tag.  To make it easy to
'   read the generated code, we tack on a line
'   return.
myresponse.Write strTableTag

End Sub
```

10. Create a new file called `listing.asp`. Add the following code to begin the heading of the page:

```
<%@ LANGUAGE="VBSCRIPT" %>

<HTML>

<HEAD>
   <TITLE>Document Title</TITLE>
</HEAD>

<BODY BGCOLOR=WHITE>
```

11. The server-side script code in `listing.asp` starts with your declaration of variables and the creation of your COM object. The `Server.CreateObject` method is used to create the object. Note that the project name, `TableTools`, is referenced and then the `TableBuilder` class is referenced. The object reference is stored in the `TB` variable.

```
<%

'   Declare our variables
Dim Row
Dim Col
Dim TB

'   Create our table gen object of the component, MyComponent
Set TB = Server.CreateObject("TableTools.TableBuilder")
```

12. In this case you indicate that the table should rotate row colors. The two colors will be green and red.

```
'   Set the flag to rotate the row colors
TB.RotateRowColors = 1

'   Set the two rotating colors
TB.RowColor1 = "RED"
TB.RowColor2 = "GREEN"
```

13. Create the table. The border is a size of **2**, cell padding is **4**, cell spacing is **3**, and width is **560** pixels.

```
'   Create the table
TB.CreateTable 2, 4, 3, 560
```

14. To create the table rows and columns, you create a double loop to generate five rows with five columns in each row. Note that for each row, no indication of rotation of color is made. The earlier property setting takes care of that. The `GenerateColumn` method shows the row and column numbers being generated.

```
'  Loop through and create five rows
For Row = 1 to 5

   '  Create our first row
   TB.StartRow

   '  Loop through and create five columns for each row
   For Col = 1 to 5

      '  Generate a column with the value of the row and
      ➥column number
      TB.GenerateColumn "Row " & Row & " - Col " & Col, "", ""

   Next

   '  End the row
   TB.EndRow

Next
```

15. Finally, the table and page end.

```
'  End the table
TB.EndTable

%>

</BODY>
</HTML>
```

How It Works

The first step is to create a standard ActiveX DLL in Visual Basic. This is really no different than creating any type of COM object DLL for use in another application. The magic is in the use of the ASP scripting context for interacting with the Web page. When a reference is made to the ASP Object Library, it expects an `OnStartPage` method that can be called with the scripting context passed as a variable. You also have the option of calling an `OnEndPage` method when the page ends.

After you have the scripting context for the calling page, you can use the full range of ASP objects within your Visual Basic application. If you want to check out and process the HTTP headers, you can do so, as well as check cookies, query parameters, form variables, and so on. As demonstrated in this How-To, you can also write HTML script code to the Web page.

Within the Web page, you simply create an instance of the COM object. As long as the DLL has been registered on the Web server with `regsvr32.exe`, the object and its methods and properties are accessible. From there the rest is fairly easy in terms of ASP script programming.

Comments

The table generated in this How-To is just a small example of what can be accomplished by building ASP-aware Visual Basic COM objects. You could extend this example to use the many different table tag settings and check for various types of browsers for support.

You can also provide easy access to any existing business objects and simply write an ASP interface wrapper on the object. As you will see in Chapter 9, "Building IIS Applications with Visual Basic 6," IIS applications function in many similar ways to the example presented here. You will learn more about integrating Visual Basic 6 into your ASP applications in Chapter 9.

COMPLEXITY
INTERMEDIATE

8.4 How do I...
Build a multipage tracking system?

COMPATIBILITY: INTERNET INFORMATION SERVER 3 AND 4

Problem

I have seen examples of how to build reports and interface with Visual Basic, but how do I begin to build more complex ASP applications that use multiple Web pages and keep state between them?

Technique

ASP technology provides a rich set of tools for building highly integrated Web applications. In previous How-To's, you reviewed accessing a database from your Web pages, as well as writing custom data back to the Web page. In this example you will build a client-tracking system that will span multiple pages and allow you to review and update client data. The key will be to review and then select the updating of a client. You will have to remember what client you were reviewing when you go to update the client's data.

Note that you will need an ODBC datasource called `clients` pointing to the database. The structure for these tables is given in the final step of this How-To.

Steps

Open and run `report.asp` using this URL:

```
http://localhost/chapter8/ht02/report.asp
```

The drop-down box shows the list of clients currently in the system. Select a client and then click Submit to review the client's data. Figure 8.6 shows the Web page.

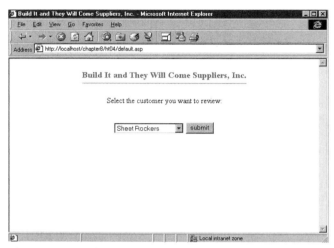

Figure 8.6 A client-listing screen

Figure 8.7 shows the client data for Sheet Rockers.

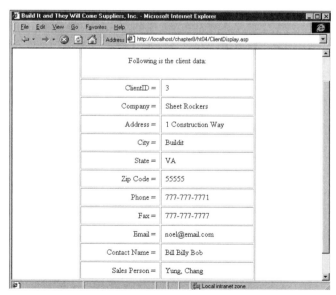

Figure 8.7 Client data display

After you review the data, you can update the client data by clicking the Update link. The form then shows the client data in text elements, as shown in Figure 8.8.

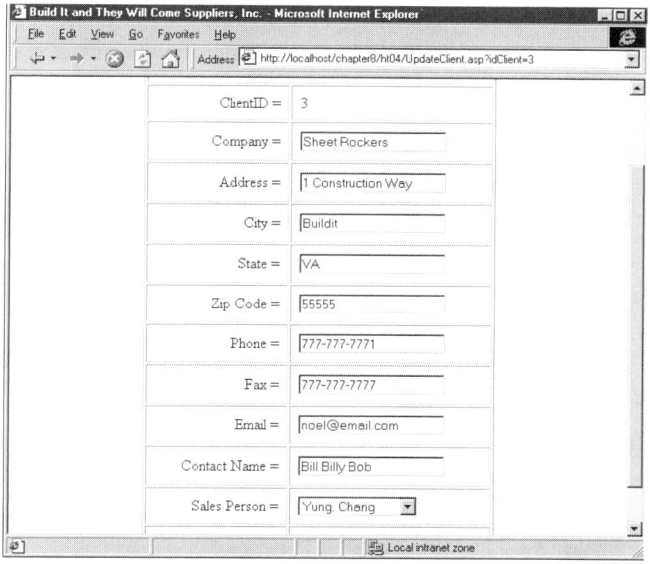

Figure 8.8 The Client Update screen

The ID for the client is in the URL for the Web page. This indicates the client data to be updated. Note that the link on the preceding screen has the ID of the client in the URL.

If you update the client and have any of the fields blank, the update form, UpdateResponse, verifies the data and gives any appropriate error messages. Figure 8.9 shows the response with no address or company name.

Complete the following steps to create this project:

1. Create a new file called default.asp. Add the following HTML code to the header of the file:

```
<html>

<head>
    <title>Build It and They Will Come Suppliers, Inc.</title>

</head>

<body bgcolor=WHITE>

<center>
```

Figure 8.9 An unsuccessful client data update

2. The following code starts the table for the page and sets up the display header. The form calling `ClientDisplay` is also set up.

```
<!-- Build the display table -->
<TABLE border=0 cellpadding=8>

<!-- Show the header -->
<tr><td align=center>

<font size=4 color=GREEN><strong>Build It and They Will Come
➥Suppliers, Inc.</strong></font>

<HR><BR>

Select the customer you want to review:<BR><BR>

</td></tr>

<!-- Set up the form -->
<tr><td align=center>

<!-- The form will post to ClientDisplay.asp -->
<form action="ClientDisplay.asp" method="post">
```

3. The ASP code starts out by declaring the database variables and then creates and Active Database Object. The connection to the database is opened, and your SQL query to return all clients is executed.

```
<%

'   Declare our variables
Dim dbClients
Dim rsClients

'   Create an Active Data Object
set dbClients = server.createobject("adodb.connection")

'   Open our database connection
dbClients.Open "dsn=Clients;uid=sa;pwd="

'   Get all of the clients from the database
set rsClients = dbclients.execute("select idClient,
➥chrCompany from clients")

%>
```

4. The select input element is started. To display the clients, the resultset, `rsClients`, is looped through to display the client name. The ID of the client is displayed in the value of the option `Select`.

```
<select name="clients">
<%

'   Loop through the clients and then fill in the select box
'   with the id of the client as the value for each option.
'   The name of the client is displayed
do until rsClients.eof

%>

<!--  Build the option with the value being the id of
      the client.  The display is the client company name
-->
<option value="<%response.write(rsClients("idClient"))%>">
  <% = response.write(rsClients("chrCompany"))%>
</option>

<%
    '   Move to the next record in the recordset
    rsClients.MoveNext

'   Loop back
Loop
```

5. Finally, the database is closed, the `select` box ends, and the HTML ending page tags are written.

```
'   Close the database connection
dbClients.Close

%>

</select>
```

continued on next page

continued from previous page

```
<!-- Show the button to submit the form -->
<input type=submit value="submit">

<!-- Close the form -->
</form>

</td></tr>
</table>

</center>
</body>
</html>
```

6. Create a new ASP file and save it as `ClientDisplay.asp`. The beginning
tags for the page are written. The table is set up to display the header for
the table.

```
<html>

<head>
    <title>Build It and They Will Come Suppliers, Inc.</title>
</head>

<body bgcolor=WHITE>

<center>

<!-- Build the display table -->
<TABLE border=1 cellpadding=8>

<!-- Display the page header -->
<tr><td align=center colspan=2 align=center>

<font size=4 color=GREEN><strong>
  Build It and They Will Come Suppliers, Inc.
</font> </strong>

<BR><BR><BR>

Following is the client data:<BR><BR>

</td></tr>
```

7. The script starts out by creating the database variables for the page. An
Active Database Object is created to connect to the client database. Then
the SQL string is executed to retrieve the record from the database.

```
<%

'  Declare our variables
Dim dbClients
Dim rsClient
Dim idClient
```

```
Dim rsSalesPerson

'  Create an Active Data Object
set dbClients = server.createobject("adodb.connection")

'  Open the database connection
dbClients.Open "dsn=Clients;uid=sa;pwd="

'  Get the client information based on the
'  id of the client which is stored in the form
'  data from the default page.
set rsClient = dbclients.execute("select * from clients
➥where idClient = " & request.form("Clients"))
```

8. The ID of the client is stored for later use. For each client data, the field label is displayed and the data for the client is displayed by accessing the resultset.

```
'  Store the id of the client
idClient = rsClient("idClient")

%>

<!-- Show the id of the client -->
<tr>
  <td align=right>ClientID = </td>
  <td>
   <% = rsClient("idClient") %>
  </td>
</tr>

<!-- Show the company name -->
<tr>
  <td align=right>Company = </td>
  <td><% = rsClient("chrCompany") %>
  </td>
</tr>

<!-- Show the address -->
<tr>
  <td align=right>Address = </td>
  <td>
    <% = rsClient("chrAddress") %>
  </td>
</tr>

<!-- Show the city -->
<tr>
  <td align=right>City = </td>
  <td>
    <% = rsClient("chrCity") %>
  </td>
</tr>

<!-- Show the state -->
<tr>
```

continued on next page

continued from previous page

```
            <td align=right>State = </td>
            <td>
                <% = rsClient("chrState")%>
            </td>
        </tr>

        <!-- Show the zip code -->
        <tr>
            <td align=right>Zip Code = </td>
            <td>
                <% = rsClient("chrZipCode") %>
            </td>
        </tr>

        <!-- Show the phone -->
        <tr>
            <td align=right>Phone = </td>
            <td>
                <% = rsClient("chrPhone") %>
            </td>
        </tr>

        <!-- Show the fax -->
        <tr>
            <td align=right>Fax = </td>
            <td>
                <% = rsClient("chrFax")%>
            </td>
        </tr>

        <!-- Show the email -->
        <tr>
            <td align=right>Email = </td>
            <td>
                <% = rsClient("chrEmail")%>
            </td>
        </tr>

        <!-- Show the contact name -->
        <tr>
            <td align=right>Contact Name = </td>
            <td>
                <% = rsClient("chrContactName")%>
            </td>
        </tr>
```

9. When you are ready to display the salesperson data, you must get the salesperson's name from the sales database. The ID of the salesperson is stored in the client record. The query then is performed based on the ID of the salesperson. After the salesperson is retrieved, the name of the salesperson is displayed.

```
<%

'   Query for the salesperson  The id of the
```

```
'   salesperson is stored in the idSalesPerson
'   value.  The query will get the name of the
'   salesperson from the SalesPerson table.
set rsSalesPerson = dbclients.execute("select * from
➥SalesPerson where idSalesPerson = " &
➥rsClient("idSalesPerson"))

%>



<!--  Display the salesperson name -->
<tr>
  <td align=right>Salesperson = </td>
<td>
  <%response.write(rsSalesPerson("chrLastName")& ", " &
  ➥rsSalesPerson("chrFirstName"))%>
  <br>
  </td>
</tr>
```

10. Build the link to the update page. It is important to set the ID of the client on the **href** link to pass along the ID of the client. The link to the default page is built and then the database is closed. Finally the table ends and the page ends.

```
<!--  Create a URL to link to the update page to allow the
    user to update the client information.  Note that on the
      URL the id of the client is stored on the parameter.
-->
<tr>
  <td align=center>
    <an href="UpdateClient.asp?idClient=<% = idClient %>">
    ➥Update</a>
  </td>

  <td align=center>
    <an href="default.asp">Home</a>
  </td>

</tr>

<%

'  Close the database
dbClients.Close

%>

</table>

</center>
</body>
</html>
```

11. Create a new ASP and save it as **UpdateClient.asp**. The following code builds the headers for the page and the beginning of the table:

```
<html>

<head>
  <title>Build It and They Will Come Suppliers, Inc.</title>
</head>

<body bgcolor=WHITE>

<center>

<!-- Start the display table -->
<TABLE border=1 cellpadding=8>


<!-- Build the header.  -->
<tr><td align=center colspan=2>

<font size=4 color=GREEN><strong>
  Build It and They Will Come Suppliers, Inc.
</font> </strong>

<BR><BR>

Following is the client data:<BR><BR>

</td></tr>

<!-- The form will call the updateresponse.asp page -->
<form action="UpdateResponse.asp" method="post">
```

12. The ASP code begins by declaring the database variables and creating an Active Data Object. The database is connected to and the client data is retrieved using an SQL query.

```
<%

'  Declare our variables
Dim dbClients
Dim rsClient
Dim rsSalespersons

'  Create the Active Data Object
set dbClients = server.createobject("adodb.connection")

'  Open the connection
dbClients.Open "dsn=Clients;uid=sa;pwd="

'  Get the client data
set rsClient = dbclients.execute("select * from clients where
➡idClient = " & request("idClient"))
```

13. The ID of the client is stored in a session variable for later access. Then a label for each field is created, and an input element for each field is created (except for the ID of the client). The value for each input element is set to the database value for that field.

```
'   Store the client id in a session variable
session("idClient") = rsClient("idClient")

%>

<!--   Show the id of the client -->
<tr>
  <td align=right>ClientID = </td>
  <td><% = rsClient("idClient")%>
  </td>
</tr>

<!--   Show the company name in a text field -->
<tr>
  <td align=right>Company = </td>
  <td><input name="company" type=text value="<% =
  ➥rsClient("chrCompany")%>">
  </td>
</tr>

<!--   Show the address in a text field -->
<tr>
  <td align=right>Address = </td>
  <td><input name="address" type=text value="<% =
  ➥rsClient("chrAddress")%>">
  </td>
</tr>

<!--   Show the city in a text field -->
<tr>
  <td align=right>City = </td>
  <td><input name="city" type=text value="<% =
  ➥rsClient("chrCity")%>">
  </td>
</tr>

<!--   Show the state in a text field -->
<tr>
  <td align=right>State = </td>
  <td><input name="state" type=text value="<% =
  ➥rsClient("chrState")%>">
  </td>
</tr>

<!--   Show the zip code in a text field -->
<tr>
  <td align=right>Zip Code = </td>
  <td><input name="zipcode" type=text value="<% =
  ➥rsClient("chrZipCode")%>">
  </td>
```

continued on next page

continued from previous page

```
      </tr>

      <!-- Show the phone in a text field -->
      <tr>
        <td align=right>Phone = </td>
        <td><input name="phone" type=text value="<% =
        ➥rsClient("chrPhone")%>">
        </td>
      </tr>

      <!-- Show the fax in a text field -->
      <tr>
        <td align=right>Fax = </td>
        <td><input name="fax" type=text value="<% =
        ➥rsClient("chrFax")%>">
        </td>
      </tr>

      <!-- Show the email in a text field -->
      <tr>
        <td align=right>Email = </td>
        <td><input name="email" type=text value="<% =
        ➥rsClient("chrEmail")%>">
        </td>
      </tr>

      <!-- Show the contact name in a text field -->
      <tr>
        <td align=right>Contact Name = </td>
        <td><input name="contactname" type=text value="<% =
        ➥rsClient("chrContactName") %>">
        </td>
      </tr>
```

14. Allow for the selection of the salesperson for the client. It is important to ensure that the current salesperson is set as the default for the **select** box. All the salespersons are selected from the database. The resultset is looped through for each salesperson. A check is done with each salesperson to see whether it matches the current assigned salesperson. If so, the option tag for that salesperson is given the selected tag.

```
<%

'  Get the list of salespeople
set rsSalespersons = dbclients.execute("select *
➥from Salesperson")

%>

<tr><td align=right>Salesperson = </td>

<td>

<!-- We need to build a list of salespeople to
```

```
        select from
-->
<select name="Salespersons">

<%

'   Loop through the salespersons
do until rsSalespersons.eof

%>

<!--  Write in the salespersons id for
    the select value
-->
<option value="<%response.write(rsSalespersons("idSalesperson"))

'   Check to see if the current salesperson in the
    ➥recordset is the
'   same as the currently assigned salesperson.  If so,
➥then select
'   the salesperson as the default.
if rsClient("idSalesperson") = rsSalespersons("idSalesperson")
➥then %>" selected>

<%else%>

">

<%

end if

'   Display their name
response.write(rsSalespersons("chrLastName")& ", " &
➥rsSalespersons("chrFirstName"))%>

</option>

<%

'   Move to the next record
rsSalespersons.movenext

loop
```

15. Finally the database is closed, the **select** element and the page is ended, the form is closed, and the appropriate tags to end the page are created.

```
'   Close the database
dbClients.Close


%>

</select>
```

continued on next page

continued from previous page

```
<br>
</td></tr>

<tr><td align=center>

<input type="submit" value="Update" name="UpdateData">

</td>

<td>
<a href="default.asp">Home</a></td>


</td></tr>

</table>

</form>

</center>

</body>

</html>
```

16. Create a new ASP and save it as **UpdateResponse.asp**. The beginning of the page is built with the appropriate header.

```
<html>

<head>
<title>Build It and They Will Come Suppliers, Inc.</title>
</head>

<body bgcolor=WHITE>

<center>

<!-- Show the header -->
<font size=4 color=GREEN><strong>
  Build It and They Will Come Suppliers, Inc.
</font> </strong>

<BR><BR><BR>
```

17. Declaring the variables for the database starts the script code. Then each form field on the calling page is checked to ensure that it is not empty. If it is, the **Flag** is set to **1** to indicate an error and the appropriate error message is written to the page.

```
<%

Dim Flag
Dim dbClients
Dim rsClients
```

```
Flag = 0

    '   Check company name
    if request.form("company") = "" then

        %>

        You did not enter in a <i>company name</i>.<br>

        <%
        Flag = 1

    End If

    '   Check address
    if request.form("address") = "" then

        %>

        You did not enter in an <i>address</i>.<br>

        <%

        Flag = 1

    End If

    '   Check city
    if request.form("city") = "" then

        %>

        You did not enter in a <i>city</i>.<br>

        <%

        Flag = 1

    End If

    '   Check state
    if request.form("state") = "" then

        %>

        You did not enter in a <i>state</i>.<br>

        <%

        Flag = 1

    End If

    '   Check zip code
    if request.form("zipcode") = "" then
```

continued on next page

continued from previous page

```
                                    %>

                                    You did not enter in a <i>zip code</i>.<br>

                                    <%

                                    Flag = 1

                                End If

                                '  Check phone number
                                if request.form("phone") = "" then

                                    %>

                                    You did not enter in a <i>phone number</i>.<br>

                                    <%

                                    Flag = 1

                                End If

                                '  Check the contact name
                                if request.form("contactname") = "" then

                                    %>

                                    You did not enter in a <i>contact name</i>.<br>

                                    <%

                                    Flag = 1

                                End If
```

18. If there were no errors on the data entered, an update query is created
with the new data entered by the user. Note that the **session** variable set
on the **ClientDisplay.asp** page storing the ID of the client is read to
ensure that you update the correct record in the database.

```
If Flag <> 1 then

    '  Create the Active Data Object
    set dbClients = server.createobject("adodb.connection")

    '  Open the database
    dbClients.Open "dsn=Clients;uid=sa;pwd="

    '  Create the record update SQL string
    strSQL = "Update Clients set " & _
    "chrCompany = '" & request.form("Company") & "', " & _
    "chrAddress = '" & request.form("Address") & "', " & _
    "chrCity = '" & request.form("City") & "', " & _
    "chrState = '" & request.form("State") & "', " & _
```

```
"chrZipCode = '" & request.form("Zipcode") & "', " & _
"chrPhone = '" & request.form("Phone") & "', " & _
"chrFax = '" & request.form("Fax") & "', " & _
"chrEmail = '" & request.form("Email") & "', " & _
"chrContactName = '" & request.form("ContactName") & "',
" & _"idSalesperson = " & request.form("Salespersons") & _
" where idClient = " & session("idClient")
```

19. The query then is executed and the database is closed. If there was an error, an appropriate error message is written to the page.

```
'   Execute the update
    set rsClients = dbclients.execute(strSQL)

'   Close the database connection
    dbClients.close

%>

<BR><BR>The update was successful.  Click <a href=
➥"default.asp">Here</a> to continue.<BR><BR>

<%

else

    %>

    <BR><BR>The update was not successful.  Click the 'back'
    ➥button on your browser to continue.<BR><BR>

    <%


End If

%>

</body>

</html>
```

20. Two database tables are required for the project. The first is for the client data, and the second is for the salespersons.

```
Clients
    idClient int IDENTITY (1, 1) NOT NULL ,
    chrCompany varchar (255) NULL ,
    chrAddress varchar (50) NULL ,
    chrCity varchar (50) NULL ,
    chrState varchar (50) NULL ,
    chrZipCode varchar (50) NULL ,
    chrPhone varchar (50) NULL ,
    chrFax varchar (50) NULL ,
    chrEmail varchar (50) NULL ,
```

continued on next page

continued from previous page

```
            chrContactName varchar (50) NULL ,
            idSalesperson int NULL


    Salesperson
            idSalesperson int NOT NULL ,
            chrFirstName varchar (50) NULL ,
            chrLastName varchar (50) NULL
```

How It Works

In this example you built a simple Web page system for maintaining client records. You have two tables of SQL Server data: one for storing the basic client data and the second for looking up salespersons to assign a salesperson to the client.

To interface with the database, you will use ADO. The real key to this project is passing data between pages in the form of state data, such as the ID of the client, or in the form of submitted HTML form data. The first page starts out by dynamically building a list of clients. This is done by looping through the recordset and listing the client's name. With each iteration, a new set of HTML **Option** tags is built. Note that the ID of the client is stored as the value of each client:

```
<option value="4">
  Wally's Lights
</option>
```

In this case, the ID for **Wally's Lights** is **4**. After the form is submitted to **ClientDisplay**, you can access the value of the selected item in the **select** box. This is done by using the **Request** object and identifying the name of the **select** box, **clients**.

The ID value then is used in building the query to return the individual client's profile data. The data then is displayed on the page. At the bottom of the page, you want to provide a link to a Web page that allows the user to edit and update the data. The URL built will include a query parameter to indicate the ID of the client:

```
http://localhost/chapter8/ht04/updateclient.asp?idClient=4
```

The parameter is **idClient** and in this case the value is **4**. On the **UpdateClient.asp** page, you can again use the **Request** object to retrieve the value of the query parameter. This allows you to build another query to return the user's data; in this case, the value of the input fields will be set to the current value in the database. An example follows:

```
<input name="company" type=text value="Wally's Lights">
```

Thus when the input text element is displayed, the current value in the database is displayed as well. The only tricky part is displaying the list of salespeople and ensuring that the current salesperson is the default. When the list of salespeople is looped through, if the ID of the salesperson equals the currently assigned salesperson, the Option tag will include the Selected attribute:

```
<option value="2" selected>

Martinez, Lupe

</option>
```

This ensures that the current salesperson is the default for the update. When the form is submitted, the action page, UpdateResponse.asp, is called and each value in the form can be reviewed by using the Request object. If there is an error, it can be displayed instead of the database being updated. If all the data appears to be correct, the database is updated with the new client data.

Note that on the ClientDisplay page, a session variable is used. Session variables allow you to carry information between pages that otherwise might be lost. In this case, you must know the ID of the client in order to update the record. By setting the variable, you then can access it on the UpdateResponse.asp page.

Comments

In this How-To you saw two ways of carrying data between pages. The first is in the URL as a query parameter. The second is as a session variable, which is really a temporary cookie. There are two more methods. In the case of a form, you can use a hidden HTML text element to store the data. Or you can use a long-term cookie to store the data. Note that you should use two methods only when the data should be stored on the user's hard drive for an extended period of time. You should avoid session variables if you do not want to use cookies. Instead, you should use query parameters and hidden text elements.

COMPLEXITY
ADVANCED

8.5 How do I...
Build reports based on ad-hoc query Web pages?

COMPATIBILITY: INTERNET INFORMATION SERVER 3 AND 4

Problem

One of the primary uses of the Web has been for intranets and data reporting. How do I build a tool that will allow my users to build ad-hoc query reports in a Web browser?

Technique

You can build an input form to take field parameters from the user. Based on those field parameters, you can build a SQL query on-the-fly to query the database and show the results. In this case you will build a fictitious **Architects** database that allows searching on architectural style, hourly rate, years in business, and sort order. Ensure that there is an ODBC DSN called **Architects** to the database for the project.

Steps

Open and run **qbe.asp** by using this URL:

`http://localhost/chapter8/ht02/report.asp`

The page shows options for selecting preferred style, hourly rate, years in business, and sort order (see Figure 8.10).

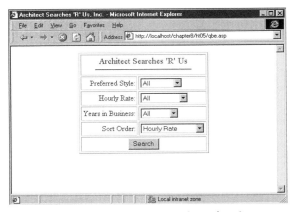

Figure 8.10 The Query Criteria Selection page

Figure 8.11 shows all the records in the database ordered by hourly rate.

Next select ranch style, with years in business greater than 6, an hourly rate greater than $400, and ordered by city. Figure 8.12 shows the results of the query and the created SQL query string.

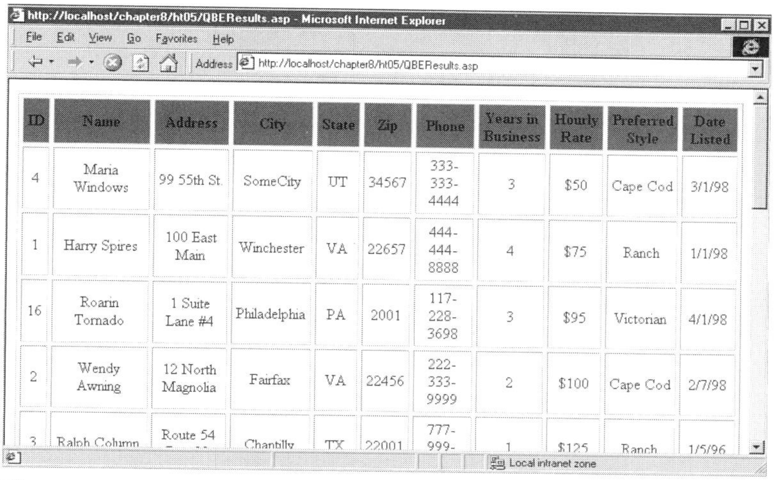

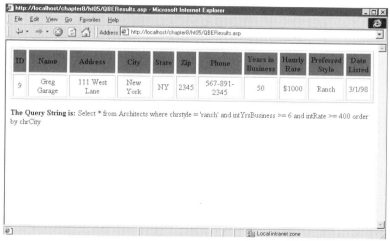

Figure 8.11 A query sorted by hourly rate with no filtering

Figure 8.12 A query sorted by city with ranch style, 6 years in business, and a rate above $400 selected

Finally, Figure 8.13 shows all the records where the style is Victorian and ordered by listing ID.

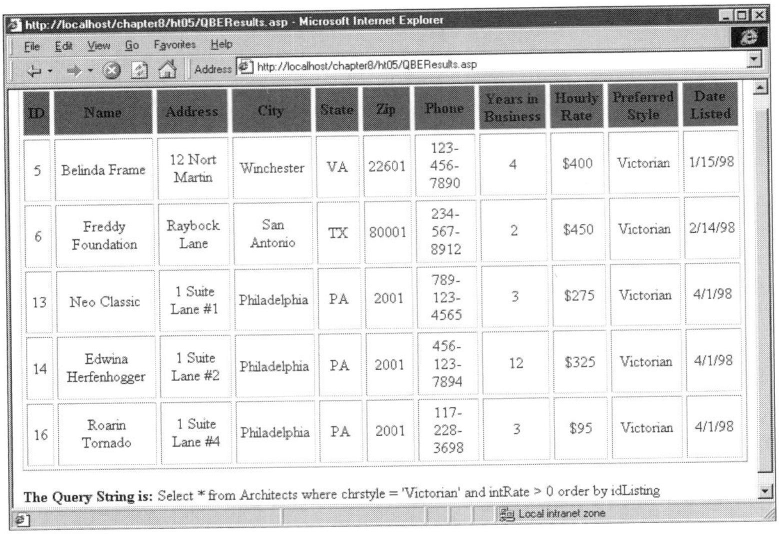

ID	Name	Address	City	State	Zip	Phone	Years in Business	Hourly Rate	Preferred Style	Date Listed
5	Belinda Frame	12 Nort Martin	Winchester	VA	22601	123-456-7890	4	$400	Victorian	1/15/98
6	Freddy Foundation	Raybock Lane	San Antonio	TX	80001	234-567-8912	2	$450	Victorian	2/14/98
13	Neo Classic	1 Suite Lane #1	Philadelphia	PA	2001	789-123-4565	3	$275	Victorian	4/1/98
14	Edwina Herfenhogger	1 Suite Lane #2	Philadelphia	PA	2001	456-123-7894	12	$325	Victorian	4/1/98
16	Roarin Tornado	1 Suite Lane #4	Philadelphia	PA	2001	117-228-3698	3	$95	Victorian	4/1/98

The Query String is: Select * from Architects where chrstyle = 'Victorian' and intRate > 0 order by idListing

Figure 8.13 A query showing all architects who prefer to build Victorian homes

Complete the following steps to create this project:

1. Create a new file and save it as `qbe.asp`. The following code sets up the HTML header for the page and the table for displaying the `select` option elements:

```
<HTML>

<Title>Architect Searches 'R' Us, Inc.</title>

<BODY>

<center>

<Table border=1 cellpadding=3 cellspacing=3>

<TR><TD align=center colspan=2>
<!--  Build the header -->
<font size=4 color=blue>Architect Searches 'R' Us</font>

<HR Width= 200 COLOR=RED>

</td></tr>

<tr><td align = right>
```

2. The form for building the select boxes is created. The page to be called is `QBEResults.asp`. This page takes the inputs from the `select` boxes and dynamically builds the query.

```
<!--  The form will call QBEResults to show the
      results of the query
-->
<form action="QBEResults.asp" method="post">

Preferred Style:

</td>

<td align=left>
```

3. Build the **select** box for **Style** with the different options.

```
<!--  Add the preferred housing styles -->
<select name="chrStyle">
<option value-"all">All</option>
<option value="ranch">Ranch</option>
<option value="Cape Cod">Cape Cod</option>
<option value="Victorian">Victorian</option>
</select>
</td></tr>

<tr><td align=right>
Hourly Rate:
</td>
```

4. Build the **select** box for **Rate** with the different options.

```
<td align=left>
<!--  Add the rate ranges -->
<select name="intRates">
<option value="0">All</option>
<option value="1">$50 to $99</option>
<option value="2">$100 to $199</option>
<option value="3">$200 to $299</option>
<option value="4">$300 to $399</option>
<option value="5">$400 and up</option>
</select>
</td></tr>

<tr><td align=right>
Years in Business:
</td>
```

5. Build the **select** box for **Years in Business** with the appropriate options.

```
<td align=left>
<!--  Add the years in business -->
<select name="intYrsBusiness">
<option value="0">All</option>
<option value="1">1 Year</option>
<option value="2">2 Years</option>
<option value="3">3 Years</option>
<option value="4">4 Years</option>
```

continued on next page

continued from previous page

```
<option value="5">5 Years</option>
<option value="6+">6+ Years</option>
</select>
</td></tr>

<tr><td align=right>
Sort Order:
</td>
```

6. Build the **select** box for the **sort** options with the appropriate values.

```
<td align=left>
<!-- Add the sort options -->
<select name="sort">
<option value="intRate">Hourly Rate</option>
<option value="intYrsBusiness">Years in Business</option>
<option value="chrCity">City</option>
<option value="idListing">ID</option>
</select>
</td></tr>

<tr><td align=center colspan=2>
<!-- Submit element to fire off the query -->
<input type=submit value="Search">
</td></tr>
</table>

</form>

</center>

</BODY>

</HTML>
```

7. Create a new file and save it as **qberesults.asp**. Add the following code to build the initial HTML for the page:

```
<HTML>

<BODY>
```

8. The **ReportArchitects** subroutine in the ASP builds the Web page for display of the records returned from the dynamically built query. The first part of the page declares the database variables.

```
<%

'   This function shows the Architect listings
'   returned from the search.
'   The parameter is the SQL string to be executed.
Sub ReportArchitects(strSearch)

Dim dbArchitects
Dim rsArchitects
```

```
Dim intCount

    '   Create an Active Data Object
    set dbArchitects = server.createobject("adodb.connection")

    '   Open our database connection
    dbArchitects.Open "dsn=Architects;uid=sa;pwd="
```

9. Execute the query to get the results from the database.

```
    '   Get all of the Architects from the database
    '   meeting our criteria.
    set rsArchitects = dbArchitects.execute(strSearch)

%>
```

10. The header for the display table is built. Note that the tags for the heading are `<TH>` to build display headers.

```
    <!--  Start the table   -->
    <table border=1 cellpadding=4 cellspacing=4>

    <!--  Show the header row -->
    <tr bgcolor="BLUE">

      <TH align=center>ID</TH>
      <TH align=center>Name</TH>
      <TH align=center>Address</TH>
      <TH align=center>City</TH>
      <TH align=center>State</TH>
      <TH align=center>Zip</TH>
      <TH align=center>Phone</TH>
      <TH align=center>Years in<BR>Business</TH>
      <TH align=center>Hourly<BR>Rate</TH>
      <TH align=center>Preferred<BR>Style</TH>
      <TH align=center>Date<BR>Listed</TH>

    </TR>
```

11. A check is done to ensure that rows were returned from the query. If not, a message is displayed indicating that no data was returned. Otherwise the resultset is looped through. For certain fields the data will be formatted appropriately for display.

```
<%

'   We first check to ensure that we
'   have data returned.
If (Not rsArchitects.BOF) Then

    '   Loop through the recordset
    Do Until rsArchitects.EOF

%><TR><%
```

continued on next page

continued from previous page

```
                           '  Loop through each field in the recordset
                              For intCount = 0 To 11
                       %><td align=center><%

                   Select Case intCount

                       ' Show the first and last name in the same table column
                       case 1
                           response.write(rsArchitects(intCount) & " " &
                           ➥rsArchitects(intCount + 1))
                           intCount = intCount + 1

                               '  Since the tenth field is the hourly rate
                               '  we want to place a '$' character in front of
                               '  it.
                       case 9
                                 '  Place the $ in front of the rate %>
                           $<% response.write(rsArchitects(intCount))

                                 '  Display the column text
                       case else
                                   response.write(rsArchitects(intCount))

                   End Select

                   %></td><%

                       Next

                       ' Move to the next row
                       rsArchitects.MoveNext

               %></TR><%

                   Loop

               Else

               %>

               <TR>
               <TD COLSPAN=9>
               No Data Returned from the Query.
               </TD>
               </tr>

               <%

               End If

               %>

                   </table>
```

12. Finally the query string is displayed.

```
<BR>
<!-- Show the query string -->
<B>The Query String is:</b>  <% = strSearch %>

<%

End Sub
```

13. The primary ASP code variables are declared for the page. The initial search string is created for pulling all fields from the database.

```
Dim strSearch
Dim intWhereFlag
Dim intYrsBusiness


'  Set the initial SQL statement to query all fields from
   ➡the houses table
strSearch = "Select * from Architects "
```

14. Next a check is done to see what styles should be pulled from the database. If something other than all styles is to be displayed, the `where` clause is added to the SQL string. A flag is set to indicate that the `where` clause has been added.

```
'  Check to see if a specific selection was made for the
'  style
If request("chrStyle") <> "All" then

    '  add on the where clause to search for the specified style
    strSearch = strSearch & "where chrstyle = '" &
    ➡request("chrStyle") & "' "

    '  Indicate the where clause has been added
    intWhereFlag = 1

End If
```

15. A check is done to see whether the years in business is between 0 and 6. If so, a check is done to see whether the `where` clause has been added. If so, the query is added on as an **and** on the query. If not, the query is added on with the `where` clause. The same checking is done if the years in business is to be 6 or greater.

```
'  Get the years in business selected
intYrsBusiness = request("intYrsBusiness")


'  Get the numerical number of rooms
intYrsBusiness = Left(intYrsBusiness, 1)
```

continued on next page

continued from previous page

```
'   Check to see if there is a specific year requested
If intYrsBusiness > 0 then


    '   Check to see if the 6+ option was selected
    If intYrsBusiness < 6   Then

        '   Check the Where flag
        If intWhereFlag = 1 then

                '   Add onto the query to search for the specified
                    ➥number of rooms
            '   Note that the 'and' clause is added if the where
                ➥was already
            '   added
                strSearch = strSearch & "and intYrsBusiness =
                ➥" & intYrsBusiness


            '   Else add the Where clause
        Else

                '   Add onto the query to search for the specified
                    ➥number of rooms
                strSearch = strSearch & " where intYrsBusiness =
                ➥" & intYrsBusiness


            '   Indicate the where clause has been added
            intWhereFlag = 1

        End if

    '   User wants to see 6+ years of experience
    Else

        '   Check the where flag
        If intWhereFlag = 1 then

                '   Search for any house with 6 or more rooms
                '   Note that the 'and' clause is added if the
                    ➥where was already
            '   added
            strSearch = strSearch & "and intYrsBusiness >=
            ➥" & intYrsBusiness


            '   No where clause has been added
        Else

                '   Search for any house with 6 or more rooms
                strSearch = strSearch & " where intYrsBusiness >=
                ➥" & intYrsBusiness


            '   Indicate the where clause has been added
            intWhereFlag = 1

        End If
```

```
        End If

    End If
```

16. Next a check is done to see what rate the user would like to see. Again a check is done to see whether the **where** clause has been added to the query. If not, the query is added. If it has been, the **add** query is added.

```
'   Check to see if the where clause has been added
If intWhereFlag = 1 then

    '   If so then we will also check the rate
    '   Note the and clause is added if the where
    '   has already been added
    strSearch = strSearch & " and intRate "

Else

    '   Add on the where clause
    strSearch = strSearch & " where intRate "

End If
```

17. Based on the rate selected, the appropriate rate range is added to the query.

```
'   Based on the rate range selected, the rate query
'   will be set appropriately.  Note the assumption
'   is made the 'where' and the 'and' clauses have been
'   added.
Select Case request("intRates")

    '   All rates
    Case 0
        strSearch = strSearch & " > 0"

        '   Set the first rate range level
        Case 1
            strSearch = strSearch & " >= 50 and intRate <= 99"

        '   Set the second rate range level
        Case 2
            strSearch = strSearch & " >= 100 and intRate <= 199"

        '   Set the third rate range level
        Case 3
            strSearch = strSearch & " >= 200 and intRate <= 299"

        '   Set the fourth rate range level
        Case 4
            strSearch = strSearch & " >= 300 and intRate <= 399"

        '   Set the last rate range level
        Case 5
            strSearch = strSearch & " >= 400"

End Select
```

18. Finally the sort order is added to the query with an **order by** clause.

```
'  Add on the 'order by' SQL clause and the field selected
strSearch = strSearch & " order by " & request("sort")

'  Call the ReportArchitects subroutine and send
'  the search string
ReportArchitects strSearch

%>

</body>

</html>
```

19. The following table definition stores the data for **Architects**:

```
Architects
    idlisting int IDENTITY (1, 1) NOT NULL ,
    chrFirstName varchar (50) NULL ,
    chrLastName varchar (50) NULL ,
    chrAddress varchar (255) NULL ,
    chrCity varchar (255) NULL ,
    chrState varchar (25) NULL ,
    chrZip varchar (25) NULL ,
    chrPhone varchar (15) NULL ,
    intYrsBusiness int NULL ,
    intRate int NULL ,
    chrStyle varchar (50) NULL ,
    dtListed datetime NULL
```

How It Works

The first thing built is an interface for the user to build queries. The interface provides a way for the user to select search and sort options and then execute a query. The **qbe.asp** page provides a series of select drop-down boxes for selecting the query parameters. The **QBEResults** page provides a fairly straightforward report for reviewing the query results.

In the **QBEResults** page, there is a global (to the ASP page) variable, **strSearch**, that stores the search string that is built to execute the user's specified query. The first parts of the code set up the basic SQL **select** statement to pull all fields from the database. After that you have to check each of the **select** elements to retrieve the selected parameter from the user. Note that the user does not have to select a parameter from the **select** elements. If users do not select a parameter, assume that they want all records for that parameter.

The first check is for the house style the user wants. If the user made a selection, a `where style` = string is attached to the current `select * from Architects` string. The equal side of the statement simply pulls the selection from the list box. For example, for a ranch style, the SQL statement that results looks like this:

```
select * from houses where style = 'ranch'
```

When the `where` clause is added, you set the `intWhere` flag to indicate that it has been added. If no style was selected, no `where` string is tacked onto your current `strSearch` variable. Next you check to see how many years in business the user wants to specify when searching for the right architect. In this case you have a little bit of a twist. First you cannot simply append the `select` box text onto your SQL statement. The left character of the Years in Business select box is needed to retrieve the actual numeric value for the number of years in business on which to search. For the `6+` option, you have to make a special check, and instead of setting `intYrsBusiness` = you need to set `intYrsBusiness >=` for the SQL query. A check is done to see whether the `where` clause was added to the search string. If not, the `where` is added. If it has been, an `and` clause is added.

Next the desired rate range is checked. First a check is again done to see whether the `where` clause was added to the string. If not, it is added; otherwise, an `and` clause is added. From there the Rate select box value is retrieved and the appropriate SQL code is built to check the rate range.

The final result of all the processing should be a properly built SQL statement that fits the user's query selection. After the search string is built, the query is processed to display the results. This is done with the `ReportArchitects` subroutine.

In the subroutine, an Active Data Object for the database query is set up. Then a connection to the database is opened. After the query is processed, a simple loop through the resultset displays the data in an HTML table. There are several formatting checks to ensure that proper data is formatted appropriately. If no data is returned from the query, a message is given to the user indicating that no architects meet the specified criteria. Finally the query is shown to display what SQL query was built to return the selected set of architects.

Comments

This is really just the start of what is possible with building highly interactive and flexible query tools. One of the ways the interface can easily be extended is to allow the user to type appropriate data into the fields for searching. Also the user might want to be able to select multiple entries for one of the fields (for example, `Ranch` and `Victorian`).

8.6 How do I...
Build an Active Server Pages client/server messaging system?

COMPATIBILITY: INTERNET INFORMATION SERVER 3 AND 4

Problem

Now that I have seen how to access databases and perform other techniques in ASP, how would I build a truly interactive system such as a client/server set of message boards for my intranet?

Technique

This How-To combines all the techniques demonstrated in this chapter plus a few new ones to build a message board system. Your system will allow for adding new messages, searching messages, and administrating the message system. Note that an ODBC DSN–named message is needed that points to the `Messages` database.

Steps

Open and run `report.asp` by using this URL:

```
http://localhost/chapter8/ht02/report.asp
```

Figure 8.14 shows the Message Board navigation page. It includes options to add a message, search all messages, search by date and message owner, and administrate the Web site.

Figure 8.15 shows the Add a Message page. Simply fill out the data and click the Submit button.

Next enter `username` in the username field and `password` in the password field to enter the administrative mode. Then click the `Show All Messages` link. Figure 8.16 shows a listing of messages with the `*ADMIN*` column visible. This column is visible only when you have successfully logged in as an administrator.

Figure 8.17 shows an individual message that can be displayed by selecting any message on the Message listing page.

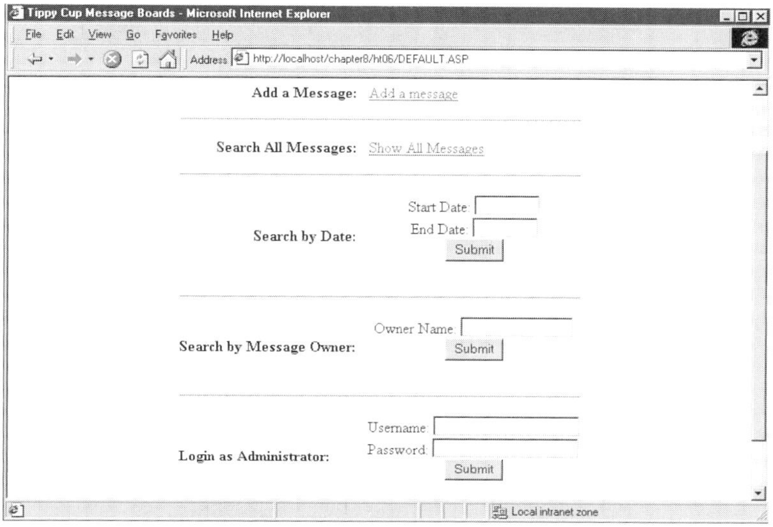

Figure 8.14 The Message Board navigation page

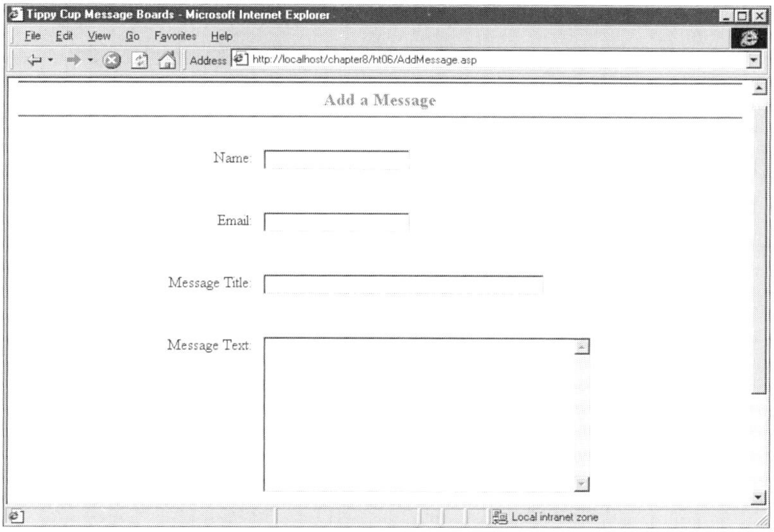

Figure 8.15 The Add a Message Web page

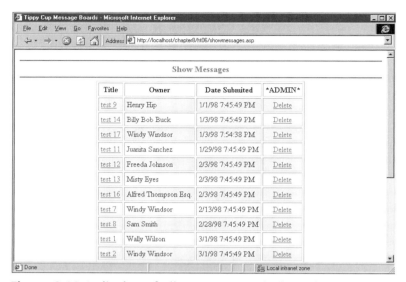

Figure 8.16 A display of all messages with the Administrator Delete option

Figure 8.17 The Message display page

To create this project, complete the following steps:

1. Create a new page and save it as **default.asp**. Add the following code to the top of the page. This code sets up the header of the page.

```
<%@ LANGUAGE="VBSCRIPT" %>

<HTML>
<HEAD>
<TITLE>Tippy Cup Message Boards</TITLE>
</HEAD>
```

```
<BODY BGCOLOR=WHITE>

<HR height=2 color=blue>

<center>


<!-- Build the header -->
<font size=4 color="GREEN">
<B>Welcome to the Tippy Cup Message Boards!</B>
<BR>
</font>

<HR height=2 color=blue><BR>
```

2. The table begins the listing of the options for the message board. The first is a link to the page for adding a message.

```
<!-- Start the table -->
<table cellspacing=4 cellpadding=4>

  <!-- Add a message option -->
<tr>
   <td align=right><B>Add a Message:</b></td>
   <td><a href="AddMessage.asp">Add a message</a></td>
</tr>


<!-- Show all messages -->
<tr>
   <td colspan=2><HR></td>
</tr>
```

3. The next link goes to the Show Messages page to display all the current messages in the page.

```
<tr>
   <td align="right">
       <b>Search All Messages:</b>
   </td>

   <td align=left>

     <a href="showmessages.asp">Show All Messages</a>


   </td>

</tr>
```

4. The next option allows you to search the message database by date. Two text input elements will take the start and end dates. Note the hidden input element, which defaults the display order to the date entered.

Finally a Submit button is displayed. Note that the link is also to the showmessages.asp page.

```
<tr><td colspan=2><HR></td></tr>

<!-- Search by date -->
<tr>
   <td align="right">
     <b>Search by Date:</b>
   </td>

   <td align=center>

      <!-- Form call to the show messages page -->
      <form action="ShowMessages.asp" method="post">

      Start Date: <input name="StartDate" value="" type="text"
      ➥size=8> <BR>

      End Date: <input name="EndDate" value="" type="text"
      ➥size=8><BR>

      <input type="hidden" name="orderby" value="dtentered">

      <input type=submit name=submit value="Submit">

      </form>

   </td>

</tr>
```

5. For users who want to look for messages by a particular message owner, you set up a form similar to the date search earlier. This time the display order also defaults to the date entered. The link is also to the showmessage.asp page.

```
<tr><td colspan=2><HR></td></tr>

<!-- Search by message owner -->
<tr>

   <td align=left>
     <B>Search by Message Owner:</B>
   </td>

   <td align=center>

      <!-- Form to call show messages by date -->
      <form action="ShowMessages.asp" method="post">

      Owner Name:

      <input name="OwnerName" value="" type="text" size=15><BR>

      <input type="hidden" value="dtentered" name="orderby">
```

```
        <input type=submit name=submit value="Submit">

        </form>

      </td>

  </tr>


  <tr><td colspan=2><HR></td></tr>
```

6. Your message system also has an administrative function. To view the administrative features of the site, you must log in. The form will post to the `login.asp` page with the username and password passed in. The password input element will not display the actual typed text but only asterisk (*) characters.

```
<!-- Login as an administrator -->
<tr>

  <td align=left>

    <B>Login as Administrator:</B>

  </td>

  <td align=center>

    <!-- Form to call the administrator login
         in page
    -->
    <form action="Login.asp" method="post">

    Username:

    <input name="UserName" value="" type="text" size=20><BR>

    Password:

    <input name="Password" value="" type="password" size=20><BR>

    <input type=submit name=submit value="Submit">

    </form>

  </td>

</tr>

</table>
```

7. Finally the page is ended with the navigation bar for the system being displayed.

```
<!-- Build the navigation bar -->
<HR height=2 color=blue>

¦ <a href="default.asp">Home</a> ¦ <a href="addmessage.asp">
Add a Message</a> ¦ <a href="showmessages.asp">
Show All Messages</a> ¦

<HR height=2 color=blue>

</center>

</BODY>
</HTML>
```

8. Create a new file and save it as **addmessage.asp**. Add the following code to the header of the page:

```
<%@ LANGUAGE="VBSCRIPT" %>

<HTML>
<HEAD>
<TITLE>Tippy Cup Message Boards</TITLE>
</HEAD>

<BODY BGCOLOR="White">


<!-- Build a header -->
<HR height=2 color=blue>

<center>

<font size=4 color="GREEN">
<B>Add a Message</B>
<BR>
</font>

<HR height=2 color=blue>>
```

9. The form will be posted to the **insertmessage.asp** page. The form consists of a series of text-input fields for name, email, message title, and message.

```
<!-- Build a form that will post the new message
     to the InsertMessage asp page
-->
<form action="InsertMessage.asp" method="post">

<!-- Begin a table for the input fields -->
<table cellpadding=4 cellspacing=4>

<!-- Name field -->
<TR>

  <td align="right" valign="top">Name:</td>
```

```
    <td align="left" valign="top"><input type="text" name=
    ➥"MessageOwner" value=""></td>

</TR>

<tr><td> </td></tr>

<!--  Email field -->
<TR>

  <TD align="right" valign="top">Email:</td>

  <TD align="left" valign="top"><input type="text" name=
  ➥"OwnerEmail" value=""></td>

</TR>

<tr><td> </td></tr>

<!--  Message field -->
<TR>

  <TD align="right" valign="top">Message Title:</TD>

  <TD align="left" valign="top"><input type=text value="" name=
  ➥"MessageTitle" size="40"></TD>

</TR>
>
<tr><td> </td></tr>

<!--  Message text area -->
<TR>

  <TD align="right" valign="top">Message Text:</TD>

  <TD align="left" valign="top"><textarea name="MessageText"
  ➥cols=40 rows=10></textarea></TD>

</TR>

<tr><td> </td></tr>

<!--  Submit button -->
<TR>

<TD COLSPAN=2 align="center"><input type=submit name=submit
➥value="Submit"></TD>

</TR>

</table>

</form>
```

10. Finally the page is ended with the footer for the page, which includes the navigation bar.

```
<!-- Navigation bar -->
<HR height=2 color=blue>

¦  <a href="default.asp">Home</a>  ¦
<a href="addmessage.asp">Add a Message</a> ¦  <a href=
➡"showmessages.asp">
Show All Messages</a> ¦

<HR height=2 color=blue>

</center>

</BODY>
</HTML>
```

11. Create a new file and save it as **InsertMessage.asp**. Note that there is no HTML code for the page—just script code. The first section of the code sets up the variables to be used on the page.

```
<%@ LANGUAGE="VBSCRIPT" %>

<%

'  Declare our variables
Dim dbMessage
Dim MessageText
Dim MessageTitle
Dim MessageOwner
Dim OwnerEmail
Dim SQL
Dim rsMessage
```

12. A database connection is created to your **Messages** database with the Active Database Object.

```
'  Create an Active Data Object
set dbMessage = server.createobject("adodb.connection")

'  Open our database connection
dbMessage.Open "dsn=Messages;uid=sa;pwd="
```

13. Next the various fields entered by the user are processed. To insert the data into a SQL Server database, all single quote (') characters must be converted into double quotes (''). The **Replace** function of VBScript is used. Also, to display the message text properly with line breaks, you must convert all carriage returns into HTML **
** tags. The **LineFeed** function does this.

```
'  Build in support for single quotes
MessageText = Replace(request("MessageText"), "'", "''")
```

```
'  Build in support for line feeds in
'  the message
MessageText = LineFeed(MessageText)

'  Build in support for single quotes
MessageTitle = Replace(request("MessageTitle"), "'", "''")

'  Build in support for single quotes
MessageOwner = Replace(request("MessageOwner"), "'", "''")

'  Build in support for single quotes
OwnerEmail = Replace(request("OwnerEmail"), "'", "''")
```

14. After the fields are processed, the SQL **Insert** statement is built to add the message to the database. After the SQL statement is built, the messages are inserted by calling the **Execute** method of the ADO connection object. Finally the page directs the browser back to the default page.

```
'  Build the SQL Statement
SQL = "insert into Messages(txtMessage, chrMessageTitle, " & _
    "chrMessageOwner, chrOwnerEmail) values('" & _
    MessageText & "', '" & _
    MessageTitle & "','" & _
    MessageOwner & "', '" & _
    OwnerEmail & "')"

'  Insert the message
set rsMessage = dbMessage.execute(SQL)

'  Go back to the home page
response.redirect("default.asp")
```

15. The **LineFeed** function loops through the text sent to it and searches for a line feed (an ASCII value of 10) and replaces it with the HTML **
** tag.

```
'  This function loops through the text
'  and will convert line feeds to HTML
'  <BR> tags
Private Function LineFeed(TextString)

        '  Check for any line feeds
        If InStr(1, TextString, chr(10)) > 0 Then

            '  Loop through the string
            For i = 1 To Len(TextString)

                '  Get the next character
                CheckChar = Mid(TextString, i, 1)

                '  Check for a line feed
                If CheckChar = chr(10) Then
                    '  Add the tagging
                    LineFeed = LineFeed & "<BR>"
                Else
                    '  Continue building the string
```

continued on next page

continued from previous page

```
                                LineFeed = LineFeed & CheckChar
                        End If
                Next
        Else
                '  Return the string
                LineFeed = TextString
        End If

End Function

%>
```

16. Create a new file and save it as **showmessages.asp**. Add the following code to the top of the page to build the page header:

```
<%@ LANGUAGE="VBSCRIPT" %>

<HTML>
<HEAD>
<TITLE>Tippy Cup Message Boards</TITLE>
</HEAD>
<BODY bgcolor="white">

<!-- Build the header -->
<HR height=2 color=blue>

<center>
<font size=4 color="GREEN">
<B>Show Messages</B>
<BR>
</font>

<HR height=2 color=blue>
```

17. The script code begins with variable declarations. An ADO database connection object is created to the **Messages** database.

```
<%

'  Declare our variables
Dim dbMessages
Dim StartDate
Dim EndDate
Dim Ownername
Dim SQL
Dim rsMessages
Dim TB

'  Create an Active Data Object
set dbMessages = server.createobject("adodb.connection")

'  Open our database connection
dbMessages.Open "dsn=Messages;uid=sa;pwd="
```

18. If the showmessages.asp page is called with a search feature of date range or message owner, the data is retrieved from the request variables. Note that these variables are empty if the page was not called with these search options.

```
'  Get the start date from the calling page
StartDate = request("StartDate")

'  Get the end date from the calling page
EndDate = request("EndDate")

'  Get the order by field from the calling page
OrderBy = request("orderby")

'  Get the ownername from the calling page
OwnerName = request("ownername")
```

19. You check to see whether the StartDate and EndDate variables are blank. If so, the date range is defaulted to well before the start of the message system, and the end date is set to a day after the current date. Also, the sort order then is set to the date.

```
'  Check to see if the start date and end
'  date are blank.  If so, then all messages
'  are to be shown.
If StartDate = "" and EndDate = "" then

  ' Set the start date back to before the application
  ' was created
  StartDate = "1/1/80"

  '  Set the end date to today plus one to ensure all current
  '  messages are retrieved
  EndDate = Date + 1


  ' Order by the date entered
  OrderBy = "dtEntered"

End If
```

20. If either of the dates entered is not valid, an error is shown.

```
'  If an invalid date was entered then an
'  error is shown
If IsDate(StartDate) = False or IsDate(EndDate) = False then

    ShowError

else
```

21. Finally the SQL statement is built to search based on the date range and sorted by the specified order. Then a check is done to see whether you are searching for a particular message owner. If you are to search for a particular message owner, the proper SQL statement is built.

```
'   Build the default SQL statement
    SQL = "select chrMessageOwner, chrMessageTitle, dtEntered,
    ➥idMessage from messages where dtEntered >= '" &
    ➥StartDate & "' and dtEntered <= '" & EndDate & "'
    ➥order by " & OrderBy

    '   If an ownername is selected then build a new query
    if OwnerName <> "" then

        '   Set the owner name to the entered name
        SQL = "select chrMessageOwner, chrMessageTitle,
        ➥dtEntered, idMessage from messages where
        ➥chrMessageOwner like '%" & OwnerName &
        ➥"%' order by " & orderby

    end if
```

22. The SQL statement is executed and the result is returned to the `rsMessages` resultset. To display the table, the `TableTools TableBuilder` COM object is used. The forecolors for the table are rotated between white and yellow.

```
'   Get all of the Messages from the database
    set rsMessages = dbMessages.execute(SQL)


    '   Create our table gen object of the component, MyComponent
    Set TB = Server.CreateObject("TableTools.TableBuilder")

    '   Set the colors to rotate between white and yellow
    TB.RotateRowColors = 1
    TB.RowColor1 = "WHITE"
    TB.RowColor2 = "YELLOW"
```

23. The table header tag is created, and the header columns for the table are created. A check is done to see whether the user has been validated as an administrator. If so, an `*ADMIN*` header column is displayed.

```
'   Create the table
    TB.CreateTable 1, 4, 3, 0

        '   Generate a column with the value a
        TB.GenerateColumn "<B>Title<B>", "Center", "Center"

        '   Generate a column with the value a
        TB.GenerateColumn "<B>Owner<B>", "Center", "Center"

        '   Generate a column with the value a
        TB.GenerateColumn "<B>Date Submitted<B>", "Center",
        ➥"Center"

    '   Check to see if the user was validated as an
```

```
' administrator
if session("validated") = "YES" then

        ' Generate a column header for the administrator
        TB.GenerateColumn "<B>*ADMIN*<B>", "Center", "Center"

end if
```

24. Now that the table is set up, you are ready to loop through the messages returned by the query. With each iteration of the loop, a table row is created. Then for each data element to be displayed, a column is generated. The first column shows the ID of the message and builds a live link to the **showmessage** page. This allows the user to see the individual message. After that, the message owner and date the message was entered are displayed.

```
' Loop through the messages
   Do until rsMessages.eof

       ' Create our first row
       TB.StartRow

           ' Generate a column with the message title
           TB.GenerateColumn "<a href="""showmessage.asp?idMessage=
                             " & _
                             rsmessages("idMessage") & """>" & _
                             rsMessages("chrMessageTitle") & _
                             "</a>", "", ""

           ' Generate a column with message owner
           TB.GenerateColumn rsMessages("chrMessageOwner"), "", ""

           ' Generate a column with the date the message
           ➡was entered
           TB.GenerateColumn rsMessages("dtEntered"), "", ""
```

25. If the user has been validated as an administrator, you show a link to the **deletemessage.asp** page. If the user clicks on this link, the message is deleted.

```
' Check to see if the administrator was validated
   if Session("Validated") = "YES" then

           ' Generate a column with an option to delete
           ➡the message
           TB.GenerateColumn "<a href="""deletemessage.asp?
           ➡idMessage=" & rsmessages("idMessage") & """>"
           ➡& "Delete </a>", "center", "center"

       end if
```

26. Finally the next row is moved to and the loop code is looped through again. If the resultset is ended, the table is ended.

```
'  Move to the next message
   rsMessages.movenext

      '  End the row
      TB.EndRow

   Loop

'  End the table
TB.EndTable


%>
```

27. Next a form is built to provide the user with sort options. The user can sort by message owner, message title, or date entered. It is important to keep the current search options when the form is submitted. Three hidden variables are set up to store the current start date, end date, and owner name.

```
<!--  Create a form to choose sort options  Note that it
      calls this same page
-->
<form method="post" action="showmessages.asp">

<B>Order by:</B>

<!--  Put in three options to sort by message owner,
      title, and date entered
-->
<input name="orderby" type="radio" value="chrMessageOwner">
➥Message Owner
<input name="orderby" type="radio" value="chrMessageTitle">
➥Message Title
<input name="orderby" type="radio" value="dtEntered">
➥Date Entered

<!--  It is important to store the start date, end date
      and owner name for any filtering of the messages
-->
<input type="hidden" name="startdate" value="<% = startdate %>">
<input type="hidden" name="enddate" value="<% = enddate %>">
<input type="hidden" name="ownername" value="<% = ownername %>">

<!--  Submit button for the form -->
<input type=submit value="Submit">

</form>

<%

End If
```

28. The ShowError subroutine displays an error to the user indicating that an invalid date has been entered.

```
'  Subroutine to show date errors
Sub ShowError

    %>

    <!-- Indicate an error in the date ->
    You have entered an invalid start or end date.
    Please try again.

    <%

End Sub

%>
```

29. Finally the page is ended with the navigation bar and ending code.

```
<!- Navigation bar -->
<HR height=2 color=blue>

¦  <a href="default.asp">Home</a>  ¦  <a href="addmessage.asp">
Add a Message</a> ¦  <a href="showmessages.asp">Show
➥All Messages</a> ¦

<HR height=2 color=blue>

</center>

</BODY>
</HTML>
```

30. Create a new file and save it as **showmessage.asp**. This page displays the selected message. Add the following code to the header of the page:

```
<%@ LANGUAGE="VBSCRIPT" %>

<HTML>
<HEAD>
<TITLE>Tippy Cup Message Board</TITLE>
</HEAD>
<BODY BGCOLOR="WHITE">


<!-- Build the header -->
<HR height=2 color=blue>

<center>
<font size=4 color="GREEN">
<B>Message</B>
<BR>
</font>

<HR height=2 color=blue>

<BR>
```

31. The script code begins with the declarations of the variables for the script. An ADO connection object is created.

```
<%

'   Declare our variables
Dim dbMessage
Dim SQL
Dim rsMessage
Dim txtMessage
Dim dtEntered

'   Create an Active Data Object
set dbMessage = server.createobject("adodb.connection")

'   Open our database connection
dbMessage.Open "dsn=Messages;uid=sa;pwd="
```

32. The SQL string is built to retrieve the specified message. The ID of the message is retrieved from the query string on the URL. Next the message data is returned by executing the query.

```
'   Build the SQL Statement
SQL = "select * from messages where idMessage = " & _
request.querystring("idMessage")

'   Get the message
set rsMessage = dbMessage.execute(SQL)

'   Get the text message
```

33. The text message and date are retrieved from the SQL statement. The table is started to display the message data.

```
txtMessage = rsMessage("txtMessage")

'   Get the date entered
dtEntered = rsMessage("dtEntered")

%>

<!-- Build our table -->
<table cellpadding=3 cellspacing=3 border=1 width=400>
```

34. The message owner, owner email, message title, message date, and message text are displayed. Note that the owner email is created as a mailto **Href**. The message text appears with appropriate line breaks.

```
<!-- Show the message owner -->
<TR>
<TD align=right><B>Message Owner:</b></td>
<!-- Show the message owner -->
<td><%=rsMessage("chrMessageOwner")%></td>
</TR>
```

```
<!-- Show the message owner's email -->
<TR>
<TD align=right><B>Message Owner Email:</b></td>
<!-- Build an email link -->
<td><A href="mailto:<%=rsMessage("chrOwnerEmail")%>">
<!-- Show the email address -->
<%=rsMessage("chrOwnerEmail")%></a></td>
</TR>

<!-- Show the message title -->
<TR>
<TD align=right><b>Message Title:</b></td>
<!-- Show the message title -->
<td><%=rsMessage("chrMessageTitle")%></td>
</TR>

<!-- Show the message date -->
<TR>
<TD align=right><b>Message Date:</b></td>
<!-- Show the date the message was entered -->
<td><% = dtEntered %></td>
</TR>

<!-- Show the message text -->
<TR>
<TD align=right><b>Message:</b></td>
<!-- Show the message text -->
<TD><% = txtMessage%></TD>
</TR>

</table>

<BR>
```

35. Finally the page is ended with a display of the navigation bar.

```
<!-- Navigation bar -->
<HR height=2 color=blue>

¦  <a href="default.asp">Home</a>  ¦  <a href="addmessage.asp">
➥Add a Message</a> ¦  <a href="showmessages.asp">
➥Show All Messages</a> ¦

<HR height=2 color=blue>

</center>


</BODY>
</HTML>
```

36. Create a new file and save it as **deletemessage.asp**. An ADO connection object is created. The SQL **delete** statement retrieves the ID of the message and deletes the message from the database. After the message is deleted, the user is redirected to the default page.

```
<%@ LANGUAGE="VBSCRIPT" %>

<%

'  Declare our variables
Dim dbMessage
Dim SQL
Dim rsMessage

'  Create an Active Data Object
set dbMessage = server.createobject("adodb.connection")

'  Open our database connection
dbMessage.Open "dsn=Messages;uid=sa;pwd="

'  Build the SQL Statement
SQL = "delete from Messages where idmessage = " &
➥request("idMessage")

'  Insert the message
set rsMessage = dbMessage.execute(SQL)

'  Go back to the home page
response.redirect("default.asp")

%>
```

37. Create a new file and save it as `login.asp`. This page checks the username and password entered by the user. If they are not correct, a page is built to notify the user that the entries are invalid. If the data is incorrect, the validated session variable is set to NO. If it is valid, it is set to YES.

```
<%@ LANGUAGE="VBSCRIPT" %>


<%

'  Check to see if the username and password is correct
If request("username") <> "username" or request("password") <>
➥"password" then

    %>

    <!-- Build a header.  Note that you must ensure that
         the header is not built in case we need to redirect
            the user when a correct username and password is
            entered
        -->
    <HTML>
    <HEAD>
    <TITLE>Tippy Cup Message Boards</TITLE>
    </HEAD>

    <BODY BGCOLOR=WHITE>
```

```
         Wrong Username and Password.  Click <a href="default.asp">
         ➡here </a> to continue.

         </BODY>
         </HTML>

         <%

         '  Store is a session variable that the user has not been
         ➡validated.
         session("validated") = "NO"

      else

         '  Store in a session variable that the user has been
            ➡validated
         session("validated") = "YES"

         '  Redirect the user back to the default page
         response.redirect("default.asp")

      end if

      %>
```

38. Create a messages database with the following fields:

```
Messages
    idMessage int IDENTITY (1, 1) NOT NULL ,
    txtMessage text NULL ,
    dtEntered datetime NULL ,
    chrMessageOwner varchar (150) NULL ,
    chrOwnerEmail varchar (50) NULL ,
    chrMessageTitle varchar (100) NULL
```

How It Works

Many key elements to this How-To code are critical. Each element relates to the issue of state and tracking information for a particular user between Web pages. Session variables are used to track the status of the user, whether or not that user is an administrator. This data is needed throughout the entire application.

You use query strings and hidden variables to carry data across different pages. In the case of reviewing messages and deleting messages, the link to those pages carries the ID of the message as a query string parameter (for example, ?id=1). This parameter is read with the request object and the querystring property. After the value is retrieved, the appropriate database query can be executed.

Hidden variables can be very critical for passing information along in a form submission. This data does not have to be visible to the user when the form is submitted but might be necessary to the targeted page. In the case of the showmessages.asp page and the search options, it is important to know the state of the page when a new sort option is selected. If the search was done by the message owner, the new sort must show the same data. The hidden variables for `StartDate`, `EndDate`, and `OrderBy` must be passed back to `showmessages.asp`.

The interaction with the database is fairly straightforward. The only wrinkle comes with the stores of multiple-line text data. It is important to convert any linefeed characters into HTML `<BR>` tags for later display. Also, if the user enters any single quotes (`'`), they should be converted to double quotes (`''`). That way the SQL statement will not be invalid because alphanumeric fields such as `text` and `varchar` require the data to be surrounded by single quotes.

Comments

This How-To demonstrates how very complete applications can be built on the Active Server Pages platform. Unlike Visual Basic, you must maintain state data between Web pages. Base Internet technology with client browsers does not provide the same kind of full-featured client technology as does a Visual Basic application. The next step for the code in this How-To is to build in a reply capability to each message.

CHAPTER 9

BUILDING IIS APPLICATIONS WITH VISUAL BASIC 6.0

9

BUILDING IIS APPLICATIONS WITH VISUAL BASIC 6.0

by Noel Jerke

How do I...

An IIS application is a Visual Basic application that uses a combination of HTML and compiled Visual Basic code in a dynamic, browser-based application. An IIS application resides on a Web server, where it receives requests from a browser, runs code associated with the requests, and returns responses to the browser (any browser). IIS applications are named for Microsoft Internet Information Server, the Web server you use to run your IIS applications. IIS applications can run in any browser, on the Internet or an intranet, and therefore make it easy to reach a broad audience.

You will find that on the face of it, IIS applications are very similar to ASP applications (see Chapter 8, "Visual Basic and Active Server Pages on the Web"). But the interface through HTML and the browser is the only similarity. With IIS applications, you can write traditional Visual Basic applications. The only difference is that instead of the standard forms interface, you build an HTML Web browser–based interface.

With IIS applications you can query databases in response to a user's request, writing information to and from records. You can also retrieve HTML pages and replace portions of them with dynamic content before sending them to the browser. The capability to dynamically create HTML elements and generate events for them on-the-fly at runtime creates a very powerful and fluid environment for building truly interactive Web-based applications.

With these or other advanced uses of IIS applications, you can perform complicated processing based on the actions users perform in the browser. IIS applications can use Visual Basic code to perform much of the same processing you might have previously done with script, CGI processing, and other methods of Internet application development such as Active Server Pages.

In this chapter, you will find extensive similarities to the coding done in Chapter 8. As you will see, however, with IIS applications, you have the full extent of the Visual Basic 6.0 programming language at your command. Unlike the limited scripting environment of Active Server Pages, you can use traditional object-oriented techniques of programming as well as your existing library of Visual Basic code.

9.1 Get Started Building IIS Applications

In Chapter 8 you saw how to build applications based on Active Server Pages with VBScript coding and server-side objects. In this How-To, you will examine the key concepts behind building IIS applications and compare them with Active Server Pages applications. You'll also look at the requirements for building and running IIS applications.

9.2 Build a Simple IIS Application

This How-To starts off your programming with a simple IIS application. You will use the Web class designer to add a custom event to your page and define the functionality of a hyperlink.

9.3 Build an IIS Application with Class Features

One of the key benefits of building IIS applications is that you can use the full programming power of Visual Basic. In this example, you will build a simple quiz that uses a class to process the user's responses.

9.4 Build an IIS Application–Based Multipage Tracking System

As you saw in Chapter 8, it is possible to build applications that span multiple pages and keep state. Internet applications do not automatically remember what a user has done between pages. With IIS applications, the same techniques are available for keeping state data across pages and building extended interactive applications. This How-To also uses the table-building COM object you built in Chapter 8.

9.5 Build an IIS Application–Based Ad-Hoc Query Report

One of the key features of Internet technology is the capability to do quick and powerful reporting. This is in large part why intranets have become so popular in the corporate world. Large databases can be developed in a central location with Internet/intranet access via corporate Web servers. In this section, you explore how to build ad-hoc query reports in an IIS application.

9.6 Build an IIS Application–Based Client/Server Messaging System

In Chapter 8, you saw how to build a complete message system with Active Server Pages technology. In this How-To, you will redevelop this application using IIS application technology. The full-featured Visual Basic language gives you extended flexibility beyond Active Server Pages in building the application.

COMPLEXITY
BEGINNING

9.1 How do I...
Get started building IIS applications?

COMPATIBILITY: VISUAL BASIC 6

Problem

I understand that in Visual Basic 6.0 I can build Internet applications that run in IIS. What are the advantages and requirements for building these applications?

Technique

An IIS application is a Visual Basic application that resides on a Web server and responds to requests from the browser. An IIS application uses HTML to present its user interface and compiled Visual Basic code to process requests and respond to events in the browser.

To the user, an IIS application appears to be made up of a series of HTML pages. To the developer, an IIS application is made up of a special type of object called a *Web class* that in turn contains a series of resources called *Web items*. The Web class acts as the central functional unit of the application, processing data from the browser and sending information to the users. You can think of Web classes as specialized classes that provide an appropriate interface for supporting the Web environment. After you create a Web class, you can easily access it in another Web class.

You define a series of procedures that determine how the Web class responds to these requests. The Web items are the HTML pages and other data the Web class can send to the browser in response to a request. For example, a hyperlink on a Web page may in fact go back to the same page with a different set of data. Or the hyperlink may go to a page that is completely created on-the-fly from your Visual Basic application. The key is that you, as the programmer, have complete control over the response of a Web page to all events.

IIS applications bear some resemblance to Active Server Pages (ASP) applications. Both types of applications present dynamic Web sites and perform their processing on the server rather than on the client. However, each has its unique advantages. Active Server Pages are for script developers interested in authoring Web pages and offer the unique capability to intermingle script with HTML. IIS applications are for Visual Basic developers building Web-based applications rather than Web pages. IIS applications allow for complicated business processing and easy access from almost any browser or platform.

If you need to build a basic Web page that does some simple processing, ASP and VBScript might be the right choice. If you are building a mission-critical business application, however, IIS applications offer the complete Visual Basic programming environment, except delivered with an HTML interface instead of a form interface.

One of the plusses of IIS applications is the capability to use IIS Active Server Pages objects such as **Request**, **Response**, and so on. You therefore have all the features of ASP applications for working in the Web environment at your disposal.

One of the challenges of the Web environment is balancing the design side as well as the technical-programming aspects. With IIS applications, the complete application can be prototyped in HTML and then imported into your IIS application for programming. You therefore have a true separation of code and HTML.

The primary system requirements for running a corporate IIS application are a production server with IIS 3.0 (preferably 4.0) running, appropriate drive space for Windows NT, and a minimum of 64MB of RAM (128MB or better is preferred). If you are running a database, you might want to run it on a separate server on the same network for added performance.

When you create an IIS application, you create its Web classes using the Webclass Designer. Web classes typically contain Web items and the code that delivers those Web items to a client. A one-to-one relationship exists between the Webclass Designer and the Web class. If you want to add more Web classes to your application, you must add more designers.

A Web class is associated with only one client (a browser on a machine) for its entire life cycle. Visual Basic creates a logical instance of the Web class for each client that accesses it. However, for each client the Web class is capable of maintaining state between requests.

Each Web class in an IIS application has an associated `.asp` (Active Server Pages) file that Visual Basic generates during the compile or debug process. The `.asp` file hosts the Web class on the Web server. In addition, it generates the Web class's runtime component when the application is first started and launches the first event in the Web class's life cycle.

The path to the ASP acts as the base URL for the Web class and its Web items. Suppose you have a decision support system that contains a Web class called `DecSupport`. Visual Basic creates an ASP called `DecSupport.asp` for the Web class when you compile the project and stores it in the specified directory, `DecSupport`, on the Web server you specify, `www.website.com`. The base URL `IDH_vbdefBaseURL@vbdef98.chm` for your Web class would be `http://www.website.com/DecSupport.asp`.

A Web class typically contains Web items it uses to provide content to the browser and expose events. A Web item can be one of two things: an HTML template file or a custom Web item.

HTML template files are HTML pages that you associate with your Web class. When the Web class receives a request, it can send the HTML pages to the browser for display. Templates differ from regular HTML pages only in that they often contain replacement areas the Web class can process before sending the page to the browser. This allows you to customize your response.

Custom Web items do not have an associated HTML page they can return to the user. Instead, a custom Web item is a programmatic resource that consists of one or more event handlers that are logically grouped together to help organize your Web application. These event handlers are called from the browser when the page loads or when a user selects an HTML element. The event handlers can generate a response to the browser or pass processing to another of the Web class's Web items.

Templates and custom Web items both expose events that the Web class processes when certain actions occur in the browser. You can write event procedures for these events using standard Visual Basic code, thus linking the actions that occur on a Web page to Visual Basic processing.

Each Web class can contain multiple templates and Web items. In most cases, you will need only one Web class in your application, but you might want to use multiple Web classes if you want to break up your application into parts that can be reused in other applications.

To run your IIS application, a Web class runtime component, MSWCRUN.DLL, helps process requests. This runtime is accessed from IIS for its processing. Your IIS application is compiled as a DLL file, which is automatically generated when the project is compiled. This DLL contains your code and is accessed by the runtime component.

Like other Visual Basic applications, an IIS application has code modules and a visual designer. IIS application objects are stored in plain text files that contain the source code of the Web class, events and property settings, and the Web items for the Web class. Visual Basic uses the extension .dsr for these files. In addition to the .dsr file, Visual Basic generates a .dsx file that contains a binary version of the application.

Comments

Building IIS applications is a new feature of Visual Basic 6 that provides a powerful way to extend your Visual Basic applications to the Internet. Over the next several sections of the chapter, you will explore how to begin building IIS applications and put the concepts outlined in this section to use.

COMPLEXITY
BEGINNING

9.2 How do I...
Build a simple IIS application?

COMPATIBILITY: VISUAL BASIC 6

Problem

Now that I have a basic idea of how IIS applications work, how can I build a simple IIS application to get started?

Technique

To get started you will build a small Web page template that will have two hyperlinks on the page. The first will call a custom event for a Web item on the page. For the second hyperlink, you will define a custom WebEvent that is called when the hyperlink is clicked on.

Steps

Open and run 9.2.vbp. Make sure that you have Internet Explorer running, and run the project. If this is the first time you have run the project, let Visual Basic add a virtual root pointing to the application (assuming you are running the Personal Web Server on Windows 95/98 or IIS 3 or 4 on Windows NT). The application then should appear in the Web browser as shown in Figure 9.1. Note the URL to the ASP page, IISProj1_WebClass1.ASP.

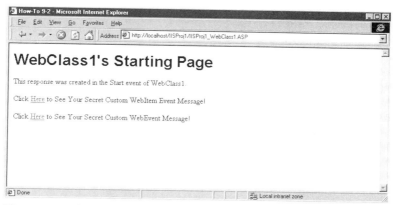

Figure 9.1 The Web page at runtime

On the Web page, you have two hyperlinks. The first calls a custom event for that hyperlink. Click on it, and you should see the hello 1 message shown in Figure 9.2.

Figure 9.2 The Hello custom Web item message

Click the browser's Back button to go to the default page. Then click the second link, which calls a custom Web event and displays the hello 2 message shown in Figure 9.3.

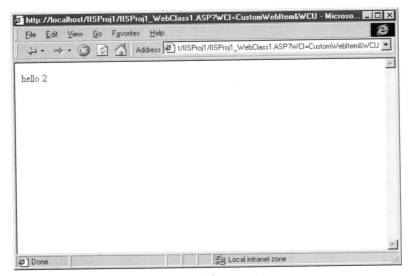

Figure 9.3 The Hello custom Web event message

Complete the following steps to create this project:

1. Start a new IIS application in Visual Basic. Name the project **IISProj1** and set the title of the application to **9.2**. On the Debugging tab, ensure that the started component is **WebClass1**.

2. Import the **9.2.htm** file. For the **HyperLink1 HREF**, double-click to create a new Web event for the hyperlink. For the second hyperlink, right-click **Custom WebItems** and choose Add Custom WebItem. Name the Web item **CustomWebItem**. Right-click the second hyperlink in the template and connect it to the custom Web item.

TIP

To get started with IIS applications, it might be easiest to copy the code from the CD-ROM and use the templates and project files as created.

3. The **9.21.htm** file is created from the **9.2.htm** file when imported as a template into the Web Class Designer. The following code sets up the header of the page:

```
<!DOCTYPE HTML PUBLIC "-//W3C//DTD W3 HTML//EN">
<HTML>
<HEAD>
<META content="text/html; charset=iso-8859.1"
➥http-equiv=Content-Type>
```

```
<TITLE>How-To 9.2</TITLE>
<META content='"MSHTML 4.72.3007.2"' name=GENERATOR>
</HEAD>
<BODY>
```

4. The first hyperlink calls the **Hyperlink1** Web event tied to this hyperlink. To tie the two together, double-click the first hyperlink in the Web Designer to create the event. Note the custom URL encoding.

```
Click <A href="IISProj1_WebClass1.ASP?WCI=Template1
➥&WCE=Hyperlink1&WCU">Here</A>
to See Your Secret Custom WebItem Event Message!
<BR><BR>
```

5. The second hyperlink calls the **CustomWebItem** custom Web event tied to this hyperlink. To create the second event, right-click **Custom WebItems** and choose Add Custom WebItem. After the event is added, name it **CustomWebItem**. To link the two together, right-click the second hyperlink in the template and choose Connect to WebItem. Then choose the Custom WebItem. Note the custom URL encoding on the HTML hyperlink to refer to the custom Web event.

```
Click <A href="IISProj1_WebClass1.ASP?WCI=CustomWebItem&WCU">
➥Here</A>
to See Your Secret Custom WebEvent Message!
</BODY></HTML>
```

6. Add the following code to the **Respond** event of the **CustomWebItem**. When the second hyperlink is clicked, this **Respond** event is fired off. In this case you are using the IIS ASP **Response** object to write the **hello 2** message back to the browser.

```
'  Code behind the custom Web item
Private Sub CustomWebItem_Respond()

'  Use the Active Server Pages Response object
'   to send a response to the browser.
Response.Write "hello 2"

End Sub
```

7. The **Template1** hyperlink event is called when the first hyperlink is clicked. In this case you use the IIS ASP **Response** object to write **hello 1** to the browser.

```
'  Code connected to the Hyperlink1 Custom Event
Private Sub Template1_Hyperlink1()

'  Use the Active Server Pages Response object
'   to send a response to the browser.
Response.Write "hello 1"

End Sub
```

8. The `Respond` event of `Template1` is called when the template is activated. In this case you use the `WriteTemplate` method to display the HTML to the browser.

```
'  Called when Template1 is set as the active item
Private Sub Template1_Respond()

'  When Template1 is set as the item our response will be
'  to write out the template.
Template1.WriteTemplate

End Sub
```

9. The `WebClass Start` event is called when the Web class is activated. In this case HTML is written to the browser, and then the next item to be processed is set to `Template1`, which activates the `Respond` event of `Template1`.

```
'  Called when the Web class is started
Private Sub WebClass_Start()

    '  Set the quote string as a character value
    Dim sQuote As String
    sQuote = Chr$(34)

    'Write a reply to the user
    With Response
        .Write "<HTML>"
        .Write "<body>"
        .Write "<h1><font face=" & sQuote & "Arial" & sQuote & _
               ">WebClass1's Starting Page</font></h1>"
        .Write "<p>This response was created in the Start
        ➥event of WebClass1.</p>"
        .Write "</body>"
        .Write "</html>"
    End With

    '  Set the next item to be Template1
    Set NextItem = Template1

End Sub
```

How It Works

This example demonstrates some of the basic features of IIS applications. The first key is using the Web Class Designer. In the designer you import the HTML prototype page, which will have programming built into it. All the tags are listed in the page or template. From there each tag can be custom programmed, including hyperlinks and forms.

As demonstrated in this example, you can build custom programming behind each event. Instead of having the hyperlink automatically jump to another page for processing, the hyperlink points to a Web event in your Web class. In the case of the examples here, each hyperlink connects to an event. In the case of `Hyperlink1`, a direct event is tied to the mouse click.

In the case of `Hyperlink2`, a custom Web item has been built that will be linked to the click of the hyperlink. The two are tied together in the Web Class Designer. You can right-click on each tag in the template page and connect the template to a custom Web event. The difference between the custom Web events and custom Web items is that Web items can be multiply connected and used in different templates. The custom event is tied directly to the particular template.

Each Web class has a startup event. In this case the Web event is the `webclass_start` event. In this event you can direct the next action in your Web class. In the Web class there is a global property, `NextItem`, that indicates the next item to be processed. For example, in your start event the next item to be processed is `Template1`. The program then fires off the `Respond` event of the next item, `Template1`. Note that when the next item is set in a procedure, the rest of the procedure is run before the `Respond` event of the next item is fired off.

To interact with the browser, the IIS object interface is at your disposal for using objects that should be familiar from Chapter 8. In this case the `Response` object is used to write HTML to the browser in the Web events.

Comments

IIS applications open up a whole new world of Internet development that combines both Active Server Pages and Visual Basic. In the next several How-To's, you will explore building more complex IIS applications. The next How-To demonstrates using a familiar feature in Visual Basic, the class, with your Web classes.

COMPLEXITY

INTERMEDIATE

9.3 How do I...

Build an IIS application with class features?

COMPATIBILITY: VISUAL BASIC 6

Problem

Now that I have seen how to build a simple IIS application, how do I use my existing code-based built-in classes with my Web class code?

Technique

To learn how to use classes with your IIS applications, you will build a simple browser-based quiz. The quiz asks three questions regarding state capitals. The actual processing of the answers is done in a class, **ProcessResponse**. Based on the results of the class, a different response is written to the browser to indicate the success of the Web user.

Steps

Open **9.3.vbp**. Make sure that you have Internet Explorer running, and run the project. If this is the first time you have run the project, let Visual Basic add a virtual root pointing to the application. The application then should appear in the Web browser as shown in Figure 9.4. Note the URL to the ASP page, **IISProj2_WebClass1.ASP**.

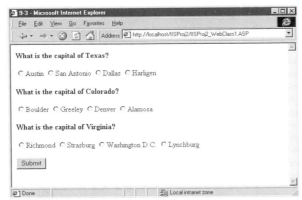

Figure 9.4 The Web form at runtime

The Web page shows three questions on the page regarding the state capitals of Texas, Colorado, and Virginia. Fill out incorrect responses to achieve the results shown in Figure 9.5.

Click Back and fill out the correct responses to the quiz (Austin, Denver, and Richmond). The response back to the user then changes as appropriate. Figure 9.6 shows the correct answer response page.

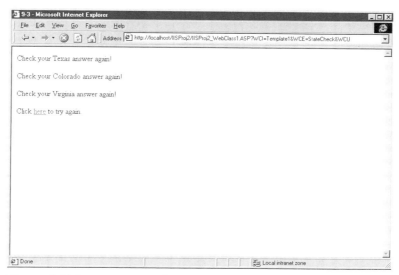

Figure 9.5 A response to incorrect answers

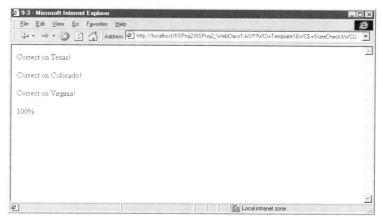

Figure 9.6 The correct answers response

To create this project, complete the following steps:

1. Start a new IIS application in Visual Basic. Name the project **IISProj2** and set the title of the application to **9.3**. On the Debugging tab, ensure that the started component is **WebClass1**.

2. Import the **9.3.htm** file.

3. Your Web page includes a form for submitting the response to the server. In this case you need a custom event for processing the response. Right-click on the form tag and add a custom event called StateCheck.

4. The 9.31.htm file is created from the 9.3.htm file when imported as a template into the Web Class Designer. The following code sets up the header of the page:

```
<!DOCTYPE HTML PUBLIC "-//W3C//DTD W3 HTML//EN">
<HTML>
<HEAD>

<META content="text/html; charset=iso-8859.1" http-equiv=
➥Content-Type>

<TITLE>9.3</TITLE>
<META content='"MSHTML 4.72.3007.2"' name=GENERATOR>

</HEAD>
<BODY>
```

5. The quiz form starts with the action pointing to the ASP for the IIS application. Note the reference to the StateCheck Web event, which is called when the form is submitted.

```
<FORM action=IISProj2_WebClass1.ASP?WCI=Template1&amp;WCE=
➥StateCheck&amp;WCU
method=post name=Texas>

<B>What is the capital of Texas?</B>

<BR><BR>
```

6. The radio button input elements for the cities in each state are set up. Note that no special notation is needed for use in the IIS application; the elements are referenced with the standard IIS Request object.

```
<INPUT name=tx type=radio value="Austin">Austin
<INPUT name=tx type=radio value="San Antonio">San Antonio
<INPUT name=tx type=radio value="Dallas">Dallas
<INPUT name=tx type=radio value="Harligen">Harligen

<BR><BR>

<B>What is the capital of Colorado?</B>

<BR><BR>

<INPUT name=co type=radio value="Boulder">Boulder
<INPUT name=co type=radio value="Greeley">Greeley
```

```
<INPUT name=co type=radio value="Denver">Denver
<INPUT name=co type=radio value="Alamosa">Alamosa

<BR><BR>

<B>What is the capital of Virginia?</B>

<BR><BR>
<INPUT name=va type=radio value="Richmond">Richmond
<INPUT name=va type=radio value="Strasburg">Strasburg
<INPUT name=va type=radio value="Washington D.C.">
➥Washington D.C.
<INPUT name=va type=radio value="Lynchburg">Lynchburg

<BR><BR>

<INPUT type=submit value=Submit>

</FORM>

</BODY></HTML>
```

7. In the IIS application project, insert a new class called `ProcessResponse`
and save it as `ProcessResponse.cls`. Add the following method,
`CheckAnswer`, to the class. This method takes in the state and city to be
checked. It then uses a `Select Case` statement to check the city response
to see whether it is the correct answer for the capital of the specified state.

```
'  Checks the answer to the specified question
Public Function CheckAnswer(state, city) As Boolean

'  Start out as false
CheckAnswer = False

'  Check which state is to be checked.
Select Case UCase(state)

    '  Texas -- Austin
    Case "TEXAS"
        If UCase(city) = "AUSTIN" Then CheckAnswer = True

    '  Virginia -- Richmond
    Case "VIRGINIA"
        If UCase(city) = "RICHMOND" Then CheckAnswer = True

    '  Colorado -- Denver
    Case "COLORADO"
        If UCase(city) = "DENVER" Then CheckAnswer = True

    '  Default to false for anything else.
    Case Else
        CheckAnswer = False

End Select

End Function
```

8. In the Web class, add the following code to the **Respond** event of **Template1**. When the **Respond** event is called (by setting it as the **NextItem**), the HTML for the template is written to the browser.

```
'  Respond event for template1
Private Sub Template1_Respond()

'  Write out the HTML for the template
Template1.WriteTemplate

End Sub
```

9. In the **StateCheck** event for the form, add the following code. The **ProcessResponse** class is instantiated for checking the state responses. The results of the check are written to a new page on-the-fly. The first step in the process is to write the HTML header for the page. You will use the **Flag** variable to track whether there are any incorrect responses. The **Request** object is used to retrieve the responses to each question. Then each response is checked with your class. With each incorrect response, an appropriate message is written to the page—likewise with each correct response. Finally, if there was an incorrect response, a link is built dynamically to refer back to the quiz page.

```
'  Process the user's responses to the
'  questions
Private Sub Template1_StateCheck()

'  Declare the variables
Dim Flag As Integer
Dim PR As ProcessResponse

'  Create an instance of the class
Set PR = New ProcessResponse

'  Write the HTML header
Response.Write "<HTML><TITLE>9.3</TITLE><BODY BGCOLOR=" &
➥Chr(34) & "white" & Chr(34) & ">"

'  Set our flag to 0
Flag = 0

'  Check the Texas answer.  Pass in the value
'  in the Texas radio button element of the form
'  using the Request object.
If PR.CheckAnswer("texas", Request("tx")) = False Then

    '  Indicate the answer was incorrect and set the flag
'  to indicate an incorrect response.
```

```
          Response.Write "Check your Texas answer again!<BR><BR>"
          Flag = 1

      Else

          '   Indicate a correct response
          Response.Write "Correct on Texas!<BR><BR>"

      End If

      '   Check the Colorado answer.  Pass in the value
      '   in the CO radio button element of the form
      '   using the Request object.
      If PR.CheckAnswer("colorado", Request("co")) = False Then

          '   Flag and indicate an incorrect response
          Response.Write "Check your Colorado answer again!<BR><BR>"
          Flag = 1

      Else

          '   Indicate a correct response
          Response.Write "Correct on Colorado!<BR><BR>"

      End If

      '   Check the Virginia answer.  Pass in the value
      '   in the VA radio button element of the form
      '   using the Request object.
      If PR.CheckAnswer("virginia", Request("va")) = False Then

          '   Flag and indicate an incorrect response.
          Response.Write "Check your Virginia answer again!<BR><BR>"
          Flag = 1

      Else

          '   Indicate a correct response.
          Response.Write "Correct on Virginia!<BR><BR>"

      End If

      '   If flag is set to 1 then
      '   there was an incorrect response
      If Flag = 1 Then

          '   Create a URL to the Template1 page
          '   using the URLFor method.
          Response.Write "Click <A HREF=""" & URLFor(Template1) & """>
          ➥here</A> to try again."

      Else
```

continued on next page

continued from previous page

```
                        '  Indicate a 100% correct response
                        Response.Write "100%"

                End If

                '  Close the HTML in the page
                Response.Write "</body></HTML>"

        End Sub

        Private Sub WebClass_Start()

                '  When the Web class starts, set the next
                '  item to be Template1 which fires the
                '  Respond event
                Set NextItem = Template1

        End Sub

        Private Sub WebItem1_Respond()

        End Sub
```

How It Works

The first step in building your application is to build a prototype Web page with the quiz form. This can be done in any HTML editor (including Notepad). After you build the basic page, you can import it into the Web Designer in your application.

The next step is to link the form to the custom Web event. When the form is submitted, the code in the custom Web event is fired off. Within this code you can create an instance of your class object, just as if you were working in any other Visual Basic application. The one key difference is the use of global classes. Remember that IIS applications do not automatically maintain state between Web pages. If you want to keep class properties accessible between Web pages, you must set the Web class property to maintain state or use some other means of tracking data (see the next set of examples).

In this case your class simply has one method for checking the correctness of a response to one of the questions. Creating and using the class is no different in an IIS application than a standard Visual Basic application. You therefore can use any business logic you might have already built into classes in your IIS applications.

Comments

The next step for this application is to have the initial HTML page constructed on-the-fly so that incorrect answers can be flagged on the page with the original responses highlighted. This requires moving away from or enhancing the original template page and tracking application state data between pages.

COMPLEXITY
INTERMEDIATE

9.4 How do I...
Build an IIS application–based multipage tracking system?

COMPATIBILITY: VISUAL BASIC 6

Problem

In the last two examples, I reviewed the basics of building IIS applications. How can I build a more complex multipage and database-driven application?

Technique

In Chapter 8 you built a client data tracking application with ASP technology. In this How-To you will create the same application in Visual Basic. Unlike the ASP application, you need only three HTML pages for your application. One page is the default for listing the clients, the second page displays the client data, and the third page allows for updating of the client data.

You will also be introduced to the use of custom tags in this How-To. Custom tags in your HTML template can be replaced with code generated in your IIS application. The `ProcessTags` event is called for a template when custom tags are found in the template. This provides a powerful and flexible means of inserting custom HTML code into a template page.

Note that you will need an ODBC datasource called `clients` pointing to the database. The last step in the section details the structure for the database required. You will need to re-create this structure in your database.

Steps

Open `9.4.vbp`. Make sure that you have Internet Explorer running, and run the project. If this is the first time you have run the project, let Visual Basic add a virtual root pointing to the application. The application then should appear in the Web browser, as shown in Figure 9.7. Note the URL to the ASP page, `IISProj3_WebClass1.ASP`.

The Web page shows a listing of clients in the drop-down list box. Select a client and click Submit. The next page shown is the client data display page (see Figure 9.8).

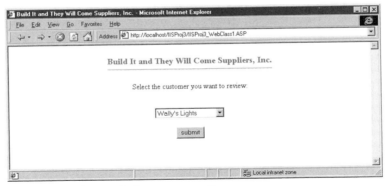

Figure 9.7 The Web form at runtime

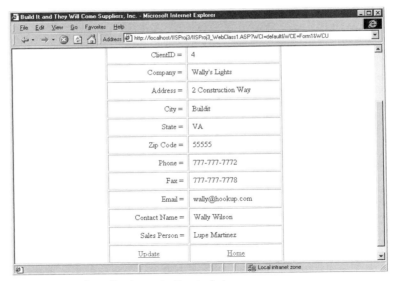

Figure 9.8 The displayed client data

The page shows the various fields and a menu of links at the bottom. To go back and select another client, click the **Home** link. To update the client's data, click the **Update** link. Figure 9.9 shows the client update screen for Wally's Lights. Update the data as appropriate and submit the page by clicking on the button at the bottom of the page. If you leave any critical fields blank, an error response is displayed.

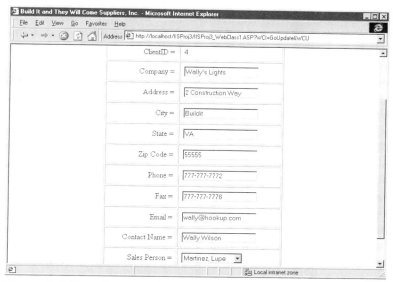

Figure 9.9 The client update form

Complete the following steps to create this project:

1. Start a new IIS application in Visual Basic. Name the project **IISProj3** and set the title of the application to **9.4**. On the Debugging tab, ensure that the started component is **WebClass1**.

2. Import the **default.htm** file, the **clientdisplay.htm** file, and the **updateclient.htm** file.

3. The form on the **default1.htm** file must be linked to a **form1** custom event. Create this by double-clicking the **Form1** tag in the Web Designer. Following is the header for the imported page:

```
<!DOCTYPE HTML PUBLIC "-//W3C//DTD W3 HTML//EN">
<HTML>
<HEAD>

<META content="text/html; charset=iso-8859.1" http-equiv=
➡Content-Type>

<TITLE>Build It and They Will Come Suppliers, Inc.</TITLE>
<META content='"MSHTML 4.72.3007.2"' name=GENERATOR>

</HEAD>

<BODY bgColor=white>

<CENTER>
```

4. The table starts by creating a display header.

```
<!-- Build the display table -->
<TABLE border=0 cellPadding=8>

    <!-- Show the header -->
    <TBODY>
    <TR>
        <TD align=middle>
            <FONT color=green size=4><STRONG>Build It and They
            Will Come Suppliers, Inc.</STRONG></FONT>
            <HR>
             <BR>Select the customer you want to review:<BR><BR>
        </TD>
    </TR>
```

5. The next row starts the form. Note the custom action, which indicates the custom event as **form1**. Also on the form is the Submit button. A custom tag, **WC@CLIENTS**, designates the display of the **select** input element. This tag will be replaced in your IIS application with the **select** box contents.

```
<!-- Set up the form -->
<TR>
    <TD align=middle><!-- The form will post to
    ➥ClientDisplay.asp -->

        <FORM action=IISProj3_WebClass1.ASP?WCI=default&amp;WCE=
        ➥Form1&amp;WCU
        method=post>

            <WC@CLIENTS>CLIENTS</WC@CLIENTS>

            <BR><BR>

            <!-- Show the button to submit the form -->
            <INPUT type=submit value=submit>

            <!-- Close the form -->
            </FORM>
    </TD>
</TR>

</TBODY>

</TABLE>

</CENTER>

</BODY>

</HTML>
```

6. The imported `clientdisplay.htm` file will have two links on the page that must be linked to custom Web items. The `Update` link will be connected to the `GoUpdate` custom Web item. The `Home` link will be connected to the `GoDefault` custom Web item. Following is the header code for the imported page:

```
<!DOCTYPE HTML PUBLIC "-//W3C//DTD W3 HTML//EN">

<HTML>
<HEAD>

<META content="text/html; charset=iso-8859.1" http-equiv=
➡Content-Type>
<TITLE>Build It and They Will Come Suppliers, Inc.</TITLE>

<META content='"MSHTML 4.72.3007.2"' name=GENERATOR>

</HEAD>

<BODY bgColor=white>

<CENTER>
```

7. The table will consist of several rows with two columns. The first column will be the label for the displayed data in the right column. Note that you are using custom replacement tags for the display of the data. These tags will be replaced with data from the database by your IIS application.

```
<!-- Build the display table -->
<TABLE border=1 cellPadding=8>

    <!-- Display the page header -->
    <TBODY>
    <TR>
        <TD align=middle colSpan=2>
            <FONT color=green size=4><STRONG>
            Build It and They Will Come Suppliers, Inc.
            </FONT></STRONG>
            <BR><BR><BR>

            Following is the client data:<BR><BR>
        </TD>
    </TR>

    <!-- Show the id of the client -->
    <TR>
        <TD align=right>ClientID = </TD>
        <TD><WC@IDCLIENT>idclient</WC@IDCLIENT> </TD>
    </TR>

    <!-- Show the company name -->
    <TR>
```

continued on next page

continued from previous page

```
            <TD align=right>Company = </TD>
            <TD><WC@CHRCOMPANY>chrcompany</WC@CHRCOMPANY> </TD>
        </TR>

        <!-- Show the address -->
        <TR>
            <TD align=right>Address = </TD>
            <TD><WC@CHRADDRESS>chraddress</WC@CHRADDRESS> </TD>
        </TR>

        <!-- Show the city -->
        <TR>
            <TD align=right>City = </TD>
            <TD><WC@CHRCITY>chrcity</WC@CHRCITY> </TD>
        </TR>

        <!-- Show the state -->
        <TR>
            <TD align=right>State = </TD>
            <TD><WC@CHRSTATE>chrstate</WC@CHRSTATE> </TD>
        </TR>

        <!-- Show the zip code -->
        <TR>
            <TD align=right>Zip Code = </TD>
            <TD><WC@CHRZIPCODE>chrzipcode</WC@CHRZIPCODE> </TD>
        </TR>

        <!-- Show the phone -->
        <TR>
            <TD align=right>Phone = </TD>
            <TD><WC@CHRPHONE>chrphone</WC@CHRPHONE> </TD>
        </TR>

        <!-- Show the fax -->
        <TR>
            <TD align=right>Fax = </TD>
            <TD><WC@CHRFAX>chrfax</WC@CHRFAX> </TD>
        </TR>

        <!-- Show the email -->
        <TR>
            <TD align=right>Email = </TD>
            <TD><WC@CHREMAIL>chremail</WC@CHREMAIL> </TD>
        </TR>

        <!-- Show the contact name -->
        <TR>
            <TD align=right>Contact Name = </TD>
            <TD><WC@CHRCONTACTNAME>chrcontactname
            ➥</WC@CHRCONTACTNAME> </TD>
        </TR>

        <!-- Display the salesperson name -->
        <TR>
```

```
            <TD align=right>Salesperson = </TD>
            <TD><WC@SALESPERSON>salesperson</WC@SALESPERSON> <BR>
            </TD>
        </TR>
```

8. The two links go directly to the IIS application ASP and indicate the custom Web item to be called.

```
        <!-- Create a URL to link to the update page to allow the
        user to update the client information. Note that on
        the URL the ID of the client is stored on the parameter.-->
        <TR>
            <TD align=middle>
                <A href="IISProj3_WebClass1.ASP?WCI=GoUpdate&WCU">
                ➥Update</A> </TD>
            <TD align=middle>
                <A href="IISProj3_WebClass1.ASP?WCI=GoDefault&WCU">
                ➥Home</A> </TD>
        </TR>

</TBODY>

</TABLE>

</CENTER>

</BODY>

</HTML>
```

9. The update client page contains two items that need custom Web items. The Save button to submit the form must be connected to the `SaveUpdate` custom Web item. The `Home` link must be connected to the `GoDefault` custom Web item. The following is the header HTML code for the page:

```
<!DOCTYPE HTML PUBLIC "-//W3C//DTD W3 HTML//EN">
<HTML>
<HEAD>

<META content="text/html; charset=iso-8859.1" http-equiv=
➥Content-Type>

<TITLE>Build It and They Will Come Suppliers, Inc.</TITLE>

<META content='"MSHTML 4.72.3007.2"' name=GENERATOR>

</HEAD>

<BODY bgColor=white>

<CENTER>
```

10. The table will be similar to the display table. Included in this table will be the submit form. Note that the action of the form is to your IIS application ASP and indicates that the `SaveUpdate` custom Web item event should be called. Once again you use custom tags to indicate to your IIS application where to insert the existing data.

```
<!-- Start the display table -->
<TABLE border=1 cellPadding=8><!-- Build the header. -->
    <TBODY>
    <TR>
        <TD align=middle colSpan=2>

            <FONT color=green size=4><STRONG>
            Build It and They Will Come Suppliers, Inc.
            </FONT></STRONG>

            <BR><BR>

            Following is the client data:<BR><BR>
        </TD>
    </TR>

    <!-- The form will call the Updateresponse.asp page -->
    <FORM action=IISProj3_WebClass1.ASP?WCI=
    ➥SaveUpdate&amp;WCU method=post>

    <!-- Show the ID of the client -->
    <TR>
        <TD align=right>ClientID = </TD>
        <TD><WC@IDCLIENT>idclient</WC@IDCLIENT></TD>
    </TR>

    <WC@CHRCOMPANY>Company</WC@CHRCOMPANY>
    <WC@CHRADDRESS>Address</WC@CHRADDRESS>
    <WC@CHRCITY>City</WC@CHRCITY>
    <WC@CHRSTATE>State</WC@CHRSTATE>
    <WC@CHRZIPCODE>ZipCode</WC@CHRZIPCODE>
    <WC@CHRPHONE>Phone</WC@CHRPHONE>
    <WC@CHRFAX>Fax</WC@CHRFAX>
    <WC@CHREMAIL>Email</WC@CHREMAIL>
    <WC@CHRCONTACTNAME>Contact Name</WC@CHRCONTACTNAME>
    <WC@SALESPERSON>Fax</WC@SALESPERSON>

    <TR>
        <TD align=middle>
            <INPUT name=UpdateData type=submit value=Update>
        </TD>
        <TD>
            <A href="IISProj3_WebClass1.ASP?WCI=SaveUpdate&WCU">
            ➥Home</A>
        </TD>
    </TR>
```

```
</TBODY>

</TABLE>

</FORM>

</CENTER>

</BODY>

</HTML>
```

11. The following set of code begins your Visual Basic IIS application code. Three recordsets are globally declared for data retrieved from the database.

```
'  Globally declare our resultset variables.
Dim rsClient
Dim rsSalesPerson
Dim rsSalesPersons
```

12. The `GetClient` subroutine retrieves a client's data from the database based on the ID of the client. Note that the ID of the client is stored in a **session** variable for later use on another Web page (the update page, typically). Also, the ID of the salesperson is stored for later reference when retrieving the name of the salesperson.

```
'  Retrieve a client from the database
Sub GetClient(idclient)

'  Declare our variables
Dim dbClients

'  Create an Active Data Object
Set dbClients = Server.CreateObject("adodb.connection")

'  Open the database connection
dbClients.Open "dsn=Clients;uid=sa;pwd="

'  Get the client information based on the
'  ID of the client that is stored in the form
'  data from the default page.
Set rsClient = dbClients.Execute("select * from clients where
➥idClient = " & idclient)

'  Store the ID of the client in a session variable
'  to keep state.
Session("idClient") = rsClient("idClient")

'  Store the ID of the salesperson in a session
'  variable for later reference.
Session("idSalesperson") = rsClient("idSalesPerson")

End Sub
```

13. The `GetSalespersons` subroutine retrieves all the salespersons from the database.

```
'  Get all salespersons
Sub GetSalespersons()

'  Declare our variables
Dim dbClients

'  Create an Active Data Object
Set dbClients = Server.CreateObject("adodb.connection")

'  Open the database connection
dbClients.Open "dsn=Clients;uid=sa;pwd="

'  Query for the salesperson.  The ID of the
'  salesperson is stored in the idSalesperson
'  value.  The query will get the name of the
'  salesperson from the Salesperson table.
Set rsSalespersons = dbClients.Execute("select *
➡from Salesperson")

End Sub
```

14. `GetSalesperson` retrieves the salesperson from the database based on the current ID of the salesperson stored in your **session** variable.

```
Sub GetSalesperson()

'  Declare our variables
Dim dbClients

'  Create an Active Data Object
Set dbClients = Server.CreateObject("adodb.connection")

'  Open the database connection
dbClients.Open "dsn=Clients;uid=sa;pwd="

'  Query for the salesperson  The ID of the
'  salesperson is stored in the idSalesperson
'  value.  The query will get the name of the
'  salesperson from the Salesperson table.
Set rsSalesPerson = dbClients.Execute("select *
➡from SalesPerson where idSalesPerson =
➡" & Session("idSalesPerson"))

End Sub
```

15. The `ProcessTag` method for the `ClientDisplay` template processes all custom tags found on the page and gives you the opportunity to replace the tag with your own data. A **Case** statement is set up to check which tag is being processed. Note that the first tag will be the `wc@idclient` tag. In this case the `GetClient` subroutine is run to get the client data. To display the data for each tag, the value of the `TagContents` parameter is set to the desired value.

```
'   Process the custom tags for displaying the client
'   data.
Private Sub clientdisplay_ProcessTag(ByVal TagName As String,
➥TagContents As String, SendTags As Boolean)

'   Check the tag name in the HTML
Select Case LCase(TagName)

    '   ID of the client
    Case "wc@idclient"
            '   Get the client data
            GetClient Request("clients")
            '   Return the ID of the client
            TagContents = rsClient("idclient")

    '   Company
    Case "wc@chrcompany"
            '   Return their company
            TagContents = rsClient("chrCompany")

    '   Address
    Case "wc@chraddress"
            '   Return their address
            TagContents = rsClient("chrAddress")

    '   City
    Case "wc@chrcity"
            '   Return their city
            TagContents = rsClient("chrCity")

    '   State
    Case "wc@chrstate"
            '   Return their state
            TagContents = rsClient("chrState")

    '   Zip Code
    Case "wc@chrzipcode"
            '   Return their zip code
            TagContents = rsClient("chrZipCode")

    '   Phone
    Case "wc@chrphone"
            '   Return their phone
            TagContents = rsClient("chrPhone")

    '   Fax
    Case "wc@chrfax"
            '   Return their fax
            TagContents = rsClient("chrFax")
```

continued on next page

continued from previous page

```
'   Email
Case "wc@chremail"
            '   Return their email
            TagContents = rsClient("chrEmail")

'   Contact Name
Case "wc@chrcontactname"
            '   Return the client contact name
            TagContents = rsClient("chrContactName")

'   Salesperson
Case "wc@salesperson"
            '   Get the salesperson for the account
            GetSalesperson
            '   Return the first and last name
            TagContents = rsSalesPerson("chrFirstName") &
➥" " & rsSalesPerson("chrLastName")

End Select

End Sub
```

16. In the `ClientDisplay` Respond event, the HTML for the template is displayed using the `WriteTemplate` method.

```
'   Respond event of the template
Private Sub clientdisplay_Respond()

'   Display the HTML
ClientDisplay.WriteTemplate

End Sub
```

17. The `Form1` event for the default template sets the next item to be displayed as the client display page.

```
'   Form1 for the default page
Private Sub default_Form1()

'   Set the next item to display the client
Set NextItem = ClientDisplay

End Sub
```

18. For the default page, the `wc@clients` tag must be processed and the select box built for all the clients. In this case, the database is opened up and the list of clients is returned. The resultset is looped through, and the options tags are built and stored in the `TagContents` parameter.

```
'   Process the default page tags
Private Sub default_ProcessTag(ByVal TagName As String,
➥TagContents As String, SendTags As Boolean)

'   Check the tag to see if the clients should
'   be shown
```

```
If LCase(TagName) = "wc@clients" Then

    ' Declare our variables
    Dim dbClients
    Dim rsClients

    ' Create an Active Data Object
    Set dbClients = Server.CreateObject("adodb.connection")

    ' Open our database connection
    dbClients.Open "dsn=Clients;uid=sa;pwd="

    ' Get all of the clients from the database
    Set rsClients = dbClients.Execute("select idClient,
    ➥chrCompany from clients")

    ' Return the beginning of the select box
    TagContents = "<select name=""clients"">"

    ' Loop through the clients and then fill in the select box
    ' with the ID of the client as the value for each option.
    ' The name of the client is displayed
    Do Until rsClients.EOF

        ' Build the option
        TagContents = TagContents & "<option value=""" &
        ➥rsClients("idClient") & """>" &
        ➥rsClients("chrCompany")

        ' Close the option
        TagContents = TagContents & "</option>"

        ' Move to the next record in the recordset
        rsClients.MoveNext

    ' Loop back
    Loop

    ' Close the database connection
    dbClients.Close

    ' Close the select box
    TagContents = TagContents & "</select>"

End If

End Sub
```

19. The `Respond` event for the default template writes out the HTML code using the `WriteTemplate` method.

```
Private Sub default_Respond()

    ' Write the page
    default.WriteTemplate

End Sub
```

20. The Respond event for the GoDefault custom Web item sets the next active item to the default template.

```
Private Sub GoDefault_Respond()

'  Set the next item to the default page
Set NextItem = default

End Sub
```

21. The Respond event for the GoUpdate custom Web item sets the next active item to the UpdateClient template.

```
Private Sub GoUpdate_Respond()

'  Set the next item to the UpdateClient page
Set NextItem = UpdateClient

End Sub
```

22. The Respond event for the SaveUpdate custom Web item first checks the validity of the data entered by the user. If any key fields are blank, a message is written to the user indicating which fields are incorrect. If everything looks good, a SQL Update statement is created to update the client's record. Note that the ID of the client is retrieved from the session variable. If the update was successful, a link is built sending the user back to the default page. The link is built using the URLFor method and indicating that the GoDefault custom Web item should be used.

```
Private Sub SaveUpdate_Respond()

'  Declare our variables
Dim Flag
Dim dbClients

'  Write the header
Response.Write "<html><head><title>Build It and They Will Come
➥Suppliers, Inc.</title></head><body bgcolor=WHITE>"
Response.Write "<center><font size=4 color=GREEN><strong>Build
➥It and They Will Come Suppliers, Inc.</font> </strong>"
Response.Write "<BR><BR><BR>"

'  Set our flag to 0
Flag = 0

    '  Check company name
    If Request.Form("company") = "" Then

        '  Indicate no company was entered
        Response.Write "You did not enter in a <i>company name
        ➥</i>.<br>"
```

```
              '  Set the flag to indicate an error
              Flag = 1

       End If

       '  Check address
       If Request.Form("address") = "" Then

              '  Indicate no address was entered
              Response.Write "You did not enter in an <i>address</i>.
              ➡<br>"
              '  Set the flag to indicate an error
              Flag = 1

       End If

       '  Check city
       If Request.Form("city") = "" Then

              '  Indicate no city was entered
              Response.Write "You did not enter in a <i>city</i>.<br>"
              '  Set the flag to indicate an error
              Flag = 1

       End If

       '  Check state
       If Request.Form("state") = "" Then

              '  Indicate no state was entered
              Response.Write "You did not enter in a <i>state</i>.<br>"
              '  Set the flag to indicate an error
              Flag = 1

       End If

       '  Check zip code
       If Request.Form("zipcode") = "" Then

              '  Indicate no zip code was entered
              Response.Write "You did not enter in a <i>zip code</i>.
              ➡<br>"
              '  Set the flag to indicate an error
              Flag = 1

       End If

       '  Check phone number
       If Request.Form("phone") = "" Then

              '  Indicate no phone number was entered
              Response.Write "You did not enter in a <i>phone number
              ➡</i>.<br>"
```

continued on next page

continued from previous page

```
                              '  Set the flag to indicate an error
                              Flag = 1

                         End If

                         '  Check the contact name
                         If Request.Form("contactname") = "" Then

                              '  Indicate no contact name was entered
                              Response.Write "You did not enter in a <i>contact name
                         ➥</i>.<br>"
                              '  Set the flag to indicate an error
                              Flag = 1

                         End If

                    If Flag <> 1 Then

                         '  Create the Active Data Object
                         Set dbClients = Server.CreateObject("adodb.connection")

                         '  Open the database
                         dbClients.Open "dsn=Clients;uid=sa;pwd="

                         '  Create the record update SQL string
                         strSQL = "Update Clients set " & _
                         "chrCompany = '" & Request.Form("Company") & "', " & _
                         "chrAddress = '" & Request.Form("Address") & "', " & _
                         "chrCity = '" & Request.Form("City") & "', " & _
                         "chrState = '" & Request.Form("State") & "', " & _
                         "chrZipCode = '" & Request.Form("Zipcode") & "', " & _
                         "chrPhone = '" & Request.Form("Phone") & "', " & _
                         "chrFax = '" & Request.Form("Fax") & "', " & _
                         "chrEmail = '" & Request.Form("Email") & "', " & _
                         "chrContactName = '" & Request.Form("ContactName") & "'
                         ➥, " & _
                         "idSalesperson = " & Request.Form("Salespersons") & _
                         " where idClient = " & Session("idClient")

                         '  Execute the update
                         Set rsClients = dbClients.Execute(strSQL)

                         '  Close the database connection
                         dbClients.Close

                         '  Indicate the update was successful
                         Response.Write "<BR><BR>The update was successful.
                         Click <a href=" & URLFor(GoDefault) & ">Here</a>
                         ➥to continue.<BR><BR>"

                    Else

                         '  Indicate the update was not successful
                         Response.Write "<BR><BR>The update was not successful.
```

```
  ➤Click the 'back' button on your browser to continue.
  ➤<BR><BR>"

End If

'  Close the page
Response.Write "</body></html>"


End Sub
```

23. The `UpdateClient ProcessTag` event replaces the tags with input
elements that have the current data defaulted. Note that the `GetClient`
method is called to retrieve the client's current data. The ID of the client is
retrieved from your **session** variable. The only twist on displaying the
sales data is the fact that you must display all the salespeople yet default to
the current salesperson. A query is performed to retrieve all the
salespeople. Then as the resultset is looped through for display, a check is
done to see which salesperson's ID matches the one stored in your
session variable. If a match is made, the option tag will have the
'**selected**' keyword inserted into the tag.

```
'  Process the tags for the UpdateClient page
Private Sub UpdateClient_ProcessTag(ByVal TagName As String,
➤TagContents As String, SendTags As Boolean)

Select Case LCase(TagName)

    '  Process the idclient tag
    Case "wc@idclient"
        '  Get the ID of the client from the session
        '  variable and retrieve the client data
        GetClient Session("idclient")
'  Display the ID of the client
        TagContents = rsClient("idclient")

    '  Process the company tag
    Case "wc@chrcompany"
        '  Start the row
        TagContents = "<tr>"
        '  Start the column to display the field name
        TagContents = TagContents & "<td align=right>Company =
➤</td>"
        '  Build an input element
        TagContents = TagContents & "<td><input name=""company""
➤type=""text"" value="
'  Display the current value
        TagContents = TagContents & Chr(34) &
        ➤rsClient("chrCompany") & Chr(34) & ">"
'  Close the row
        TagContents = TagContents & "</td></tr>"

    '  Process the address tag
    Case "wc@chraddress"
```

continued on next page

continued from previous page

```
                                   '   Start the row
                                   TagContents = "<tr>"
                                   '   Start the column to display the field name
                                   TagContents = TagContents & "<td align=right>
                               ➥Address = </td>"
                                   '   Start the input element
                                   TagContents = TagContents & "<td><input name=""address"
                               ➥" type=""text"" value=" & Chr(34) &
                               ➥rsClient("chrAddress") & Chr(34) & ">"
                   '   End the column
                                   TagContents = TagContents & "</td></tr>"

                           '   Process the city tag
                           Case "wc@chrcity"
                                   '   Start the row
                                   TagContents = "<tr>"
                                   '   Show the city field name
                                   TagContents = TagContents & "<td align=right>City =
                               ➥</td>"
                                   '   Build the input element and show the default value
                                   TagContents = TagContents & "<td><input name=""city""
                               ➥type=""text"" value=" & Chr(34) &
                               ➥rsClient("chrCity") & Chr(34) & ">"
                   '   End the row
                                   TagContents = TagContents & "</td></tr>"

                           '   Start the state field
                           Case "wc@chrstate"
                                   '   Start the row
                                   TagContents = "<tr>"
                                   '   Display the field name
                                   TagContents = TagContents & "<td align=right>State =
                               ➥</td>"
                                   '   Build the input element and show the default value
                                   TagContents = TagContents & "<td><input name=""state""
                               ➥type=""text"" value=" & Chr(34) &
                               ➥rsClient("chrState") & Chr(34) & ">"
                                   '   End the row
                                   TagContents = TagContents & "</td></tr>"

                           '   Process the ZIP code tag
                           Case "wc@chrzipcode"
                                   '   Start the row
                                   TagContents = "<tr>"
                                   '   Show the field name
                                   TagContents = TagContents & "<td align=right>Zip Code =
                               ➥</td>"
                                   '   Build the input element and show the default value
                                   TagContents = TagContents & "<td><input name=""zipcode""
                               ➥type=""text"" value=" & Chr(34) &
                               ➥rsClient("chrZipCode") & Chr(34) & ">"
                   '   End the row
                                   TagContents = TagContents & "</td></tr>"

                           '   Process the phone tag
                           Case "wc@chrphone"
                                   '   Start the row
```

```
      TagContents = "<tr>"
      '   Show the field name
      TagContents = TagContents & "<td align=right>Phone =
   ➥</td>"
      '   Build the input element and show the default value
      TagContents = TagContents & "<td><input name=""phone""
   ➥type=""text"" value=" & Chr(34) &
   ➥rsClient("chrPhone") & Chr(34) & ">"
'   End the row
      TagContents = TagContents & "</td></tr>"

   '   Process the fax tag
   Case "wc@chrfax"
      '   Start the row
      TagContents = "<tr>"
      '   Show the field name
      TagContents = TagContents & "<td align=right>Fax =
   ➥</td>"
      '   Build the input element and show the default value
      TagContents = TagContents & "<td><input name=""fax""
   ➥type=""text"" value=" & Chr(34) &
   ➥rsClient("chrFax") & Chr(34) & ">"
'   End the row
      TagContents = TagContents & "</td></tr>"

   '   Process the email tag
   Case "wc@chremail"
      '   Start the row
      TagContents = "<tr>"
      '   Show the field name
      TagContents = TagContents & "<td align=right>Email =
   ➥</td>"
      '   Build the input element and show the default value
      TagContents = TagContents & "<td><input name=""email""
   ➥type=""text"" value=" & Chr(34) &
   ➥rsClient("chrEmail") & Chr(34) & ">"
'   End the row
      TagContents = TagContents & "</td></tr>"

   '   Process the contact name tag
   Case "wc@chrcontactname"
      '   Start the row
      TagContents = "<tr>"
      '   Show the field name
      TagContents = TagContents & "<td align=right>
   ➥Contact Name = </td>"
      '   Build the input element and show the default value
      TagContents = TagContents & "<td><input name="
   ➥"contactname"" type=""text"" value=" &
   ➥Chr(34) & rsClient("chrContactName") & Chr(34)
   ➥& ">"
'   End the row
      TagContents = TagContents & "</td></tr>"

   '   Process the phone tag
   Case "wc@chrphone"
```

continued on next page

continued from previous page

```
              ' Start the row
          TagContents = "<tr>"
              ' Show the field name
          TagContents = TagContents & "<td align=right>Phone =
          ➥</td>"
              ' Build the input element and show the default value
          TagContents = TagContents & "<td><input name=""phone""
          ➥type=""text"" value=" & Chr(34) &
          ➥rsClient("chrPhone") & Chr(34) & ">"
      ' End the row
          TagContents = TagContents & "</td></tr>"

          ' Process the salesperson tag
      Case "wc@salesperson"

              ' Get the assigned salesperson
          GetSalesperson

              ' Start the row and show the field name
          TagContents = "<tr><td align=right>Salesperson = </td>
          ➥<td>"

              ' Start the select box
          TagContents = TagContents & "<select name="
          ➥"Salespersons"">"

              ' Get all the salespersons
           GetSalespersons

              ' Loop through the salespersons
          Do Until rsSalespersons.EOF

                  ' Build the option and set the value to be the ID
                  ' of the current salesperson
              TagContents = TagContents & "<option value=" &
              ➥Chr(34) & rsSalespersons("idSalesperson")

                  ' Check to see if the current salesperson in the
                  ' recordset is the
          ' same as the currently assigned salesperson.  If so, then
                  ' select the salesperson as the default.
              If rsClient("idSalesperson") =
              ➥rsSalespersons("idSalesperson") Then
                  TagContents = TagContents & Chr(34) &
                  ➥" selected>"
              Else
                  TagContents = TagContents & Chr(34) & ">"
              End If

                  ' Display their name
              TagContents = TagContents & rsSalesPersons
              ➥("chrLastName") & ", " &
              ➥rsSalesPersons("chrFirstName")

                  ' End the option
              TagContents = TagContents & "</option>"
```

```
                        '   Move to the next record
                        rsSalespersons.MoveNext

                        Loop

                        '   End the select and the row
                        TagContents = TagContents & "</select><br></td></tr>"

                End Select

        End Sub
```

24. The `Respond` event of the `UpdateClient` template writes the HTML code for the template using the `WriteTemplate` method.

```
Private Sub UpdateClient_Respond()

'   Write the template
UpdateClient.WriteTemplate idclient

End Sub
```

25. When the class is started, the next item is set to the default template.

```
Private Sub WebClass_Start()

        '   Set the next item to the default page
        Set NextItem = default

End Sub
```

26. Two database tables are required for the project. The first is for the client data, and the second is for the salespersons. You will need to re-create these tables and fields in your database.

```
Clients
        idClient int IDENTITY (1, 1) NOT NULL ,
        chrCompany varchar (255) NULL ,
        chrAddress varchar (50) NULL ,
        chrCity varchar (50) NULL ,
        chrState varchar (50) NULL ,
        chrZipCode varchar (50) NULL ,
        chrPhone varchar (50) NULL ,
        chrFax varchar (50) NULL ,
        chrEmail varchar (50) NULL ,
        chrContactName varchar (50) NULL ,
        idSalesperson int NULL



Salesperson
        idSalesperson int NOT NULL ,
        chrFirstName varchar (50) NULL ,
        chrLastName varchar (50) NULL
```

How It Works

In this example you built an IIS application for maintaining client records. You have two tables of SQL Server data: one for storing the basic client data and the second to look up a salesperson to assign a salesperson to the client.

One of the keys to understanding this application is the use of custom events and custom Web items. Specifically you have a custom event, `Form1`, that is called when the update form is submitted. The code in the form then checks the data and builds a custom page of error messages if data was entered incorrectly, or it submits the data to the database.

The `GoDefault` and `GoUpdate` custom Web items show how to use Web item code for multiuse. Unlike a custom event, which is tied to a particular set of template HTML code, a custom Web item can be tied to several different pieces of HTML code. In this case the navigation to the update and default pages can be tied to different links.

The second key is the use of custom tags. Custom tags allow you to dynamically generate HTML in the location of the tag on the Web page template. When the template is processed and custom tags are found, the `ProcessTag` event is called. In this example, for each tag on the page, a database call is made to return the appropriate data to be displayed. For the client display and `UpdateClient` templates, the information for the client is displayed. Note the salesperson data displayed in a `select` element list box for the `UpdateClient` template. That entire set of code is returned to the browser. The same is true for displaying the list of clients on the default template.

The third key is the use of session variables to maintain state. When a client's data is displayed, you need to know the ID of the client if the user selects the Update option. To show the update data for the specified client and to be able to update that record, you need to know that client's ID. Note that the ID of the client also can be stored on the URL linking to the update page as a query parameter. You also store the ID of the salesperson in a session variable for easy reference on the update page.

For database connectivity, the Active Data Object is used the same as it was in ASP. This allows you to easily interact with your database from Visual Basic. Note that the connections do not stay open between pages. Thus, you cannot keep the client display resultset around for later updating on the update page.

Comments

In the original ASP version in Chapter 8, you had an additional page for validating and updating the client data on an update. Note that in your application here, the code is internalized into Visual Basic and a page is generated on-the-fly for error generation. If you wanted to, you could have reshown the update template with the original data entered by the user displayed and the appropriate field highlighted. You could do this by generating that page on-the-fly or adding custom tags to the page to show an error message symbol if there is an error in a field.

COMPLEXITY
INTERMEDIATE

9.5 How do I...
Build an IIS application–based ad-hoc query report?

COMPATIBILITY: VISUAL BASIC 6

Problem

In Chapter 8 I built an ad-hoc query system with ASP. How can I build the same system with a Visual Basic IIS application?

Technique

You'll add a new twist to your IIS applications. In this case you must generate custom user events on-the-fly. Your search page will consist of several select boxes with different search criteria options on your **Architects** database. The resulting report page will show a listing of the architects, with a link to a page to show the individual architect's data. Those links must call custom user events in your IIS application. These links cannot be initially created in a template file because the results will change based on the query.

URLFor is used to specify the *uniform resource locator* (URL) the system needs to reference a Web class's HTML template or Web item in the browser. It can also be used to create custom events on-the-fly in a Web page, such as links to data in a database.

Steps

Open **9.5.vbp**. Make sure that you have Internet Explorer running, and run the project. If this is the first time you have run the project, let Visual Basic add a virtual root pointing to the application. The application then should appear in the Web browser as shown in Figure 9.10. Note the URL to the ASP page, **IISProj5_WebClass1.ASP**.

The Web page shows a listing of search options on the database in the **select** element drop-down lists. Select a Preferred Style of Ranch, an Hourly Rate between $50 and $99, and order it by the number of Years in Business. Figure 9.11 shows the results of the search sorted by city. The result is Harry Spires. Note the SQL query that is generated at the bottom of the page.

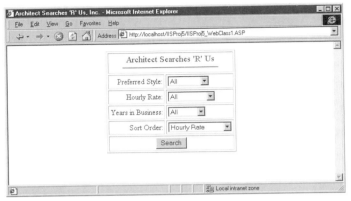

Figure 9.10 The architect's query page

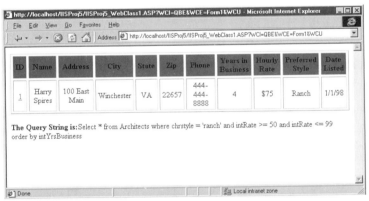

Figure 9.11 A query sorted by city with ranch style, rate between $50 and $99, and ordered by years in business

Next return to the main page and allow the defaults of All to be set. Figure 9.12 shows the resulting listing. Click on the ID of one of the architects to see an individual data listing.

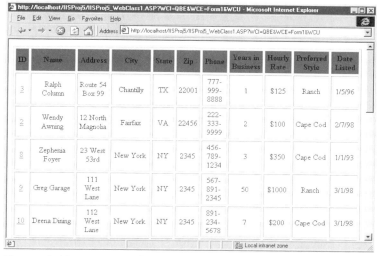

Figure 9.12 A query of all architects ordered by ID

Complete the following steps to create this project:

1. Start a new IIS application in Visual Basic. Name it **IISProj5** and set the title of the application to **9.5**. On the Debugging tab, ensure that the started component is **WebClass1**.

2. Import the **qbe.htm** file and the **qberesults.htm** file.

3. The Query by Example (QBE) template file must have a custom event connected to the **Form1** tag. This event processes the request. The following is the HTML header code for the template:

```
<!DOCTYPE HTML PUBLIC "-//W3C//DTD W3 HTML//EN">
<HTML>
<HEAD>

<META content="text/html; charset=iso-8859.1" http-equiv=
➥Content-Type>

<TITLE>Architect Searches 'R' Us, Inc.</TITLE>

<META content='"MSHTML 4.72.3007.2"' name=GENERATOR>

</HEAD>

<BODY>

<CENTER>
```

4. The table starts out with a header to the page. A series of **select** element drop-down list boxes is created with the appropriate search options. Note that the action of your form is to the ASP for your IIS application. The custom event to be called in your application is **Form1**.

```
<TABLE border=1 cellPadding=3 cellSpacing=3>
    <TBODY>
    <TR>
        <TD align=middle colSpan=2>
        <!-- Build the header -->
        <FONT color=blue size=4>Architect Searches 'R' Us</FONT>
            <HR color=red width=200>
        </TD>
    </TR>
    <TR>
        <TD align=right>
        <!-- The form will call QBEResults to show the results
        ➡ of the query -->
<FORM action=IISProj5_WebClass1.ASP?WCI=QBE&amp;
➡WCE=Form1&amp;WCU
            method=post>

        Preferred Style:
        </TD>
        <TD align=left>
            <!-- Add the preferred housing styles -->
            <SELECT name=chrStyle>
                    <OPTION selected value-"all">All
                    <OPTION value=ranch>Ranch
                    <OPTION value="Cape Cod">Cape Cod
                    <OPTION value="Victorian">Victorian
            </SELECT>
        </TD>
    </TR>
    <TR>
        <TD align=right>Hourly Rate:
        </TD>
        <TD align=left>
            <!-- Add the rate ranges -->
            <SELECT name=intRates>
                    <OPTION selected value=0>All
                    <OPTION value=1>$50 to $99
                    <OPTION value=2>$100 to $199
                    <OPTION value=3>$200 to $299
                    <OPTION value=4>$300 to $399
                    <OPTION value=5>$400 and up
            </SELECT>
        </TD>
    </TR>
    <TR>
```

```
            <TD align=right>Years in Business: </TD>
            <TD align=left>
                <!-- Add the years in business -->
                <SELECT name=intYrsBusiness>
                        <OPTION selected value=0>All
                        <OPTION value=1>1 Year
                        <OPTION value=2>2 Years
                        <OPTION value=3>3 Years
                        <OPTION value=4>4 Years
                        <OPTION value=5>5 Years
                        <OPTION value=6+>6+ Years</SELECT>
            </TD>
        </TR>
        <TR>
            <TD align=right>Sort Order: </TD>
            <TD align=left>
                <!-- Add the sort options -->
                    <SELECT name=sort>
                        <OPTION selected value=intRate>Hourly Rate
                        <OPTION value=intYrsBusiness>Years
                        ➥in Business
                        <OPTION value=chrCity>City
                        <OPTION value=idListing>ID</SELECT>
            </TD>
        </TR>
        <TR>
            <TD align=middle colSpan=2>
                <!-- Submit element to fire off the query -->
                <INPUT type=submit value=Search>
            </TD>
        </TR>

    </TBODY>

    </TABLE>

    </FORM>

    </CENTER>

    </BODY>

    </HTML>
```

5. The QBE results template page is fairly simple. The key is the two replacement tags for the page. The first tag is the report results. The second tag is the query for the page. The primary table for the data display is created. Note that you can generate the complete template on-the-fly if you prefer.

```html
<!DOCTYPE HTML PUBLIC "-//W3C//DTD W3 HTML//EN">
<HTML>
<HEAD>

<META content="text/html; charset=iso-8859.1"
➥http-equiv=Content-Type>

<META content='"MSHTML 4.72.3007.2"' name=GENERATOR>

</HEAD>

<BODY>

<!-- Start the table -->
<TABLE border=1 cellPadding=4 cellSpacing=4>

    <!-- Show the header row -->
    <TBODY>
    <TR bgColor=blue>
        <TH align=middle>ID</TH>
        <TH align=middle>Name</TH>
        <TH align=middle>Address</TH>
        <TH align=middle>City</TH>
        <TH align=middle>State</TH>
        <TH align=middle>Zip</TH>
        <TH align=middle>Phone</TH>
        <TH align=middle>Years in<BR>Business</TH>
        <TH align=middle>Hourly<BR>Rate</TH>
        <TH align=middle>Preferred<BR>Style</TH>
        <TH align=middle>Date<BR>Listed</TH>
    </TR>

    <WC@RESULTS>Results</WC@RESULTS>

</TBODY>

</TABLE>

<BR>

<!-- Show the query string -->

<B>

The Query String is:</B>

<WC@QUERYSTRING> Query String</WC@QUERYSTRING>

</BODY>

</HTML>
```

6. Place the following code in the Visual Basic application. There is one global variable for storing the search string.

```
'   Globally store the search string
Dim strSearch
```

7. The `BuildSearchString` function takes the selections of the user and builds the appropriate SQL search string. Note that the code for this section is similar to the code presented in Chapter 8. The primary concept is to build the proper SQL string by checking each search option. The key is the placement of the `where` clause in the search string. It cannot be placed until the first set of criteria is set. The `intWhereFlag` indicates when the `where` clause has been added.

```
'   Subroutine to build the search string
Private Sub BuildSearchString()

'   Declare our variables
Dim intWhereFlag
Dim intYrsBusiness
Dim chrYrsBusiness

'   Set the initial SQL statement to query all fields from
'   the houses table
strSearch = "Select * from Architects "

'   Check to see if a specific selection was made for the
'   style
If Request("chrStyle") <> "All" Then

    '   add on the where clause to search for the specified style
    strSearch = strSearch & "where chrstyle = '" &
    ➥Request("chrStyle") & "' "

    '   Indicate the where clause has been added
    intWhereFlag = 1

End If

'   Get the years in business selected
chrYrsBusiness = Request("intYrsBusiness")

'   Get the numerical number of years in business
intYrsBusiness = Val(Mid(chrYrsBusiness, 1, 1))

'   Check to see if there is a specific year requested
If intYrsBusiness > 0 Then

    '   Check to see if the 6+ option was selected
    If intYrsBusiness < 6 Then
```

continued on next page

continued from previous page

```
      '  Check the Where flag
     If intWhereFlag = 1 Then

         '  Add onto the query to search for the specified years
         '  in business
         '  Note that the 'and' clause is added if the where was
         '  already added
         strSearch = strSearch & "and intYrsBusiness = " &
         ➡intYrsBusiness

      '  Else add the Where clause
     Else

             '  Add onto the query to search for the specified
             '  number of rooms
             strSearch = strSearch & " where intYrsBusiness = " &
             ➡intYrsBusiness

         '  Indicate the where clause has been added
         intWhereFlag = 1

     End If

  '  User wants to see 6+ years of experience
  Else

     '  Check the where flag
     If intWhereFlag = 1 Then

             '  Search for any house with 6 or more rooms
             '  Note that the 'and' clause is added if the where
             '  was already added
             strSearch = strSearch & "and intYrsBusiness >= " &
             ➡intYrsBusiness

      '  No where clause has been added
     Else

             '  Search for any business that has been in business
             '  more than 6 years
             strSearch = strSearch & " where intYrsBusiness >= " &
             ➡intYrsBusiness

             '  Indicate the where clause has been added
             intWhereFlag = 1

     End If


  End If

End If
```

```
'   Check to see if the where clause has been added
If intWhereFlag = 1 Then

    '   If so then we will also check the rate
    '   Note the and clause is added if the where
    '   has already been added
    strSearch = strSearch & " and intRate "
Else

    '   Add on the where clause
    strSearch = strSearch & " where intRate "

End If


'   Based on the rate range selected, the rate query
'   will be set appropriately.  Note the assumption
'   is made the 'where' and the 'and' clauses have been
'   added.
Select Case Request("intRates")

    '   All rates
    Case 0
        strSearch = strSearch & " > 0"

        '   Set the first rate range level
        Case 1
            strSearch = strSearch & " >= 50 and intRate <= 99"

        '   Set the second rate range level
        Case 2
            strSearch = strSearch & " >= 100 and intRate <= 199"

        '   Set the third rate range level
        Case 3
            strSearch = strSearch & " >= 200 and intRate <= 299"

        '   Set the fourth rate range level
        Case 4
            strSearch = strSearch & " >= 300 and intRate <= 399"

        '   Set the last rate range level
        Case 5
            strSearch = strSearch & " >= 400"

End Select


'   Add on the 'order by' SQL clause and the field selected
strSearch = strSearch & " order by " & Request("sort")

End Sub
```

8. The ShowResults function retrieves the data from the database and builds the appropriate display table for insertion into the template. Note that the link to the single architect listing uses the URLFor function with two results. The first result is the name of the template page to process the link, and the second result is the ID for the architect. This creates a custom user event on the page. QBEResults processes the UserEvent when the link is clicked. The HTML code built in the function is returned for display.

```
Private Function ShowResults() As String

'   This function shows the Architect listings returned
'   from the search.
'   The parameter is the SQL string to be executed.
Dim dbArchitects
Dim rsArchitects
Dim intCount

'   Create an Active Data Object
Set dbArchitects = Server.CreateObject("adodb.connection")

'   Open our database connection
dbArchitects.Open "dsn=Architects;uid=sa;pwd="

'   Get all of the Architects from the database
'   meeting our criteria.
Set rsArchitects = dbArchitects.Execute(strSearch)

    '   We first check to ensure that we
    '   have data returned.
    If (Not rsArchitects.EOF) Then

        ' Loop through the recordset
        Do Until rsArchitects.EOF

        results = results & Chr(10) & Chr(13) & "<TR>"

            '   Loop through each field in the recordset
            For intCount = 0 To 11
            results = results & "<td align=center>"

        '   Build a different result display depending on
        '   the field.
        Select Case intCount

            '   Build an href on the ID
            Case 0
                results = results & "<a href=" &
                ➡URLFor(QBEResults,
                ➡CStr(rsArchitects(intCount))) & ">" &
                ➡rsArchitects(intCount) & "</a>"

            '   Show the first and last name in the same
            '   table column
```

```
                        Case 1
                            results = results & (rsArchitects(intCount)
                            ➥& " " & rsArchitects(intCount + 1))
                           intCount = intCount + 1

                        '  Since the tenth field is the hourly rate
                        '  we want to place a '$' character in front of
                        '  it.
                        Case 9
                            '  Place the $ in front of the rate %>
                            results = results & ("$" &
                            ➥rsArchitects(intCount))

                        '  Display the column text
                        Case Else

                            '  Display the text
                            results = results & (rsArchitects(intCount))

                    End Select

                    '  End the column
                    results = results & "</td>"

                Next

                '  Move to the next row
                rsArchitects.MoveNext

                '  Close the row
                results = results & "</TR>"

            Loop

        Else

            '  Indicate no data was returned from the query
            results = results & "<TR><TD COLSPAN=9>No Data Returned
            ➥from the Query.</TD></tr>"

        End If

        '  Return the result string
        ShowResults = results

    End Function
```

9. The Respond event of the custom Web item, Architect, creates a page on-the-fly to display an architect's data. The ID for the architect is retrieved from a session variable. Note that a link is built at the end of the page with the URLFor method, with the link being to the custom Web item, GoSearch.

```
Private Sub Architect_Respond()

Response.Write "<HTML><TITLE>Architects 'R' Us</title>"
Response.Write "<body>"

'  Create an Active Data Object
Set dbArchitects = Server.CreateObject("adodb.connection")

'  Open our database connection
dbArchitects.Open "dsn=Architects;uid=sa;pwd="

'  Get all of the architects from the database
'  meeting our criteria.
Set rsArchitects = dbArchitects.Execute("select *
➥from architects where idlisting = " & Session("architect"))

'  Build the display table
Response.Write "<table border=1 cellpadding=2 cellspacing=2>"
Response.Write "<tr><td align=right>First Name:</td>"
Response.Write "<td>" & rsArchitects("chrFirstName") & "</td>
➥</tr>"
Response.Write "<tr><td align=right>Last Name:</td>"
Response.Write "<td>" & rsArchitects("chrLastName") & "</td>
➥</tr>"
Response.Write "<tr><td align=right>Address:</td>"
Response.Write "<td>" & rsArchitects("chrAddress") & "</td>
➥</tr>"
Response.Write "<tr><td align=right>City:</td>"
Response.Write "<td>" & rsArchitects("chrCity") & "</td></tr>"
Response.Write "<tr><td align=right>State:</td>"
Response.Write "<td>" & rsArchitects("chrState") & "</td></tr>"
Response.Write "<tr><td align=right>Zip Code:</td>"
Response.Write "<td>" & rsArchitects("chrZip") & "</td></tr>"
Response.Write "<tr><td align=right>Phone:</td>"
Response.Write "<td>" & rsArchitects("chrPhone") & "</td></tr>"
Response.Write "<tr><td align=right>Years in Business:</td>"
Response.Write "<td>" & rsArchitects("intYrsBusiness") & "</td>
➥</tr>"
Response.Write "<tr><td align=right>Hourly Rate:</td>"
Response.Write "<td>" & rsArchitects("intRate") & "</td></tr>"
Response.Write "<tr><td align=right>Style:</td>"
Response.Write "<td>" & rsArchitects("chrStyle") & "</td></tr>"
Response.Write "<tr><td align=right>Date Listed:</td>"
Response.Write "<td>" & rsArchitects("dtListed") & "</td></tr>"
Response.Write "</table><BR><BR>"

'  Build a link using the URLFor method to the
'  GoSearch event
Response.Write "Click <a href=" & URLFor(GoSearch) & ">here
➥</a> to search again."

'  Write then end of the page
Response.Write "</body></html>"

End Sub
```

10. The `Respond` event of `GoSearch` sets the next item to be the QBE search template page.

```
Private Sub GoSearch_Respond()

'  Set the next item to the QBE form
Set NextItem = QBE

End Sub
```

11. The `Form1` custom Web event sets the next item to be the results page.

```
Private Sub QBE_Form1()

'  Set the next item to the QBEResults page
Set NextItem = QBEResults

End Sub
```

12. The `Respond` event of the QBE search template page writes the HTML out for the page.

```
Private Sub QBE_Respond()

'  Write the template
QBE.WriteTemplate

End Sub
```

13. The `ProcessTag` event for the results page calls the `BuildSearchString` procedure to build the search string. Then the `ShowResults` function is called to build the HTML rows for display. The query string is displayed at the end of the page.

```
Private Sub QBEResults_ProcessTag(ByVal TagName As String,
➥TagContents As String, SendTags As Boolean)

'  Process the tags
Select Case LCase(TagName)

    '  Process the results tag
    Case "wc@results"
        '  Build the search string
        BuildSearchString
        '  Show the results
        TagContents = ShowResults

    '  Process the query string tag
    Case "wc@querystring"
        '  Display the results
        TagContents = strSearch

End Select

End Sub
```

14. The `Respond` event for the results page uses the `WriteTemplate` method to write out the HTML for the page.

```
Private Sub QBEResults_Respond()

'  Write the template
QBEResults.WriteTemplate

End Sub
```

15. The `UserEvent` event is called in response to a custom user event on a Web page. In this case, the links to an individual architect's listing on the results page are created on-the-fly. In this case the `EventName` will be the ID of the architect. The ID is stored in the `Architect` session variable, and the next item is set to the `Architect` custom Web item. This custom Web item then builds the page on-the-fly to show the data based on the value of the session variable.

```
Private Sub QBEResults_UserEvent(ByVal EventName As String)

'  Store the event in the architect session variable
Session("architect") = EventName

'  Set the next item to be the architect
'  event
Set NextItem = Architect

End Sub
```

16. When the Web class is started, the next item is set to the QBE search template page.

```
Private Sub WebClass_Start()

    '  Set the next item to be the QBE page
    Set NextItem = QBE

End Sub
```

17. The following table stores the data for the architects. You will need to re-create the table and fields in your ODBC compliant database.

```
Architects
    idlisting int IDENTITY (1, 1) NOT NULL ,
    chrFirstName varchar (50) NULL ,
    chrLastName varchar (50) NULL ,
    chrAddress varchar (255) NULL ,
    chrCity varchar (255) NULL ,
    chrState varchar (25) NULL ,
    chrZip varchar (25) NULL ,
    chrPhone varchar (15) NULL ,
    intYrsBusiness int NULL ,
    intRate int NULL ,
    chrStyle varchar (50) NULL ,
    dtListed datetime NULL
```

How It Works

This particular example shows clearly the benefits of using IIS applications over ASP applications. In this case you can more readily encapsulate your code for building the search string and the results page in your Visual Basic application. In fact, if you had extended routines for building SQL queries and building custom searches, these could be readily incorporated into your IIS application.

There is one new wrinkle introduced into the example from the earlier IIS application code. The problem is generating custom Web events such as links on-the-fly. The solution is the creation of custom user events using the URLFor method. In this case you are creating a custom link to the QBEResults page with a parameter that names the event. In this case the parameter is the ID of the architect. In the Web browser the link would look like this:

```
http://localhost/IISProj5/IISProj5_WebClass1.ASP?WCIID=1283&WCE=4
```

WCIID is the unique identifier for the QBEResults template. The WCE in this case is actually the ID for the architect. After the link is clicked, the UserEvent event is called for the QBEResults template. Then the ID of the architect is stored in a session variable, and the next item set is to the Architect Web item for display of the data.

Note that the QBE results template page is fairly simple. The HTML code in the page could be replaced with code in the Visual Basic application and the template not imported at all.

Comments

To make the code more efficient, try to replace the custom user event to the Architect custom Web item instead of QBEResults. Then in the UserEvent for Architect, build the display page on-the-fly. This saves the use of the session variable for storing the ID of the architect.

COMPLEXITY
ADVANCED

9.6 How do I...
Build an IIS application–based client/server messaging system?

COMPATIBILITY: VISUAL BASIC 6

Problem

Now that I have seen how to access databases and perform other techniques in IIS applications, how can I build a truly interactive system, such as a client/server set of message boards for my intranet?

Technique

This How-To combines all the techniques demonstrated in this chapter plus a few new ones to build an IIS application–based message board system. Your system will allow for adding new messages, searching messages, and administrating the message system. Note that an ODBC DSN–named message is needed that points to the **Messages** database. The last step in this How-To outlines the database structure needed.

Steps

Open **9.6.vbp**. Ensure that you have Internet Explorer running, and run the project. If this is the first time you have run the project, let Visual Basic add a virtual root pointing to the application. The application then should appear in the Web browser as shown in Figure 9.13. Note the URL to the ASP page, **IISProj6_WebClass1.ASP**.

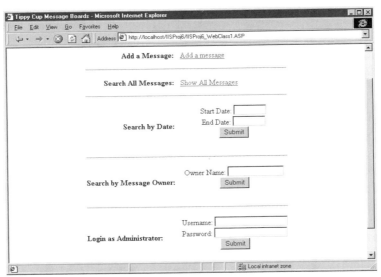

Figure 9.13 The message option select page

The initial page is the listing for accessing the message boards. In the message boards you can add a message, show all messages, search for messages by date, search for messages by owner, and log in as an administrator. Click **Add a message** to add a message (see Figure 9.14).

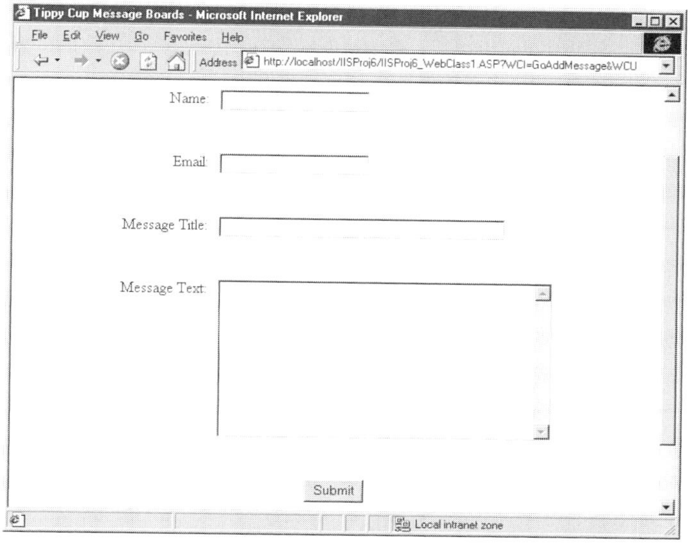

Figure 9.14 The add message page

First log in as an administrator with the username of `username` and password of `password`. To review messages click `Show All Messages` to list all the messages. Figure 9.15 shows the listing of messages sorted by date submitted. Note the `*ADMIN*` column for deleting messages.

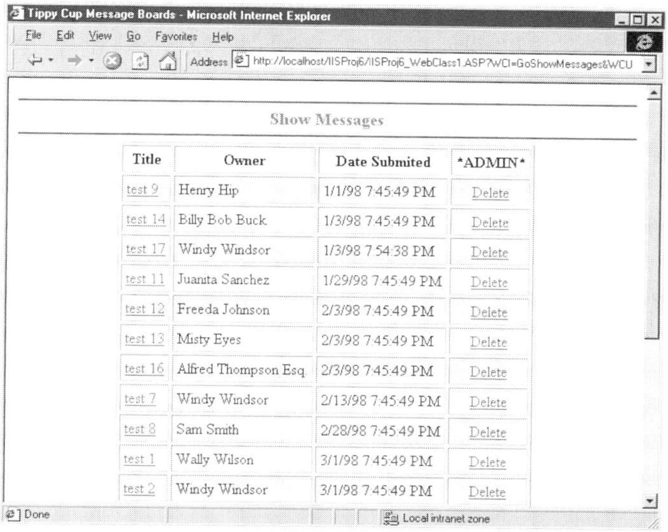

Figure 9.15 Listing messages with the Administrative option ordered by date submitted

Next, put in the date range for January of 1998 and submit the request. Figure 9.16 shows the listing sorted by owner name. Also, the *ADMIN* column is still available because you are logged in as an administrator. To see an individual message, click on the title of the message.

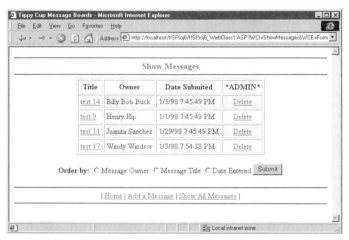

Figure 9.16 Displaying messages for January ordered by owner name

To create this project, complete the following steps:

1. Start a new IIS application in Visual Basic. Name the project IISProj6 and set the title of the application to **9.6**. On the Debugging tab, ensure that the started component is WebClass1.

2. Import the default.htm file, AddMessage.htm, ShowMessage.htm, and ShowMessages.htm. Also included in the project but documented in Chapter 8 is the TableBuilder class. You will use this class to build various tables in your application. This is an excellent example of how existing Visual Basic code can be used within your IIS applications.

3. The default template page will need two custom events tied to it. The first event is for the first two forms, which connect to the Form1 event. The second event is a connection to the Form3 event with the form for submitting administrator information.

```
<!DOCTYPE HTML PUBLIC "-//W3C//DTD W3 HTML//EN">
<HTML>
<HEAD>

<META content="text/html; charset=iso-8859-1"
➡http-equiv=Content-Type>

<TITLE>Tippy Cup Message Boards</TITLE>
```

```
<META content='"MSHTML 4.72.3007.2"' name=GENERATOR>

</HEAD>

<BODY bgColor=white>

<HR color=blue height = 2>

<CENTER>

<!-- Build the header -->
<FONT color=green size=4>
<B>Welcome to the Tippy Cup Message Boards!</B> <BR></FONT>

<HR color=blue height = 2>

<BR>
```

4. The table begins the listing of message board options. Note that the **Add Message** option is a link to the **GoAddMessage** custom Web item. The **SearchAllMessages** link goes to the **GoShowMessages** custom Web item. The three forms link to the **Form1** and **Form3** custom Web events.

```
<!-- Start the table -->
<TABLE cellPadding=4 cellSpacing=4>

<!-- Add a message option -->
   <TBODY>
   <TR>
      <TD align=right><B>Add a Message:</B></TD>
      <TD>
         <A href="IISProj6_WebClass1.ASP?WCI=
         ➥GoAddMessage&WCU">
         Add a message</A>
      </TD>
   </TR>
   <!-- Show all messages -->
   <TR>
      <TD colSpan=2>
         <HR>
      </TD>
   </TR>
   <TR>
      <TD align=right><B>Search All Messages:</B> </TD>
      <TD align=left>
         <A href="IISProj6_WebClass1.ASP?WCI=
         ➥GoShowMessages&WCU">
         Show All Messages</A></FORM>
      </TD>
   </TR>
   <TR>
      <TD colSpan=2>
         <HR>
         </TD>
   </TR>
```

continued on next page

continued from previous page

```
<!-- Search by date -->
<TR>
    <TD align=right><B>Search by Date:</B> </TD>
    <TD align=middle>
        <!-- Form call to the show messages page -->
        <FORM action=IISProj6_WebClass1.ASP?WCI=default&amp;
        ➥WCE=Form1&amp;WCU
        method=post>
            Start Date: <INPUT name=StartDate size=8> <BR>
            End Date: <INPUT name=EndDate size=8><BR>
            <INPUT name=orderby type=hidden value=dtentered>
            <INPUT name=submit type=submit value=Submit>
            ➥</FORM>
    </TD>
</TR>
<TR>
    <TD colSpan=2>
        <HR>
    </TD>
</TR>
<!-- Search by message owner -->
<TR>
    <TD align=left><B>Search by Message Owner:</B> </TD>
    <TD align=middle>
        <!-- Form to call show messages by date -->
        <FORM action=IISProj6_WebClass1.ASP.ASP?WCI=
        ➥default&amp;WCE=Form2&amp;WCU
        method=post>
        Owner Name: <INPUT name=OwnerName size=15><BR>
        <INPUT name=orderby type=hidden value=dtentered>
         <INPUT name=submit type=submit value=Submit>
        </FORM>
    </TD>
</TR>
<TR>
    <TD colSpan=2>
        <HR>
    </TD>
</TR>
<!-- Login as an administrator -->
<TR>
    <TD align=left><B>Login as Administrator:</B> </TD>
    <TD align=middle>
        <!-- Form to call the administrator login in page-->
        <FORM action=IISProj6_WebClass1.ASP?WCI=default&amp;
        ➥WCE=Form3&amp;WCU
        method=post>
        Username: <INPUT name=UserName><BR>
        Password: <INPUT name=Password type=password><BR>
        <INPUT name=submit type=submit value=Submit>
        </FORM>
    </TD>
</TR>

</TBODY>
</TABLE>
```

5. The navigation bar builds three links to the custom Web items. These Web items are used multiple times on navigation bars used throughout the message board pages. The home page links to the default template. The **Add Message** option links to the **GoAddMessage** custom Web item. And finally the **Show Messages** link goes to the **GoShowMessages** custom Web item.

```
<!-- Build the navigation bar -->
<HR color=blue height = 2>
¦ <A href="IISProj6_WebClass1.ASP?WCI=default&WCU">Home</A>
¦ <A href="IISProj6_WebClass1.ASP?WCI=GoAddMessage&WCU">
➥Add a Message</A>
¦ <A href="IISProj6_WebClass1.ASP?WCI=GoShowMessages&WCU">
➥Show All Messages</A>
¦ <HR color=blue height = 2>

</CENTER>

</BODY>

</HTML>
```

6. The Add Message page is primarily HTML, which builds an input form for the new message. The link connects to a custom Web event, **Form1**. The navigation bar follows the same model as built on the default page.

```
<!DOCTYPE HTML PUBLIC "-//W3C//DTD W3 HTML//EN">
<HTML>
<HEAD>

<META content="text/html; charset=iso-8859.1" http-equiv=
➥Content-Type>

<TITLE>Tippy Cup Message Boards</TITLE>

<META content='"MSHTML 4.72.3007.2"' name=GENERATOR>

</HEAD>

<BODY bgColor=white>

<!-- Build a header -->
<HR color=blue height = 2>

<CENTER>

<FONT color=green size=4><B>Add a Message</B> <BR></FONT>

<HR color=blue height = 2>
```

continued on next page

continued from previous page

```
<!-- Build a form that will post the new message to the
➡InsertMessage asp page-->


<FORM action=Project1_WebClass1.ASP?WCI=AddMessage&amp;
➡WCE=Form1&amp;WCU
method=post>

<!-- Begin a table for the input fields -->

<TABLE cellPadding=4 cellSpacing=4>

    <!-- Name field -->
    <TBODY>
    <TR>
        <TD align=right vAlign=top>Name:</TD>
        <TD align=left vAlign=top>
            <INPUT name=MessageOwner>
        </TD>
    </TR>
    <TR>
        <TD> </TD>
    </TR>

    <!-- Email field -->
    <TR>
        <TD align=right vAlign=top>Email:</TD>
        <TD align=left vAlign=top>
            <INPUT name=OwnerEmail>
        </TD>
    </TR>
    <TR>
        <TD> </TD></TR>

    <!-- Message field -->
    <TR>
        <TD align=right vAlign=top>Message Title:</TD>
        <TD align=left vAlign=top>
            <INPUT name=MessageTitle size=40>
        </TD>
    </TR>
    <TR>
        <TD> </TD></TR><!-- Message text area -->
    <TR>
        <TD align=right vAlign=top>Message Text:</TD>
        <TD align=left vAlign=top>
            <TEXTAREA cols=40 name=MessageText rows=10>
            </TEXTAREA>
        </TD>
    </TR>
    <TR>
        <TD> </TD>
    </TR>
    <!-- Submit button -->
    <TR>
        <TD align=middle colSpan=2>
            <INPUT name=submit type=submit value=Submit>
```

```
            </TD>
        </TR>

    </TBODY>

    </TABLE>

    </FORM>

    <!--  Navigation bar -->
    <HR color=blue height = 2>
    ¦ <A href="IISProj6_WebClass1.ASP?WCI=GoDefault&WCU">Home</A>
    ¦ <A href="IISProj6_WebClass1.ASP?WCI=GoAddMessage&WCU">
    ➥Add a Message</A>
    ¦ <A href="IISProj6_WebClass1.ASP?WCI=GoShowMessages&WCU">
    ➥Show All Messages</A>
    ¦ <HR color=blue height = 2>

    </CENTER>

    </BODY>

    </HTML>
```

7. The ShowMessages page builds an HTML framework for displaying the
listing of the messages. The primary table is built using the
`http://localhost/iisProj6/iisProj6_WebClass1.asp?WCI=GoShowMes`
`sages&WCU` tag.

```
<!DOCTYPE HTML PUBLIC "-//W3C//DTD W3 HTML//EN">
<HTML>
<HEAD>

<META content="text/html; charset=iso-8859.1" http-equiv=
➥Content-Type>

<TITLE>Tippy Cup Message Boards</TITLE>

<META content='"MSHTML 4.72.3007.2"' name=GENERATOR>

</HEAD>

<BODY bgColor=white>

<!--  Build the header -->

<HR color=blue height = 2>

<CENTER>

<FONT color=green size=4><B>Show Messages</B> <BR></FONT>

<HR color=blue height = 2>

<WC@SHOWMESSAGES>Show Messages</WC@SHOWMESSAGES>
```

8. A search form is created for ordering the listing of messages on the page. The form links to a custom Web event, `Form1`. Also included on the form are three hidden variables that store the start date, end date, and owner name. Finally the navigation bar is displayed.

```
<!-- Create a form to choose sort options  Note that it
➥calls this same page-->
<FORM action=IISProj6_WebClass1.ASP?WCI=ShowMessages&amp;
➥WCE=Form1&amp;WCU
method=post>

<B>Order by:</B>

<!-- Put in three options to sort by message owner, title,
➥and date entered-->
<INPUT name=orderby type=radio value=chrMessageOwner>
➥Message Owner
<INPUT name=orderby type=radio value=chrMessageTitle>
➥Message Title
<INPUT name=orderby type=radio value=dtEntered>Date Entered

<!-- It is important to store the start date, end date and
➥owner name for any filtering of the messages-->

<WC@HIDDENVARS> Hidden Variables</WC@HIDDENVARS>

<!-- Submit button for the form -->
<INPUT type=submit value=Submit>

</FORM>

<!- Navigation bar -->
<HR color=blue height = 2>
┊ <A href="IISProj6_WebClass1.ASP?WCI=GoDefault&WCU">Home</A>
┊ <A href="IISProj6_WebClass1.ASP?WCI=GoAddMessage&WCU">
➥Add a Message</A>
┊ <A href="IISProj6_WebClass1.ASP?WCI=GoShowMessages&WCU">
➥Show All Messages</A>
┊
┊
<HR color=blue height = 2>

</CENTER>

</BODY>

</HTML>
```

9. The show message page lists the data for the message. Each data field is set up as a custom tag that is replaced with the live data. The navigation bar is displayed last.

```
<!DOCTYPE HTML PUBLIC "-//W3C//DTD W3 HTML//EN">
<HTML>
<HEAD>

<META content="text/html; charset=iso-8859.1" http-equiv=
➥Content-Type>

<TITLE>Tippy Cup Message Board</TITLE>

<META content='"MSHTML 4.72.3007.2"' name=GENERATOR>

</HEAD>

<BODY bgColor=white>

<!-- Build the header -->

<HR color=blue height = 2>

<CENTER>

<FONT color=green size=4><B>Message</B> <BR></FONT>

<HR color=blue height = 2>
<BR>

<!-- Build our table -->
<TABLE border=1 cellPadding=3 cellSpacing=3 width=400>

    <!-- Show the message owner -->
    <TBODY>
    <TR>
        <TD align=right><B>Message Owner:</B></TD>
        <!-- Show the message owner -->
        <TD>
            <WC@CHRMESSAGEOWNER>Message Owner</WC@MESSAGEOWNER)
        </TD>
    <!-- Show the message owner's email -->
    <TR>
        <TD align=right><B>Message Owner Email:</B></TD>
        <!-- Build an email link -->
        <TD><WC@CHROWNEREMAIL>Owner Email</WC@OWNEREMAIL></TD>
    </TR>
    <!-- Show the message title -->
    <TR>
        <TD align=right><B>Message Title:</B></TD>
        <!-- Show the message title -->
        <TD><WC@CHRMESSAGETITLE>Message Title</WC@MESSAGETITLE>
        </TD>
    </TR>
    <!-- Show the message date -->
    <TR>
        <TD align=right><B>Message Date:</B></TD>
        <!-- Show the date the message was entered -->
```

continued on next page

continued from previous page

```
                          <TD><WC@DTENTERED>Date Entered</WC@DTENTERED></TD>
                    </TR>
                    <!--  Show the message text -->
                    <TR>
                        <TD align=right><B>Message:</B></TD>
                        <!--  Show the message text -->
                        <TD><WC@TXTMESSAGE>Message</WC@TXTMESSAGE></TD>
                    </TR>

            </TBODY>

            </TABLE>

            <BR>

            <!--  Navigation bar -->
            <HR color=blue height = 2>
            ¦ <A href="default.asp">Home</A>
            ¦ <A href="addmessage.asp">Add a Message</A>
            ¦ <A href="showmessages.asp">Show All Messages</A>
            ¦   <HR color=blue height = 2>

            </CENTER>

            </BODY>

            </HTML>
```

10. Add the following code to the Visual Basic application. The `rsMessages`
and `rsMessage` resultset store the message data retrieved from the
database. The start date, end date, and message owner are stored globally
for reference. The `BadDate` variable stores a bad date entered into the
system.

```
Option Explicit

'  Global messages recordset
Dim rsMessages

'  Keep the start date, end date and message owner global
Dim StartDate
Dim EndDate
Dim OwnerName

'  Store the bad date
Dim BadDate

'  Global recordset for the message
Dim rsMessage


Dim txtMessage
Dim dtentered
```

11. The `GetMessage` subroutine retrieves the data for the message based on the ID of the message. The message data is stored in the global variables.

```
'   Get the message based on the ID of the message
Sub GetMessage(idMessage)

'   Declare our variables
Dim dbMessage
Dim SQL

'   Create an Active Data Object
Set dbMessage = Server.CreateObject("adodb.connection")

'   Open our database connection
dbMessage.Open "dsn=Messages;uid=sa;pwd="

'   Build the SQL Statement
SQL = "select * from messages where idMessage = " & idMessage

'   Get the message
Set rsMessage = dbMessage.Execute(SQL)

'   Get the text message
txtMessage = rsMessage("txtMessage")

'   Get the date entered
dtentered = rsMessage("dtEntered")

End Sub
```

12. The `GetMessages` function retrieves messages based on the date range or the message owner. If a bad date is entered, the global **BadDate** flag is set to **True**. Otherwise you build the appropriate SQL statement for searching a date range or searching by message owner.

```
'   Get messages based on user selections
Sub GetMessages()

'   Declare our variables
Dim dbMessages
Dim SQL As String
Dim OrderBy As String

'   Create an Active Data Object
Set dbMessages = Server.CreateObject("adodb.connection")

'   Open our database connection
dbMessages.Open "dsn=Messages;uid=sa;pwd="

'   Get the start date from the calling page
StartDate = Request("StartDate")
```

continued on next page

continued from previous page

```vb
    ' Get the end date from the calling page
    EndDate = Request("EndDate")

    ' Get the order by field from the calling page
    OrderBy = Request("orderby")

    ' Get the ownername from the calling page
    OwnerName = Request("ownername")

    ' Check to see if the start date and end
    ' date are blank.  if so, then all messages
    ' are to be shown.
    If StartDate = "" And EndDate = "" Then

        ' Set the start date back to before the application
        ' was created
        StartDate = "1/1/80"

        ' Set the end date to today plus one to ensure all current
        ' messages are retrieved
        EndDate = Date + 1

        ' Order by the date entered
        OrderBy = "dtEntered"

    End If

    ' If an invalid date was entered then an
    ' error is shown
    If IsDate(StartDate) = False Or IsDate(EndDate) = False Then

        BadDate = True

    Else

        ' Build the default SQL statement
        SQL = "select chrMessageOwner, chrMessageTitle, dtEntered,
        ➥idMessage from messages where dtEntered >= '" &
        ➥StartDate & "' and dtEntered <= '" & EndDate &
        ➥"' order by " & OrderBy

        ' If an ownername is selected then build a new query
        If OwnerName <> "" Then

            ' Set the owner name to the entered name
            SQL = "select chrMessageOwner, chrMessageTitle,
            ➥dtEntered, idMessage from messages where
            ➥chrMessageOwner like '%" & OwnerName &
            ➥"%' order by " & OrderBy

        End If

        ' Get all of the Messages from the database
        Set rsMessages = dbMessages.Execute(SQL)

    End If

End Sub
```

13. The `DisplayMessage` function builds the appropriate HTML code for displaying the results of the query on the **Messages** database. Note that you are using the **TableBuilder** class to create the table. A check is done in the process to see whether the user has been validated as an administrator of the system. If so, an additional column is displayed for deleting the message. Note that the link to the **ShowMessage** template for reviewing a single message is created using the **URLFor** method. In this case you create a custom user event by giving the event name as the ID of the message. Thus when the link is clicked on, the **UserEvent** event of the **ShowMessage** template is called with the ID of the message.

```
Private Function DisplayMessages() As String

Dim TB As TableBuilder

'  Check to see if a bad date range was entered
If BadDate = True Then

    '  Display an error message
    DisplayMessages = "You have entered an invalid start or
    ➥end date.  Please try again."

    '  Exit the function
    Exit Function

End If

'  Create our table gen object of the component, MyComponent
Set TB = New TableBuilder

'  Set the colors to rotate between white and yellow
TB.RotateRowColors = 1
TB.RowColor1 = "WHITE"
TB.rowcolor2 = "YELLOW"

'  Create the table
DisplayMessages = TB.CreateTable(1, 4, 3, 0)

    '  Generate a column with the value a
    DisplayMessages = DisplayMessages & TB.GenerateColumn
    ➥("<B>Title<B>", "Center", "Center")

    '  Generate a column with the value a
    DisplayMessages = DisplayMessages & TB.GenerateColumn
    ➥("<B>Owner<B>", "Center", "Center")

    '  Generate a column with the value a
    DisplayMessages = DisplayMessages & TB.GenerateColumn
    ➥("<B>Date Submitted<B>", "Center", "Center")

'  Check to see if the user was validated as an administrator
If Session("validated") = "YES" Then
```

continued on next page

continued from previous page

```
                            ' Generate a column header for the administrator
                            DisplayMessages = DisplayMessages & TB.GenerateColumn
                         ➡("<B>*ADMIN*<B>", "Center", "Center")

           End If

           ' Loop through the messages
           Do Until rsMessages.EOF

             ' Create our first row
             DisplayMessages = DisplayMessages & TB.StartRow

               ' Generate a column with the message title
               DisplayMessages = DisplayMessages & TB.GenerateColumn
            ➡("<a href=" & URLFor(ShowMessage, CStr(rsMessages
            ➡("idMessage"))) & ">" & rsMessages("chrMessageTitle")
            ➡& "</a>", "", "")

               ' Generate a column with message owner
               DisplayMessages = DisplayMessages & TB.GenerateColumn(CStr
            ➡(rsMessages("chrMessageOwner")), "", "")

               ' Generate a column with the date the message was entered
               DisplayMessages = DisplayMessages & TB.GenerateColumn(CStr
            ➡(rsMessages("dtEntered")), "", "")

           ' Check to see if the administrator was validated
           If Session("Validated") = "YES" Then

               ' Generate a column with an option to delete the message
               DisplayMessages = DisplayMessages & TB.GenerateColumn
            ➡("<a href=" & URLFor(DeleteMessage, CStr(rsMessages
            ➡("idMessage"))) & ">" & "Delete </a>",
            ➡"center", "center")

           End If

           ' Move to the next message
           rsMessages.MoveNext

             ' End the row
             DisplayMessages = DisplayMessages & TB.EndRow

           Loop

           ' End the table
           DisplayMessages = DisplayMessages & TB.EndTable

           End Function
```

14. The Form1 event of AddMessage adds the message to the database. The data is retrieved from the form and reviewed for insertion. Note that a check is done to ensure that all single quotes (') are double quoted for proper insertion, and a check is done to ensure that all line breaks are converted to HTML `<BR>` tags for display with the `LineFeed` function.

```
Private Sub AddMessage_Form1()

' Declare our variables
Dim dbMessage
Dim MessageText As String
Dim MessageTitle As String
Dim MessageOwner As String
Dim OwnerEmail As String
Dim SQL As String
Dim rsMessage

' Create an Active Data Object
Set dbMessage = Server.CreateObject("adodb.connection")

' Open our database connection
dbMessage.Open "dsn=Messages;uid=sa;pwd="

' Build in support for single quotes
MessageText = Replace(Request("MessageText"), "'", "''")

' Build in support for line feeds in
' the message
MessageText = LineFeed(MessageText)

' Build in support for single quotes
MessageTitle = Replace(Request("MessageTitle"), "'", "''")

' Build in support for line feeds in
' the message
MessageTitle = LineFeed(MessageTitle)

' Build in support for single quotes
MessageOwner = Replace(Request("MessageOwner"), "'", "''")

' Build in support for line feeds in
' the message
MessageOwner = LineFeed(MessageOwner)

' Build in support for single quotes
OwnerEmail = Replace(Request("OwnerEmail"), "'", "''")

' Build in support for line feeds in
' the message
OwnerEmail = LineFeed(OwnerEmail)

' Build the SQL Statement
SQL = "insert into Messages(txtMessage, chrMessageTitle, " & _
      "chrMessageOwner, chrOwnerEmail) values('" & _
      MessageText & "', '" & _
      MessageTitle & "','" & _
```

continued on next page

continued from previous page

```
                    MessageOwner & "', '" & _
                    OwnerEmail & "')"

            '   Insert the message
            Set rsMessage = dbMessage.Execute(SQL)

            '   Go back to the home page
            Set NextItem = default

            End Sub
```

15. The `LineFeed` function looks for line breaks in the passed text, and an HTML line break `<BR>` is inserted into the text.

```
'   This function loops through the text
'   and will convert line feeds to HTML
'   <BR> tags
Private Function LineFeed(TextString)

'   Check for any line feeds
If InStr(1, TextString, Chr(10)) > 0 Then

    '   Loop through the string
    For i = 1 To Len(TextString)

        '   Get the next character
        CheckChar = Mid(TextString, i, 1)

        '   Check for a line feed
        If CheckChar = Chr(10) Then
            '   Add the tagging
            LineFeed = LineFeed & "<BR>"
        Else
            '   Continue building the string
            LineFeed = LineFeed & CheckChar
        End If
    Next
Else
    '   Return the string
    LineFeed = TextString
End If

End Function
```

16. The `Respond` event of `AddMessage` calls the `WriteTemplate` method to display the page.

```
Private Sub AddMessage_Respond()

'   Write the template
AddMessage.WriteTemplate

End Sub
```

17. The Form1 event sets the next item to the ShowMessages template.

```
Private Sub default_Form1()

'  Set the next item to show the messages
Set NextItem = ShowMessages

End Sub
```

18. The Form3 custom event checks the username and password entered into the administrator form. If the username and password have been properly entered, the validated session variable is set to YES; if not, it is set to NO.

```
Private Sub default_Form3()

'  Check to see if the username and password are correct
If Request("username") <> "username" And Request("password")
➥<> "password" Then

    '  Write the header
    Response.Write "<HTML><HEAD><TITLE>Tippy Cup Message Boards
    ➥</TITLE></HEAD><BODY BGCOLOR=WHITE>"

    '  Indicate the wrong info was entered
    Response.Write "Wrong Username and Password.  Click
    ➥<a href=" & URLFor(default) & "> here </a> to continue."

    '  Write the close of the page
    Response.Write "</BODY></HTML>"

    '  Store is a session variable that the user has not
    '  been validated.
    Session("validated") = "NO"

Else

    '  Store in a session variable that the user has
    '  been validated
    Session("validated") = "YES"

    '  Redirect the user back to the default page
    Set NextItem = default

End If

End Sub
```

19. The Respond event of the default template writes the HTML to the page.

```
Private Sub default_Respond()

'  Write the template
default.WriteTemplate

End Sub
```

20. The `DeleteMessage` custom Web item's `UserEvent` is called to delete the appropriate message from the database. The `EventName` will be the ID of the message to be deleted. After the message is deleted, the next item is set to the default template page.

```
Private Sub DeleteMessage_UserEvent(ByVal EventName As String)

'   Declare our variables
Dim dbMessage
Dim SQL As String
Dim rsMessage

'   Create an Active Data Object
Set dbMessage = Server.CreateObject("adodb.connection")

'   Open our database connection
dbMessage.Open "dsn=Messages;uid=sa;pwd="

'   Build the SQL Statement
SQL = "delete from Messages where idmessage = " & EventName

'   Insert the message
Set rsMessage = dbMessage.Execute(SQL)

'   Go back to the home page
Set NextItem = default

End Sub
```

21. The `GoAddMessage` custom Web item `Respond` event sets the next item to the `AddMessage` template.

```
Private Sub GoAddMessage_Respond()

'   Set the next item to AddMessage
Set NextItem = AddMessage

End Sub
```

22. The `GoDefault` custom Web item sets the next item to be the default template.

```
Private Sub GoDefault_Respond()

'   Set the next item to default
Set NextItem = default

End Sub
```

23. The `GoShowMessages` custom Web item sets the next item to be the `ShowMessages` template.

```
Private Sub GoShowMessages_Respond()

'   Set the next item to show messages
Set NextItem = ShowMessages

End Sub
```

24. The `ShowMessage ProccessTag` event processes the tags on the `ShowMessage` page to show the data for the message. Each tag is read, and the data from the resultset is retrieved and returned to the browser.

```
Private Sub ShowMessage_ProcessTag(ByVal TagName As String,
➥TagContents As String, SendTags As Boolean)

'   Process the tags
Select Case LCase(TagName)

    '   Process the text message
    Case "wc@txtmessage"
        '   Write out the message
        TagContents = txtMessage

    '   Process the Message Owner
    Case "wc@chrmessageowner"
        '   Write out the Message Owner
        TagContents = rsMessage("chrMessageOwner")

    '   Process the Owner Email
    Case "wc@chrowneremail"
        '   Write out the Owner Email
        TagContents = rsMessage("chrOwnerEmail")

    '   Process the Message Title
    Case "wc@chrmessagetitle"
        '   Write the Message Title
        TagContents = rsMessage("chrMessageTitle")

    '   Process the Date Entered
    Case "wc@dtentered"
        '   Write out the date entered
        TagContents = dtentered

End Select

End Sub
```

25. The `ShowMessage Respond` event calls the `WriteTemplate` method to display the HTML for the page.

```
Private Sub ShowMessage_Respond()

'   Write the template
ShowMessage.WriteTemplate

End Sub
```

26. The `ShowMessage` user event is called when the link on the `ShowMessages` page is clicked. The `EventName` will be the ID of the message. The data for the message is retrieved using the `GetMessage` subroutine. Then `NextItem` is set to the `ShowMessage` template.

```
Private Sub ShowMessage_UserEvent(ByVal EventName As String)

'  Get the message for the ID in the event name
GetMessage CInt(EventName)

'  Set the next item to ShowMessage
Set NextItem = ShowMessage

End Sub
```

27. The form for `ShowMessages` calls the `ShowMessages` page to set the new sort order for the messages.

```
Private Sub ShowMessages_Form1()

'  Set the next item to ShowMessage
Set NextItem = ShowMessages

End Sub
```

28. The `ShowMessages ProcessTag` event builds the display of the messages based on the query. The messages are retrieved in the `GetMessages` function. The HTML is built in the `DisplayMessages` function. The hidden variables for storing the original search parameters are also built. These ensure that the same search parameters are used if the user selects a different sort option.

```
Private Sub ShowMessages_ProcessTag(ByVal TagName As String,
➥TagContents As String, SendTags As Boolean)

'  Process the tags
Select Case LCase(TagName)

    Case "wc@showmessages"
        '  Get the messages
        GetMessages

        '  Write out the content
        TagContents = DisplayMessages

    Case "wc@hiddenvars"
        '  Create the hidden variables for storing page data
        TagContents = "<input type=""hidden"" name=""startdate""
        ➥value=" & Chr(34) & StartDate & Chr(34) & ">"
TagContents = TagContents & "<input type=""hidden"" name=
➥""enddate"" value=" & Chr(34) & EndDate & Chr(34) & ">"
```

```
TagContents = TagContents & "<input type=""hidden"" name=
➥""ownername"" value=" & Chr(34) & OwnerName & Chr(34) & ">"

End Select

End Sub
```

29. The `Respond` event of the `ShowMessages` template writes the HTML to the page using `WriteTemplate`.

```
Private Sub ShowMessages_Respond()

'  Write the template
ShowMessages.WriteTemplate

End Sub
```

30. When the Web class is started, `NextItem` is set to the default template.

```
Private Sub WebClass_Start()

    '  Set the next item to default
    Set NextItem = default

End Sub
```

31. Create a messages database table with the following fields on your system. Ensure your ODBC database source points to the database.

```
Messages
    idMessage int IDENTITY (1, 1) NOT NULL ,
    txtMessage text NULL ,
    dtEntered datetime NULL ,
    chrMessageOwner varchar (150) NULL ,
    chrOwnerEmail varchar (50) NULL ,
    chrMessageTitle varchar (100) NULL
```

How It Works

This How-To pulls all the pieces of an IIS application into one example. The application first starts out with a series of HTML templates to provide the framework for the interface. And you even throw into the pot the table-building class built in Chapter 8 to make your life a bit easier when building the colorful message list display.

After the HTML templates are imported and all appropriate custom Web events and custom Web items are created and connected, you are ready to begin coding the application. The default template is the key to the site. From there you can add messages, show messages, search messages, and administrate messages. Note the standard navigation bar on the pages. Each page's navigation bar has links to three custom Web items: `GoDefault`, `GoAddMessage`, and `GoShowMessages`.

The task of adding a message is fairly straightforward. The template form only contains the standard navigation and a form that links back to a custom Web event. The code in the event simply takes the data entered and inserts it into the database.

The searching of messages takes place in three ways. The first is to show all messages. The second is to search by date range, and the third is to search by owner name. All three use the same set of code. Your `GetMessages` subroutine retrieves the search data and builds the appropriate SQL query. After the messages are retrieved, the `DisplayMessages` function is called. This builds the display table using the `TableBuilder` tools. Note that the links to review a message and delete a message create custom user events using the IDs of the messages and the `URLFor` method.

After the `Display Message` link is clicked on the `ShowMessages` page, the `ShowMessage` template is called with the `UserEvent` name, which is the ID of the message. The data for the message is retrieved from the database and the message is displayed. If the `Delete` link is clicked on, the `DeleteMessage UserEvent` event is called with the ID of the message. The message then is deleted from the database.

This How-To demonstrates how full-fledged client/server Internet applications can be built using Microsoft's new IIS applications technology. Your existing Visual Basic applications can easily add a Web class interface to the existing business logic code and then be accessible on your corporate intranet or publicly on your Internet site.

Comments

Consider adding to your application features for building reply-to capabilities for a message and adding multithreaded discussion capabilities. The same suggestion was made in Chapter 8 with the ASP version of this application. You might find that the capability to build a truly robust message board application is much easier with a full-fledged programming environment such as Visual Basic behind you rather than the limited scripting environment provided in ASP.

CHAPTER 10

REPORTING AND DATA CONNECTION SUPPORT

10

REPORTING AND DATA CONNECTION SUPPORT

by Don Kiely

How do I...

10.1 **Create a report using Crystal Reports?**

10.2 **Create a detailed grouped report without Crystal Reports?**

10.3 **Create a multiple query report using Word 97 and ActiveX?**

10.4 **Create a pivot table and chart using Excel 97 and ActiveX?**

This chapter provides a series of How-To's for the decision-support aspect of client/server development and offers special solutions crafted around the use of Visual Basic 6, Microsoft Office, and Crystal Reports.

The How-To's in this chapter use different datasources to generate the reports, including single Access `.MDB` files and remote data from a SQL Server. The source of the data doesn't really make much difference; however, all the techniques are easily changed for any source. The biggest differences are in how errors with the connection to the data are handled. When using the Jet Engine's Data Access Objects (DAOs), errors must be handled differently than with Remote Data Objects (RDOs).

The four How-To's in this chapter provide a foundation for a variety of reporting techniques to use in your client/server applications. The methods you choose depend largely on how much control you want to give users over the final report and the resources available on the end-users' computers, such as whether they have Microsoft Office available.

10.1 Create a Report Using Crystal Reports

The Crystal Reports report generator included with Visual Basic and most Microsoft database products gives you everything in a single package: a standalone report generator, a custom control you can use to run reports from a Visual Basic application, and an API for more control over a report. This How-To shows the creation of a database report using the Crystal Reports designer program.

10.2 Create a Detailed Grouped Report Without Crystal Reports

At times, none of the packaged database reporting systems will work for your application, perhaps because they don't handle your situation very well, such as reports that don't easily fit into a row-and-column format or that require special processing beyond the capability of the Crystal print engine. Or you might not want to deliver the required megabytes of support files with your applications. This How-To shows how you can use the Windows RichTextBox control to create complex reports grouped on the records in a different table than the one used for the main body of data.

10.3 Create a Multiple Query Report Using Word 97 and ActiveX

For client/server databases of anything more than trivial size, performance is always an issue. A busy network, while it is waiting for data to return from the server, can make your application seem sluggish to the end user, even if you tell the end user the reason for the delay. Using a multiple query can significantly improve the speed of queries to database servers. This How-To demonstrates a multiple query, using Microsoft Word to generate a report document with three sections resulting from each of the multiple queries sent to the server.

10.4 Create a Pivot Table and Chart Using Excel 97 and ActiveX

A pivot table is a useful technique for analyzing and filtering data contained in many records. This How-To focuses on querying a database and formatting the data to produce a pivot table and chart using OLE and Microsoft Excel.

10.1 How do I...
Create a report using Crystal Reports?

COMPATIBILITY: VISU,

Problem

I must create a quick report to summarize data in our client/server system and distribute it enterprise-wide with my application. How can I standard report quickly and easily?

Technique

The Crystal Reports program—included with Visual Basic since version 3 added database support—is a powerful and flexible report tool. The user interface is a bit quirky, however, so be prepared to spend some time fussing with your report to get it just the way you want it. This How-To exercises many of Crystal Report's design features, but many more are hidden in its menus and dialog boxes. The best way to become comfortable with these features is to experiment and try different ways of accomplishing things.

Because Visual Basic now has its own report writer and object, Crystal Reports is not automatically installed with Visual Basic 6, but you can find the installation program on the Visual Studio CD-ROM—number 1 under `\Common\Tools\VB\Crysrept` (it should be in a similar location on the standalone Visual Basic Installation CD-ROM). Be sure to read the `Readme.txt` file before installing Crystal Reports, and install it after you install Visual Basic so that it can register itself as an add-in in the Visual Basic Add-In menu. The version included with Visual Basic 6 is similar to the version distributed with Visual Basic 5, so if you've worked with that version, you'll be right at home.

So why should you consider using Crystal Reports instead of Visual Basic's data report? Crystal Reports has been available for years, so its interface and tools are more robust, and many developers have wrangled with its quirks long enough to feel comfortable with it. It allows you to save reports in various formats and provides tools for distributing reports throughout an enterprise. Visual Basic's data report is limited as far as the ActiveX controls you can use with it, limiting your capability to thoroughly customize a report. However, for most basic application report generation, Visual Basic's data report probably has all the features you need.

10.1 How do I...

Create a report using Crystal Reports?

Problem

I must create a quick report to summarize data in our client/server database system and distribute it enterprise-wide with my application. How can I create a standard report quickly and easily?

Technique

The Crystal Reports program—included with Visual Basic since version 3 added database support—is a powerful and flexible report tool. The user interface is a bit quirky, however, so be prepared to spend some time fussing with your report to get it just the way you want it. This How-To exercises many of Crystal Report's design features, but many more are hidden in its menus and dialog boxes. The best way to become comfortable with these features is to experiment and try different ways of accomplishing things.

Because Visual Basic now has its own report writer and object, Crystal Reports is not automatically installed with Visual Basic 6, but you can find the installation program on the Visual Studio CD-ROM—number 1 under \Common\Tools\VB\Crysrept (it should be in a similar location on the standalone Visual Basic Installation CD-ROM). Be sure to read the Readme.txt file before installing Crystal Reports, and install it after you install Visual Basic so that it can register itself as an add-in in the Visual Basic Add-In menu. The version included with Visual Basic 6 is similar to the version distributed with Visual Basic 5, so if you've worked with that version, you'll be right at home.

So why should you consider using Crystal Reports instead of Visual Basic's data report? Crystal Reports has been available for years, so its interface and tools are more robust, and many developers have wrangled with its quirks long enough to feel comfortable with it. It allows you to save reports in various formats and provides tools for distributing reports throughout an enterprise. Visual Basic's data report is limited as far as the ActiveX controls you can use with it, limiting your capability to thoroughly customize a report. However, for most basic application report generation, Visual Basic's data report probably has all the features you need.

TIP

To use Visual Basic's data report, open a project and choose Add Data Report from the Project menu. The data report appears as a designer, and you create a report much like you create a form.

Steps

The steps in this How-To show in detail how to create a report that lists the publishers and titles in the **BIBLIO.MDB** database included with Visual Basic. Upon completion, the report looks like Figure 10.1.

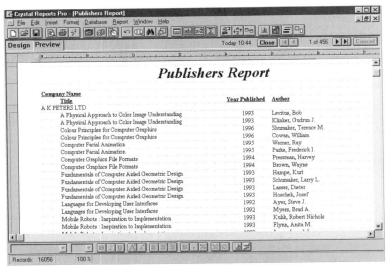

Figure 10.1 Print preview of the finished publishers report

In the Crystal Reports window, choose Open from the File menu and select the **PUBS.RPT** report to open and run a report in Crystal Reports. Click the Print icon on the toolbar, or choose Print from the File menu to print the report. To preview the report onscreen, click the Print Preview icon on the toolbar, or choose Print Preview from the File menu. Complete the following steps to create this project:

1. Start Crystal Reports by choosing Microsoft Visual Studio 6.0, Microsoft Visual Basic 6.0, Crystal Reports from the Start menu (depending on your installation, it might be located under another menu item).

2. In the Crystal Reports window, choose Options from the File menu. In the File Options dialog box that appears, select the New Report tab, as shown in Figure 10.2. Make sure that the Use Report Gallery for New Reports check box is enabled. Set the Report Directory field to the default location where you want to save reports.

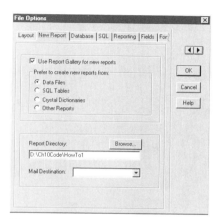

Figure 10.2 Setting the New Report options in the File Options dialog box

3. Select the Reporting tab and make sure that the Refresh Data on Every Print check box is disabled so that the underlying query isn't run every time you preview the report as you put it together (see Figure 10.3).

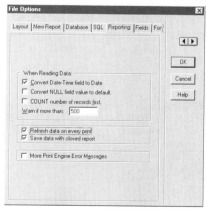

Figure 10.3 Setting the Reporting options in the File Options dialog box

4. Select the Layout tab (see Figure 10.4). You might want to experiment with the Show Field Names check box to see which you prefer as you design your report: a cluttered report with the field names showing or a clean report with less information.

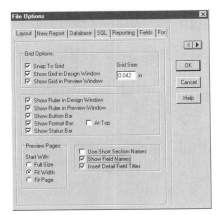

Figure 10.4 Setting the Layout options in the File Options dialog box

As you design reports in Crystal Reports, be sure to periodically save your work by choosing Save from the File menu.

5. Click the New Report toolbar button or choose New from the File menu. The Create New Report dialog box shown in Figure 10.5 appears. This dialog box lists a number of wizards—called *experts*—you can use to create different kinds of reports. Click the Standard button in the Choose an Expert section.

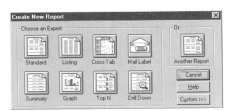

Figure 10.5 The Create New Report dialog box

6. When the Create Report Expert dialog box appears, the Step 1: Tables tab is selected so that you can select the database file used for the report (see Figure 10.6). Click the Data File button and select the `BIBLIO.MDB` database file located in your Visual Basic program directory, usually `C:\Program Files\Microsoft Visual Studio\VB98\`. Click Done after you select the file; Crystal Reports lets you add files if you want, but this How-To uses only one. After a moment, the dialog box lists the tables in the database and switches automatically to Step 2: Links.

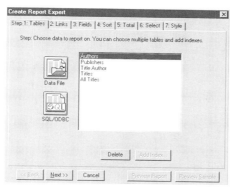

Figure 10.6 Use Step 1: Tables in the Create Report Expert to select the database

7. On the Step 2: Links tab, Crystal Reports shows all the relationships defined between the tables of the database (see Figure 10.7). If the existing relationships in the database are not adequate for the report, add and edit them here. For this How-To, the default relationships are adequate.

TIP

You can also modify the relationships afterward by using the Database menu on the menu bar/Visual Linking Expert command. You can see and do a lot of cool things with this step of the screen or menu item, such as viewing indexes, modifying relationships, adding new data files, or linking to ODBC databases, to name a few.

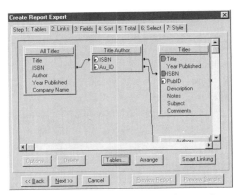

Figure 10.7 Use Step 2: Links in the
Create Report Expert dialog box to
maintain relationships between
tables

8. Select the Step 3: Fields tab or click Next, and then select the fields you
want to include in the table. This step uses standard Windows selection
methods, so you can add fields to the report by any of the following
methods:

✔ Double-clicking the field

✔ Clicking the field and then clicking the Add button

✔ Selecting multiple fields by Ctrl-clicking each one and then clicking the
Add button

Use one of these methods to add the fields listed in Table 10.1 to the
report. When you're finished, the dialog box should look like Figure 10.8.

Table 10.1 Fields from the Biblio database used in the report

TABLE NAME	FIELD NAME
Publishers	Company Name
Titles	Title
	Year Published
Authors	Author

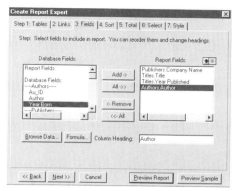

Figure 10.8 Use Step 3: Fields in the Create Report Expert dialog box to select the data fields you want to include in the report

9. Select the Step 4: Sort tab or click Next. Most database reports should be grouped and printed in some logical order, and this report groups all of a single publisher's titles together under the publisher's name. Add `Publishers.Company Name` to the Group Fields list box. Then add the `Titles.Title` field so that each publisher's books are listed alphabetically. The order in which you add these fields is important because that determines how the records are sorted in the final report. Figure 10.9 shows the Create Report Expert dialog box at this point. Both of these fields should sort in ascending order, so accept that as the default in the Order list box.

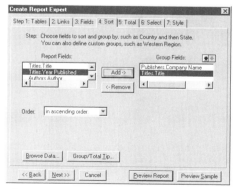

Figure 10.9 Use Step 4: Sort in the Create Report Expert dialog box to control the order in which records are printed

10. Select the Step 5: Total tab or click Next. If this were a report with values such as money or counts of things, Crystal Reports would add group and grand totals to the report. In this case, however, totals aren't meaningful for any fields. Crystal Reports does try to be helpful, though, by adding the numeric Year Published field to the Total Fields list on the **Publishers.Company Name** tab, and **Titles.Year Published** on the **Titles.Title** tab. Because the sum of years is meaningless, click on the field and then click Remove on each of these tabs. Also disable the Add Grand Totals check box. The Create Report Expert dialog box should now look like Figure 10.10.

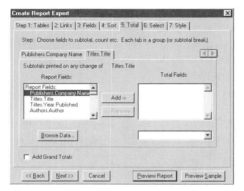

Figure 10.10 Use Step 5: Total to add group and grand totals to the report

11. Select the Step 6: Select tab or click Next to move to the next step, as shown in Figure 10.11. If you are interested in only a subset of the records in the tables you've selected, you can select them here. When you add a field to the Select Fields list, options appear below for entering the criteria to use for the selection. For this report, you don't want any subsets. Because Crystal Reports hasn't made any selections for you, nothing needs to be done.

12. Select the Step 7: Style tab or click Next. Enter a report title, **Publishers Report**, in the Title text box. Crystal Reports creates reports as simple or as fancy as you want, using various combinations of highlighting, font sizes, shading, and other effects. Leave the selection as Standard in the Style box unless you want to experiment with other looks for the report. Just be aware that if you choose another style, your final report probably will not look like the report created in this How-To. As you select each report style, a vague approximation of the report appearance is displayed to the right of the Style list, as shown in Figure 10.12. You can also add an image to the report by clicking the button showing the two mountains and rising sun.

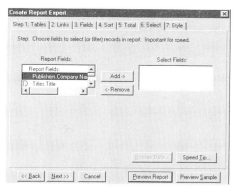

Figure 10.11 Use Step 6: Select to filter records for the report

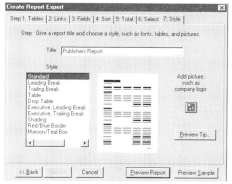

Figure 10.12 Use Step 7: Style to select among the predesigned report styles

13. Click the Preview Sample button at the lower-right side of the Create Report Expert dialog box. The dialog box disappears and another appears letting you select to use all the records in the tables for the sample or just a limited number. Leave the default selected, All the Records, and click OK to produce the sample report; this can take some time if the number of records is large, as it is in this case. The window shown in Figure 10.13 appears, letting you examine your results so far. You might want to choose

Zoom from the Report menu to get a clearer look at the contents of the report. Although Crystal Reports makes a valiant attempt to create a good report, it isn't yet perfect, so the next step is to make some adjustments to produce the desired result.

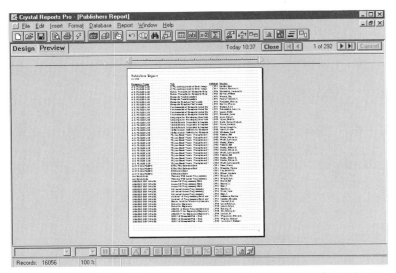

Figure 10.13 After the Create Report Expert completes its work, you can preview the report so far

14. Before starting to make some customizations, this is a good time to save the report. Choose Save from the File menu or click the Disk icon, and save the report as PUBS.RPT.

15. Go to design mode by selecting the Design tab. Take a moment to poke around the Design view. Notice that the left side of the view has a wide gray area divided into sections. Each of these sections has a particular function within the report, as described in Table 10.2.

Table 10.2 Crystal Reports sections

SECTION	DESCRIPTION
Title	Prints the information here only on the first page of the report
Page Header	Prints the fields located here at the top of every page
#1: Company Name	Prints the company name at the beginning of each company's records
#2: Year Published	Prints at the beginning of each different year (this report will not use this section)
Details	Prints each title, grouped by publisher

SECTION	DESCRIPTION
#2: Year Published	Prints at the end of each different year (this report will not use this section)
#1: Company Name	Prints the company name at the end of each company's records
Page Footer	Prints the fields located here at the bottom of every page
Summary	Prints the information here only on the last page of the report

16. The default report layout does not include the Company Name and Year Published groups, or *bands*, so you must add them. Choose Group Section from the Insert menu; the Insert Group Section dialog box appears, as shown in Figure 10.14.

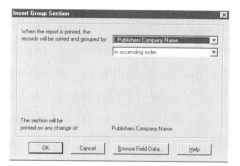

Figure 10.14 The Insert Group Section dialog box lets you create new grouping bands in the report

Crystal Reports automatically selects `Publishers.Company Name` to be grouped and sorted in ascending order, so click OK to accept this selection. The report's Design view should now look like Figure 10.15.

17. The default left and right margins for this report are 0.25". This report isn't terribly cluttered, so start by increasing the margins to 0.5" on each side. Choose Page Margins from the File menu, set the left and right margins to 0.5", and click OK.

WARNING

Crystal Reports has a nasty habit of making inaccessible fields that are outside the printable area of the page. So be sure to move any fields that might otherwise disappear before changing the margins.

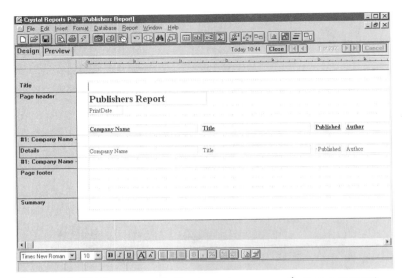

Figure 10.15 The report's Design view now shows a report band for grouping by company name

18. The next thing to do is to get rid of a few extraneous fields that Crystal Reports added to the report. (Some of these elements might not have been added to the report, whereas others might have been added that aren't mentioned here. Crystal Services seems to be constantly refining the product, so your mileage might vary.) Even though you told Crystal Reports not to add totals, it added a Total field for the years, so delete the field that looks like -5,555,555.55 (assuming that you set the options described at the beginning of this How-To) and the label to the left of it by selecting the fields and pressing Del.

19. Delete the extra Company Name field in the group footer section. Remember when you told Crystal Reports to group by company names and titles? Crystal Reports adds this extra field so that the company name prints at the end of each company's records. A nice touch but not necessary for this type of report.

In some instances, you don't have this extra Company Name field, but the field is in the Detail section, so the company name prints repeatedly with each book title. Drag the Company Name field to the #1: Company section in the same horizontal position. Now the company name will print only at the beginning of that company's titles.

20. After listing each publisher's titles, the report should state the number of titles for that publisher. This step adds two fields so that `Title count for <publisher name>: #` prints. Start by selecting one of the fields in the Details section of the report. Add the title count by choosing Summary from the Insert menu. In the top combo box, select Count. `Group #1: Publishers.Company Name -A` should already appear in the second combo box. Click OK. The field appears in the bottom #1: Company Name section. Move it so that the field's right edge is at the right margin, and narrow it to hold three or four characters.

21. Add the text for the title count by choosing Formula Field from the Insert menu. Name the field `PublisherSubTotal` and click OK. In the Edit Formula: `@PublisherSubTotal` dialog box, enter the following:

```
"Title count for "  + TrimRight({Publishers.Company Name})
➥+ ": "
```

Then click Check and click OK. This code creates a string that prints in the report, combining the text in the double quotes with the trimmed contents of the `Publishers.Company Name` field in the database. Position the new field so that its right edge just touches the `Count of Titles.Title` field in the Page Footer section of the report. Extend the left edge of the field to the report's left margin so that there is room for any length of company name.

The formula syntax in Crystal Reports is generally similar to that in Visual Basic, but is just different enough to sometimes be confusing. For example, database field names must be delimited with curly brackets {} as shown in the preceding code. Crystal will handle creating formulas with the correct syntax if you use the Edit Formula dialog box, as described here.

22. This step might vary a bit, depending on whether you have a report section showing named #2: Year Published. Crystal Reports created one or two grouping fields based on company name and title, as indicated by the `#1: Company Name` and `#2: Year Published` headings in the gray area to the left of the report fields. The report doesn't need to include any data there, nor should there be spaces between titles. Right-click on both the header (first or top) #2: Year Published heading in the gray area, and select Hide Section. Do the same for the footer (second or bottom) #2: Year Published heading. At this point, the report should look like Figure 10.16.

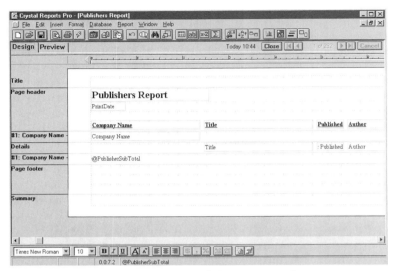

Figure 10.16 The Design view of the report after some changes have been made

23. If necessary, scroll to the right of the report so that the `Page Number` field in the Page Footer section is showing. The default page number simply says `1`, but this report should show `Page 1`. Unfortunately, Crystal Reports has no easy way to add text to the page number, so use a formula field with the `ToText` function, which is a Crystal Reports function to convert a number to text. Choose Formula Field from the Insert menu and name the field `PageNumber`. Enter this code in the Edit Formula dialog box, which creates a string of the form `Page 1` by combining `"Page"` with the page number converted to text:

```
"Page " + ToText (PageNumber, 0)
```

The Edit Formula dialog box looks like Figure 10.17 when you are ready to accept the formula. (Notice that you can select fields, functions, and operators using the list boxes at the top of this dialog box.) Click Check and click OK, positioning the new field on the middle line of the Page Footer section of the report, with its right edge at the right margin. Click on the previously existing page number field and press Del to delete it.

24. To look its best, the page number should appear right-justified in the field, but by default it is left-justified. Right-click the `PageNumber` field and choose Change Format from the shortcut menu. Change the alignment to Right and click OK.

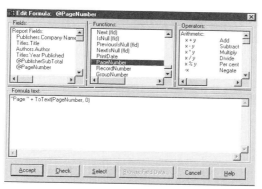

Figure 10.17 Entering a formula to print a formatted page number on each page

25. Scroll back to the left side of the report if necessary. Crystal Reports set up the report so that the publisher's name prints on the same line as every book. Because it really needs to print only once at the beginning of each list of titles, delete that field from the Details section of the report. Be careful not to delete the bold `Company Name` heading in the #1: Company Name section.

26. Rearrange the fields on the Details line so that the `Title` prints about a half-inch from the left side of the report, the `Year Published` prints to the right of the title, and the `Author Name` prints to the right of that. Resize the fields and space them as you prefer. You can switch back and forth between the Design view and Preview to see how things look and then make adjustments. When you are done, move the header fields at the bottom of the Page Header section of the report so that the proper heading is positioned over the correct field, as shown in Figure 10.18. Move the `Company Name` header one line up so that it is above the `Title` header.

27. The default for the report title is to print it at the top of every page, so Crystal Reports puts it in the Page Header section. For this report, the title should appear only on the first page, so move the field to the Title section of the report by dragging it with the left mouse button. While you're at it, delete the date field or move it to a more convenient location on the report, such as in the Page Footer or Summary section.

28. The Page Header section now has two blank lines between the report title and the column headers. Select all the column headers by clicking on one and pressing Ctrl while clicking on the others, and move them as a group up one line. Then drag the bottom line of the Page Header section up as far as it will go, immediately below the column header fields.

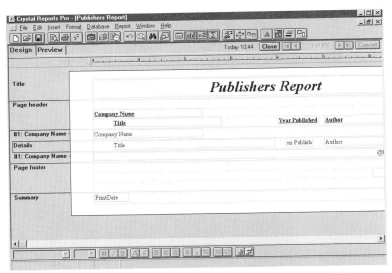

Figure 10.18 Crystal Reports' Design window for Publishers Report

29. Spruce up the report by changing fonts and field alignments. Start by right-clicking on the report header (do this before widening the field so that the right edge of the field will not disappear beyond the right margin when you enlarge the font) and choose Change Font from the shortcut menu. Set the font to 24-point bold italic. Click OK and right-click on the field again. Choose Change Format from the shortcut menu, and set Alignment to Centered. Click OK. Finally, drag the right edge of the field to the right margin of the report so that it is centered across the entire width of the report.

30. Set the properties listed in Table 10.3 for the rest of the fields; leave the defaults for the other properties and fields not listed. Remember to right-click on the field you want to edit, and choose Change Format to change the alignment and to make other related changes; choose Change Font to change the font. The Print on Multiple Lines option for the `Titles.Title` field prints the whole title on as many lines as it takes, so none of the titles are hidden.

Table 10.3 Publishers report fields and formatting

REPORT ELEMENT	VALUES
Report header	Centered alignment
Year header	Centered alignment
`Titles.Title`	Print on multiple lines

REPORT ELEMENT	VALUES
Titles.Year Published	Centered alignment, no thousands separator
Count of Titles.Title	Left alignment, no negative
@PublisherSubtotal	Right alignment
@PageNumber	Right alignment

31. Test the layout of the report by clicking the Print Preview button on the toolbar or by choosing Print Preview from the File menu.

How It Works

The Crystal Reports engine takes the report format that you create and combines it with data at runtime to produce the report.

Comments

Although the user interface of Crystal Reports can be frustrating to work with, it is quite flexible. Even if there isn't an obvious way to do any given formatting feature using Crystal Reports' built-in functions (such as ToText, which was used in this How-To), you can usually achieve the effect you want by designing your database queries at the back end of the server system or by using Crystal Reports' scripting language. The script is similar to Visual Basic code but different enough so that you will have some work getting used to it. To help you, Crystal Reports provides list boxes for many selections. Because the product is available for almost every database server you're likely to encounter, you will have to learn its idiosyncrasies only once.

COMPLEXITY
ADVANCED

10.2 How do I...

Create a detailed grouped report without Crystal Reports?

COMPATIBILITY: VISUAL BASIC

Problem

I need to print a highly customized database report but cannot use Crystal Reports because of its quirks and all the files I would need to distribute with my application. I can use the Visual Basic Printer object, but that means writing a lot of code to specify every detail of layout. How can I put together an attractive report with native Visual Basic and Windows tools with enough flexibility to allow record groupings?

Technique

This How-To combines the Windows RichTextBox control with a couple of API calls to produce a What-You-See-Is-What-You-Get (WYSIWYG) display that shows what will be printed. It is far easier to code a report this way than to use the Visual Basic `Printer` object, and this method does not require that any large files be included with your application. Another option is to use the Visual Basic Data Report, but even that requires that you stick to fairly simple reports. For complete flexibility, there just isn't any better way than coding your own, as demonstrated in this How-To.

Grouping records is a powerful relational database technique that lets you create and display a hierarchy of data. In this How-To, the report groups books by authors—that is, it lists an author's name and then groups that author's books under his or her name. In theory, you can use any number of grouping levels, depending on the type of data you want in the report.

Steps

Open and run the `RTFPRINT.VBP` project file. The Database Report window appears, as shown in Figure 10.19.

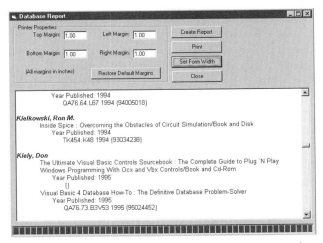

Figure 10.19 The Windows RichTextBox control provides a handy way to produce database reports with a Print Preview feature

Set the margins for the report or accept the default one-inch margins. Click Create Report and watch as the report is generated in the RichTextBox window. When the report is complete, click Set Form Width to size the form to the actual width of the report based on your settings. Then click Print to send the report to the default printer.

To create this project, complete the following steps:

1. Create a new project and name it `RTFPRINT.VBP`.

2. Choose Components from the Project menu and select the following custom controls:

> Microsoft Common Dialog Control 6.0
>
> Microsoft RichTextBox Control 6.0
>
> Microsoft Windows Common Controls 6.0

Uncheck all other controls so that your project isn't cluttered with controls you aren't using and the Setup Wizard doesn't include a lot of dead weight with your application.

3. Choose References from the Project menu and select the following references:

> Microsoft Visual Basic for Applications
>
> Visual Basic Runtime Objects and Procedures
>
> Visual Basic Objects and Procedures
>
> Microsoft DAO 3.51 Object Library

Uncheck all other references so that your project isn't cluttered with DLLs you aren't using and the Setup Wizard doesn't include a lot of dead weight with your application.

4. Name the default form `frmPrint` and save the file as `RTFPRINT.FRM`. Add the controls as shown in Figure 10.19, setting the properties listed in Table 10.4.

Table 10.4 Objects and properties for `RTFPRINT.FRM`

OBJECT	PROPERTY	SETTING
Form	Name	frmPrint
	Caption	"Form1"
CommandButton	Name	cmdSetFormWidth
	Caption	"Set Form Width"
CommandButton	Name	cmdCreateReport
	Caption	"Create Report"
Frame	Name	fraSettings
	Caption	"Printer Properties"
CommandButton	Name	cmdDefaults
	Caption	"Restore Default Margins"

continued on next page

Table 10.4 continued

OBJECT	PROPERTY	SETTING
TextBox	Name	txtRightMargin
TextBox	Name	txtLeftMargin
TextBox	Name	txtTopMargin
TextBox	Name	txtBottomMargin
Label	Name	Label5
	Caption	"(All margins in inches)"
Label	Name	Label4
	Alignment	1 'Right Justify
	Caption	"Bottom Margin:"
Label	Name	Label3
	Alignment	1 'Right Justify
	Caption	"Top Margin:"
Label	Name	Label2
	Alignment	1 'Right Justify
	Caption	"Right Margin:"
Label	Name	Label1
	Alignment	1 'Right Justify
	Caption	"Left Margin:"
CommandButton	Name	cmdClose
	Caption	"Close"
CommandButton	Name	cmdPrint
	Caption	"Print"
ProgressBar	Name	progBar
	Align	2 'Align Bottom
CommonDialog	Name	cdDB
RichTextBox	Name	rtb1
	HideSelection	0 'False
	ReadOnly	-1 'True
	ScrollBars	2 - rtfVertical

5. Add the following code to the Declarations section of the form. `Option Explicit` tells Visual Basic to make sure that you declare all variables and objects before using them in order to avoid naming problems. The two module-level variables will contain a reference to the database file used for the report and RichTextBox's line width so that it can be kept consistent throughout the report.

```
Option Explicit

Dim mDB As Database
Dim mlLineWidth As Long
```

6. Add the following code to the form's **Load** event procedure. The code calls the **cmdDefaults Click** event procedure to format the initial defaults for the page margins.

```
Private Sub Form_Load()
    'Initialize Form and Command button
    Me.Caption = "Database Report"

    cmdDefaults_Click

End Sub
```

7. By including code in the form's **Resize** event procedure, the RichTextBox shrinks or expands to fit the form any time the form is resized. This is handy for the **cmdSetFormWidth** button, which sizes the form to show the full width of the text in the control if the monitor and resolution allow it.

```
Private Sub Form_Resize()
Dim lTop As Long
Dim lHeight As Long
Dim lWidth As Long

    'Position the RTF on form
    lTop = fraSettings.Top + fraSettings.Height + 200
    lWidth = Me.ScaleWidth - 200
    lHeight = progBar.Top - lTop - 100
    rtb1.Move fraSettings.Left, lTop, lWidth, lHeight

End Sub
```

8. Add this code to the **Click** event of the **cmdDefaults** command button, which gives the end user an easy way to return to the document's starting state of one-inch margins, in case the end user makes changes and then later decides that the defaults were okay. The form's **Load** event uses this procedure to set the initial defaults.

```
Private Sub cmdDefaults_Click()
'Set the default margins to one inch
    txtTopMargin.Text = "1.00"
    txtBottomMargin.Text = "1.00"
    txtLeftMargin.Text = "1.00"
    txtRightMargin.Text = "1.00"

End Sub
```

9. The code in the `GotFocus` events of each of the text boxes makes it easier for the end user to edit the margins for the report. As the end user tabs among the text boxes, the code highlights the current entry so that the end user doesn't need to select the text before making a change. The `LostFocus` event code formats new entries in the margin text boxes in the format "`0.00`" so that the information stays uniform in appearance. You can also add error-checking code to these events to prevent settings that allow no area on the page for text, for example.

```
Private Sub txtTopMargin_GotFocus()
    txtTopMargin.SelStart = 0
    txtTopMargin.SelLength = Len(txtTopMargin.Text)
End Sub

Private Sub txtBottomMargin_GotFocus()
    txtBottomMargin.SelStart = 0
    txtBottomMargin.SelLength = Len(txtBottomMargin.Text)
End Sub

Private Sub txtleftMargin_GotFocus()
    txtLeftMargin.SelStart = 0
    txtLeftMargin.SelLength = Len(txtLeftMargin.Text)
End Sub

Private Sub txtrightMargin_GotFocus()
    txtRightMargin.SelStart = 0
    txtRightMargin.SelLength = Len(txtRightMargin.Text)
End Sub

Private Sub txtTopMargin_LostFocus()
    txtTopMargin.Text = Format$(Str(Val(txtTopMargin.Text)), _
        "#0.00")
End Sub

Private Sub txtbottomMargin_LostFocus()
    txtBottomMargin.Text = Format$(Str( _
        Val(txtBottomMargin.Text)), "#0.00")
End Sub

Private Sub txtleftMargin_LostFocus()
    txtLeftMargin.Text = Format$(Str( _
        Val(txtLeftMargin.Text)), "#0.00")
End Sub

Private Sub txtrightMargin_LostFocus()
    txtRightMargin.Text = Format$(Str( _
        Val(txtRightMargin.Text)), "#0.00")
End Sub
```

10. Add the `SetupRTB` and `NormalRTF Sub` procedures, which set the RichTextBox to different formats. The `SetupRTB Sub` procedure sets the RichTextBox control to a uniform beginning state. Putting this code into a single procedure avoids the need to change formatting commands in many places throughout the form's code. Any time the code makes changes to the formatting, such as by entering bold text, **NormalRTF** sets it back to its normal state.

SetupRTB makes a call to the **WYSIWYG_RTF** procedure in the **RTFPRINT.BAS** code module. **WYSIWYG_RTF** establishes the line width for the text in the RichTextBox given the margins set in the form's code. It also sets the length of the line of text to appear the same in the RichTextBox and on the printer.

```
Private Sub SetupRTB()
Dim lLeftMargin As Long
Dim lRightMargin As Long

    rtb1.Text = ""

    'Set the RTF box to its normal formatting
    NormalRTF

    'Tell the RTF to base its display off of the printer
    '1440 Twips=1 Inch
    lLeftMargin = Val(txtLeftMargin.Text) * 1440
    lRightMargin = Val(txtRightMargin.Text) * 1440
    mlLineWidth = WYSIWYG_RTF(rtb1, lLeftMargin, lRightMargin)

End Sub

Private Sub NormalRTF()
'Reset the RTF box to our chosen default
    rtb1.SelAlignment = rtfLeft
    rtb1.SelBold = False
    rtb1.SelItalic = False
    rtb1.SelFontName = "Arial"
    rtb1.SelFontSize = 10
End Sub
```

11. Add a **LoadDB** function procedure to the **frmPrint** form and enter the code that follows. This function locates the **BIBLIO.MDB** database included with Visual Basic. It starts by checking to see whether a file location was stored in the Registry when this program was run previously, under the **VB6CSHT** key under the application's **.EXE** name. If there is no entry or if the file isn't at the specified location, it uses the form's common dialog control to prompt the end user for the file's location. If the end user cancels the dialog box, the code pops up a warning message box and ends the procedure. Otherwise, the procedure opens the database, stores the file location in the Registry, and sets the function's return value to the name of the file.

```
Public Function LoadDB(sDefaultFile As String) As String
'Returns the full file name if it can be found
Dim sAppFile As String

    sAppFile = GetSetting("VB6CSHT", App.EXEName, "DBPath", _
        sDefaultFile)

    If Len(Dir(sAppFile)) = 0 Then
        cdDB.InitDir = sDefaultFile
        cdDB.FileName = "biblio.mdb"
        cdDB.DialogTitle = "Open VB Biblio Database"
        cdDB.Filter = "Access (*.mdb)¦*.mdb¦All Files (*.*)¦*.*"
        cdDB.Flags = cdlOFNPathMustExist + cdlOFNFileMustExist
        cdDB.ShowOpen
        sAppFile = cdDB.FileName
        If Len(Dir(sAppFile)) = 0 Or Mid$(sAppFile, 3, 1) <> "\" _
            Then
            'No file selected
            MsgBox "No file selected. Ending application.", _
                vbCritical, "No Database Selected"
            LoadDB = ""
            cmdClose_Click
            Exit Function
        End If
    End If

    'It is here, so open it
    Set mDB = OpenDatabase(sAppFile, False, False)

    'Save the file name and location for next execution
    SaveSetting "VB6CSHT", App.EXEName, "DBPath", sAppFile

    LoadDB = sAppFile
End Function
```

12. Add the following code to the cmdCreateReport_Click event procedure, which generates the report in the RichTextBox control. It starts by opening the BIBLIO.MDB database using the LoadDB procedure. Then it sets up the RichTextBox with the starting format. It then calls the PrintReportHeader to print the report name, in this case using bold italics, to print "Author's Bibliography List".

This procedure uses two SQL statements to manage grouping titles for each author. The first SQL statement simply retrieves the contents of the Authors table, sorted by the author name. The names are in the form "Last Name, First Name" in this database, so this puts the authors in alphabetical order without any string concatenation. This recordset, rsAuthors, then is used for the main Do While loop.

Inside the author's loop, another SQL statement retrieves the author's titles from the Titles table. If this author has any titles, the PrintAuthor procedure is used to print the data. With each run through the author's loop, the code updates the form's progress bar.

```
Private Sub cmdCreateReport_Click()
Dim sSQLAuthors As String
Dim sSQLTitles As String
Dim sSQL As String
Dim rsAuthors As Recordset
Dim rsTitles As Recordset
Dim i As Long

   rtb1.SetFocus

   'Open the database
   LoadDB _
      "c:\Program Files\Microsoft Visual Studio\vb98\biblio.mdb"

   'Set up the rich text box for the report
   SetupRTB
   PrintReportHeader

   'Create the authors query statement
   sSQLAuthors = "SELECT * FROM Authors WHERE Author LIKE 'K*' "
   ➡& "ORDER BY Author"

   Set rsAuthors = mDB.OpenRecordset(sSQLAuthors, _
      dbOpenSnapshot)

   progBar.Min = 0
   progBar.Max = rsAuthors.RecordCount
   progBar.Value = 0
   i = 0

   Do While Not rsAuthors.EOF
      sSQLTitles = "SELECT * FROM Titles " _
         & "INNER JOIN [Title Author] " _
         & "ON Titles.ISBN = [Title Author].ISBN " _
         & "WHERE ([Title Author].Au_ID) = "
         ➡& rsAuthors("Au_ID")
         & & " ORDER BY Titles.Title;"
      Set rsTitles = mDB.OpenRecordset(sSQLTitles, _
         dbOpenSnapshot)

'       rsTitles.MoveLast
      If rsTitles.RecordCount Then
         PrintAuthor rsAuthors, rsTitles
      End If

      rsAuthors.MoveNext

      i = i + 1
      progBar.Value = i
   Loop

End Sub
```

13. The `PrintReportHeader Sub` procedure is the first of two procedures called by `cmdCreateReport` to print a report element. Isolating code like this makes it easier to write understandable code and localizes the formatting code you will likely need to tweak. This procedure sets the formatting options for the report title, prints the title, returns the formatting to normal by calling the `NormalRTF` procedure, and adds a date to the report. Note that all of the RichTextBox control's formatting options are set through its methods.

```
Private Sub PrintReportHeader()

    rtb1.SelAlignment = rtfCenter
    rtb1.SelBold = True
    rtb1.SelItalic = True
    rtb1.SelFontSize = 24

    rtb1.SelText = "Author's Bibliography List" _
        & vbCrLf & vbCrLf

    NormalRTF
    rtb1.SelText = Format$(Now, "Medium Date") & " " _
        & Format$(Now, "Medium Time") & vbCrLf & vbCrLf

End Sub
```

14. `cmdCreateReport` calls the `PrintAuthor Sub` procedure to print the author group header name and the list of titles. The code starts by printing the author name in bold italic and then changes back to the normal text. The `Do While` loop prints each of the author's titles, year published, and comments. Note that by using the RichTextBox control, you don't have to write code to break lines at logical places as you would when using Visual Basic's `Printer` object. The RichTextBox handles all that for you, and you can fine-tune it by setting the margin widths and using the `SelIndent` property of the RichTextBox.

```
Private Sub PrintAuthor(rsAuthors, rsTitles)
'Print each author's information. Assumes that the
'desired formatting is set before calling, and that
'line spacing before is set.
Dim sText As String

    rtb1.SelBold = True
    rtb1.SelItalic = True
    rtb1.SelText = rsAuthors("Author") & vbCrLf
    rtb1.SelBold = False
    rtb1.SelItalic = False

    rtb1.SelRightIndent = 720 'Half inch

    rsTitles.MoveFirst
    Do While Not rsTitles.EOF
```

```
rtb1.SelIndent = 720 'Half inch
rtb1.SelText = rsTitles("Title") & vbCrLf
rtb1.SelIndent = 1080

If Not IsNull(rsTitles("Year Published")) Then
    rtb1.SelText = "Year Published: " _
        & rsTitles("Year Published") & vbCrLf
End If

rtb1.SelIndent = 1440
If Not IsNull(rsTitles("Comments")) Then
    rtb1.SelText = rsTitles("Comments") & vbCrLf
End If

rsTitles.MoveNext
    Loop

rtb1.SelText = vbCrLf
rtb1.SelIndent = 0
rtb1.SelRightIndent = 0

End Sub
```

15. As a convenience to the end user, the cmdSetFormWidth_Click event resizes the form to show the report as it will appear when printed, including line breaks. If the monitor is not wide enough to show the full width of the form, the form is sized to the width of the monitor. If for any reason mlLineWidth hasn't yet been set, the form is not changed.

```
Private Sub cmdSetFormWidth_Click()
'Set the form width to match the line width, but only
'if mlLineWidth has been set.
Dim lWidth As Long

    If mlLineWidth Then
        lWidth = mlLineWidth + 200
        If lWidth > Screen.Width Then
            lWidth = Screen.Width
        End If

        If Me.WindowState = vbNormal Then
            Me.Width = lWidth
        End If

    End If
End Sub
```

16. Add the cmdPrint_Click event procedure to the form to send the report to the printer. Using the same margins used to create the report in the RichTextBox, the procedure calls the PrintRTF function in RTFPRINT.BAS (created in step 18). PrintRTF is roughly the equivalent of the cmdCreateReport_Click event procedure but sends the output to the printer.

```
Private Sub cmdPrint_Click()
Dim lLeftMargin As Long
Dim lRightMargin As Long
Dim lTopMargin As Long
Dim lBottomMargin As Long

    '1440 Twips=1 Inch
    lLeftMargin = Val(txtLeftMargin.Text) * 1440
    lRightMargin = Val(txtRightMargin.Text) * 1440
    lTopMargin = Val(txtTopMargin.Text) * 1440
    lBottomMargin = Val(txtBottomMargin.Text) * 1440

    ' Print the contents of the RichTextBox with a one
    'inch margin
    PrintRTF rtb1, lLeftMargin, lTopMargin, _
        lRightMargin, lBottomMargin ' 1440 Twips = 1 Inch
End Sub
```

17. Add the following code to the **Click** event of the **cmdClose** command button. This code ends the application by unloading the form.

```
Private Sub cmdClose_Click()
    Unload Me
End Sub
```

18. Add a new code module to the project by choosing Add Module from the Project menu, and save it as **RTFPRINT.BAS**. The following code is adapted from Microsoft KnowledgeBase article Q146022. It provides some handy routines for printing formatted text from the RichTextBox control.

19. Add the following code to the Declarations section of the code module. **Option Explicit** tells Visual Basic to make sure you declare all variables and objects before using them in order to avoid naming problems.

```
Option Explicit
```

20. Add the following code to the Declarations section of the code module. The three user-defined types and the constants are used with the three Windows API functions, which give access to various properties of the RichTextBox in order to print the contents as they appear onscreen.

```
Private Type Rect
    Left As Long
    Top As Long
    Right As Long
    Bottom As Long
End Type

Private Type CharRange
    cpMin As Long  ' First character of range (0 for start of doc)
```

```
      cpMax As Long   ' Last character of range (-1 for end of doc)
   End Type

   Private Type FormatRange
      hdc As Long         ' Actual DC to draw on
      hdcTarget As Long   ' Target DC for determining text formatting
      rc As Rect          ' Region of the DC to draw to (in twips)
      rcPage As Rect      ' Region of the entire DC (in twips)
      chrg As CharRange   ' Range of text to draw
   End Type

   Private Const WM_USER As Long = &H400
   Private Const EM_FORMATRANGE As Long = WM_USER + 57
   Private Const EM_SETTARGETDEVICE As Long = WM_USER + 72
   Private Const PHYSICALOFFSETX As Long = 112
   Private Const PHYSICALOFFSETY As Long = 113

   Private Declare Function GetDeviceCaps Lib "gdi32" ( _
      ByVal hdc As Long, ByVal nIndex As Long) As Long
   Private Declare Function SendMessage Lib "USER32" _
      Alias "SendMessageA" _
      (ByVal hWnd As Long, ByVal msg As Long, ByVal wp As Long, _
      lp As Any) As Long
   Private Declare Function CreateDC Lib "gdi32" _
      Alias "CreateDCA" _
      (ByVal lpDriverName As String, ByVal lpDeviceName As String, _
      ByVal lpOutput As Long, ByVal lpInitData As Long) As Long
```

21. Add the code for the `WYISWYG_RTF` function procedure, which sets an RTF
control to display as it would print on the default printer.

```
Public Function WYSIWYG_RTF(RTF As RichTextBox, _
   LeftMarginWidth As Long, _
   RightMarginWidth As Long) As Long
   Dim LeftOffset As Long
   Dim LeftMargin As Long
   Dim RightMargin As Long
   Dim LineWidth As Long
   Dim PrinterhDC As Long
   Dim r As Long

   ' Start a print job to initialize printer object
   Printer.Print Space(1)
   Printer.ScaleMode = vbTwips

   ' Get the offset to the printable area on the page in twips
   LeftOffset = Printer.ScaleX(GetDeviceCaps(Printer.hdc, _
      PHYSICALOFFSETX), vbPixels, vbTwips)

   ' Calculate the Left and Right margins
   LeftMargin = LeftMarginWidth - LeftOffset
   RightMargin = (Printer.Width - RightMarginWidth) - LeftOffset
```

continued on next page

continued from previous page

```
                        ' Calculate the line width
                        LineWidth = RightMargin - LeftMargin

                        ' Create an hDC on the Printer pointed to by the
                        'Printer object
                        ' This DC needs to remain for the RTF to keep up the
                        'WYSIWYG display
                        PrinterhDC = CreateDC(Printer.DriverName, _
                           Printer.DeviceName, 0, 0)

                        ' Tell the RTF to base its display off of the printer
                        '    at the desired line width
                        r = SendMessage(RTF.hWnd, EM_SETTARGETDEVICE, PrinterhDC, _
                           ByVal LineWidth)

                        ' Abort the temporary print job used to get printer info
                        Printer.KillDoc

                        WYSIWYG_RTF = LineWidth
                     End Function
```

22. Add the code for the **PrintRTF** procedure. This code prints the contents of a RichTextBox control using the specified margins.

```
Public Sub PrintRTF(RTF As RichTextBox, _
        LeftMarginWidth As Long, _
        TopMarginHeight As Long, _
        RightMarginWidth As Long, _
        BottomMarginHeight As Long)
    Dim LeftOffset As Long, TopOffset As Long
    Dim LeftMargin As Long, TopMargin As Long
    Dim RightMargin As Long, BottomMargin As Long
    Dim fr As FormatRange
    Dim rcDrawTo As Rect
    Dim rcPage As Rect
    Dim TextLength As Long
    Dim NextCharPosition As Long
    Dim r As Long

    ' Start a print job to get a valid Printer.hDC
    Printer.Print Space(1)
    Printer.ScaleMode = vbTwips

    ' Get the offset to the printable area on the page in twips
    LeftOffset = Printer.ScaleX(GetDeviceCaps(Printer.hdc, _
        PHYSICALOFFSETX), vbPixels, vbTwips)
    TopOffset = Printer.ScaleY(GetDeviceCaps(Printer.hdc, _
        PHYSICALOFFSETY), vbPixels, vbTwips)

    ' Calculate the Left, Top, Right, and Bottom margins
    LeftMargin = LeftMarginWidth - LeftOffset
    TopMargin = TopMarginHeight - TopOffset
    RightMargin = (Printer.Width - RightMarginWidth) - LeftOffset
```

```
            BottomMargin = (Printer.Height - BottomMarginHeight) _
                - TopOffset

            ' Set printable area rect
            rcPage.Left = 0
            rcPage.Top = 0
            rcPage.Right = Printer.ScaleWidth
            rcPage.Bottom = Printer.ScaleHeight

            ' Set rect in which to print (relative to printable area)
            rcDrawTo.Left = LeftMargin
            rcDrawTo.Top = TopMargin
            rcDrawTo.Right = RightMargin
            rcDrawTo.Bottom = BottomMargin

            ' Set up the print instructions
            ' Use the same DC for measuring and rendering
            fr.hdc = Printer.hdc
            fr.hdcTarget = Printer.hdc   ' Point at printer hDC
            ' Indicate the area on page to draw to
            fr.rc = rcDrawTo
            fr.rcPage = rcPage              ' Indicate entire size of page
            fr.chrg.cpMin = 0              ' Indicate start of text through
            fr.chrg.cpMax = -1            ' end of the text

            ' Get length of text in RTF
            TextLength = Len(RTF.Text)

            ' Loop printing each page until done
            Do
               ' Print the page by sending EM_FORMATRANGE message
               NextCharPosition = SendMessage(RTF.hWnd, EM_FORMATRANGE,
               ➥True, fr)
               If NextCharPosition >= TextLength Then Exit Do
               'If done then exit
               fr.chrg.cpMin = NextCharPosition
               ' Starting position for next page
               Printer.NewPage                    ' Move on to next page
            Loop

            ' Commit the print job
            Printer.EndDoc

            ' Allow the RTF to free up memory
            r = SendMessage(RTF.hWnd, EM_FORMATRANGE, False,
            ➥ByVal CLng(0))
        End Sub
```

23. In the Tools Project Options menu, choose Project Options from the Tools menu and set the startup form to frmPrint. You can also set an application description, but that is not required for the operation of this application.

How It Works

The code in this How-To uses code from the Microsoft KnowledgeBase article Q146022 about setting up the RichTextBox control for WYSIWYG printing. The `WYSIWYG_RTF` procedure uses a Windows device context (DC) to send an `EM_SETTARGETDEVICE` message to the RichTextBox control to base its display on a printer DC, so the procedure returns the length of each line. The `PrintRTF` then uses an `EM_FORMATRANGE` message to send a page at a time to the printer.

The `PrintHeader` and `PrintAuthor Sub` procedures demonstrate one way to format and add text to the RichTextBox control for repeating information of a database table grouped in this case by author. Using the RichTextBox gives you complete control and flexibility as to how you present the information, nested as deeply as you want, without the constraints of report writing tools. You can achieve a similar degree of flexibility by using OLE and a word processor such as Word for Windows or WordPerfect, but then all users must have access to a copy of the word processor. Because the RichTextBox control is included with Windows 95 and NT, you don't need to include any other files or programs with your application.

Comments

Before Visual Basic 4, the only option you had to print any type of document was the Visual Basic `Printer` object if you didn't want to use a third-party product. Programming a database report with the `Printer` object was tortuous at best because you had to keep track of your current location and where you were on the page, and you had to code for line breaks in the right places. The new Data Report Designer introduced in Visual Basic 6 is far better in most respects than Crystal Reports, but it limits you in some ways, stifling your creativity if you have a flair for the flamboyant.

In theory, you could use the regular Windows text box in the same way as the RichTextBox in this How-To, but the text box doesn't let you set different fonts and format different text in the document. It was also limited to 32KB of text, although you could actually expand that to almost 64KB. The text box option just isn't viable for a modern application.

The RichTextBox control provides many features needed for a database report. Besides handling line breaks, it lets you format the text almost any way you want. The first incarnation of the control has some fairly serious bugs, none of which affect this How-To, but it limits your capability to add graphics to a report. The control also has hooks to save the text to an `.RTF` disk file so that you don't have to code to save files. Probably the best part of the control is that it can handle unlimited text sizes.

COMPLEXITY
INTERMEDIATE

10.3 How do I...

Create a multiple query report using Word 97 and ActiveX?

COMPATIBILITY: VISUAL BASIC

Problem

I have several queries that I need to send to an ODBC datasource to produce a database report. But sending each query, producing its report, and then sending the next query is slow. How can I consolidate the dissimilar queries to produce my report more quickly?

Technique

Microsoft Access's Jet Engine and most back-end database servers support multiple queries and multiple resultsets. Using multiple queries can have a dramatic effect on your application's performance because sending multiple queries together in a single call to the back-end database system can obtain all the information needed to populate resultsets in your application. This How-To demonstrates combining multiple queries with Visual Basic's Remote Data Objects (RDOs) sent all at once to SQL Server—although the technique works with any database server that supports multiple queries—and using Microsoft Word to produce a custom database report via OLE.

Steps

Open and run the MULTIQ.VBP Visual Basic project file. The Multiple Query Report dialog box appears, and the application makes a connection to the Books Available datasource linked to the PUBS SQL Server sample database (see Figure 10.20).

The application then starts Microsoft Word and gets a Word.Basic OLE object used to create the report. Click Create Report to generate the three-part database report: a list of publishers, authors, and titles in the database. When the report is finished, as shown in Figure 10.21, the application activates Word so that you can preview, edit, and print the document.

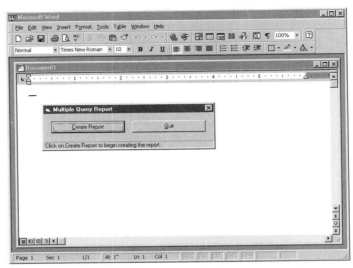

Figure 10.20 Using a Visual Basic form to create a database report based on a multiple `rdoResultset` query

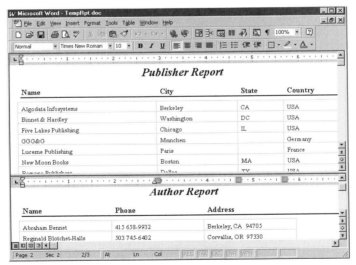

Figure 10.21 Using multiple queries and Microsoft Word to produce a database report

Return to the MultiQ application and click Quit to exit the application and leave Word running. Complete the following steps to create this project. This

How-To uses an ODBC SQL Server driver and the sample PUBS database included with SQL Server. You can use any other ODBC datasource or database, but you will need to change the fields connected to the form's text boxes.

1. Create a datasource name in ODBC for the PUBS database. Previous versions of ODBC required that you use the ODBC Data Source Administrator, **ODBCAD32.EXE**, usually located in the Windows System directory in Windows 95 or the System32 directory in Windows NT. The latest versions of ODBC install the Administrator as a Control Panel applet, listed as 32bit ODBC or simply as ODBC. (If you are using an older version of ODBC, the steps you take will differ from those listed here. Check the ODBC documentation for information.) ODBC Administrator displays the ODBC Data Source Administrator dialog box, as shown in Figure 10.22. Here you define and maintain datasource names available on this system.

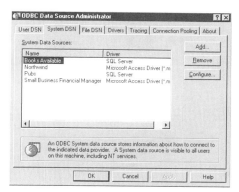

Figure 10.22 The ODBC Data
Source Administrator dialog box

2. Select the System DSN tab so that the datasource name you are about to create will be available to any user on the system. Click Add, and the Create a New Data Source dialog box appears. The driver you need will be listed as something like SQL Server or SQL Server (32-bit). Click this driver and then click Finish. The Create a New Data Source to SQL Server Wizard appears. Each ODBC driver has its own version of this wizard, prompting for the particular information the driver needs to make a connection with its database. Enter the information shown in Table 10.5 as you step through the wizard. For any items not listed in the table, use the defaults. You might have to adjust other entries not listed in the table for your system setup. When you reach the last screen in the wizard, click Finish to create the datasource name.

Table 10.5 Setup information for the books available datasource name

PROMPT	INFORMATION TO ENTER
Data Source Name	Books Available
Description	Optional description information to identify the datasource
Server	The server where SQL Server is located
Database Name	PUBS
Login ID authenticity	Check with your database administrator for this information
Default Database	Mark the check box to enable the list box PUBS

3. The ODBC Microsoft SQL Server Setup dialog box appears, as shown in Figure 10.23. The text box lists all the settings for this new datasource name. Click Test Data Source to test the connection to SQL Server. If you receive an error message, go back and verify the settings, particularly those for authenticating the login ID. Click OK when everything works.

Figure 10.23 Using the ODBC Microsoft SQL Server Setup dialog box to validate and test a new datasource name

4. The new Books Available datasource name appears in the Data Sources window as something like Books Available with a driver listed as SQL Server. Click OK to end the ODBC Data Source Administrator.

5. Start Visual Basic. Create a new project called MULTIQ.VBP. Add the form ERRORRDO.FRM (see How-To 2.1 in Chapter 2 for a description of this form) using Visual Basic's Add File command from the Project menu. This form handles RDO errors.

6. Choose Components from the Project menu and select the following custom controls:

> Microsoft Common Dialog Control 6.0
>
> Microsoft Windows Common Controls 6.0

Disable all the other check boxes so that your project isn't cluttered with controls you aren't using and the Setup Wizard doesn't include a lot of dead weight with your application.

7. Choose References from the Project menu and select the following references:

> Microsoft Visual Basic for Applications
>
> Visual Basic Runtime Objects and Procedures
>
> Microsoft Remote Data Object 2.0

Disable all the other check boxes so that your project isn't cluttered with DLLs you aren't using and the Setup Wizard doesn't include a lot of dead weight with your application.

8. Add the controls shown in Figure 10.20 to the form in the new project, with the property settings listed in Table 10.6. Save the form as `MULTIQ.FRM`.

Table 10.6 Objects and properties for `MULTIQ.FRM`

OBJECT	PROPERTY	SETTING
Form	Name	frmMultiQuery
	BackColor	&H00C0C0C0&
	Caption	"Multiple Query Report"
CommandButton	Name	cmdReport
	Caption	"&Create Report"
	Default	-1 'True
CommandButton	Name	cmdQuit
	Caption	"&Quit"
StatusBar	Name	StatusBar1
	Align	2 'Align Bottom
	AlignSet	-1 'True
	Style	1
	SimpleText	""

9. Add the following code to the Declarations section of the form. `Option Explicit` tells Visual Basic to make sure that you declare all variables and objects before using them in order to avoid naming problems. The `mobjWord` object variable holds the OLE object obtained from Microsoft Word. The `mColumn` array variables are used in the three different parts of the report to format tabs and table columns. The third set of variables are the RDOs used to make the connection with the Books Available SQL Server datasource.

```
Option Explicit

Dim mobjWord As Object

Dim mColumnTabs() As String
Dim mColumnHeaders() As String
Dim mColumnWidths() As String

'Remote Data Object variables
Private mrdoEnv As rdoEnvironment
Private mrdoConn As rdoConnection
Private mrdoRS As rdoResultset
```

10. Add the following code to the form's **Load** event procedure. This procedure does two primary tasks in preparation for creating the report: It makes the connection to the Books Available datasource and gets an OLE object from Microsoft Word. If the datasource cannot be connected, the form unloads itself and ends the application.

```
Private Sub Form_Load()
Dim iSaveCursor As Integer

    cmdReport.Enabled = False
    cmdQuit.Enabled = False

    iSaveCursor = Me.MousePointer
    Me.MousePointer = vbHourglass

    Me.Show
    Me.Refresh

    'Open the Books Available data source
    Status "Connecting to Books Available data source."
    If Not OpenDataSource() Then
       MsgBox "Couldn't open Books Available data source. " _
          & "Ending application.", vbOKOnly, "Data Source Error"
       Unload Me
       Exit Sub
    End If
```

The next set of code makes the connection to Word by first starting Word itself. This isn't strictly necessary, but in this case, the application uses the Word user interface to display the report, let the end user make changes, and print the report. These tasks can just as easily be controlled from your application by manipulating the Word object; the `GetObject` and `CreateObject` methods then start an invisible instance of Word.

```
'Create a Microsoft Word object
   DoEvents
   Status "Starting Word."
   If Not StartWord() Then
      MsgBox "Couldn't start Word for Windows. " _
         & "Ending application.", vbOKOnly, "Error Starting Word"
      Unload Me
      Exit Sub
   End If
```

After Word starts, `GetObject` gets a `Word.Basic` object and sets it to the `mobjWord` object variable.

```
Status "Creating a Word object"
   Set mobjWord = GetObject("", "Word.Basic")

   cmdReport.Enabled = True
   cmdQuit.Enabled = True

   Status "Click on Create Report to begin creating the report."
   Me.MousePointer = iSaveCursor

End Sub
```

11. Add the `OpenDataSource` function procedure. This is the procedure that opens the connection to the Books Available datasource using Visual Basic's RDOs. After making the connection using the `OpenConnection` method, the `rdoDefaultCursorDriver` is set to `rdUseServer`. `rdUseServer` tells the RDO to use the back-end SQL Server database to manage the resultset cursors, which will be retrieved one at a time.

The SQL statement in the code contains three queries. The first retrieves all the publisher names from the Publisher table and sorts them on `pub_name`. The second retrieves the list of authors from the Authors table and sorts the list by last name and then first name. The third query retrieves a list of titles from the Titles table, pulling the associated publisher data from the Publisher table. Note that in the final `sSQL` string, the three queries are separated by semicolons. You can use an essentially unlimited number of queries, not all of which need to be the same type. You just as easily could have included an **UPDATE** query to update a publisher's address at the same time.

When the SQL statement is ready, the code creates a prepared statement to generate a **psBooks** statement in SQL Server. You can also directly use the **OpenResultset** statement without using a prepared statement.

In case of an error while making the remote data connection, the **frmRDOErrors** displays the full error returned by SQL Server, the ODBC driver, and the RDO. Because any tier along the connection path can raise an error, you must be sure to obtain all errors to pinpoint the problem. See How-To 2.1 in Chapter 2 for more details about this procedure.

```
Private Function OpenDataSource()
Dim sSQL As String
Dim rdoPS As rdoPreparedStatement

    'Allocate an ODBC environment handle
    Set mrdoEnv = rdoEnvironments(0)
    Set mrdoConn = mrdoEnv.OpenConnection("Books Available", _
        rdDriverComplete, False, "ODBC;UID=sa;PWD=")
    rdoDefaultCursorDriver = rdUseServer

    sSQL = "SELECT * FROM publishers ORDER BY pub_name; "
    sSQL = sSQL & "SELECT * FROM authors " _
        & "ORDER BY au_lname, au_fname; "
    sSQL = sSQL & _
        "SELECT titles.*, publishers.* " _
        & "FROM titles, publishers " _
        & "WHERE publishers.pub_id = titles.pub_id " _
        & "ORDER BY titles.Title ASC;"

    On Error GoTo OpenDataSourceError
    Set rdoPS = mrdoConn.CreatePreparedStatement("psBooks", "")
    rdoPS.SQL = sSQL
    rdoPS.RowsetSize = 1

    Set mrdoRS = rdoPS.OpenResultset(rdOpenForwardOnly)
    'Set mrdoRS = mrdoConn.OpenResultset(sSQL, rdOpenForwardOnly)
    OpenDataSource = True
    Exit Function

OpenDataSourceError:
    frmRDOErrors.ErrorColl = rdoErrors
    OpenDataSource = False

End Function
```

12. Add the **StartWord** function procedure code that follows. This procedure starts Word so that the end user can use its features to modify and print the report rather than code these features into the Visual Basic application. The procedure starts by using the Windows API function **FindExecutable** to find the program associated in the Registry with ***.DOC** files. Because this function requires a full filename of a Word document, you use the

TempRpt.doc file generated by this How-To's program, located in the application directory. There are other ways to get this information, such as by searching the Registry, but this technique is reliable in most cases because most end users will not change the association established by the Word installation program.

FindExecutable returns error codes between 0 and 32, so if the result code is greater than 32, sFileName contains the full path and filename for Word. The code strips the terminating null character from this string and then uses Visual Basic's Shell function to start Word. The AppActivate statement sets focus to Word. Then the form's SetFocus method returns to the MultiQ application so that the end user can start generating the report.

```
Private Function StartWord()
Dim sFileName As String
Dim iResult As Integer
Dim lResult As Long

    sFileName = Space$(128)
    iResult = FindExecutable("TempRpt.doc", App.Path, sFileName)

    If iResult > 32 Then
        sFileName = Left$(sFileName, Len(sFileName) - 1)
        lResult = Shell(sFileName, vbNormalNoFocus)
        StartWord = True
        AppActivate App.Title
        Me.SetFocus
    Else
        StartWord = False
    End If

End Function
```

13. After the connection to Books Available is made and Word has started, the end user can click the cmdReport command button to generate the report. Add the following code to the button's Click event procedure. The procedure starts by using the mobjWord object's DocRestore method to restore the active document's MDI child window in case it is minimized or maximized. If it is minimized, the end user isn't able to see the report as it is generated; if it is maximized, you cannot use the AppActivate statement to switch to Word because the document's name will be in the title bar.

The next bit of code sets the page formatting for all three of the reports. By setting these properties before adding any text to the document, the changes will apply to all three reports.

The code then generates the three reports in succession. The mrdoRS resultset variable contains the first of the three resultsets from the multiple query created in the OpenDataSource function. After the code is finished with the first rdoResultset, it uses the MoreResults method to check whether there are more results (no surprise there). But `MoreResults` also closes the first `rdoResultset`, making the second `rdoResultset` active and available for use. This is an example of how the RDO manages the SQL Server cursors for your application.

The rest of the code in this procedure saves the report, using a `TEMPRPT.DOC` filename, after first turning off Word's Summary prompt so that the dialog box won't appear. It then moves to the top of the document and makes Word the active application so the end user can review the report.

```
Private Sub cmdReport_Click()
Dim sFileName As String
Dim iSaveCursor As Integer

    iSaveCursor = Me.MousePointer
    Me.MousePointer = vbHourglass

    cmdReport.Enabled = False

    Status "Creating a new Word document"
    mobjWord.FileNew
    'Restore the document so we can use AppActivate
    'with "Microsoft Word"
    On Error Resume Next
    mobjWord.DocRestore
    On Error GoTo 0

    With mobjWord
        .FilePageSetup TopMargin:="0.8" + Chr$(34), _
            BottomMargin:="0.8" + Chr$(34), _
            LeftMargin:="0.75" + Chr$(34), _
            RightMargin:="0.75" + Chr$(34), _
            ApplyPropsTo:=0, _
            DifferentFirstPage:=0
    End With

    PrintPublishers

    If mrdoRS.MoreResults Then
        mobjWord.EndOfDocument
        mobjWord.insertbreak Type:=2 'Break, new page
        PrintAuthors
    End If
    If mrdoRS.MoreResults Then
        mobjWord.EndOfDocument
        mobjWord.insertbreak Type:=2 'Break, new page
        PrintTitles
    End If

    'Save the Word document
    mobjWord.ToolsOptionsSave SummaryPrompt:=0

    sFileName = App.Path & "\TempRpt.doc"
    'Word won't let us save over an existing document
```

```
        If Len(Dir(sFileName)) Then
            Kill sFileName
        End If
        mobjWord.FileSaveAs Name:=sFileName

        Status "Report complete"
        mobjWord.StartOfDocument
        AppActivate "Microsoft Word"
        Me.MousePointer = iSaveCursor

End Sub
```

14. The next several procedures generate the three reports, using the
`mobjWord` object variable and its methods and properties to format and
insert text. First you'll look at the three procedures that generate the
reports and then you'll examine the support procedures. The first report
lists the publishers, so enter this code for the `PrintPublishers Sub`
procedure. The procedure uses the `mColumnTabs`, `mColumnHeaders`, and
`mColumnWidths` arrays to set up the columns used for each field in the
report. `mColumnTabs` sets the widths of the columns based on the tab
spacing of the column header. The `SetColumnWidths` procedure uses this
array to calculate the table's column widths.

The next set of code uses these arrays to print the report header and footer
for the Publishers report, adding the `SortaMarvelous Software` company
name to the bottom of the report. The `TableInsertTable` Word function
inserts a table into the document. The code then formats the column
widths of the new table using the `mColumnWidths` array.

After the table is formatted properly, a `Do While` loop moves through the
current `mrdoRS rdoResultset`, adding field data to each cell in the table.
Note that because the `mrdoRS` was created as a forward-only cursor to be
more efficient, you cannot move back and forth through the
`rdoResultset`. For example, if you try to use the `MoveFirst` method on
the `mrdoRS` object, the RDO generates an error even if you are at the first
record.

```
Private Sub PrintPublishers()
Dim sTitle As String
Dim iColumns As Integer
Dim i As Integer
Dim sInsertText As String
Dim iColCount As Integer

    sTitle = "Publisher Report"
    Status "Setting up report"

    'Set up standard layout information
    iColCount = 4
    ReDim mColumnTabs(iColCount - 1)
```

continued on next page

continued from previous page

```
mColumnTabs(0) = "3.0"
mColumnTabs(1) = "4.75"
mColumnTabs(2) = "5.75"
mColumnTabs(3) = "7.0"

ReDim mColumnHeaders(iColCount)
mColumnHeaders(0) = "Name"
mColumnHeaders(1) = "City"
mColumnHeaders(2) = "State"
mColumnHeaders(3) = "Country"

ReDim mColumnWidths(iColCount)
SetColumnWidths

Status "Inserting header and footer information"

'PrintHeader sTitle, mColumnTabs(), mColumnHeaders()
PrintFooter "SortaMarvelous Software, Inc."
PrintReportTitle sTitle
PrintColHeaders mColumnTabs(), mColumnHeaders()

'Start printing the report
Status "Adding data to report"

mobjWord.TableInsertTable NumColumns:=iColCount, _
NumRows:=2, _
InitialColWidth:="2 in"

For i = 0 To iColCount
   With mobjWord
      .TableSelectColumn
      .TableColumnWidth ColumnWidth:=mColumnWidths(i)
      .NextCell
      .NextCell
   End With
Next

'Format the paragraph height
mobjWord.TableSelectTable
mobjWord.FormatParagraph Before:="6 pt"

'Select the first cell in the table
'mobjWord.TableSelectColumn
mobjWord.NextCell

Do While Not mrdoRS.EOF
   With mobjWord
      sInsertText = mrdoRS("pub_name") & ""
      .Insert sInsertText
      .NextCell
      sInsertText = mrdoRS("City") & ""
      .Insert sInsertText
      .NextCell
      sInsertText = mrdoRS("State") & ""
      .Insert sInsertText
```

```
            .NextCell
            sInsertText = mrdoRS("Country") & ""
            .Insert sInsertText
            .NextCell
            .TableInsertRow
        End With
        mrdoRS.MoveNext
    Loop

End Sub
```

15. Add the following code for the **PrintAuthors Sub** procedure. This procedure works like the **PrintPublishers** procedure, changing only to use the fields from the Authors table.

```
Private Sub PrintAuthors()
Dim sTitle As String
Dim iColumns As Integer
Dim i As Integer
Dim sInsertText As String
Dim iColCount As Integer

    sTitle = "Author Report"
    Status "Setting up report"

    'Set up standard layout information
    iColCount = 3
    ReDim mColumnTabs(iColCount - 1)
    mColumnTabs(0) = "2.0"
    mColumnTabs(1) = "4.0"
    mColumnTabs(2) = "6.0"

    ReDim mColumnHeaders(iColCount)
    mColumnHeaders(0) = "Name"
    mColumnHeaders(1) = "Phone"
    mColumnHeaders(2) = "Address"

    ReDim mColumnWidths(iColCount)
    SetColumnWidths

    Status "Inserting header and footer information"

'    PrintHeader sTitle, mColumnTabs(), mColumnHeaders()
'    PrintFooter "SortaMarvelous Software, Inc."
    PrintReportTitle sTitle
    PrintColHeaders mColumnTabs(), mColumnHeaders()

    'Start printing the report
    Status "Adding data to report"

    mobjWord.TableInsertTable NumColumns:=iColCount, _
    NumRows:=2, _
    InitialColWidth:="2 in"
```

continued on next page

continued from previous page

```
For i = 0 To iColCount
    With mobjWord
        .TableSelectColumn
        .TableColumnWidth ColumnWidth:=mColumnWidths(i)
        .NextCell
        .NextCell
    End With
Next

'Format the paragraph height
mobjWord.TableSelectTable
mobjWord.FormatParagraph Before:="6 pt"

'Select the first cell in the table
'mobjWord.TableSelectColumn
mobjWord.NextCell

Do While Not mrdoRS.EOF
    With mobjWord
        sInsertText = mrdoRS("au_fname") & " " _
            & mrdoRS("au_lname") & ""
        .Insert sInsertText
        .NextCell
        sInsertText = mrdoRS("phone") & ""
        .Insert sInsertText
        .NextCell
        sInsertText = mrdoRS("city") & ", " _
            & mrdoRS("state") & "  " _
            & mrdoRS("zip") & ""
        .Insert sInsertText
        .NextCell
        .TableInsertRow
    End With
    mrdoRS.MoveNext
Loop

End Sub
```

16. Add the following code for the **PrintTitles Sub** procedure. This procedure again works much like the **PrintPublishers** procedure but has a few new twists to better format the numerical data included in this part of the report, using Visual Basic's **Format$** function to add dollar signs and percent signs and to keep the numbers aligned vertically.

```
Private Sub PrintTitles()
Dim sTitle As String
Dim iColumns As Integer
Dim i As Integer
Dim sInsertText As String
Dim iColCount As Integer

    sTitle = "Titles Report"
    Status "Setting up report"
```

```
'Set up standard layout information
iColCount = 6
ReDim mColumnTabs(iColCount - 1)
mColumnTabs(0) = "2.0"
mColumnTabs(1) = "3.65"
mColumnTabs(2) = "4.25"
mColumnTabs(3) = "5.0"
mColumnTabs(4) = "6.0"
mColumnTabs(5) = "7.0"

ReDim mColumnHeaders(iColCount)
mColumnHeaders(0) = "Title"
mColumnHeaders(1) = "Publisher"
mColumnHeaders(2) = "Price"
mColumnHeaders(3) = "Advance"
mColumnHeaders(4) = "Royalty"
mColumnHeaders(5) = "YTD Sales"

ReDim mColumnWidths(iColCount)
SetColumnWidths

Status "Inserting header and footer information for titles."

PrintReportTitle sTitle
PrintColHeaders mColumnTabs(), mColumnHeaders()

'Start printing the report
Status "Adding data to report"

mobjWord.TableInsertTable NumColumns:=iColCount, _
NumRows:=2, _
InitialColWidth:="2 in"

For i = 0 To iColCount
    With mobjWord
        .TableSelectColumn
        .TableColumnWidth ColumnWidth:=mColumnWidths(i)
        .NextCell
        .NextCell
    End With
Next

'Format the paragraph height
mobjWord.TableSelectTable
mobjWord.FormatParagraph Before:="6 pt"

'Select the first cell in the table
'mobjWord.TableSelectColumn
mobjWord.NextCell

Do While Not mrdoRS.EOF
    With mobjWord
        sInsertText = mrdoRS("title") & ""
        .Insert sInsertText
        .NextCell
```

continued on next page

continued from previous page

```
                                sInsertText = mrdoRS("pub_name") & ""
                                .Insert sInsertText
                                .NextCell
                                sInsertText = Format$(mrdoRS("price"), "Currency")
                                .RightPara
                                .Insert sInsertText
                                .NextCell
                                sInsertText = Format$(mrdoRS("advance"), "$#,##0")
                                .RightPara
                                .Insert sInsertText
                                .NextCell
                                sInsertText = Format$(mrdoRS("royalty") / 100, "#0%")
                                .RightPara
                                .Insert sInsertText
                                .NextCell
                                sInsertText = Format$(mrdoRS("ytd_sales"), "$#,##0")
                                .RightPara
                                .Insert sInsertText
                                .NextCell
                                .TableInsertRow
                        End With
                        mrdoRS.MoveNext
                Loop

        End Sub
```

17. The `SetColumnWidths` Sub procedure is the first of the support procedures used in all three of the report sections. This procedure takes the tabs set in the `mColumnTabs` array (which are text values) to easily use them with the `mobjWord` object, and it calculates the distances between them to set the column widths.

```
Private Sub SetColumnWidths()
    Dim i As Integer
    For i = LBound(mColumnTabs) To UBound(mColumnTabs)
        If i Then
            mColumnWidths(i) = Str$(Val(mColumnTabs(i)) _
                - Val(mColumnTabs(i - 1)))
        Else
            mColumnWidths(i) = mColumnTabs(i)
        End If
    Next
End Sub
```

18. Add the following code for the `PrintHeader` Sub procedure. This code uses the `ViewHeader` and `ToggleHeaderFooterLink` to add headers and footers to this part of the report. It also calls the `PrintColHeaders` procedure to add column headings.

```
Private Sub PrintHeader(Title As String, Tabs() As String, _
ColHeaders() As String)
Dim i As Integer

    'Insert the report header
    With mobjWord
       .ViewHeader
       .ToggleHeaderFooterLink
       .FormatTabs ClearAll:=1
       .FormatTabs Position:="7.0" + Chr$(34), _
          DefTabs:="0.5" + Chr$(34), _
          Align:=2
       .StartOfLine
       .SelectCurSentence
       .CharRight 1, 1
       .FormatFont Points:="12", _
          Font:="Times New Roman", _
          Bold:=1
       .StartOfLine
       .Insert Title + Chr$(9)
       .InsertDateTime DateTimePic:="d' 'MMMM', 'yyyy", _
          InsertAsField:=0
       .InsertPara
       .InsertPara
    End With

    PrintColHeaders Tabs(), ColHeaders()

    mobjWord.ViewHeader    'Closes if it is open

    'Give it a chance to catch up
    DoEvents

End Sub
```

19. Add the following code to the **PrintFooter Sub** procedure. This procedure is similar to the **PrintHeader** procedure.

```
Private Sub PrintFooter(Company As String)

    'Insert the report footer
    mobjWord.ViewFooter
    mobjWord.FormatTabs ClearAll:=1
    mobjWord.FormatTabs Position:="7.0" + Chr$(34), _
       DefTabs:="0.5" + Chr$(34), _
       Align:=2, _
       Leader:=0
    mobjWord.StartOfLine
    mobjWord.Insert Company + Chr$(9) + "Page "
    mobjWord.InsertPageField
    mobjWord.SelectCurSentence
    mobjWord.FormatFont Points:="12", _
```

continued on next page

continued from previous page

```
            Font:="Times New Roman", _
            Bold:=1

    mobjWord.ViewFooter

    'Give it a chance to catch up
    DoEvents

End Sub
```

20. The `PrintReportTitle` `Sub` procedure prints the report title for this section of the report, printing the name in bold and nonitalic text.

```
Private Sub PrintReportTitle(Title As String)
    With mobjWord
        .InsertPara
        .LineUp
        .Insert Title
        .StartOfLine
        .SelectCurSentence
        .FormatFont Points:="18", _
            Font:="Times New Roman", _
            Bold:=1, _
            Italic:=1
        .CenterPara

        .FormatBordersAndShading ApplyTo:=0, _
            Shadow:=0

        'Leave the cursor on the following line
        .LineDown
    End With

    'Give it a chance to catch up
    DoEvents

End Sub
```

21. Add the following code for the `PrintColHeaders` `Sub` procedure. Using the column arrays, this procedure inserts the column headers for this part of the report.

```
Private Sub PrintColHeaders(Tabs() As String, _
ColHeaders() As String)
Dim i As Integer
Dim iAlign As Integer

    'Assumes cursor is at the beginning of the proper location
    mobjWord.InsertPara
    mobjWord.LineUp
    mobjWord.FormatParagraph Before:="12 pt", _
        After:="6 pt"

    For i = 0 To UBound(Tabs)
        Select Case Right$(Tabs(i), 1)
```

```
            Case "R"
               iAlign = 2 'Right align
               Tabs(i) = Left$(Tabs(i), Len(Tabs(i)) - 1)
            Case "C"
               iAlign = 1 'Center align
               Tabs(i) = Left$(Tabs(i), Len(Tabs(i)) - 1)
            Case "D"
               iAlign = 3 'Decimal align
               Tabs(i) = Left$(Tabs(i), Len(Tabs(i)) - 1)
            Case "B"
               iAlign = 4 'Bar
               Tabs(i) = Left$(Tabs(i), Len(Tabs(i)) - 1)
            Case Else
               iAlign = 0 'Left align
         End Select

         mobjWord.FormatTabs Position:=Tabs(i) + Chr$(34), _
            Align:=iAlign
      Next
      For i = 0 To UBound(ColHeaders) - 1
         mobjWord.Insert ColHeaders(i) + Chr$(9)
      Next

      With mobjWord
         .StartOfLine
         .SelectCurSentence
         .CharRight 1, 1
         .FormatFont Points:="12", _
            Font:="Times New Roman", _
            Bold:=1
         .FormatBordersAndShading ApplyTo:=0, _
            BottomBorder:=2
         .LineDown
      End With

      'Give it a chance to catch up
      DoEvents

   End Sub
```

22. Add the following code to the **Status Sub** procedure. At various points
throughout the application, status messages are sent to the **StatusBar**
control at the bottom of the form to keep the end user apprised of what is
happening.

```
Sub Status(sCaption)
   StatusBar1.SimpleText = sCaption
   StatusBar1.Refresh
End Sub
```

23. Add the following code for the **cmdQuit** command button's **Click** event
procedure and the form's **Unload** event procedure. This code ends the
application by unloading the form and setting the module-level object
variables to **Nothing**.

```
Private Sub cmdQuit_Click()
    Status "Ending application"
    Unload Me
End Sub

Private Sub Form_Unload(Cancel As Integer)
    'Shut down Word
    Set mobjWord = Nothing

    Set mrdoEnv = Nothing
    Set mrdoConn = Nothing
    Set mrdoRS = Nothing

End Sub
```

24. Add a new code module to the project by choosing Add Module from the Project menu. Save the file as COMMON.BAS and set its module name in the property's window as basCommon.

25. Add the following code to the Declarations section of the module. The sole purpose of the code module is to contain the Declare statement for the FindExecutable API function.

```
Option Explicit

Declare Function FindExecutable Lib "shell32.dll" _
    Alias "FindExecutableA" (ByVal lpFile As String, _
    ByVal lpDirectory As String, _
    ByVal lpResult As String) As Long
```

26. In the Tools Project Options menu, choose Project Options from the Tools menu and set the startup form to frmMultiQuery. You can also set an application description, but that is not required for the operation of this application.

How It Works

Many back-end database servers enable you to create multiple query strings that contain more than one query. One of the advantages of this technique is that it reduces the amount of network traffic because only one SQL statement string is sent to the database server, which can also manage the cursor for the resultsets. This How-To used a SQL string that looks like the following with all the Visual Basic operators used in the code stripped away:

```
SELECT * FROM publishers ORDER BY pub_name;
SELECT * FROM authors ORDER BY au_lname, au_fname;
SELECT titles.*, publishers.* FROM titles, publishers
    WHERE publishers.pub_id = titles.pub_id
    ORDER BY titles.Title ASC;"
```

Here is another example of a valid multiple query string that uses different types of queries in the same string:

```
SELECT * FROM publishers ORDER BY pub_name;
UPDATE Publishers SET City = 'Fairbanks' WHERE pub_id = '1389';
SELECT titles.*, publishers.* FROM titles, publishers
   WHERE publishers.pub_id = titles.pub_id
   ORDER BY titles.Title ASC;"
```

Some SQL Server stored procedures return multiple resultsets; you use the same technique with `MoreResults` with this type of query.

`MoreResults` clears the current `rdoResultset` and returns a Boolean value that indicates whether one or more additional resultsets are waiting. If there are no additional resultsets to process, the `MoreResults` method returns `False` and the RDO's `BOF` and `EOF` properties are set to `True`. Using the `MoreResults` method flushes the current `rdoResultset`, so be sure that you are finished with the current resultset before using the `MoreResults` method. You can also use the RDO's `Cancel` method to flush the contents of an `rdoResultset`, but `Cancel` also flushes any additional resultsets not yet processed.

Comments

The `FindExecutable` API function used in this How-To is only one way to find the WinWord application associated in Windows with a `.DOC` file. Using this method assumes that the end user hasn't changed the association for `.DOC` files, and this is probably a pretty safe assumption. You can always fall back on other methods, such as prompting the end user for the `.EXE` file location, searching the Windows Registry directly, or even searching the hard drive directly. In any event, you should include code for the possibility that the computer doesn't have access to Word either locally or over the network via remote automation. You can include this check in your application or the installation program.

Most of the rest of the code in this How-To manages the `Word.Basic` object variable `mobjWord`. It's a lot of code but is still far less than trying to code the same features using the Visual Basic `Printer` object, taking advantage of the features built into Microsoft Word or any other word processor of choice. The use of the `Word.Basic` object is designed to use the monolithic object in Word 7.0 and earlier versions. Later versions of Word use a more complex object model that gives you finer control over the objects, but it should still work with this code.

If the format of the data presentation is known beforehand, you can create a Word document that serves as a template. This document would include fields and bookmarks, which can then be called from VB to place the resultset accordingly.

COMPLEXITY
ADVANCED

10.4 How do I...
Create a pivot table and chart using Excel 97 and ActiveX?

COMPATIBILITY: VISUAL BASIC

Problem

I have a large database of information that includes many pieces of data for each of the company's salespeople, tracking their performance over the last 10 years. How can I analyze the data using Visual Basic to put it into a meaningful form and display it in such a way that even top management can use and understand it?

Technique

The code in this How-To demonstrates creating a pivot table and chart using a Visual Basic RDO to query a SQL Server database, adding the data to an Excel worksheet using a worksheet OLE object provided by Excel, and creating a chart based on the pivot table—again through OLE. The code keeps the table and chart logic separate so that you can easily create just a pivot table without a chart.

A pivot table is one way to display data that has a relatively small set of entities, each of which has a relatively high number of pieces of data in the database. A pivot table summarizes, or cross-tabulates, large amounts of data. For example, you might have a table with the percentage population change for the 10 largest cities in the country for each of the last 15 years. By using a pivot table, you can display the data to show how the population changed by year or by city.

Steps

Start Microsoft Excel and open and run the **PIVOT.VBP** Visual Basic project file. The project's Data Analysis form appears, and the application obtains a worksheet object from the Excel Object Library (see Figure 10.24).

Figure 10.24 Using a Visual Basic form to create a pivot table and chart with Microsoft Excel

Click Load Spreadsheet; the application connects to the Books Available SQL Server database, producing the data and pivot table shown in Figure 10.25.

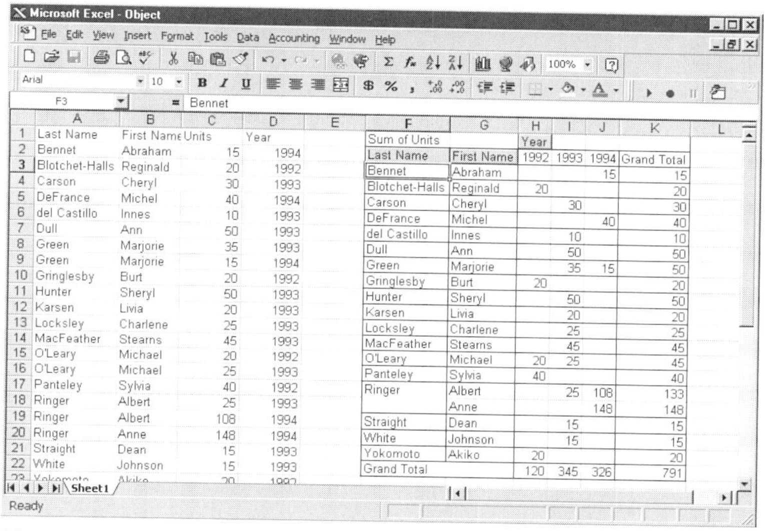

Data table (columns A–D):

Last Name	First Name	Units	Year
Bennet	Abraham	15	1994
Blotchet-Halls	Reginald	20	1992
Carson	Cheryl	30	1993
DeFrance	Michel	40	1994
del Castillo	Innes	10	1993
Dull	Ann	50	1993
Green	Marjorie	35	1993
Green	Marjorie	15	1994
Gringlesby	Burt	20	1992
Hunter	Sheryl	50	1993
Karsen	Livia	20	1993
Locksley	Charlene	25	1993
MacFeather	Stearns	45	1993
O'Leary	Michael	20	1992
O'Leary	Michael	25	1993
Panteley	Sylvia	40	1992
Ringer	Albert	25	1993
Ringer	Albert	108	1994
Ringer	Anne	148	1994
Straight	Dean	15	1993
White	Johnson	15	1993
Yokomoto	Akiko	20	1992

Pivot table (Sum of Units):

Last Name	First Name	1992	1993	1994	Grand Total
Bennet	Abraham			15	15
Blotchet-Halls	Reginald	20			20
Carson	Cheryl		30		30
DeFrance	Michel			40	40
del Castillo	Innes		10		10
Dull	Ann		50		50
Green	Marjorie		35	15	50
Gringlesby	Burt	20			20
Hunter	Sheryl		50		50
Karsen	Livia		20		20
Locksley	Charlene		25		25
MacFeather	Stearns		45		45
O'Leary	Michael	20	25		45
Panteley	Sylvia	40			40
Ringer	Albert		25	108	133
	Anne			148	148
Straight	Dean		15		15
White	Johnson		15		15
Yokomoto	Akiko	20			20
Grand Total		120	345	326	791

Figure 10.25 A pivot table using an RDO and Microsoft Excel

The data on the left is the result of the query added to the worksheet, and the table on the right is the pivot table based on the data. Return to the Pivot application and click Create Chart to create a stacked column chart in Excel, as shown in Figure 10.26.

Click Quit to quit the application. To create this project, complete the following steps. This How-To uses an ODBC SQL Server driver and the sample PUBS database included with SQL Server. You can use any other ODBC datasource or database, but you will need to change the fields connected to the form's text boxes.

1. Create a datasource name in ODBC for the PUBS database. Previous versions of ODBC required that you use the ODBC Data Source Administrator, **ODBCAD32.EXE**, usually located in the Windows System directory in Windows 95 or the System32 directory in Windows NT. The latest versions of ODBC install the Administrator as a Control Panel applet, listed as 32bit ODBC or simply as ODBC. (If you are using an older version of ODBC, the steps you take will differ from those listed here. Check the ODBC documentation for information.) ODBC Administrator loads the ODBC Data Source Administrator dialog box (refer to Figure 10.22). Here you define and maintain datasource names available on this system.

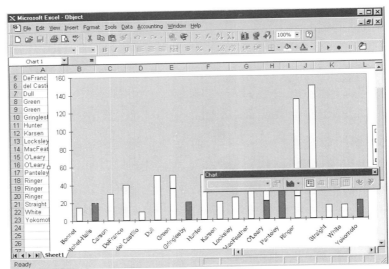

Figure 10.26 Creating an editable chart based on the pivot
table

2. Select the System DSN tab so that the datasource name you are about to
create will be available to any user on the system. Click Add so that the
Create a New Data Source window appears. The driver you need will be
listed as something like SQL Server or SQL Server (32-bit). Click this
driver, and then click Finish. The Create a New Data Source to SQL Server
Wizard appears. Each ODBC driver has its own version of this wizard,
prompting for the particular information the driver needs to make a
connection with its database. Enter the information shown in Table 10.5
as you step through the wizard. For any items not listed in the table, use
the defaults. You might have to adjust other entries not listed in the table
for your system setup. When you reach the last screen in the wizard, click
Finish to create the datasource name.

3. The ODBC Microsoft SQL Server Setup dialog box appears (refer to Figure
10.23). The text box lists all the settings for this new datasource name.
Click Test Data Source to test the connection to SQL Server. If you receive
an error message, go back and verify the settings, particularly those for
authenticating the login ID. Click OK when everything works.

4. The new Books Available datasource name appears in the Data Sources
window as something like Books Available with a driver listed as SQL
Server. Click OK to end the ODBC Data Source Administrator.

5. Start Visual Basic. Create a new project called `PIVOT.VBP`. Add the form `ERRORRDO.FRM` (see the introduction to Chapter 2 for a description of this form) by choosing Add from the File menu. This form handles RDO errors.

6. Choose Components from the Project menu and select the following custom controls:

> Microsoft Common Dialog Control 6.0
>
> Microsoft Windows Common Controls 6.0

Disable all the other check boxes so that your project isn't cluttered with controls you aren't using and the Setup Wizard doesn't include a lot of dead weight with your application.

7. Choose References from the Project menu and select the following references:

> Microsoft Visual Basic for Applications
>
> Visual Basic Runtime Objects and Procedures
>
> Visual Basic objects and procedures
>
> Microsoft Excel 8.0 Object Library
>
> Microsoft Remote Data Object 2.0

Disable all the other check boxes so that your project isn't cluttered with DLLs you aren't using and the Setup Wizard doesn't include a lot of dead weight with your application.

8. Add the controls shown in Figure 10.24 to the form in the new project, with property settings listed in Table 10.7. Save the form as file `PIVOT.FRM`.

Table 10.7 Objects and properties for `PIVOT.FRM`

OBJECT	PROPERTY	SETTING
Form	Name	frmPivot
	Caption	"Data Analysis"
CommandButton	Name	cmdChart
	Caption	"Create Chart"
CommandButton	Name	cmdLoadSS
	Caption	"&Load Spreadsheet"
	Enabled	0 'False

continued on next page

Table 10.7 continued

OBJECT	PROPERTY	SETTING
CommandButton	Name	cmdQuit
	Caption	"&Quit"
	Default	-1 'True
StatusBar	Name	StatusBar1
	Align	2 'Align Bottom
	AlignSet	-1 'True
	Style	1 SimpleText

9. Add the following code to the Declarations section of the form. `Option Explicit` tells Visual Basic to make sure that you declare all variables and objects before using them in order to avoid naming problems. The `mobjExcel` object variable holds the worksheet OLE object obtained from Microsoft Excel. The set of `mrdo` variables consists of the RDOs used to make the connection with the Books Available SQL Server datasource.

```
Option Explicit

'PRIVATE: ****************************************
'Private data members

'Object variable for Excel worksheet
Dim mobjExcel As Object

'Remote Data Object variables
Private mrdoEnv As rdoEnvironment
Private mrdoConn As rdoConnection
Private mrdoRS As rdoResultset
```

10. Enter the following code in `frmPivot`'s `Load` event procedure. The main purpose of this procedure is to get a worksheet OLE object from Excel's object library.

```
Private Sub Form_Load()
    cmdLoadSS.Enabled = False
    cmdChart.Enabled = False
    cmdQuit.Enabled = True

    Me.Show
    Me.Refresh

    'Create a Microsoft Excel object
    Status "Creating an Excel object"
    Set mobjExcel = CreateObject("Excel.Sheet")

    Status "Click on Load Spreadsheet to begin creating the
report."
    cmdLoadSS.Enabled = True
End Sub
```

11. Add the following code to the **Click** event procedure of the **cmdLoadSS** command button. After the form is loaded and **mobjExcel** contains a reference to a worksheet object, this procedure reads the database information and adds it to a database area of an Excel spreadsheet.

The **OpenDataSource** procedure, discussed later, makes the connection to the Books Available datasource. If the connection isn't made for any reason, this function returns **False**, the end user is notified, and the **Sub** procedure exits.

The next bit of code loops through the **rdoColumns** collection of the **mrdoRS** rdoResultSet, adding each field's name to the top of a column in the Excel worksheet. The **iRowNo** variable keeps track of the current row in the spreadsheet when the data from the resultset is added to the sheet.

The **Do While** loop then steps through the resultset containing the data for the pivot table, adding each record to a row in the worksheet. This example is fairly generic so that it works with any number of fields in the resultset.

The next section of code selects the area of the worksheet containing the data just added. In the later call to Excel's **PivotTableWizard** method, you can specify an area containing the data as a range, or the method uses the database named **range** by default. In this example, you define the database range name and then redefine **sRange** to the location where you want to place the pivot table. Be careful not to overwrite any of the data used for the pivot table; the generated table will use the changed data, resulting in garbage in the table.

The next section of code uses the **PivotTableWizard** method to create the actual pivot table, which is named **AuthorsPivot**. The **SourceType** parameter tells Excel to use an Excel database for the source data. You can also make an ODBC connection directly through Excel, specify a range in the worksheet, or use another pivot table. Because I'm the paranoid type, I've specified the database named **range** for the **SourceData** parameter, even though this is the default for a **SourceType** of **xlDatabase**.

After the pivot table is created, you must specify which fields the table uses for its different parts. **RowFields** is the data contained in the row headings, and **ColumnFields** is for the columns.

Setting the table's **DataFields** is a less-than-intuitive process given the nice simple **AddFields** method. Even though the **Units** field hasn't explicitly been added to the pivot table's fields, use the **PivotFields** (**Units**) method to return a reference to this object and set its orientation to **xlDataField**. This sets the data used in the main body of the table to the **Units** field, summing the units for the total number by author and year.

By default, the `PivotTableWizard` includes a subtotal line for each unique `RowFields` line. Because this pivot table has only one author on each line, turn off the subtotals, which clutter the table needlessly. Setting the `Subtotals` array to all `False` values completely turns off subtotals. See the Access documentation for more information about the `Subtotals` property.

```
Private Sub cmdLoadSS_Click()
Dim iSaveCursor As Integer
Dim aConnect(1) As String
Dim sSQL As String
Dim irowNo As Integer
Dim j As Integer
Dim sRange As String

    iSaveCursor = Me.MousePointer
    Me.MousePointer = vbHourglass

    'Open the Books Available data source
    Status "Connecting to Books Available data source."
    If Not OpenDataSource() Then
        Status "Unable to connect to the Books Available data
        ➥source."
        MsgBox "Couldn't open Books Available data source. " _
            & "Ending application.", vbOKOnly, "Data Source Error"
        Unload Me
        Exit Sub
    End If

    cmdLoadSS.Enabled = False

    'At the end of the loop, iRowNo will have the last row
    'of the range of cells and j will hold the number of
    'columns.
    irowNo = 1
    Status "Adding column names to pivot table data."
    For j = 0 To mrdoRS.rdoColumns.Count - 1
        mobjExcel.Worksheets(1).Cells(irowNo, j + 1).
        ➥Value = mrdoRS.rdoColumns(j).Name
    Next

    Do While Not mrdoRS.EOF
        irowNo = irowNo + 1
        Status "Adding row to pivot table data: " _
            & mrdoRS.rdoColumns("Last Name").Value
        For j = 0 To mrdoRS.rdoColumns.Count - 1
            mobjExcel.Worksheets(1).Cells(irowNo, j + 1).
            ➥Value = mrdoRS.rdoColumns(j).Value
        Next
        mrdoRS.MoveNext
    Loop

    With mobjExcel.Worksheets(1)
        Status "Defining the Database range."
```

```
            sRange = "$A1:$" & Chr(Asc("A") + j - 1)
            ➥& LTrim(Str(irowNo))
            .Range(sRange).Name = "Database"
            sRange = Chr(Asc("A") + j + 1) & "1"
            .Range(sRange).Select

            Status "Adding the pivot table to the worksheet."
            .PivotTableWizard SourceType:=xlDatabase, _
                SourceData:="Database", TableName:="AuthorsPivot", _
                RowGrand:=True, ColumnGrand:=True

            Status "Adding fields to pivot table."
            .PivotTables(1).AddFields _
                RowFields:=Array("Last Name", "First Name"), _
                ColumnFields:=Array("Year"), _
                AddToTable:=True

            Status "Setting the data field for the pivot table."
            .PivotTables(1).PivotFields("Units").Orientation =
            ➥xlDataField

            sRange = Chr(Asc("A") + j + 1) & "3"
            .Range(sRange).Select

            Status "Turning off the subtotal lines for each row."
            .PivotTables(1).PivotFields("Last Name").Subtotals = _
                Array(False, False, False, False, False, False, _
                False, False, False, False, False, False)

        End With

        Status "Pivot table completed."
        DoEvents
        mobjExcel.Application.Visible = True
        Me.MousePointer = iSaveCursor
        cmdChart.Enabled = True
        cmdLoadSS.Enabled = False

    End Sub
```

12. Add the `OpenDataSource` function procedure. This is the procedure that opens the connection to the Books Available datasource using Visual Basic's RDOs.

The code puts the **SQL SELECT** statement in the **sSQL** string variable. This query summarizes data in the Authors, Sales, and Titles tables in the PUBS database to create a resultset that contains a record for each author for every year in which he or she had sales. The data in the source tables ranges from 1992 to 1994, so each author could have zero to three records in the resultset. See the "How It Works" section later for more information about this process.

```
Private Function OpenDataSource()
Dim sSQL As String
Dim rdoPS As rdoPreparedStatement

    'Allocate an ODBC environment handle
    On Error GoTo OpenDataSourceError
    Set mrdoEnv = rdoEnvironments(0)
    Set mrdoConn = mrdoEnv.OpenConnection("Books Available", _
        rdDriverComplete, False, "ODBC;UID=sa;PWD=")

    sSQL = "SELECT authors.au_lname 'Last Name', " _
        & "authors.au_fname 'First Name', " _
        & "Sum(sales.qty) 'Units', " _
        & "datepart(year,(sales.ord_date)) 'Year' " _
        & "FROM authors, sales, titleauthor " _
        & "WHERE titleauthor.au_id = authors.au_id " _
        & "AND titleauthor.title_id = sales.title_id " _
        & "GROUP BY authors.au_lname, authors.au_fname, " _
        & "datepart(year,(sales.ord_date)) " _
        & "ORDER BY authors.au_lname, authors.au_fname"

    Set mrdoRS = mrdoConn.OpenResultset(sSQL, rdOpenForwardOnly)
    OpenDataSource = True

    Exit Function

OpenDataSourceError:
    frmRDOErrors.ErrorColl = rdoErrors
    OpenDataSource = False
End Function
```

13. After the pivot table is created in Excel, the **cmdLoadSS** enables the **cmdChart** button on the form. Add the following code to the **cmdChart** command button's **Click** event procedure. This procedure uses the new pivot table to create the bar chart shown in Figure 10.26.

The code sets up the parameters needed by the Excel **ChartWizard** method to create the bar chart. Because the Excel sheet is a new worksheet and the code in this application just created a single pivot table, this code references the first and only pivot table, **PivotTables(1)**. The **TableRange1** method returns a reference to the full area of the table less any page fields (this How-To doesn't use page fields). A companion method, **TableRange2**, selects the entire table—including the page fields. But **TableRange1** includes the row and column totals that you don't want to include in the chart, because those larger numbers skew the results and make the chart harder to use. This means using the **Selection.Row** and **.Column** properties, along with a count of the columns in the range (the pivot table) to determine the size of the range and reduce it by one row and one column. After you have this information, you rebuild the **sRange** string variable to specify the range to be included in the chart.

The code can at last call the **ChartWizard** method to create the chart, using the edited range of the table and a column chart of type 3 (stacked bars).

```
Private Sub cmdChart_Click()
Dim iRow As Integer
Dim iCol As Integer
Dim iRowCount As Integer
Dim iColCount As Integer
Dim sRange As String
Dim iSaveCursor As Integer

    iSaveCursor = Me.MousePointer
    Me.MousePointer = vbHourglass

    With mobjExcel.Worksheets(1)
        'Select the pivot table
        .PivotTables(1).TableRange1.Select

        'TableRange1 includes cells we don't want,
        'so get the range of cells and cut it down
        'to exclude the row and column totals, and the
        'fields at the top of the table.
        iRow = .Application.Selection.Row
        iCol = .Application.Selection.Column
        iRowCount = .Application.Selection.Rows.Count
        iColCount = .Application.Selection.Columns.Count

        sRange = Chr(Asc("A") + iCol - 1) _
            & LTrim(Str(iRow + 1)) & ":" _
            & Chr(Asc("A") + iCol + iColCount - 3) _
            & LTrim(Str(iRow + iRowCount - 2)))
        .Range(sRange).Select

        'Add the chart.
        .ChartObjects.Add(40, 40, 575, 325).Select
        .Application.CutCopyMode = False
        .Application.ActiveChart.ChartWizard Source:=
    ➡.Range(sRange), _
            Gallery:=xlColumn, Format:=3, PlotBy:=xlColumns, _
            CategoryLabels:=1, SeriesLabels:=1, HasLegend:=1
    End With

    Status "Pivot chart completed."
    DoEvents
    mobjExcel.Application.Visible = True
    Me.MousePointer = iSaveCursor
    cmdChart.Enabled = False
End Sub
```

14. Add the following code to the **cmdQuit** command button's **Click** event to unload the form and thus end the application:

```
Private Sub cmdQuit_Click()
    Unload Me
End Sub
```

15. Add the following code to the form's `Unload` event procedure. This code sets the object and RDO variables to `Nothing`, releasing their memory. In most cases, it is best to release these variables in the form's `Unload` event so that they are explicitly released even if the form isn't closing as a result of the end user clicking Quit.

```
Private Sub Form_Unload(Cancel As Integer)
    'Release the module-level variable objects.
    Set mrdoEnv = Nothing
    Set mrdoConn = Nothing
    Set mrdoRS = Nothing
    Set mobjExcel = Nothing
End Sub
```

16. In the Tools Project Options menu, choose Project Options from the Tools menu and set the startup form to `frmPivot`. You can also set an application description, but that is not required for the operation of this application.

How It Works

A pivot table is a useful way to analyze data that consists of multiple records for each entity of interest, with a couple of characteristics for each entity. Table 10.8 lists the results of the query used in the code for this How-To, for example:

```
SELECT authors.au_lname 'Last Name', authors.au_fname 'First Name',
    Sum(sales.qty) 'Units', datepart(year,(sales.ord_date)) 'Year'
FROM authors, sales, titleauthor
WHERE titleauthor.au_id = authors.au_id
    AND titleauthor.title_id = sales.title_id
GROUP BY authors.au_lname, authors.au_fname, datepart(year,(sales.ord_date))
ORDER BY authors.au_lname, authors.au_fname
```

This SQL statement takes a first step in summarizing the data into a form that can easily be used by Excel's Pivot Table Wizard. Notice that several authors have more than one record in the table, meaning that their books had at least one sale in each of the years. This format makes analyzing the data very difficult—all the more so when you are working with thousands of rows of data, such as when an individual author might have dozens of records in the data.

Table 10.8 Data from the PUBS SQL Server database

LAST NAME	FIRST NAME	UNITS	YEAR
Bennet	Abraham	15	1994
Blotchet-Halls	Reginald	20	1992
Carson	Cheryl	30	1993
DeFrance	Michel	40	1994
del Castillo	Innes	10	1993

LAST NAME	FIRST NAME	UNITS	YEAR
Dull	Ann	50	1993
Green	Marjorie	35	1993
Green	Marjorie	15	1994
Gringlesby	Burt	20	1992
Hunter	Sheryl	50	1993
Karsen	Livia	20	1993
Locksley	Charlene	25	1993
MacFeather	Stearns	45	1993
O'Leary	Michael	20	1992
O'Leary	Michael	25	1993
Panteley	Sylvia	40	1992
Ringer	Albert	25	1993
Ringer	Albert	108	1994
Singer	Anne	148	1994
Straight	Dean	15	1993
White	Johnson	15	1993
Yokomoto	Akiko	20	1992

The resulting pivot table, shown in Table 10.9, provides a format much easier to analyze. In one glance, you can see each author's yearly sales.

Table 10.9 Pivot table generated from data in Table 10.8

LAST NAME	FIRST NAME	1992	1993	1994	GRAND TOTAL
Bennet	Abraham	0	0	15	15
Blotchet-Halls	Reginald	20	0	0	20
Carson	Cheryl	0	30	0	30
DeFrance	Michel	0	0	40	40
del Castillo	Innes	0	10	0	10
Dull	Ann	0	50	0	50
Green	Marjorie	0	35	15	50
Gringlesby	Burt	20	0	0	20
Hunter	Sheryl	0	50	0	50
Karsen	Livia	0	20	0	20
Kiely	Don	50	75	95	220
Locksley	Charlene	0	25	0	25
MacFeather	Stearns	0	45	0	45

continued on next page

Table 10.9 continued

LAST NAME	FIRST NAME	1992	1993	1994	GRAND TOTAL
O'Leary	Michael	20	25	0	45
Panteley	Sylvia	40	0	0	40
Ringer	Albert	0	25	108	133
Singer	Anne	0	0	148	148
Straight	Dean	0	15	0	15
White	Johnson	0	15	0	15
Yokomoto	Akiko	20	0	0	20
Grand Total		170	420	421	1011

Most of the hard work in producing the pivot table takes place within Excel, so the Visual Basic code in this How-To serves mostly to read data and place it into the spreadsheet. Then the code calls the Excel Pivot Table Wizard to create the table. The Excel Chart Wizard then charts the pivot table. This is an example of producing relatively simple code by using the sophisticated features of an OLE server—in this case, Excel.

GLOSSARY

by George Szabo

action query   A query that makes changes, either administrative or manipulative, to a record or records with a single request. Here are some keywords used in action queries: `INSERT`, `UPDATE`, and `DELETE`. Action queries can also use stored procedures.

Active Data Object (ADO)   An automation object that can retrieve, update, and create records in any OLE database provider. This includes ODBC databases. ADO is a data-access method meant to replace Data Access Object (DAO) and Remote Data Object (RDO) over the next several releases. *See also* open database connectivity (ODBC) and remote data object (RDO).

ActiveX Automation Server   An application (ActiveX EXE or library ActiveX DLL) based on the Component Object Model (COM) that provides an ActiveX interface by which clients can access services the server provides in the form of methods and properties. This is also referred to as an *ActiveX component. See also* Component Object Model (COM).

Application Programming Interface (API)   A set of routines available in an application that programmers can use to design application interfaces. Visual Basic allows access to APIs through the `Declare` statement.

asynchronous   A situation in data access in which a client can make a request of the server, and control is returned to the client prior to the completion of the task. After the query is processed, the client is notified.

authentication   The process of verifying a user's login ID and password.

back end   In a client/server system, the back end is synonymous with the database engine that resides on the server or host. The database engine or back end processes SQL requests and stores and retrieves data.

binding   Associates a default or rule with a column or datatype. The `rdoQuery` provides object support for the attributes that have been defined for a parameter. Among other things, this includes enforcing the datatype of a parameter.

buffer   A reserved area in memory designated to hold the value of a file or variable. One type of buffer is a cache that holds data during input/output (I/O) transfers.

business rules   An organization's operating procedures that must be followed to ensure a correctly run business. The implementation of business rules is designed to maintain accuracy and integrity of the database from the business perspective. A business rule may be that credit cannot be extended to anyone with a balance due, for example.

Cartesian product   Named after the French mathematician and philosopher René Descartes. A Cartesian product describes the result of a join that generates all possible combinations of rows and columns from each table referenced in the SQL statement. The number of rows in a Cartesian product of two tables is equal to the number of rows in the first table times the number of rows in the second table, and so on.

cascading delete   A delete in which all related database rows or columns are deleted. This is often implemented as a trigger in a database.

case sensitivity   With regard to SQL statement submission, case sensitivity specifies whether the query engine will regard the same table name spelled with a different number of lower- and uppercase letters as matching. The Microsoft SQL Server default installation is not case sensitive.

child   Within the Windows environment, *child* is a synonym for an MDI child window. With the introduction of class modules to Visual Basic, *child* can also describe an object related to but lower in the object hierarchy than a parent object.

class module   Used in Visual Basic to define classes and their properties and methods. A class module defines a single class. You must create a class module for each class you want to define. *See also* method, property.

clause   The portion of a SQL statement that begins with a keyword. The keyword names the basic operation that will be performed. `WHERE` is a common keyword, and the `WHERE` clause contains conditions that restrict the retrieval of records.

client   The user of a service provided by a server. A client is commonly a front-end application. Many people refer to the computer hosting the application as the client, but this should actually be referred to as the *client computer.*

client/server   An architecture founded on the concept of dividing a process between two separate entities—a client and a server. Client/server most commonly refers to a database system. Within this type of client/server system, the client application presents and manipulates data on the client's workstation and the server services the client requests for storing, deleting, and retrieving data. *See also* client, server.

CLSID (class ID)   The unique identification key assigned to all class objects when they are created. The class ID value size is 128 bits and is used to uniquely identify the class through the Registry. *See also* Registry.

clustered index   An index type available in SQL Server and other back-end databases. The order of the key values is the same as the physical order of the corresponding rows that exist in the table. Clustered indexes are associated with high overhead and fast retrieval of data. Note that this definition is specific to SQL Server.

column   The smallest meaningful unit of information in a database when defined as synonymous with *field*. A column can also represent all values in a table that have a common attribute. An example is a ZIP code field in a table filled with addresses.

commit   A process by which data is written to disk. Transaction processing often requires that a variety of changes to data occurs as a unit. A commit occurs either under programmer control or database engine control at the successful completion of the specified transaction task.

Component Object Model (COM)   A standard that defines a set of component interfaces supported at the system level. This object model is designed to allow complete interoperability between components, regardless of language or vendor.

concurrency   The capability to allow multiple clients to access the same data—whether a table, row, or field—at the same time without causing a collision.

connection   The channel of communication established between a client and a back-end database engine. A client can have one or more connections. Each connection allows the submission of requests and the retrieval of results. A connection allows sequential execution. A new request cannot be submitted via a connection until the previous request is completely processed or canceled. *See also* client.

cursor   The pointer to a record in a SQL resultset. The cursor concept was introduced to SQL database engines to mimic record-oriented access methods. Cursors allow the manipulation of data by rows rather than by sets. The use of cursors allows multiple operations to be executed row by row on the results of a query. Cursors can be executed on the server side or maintained on the client side of a client/server scenario. *See also* client, client/server, and server.

Data Access Objects (DAO)   An object model that provides access to Microsoft Jet engine databases (MDB files) as well as ISAM databases and any ODBC data source.

data definition language (DDL)   The portion of the Structured Query Language (SQL) that allows you to create, manipulate, and delete objects such as tables, indexes, and so on in a database. *See also* Structured Query Language (SQL).

data remoting   A method of moving data from a server to a client application or Web page, where it can be manipulated on the client. After remoting is complete, updates can be returned to the server in a single round trip.

database   An organized collection of information. The data is stored in tables; other objects such as stored procedures and triggers are also organized within the database. A database provides for a logical as well as physical grouping of related information and allows searching, sorting, and recombining of this data.

database device   A physical file that can house one or more databases. One database can be stored on several devices. This definition is specific to SQL Server.

database management system (DBMS)   A computer-maintained repository of data that allows users to insert, update, and delete data, as well as to generate reports and perform other data management-related tasks.

database manipulation language (DML)   A subset of the SQL language used to retrieve and manipulate data stored in a database. The primary DML statement is a SELECT. *See also* SELECT and Structured Query Language (SQL).

database object   Any one of the components found in a database. These components are tables, indexes, procedures, views, defaults, triggers, constraints, and rules.

database object owner   The user who creates a database object. The owner of an object can grant permissions to others with regard to the object. Database object ownership cannot be transferred. This is different from the owner of the database because ownership of the database can be reassigned to a different user.

DB-Library (DBLIB)   An API to Microsoft SQL Server. Transact-SQL statements can be transmitted to the SQL Server engine via the DBLIB.DLL for execution. Note that the SQL Server ODBC driver does not use DBLIB.DLL to process iterations with SQL Server. *See also* Application Programming Interface (API) and Transact-SQL (T-SQL).

deadlock   A situation that occurs when two users who have a data page locked within a database simultaneously try to lock each other's page of information. A deadlock is created because each user is waiting for the other to release the lock he has on his own page of data. SQL Server detects the occurrence of deadlocks and kills one of the user's processes. *See also* livelock.

decision support system (DSS)   Uses data and exploits computing resources to provide support for decision analysis and other decision-related activities. A DDS usually requires just read-only access to data. In many cases, companies are creating separate data warehouses to facilitate this type of analysis without impacting their production database operations.

denormalization   The act of combining two or more relational tables into a single flat table with data from both. Denormalization of data tables is common when constructing data warehouses. In certain cases denormalization can improve performance by reducing the number of joins needed to retrieve information.

dependent object   An object that cannot be instantiated directly by a user. The dependent object exists as part of a larger component object, which is responsible for creating and releasing the dependent object as it is needed to fulfill the greater component's service. An invoice component object may have a dependent detail object that contains detailed information for each line of the invoice object, for example. By itself, the detail line means nothing and therefore is implemented as a dependent object. *See also* instantiate.

distributed component object model (DCOM)   Another name for what previously was referred to as *Network OLE*. DCOM is a protocol that allows applications to make object-oriented remote procedure calls (RPCs) in distributed computing environments (DCEs).

distributed computing environments (DCE)   The Open Software Foundation's specification for a set of integrated services, including security services, distributed files systems, and remote procedure calls. Microsoft Remote Procedure Calls (RPC) are based on the OSF-DCE RPC standard.

domain   A collection of computers grouped together for administrative purposes within the NT environment. A domain shares a single common security database and allows for the centralized control of resources. A single network server is designated as the domain controller and houses the security database.

dynamic link library (DLL)   A collection of executable routines. These routines usually are grouped by the services they provide. `.DLL` is the extension of the physical filename. DLLs load and execute within the same thread of execution as the instantiating client application. *See also* instantiate, thread.

encapsulate   To contain and hide information about an object's internal implementation. This pertains to data structures as well as code. Encapsulation isolates an object's internal complexity from the object's use and operation within the greater application. As an example, an application asking a business component object to validate a credit card number does not need to know how this was actually accomplished, but only whether the number was approved.

exclusive lock   A lock applied to a database table during `INSERT`, `UPDATE`, and `DELETE` operations. An exclusive lock prevents any other transaction from getting a lock on that table until the original lock is released.

fifth normal form   A rule for relational databases that a table divided into multiple tables must be capable of being reconstructed, via one or more `JOIN` statements, to its exact original structure. *See also* `JOIN`.

first normal form   A rule for relational databases that requires tables to be flat. Flat tables can contain only one data value set per row. Members of the data value set are called *data cells*, are contained in one column of the row, and must have only one value. Data cells are often referred to as *fields*.

flow control   Conditional expressions that control the flow of execution of statements that exist within the code of an application or procedure.

foreign key   A column or collection of columns that must match a column or columns designated as a primary key in another table. Unlike primary keys, foreign keys do not need to be unique. *See also* primary key.

fourth normal form   A rule for relational databases requiring that only related data entities are included in a single table. Additionally, tables cannot contain data related to more than one data entity when many-to-one relationships exist among the entities.

front end   An application used by a client to access any database engine or to present information to the user. A Visual Basic application is often a front end for a database. *See also* client.

gateway   A software product used on a network to allow networks or computers running dissimilar protocols to communicate. A gateway provides transparent access to a variety of foreign database management systems. A SQL Server can be used as a gateway to DB2 database files. *See also* Database Management System (DBMS).

Globally Unique Identification Key (GUID)   Identifies ActiveX components and their interfaces in the Registry. GUIDs are mechanisms defined by the Component Object Model. *See also* Component Object Model (COM).

handle   An address system that allows programmers to use structures created by the ODBC API. These structures consist of stored parameters, errors, and returned arguments. Three types of objects have handles within the ODBC API: environment, connection, and statement. These handles are available also when working with the Remote Data Object (RDO) layer. *See also* Application Programming Interface (API), open database connectivity (ODBC), and remote data object (RDO).

in-process   This term is used with the creation of software components referred to as *servers*. An in-process server is one in which the code executes in the same process space as the client application. Starting with Visual Basic 4, you can create in-process servers as ActiveX DLLs. *See also* client/server and server.

index   A database object that provides a cross-reference of one or more columns in a table to provide quick access to data.

instantiate   The act of creating an instance of an object. Instantiation brings an object into existence for use by the instantiating application or component. After all references to the object are dropped, the object terminates.

Internet database connector   A program distributed with Microsoft's Internet Information Server and Front Page's Personal Web Server that allows for the submission of SQL statements to any ODBC datasource. The Internet database connector is found in `HTTPODBC.DLL` and runs as an in-process server, which provides enhanced speed of query submission and formatting of results. *See also* in-process.

JET database engine   JET stands for Joint Engine Technology and is a database management system that stores and retrieves data in user and system databases. The JET database engine provides data access functionality to other systems like Microsoft Access and Visual Basic.

JOIN   A keyword used in SQL syntax to allow the combination of two or more tables into a resultset. This is based mostly on the use of primary and foreign keys. *See also* resultset.

keyset   A set of values used to access specific records in a database. A keyset can be maintained by the server, or it can be maintained using ODBC–maintained cursors.

livelock   When a request for an exclusive lock is denied repeatedly because of several overlapping shared locks that currently exist, a livelock is created. An exclusive lock is a request for read/write access to the data page, while the shared locks are read-only access.

marshaling   The process of packaging interface parameters and sending them across process boundaries. In the mainframe environment, keystrokes are marshaled from the terminal to the host. With regard to remote automation, requests are marshaled to remotely deployed objects. *See also* remote automation.

method   A procedure that performs a specific task as part of an object by which it is exposed.

Microsoft Database (MDB)   A format used by Microsoft Access and *Joint Engine Technology* (JET). Unlike dBASE data files, the MDB allows for storage of database-related objects, including queries, reports, forms, macros, and code.

mission-critical   Refers to specific systems in a business that cannot fail. If these systems fail, the company cannot conduct any business. An airline reservation system is a mission-critical system, as is an air traffic controller application.

multiuser With regard to data, the capability of a front-end application or back-end database engine to allow multiple users to access data stored in a single table or set of tables simultaneously. *See also* back end and front end.

normal forms A set of five rules used to design relational databases. Five normal forms are generally accepted in the creation of relational databases. *See also* first normal form through fifth normal form.

normalization The act of removing redundancy from a database design. *See also* first normal form through fifth normal form and normal forms.

NT file storage (NTFS) A file storage management system available for the NT operating system. NTFS provides a much higher level of security over access to a computer's resources as well as methods for file system recovery. All files are treated as objects with user- and system-defined attributes. NTFS also supports long filenames.

null In SQL terms, *null* refers to a field with no assigned value. This is not the same as zero for numeric data or an empty string for a character field. When defining the attributes of a field in a table, it is possible to prevent the addition of a new record with a null value.

object Within the back-end database, an *object* refers to any one of a number of database components: table, view, index, trigger, constraint, default, rule, procedure, or user-defined datatype. Within the Component Object Model, an object refers to a component. *See also* back end, Component Object Model (COM).

online analytical processing (OLAP) A high-end, analysis-oriented DBMS application that allows for process-intensive analysis of data warehouse information. *See also* Database Management System (DBMS).

online transaction processing (OLTP) Refers to high-end applications that are optimized for transaction-oriented DBMSs such as airline reservation systems or *automated teller machine* (ATM) operations. *See also* Database Management System (DBMS).

open database connectivity (ODBC) A standard API and protocol that is database independent. Using ODBC allows a programmer to develop applications using a standard set of syntax that can be directed to any ODBC-compliant datasource. *See also* Application Programming Interface (API).

optimizer The component of a database engine responsible for finding the optimal plan for processing a query.

out-of-process Refers to an ActiveX server that runs in a separate process space from the client requesting services. In Visual Basic, this equates to the ActiveX EXE component and how it operates. *See also* in-process.

page A virtual storage system for data within the database. In Microsoft Access and Microsoft SQL Server, a page is a fixed length and is equal to 2KB. It is important to note that because locking is performed on a page level and not on a row or record level, two or more records could be locked by locking one page. This is because a single record may be less than 2KB.

parameter query A query that requires the client submitting the query to specify values at the time of submission. A *parameter* is the equivalent of an *argument*.

partitioning A method for encapsulating an application's functionality into components and making it deployable. After an application is partitioned into components, the components can be deployed across networks on another machine transparent to the client application. This allows the integration of more hardware into the application's execution, which supports the benefits of distributed processing.

persistent data   Data stored in a database in a physical form rather than just in memory. Data stored in tables in a database system is considered persistent data.

persistent objects   Objects stored in a database in a physical form rather than just in memory.

prepared statement   A precompiled request submitted by a client for temporary storage by a back-end database engine. The ODBC API uses the `SQLPrepare` function to submit SQL statements to the back end that will be used over and over during a single session. Allowing the engine to precompile the statement enables faster execution each time the statement is called. A prepared statement can accept parameters each time it is called. When the connection is dropped, the statement is released. *See also* back end.

primary key   The column or columns that uniquely identify each row in a table. The primary key cannot contain any duplicate values. This key is used when joining to other tables to find additional related data. The primary key field must never be null. *See also* foreign key.

property   One of the two main characteristics of an object (the other is method). A property can be read-only, write-only, or read/write. Properties are defined in Visual Basic by creating `GET`, `LET`, or `SET` procedures in a class module. Public variables declared in the declaration section of a class module also become properties of the component object.

proxy   An object that packages parameters for an interface in preparation for a remote method call. A proxy runs in the address space of the client and communicates with a corresponding stub in the receiver's address space on a remote machine. *See also* stub.

query   A request that can result in the retrieval or manipulation of records in a database. SQL is the de facto standard as a universal query language, but other proprietary languages do exist. *See also* Structured Query Language (SQL).

recursion   A situation in which a function or procedure calls itself. This can cause unpredictable results in Visual Basic and is discouraged.

referential integrity   A set of rules created to establish and maintain the relationship between related tables. Referential integrity is enforced whenever records are added, modified, or deleted to ensure that table relations are not violated.

Registry   A database repository found in Windows NT and Windows 95 used to store information relating to system and application configuration. The Registry also serves as a warehouse for container and ActiveX server information.

remote automation   Through the use of *remote procedure calls* (RPCs), remote automation allows access to an ActiveX component on a remote machine. This technology employs a technique involving the use of local proxies and an application called the Remote Automation Manager to marshal requests over a network. *See also* proxy, remote procedure call (RPC).

remote data object (RDO)   A thin layer that sits on top of the ODBC API, providing a simplified object model to assist in programming data access. The objects of RDO closely resemble those of the Data Access Objects found in JET.

remote data service (RDS)   Provides client-side caching of recordset objects. By doing this, the amount of network round trips is minimized. RDS also provides a data-binding mechanism to display recordset objects in data-bound controls on a Web page.

remote procedure call (RPC)   The invocation of a stored procedure on a remote server from a procedure on another server. RPCs play an important role in the communication between local and remote ActiveX automation servers.

resultset   The rows or return values provided in response to a query submitted against a database.

rollback   A term used in transaction processing that allows any partial transactions to be returned to their original state. Because a transaction can have many parts, and all parts must succeed in order for the transaction to be valid, rollback provides a way to reverse transactions that do not succeed in their entirety.

row   Another name for record. Refers to a single entity of a database table that contains each of the columns of data cells defined for the table.

rule   Defines what data can be entered into a column. A rule is a database object and is bound to a specific column. The `INSERT` and `UPDATE` statements trigger the execution of the validation information stored in a rule associated with any given column in a table. Limit and list checking are available to a rule implementation.

second normal form   A rule for relational databases stating that columns that are not key fields must be related to the key field. This means that a row cannot contain values in a field that do not pertain to the value of the key field. In an orders table, for example, the columns of each row must pertain only to the order for which the order number is the key field.

SELECT   A SQL statement used to retrieve records from a database. The `SELECT` statement can include one or many tables and is often accompanied by a `WHERE` clause that restricts the resultset.

server   A machine on a network designated to provide centralized resource services. A server can share files and printers or house a DBMS such as SQL Server. A server also refers to an application (such as a database engine) that services requests from other applications. *See also* client/server, Database Management System (DBMS).

stored procedure   A precompiled set of instructions that a database engine can execute. A stored procedure can contain anything from a single action query that returns no records to a query that returns multiple resultsets. In addition to SQL statements, stored procedures can contain control-of-flow statements. *See also* flow control.

Structured Query Language (SQL)   This language has become a de facto standard for relational databases. It was originally developed by IBM for use with its mainframe computer systems. Currently an ANSI-standard SQL definition exists for every computer system. SQL can be used to query and manipulate data, as well as to manage objects within a relational database.

stub   An object that unbundles parameters that have been marshaled across processes from a remote machine. After the parameters are unbundled, the stub makes the requested method call to the interface. A stub runs in the same address space as the receiver. *See also* marshaling.

subquery   A `SELECT` statement that is nested inside another SQL statement. Subqueries can be used in `SELECT`, `INSERT`, `UPDATE`, or `DELETE` statements. You can also use a subquery inside another subquery.

table   Similar to a database file. A table is a unit of data storage in a relational database system. A table consists of rows and columns that represent individual data records.

third normal form   The rule for relational databases stating that a column that is not a key column cannot be dependent on another column that is not a key column.

thread   The part of a process that can run as an object or an entity. A thread is made up of a stack, the state of the CPU registers, and an entry in the system scheduler's execution list. In other words, it executes separately.

Transact-SQL (T-SQL)   A standard language for communicating with SQL Server. Transact-SQL is an enhanced version of SQL, complete with syntax to perform data definitions as well as manipulation. Stored procedures allow Transact-SQL to implement control-of-flow syntax as well. *See also* flow control, Structured Query Language (SQL).

transaction   A collection of database actions that represents a unit of work. A transaction must be completed in its entirety or rolled back to its original state. *See also* rollback.

transfer control protocol/Internet protocol (TCP/IP)   The basic transport mechanism for the Internet. TCP/IP was originally developed by the U.S. military to create a secure network in case of atomic attack.

trigger   A database object that is much like a stored procedure. Triggers are executed in response to an action such as an `INSERT`, an `UPDATE`, or a `DELETE`. It is often the function of a trigger to maintain referential integrity, among other things. *See also* referential integrity.

universally unique identification key (UUID)   Identifies ActiveX components and their interfaces. A UUID is a mechanism defined by the DCOM. *See also* Distributed Component Object Model (DCOM).

UPDATE   A SQL statement that allows the addition, deletion, or changing of data in one or many tables.

view   A virtual table. A view or virtual table is created as a collection of columns from one or more tables, referred to as *base tables*. It is possible to create a view based on another view. A view is referred to as a *virtual table,* because although you can see the data in the view structure, the data still physically resides in the base table.

wide area network (WAN)   A system that allows for the connection of multiple computers in geographically disparate locations through the use of leased data lines or switched telephone networks. Optical lines are becoming very popular for this type of network configuration.

B

CLIENT/SERVER DATABASE RESOURCES

by David Jung

This appendix provides information on various client/server support products and tools, as well as a list of areas of support on various online services and user groups.

ActiveX

The first method of expanding Visual Basic was through the use of custom controls called *Visual Basic Extensions* (VBXs). As Visual Basic evolved, the controls became more enriched, and Visual Basic's use of controls increased. The use of OLE controls or OCXs started to appear, and Microsoft Access 2.0 was the first product to use them. When Visual Basic 4.0 was released in 1995, all VBX controls were migrated into OCX controls in both 16- and 32-bit versions. Early in 1996, Microsoft announced a technology known as *ActiveX*. Its first associations were related to technologies regarding the Internet and applications that would use the Internet as their connectivity layer. As the specifications became further defined, the inclusion of OCXs was made. Currently, ActiveX technology does not refer to just Internet technology or OLE control technology. It encompasses both technologies, as well as OLE embedding and automation. For more information on ActiveX technology, refer to the Microsoft ActiveX SDK.

In this section, it would be impossible to list all the ActiveX controls and the independent software vendors who developed them. You can refer to several Web sites and mail-order companies for this information. Table B.1 lists some of the Internet Web sites you can refer to for more information.

Table B.1 Web sites that reference ActiveX

URL	DESCRIPTION
http://www.activex.com	Sponsored by Cnet; an ActiveX control library
http://www.active-x.com	A site dedicated to providing information about ActiveX for developers
http://www.activex.org	The ActiveX working group formed to provide direction for the ActiveX standard as it is implemented on multiple platforms and operating systems
http://www.microsoft.com/activex	Microsoft site dedicated to ActiveX resources
http://www.pparadise.com	Mail-order company that sells thousands of ActiveX controls and development tools
http://www.componentsource.com	ComponentSource: Mail-order company that sells thousands of ActiveX controls and development tools
http://www.vbextras.com	Mail-order company that sells thousands of ActiveX controls and development tools

BackOffice Products

This category is for products that will assist you with your development with Microsoft BackOffice products. Microsoft BackOffice products consist of Microsoft SQL Server, Microsoft Internet Information Server, Microsoft Exchange, Microsoft SMS (Systems Management Server), Microsoft Transaction Server, Microsoft Index Server, and so on.

Brio Technology, Inc.
650 Castro St., Suite 500
Mountain View, CA 94041
Tel: (415) 961-4110
    (800) TRY-BRIO
Fax: (415) 961-4572
Web: http://www.brio.com

BrioQuery

BrioQuery Enterprise is a graphical-analysis tool designed for data warehousing with integrated charting, querying, and reporting capabilities. It is based on three separate tools: BrioQuery Designer, BrioQuery Explorer, and BrioQuery Navigator. BrioQuery Designer is intended for database administrators (DBAs) to design and maintain data models and standard queries. Designer allows the DBA to establish security restrictions on database tables, views, and other database objects. BrioQuery Explorer is designed for users as a query tool. BrioQuery Navigator is designed for users who will be viewing the reports and queries developed by the BrioQuery Explorer. All three components are sold individually and are available on the Macintosh, Windows, and UNIX operating systems.

DataEdit System

DataEdit System resides in your relational database system. It includes a data-entry forms-building program with a built-in SQL generator and uses a centralized data model to ensure data integrity. The DataEdit System is based on three components: DataEdit, DataEdit Designer, and DataEdit Client. DataEdit is the development tool you use to create forms and applications for your users to interact with. DataEdit Designer is the development tool you use to create your data model. Database Client is the software you install on every user's machine to execute the applications developed using DataEdit. DataEdit and DataEdit Designer are sold as a single product. This product is available for both the Macintosh and Windows operating systems.

Informix
4100 Bohannon Drive
Menlo Park, CA 94025
Tel: (650) 926-6300
Web: http://www.informix.com

Data Director

Data Director is a powerful data-management platform that is fully integrated with Visual Basic to improve the time-to-market interval for client/server applications by increasing developer productivity.

Logic Works, Inc.
University Square at Princeton
111 Campus Drive
Princeton, NJ 08540
Tel: (800) 78ERWIN
Web: http://www.logicworks.com

ERwin/Desktop

ERwin/Desktop for Visual Basic is a full development life-cycle tool. It handles data modeling through the use of *entity-relationship diagrams* (ERDs), generates Microsoft Access database structures based on the ERDs, and builds a Visual Basic prototype application based on your ERDs and business rules. It also has the capability to reverse-engineer your existing Microsoft Access databases into data models and then generate your Visual Basic prototype.

ERwin/ERX

In addition to everything that ERwin/Desktop does, ERwin/ERX also has the capability to create the database objects for many of the major back-end databases, such as Microsoft SQL Server, Sybase, Oracle, Informix, and DB2. It can also generate database classes to be integrated with development environments like Visual Basic and PowerBuilder.

Sheridan Software Systems

35 Pinelawn Rd.

Melville, NY 11747

Tel: (516) 753-0985

Fax: (516) 753-3661

Web: http://www.shersoft.com

CompuServe: GO SHERIDAN

sp_Assist

sp_Assist is a development tool for SQL Server to allow DBAs to quickly create, maintain, and manage database objects, such as stored procedures, triggers, tables, indexes, and so on. It also generates Visual Basic code to call queries and stored procedures defined by sp_Assist.

Sylvain Faust, Inc.

880 Boulevard de la Carriere

Hull, Quebec, J8Y 6T5 Canada

Tel: (800) 567-9127

 (819) 778-5045

Fax: (819) 778-7943

Web: http://www.sfi-software.com

SQL-Programmer for Windows

SQL-Programmer is a "test while you edit" development environment featuring a unique virtual editor. It replaces command-line ISQL programming with live editing, creation, testing, and impact assessment with all database objects, such as stored procedures, triggers, views, and so on. It features multiple SQL Server connections, including support for Sybase System 10 and SQL Server 6.0 and team programming. It has an Automatic SQL Server System Documentation generation feature that creates 16 standard reports and full ISQL scripts that can be used by other relational database systems.

Sybase Inc., Powersoft Business Group
6475 Christie Ave.
Emeryville, CA 94608-1050
Tel: (800) 879-2273
Fax: (800) 792-7329
Web: http://www.powersoft.com

PowerDesigner

PowerDesigner is an integrated modeling solution for analysis, database construction, and model-driven development. Six tools—ProcessAnalyst, DataArchitect, AppModeler, WarehouseArchitect, MetaWorks, and Viewer—allow developers to choose the appropriate language, computing model, and architecture that makes the most sense for each component of their projects.

Database Connectivity

In a distributed environment, your database connectivity is an important link to a successful project. This category lists components and their manufacturers that provide a connection layer to your database.

Intelligent Objects Corp.
47 Stonewall St.
Cartersville, GA 30120
Tel: (770) 382-6585
    (800) 876-6585
Fax: (770) 382-6374
Web: http://www.intelligent-objects.com

SQL Objects

SQL Objects Database Class Library is an award-winning tool that allows you to fully use database independence under OS/2, Windows NT, Windows 95, and many flavors of UNIX by enabling easy cross-platform development. SQL Objects gives you drivers for Oracle, Sybase, SQL Server, SQL Base, Watcom SQL, Informix, DB2/2, NetWare SQL, Btrieve, and many more. Also included is ODBC Objects (this adds a class library to your ODBC development; it also allows you to access any database Intelligent Objects Corp. doesn't have native drivers for).

SQL OLE!

SQL OLE! is a complete high-level API that provides DBMS-independent access, query, and data-handling methods to rapidly build applications. SQL OLE! provides the database independence your application needs (without having to rely on ODBC). SQL OLE! provides access to Oracle, SQL Server, Sybase, Informix, Watcom SQL,

DB2/2, SQL Base, and many more. Also included is ODBC Objects (which allows you to access any database Intelligent Objects Corp. doesn't have native drivers for).

ODBC Objects

ODBC Objects is an ODBC class library for any ODBC driver. ODBC Objects will assist you with your development by leveling out the inconsistencies of ODBC as well as using Intelligent Objects Corp.'s database classes for your ODBC development.

Intersolv

9420 Key West Ave.

Rockville, MD 20850

Tel: (301) 838-5000

(800) 547-7827

Fax: (301) 838-5064

Web: http://www.intersolv.com

Intersolv DataDirect ODBC Pack

Intersolv DataDirect ODBC Pack is a comprehensive suite of ODBC drivers that connect ODBC-compliant applications across multiple platforms to all major databases and gateways. These database drivers allow you to seamlessly access information from any ODBC-based application. DataDirect ODBC Pack drivers provide a consistent level of ODBC implementation. All DataDirect ODBC drivers support the ODBC-Core, Level-1, and primary Level-2 functions.

Microsoft Corporation

One Microsoft Way

Redmond, WA 98052

Tel: (800) 426-9400

Web: http://www.microsoft.com

Active Database Connector (ADC)

This is a key piece of Microsoft's Internet client/server technology for building useful intranet applications that mimic existing client/server systems' capability to handle live data. This software links Microsoft's Internet Explorer Web browser to server databases across the Internet. Current Web-based applications can present only a static view of data retrieved from databases. Through ADC, developers can build applications that cache database information locally on the client machines, thus improving the performance of applications by distributing the workload across the application environment.

Sequiter Software Inc.

9644-54 Ave., Suite 209

Edmonton, Alberta T6E 5V1 Canada

Tel: (403) 436-2999

Fax: (403) 436-2999

Email: info@sequiter.com

Web: http://www.sequiter.com

CodeBase

CodeBase 6 is a high-performance database engine designed for developers who need maximum speed in their applications without giving up huge amounts of system resources to get it. CodeBase 6 meets this need by combining a small, fast database library with an easy-to-use API that integrates seamlessly with multiple programming languages. It is multiuser-xBASE compatible, completely portable, and fully scaleable between single-user, multiuser, and client/server. It also includes a complete set of RAD tools and full source code for the library.

Simba Technologies

885 Dunsmuir St., Suite 400

Vancouver, BC Canada V6C 1N8

Tel: (604) 601-5300

 (800) 388-4933 (in North America)

Fax: (604) 601-5320

Email: info@simba.com

Web: http://www.simba.com

SimbaExpress and SimbaEngine for JDBC

SimbaExpress and SimbaEngine for JDBC are ODBC and 100 percent Pure Java JDBC connectivity solutions, including server and desktop-based drivers for high performance and manageable Internet data access. A common theme with all Simba's family of products is their capability to support the Microsoft data access interfaces: ADO, RDO, and OLE DB.

Enabling Technology-Development Tools

This category is for products that will allow you to leverage your client/server development.

Advantageware Inc.

425 Madison Avenue, Suite 1700

New York, NY 10017-1155

Tel: (212) 319-1903

(888) 858-0800

Fax: (212) 319-1016

Web: http://www.advantageware.com

VB Advantage

VB Advantage is a powerful Visual Basic development productivity utility that enhances the Visual Basic design-time environment. VB Advantage's mission is to give you an easy way to have and create design-time tools that let you exploit the powerful features within Visual Basic and give you function and features not available in Visual Basic.

Crescent Software, Division of Progress Software Corporation

14 Oak Park

Bedford, MA 01730

Tel: (800) 352-2742

Web: http://www.progress.com/crescent

EnQuiry

EnQuiry is a point-and-click solution to SQL query-building and data-bound control layout. As a well-integrated add-in application to Visual Basic, EnQuiry can take you away from the time-consuming tasks of database access and form layout. With EnQuiry, query generation, query preview, and form layout have become a single speedy process.

Integra Technology International

70-15 Austin St., 3rd Floor

Forest Hills, NY 11375

Tel: (718) 793-7963

(800) 535-3267

Fax: (718) 793-9710

Integra VDB for Visual Basic

Integra VDB for Visual Basic is a graphical database builder to help build client/server applications easily, quickly, and often with virtually no code. It consists of database custom controls, a database class library, database functions, a visual query builder, a visual data manager, and an SQL engine based on the ANSI SQL 92 standard. It comes in two editions: Desktop and Client/Server. The Desktop Edition supports Microsoft Access, FoxPro, Btrieve, dBASE, Paradox, and Integra SQL. The Client/Server Edition supports all the Desktop Edition databases, as well as other database systems that support ODBC, such as DEC Rdb, SQL 400, DB2, Oracle, Sybase, Microsoft SQL Server, Ingres, Informix, Watcom SQL, and others.

Microsoft Corporation
One Microsoft Way
Redmond, WA 98052
Tel: (800) 426-9400
Web: http://www.microsoft.com

Microsoft Visual Basic 6.0, Enterprise Edition

Visual Basic makes it possible to create 32-bit multitiered client/server applications with true distributed processing within the application. The foundation for this distributed process is OLE. OLE already has become the industry standard for application interoperability on the desktop. In Visual Basic 6.0, you can create ActiveX Automation Servers for application interoperability. Through this capability, you can create OLE-based business objects that can be used across development environments. Remote data access has been enhanced through the use of a remote data control and the remote data object. You can create ActiveX controls that contain business logic for use over the Internet or within your intranet. ActiveX documents can help you develop applications that are browser-centric rather than form-centric. WebClasses and DHTML components can easily be created in this version. Management of team development can be done directly through the Visual Basic design environment with the integrated Microsoft Visual SourceSafe version control system.

Microsoft Visual C++ 6.0

Visual C++ is a development system that provides tools to help you take advantage of the power of code reuse. Key pieces of the reuse architecture are the Component Gallery, customizable AppWizards, and *Microsoft Foundation Class* (MFC) extensions. The Component Gallery contains reusable C++ components and OLE controls shareable with other tools. The AppWizard allows you to create and use templates to jump-start application development. MFC extensions are dynamic link libraries that extend MFC libraries by deriving new custom classes. Through the use of Visual C++, you can extend your client/server development by using it to build middle-tier components.

NuMega Technologies
9 Townsend West
Nashua, NH 03063
Tel: (603) 578-8400
    (800) 4-NUMEGA
Fax: (603) 578-8401
Web: http://www.numega.com

NuMega DevPartner Studio

NuMega DevPartner Studio, the SmartDebugging companion for Visual Studio, accelerates team development of components and applications, whether they are developed in Visual C++, Visual Basic, or Visual J++, for the enterprise or the Internet. This suite of tools automatically detects, diagnoses, and facilitates the resolution of software bugs and performance problems.

Rational Software
18880 Homestead Rd.
Cupertino, CA 95014
Tel: (408) 863-9900
    (800) 728-1212
Fax: (408) 863-4120
Web: http://www.rational.com

Rational Rose

Rational Rose is a graphical component modeling and development tool that enables organizations both to model software applications that meet current business needs and to evolve them easily as new requirements emerge. It allows developers to step back and graphically visualize their applications using the industry-standard notation, the *Unified Modeling Language* (UML). It integrates into the Microsoft Repository, which is part of Microsoft's Data Warehousing Framework. It also includes multilanguage development support for C++, Java, and Visual Basic, letting you create components/classes in mixed languages from the modeled components.

Sheridan Software Systems
35 Pinelawn Rd.
Melville, NY 11747
Tel: (516) 753-0985
Fax: (516) 753-3661
Web: http://www.shersoft.com

VBAssist

VBAssist is a set of productivity tools that seamlessly integrate into the Visual Basic development environment. VBAssist has been totally re-architected to take maximum advantage of Visual Basic's 32-bit environment.

Siemens Nixdorf Information Systems
200 Wheeler Rd.
Burlington, MA 01803

Tel: (617) 273-0480
Fax: (617) 221-0231
Web: http://usa.siemens.com

ComUnity Visual Framework

This is a comprehensive business application development environment for Visual Basic. The ComUnity Visual Framework facilitates the building and deployment of extensible multitier applications out of reusable ActiveX components, enabling developers to focus on business logic and presentation customization.

WhippleWare
20 Cedar St.
Charleston, MA 02129
Tel: (617) 242-2511
　　(800) 241-8727
Fax: (617) 241-8496
Web: http://www.whippleware.com

VB Compress Pro

VB Compress Pro analyzes your project from top to bottom and reports in detail on what it finds. It also creates an optimized copy of your code without a single unnecessary byte.

Internet

The Internet has become a very natural extension of the client/server environment. This category depicts resources that allow you to leverage your client/server components over the Internet. A number of other Java development environments are available in addition to the ones mentioned in this section. The ones mentioned here contain ActiveX-enabled Java Virtual Machines, which allow you to make COM objects in Java where other Java development environments cannot.

Halcyon Software
1590 La Pradera Drive
Campbell, CA 95008
Tel: (408) 378-9898
Fax: (408) 378-9935
Email: info@halcyonsoft.com
Web: http://www.halcyonsoft.com

Instant Java for Basic

Instant Java for Basic (IJ4B) is a 4GL development tool compatible with Visual Basic. It allows you to easily migrate existing Visual Basic applications to Java platforms. The Professional Edition of IJ4B contains support for data controls, data access objects (DAO), and remote data objects (RDO). It also enables you to create 100 percent Pure Java solutions without learning the Java language or a new Java Integrated Development Environment (IDE).

Instant Installer

This lightweight, 100% Pure Java certified, full-featured integrated application deployment and distribution solution for Java simplify cross-platform installation. Developers can create single-step installation files that can be executed on any Java-enabled platform. Instant Installer provides support for several installation features, including algorithm-based serial number generation, creating and saving multiple distribution configurations, installation options (for example, Compact, Typical, Custom), promotional side screens during installation, Java Virtual Machine auto detection, and more.

Microsoft Corporation
One Microsoft Way
Redmond, WA 98052
Tel: (800) 426-9400
Web: http://www.microsoft.com

Microsoft Visual J++

This product is a Java development tool using Microsoft's Developer Studio IDE. It is optimized for both novice and experienced Java developers. It contains wizards to help developers create applications that take advantage of animation sequences, forms, databases, multiple threads, and more. It includes a Java source compiler that drastically cuts build time with its capability to compile up to 10,000 lines of code per second.

Microsoft Visual Basic 6.0 Custom Control Edition

This product is designed specifically to be the easiest and fastest way to create ActiveX components. Unlike its full-version counterparts, the Custom Control Edition can be used only to create ActiveX controls; it cannot be used to create standalone applications. It is free and available for download from the Internet.

SuperCede, Inc.
110–110th Ave. NE
Bellevue, WA 98004-5840
Tel: (425) 462-7242
     (800) 365-8553
Web: http://www.supercede.com

SuperCede for Java

SuperCede provides the highest Java performance when you need it, with the first native compiler for the Intel/Win32 platform. Plus, SuperCede is the only compiler with complete support for JDK 1.1, including compilation from both source and bytecode—even dynamic loading of class files into native executables. Of course, you can generate portable class files whenever you need portability.

Symantec Corp.

10201 Torre Ave.

Cupertino, CA 95014

Tel: (800) 441-7234

Web: http://www.symantec.com

Visual Café for Java

Visual Café is a rapid Java development environment. Through the use of drag-and-drop, a comprehensive component library, and an extensive Java toolset, application development time is drastically reduced. Visual Café also is available in a Pro version. The Pro version includes all the features of Café, as well as database connectivity through the use of Symantec dbANYWHERE Workgroup Server, a middleware database server.

TVObjects

29 Emmons Drive

Princeton, NJ 08540

Tel: (609) 514-1444

Fax: (609) 514-1004

Web: http://www.tvobjects.com

Applet Designer

This add-in allows Visual Basic developers to create Java applets from within their Visual Basic environment. You create an application through the Visual Basic development environment, and Applet Designer saves your form and code module with a .JAV extension. Then you click Applet Designer's Make Applet button, and it converts your Visual Basic code into Java code. At this point, you need to compile the Java-generated code with a Java compiler, such as Microsoft Visual J++ or Symantec Visual Café. Applet Designer is available in three versions: Applet Designer, Applet Designer Professional, and Applet Designer Enterprise. The Professional edition does all that was just mentioned, and it includes Java database connectivity code based on Visual Basic's data access object. It ships with Sun's Java Developer's Kit. The Enterprise edition also supports industry-standard CORBA.

Internet Servers

With the Internet playing a large role in distributed application development, the need for more robust Internet servers has increased. No longer are Internet servers residing only on UNIX servers, but also on Windows NT and Windows 95 servers.

Microsoft Corporation

One Microsoft Way

Redmond, WA 98052

Tel: (800) 426-9400

Web: http://www.microsoft.com/iis

Microsoft Internet Information Server

The Microsoft *Internet Information Server* (IIS) is an Active Server fully integrated into Windows NT Server. IIS security is tied into NT Server's, which makes managing users and resources easier. Its toolset includes content creation and management with Microsoft FrontPage, context indexing with Microsoft Index Server, database connectivity through ODBC, *common gateway interface* (CGI) support, and integration with Microsoft BackOffice products. It also is capable of server-side scripting, which enables developers to create Web applications that dynamically build HTML documents on the server before they are sent across the wire to the user's browser. These documents are called *active server pages*. A server-side scripted application does not rely on just one language but can be developed using JavaScript, VBScript, HTML, Perl, and CGI.

Netscape Communications

501 E. Middlefield Rd.

Mountain View, CA 94043

Tel: (415) 937-2555

Web: http://www.netscape.com

Netscape SuiteSpot

SuiteSpot is a suite of five integrated servers that allows your business and network to communicate using Internet technology. It includes the following servers: Netscape Enterprise Server, Netscape Proxy Server, Netscape Catalog Server, Netscape News Server, and Netscape Mail Server. It also includes the LiveWire Pro development environment. Its integrated management services include SNMP versions 1 and 2, and SSL 3.0-based security. It also provides database support through native drivers for Informix, Oracle, and Sybase, as well as database connectivity through ODBC.

O'Reilly & Associates
101 Morris St.
Sebastopol, CA 95472
Tel: (800) 998-9938
Web: http://www.ora.com

WebSite

WebSite is an Internet server that not only works with Windows NT but Windows 95 as well. It's available in two editions: WebSite and WebSite Professional. Both allow you to publish and maintain your HTML documents, control user access, and use CGI to access applications within your HTML documents. The latest version comes with the capability to use Visual Basic to create Web-based applications. WebSite Professional not only has CGI support, but Java and Microsoft ISAPI compatibility as well. It also includes database connectivity through the use of ColdFusion, a powerful application package with templates and a software development kit.

Microsoft Visual Basic for Applications

Visual Basic for Applications (VBA) is Microsoft's vision for one common macro language. Built on the foundation of Visual Basic, VBA is a shared development environment that enables developers for Microsoft Office and other applications featuring VBA to create custom business solutions. VBA's development environment includes a lot of the same features that come with Visual Basic, such as the VBA language engine and an IDE. The only thing VBA cannot do is generate standalone components, such as a standard EXE or ActiveX object.

VBA is available in products such as Microsoft Office 97, Microsoft Project, Visio Corp.'s Visio products, and Autodesk's AutoCAD. By incorporating VBA into your client/server application, your customers can extend your application without having to modify your core components.

Mystic River Software
142 North Rd.
Sudbury, MA 01776
Tel: (978) 371-1100
Fax: (978) 371-1818
Web: http://www.mysticriver.com

Mystic River's PowerPack

Mystic River's PowerPack is an automated developer's toolkit that allows ISVs (Independent Software Vendors) and corporate MIS departments to incorporate VBA scripting technology into programs written in C++ or Visual Basic 5.0. It comes with a set of tools that let developers plant VBA quickly and effectively into Visual

Basic and C++ applications a full order of magnitude faster than could be achieved with the VBA SDK alone.

Summit Software
4933 Jamesville Road
Jamesville, NY 13078-9428
Tel: (315) 445-9000
Fax: (315) 445-9567
Email: info@summsoft.com
Web: http://www.summsoft.com

Summit VBA Access Object

The Summit *VBA Access Object* (VAO) is an ActiveX component that makes it easy to add Microsoft VBA to Visual Basic applications.

Summit VBA Framework for MFC

The Summit *VBA Framework for MFC* (VBFX) is a set of MFC-derived classes that greatly simplifies the task of integrating Visual Basic, Applications Edition into an MFC application. In the same way that MFC makes it relatively easy for you to access the powerful features of OLE, the MFC-derived classes in VBFX make it easy for you to use VBA's many features without having to learn the intricacies of VBA's COM-based interfaces and services. VBFX supports the MFC document/view architecture while allowing your MFC application to host OLE controls that interact with VBA. Your application uses VBFX as a set of base classes, which are in turn derived from standard MFC classes.

Report Writers

Report writers access data stored in database tables and allow users to manipulate the information in a more useful and informative manner.

Strategic Reporting Systems, Inc.
3 Centennial Drive, Suite G
Peabody, MA 01960
Tel: (978) 531-0905
Fax: (978) 531-1007
Web: http://www.srs-inc.com

ReportSmith

ReportSmith is a reporting and query tool that lets you interact with data directly. ReportSmith takes a different approach to reports; it creates reports by allowing you to work with live data to give a true *what you see is what you get* (WYSIWYG) environment.

Concentric Data Systems, Inc.

110 Turnpike Rd.

Westborough, MA 01581

Tel: (508) 366-1122

   (800) 325-9035

Fax: (508) 366-2954

Web: http://www.infointf.com/rrinfo.htm

R&R Report Writer for Windows, SQL Edition

R&R Report Writer lets you select, analyze, summarize, and present data from client/server databases. No knowledge of SQL syntax or programming is necessary. Through the use of menus, data selection automatically generates the SQL statements for you. Customizable report wizards make creating new reports easy for any user. R&R can be incorporated into almost any application through the use of runtime EXE, DLL, and VBX modules.

Data Dynamics

2600 Tiller Lane

Columbus, OH 43231

Tel: (614) 895-3142

Fax: (614) 899-2943

Email: info@datadynamics.com

Web: http://www.datadynamics.com

ActiveReports

ActiveReports combines the power and ease of use of Visual Basic with advanced ActiveX Designer Component technology to provide the ultimate report designer for Visual Basic developers. ActiveReports is fully integrated in the Visual Basic programming environment; it feels and works like Visual Basic—no more cryptic scripts or workarounds. It provides a fully open architecture that lets you use Visual Basic code, ActiveX, and OLE objects in your reports so that you can handle the toughest reports without limits.

Microsoft Corporation

One Microsoft Way

Redmond, WA

Tel: (800) 426-9400

Web: http://www.microsoft.com

Microsoft Access

Microsoft Access on its own can be used to develop multiuser applications. By incorporating it as one of your client/server tools, you can use it as part of your business objects. Microsoft Access now demonstrates its reporting capabilities as an OLE object.

ProtoView
2540 Route 130
Cranbury, NJ 08512
Tel: (609) 655-5000
   (800) 231-8588
Fax: (609) 655-5353
Web: http://www.protoview.com

ScreenPrinter

ProtoView ScreenPrinter is an ActiveX control that developers can use to add screen-printing capabilities to their applications using as little as one line of code. Invisible at runtime, the ScreenPrinter exposes methods and properties that can be invoked programmatically (through button clicks or menu selections by the end user) to capture and possibly print a screen.

Seagate Software Information Management Group
1095 West Pender St., 4th Floor
Vancouver BC Canada V6E 2M6
Tel: (604) 681-3435
   (800) 677-2340 (in North America)
Fax: (604) 681-2934
Web: http://www.seagatesoftware.com/

Crystal Reports

Crystal Reports combines ease of use with the report-design and data-analysis features that make reporting tasks really efficient. Whether it's Web reporting that leverages existing skills, flexible report integration within applications, or presentation-quality reports from any database, Seagate Crystal Reports 6 is the only tool you need. Its page-on-demand, thin-wire architecture ensures superior Web response time.

VideoSoft
5900 Hollis St., Suite T
Emeryville, CA 94608
Tel: (510) 595-2400
   (888) ACTIVEX
Fax: (510) 595-2424
Web: http://www.videosoft.com

VSReport

VSReport allows you to print Microsoft Access-created reports without having Access or its runtime DLLs installed on the user's machine. This ActiveX control permits you to use the industry's leading report designer, Access, to create your reports and then print them using Visual Basic or any ActiveX container.

Transaction Servers

For years, mainframe applications took advantage of transaction servers to manage the execution of applications and resources across the enterprise. With the reintroduction of distributed processing and applications at the personal computer network level, transaction servers are being introduced to a new generation of application developers.

IBM Corp.

1133 Westchester Ave.

White Plains NY 10604

Tel: (800) 426-3333

Web: http://www.ibm.com

Transaction Server for Windows NT

This transaction-processing solution provides CICS functionality for business-critical applications that will help leverage client/server applications and extend application capabilities to meet future business requirements. It's a robust, enterprise-wide process coordinator and integrator of servers across the network. It includes five basic components: CICS for Windows NT Server; CICS clients that support OS/2, DOS, Windows 3.x, Macintosh, Windows 95, and Windows NT operating systems; Encina for Windows NT; Encina Clients for AIX and Windows NT; and CICS Client for AIX.

Microsoft Corporation

One Microsoft Way

Redmond, WA 98052

Tel: (800) 426-9400

Web: http://www.microsoft.com

Microsoft Transaction Server

This Active Server is a key component to Microsoft's Active Server lineup. Applications designed for the Internet using Microsoft Internet Information Server to Visual Basic applications developed for DCOM can take advantage of this server. Its components include transaction-process monitoring, transaction-resource scaleability, component configuration, and security services. It is available free as part of the Windows NT Option Pack.

Progress Software Corp.

14 Oak Park

Bedford, MA 01730

Tel: (800) 477-6473

Web: http://webspeed.progress.com

WebSpeed Transaction Server

The WebSpeed Transaction Server is a Web-based transaction-processing environment that ensures the integrity of your database transaction. It contains three components: Messenger, Transaction Broker, and Transaction Agent. The Messenger is compatible with any CGI-compliant Web server. Its purpose is to transfer data directly between the Web server and the Transaction Agent during a single transaction. The Transaction Broker manages the pool of Transaction Agents and maintains the status information of Web requests. This eliminates the overhead of starting a new agent for each user request, and it dynamically increases the agent pool size when resources start to get low. The Transaction Agent executes Web objects and database transactions, and dynamically merges data into HTML format to build Web documents in real time.

NOTE

In no way are any of the authors endorsing any of these products; nor is this a complete list of client/server database resources. Many of the vendors' Web sites refer to other client/server products through links. This portion of the appendix is just to give you a good place to start.

CompuServe/Internet/World Wide Web Support

A popular form of getting support from peers is through electronic sources such as CompuServe or the Internet. The support areas listed here are a very small representation of the online support available. To find more online support, go to any of the Web sites listed here and look for links to other Visual Basic Web sites.

ADVANCED VISUAL BASIC

http://www.duke-net.com/vb

CALIFORNIA STATE UNIVERSITY, SAN MARCOS

http://coyote.csusm.edu/cwis/winworld/vbasic.html

CODD MULTIMEDIA HOME PAGE—HOME OF VB ONLINE

Web: `http://www.vbonline.com`

CompuServe: GO BASIC

FAWCETTE TECHNICAL PUBLISHINGS

Web: `http://www.windx.com`

CompuServe: GO VBPJ

GO WINCOMPA

GO WINCOMPB

GO WINCOMPC

GARY 'N CARL'S VISUAL BASIC HOME PAGE

`http://www.apexsc.com/vb`

GARY BEENE'S VISUAL BASIC WORLD

`http://www.iadfw.net/gbeene/visual.html`

MICROSOFT CORPORATION

`http://www.microsoft.com/msdn`

`http://www.microsoft.com/support`

VB TIPS & TRICKS HOME PAGE

`http://www.apexsc.com/vb/davem/vbtt.html`

Visual Basic User Groups

AMATEUR COMPUTER GROUP OF NEW JERSEY (ACGNJ)

Jim Wong

113 Mt. Arlington Blvd.

Landing, NJ 07850

Phone: (201) 398-2087

ATLANTA VISUAL BASIC USER'S GROUP

Andy Dean, Paul Goldsman

946 Glen Arden Way, NE

Atlanta, GA 30306

Phone: (404) 874-6938

Fax: (404) 872-1286

CompuServe: 71233,1412

Web: `http://www.mindspring.com/~andyd/avbug.html`

AUSTRALIAN VISUAL BASIC USER'S GROUP

Mark Henry

Information Technology

3/489 Swanston St.

Melbourne, Vic 3000

Australia

Phone: 61-3-9623-3262 (business hours)

61-3-9877-5969 (after hours)

Fax: 61-3-9894-2738

BBS: 61-3-9761-4043

BAY AREA VISUAL BASIC USER GROUP

Gustavo Eydelsteyn

2625 Alcatraz Ave. #271

Berkeley, CA 94705

Phone: (510) 547-7295

BELLEVILLE AREA VISUAL BASIC UG

Robert Morris

507 North Fourth St.

Mascoutah, IL 62258

Phone: (618) 566-7505

BIG BLUE AND COUSINS—VISUAL BASIC

Victoria, BC V8R 6S4

Elliott Building

Phone: (604) 382-3934

BOSTON COMPUTER SOCIETY VB-SIG

John Barrie

30 Clark St.

Holden, MA 01520

Phone: (508) 829-2181

CompuServe: 70373,2241

Web: http://www.bcs.org/

CALGARY VISUAL BASIC UG

Jean Paradis

3100-150 6th Ave. SW

Calgary, Alberta, Canada T2P 4M5

Phone: (403) 234-2929

Web: http://www.iadfw.net/gbeene/calgary.html

CAPITAL DISTRICT USER GROUP

Jeff Polansky, President

420 Sand Creek Road, Suite 132

Albany, NY 12205

Phone: (518) 459-8536, ext. 19

CompuServe: 73114,2754

CAPITAL PC UG

Charles Kelly

3613 Rose Lane

Annandale, VA 20550

Phone: (202) 357-9796

Fax: (703) 642-2329

Web: http://cpcug.org/user/windows

CENTRAL FLORIDA VB UG

Chris Douglas

Route 3, Box 55W

Aachua, FL 32615

CENTRAL TEXAS PC USER'S GROUP

http://www.ctpcug.com/newsltr/9506/sigs.htm

CHARLOTTE AREA VB USERS GROUP

Gary Baker

102 Higgins Court

Huntersville, NC 28078

CompuServe: 75505,1114

Web: http://www.iadfw.net/gbeene/charlott.html

CHARLOTTE VISUAL BASIC USERS GROUP

Tim Booker

One Nations Bank Plaza, Suite 3710

Charlotte, NC 28280

Phone: (704) 375-5788

Fax: (704) 375-5699

CHICAGO COMPUTER SOCIETY

Allan Wolff

1560 North Sandburg Terrace, Suite 1715

Chicago, IL 60610

Phone: (312) 787-8966

CHICAGO CORPORATE VISUAL BASIC USER GROUP

http://www.ccvbug.org

COMPUTER EXPERTS OF NORTHERN CALIFORNIA—VISUAL BASIC

1266 Sir Francis Drake

Kentfield, CA 94904-1005

Phone: (415) 925-9880

COMPUTER LANGUAGE SOCIETY

Bill Sharpe
455 Lincoln Blvd.
Santa Monica, CA 90402
Phone: (310) 451-9598

CONNECTICUT VISUAL BASIC SPECIAL INTEREST GROUP

North Haven, CT
Phone: (203) 239-6874
Fax: (203) 239-6874
Web: http://www.vb-bootcamp.com/

DANBURY AREA COMPUTER SOCIETY—VISUAL BASIC

Danbury, CT
Phone: (203) 791-2283

DES MOINES VB USERS GROUP

Tej Dhawan
5233 Walnut St.
West Des Moines, IA 50265

DIABLO VALLEY PC UG

Steve Israel
3687 Mt. Diablo Blvd., Suite 350
Lafayette, CA 94549

EDMONTON VB/ACCESS DEVELOPERS SIG

Nisku, Alberta
Phone: (403) 955-3065

GOLD COAST USER GROUP

Joe Homnick

Maureen Callery

2300 Glades Rd.

Suite 150 Tower West

Boca Raton, FL 33431

Phone: (407) 368-0010

Fax: (407) 347-0765

GOTHAM NEW YORK PC CORPORATION—VISUAL BASIC

New York, NY

Phone: (212) 686-6972

GREATER CLEVELAND PC USERS GROUP—VISUAL BASIC

Cleveland, OH

Phone: (216) 781-4132

HARTFORD VISUAL BASIC UG

Daniel Mezick

New Technology Solutions

6 Robin Court, Suite 720

North Haven, CT 06473

Phone: (203) 239-6874

HEARTLAND WINDOWS PC UG

Ken Neal

10201 W. 89th Terrace

Overland Park, KS 66212

Phone: (913) 541-0591

HOUSTON AREA LEAGUE

Fred Thorlin
10819 Lakeside Forest Lane
Houston, TX 77042-1025
Phone: (713) 784-8906
Web: http://www.hal-pc.org/

HOUSTON VB SIG

Robert D. Thompson
3215 Mulberry Hill Lane
Houston, TX 77084
Phone: (713) 398-9042

INDIANAPOLIS COMPUTER SOCIETY

Bill Seltzer
2064 Emily Dr.
Indianapolis, IN 46260
Web: http://www.otisnet.com/ICS/ics.htm

IVBUG (THE IRISH VISUAL BASIC USERS GROUP)

Donal P Higgins
c/o Carmichael House
60 Lower Baggot St.
Dublin 2
Ireland
Phone: 353-1-676-2240
Fax: 353-1-676-2447

IVY TECH TERRE HAUTE REGION 7 VB USER GROUP

7999 US Highway 41
Terre Haute, IN 47802
Web: http://www.ivy.tec.in.us/haute/thaute.htm

KANSAS CITY HEARTLAND USER'S GROUP VB SIG

Belton, MO

Phone: (816) 322-1845

KENTUCKY/INDIANA PC UG

Tim Landgrave

200 Whittington Parkway, Suite 100A

Louisville, KY 40222

LAS VEGAS PC USERS GROUP—VISUAL BASIC

3200 E. Cheynne Ave.

Las Vegas, NV 89119

Phone: (702) 736-3788

LONDON LIFE VISUAL BASIC UG

Stephen Baldock, Consultant

255 Dufferin Ave.

London, Ontario

N6A 4K1 Canada

Phone: (519) 432-2000, ext. 4429

Fax: (519) 432-3862

Web: http://www.iadfw.net/gbeene/london.html

LONG ISLAND PC USERS GROUP—VISUAL BASIC

235 Pinelawn Rd.

Baldwin, NY 11510-1031

Phone: (516) 223-1761

LOS ANGELES VISUAL BASIC USERS GROUP

Covina, CA

Phone: (818) 332-8879

MADISON PC UG

Peter Welter
1225 W. Dayton St., Room 1229
Madison, WI 53706
Phone: (608) 263-3447

MARYLAND VISUAL BASIC USER GROUP

College Park, MD
Phone: (301) 405-2977
Fax: (301) 314-9198

MELBOURNE PC USER GROUP—BASIC PROGRAMMING

South Melbourne, VIC
Phone: (613) 699-622
Web: http://www.melbpc.org.au/

MEMPHIS PC USERS GROUP, INC.—VISUAL BASIC

5983 Macon Cove
Memphis, TN 38124-1756
Phone: (901) 375-4316

MEXICAN VB USER GROUP

http://www.iadfw.net/gbeene/mexico.html

MILWAUKEE AREA VISUAL BASIC USERS' GROUP

Arthur Edstrom
P.O. Box 28
Waterford, WI 53815-0028
Phone: (414) 534-5181 (daytime)
      (414) 534-3440 (evening)
CompuServe: 75410,2203

MONTREAL-GROUPE D'ENTRAIDE VISUAL BASIC

`http://www.login.net/gvbm/vb.htm`

NAPA VALLEY PC UG

Frank Sommer
1253 Monticello Rd.
Napa, CA 94558
Phone: (707) 258-2509
Web: `http://community.net/~stevefc/vb.html`

NORTH ORANGE COUNTY COMPUTER CLUB

Bill Hines
712 N. Clinton
Orange, CA 92667
Phone: (714) 633-4874

NORTH TEXAS PC UG

Woody Pewitt
3200 W. Pleasant Run Rd., Suite 328
Lancaster, TX 75146-1046
Phone: (214) 230-3485

NORTH TEXAS PC UG (BEGINNERS GROUP)

Jim Carter
1112 Pueblo Drive
Richardson, TX 75080
Phone: (214) 235-5968

NYPC VISUAL BASIC SIG

David Kulick
147–51 72nd Road, #3F
Flushing, NY 11367
Phone: (718) 261-0285

OKLAHOMA CITY PC USERS GROUP—VISUAL BASIC

1900 Spring Lake Drive
Oklahoma City, OK 73157-2027
Phone: (405) 791-0894

ORANGE COAST IBM PC UG

Wendy Sarrett
3700 Park View Lane #22D
Irvine, CA 92715
Phone: (714) 966-3925

ORANGE COUNTY VISUAL BASIC UG

Irvine, CA
Web: http://www.ocvbug.org

PACIFIC NORTHWEST PC UG

Sean Bleichschmidt
9602 NE 35th Place
Bellevue, WA 98004
Phone: (206) 462-8395

PACIFIC NORTHWEST PC UG

Richard Buhrer
1202 East Pike St. #665
Seattle, WA 98122
Phone: (206) 324-9024

PASADENA IBM USERS GROUP

Rod Ream and David Jung
2026 South 6th St.
Alahambra, CA 91830
Phone: (626) 280-6850
Web: http://www.pibmug.org/sigs/vbsig.html

PC USERS' GROUP INC. (ACT)—VISUAL BASIC

Belconnen, ACT 2616 Australia
Phone: (616) 239-6511

PHILADELPHIA AREA COMPUTER SOCIETY

Steve Longo
c/o LaSalle University
1900 West Olney
Philadelphia, PA 19141
Phone: (215) 951-1255

PHOENIX PC UG

P.O. Box 35637
Phoenix, AZ 85069-5637
Phone: (602) 222-8511
BBS: (602) 222-5491
Web: http://www.phoenixpcug.org/

PINELLAS IBM PC UG

Thomas Kiehl
14155 102nd Ave. N
Largo, FL 34644

PORTABLE COMPUTING UG

Virginia Benedict
208 E. 51 St. #366
New York, NY 10022
Phone: (212) 348-0690

PORTLAND VISUAL BASIC USER GROUP

Hillsburo, OR 97123
Phone: (503) 628-0705
Fax: (503) 628-6005
Web: http://www.teleport.com/~pdxvbug/

POUGHKEEPSIE IBM CLUB MICROCOMPUTER CLUB—BASIC

Hyde Park, NY

Phone: (914) 229-6551

QUEENSLAND VB GROUP

---

http://www.odyssey.com.au/vb/index.html

RESEARCH TRIANGLE PARK VB USER GROUP

Bob Canavan

c/o Fonville Morisey Realtors

3600 Glennwood Ave., Suite 150

Raleigh, NC 27612

Phone: (919) 781-7809

RICHMOND ACCESS/VISUAL BASIC DEVELOPERS' FORUM

Glen Allen, VA

Phone: (804) 273-6244

Fax: (804) 273-1804

SACRAMENTO PC UG—VB/ACCESS

Larry Clark

345 Prewett Drive

Folsom, CA 95630

Phone: (916) 983-3950

Web: http://www.iadfw.net/gbeene/mento.html

ST. LOUIS USER GROUP FOR THE PC—BASIC

St. Louis, MO 63169-0099

Phone: (314) 458-9597

ST. LOUIS VISUAL BASIC USERS GROUP

Brian Back
2066 Willow Leaf
St. Louis, MO 63131
Phone: (314) 984-8779
Email: brianb@mo.net

SAN DIEGO VISUAL BASIC USERS GROUP

7480 Mission Valley Rd.
La Jolla, CA 92037
Phone: (619) 459-5535
Fax: (619) 459-5535
Web: http://www.apexsc.com/vb/davem/sdvbug.html

SAN FERNANDO VALLEY VISUAL BASIC USERS GROUP

http://www.instanet.com/~mdorris

SAN FRANCISCO SOFTWARE FORUM'S VB-SIG

Dov Gorman
1164 18th St.
San Francisco, CA
Phone: (415) 552-3859
Web: http://www.softwareforum.org

SANTA CLARITA VALLEY PC GROUP—VISUAL BASIC

Canyon Country, CA
Phone: (805) 252-8852

SILICON VALLEY SOFTWARE FORUM'S VB-SIG

Allan Colby
107 Lake Rd.
Portola Valley, CA 94028-8116
Phone: (415) 851-4567
Web: http://www.softwareforum.org

SOFTWARE FORUM

Barbara Cass
Phone: (415) 854-7219
Web: http://www.softwareforum.org/

SOUTH FLORIDA DATABASE AND DEVELOPERS GROUP VB/ACCESS SIG

Coconut Grove, FL
Phone: (305) 858-8200
Fax: (305) 858-3719
Web: http://www.shadow.net/~datachem/sfddg12.html

SPACE COAST PC USERS GROUP—VISUAL BASIC

---

308 Forest Ave.
Cocoa, FL 32923-0369
Phone: (407) 254-1926

STATE COLLEGE AREA VISUAL BASIC USERS GROUP

---

c/o Blue Mountain Software
W. David Raike
208 West Hamilton Ave.
State College, PA 16810
Phone: (814) 234-2417

TAMPA BAY COMPUTER SOCIETY

Clearwater, FL
Phone: (813) 443-4433
Web: http://www.iadfw.net/gbeene/tampa.html

TC/PC VB-SIG

Bill Rothermal
3629 Sumter Ave. S.
St. Louis Parl, MN 55426-4007
Phone: (612) 935-0513

TORONTO VB USERS GROUP

Dwayne Lamb

3555 Don Mill Rd.

Suite 6-1705

North York, ON, Canada, M2H 3N3

Phone: (416) 499-1978

Fax: (416) 499-1681

Email: mrsheep@visualbyte.com

TORONTO WINDOWS UG

Don Roy

6327 Atherley Crescent

Mississaugua, ONT, Canada, L5N 2J1

Phone: (416) 826-0320

TUCSON COMPUTER SOCIETY

Bruce Fulton

516 East Mabel

Tucson, AZ 85705

Phone: (602) 577-7700

CompuServe: 73510,3550

Web: http://www.azstarnet.com/public/nonprofit/tcs

TULSA COMPUTER SOCIETY—VISUAL BASIC

Tulsa, OK

Phone: (918) 622-3417

TWIN CITIES PC UG, INC.—ACCESS/VISUAL BASIC PROFESSIONAL

Edina, MN 55424

Phone: (612) 229-5850

UK VISUAL BASIC USER GROUP

Jeff Cabrie

15 Mount Way

Chepstow

Gwent

NP6 5NF England

Phone: 44-0291-620720

Fax: 44-0291-627320

Web: http://www.exe.co.uk/home/vbug.html

UNIVERSITY OF MARYLAND VISUAL BASIC USER GROUP

http://wonderland.dial.umd.edu/documents/VisualBasic/AboutVBUG.html

UTAH COMPUTER SOCIETY—VISUAL BASICS

Jim Murtha

P.O. Box 510811

Salt Lake City, UT 84151

Phone: (801) 521-7830

BBS: (801) 521-5009

Web: http://www.ucs.org

VB LARGE USERS GROUP

Englewood, NJ 07631

Phone: (201) 816-8900

Fax: (201) 816-1644

VB LARGE USERS GROUP—NYC

George Febish

50 East Palisade Ave., Suite 411

Englewood, NJ 07631

Phone: (201) 816-8900

Fax: (201) 816-1644

VBSPECIALISTS

Lewisville, TX 75067

Phone: (214) 315-7528

VB.UG

Louisville, KY 40222

Phone: (502) 327-0333

Fax: (502) 327-7418

VBUG MEXICO

Alberto Curiel

Torres Adalid 707-302

Mexico D.F. 03100

Phone: (608) 742-5373

VISUAL BASIC DEVELOPER NETWORK

John Chemla

10300 South Cicero

Oak Lawn, IL 60453

Phone: (708) 430-2819

Fax: (708) 430-3643

CompuServe: 72066,3035

Web: `http://d_us.pd.mcs.net/vbdn`

VISUAL DEVELOPER'S GROUP (VISDEV—AN ONLINE USER GROUP)

`http://www.galstar.com/~qt2/visdev.html`

VISUAL BASIC GROEP (DUTCH)

`http://www.xs4all.nl/~treffers/vbgg.htm`

VISUAL BASIC MILWAUKEE

Waterford, WI 53185-0028

Phone: (414) 534-4309

Fax: (414) 534-7809

VISUAL BASIC USERS OF NOVA SCOTIA

Enfield, NS

Phone: (902) 883-1010

Fax: (902) 883-8586

VDUNY—VISUAL DEVELOPER OF UPSTATE NEW YORK

Robert H. Mowery III

c/o SofTech Multimedia, Inc.

79 Springfield Ave.

Rochester, NY 14609-3607

Phone: (716) 288-5830

Fax: (716) 482-7105

Web: http://www.frontiernet.net/~softech/vduny/

WESTCHESTER PC USERS GROUP VB SIG

Michael Lee

Dictaphone Corp.

3191 Broadbridge Rd.

Stratford, CT 06497

WPCUG hotline: (914) 962-8022 for the latest on the Sigs

Phone: (203) 381-7138 (day)

CompuServe: 75720,1221

Web: http://www.wpcug.org/

WINNIPEG PC UG

Darryl Draeger

61 Amundsen Bay

Winnipeg, MB, Canada, R3K0V1

Phone: (204) 831-7163

WINDOWS ON THE ROCKIES USER GROUP—VISUAL BASIC

Highlands Ranch, CO 80126

Phone: (303) 470-6504

Fax: (303) 449-7525

Windows NT/BackOffice User Groups

ADVANCED SYSTEMS USER GROUP

Annandale, VA 22003

Phone: (703) 642-2329

Web: http://cpcug.org/user/ckelly/new_asug.html

AETNA DATABASE USER GROUP

Hartford, CT 06156

Phone: (203) 273-2016

Fax: (203) 273-2016

ANCHORAGE WINDOWS NT USERS GROUP

http://www.rmm.com/awntug/

ARIZONA SOCIETY FOR COMPUTER INFORMATION INC.

Phoenix, AZ

Phone: (602) 978-9031

ASSOCIATION OF DATABASE DEVELOPERS

Oakland, CA

Phone: (415) 281-5638

ATLANTA BACKOFFICE USERS GROUP

Atlanta, GA

Phone: (404) 233-5500

Fax: (404) 233-9698

BELLEVUE DATABASE USERS

Omaha, NE

Phone: (402) 592-9620

Fax: (402) 593-0886

BOSTON COMPUTER SOCIETY WINDOWS NT USERS GROUP

Email: wihl@shore.net

Web: http://www.shore.net/~wihl/nentug.html

BRISBANE NT USER GROUP

Email: dkowald@ozemail.com.au

Web: http://www.ozemail.com.au/~dkowald/bntug.htm

CANBERRA—MICROSOFT SYSTEMS USER GROUP

neil.pinkerton@cao.mts.dec.com

CENTRAL TEXAS PC USERS' GROUP, INC.—DATABASE

26th Red River

Austin, TX 78766

Phone: (512) 343-7258

CHAMPAIGN-URBANA NT USERS GROUP

Email: kashi@uiuc.edu

Web: http://www.cofsci.uiuc.edu/~kashi

CHATTANOOGA–RIVER VALLEY NT USERS GROUP

james@press.southern.edu

CHICAGO AREA NT BUSINESS USERS GROUP

Oak Brook, IL

Phone: (708) 368-7000

Fax: (708) 368-7090

CHICAGO, GREAT LAKES SQL SERVER USER GROUP

Don_Opperthauser@rdisoft.com

COLORADO SPRINGS PC USERS GROUP—WINDOWS NT

Colorado Springs, CO

Phone: (719) 578-2215

COMPUNET COMPUTER CLUB—DATABASE

Sardinia, OH

Phone: (513) 446-2202

COMPUTER EXPERTS OF NORTHERN CALIFORNIA—DATABASE

1266 Sir Francis Drake

Kentfield, CA 94904-1005

Phone: (415) 925-9880

CROSSROADS COMPUTER CLUB—DATABASE

Alexandria, LA

Phone: (318) 487-4078

DANBURY AREA COMPUTER SOCIETY—DATABASE

Danbury, CT

Phone: (203) 791-2283

DATABASE DEVELOPERS GROUP

Peoria, AZ

Phone: (602) 977-2177

DEVELOPERS' SIG

djs@cnj.digex.net

DIABLO VALLEY PC USERS GROUP WINDOWS NT

Walnut Creek, CA

Phone: (510) 943-1367

DUBLIN DATABASE USER GROUP

Dublin, OH
Phone: (614) 766-9828

FRENCH NT USERS GROUP

http://fwntug.esf.org/

GOLDEN GATE COMPUTER SOCIETY—DATABASE SIG

618 B St.
San Rafael, CA 94901
Phone: (415) 454-5556

GOTHAM NEW YORK PC CORPORATION—NT DEVELOPERS

New York, NY
Phone: (212) 686-6972

GREAT LAKES SQL SERVER USERS GROUP, THE

Buffalo Grove, IL
Phone: (847) 609-8783
Fax: (847) 419-0190
Web: http://www.glssug.com/glssug/

GREATER CLEVELAND PC USERS GROUP—DATABASE

Cleveland, OH
Phone: (216) 781-4132

GROUPWARE & DATA BASES

100 Mill Plain Rd.
Danbury, CT
Phone: (914) 892-9030
Fax: (914) 892-9068

HUNTSVILLE PC USER GROUP, INC.—DATABASES

Huntsville, AL

Phone: (205) 883-4154

INDIANA UNIVERSITY WINDOWS NT USERS GROUP, IUWNTUG

http://www.iuinfo.indiana.edu/nt/

INTERIOR ALASKA WINDOWS NT USERS GROUP

http://www.iawntug.org/iawntug/

THE INTERNATIONAL WINDOWS NT USERS GROUP

http://www.iwntug.org/

KANSAS CITY WINDOWS NT USERS GROUP

srodgers@kumc.edu

LONG BEACH IBM USERS GROUP—DATABASE

5155 E. Pacific Coast Hwy.

Lakewood, CA

Phone: (310) 420-3670

LOS ANGELES WINDOWS NT/MICROSOFT NETWORKING USERS GROUP

http://www.bhs.com/lantug/

MADISON PC USER'S GROUP—DATABASE

5445 Cheryl Parkway

Madison, WI 53701

Phone: (608) 231-2725

MELBOURNE PC USER GROUP—DBMS

Phone: (613) 699-6222

Web: http://www.melbpc.org.au/

MELBOURNE–AUSTRALIAN NT USERS GROUP

rcomg@chudich.cse.rmit.edu.au

MEMPHIS PC USERS GROUP, INC. DATABASE USERS

5983 Macon Cove
Memphis, TN 38124-1756
Phone: (901) 375-4316

MICROSOFT DATABASES USER GROUP OF SAN DIEGO

Oceanside, CA
Phone: (619) 433-7374
Fax: (619) 433-0776

MICROSOFT NETWORKING SIG

deborahl@microsoft.com

MINNEAPOLIS–WINDOWS NT USERS GROUP

quadling@mnhepo.hep.umn.edu

NEW YORK CITY NT DEVELOPERS SIG

lee_t@access.digex.net
iams@smosna.cs.nyu.edu

NORTH ORANGE COUNTY COMPUTER CLUB—DATABASE

333 N. Glassell St.
Orange, CA 92665
Phone: (714) 645-5950

NORTH TEXAS SQL SERVER USER GROUP

Plano, TX
Phone: (214) 509-6137
Fax: (214) 509-3509

NT USER'S GROUP ST. LOUIS

St. Louis, MO

Phone: (314) 997-4700

Fax: (314) 997-5426

NW DATABASE SOCIETY

James Erickson

10305 SW Denney Rd. #8

Beaverton, OR 97005

Phone: (503) 626-8485

OKLAHOMA COMPUTER SOCIETY—DATABASE

Stillwater, OK

Phone: (405) 372-6800

ONTARIO NT USERS GROUP

http://www.ontug.org/

ORANGE COAST IBM PC USER GROUP—DATABASE REVIEW

Costa Mesa, CA

Phone: (714) 843-2048

Web: http://www.wecom.com/~ocipug/

ORANGE COUNTY NT USERS GROUP

Attn: Ed Roberts

18551 Von Karman Ave.

Irvine, CA 92612-1510

Web: http://www.ocntug.org/

ORANGE COUNTY SQL SERVER DEVELOPERS GROUP

Taco Bell Office

17901 Von Karman Ave.

Irvine, CA 92614

Phone: (714) 831-6856
Fax: (714) 831-1456

PACIFIC NORTHWEST IBM PC USER GROUP—WINDOWS NT

Bellevue, WA
Phone: (206) 728-7075

PACIFIC NORTHWEST SQL SERVER UG

Bellevue, WA
Phone: (206) 467-5651

PC USERS' GROUP INC. (ACT)—PC DATABASE DEVELOPERS

Belconnen, ACT
Phone: (616) 239-6511

PC USERS' GROUP OF JACKSONVILLE—DATABASE

2800 North University Blvd.
Jacksonville, FL 32247-7197
Phone: (904) 221-5628

PERSONAL COMPUTER CLUB OF SUN LAKES—DATABASE

Banning, CA
Phone: (909) 845-5822

PHILADELPHIA AREA COMPUTER SOCIETY—SQL

Philadelphia, PA
Phone: (215) 951-1255

PHILADELPHIA NT USERS GROUP

aengel@netaxs.com

PHOENIX PCUG WINDOWS NT SIG

Phoenix, AZ

Phone: (602) 222-8511

Web: http://www.phoenixpcug.org/

PORTLAND AREA WINDOWS NT USER GROUP

Email: andreas@mail.inprot.com

Web: http://www.inprot.com/NT

PORTLAND OREGON SQL USER GROUP

Hillsburo, OR

Phone: (503) 628-0705

Fax: (503) 628-6005

PORTLAND PC USERS GROUP—DATABASE

1819 NW Everett

Portland, OR 97205

Phone: (503) 226-4143

Web: http://odin.cc.pdx.edu/~psu01435/cgi/ppcug.cgi

POUGHKEEPSIE IBM CLUB MICROCOMPUTER CLUB—DATABASE

Hyde Park, NY

Phone: (914) 229-6551

PROFESSIONAL DBMS DEVELOPERS

Hermsillo, Sonora

Phone: (621) 546-8600

ROCKY MOUNTAIN WINDOWS NT USERS GROUP

Louisville, CO

Phone: (303) 673-2935

Web: http://budman.cmdl.noaa.gov/RMWNTUG/RMWNTUG.HTM

SAN DIEGO COUNTY WINDOWS NT USERS GROUP

http://www.bhs.com/sdug/

SARASOTA PERSONAL COMPUTER USER GROUP, INC.—DATABASE

4826 Ashton Rd.
Sarasota, FL 34232
Phone: (941) 377-4072

SILICON NORTHWEST DATABASE PROFESSIONALS

Seattle, WA
Phone: (206) 781-0225

SOUTHEAST FLORIDA DATABASE DEVELOPER'S GROUP

http://www.shadow.net/~datachem/sfddg12.html

SWISS NT USERS GROUP

deffer@eunet.ch

SYDNEY NT USER'S GROUP

robg@pactok.peg.apc.org

TRIANGLE NT USERS GROUP

Raleigh, NC
Phone: (919) 510-6970
Fax: (919) 510-6971
Email: tntug@networks.com
Web: http://www.nando.net/ads/ncs

TULSA COMPUTER SOCIETY—DATABASE

Tulsa, OK
Phone: (918) 622-3417

TWIN CITIES PC UG, INC.—CLIENT SERVER

Edina, MN

Phone: (612) 229-5850

WASHINGTON DC MICROSOFT SQL SERVER USERS GROUP

Sterling, VA

Phone: (703) 356-1717

Fax: (703) 356-3009

WINDOWS NT USER GROUP OF INDIANAPOLIS

http://www.wintugi.org/

INDEX

995
VISUAL BASIC 6 CLIENT/SERVER HOW-TO

995

995

995

I

Doing Objects in Visual Basic 6

—*Deborah Kurata*

Doing Objects in Visual Basic 6 is an intermediate-level tutorial that begins with the fundamentals of OOP. It advances to the technical aspects of using the Visual Basic IDE to create objects and interface with databases, Web sites, and Internet applications. This revised edition features more technical information than the last edition and specifically highlights the features of the new release of Visual Basic.

Price: $49.99 US/$46.18 CDN
ISBN: 1-56276-577-9

User Level: Intermediate–Expert
560 pages

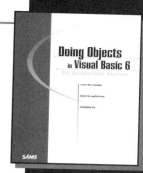

Dan Appleman's Developing COM/ActiveX Components with Visual Basic 6

—*Dan Appleman*

Dan Appleman's Developing COM/ActiveX Components with Visual Basic 6 is a focused tutorial for learning component development. It teaches you the programming concepts and the technical steps needed to create ActiveX components. Dan Appleman is one of the foremost developers in the Visual Basic community and is the author whom Visual Basic programmers recommend to their friends and colleagues. He consistently delivers on his promise to break through the confusion and hype surrounding Visual Basic and ActiveX and goes beyond the basics to show you common pitfalls and practical solutions for key problems.

Price: $49.99 US/$71.95 CDN
ISBN: 1-56276-576-0

User Level: Intermediate
850 pages

COMING SOON

The Waite Group's Visual Basic 6 How-To

—Eric Brierley, et al

Written in The Waite Group's proven question-and-answer format, *The Waite Group's Visual Basic 6 How-To* is a programmer-oriented, problem-solving guide that teaches you how to enhance your Visual Basic skills. Chapters are organized by topic and divided into How-To's. Each How-To describes a problem, develops a technique for solving the problem, presents a step-by-step solution, furnishes relevant tips, comments, and warnings, and presents alternative solutions where applicable. You learn expanded coverage of Visual Basic 6 and how to take advantage of new interface options and Windows APIs, how to build multitier Web-based applications, how to use Advanced Data Objects (ADO), and much more, including Internet topics.

Price: $39.99 US/$57.95 CDN ***User Level: Intermediate***
ISBN: 1-57169-153-7 *800 pages*

The Waite Group's Visual Basic 6 Database How-To

—Eric Winemiller and Jason R. Roff

Written in The Waite Group's proven question-and-answer format, *The Waite Group's Visual Basic 6 Database How-To* is an updated edition of *Visual Basic How-To*, which has sold over 50,000 copies and won the Visual Basic Programmer's Journal Reader's Choice Award in 1995. You learn expanded coverage of Visual Basic 6, including Internet topics and lots of all new How-To's.

Price: $39.99 US/$57.95 CDN ***User Level: Intermediate–Advanced***
ISBN: 1-57169-152-9 *1,100 pages*

Add to Your Sams Library Today with the Best Books for Programming, Operating Systems, and New Technologies

To order, visit our Web site at www.mcp.com or fax us at

1-800-835-3202

ISBN	Quantity	Description of Item	Unit Cost	Total Cost
1-56276-577-9		Doing Objects in Visual Basic 6	$49.99	
1-56276-576-0		Dan Appleman's Developing COM/ActiveX Components with Visual Basic 6	$49.99	
1-57169-153-7		The Waite Group's Visual Basic 6 How-To	$39.99	
1-57169-152-9		The Waite Group's Visual Basic 6 Database How-To	$39.99	
		Shipping and Handling: See information below.		
		TOTAL		

Shipping and Handling

Standard	$5.00
2nd Day	$10.00
Next Day	$17.50
International	$40.00

201 W. 103rd Street, Indianapolis, Indiana 46290   1-800-835-3202 — FAX

Book ISBN 0-57169-154-5

WHAT'S ON THE DISC

The companion CD-ROM contains all the authors' sace code, samples from the book, and many third-party software products.

Windows 95/NT 4 Installation Instructions

1. Insert the CD-ROM disc into your CD-ROM drive.

2. From the Windows 95 desktop, double-click the My Computer icon.

3. Double-click the icon representing your CD-ROM drive.

4. Double-click the icon titled SETUP.EXE to run the installation program.

NOTE

If Windows 95 is installed on your computer and you have the AutoPlay feature enabled, the SETUP.EXE program starts automatically whenever you insert the disc into your CD-ROM drive.